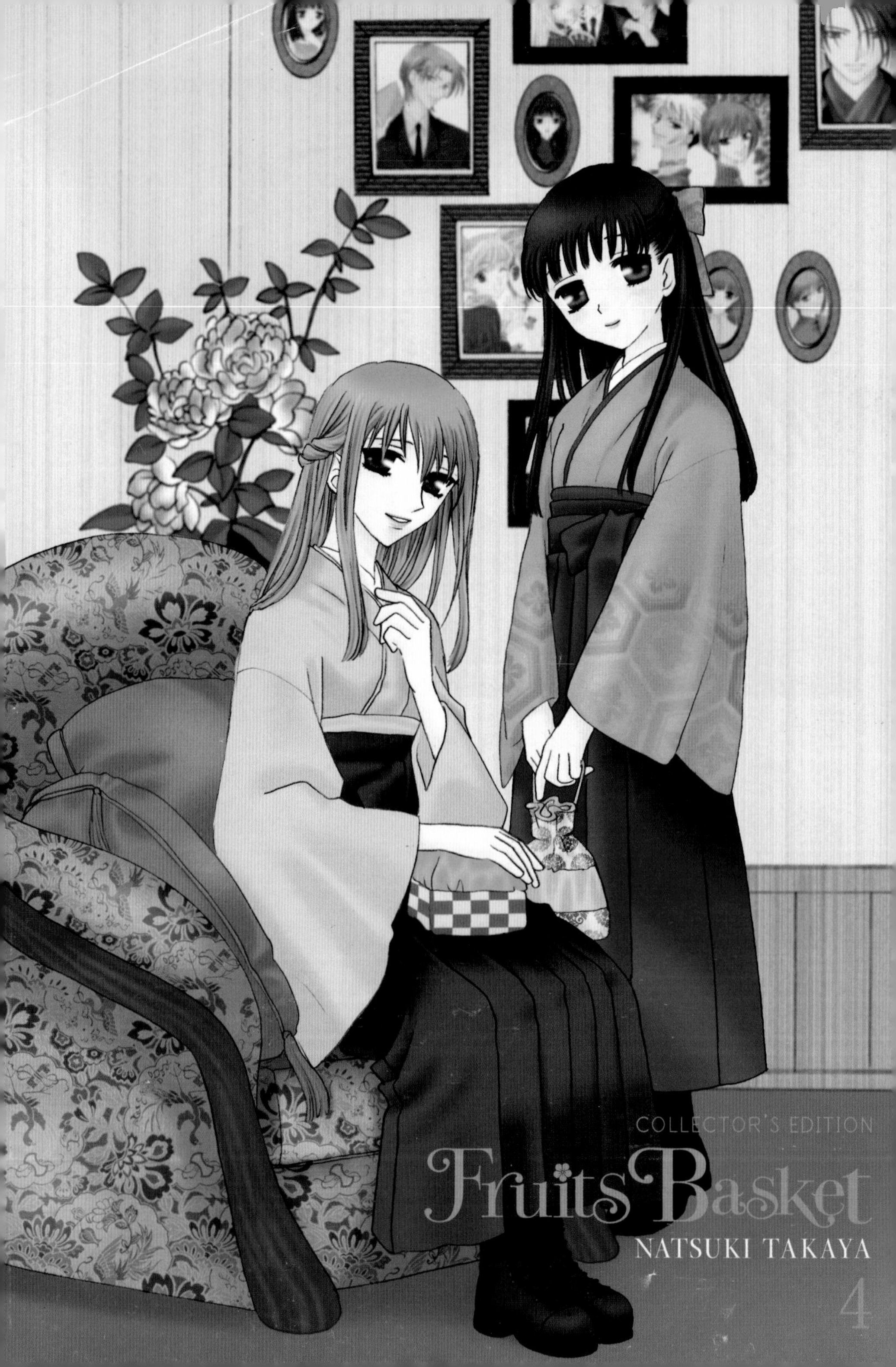
COLLECTOR'S EDITION
Fruits Basket
NATSUKI TAKAYA
4

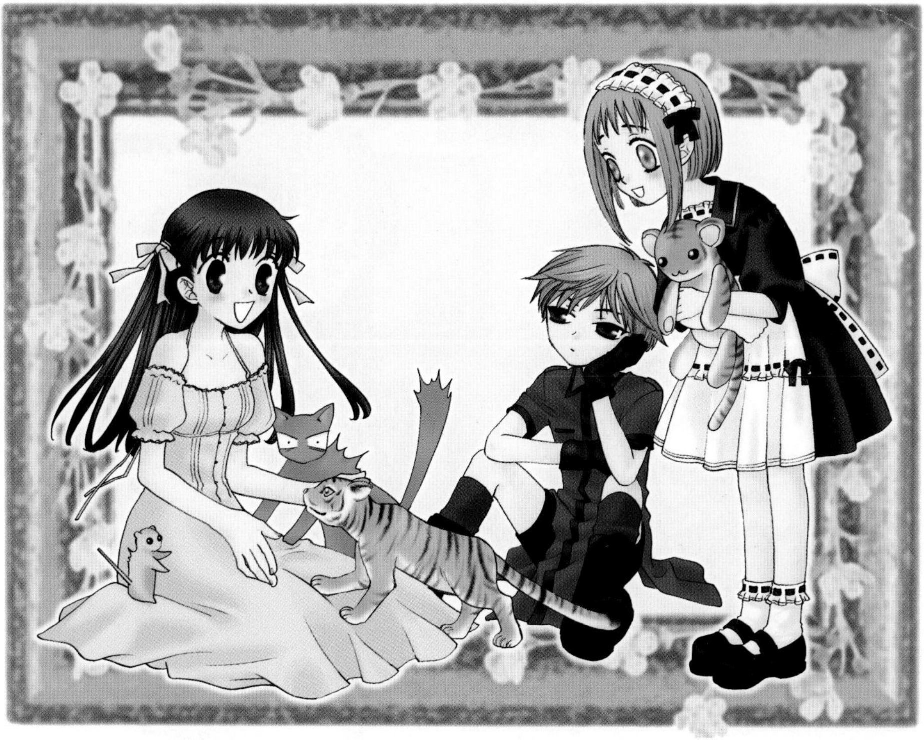
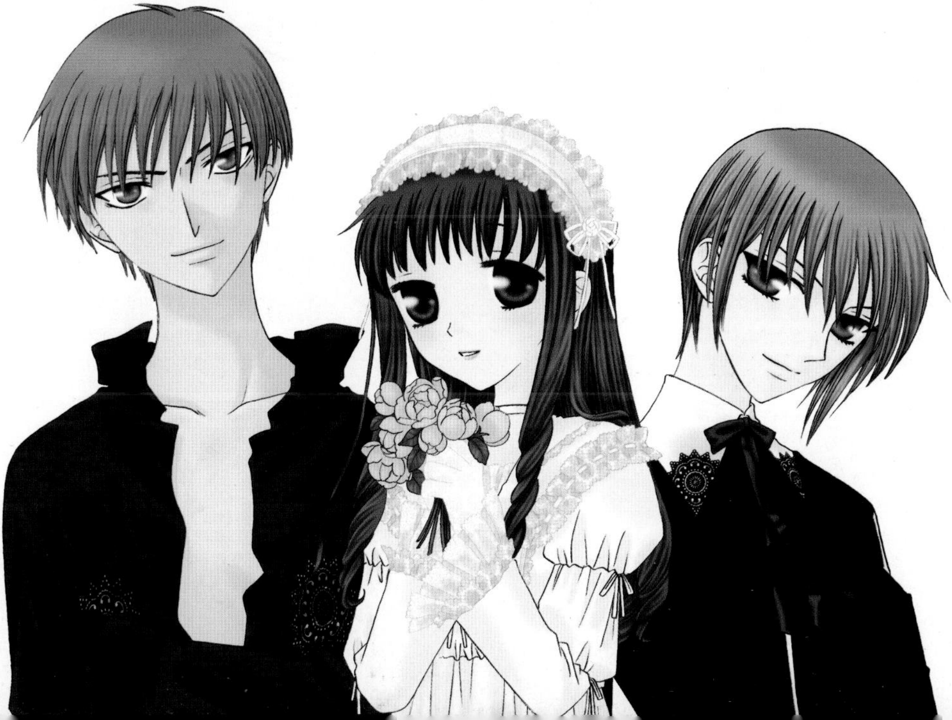

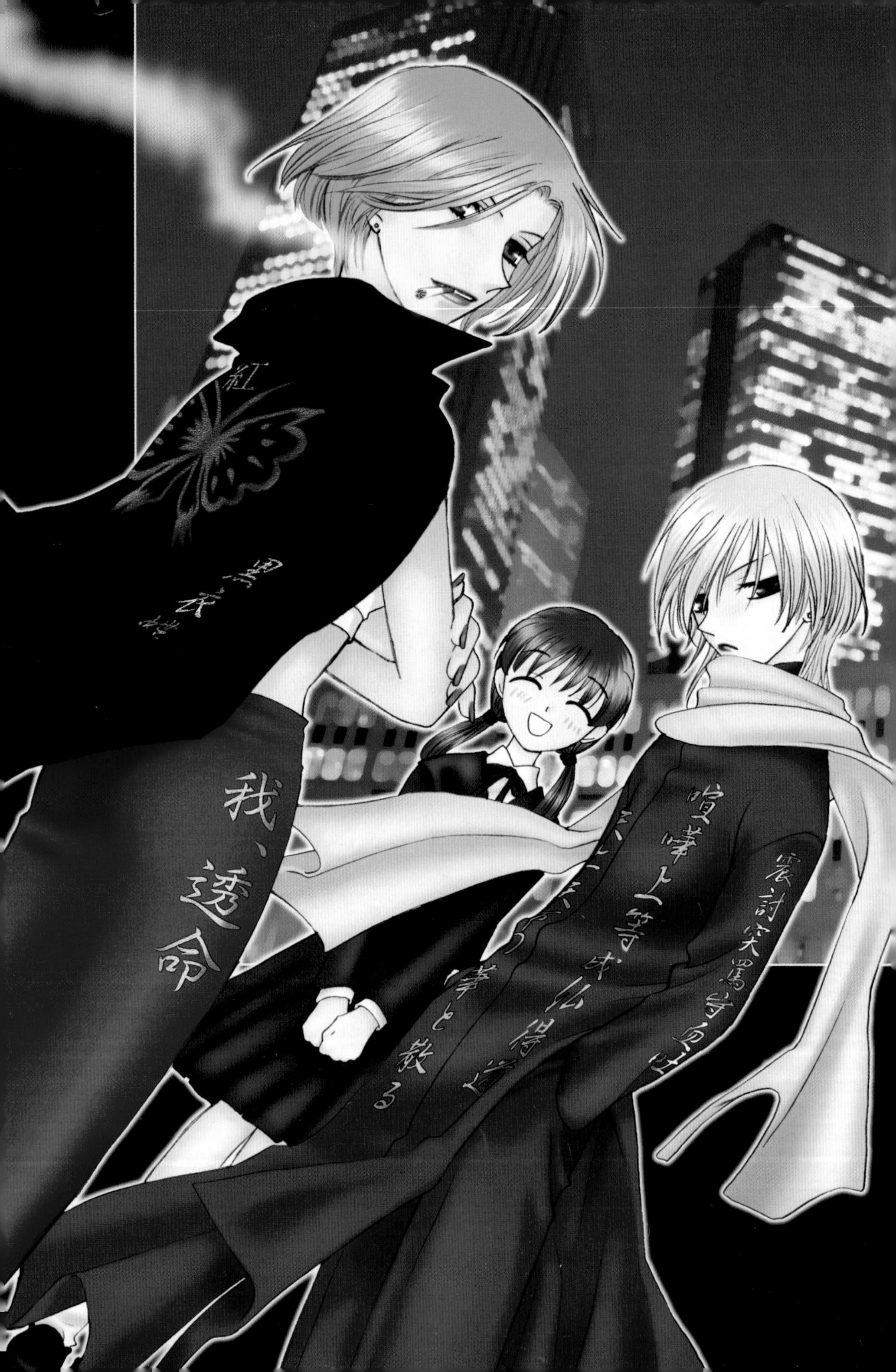
紅
我、透命
喧嘩上等

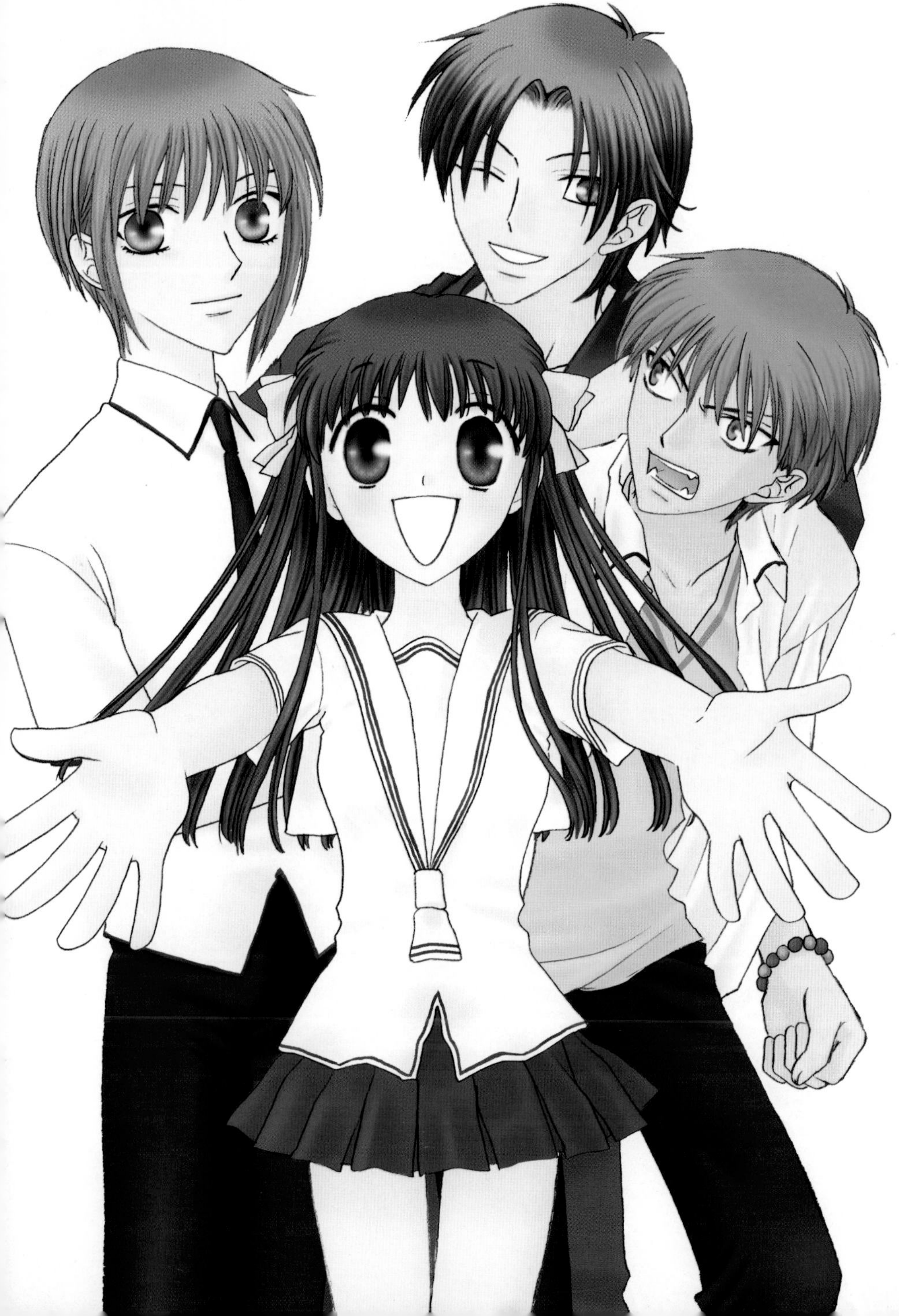

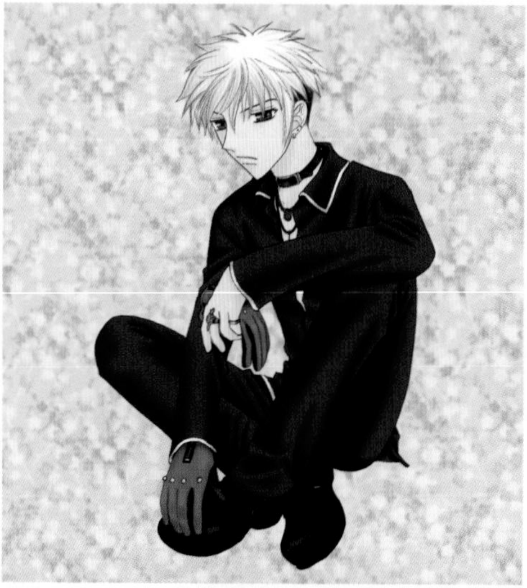
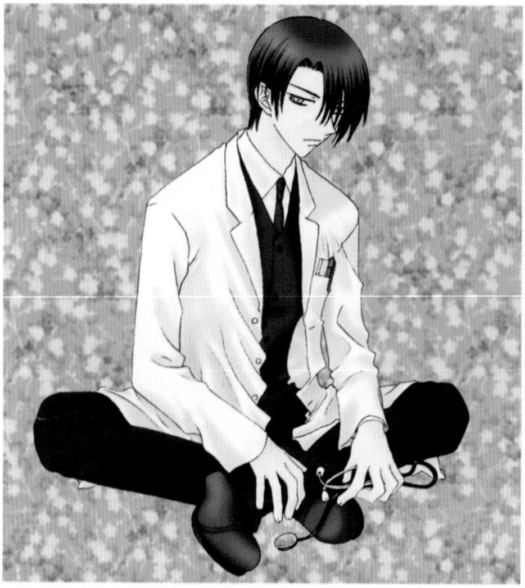
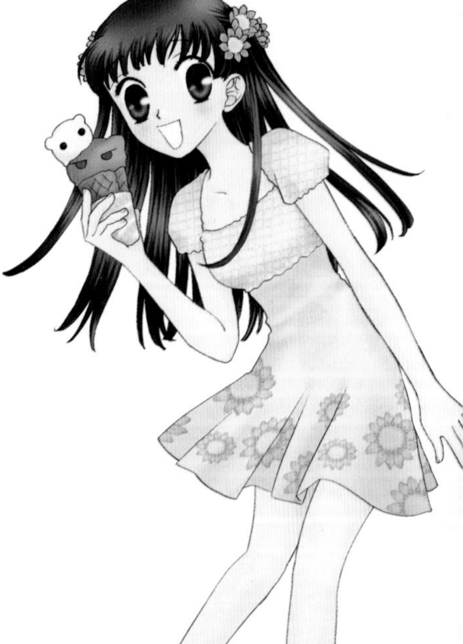
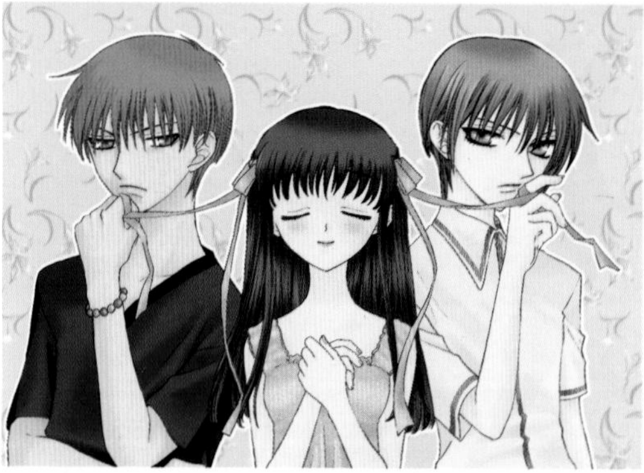
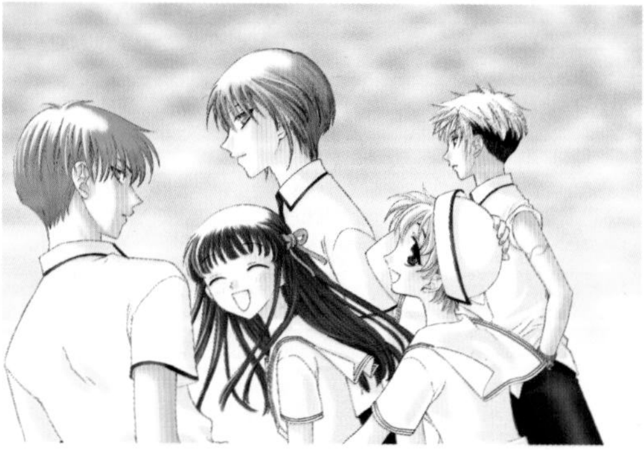

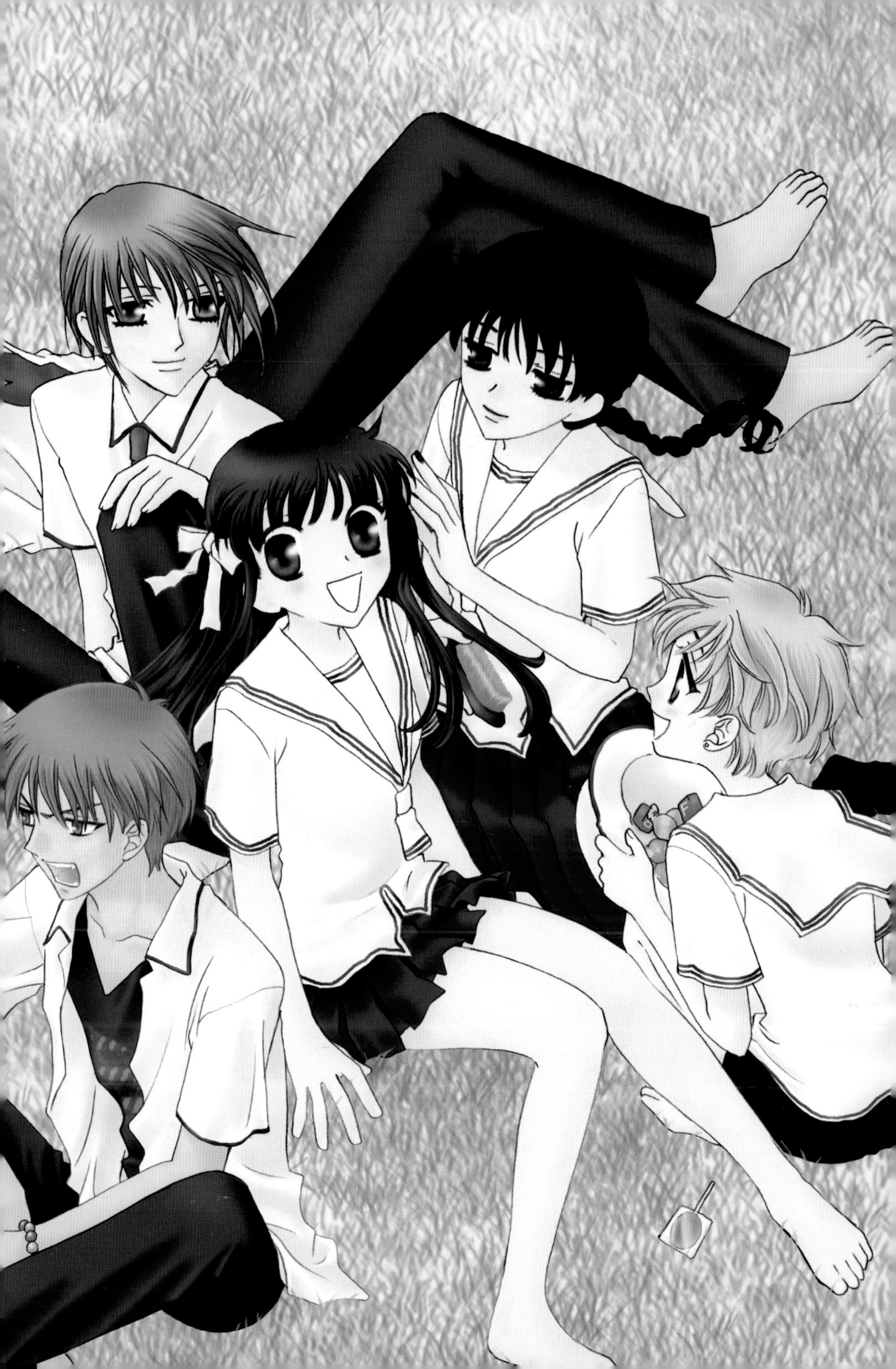

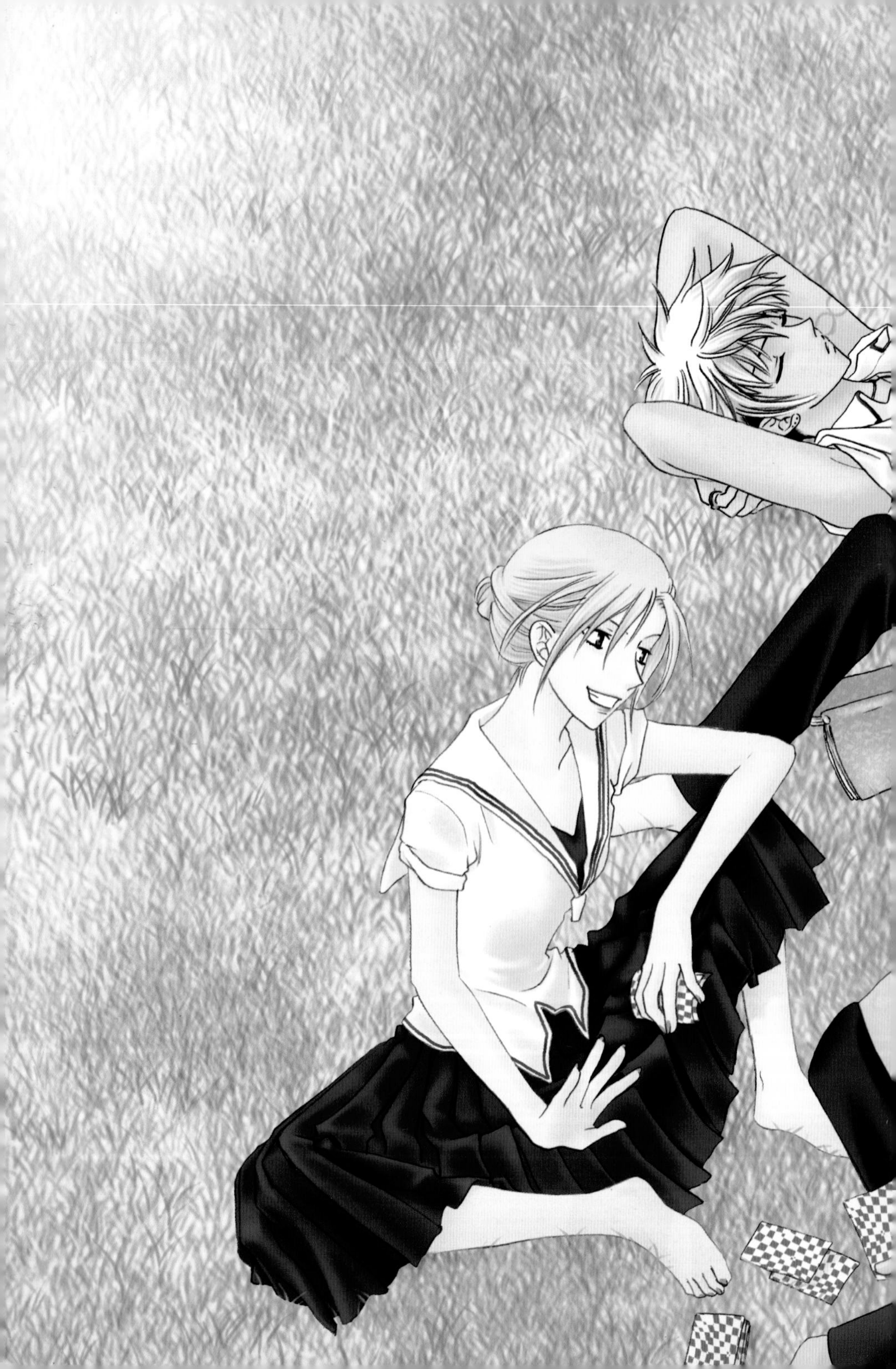

TABLE OF CONTENTS

COLLECTOR'S EDITION

Fruits Basket 4

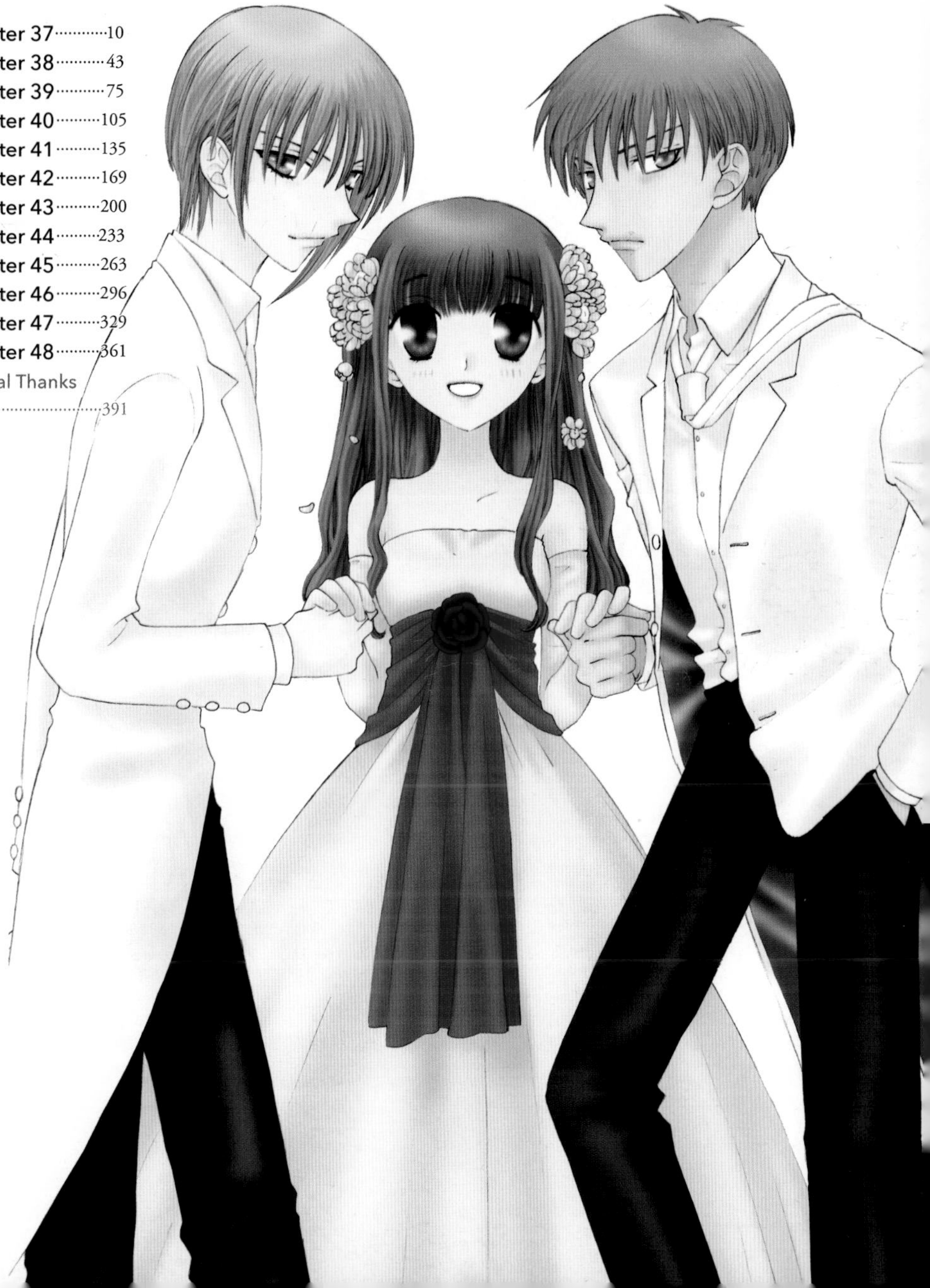

COLLECTOR'S EDITION

Fruits Basket

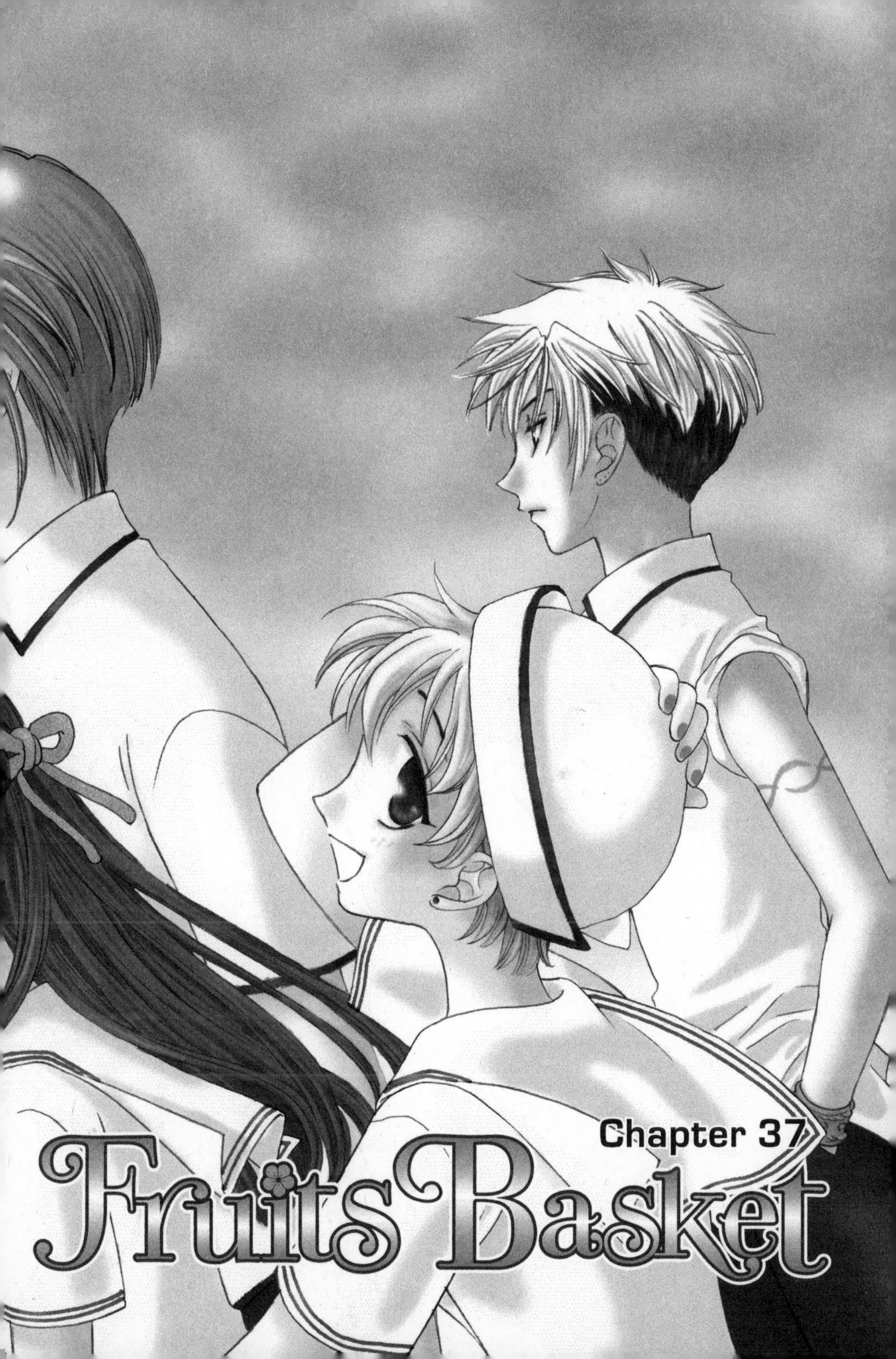
Chapter 37
Fruits Basket

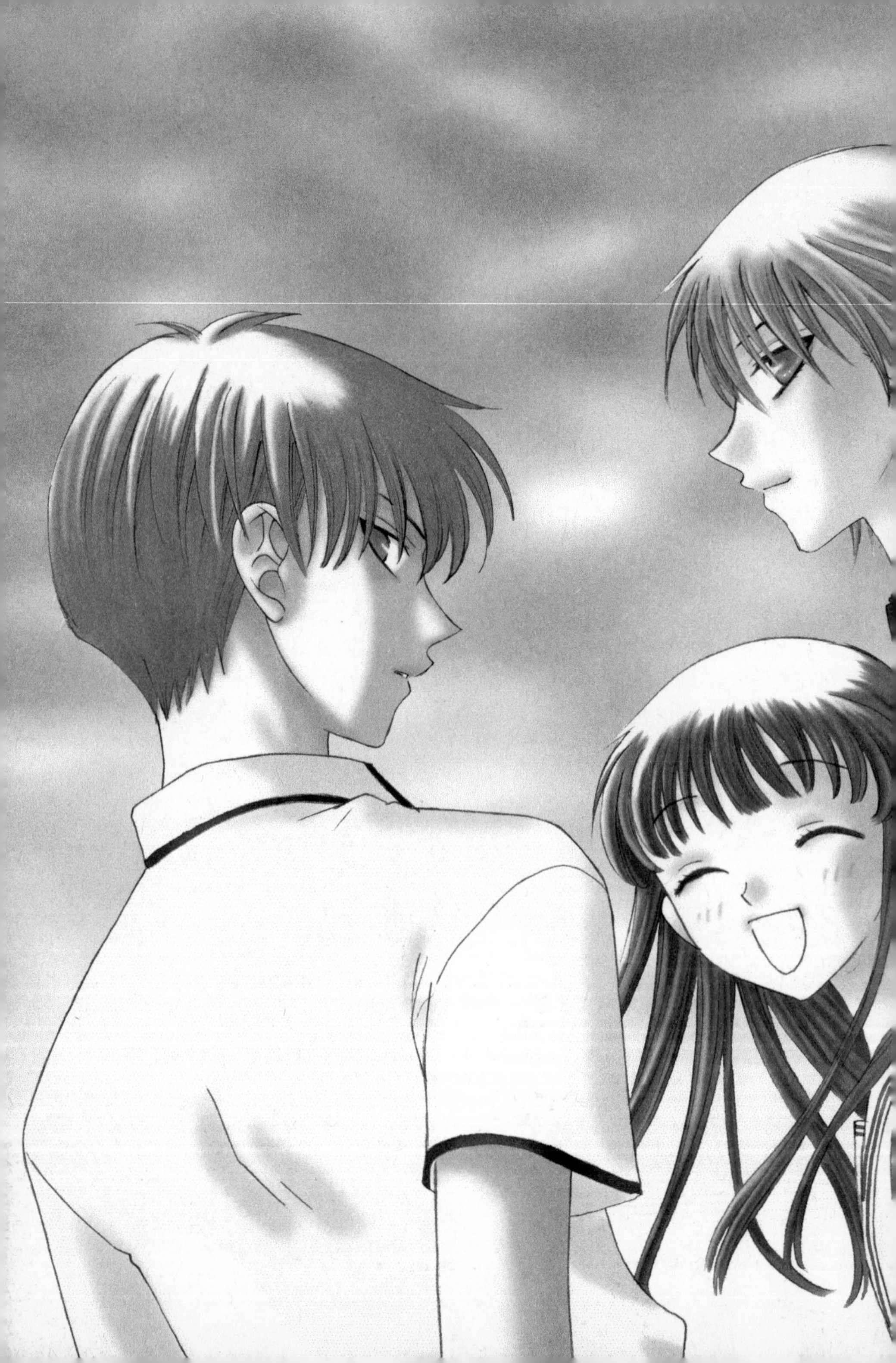

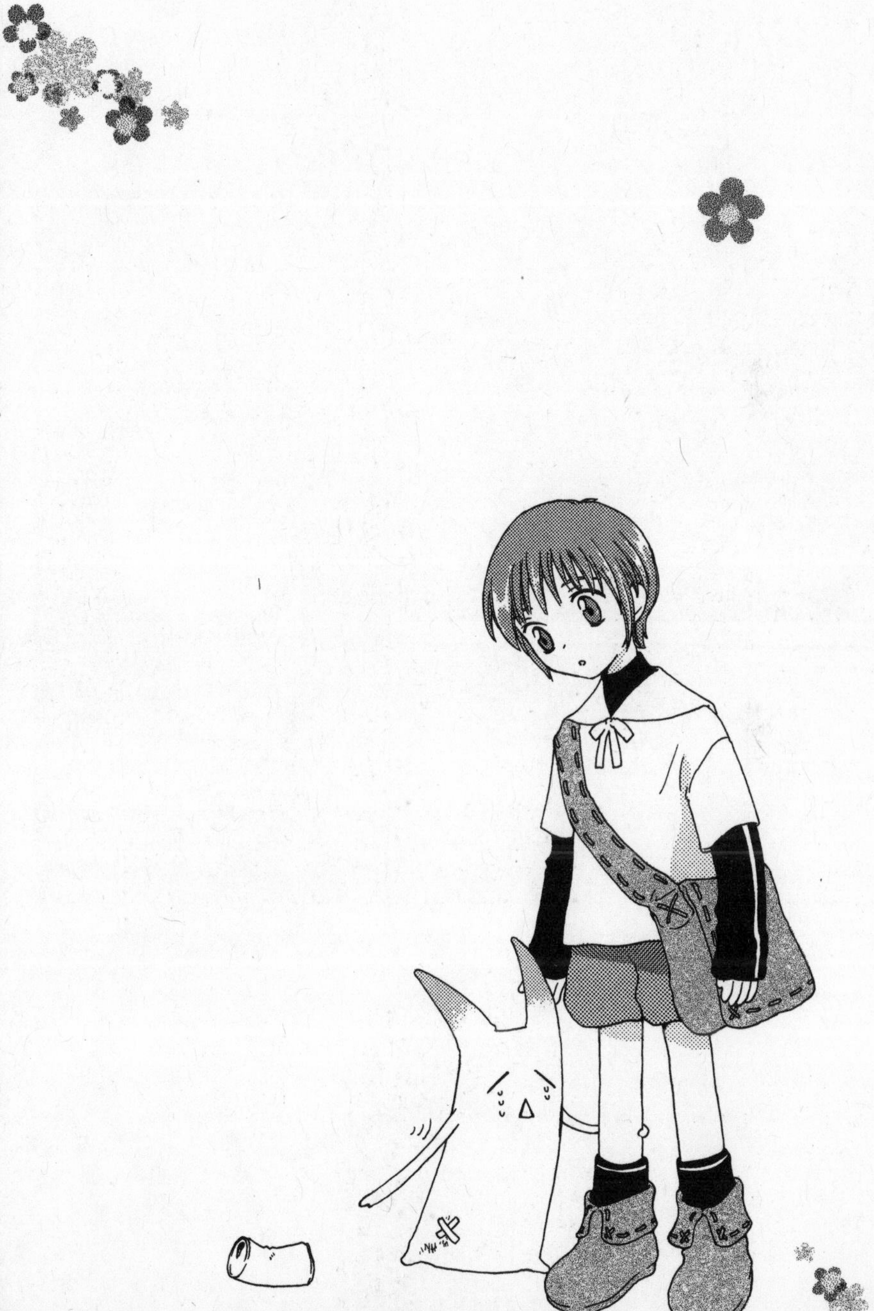

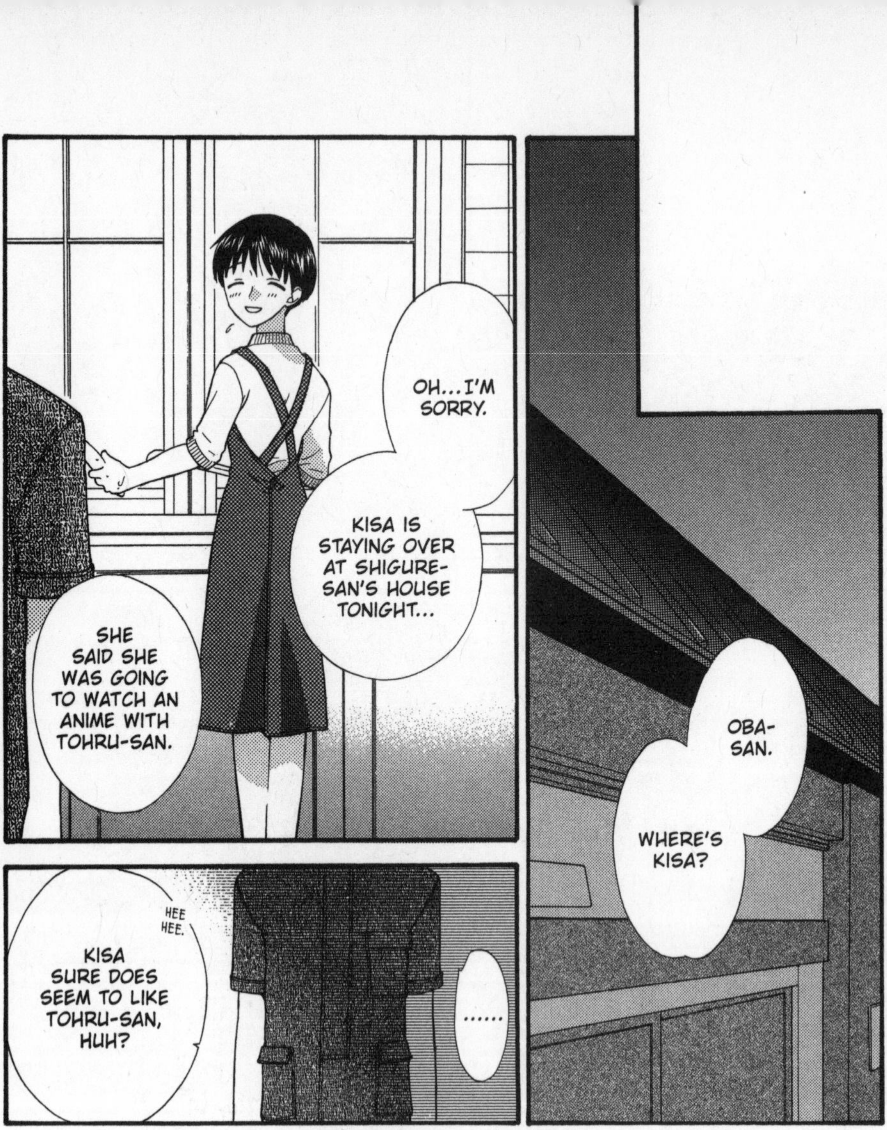
OBA-SAN.
WHERE'S KISA?
OH...I'M SORRY.
KISA IS STAYING OVER AT SHIGURE-SAN'S HOUSE TONIGHT...
SHE SAID SHE WAS GOING TO WATCH AN ANIME WITH TOHRU-SAN.
......
HEE HEE.
KISA SURE DOES SEEM TO LIKE TOHRU-SAN, HUH?

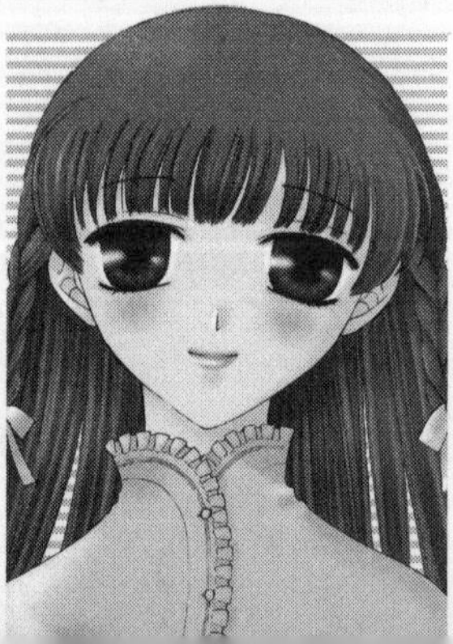

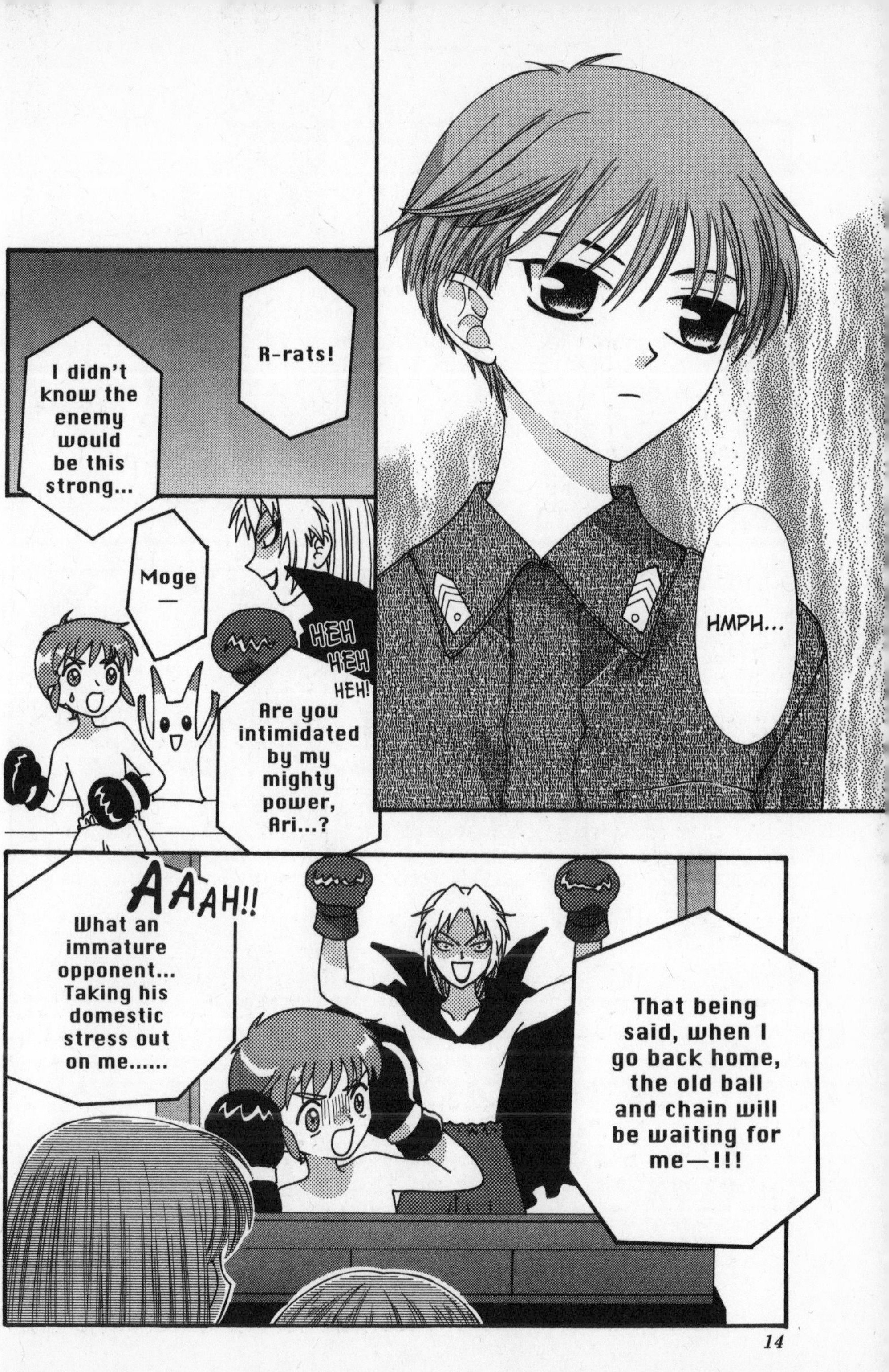
HMPH...
R-rats!
I didn't know the enemy would be this strong...
HEH HEH HEH!
Are you intimidated by my mighty power, Ari...?
Moge —
That being said, when I go back home, the old ball and chain will be waiting for me—!!!
AAAH!!
What an immature opponent... Taking his domestic stress out on me......

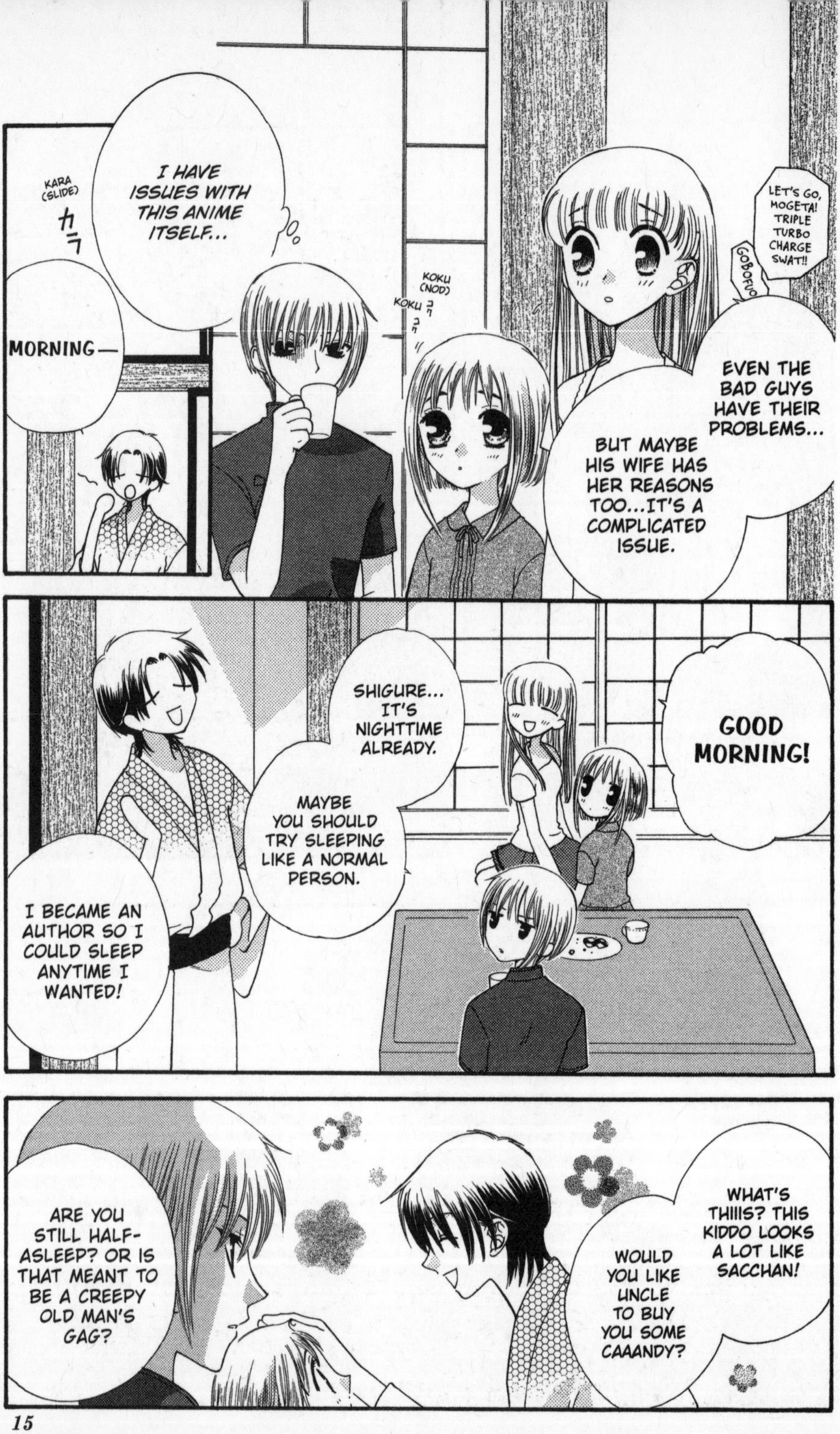
LET'S GO, MOGETA! TRIPLE TURBO CHARGE SWAT!!
GOBOFUO
EVEN THE BAD GUYS HAVE THEIR PROBLEMS...
BUT MAYBE HIS WIFE HAS HER REASONS TOO...IT'S A COMPLICATED ISSUE.
KOKU KOKU (NOD)
コク コク
I HAVE ISSUES WITH THIS ANIME ITSELF...
KARA (SLIDE)
カラ
MORNING—
GOOD MORNING!
SHIGURE... IT'S NIGHTTIME ALREADY.
MAYBE YOU SHOULD TRY SLEEPING LIKE A NORMAL PERSON.
I BECAME AN AUTHOR SO I COULD SLEEP ANYTIME I WANTED!
WHAT'S THIIIS? THIS KIDDO LOOKS A LOT LIKE SACCHAN!
WOULD YOU LIKE UNCLE TO BUY YOU SOME CAAANDY?
ARE YOU STILL HALF-ASLEEP? OR IS THAT MEANT TO BE A CREEPY OLD MAN'S GAG?

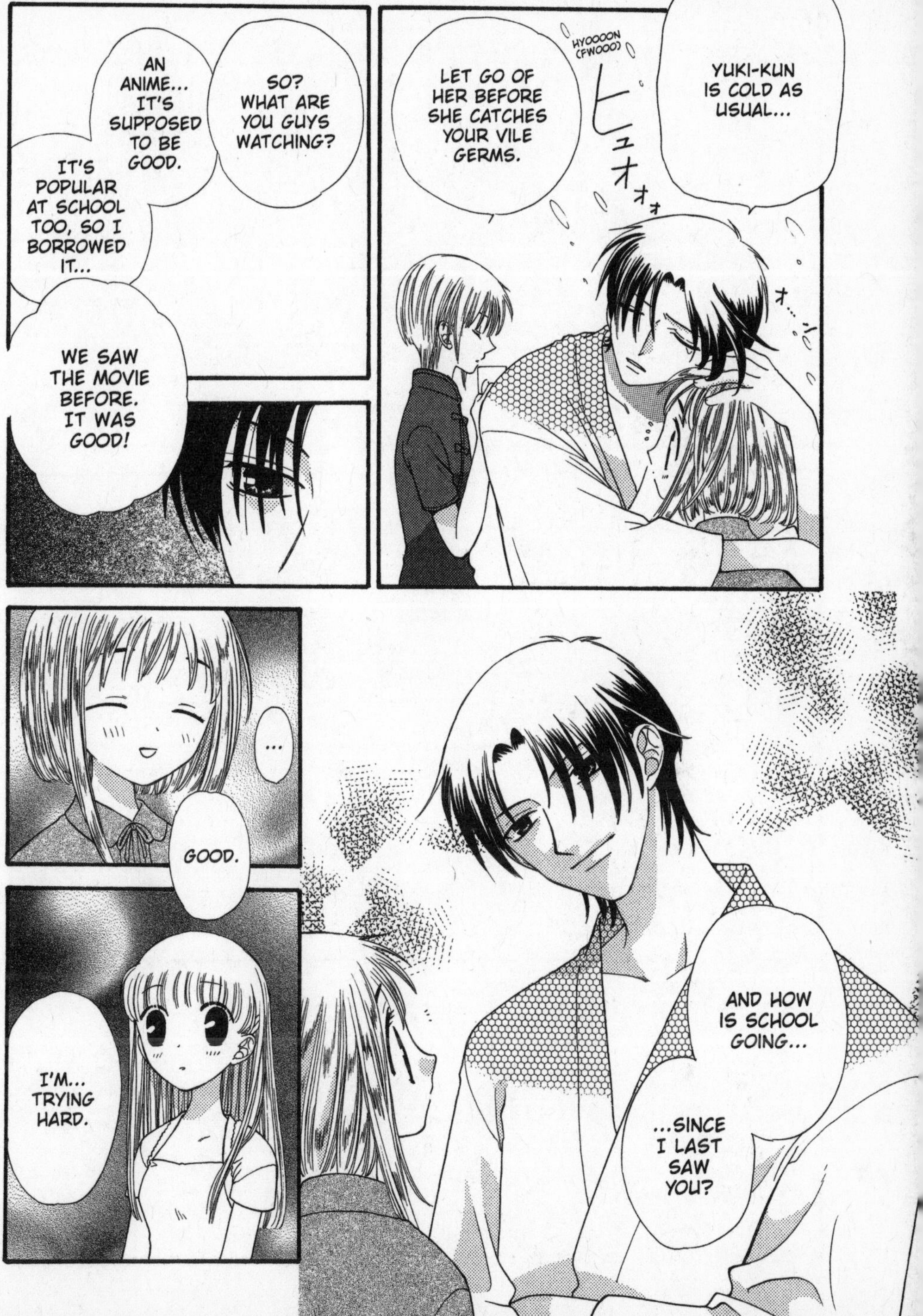
YUKI-KUN IS COLD AS USUAL...
HYOOOON (FWOOO)
ヒュオォ
LET GO OF HER BEFORE SHE CATCHES YOUR VILE GERMS.
SO? WHAT ARE YOU GUYS WATCHING?
AN ANIME... IT'S SUPPOSED TO BE GOOD.
IT'S POPULAR AT SCHOOL TOO, SO I BORROWED IT...
WE SAW THE MOVIE BEFORE. IT WAS GOOD!
AND HOW IS SCHOOL GOING...
...SINCE I LAST SAW YOU?
...
GOOD.
I'M... TRYING HARD.

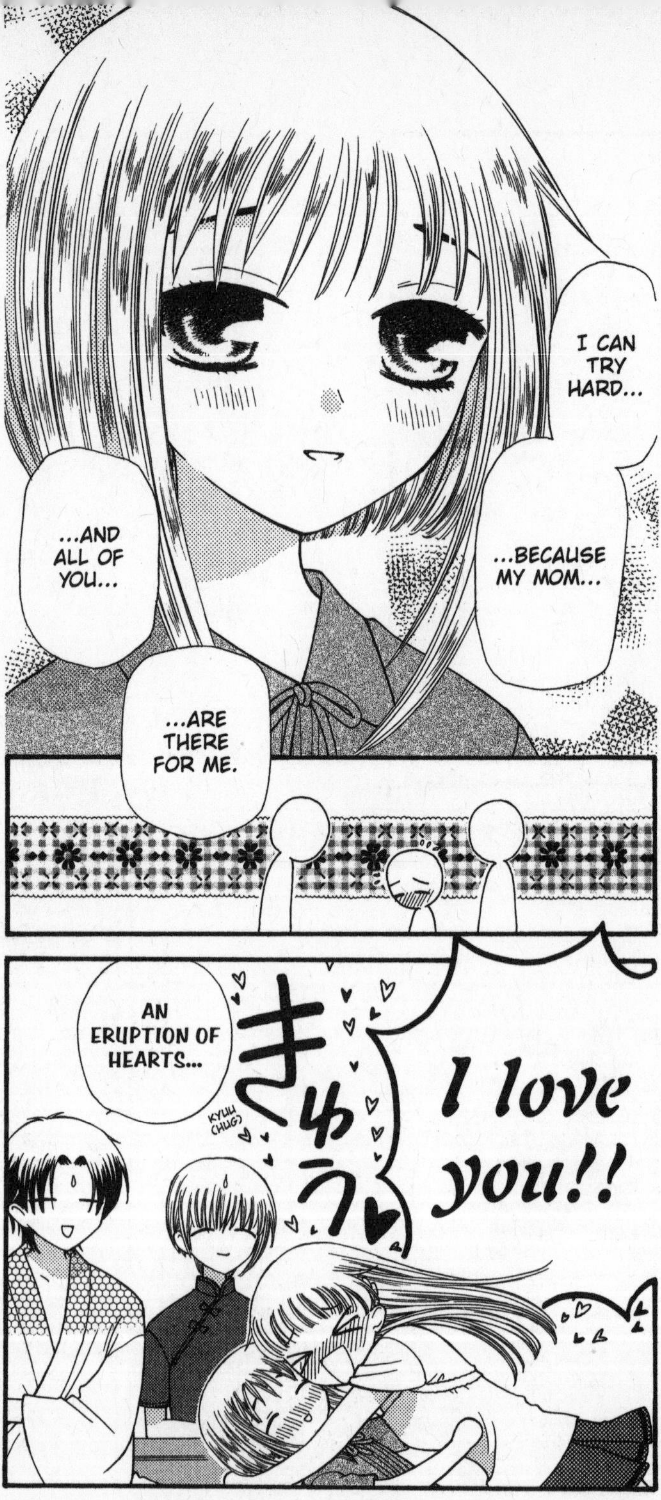
I CAN TRY HARD...
...BECAUSE MY MOM...
...AND ALL OF YOU...
...ARE THERE FOR ME.
I love you!!
きゅう
KYUU (HUG)
AN ERUPTION OF HEARTS...
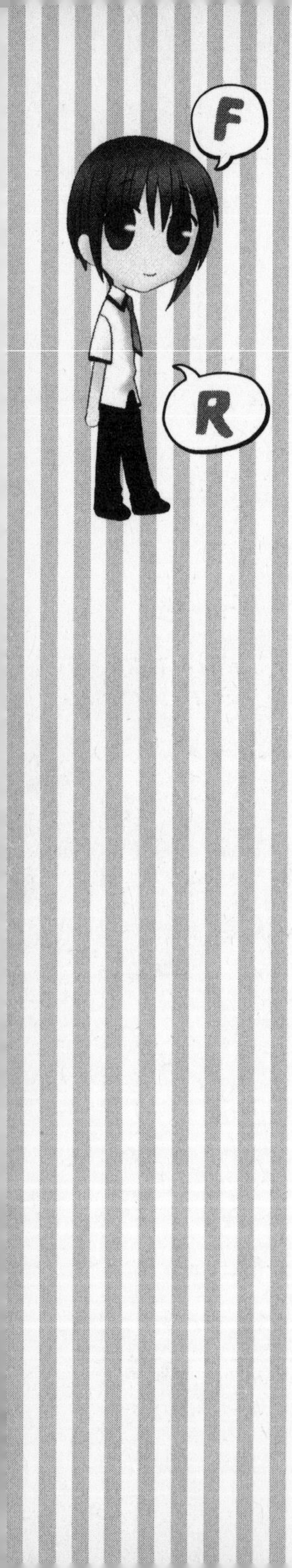
F
R

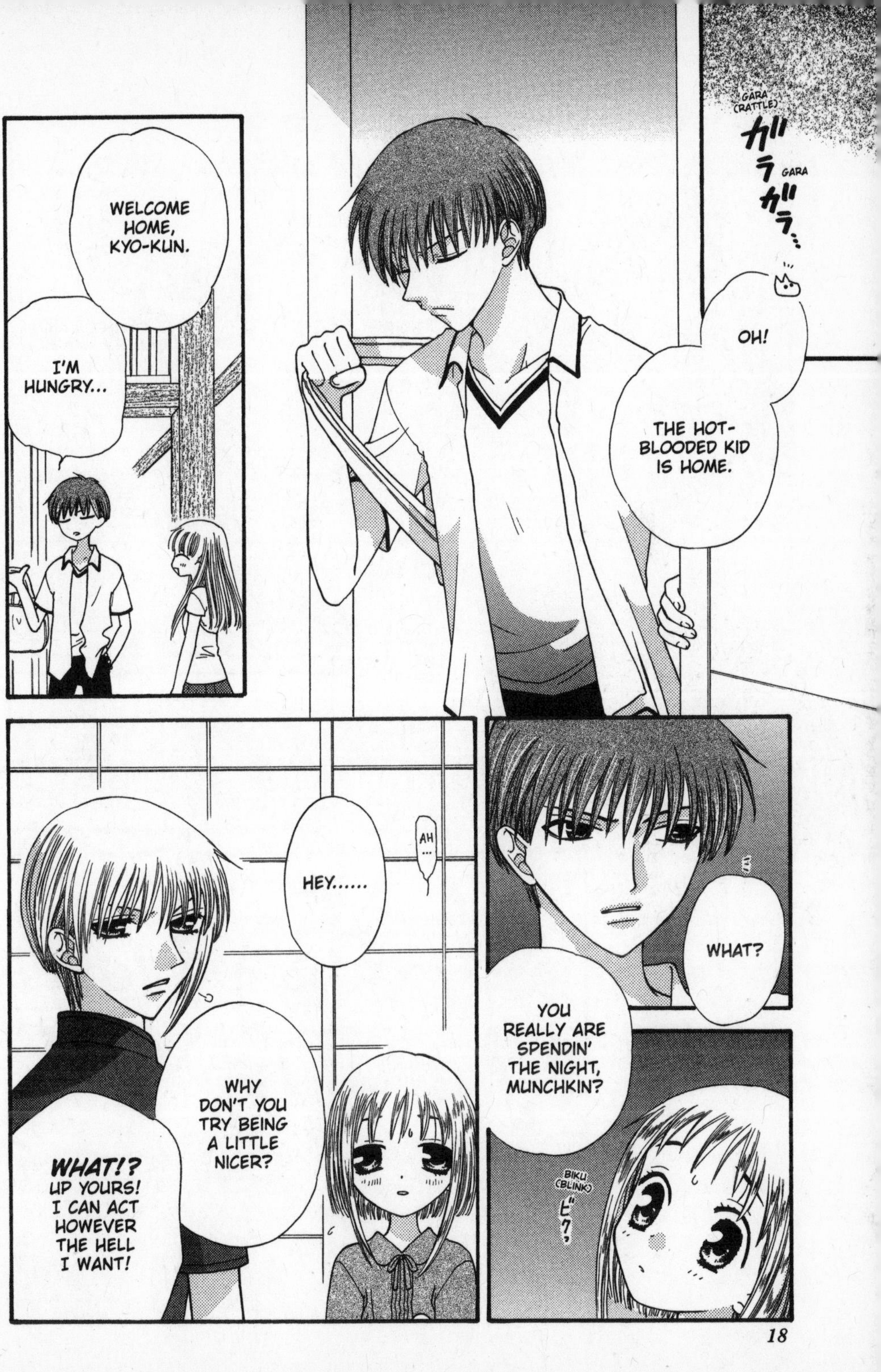
GARA (RATTLE)
ガラ GARA ガラ…
OH!
THE HOT-BLOODED KID IS HOME.
WELCOME HOME, KYO-KUN.
I'M HUNGRY...
WHAT?
YOU REALLY ARE SPENDIN' THE NIGHT, MUNCHKIN?
BIKU (BLINK) ビクッ
AH ...
HEY......
WHY DON'T YOU TRY BEING A LITTLE NICER?
WHAT!? UP YOURS! I CAN ACT HOWEVER THE HELL I WANT!

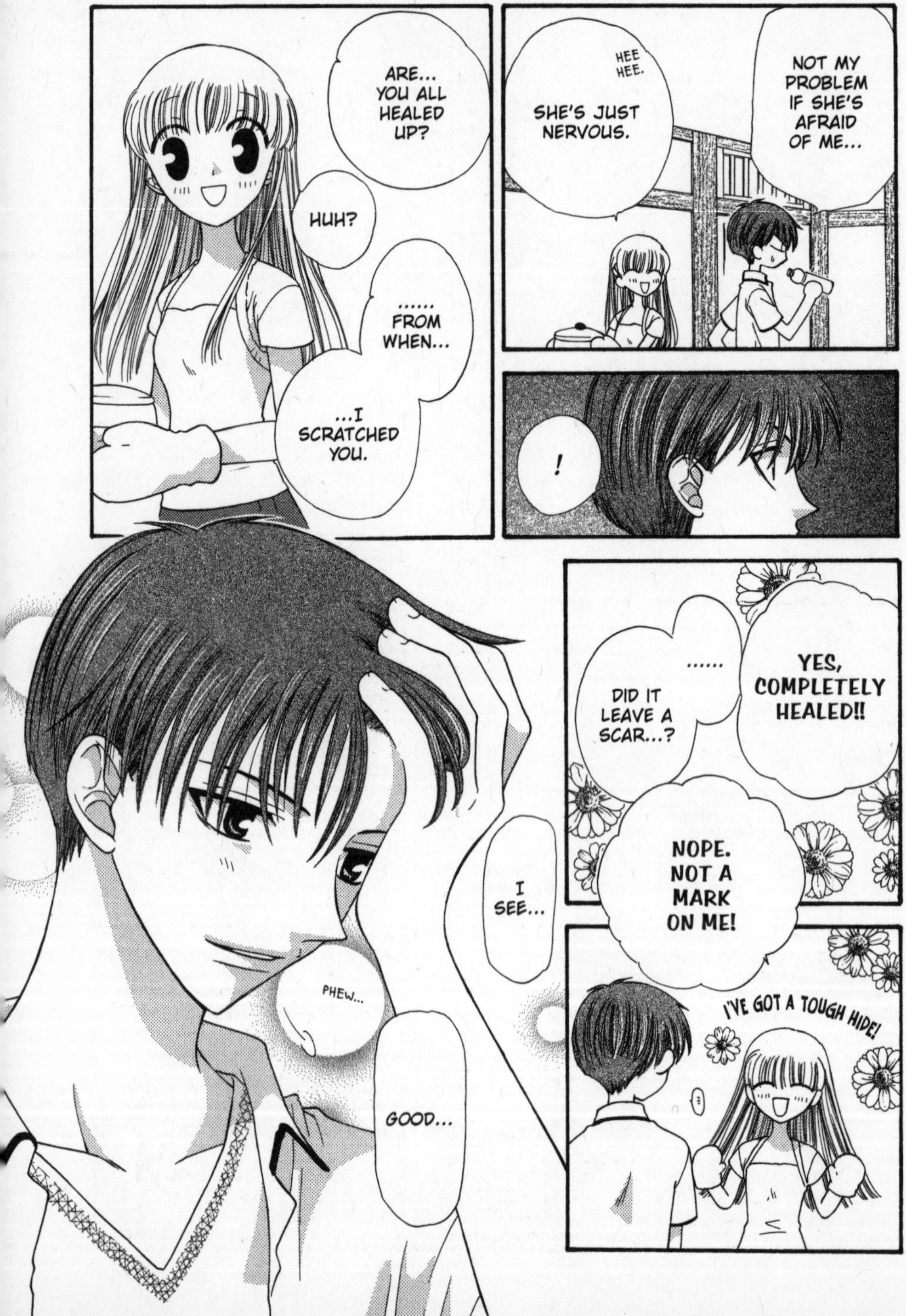
NOT MY PROBLEM IF SHE'S AFRAID OF ME...
HEE HEE.
SHE'S JUST NERVOUS.
!
ARE... YOU ALL HEALED UP?
HUH?
...... FROM WHEN...
...I SCRATCHED YOU.
YES, COMPLETELY HEALED!!
......
DID IT LEAVE A SCAR...?
NOPE. NOT A MARK ON ME!
I'VE GOT A TOUGH HIDE!
I SEE...
PHEW...
GOOD...

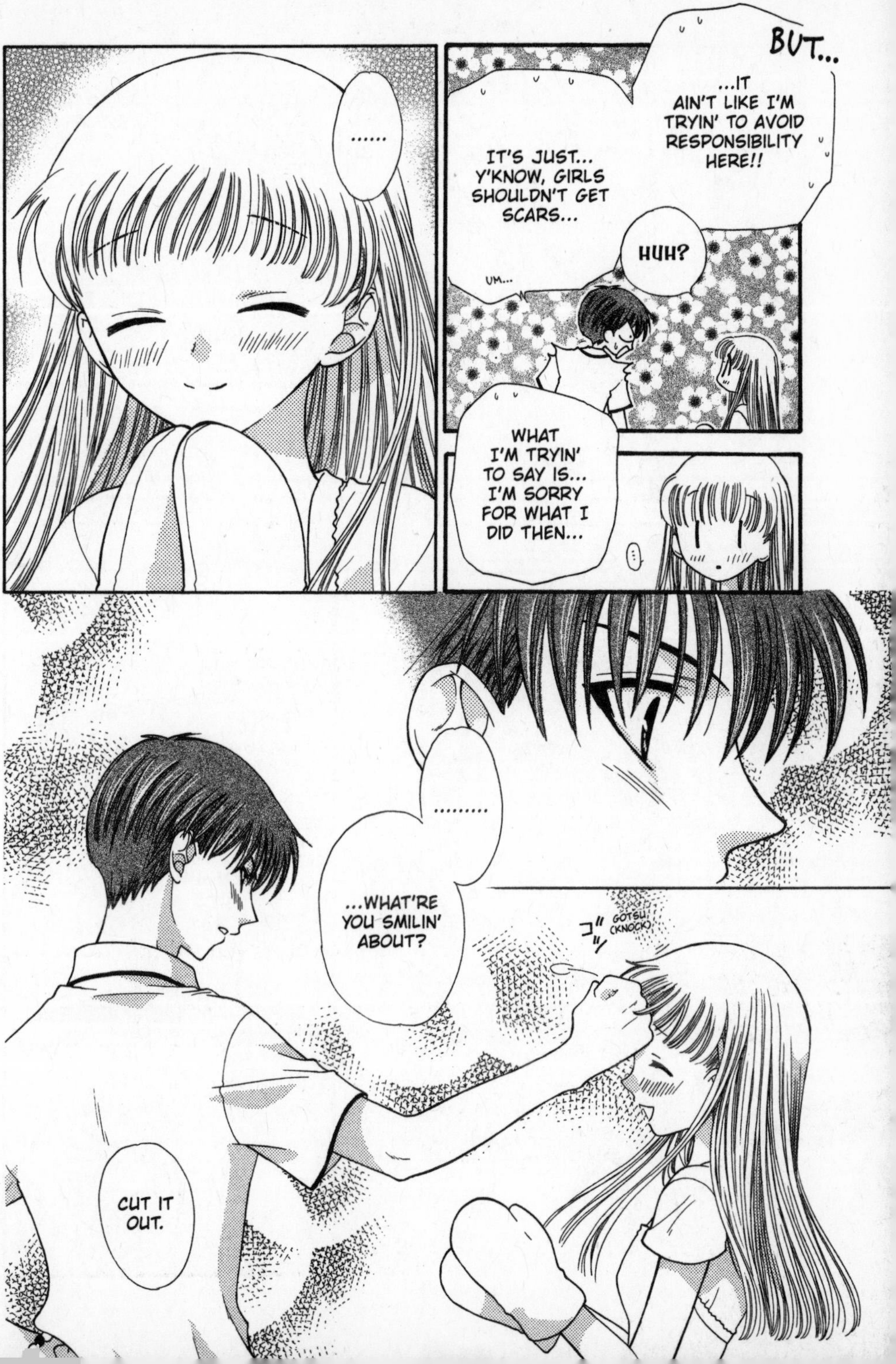

BUT...
...IT AIN'T LIKE I'M TRYIN' TO AVOID RESPONSIBILITY HERE!!
IT'S JUST... Y'KNOW, GIRLS SHOULDN'T GET SCARS...
HUH?
UM...
WHAT I'M TRYIN' TO SAY IS... I'M SORRY FOR WHAT I DID THEN...
!
......
....
...WHAT'RE YOU SMILIN' ABOUT?
GOTSU (KNOCK)
CUT IT OUT.

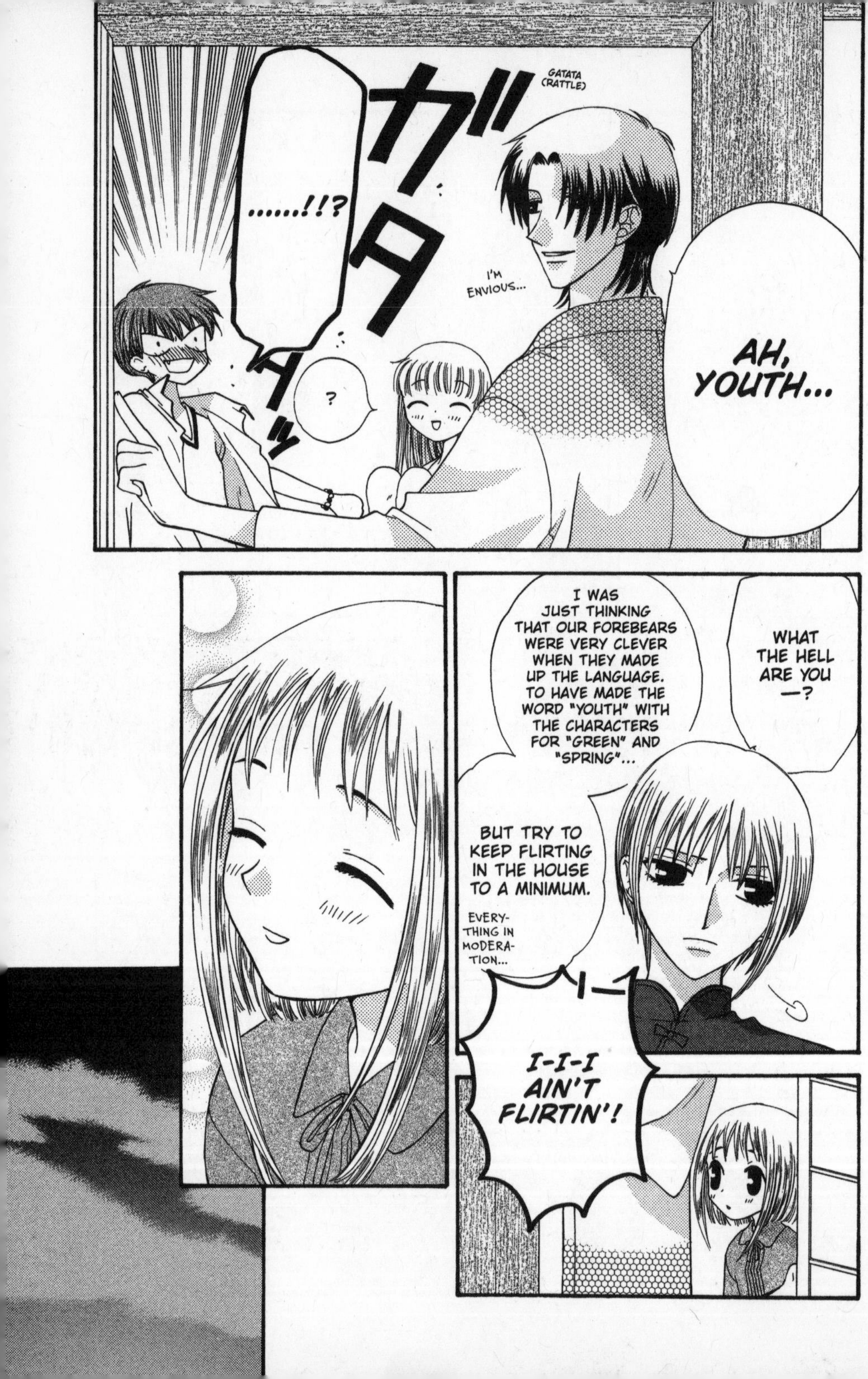
AH, YOUTH...
GATATA (RATTLE)
I'M ENVIOUS...
......!!?
?
WHAT THE HELL ARE YOU—?
I WAS JUST THINKING THAT OUR FOREBEARS WERE VERY CLEVER WHEN THEY MADE UP THE LANGUAGE. TO HAVE MADE THE WORD "YOUTH" WITH THE CHARACTERS FOR "GREEN" AND "SPRING"...
BUT TRY TO KEEP FLIRTING IN THE HOUSE TO A MINIMUM.
EVERY-THING IN MODERA-TION...
I-I-I AIN'T FLIRTIN'!

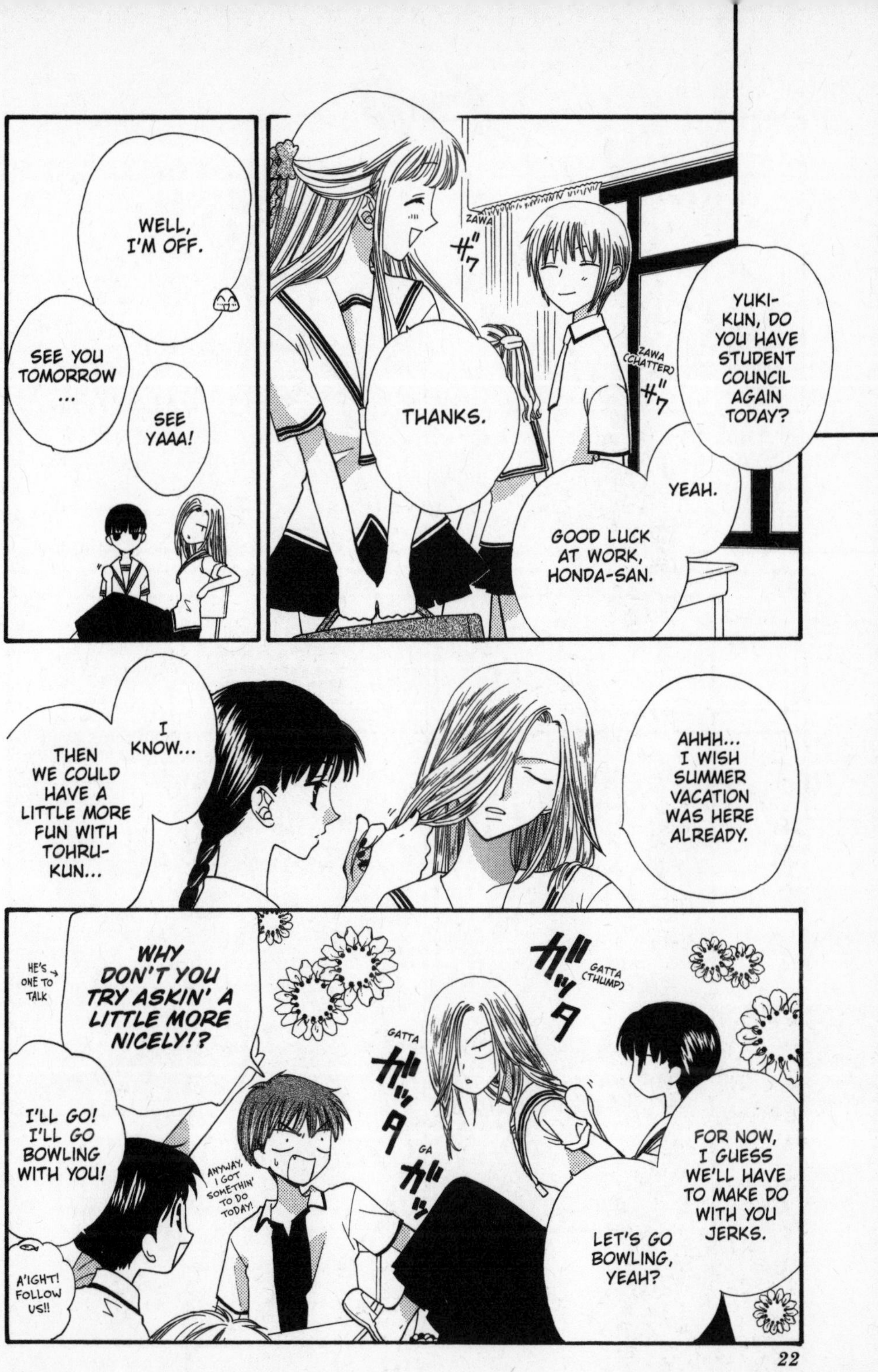
YUKI-KUN, DO YOU HAVE STUDENT COUNCIL AGAIN TODAY?
ZAWA (CHATTER)
YEAH.
GOOD LUCK AT WORK, HONDA-SAN.
ZAWA
THANKS.
WELL, I'M OFF.
SEE YAAA!
SEE YOU TOMORROW ...
AHHH... I WISH SUMMER VACATION WAS HERE ALREADY.
I KNOW...
THEN WE COULD HAVE A LITTLE MORE FUN WITH TOHRU-KUN...
GATTA (THUMP)
FOR NOW, I GUESS WE'LL HAVE TO MAKE DO WITH YOU JERKS.
LET'S GO BOWLING, YEAH?
GATTA
GA
WHY DON'T YOU TRY ASKIN' A LITTLE MORE NICELY!?
HE'S ONE TO TALK
ANYWAY, I GOT SOMETHIN' TO DO TODAY!
I'LL GO! I'LL GO BOWLING WITH YOU!
A'IGHT! FOLLOW US!!

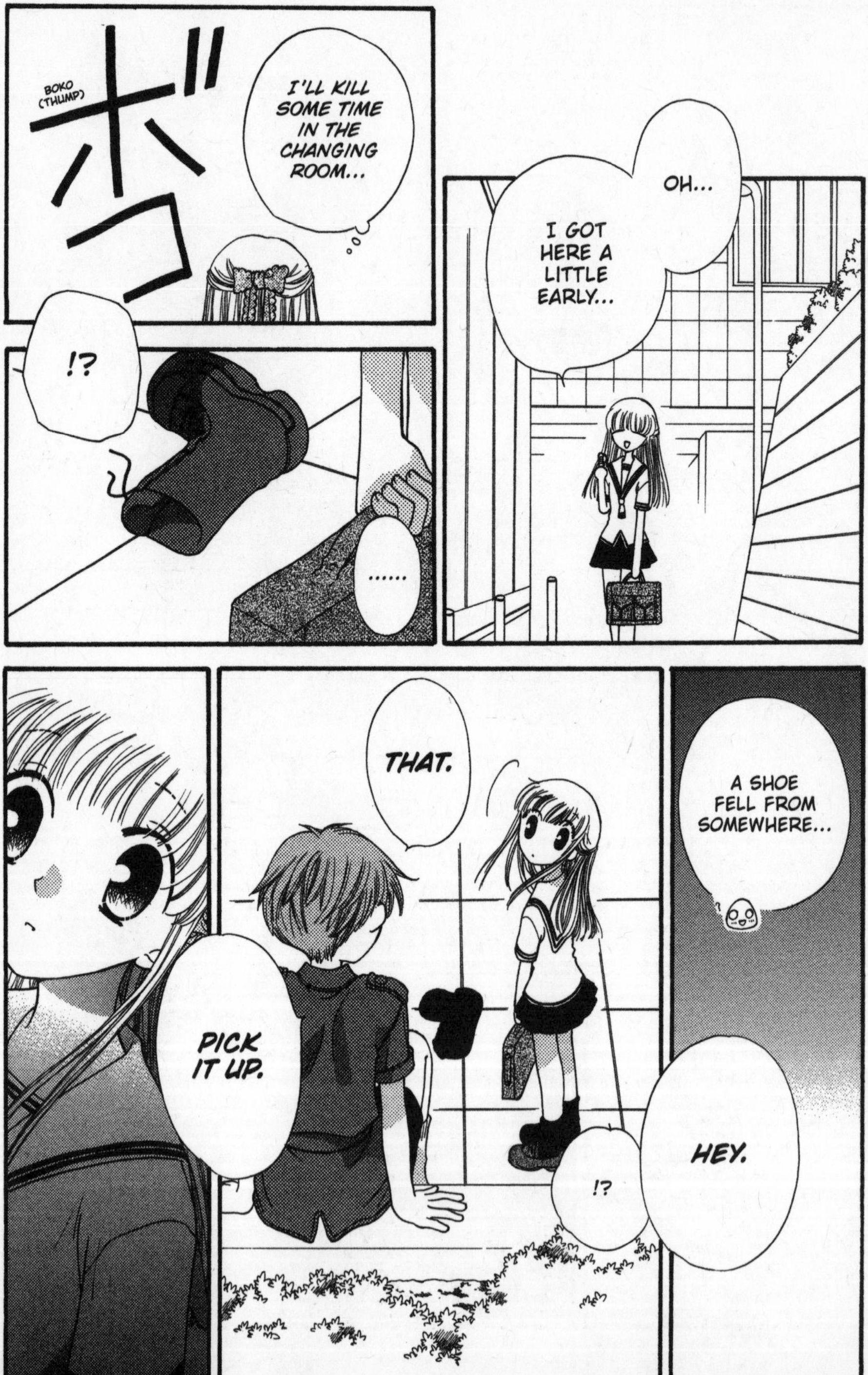

OH...
I GOT HERE A LITTLE EARLY...
I'LL KILL SOME TIME IN THE CHANGING ROOM...
BOKO (THUMP)
!?
......
A SHOE FELL FROM SOMEWHERE...
HEY.
!?
THAT.
PICK IT UP.

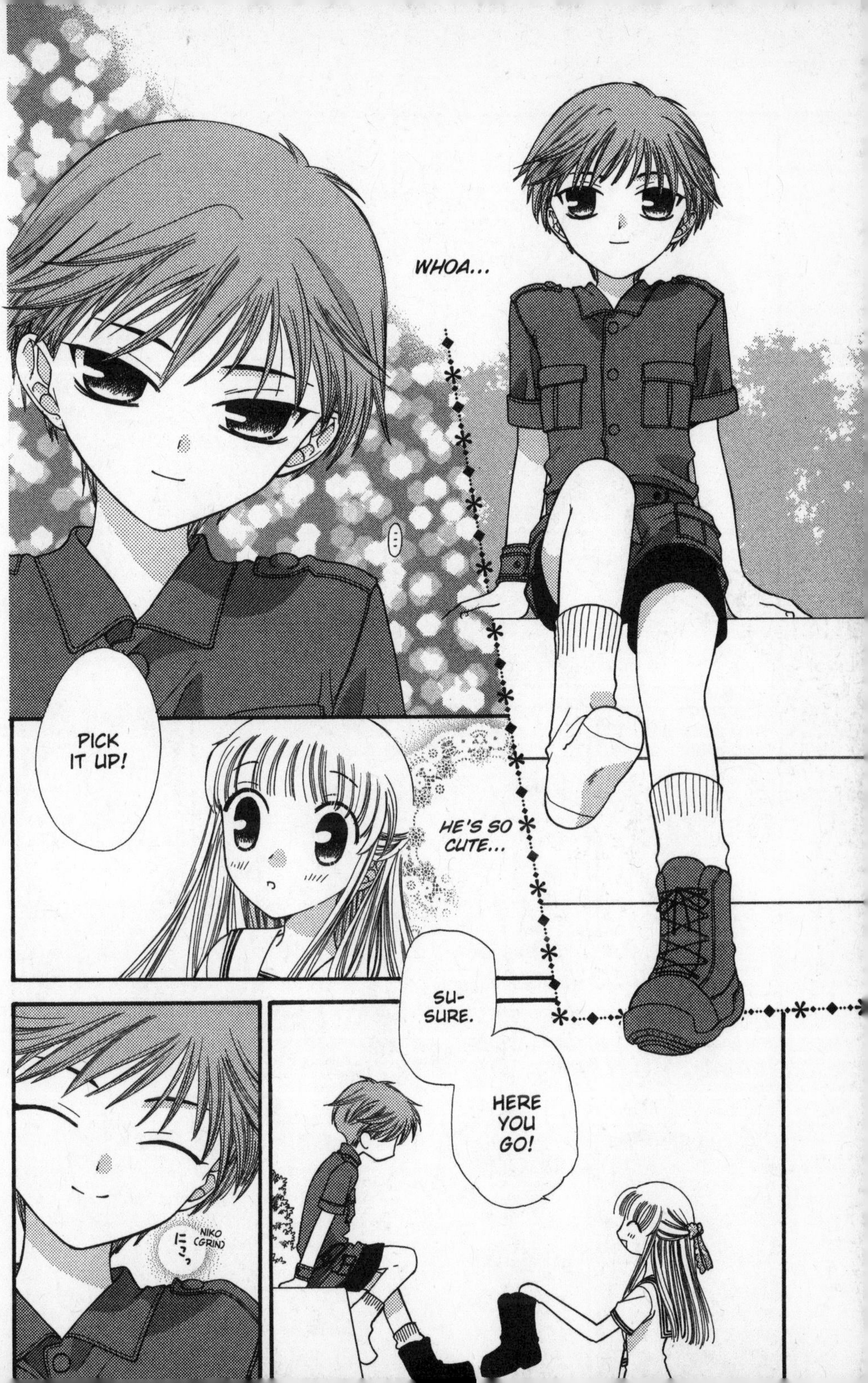
WHOA...
...
PICK IT UP!
HE'S SO CUTE...
SU-SURE.
HERE YOU GO!
にこっ
NIKO (GRIN)

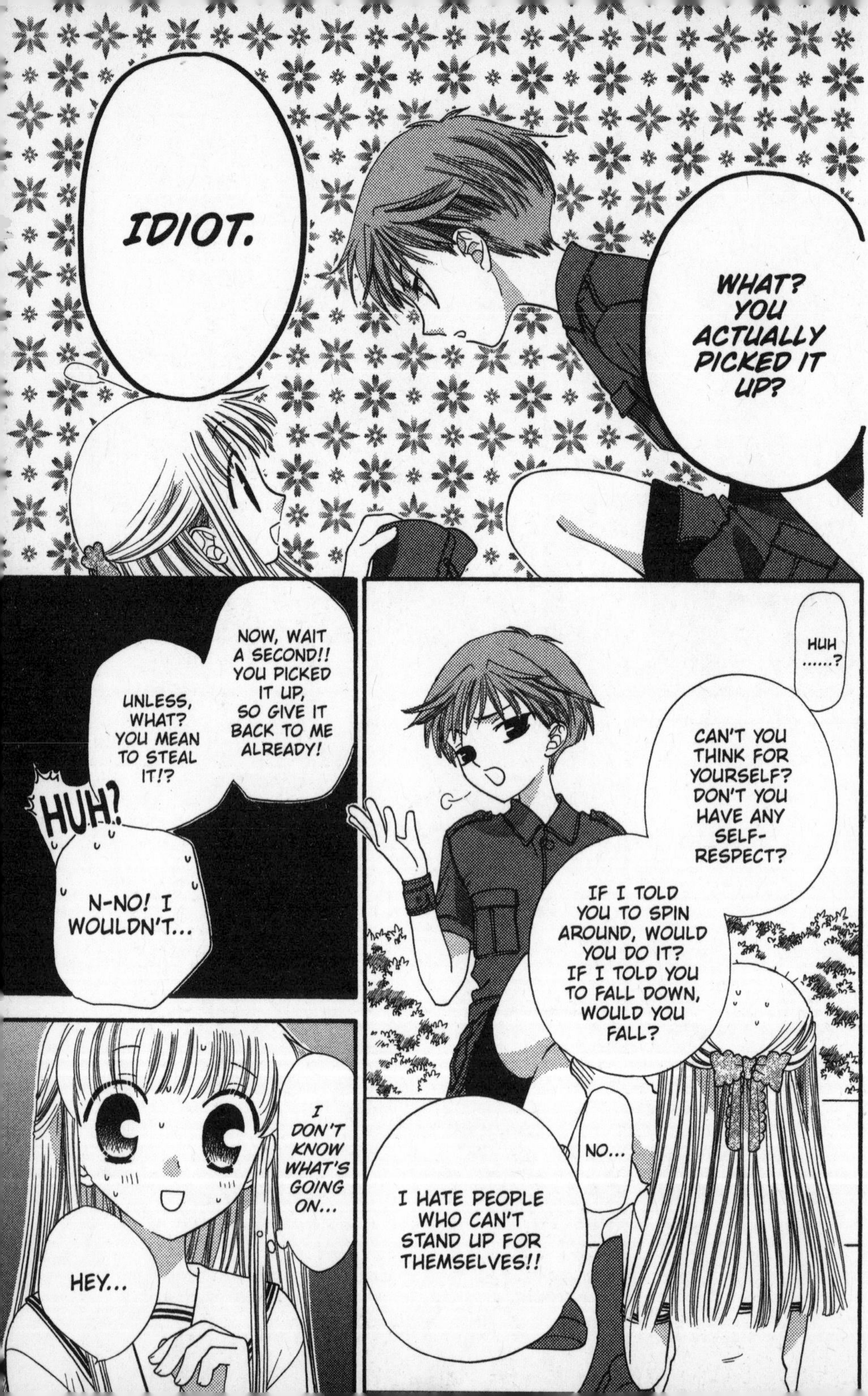
WHAT? YOU ACTUALLY PICKED IT UP?
IDIOT.
HUH ......?
CAN'T YOU THINK FOR YOURSELF? DON'T YOU HAVE ANY SELF-RESPECT?
IF I TOLD YOU TO SPIN AROUND, WOULD YOU DO IT? IF I TOLD YOU TO FALL DOWN, WOULD YOU FALL?
NO...
I HATE PEOPLE WHO CAN'T STAND UP FOR THEMSELVES!!
NOW, WAIT A SECOND!! YOU PICKED IT UP, SO GIVE IT BACK TO ME ALREADY!
UNLESS, WHAT? YOU MEAN TO STEAL IT!?
HUH?
N-NO! I WOULDN'T...
I DON'T KNOW WHAT'S GOING ON...
HEY...

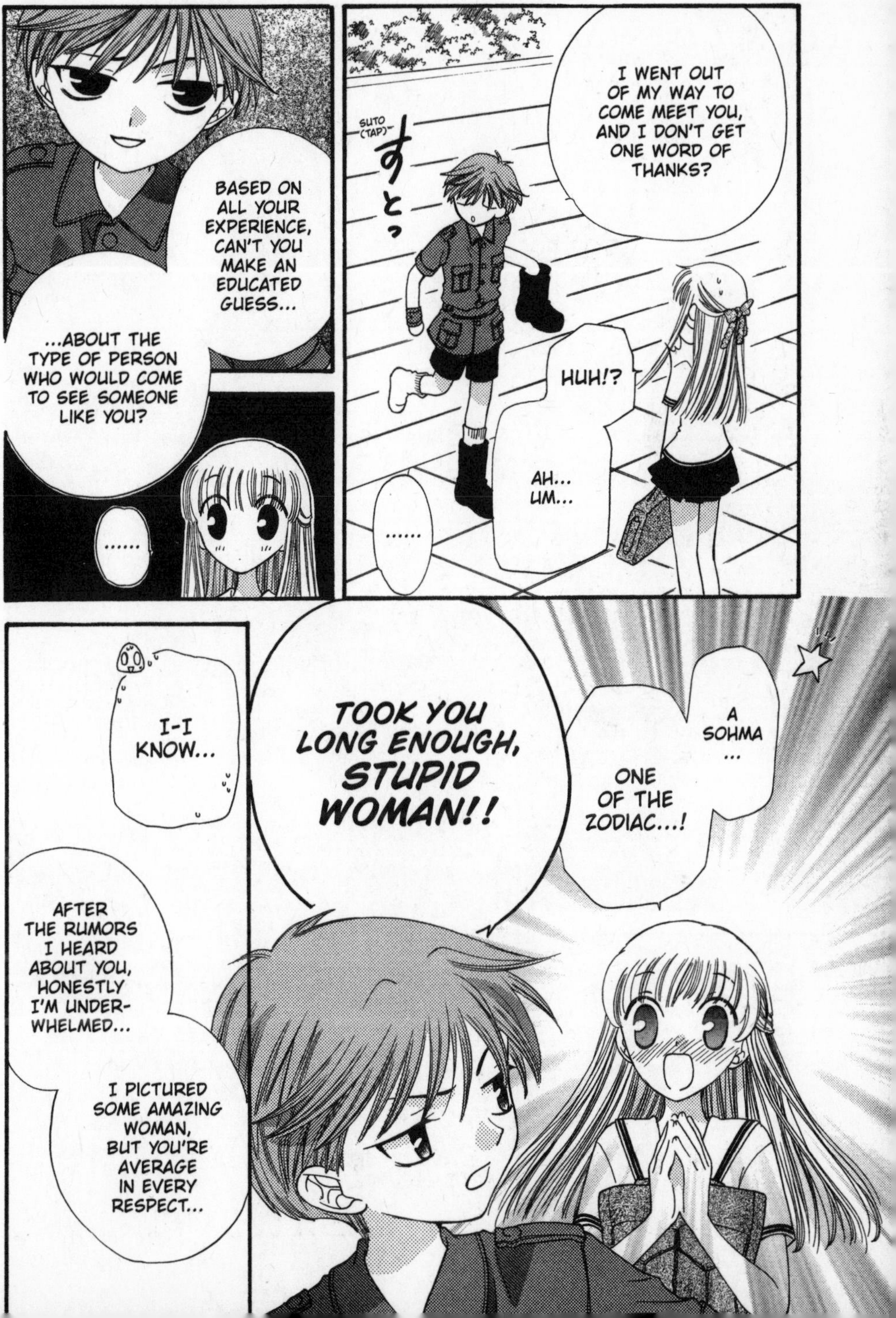
I WENT OUT OF MY WAY TO COME MEET YOU, AND I DON'T GET ONE WORD OF THANKS?
SUTO (TAP)
すとっ
HUH!?
AH... UM...
......
BASED ON ALL YOUR EXPERIENCE, CAN'T YOU MAKE AN EDUCATED GUESS...
...ABOUT THE TYPE OF PERSON WHO WOULD COME TO SEE SOMEONE LIKE YOU?
......
A SOHMA ...
ONE OF THE ZODIAC...!
TOOK YOU LONG ENOUGH, STUPID WOMAN!!
I-I KNOW...
AFTER THE RUMORS I HEARD ABOUT YOU, HONESTLY I'M UNDER-WHELMED...
I PICTURED SOME AMAZING WOMAN, BUT YOU'RE AVERAGE IN EVERY RESPECT...

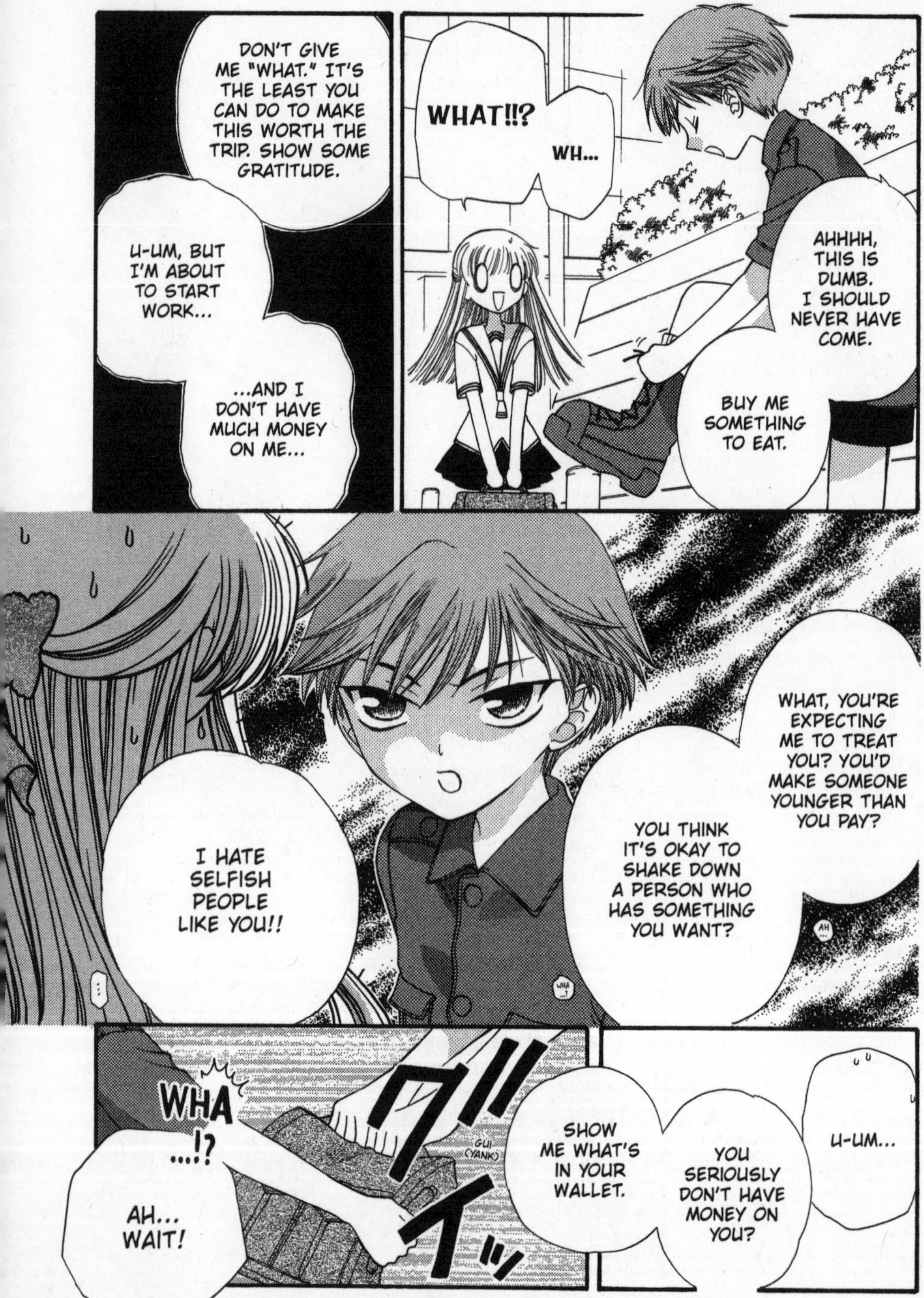
AHHHH, THIS IS DUMB. I SHOULD NEVER HAVE COME.
BUY ME SOMETHING TO EAT.
WH...
WHAT!!?
DON'T GIVE ME "WHAT." IT'S THE LEAST YOU CAN DO TO MAKE THIS WORTH THE TRIP. SHOW SOME GRATITUDE.
U-UM, BUT I'M ABOUT TO START WORK...
...AND I DON'T HAVE MUCH MONEY ON ME...
WHAT, YOU'RE EXPECTING ME TO TREAT YOU? YOU'D MAKE SOMEONE YOUNGER THAN YOU PAY?
YOU THINK IT'S OKAY TO SHAKE DOWN A PERSON WHO HAS SOMETHING YOU WANT?
AH...
WHA...?
I HATE SELFISH PEOPLE LIKE YOU!!
U-UM...
YOU SERIOUSLY DON'T HAVE MONEY ON YOU?
SHOW ME WHAT'S IN YOUR WALLET.
GUI (YANK)
WHA...!?
AH... WAIT!

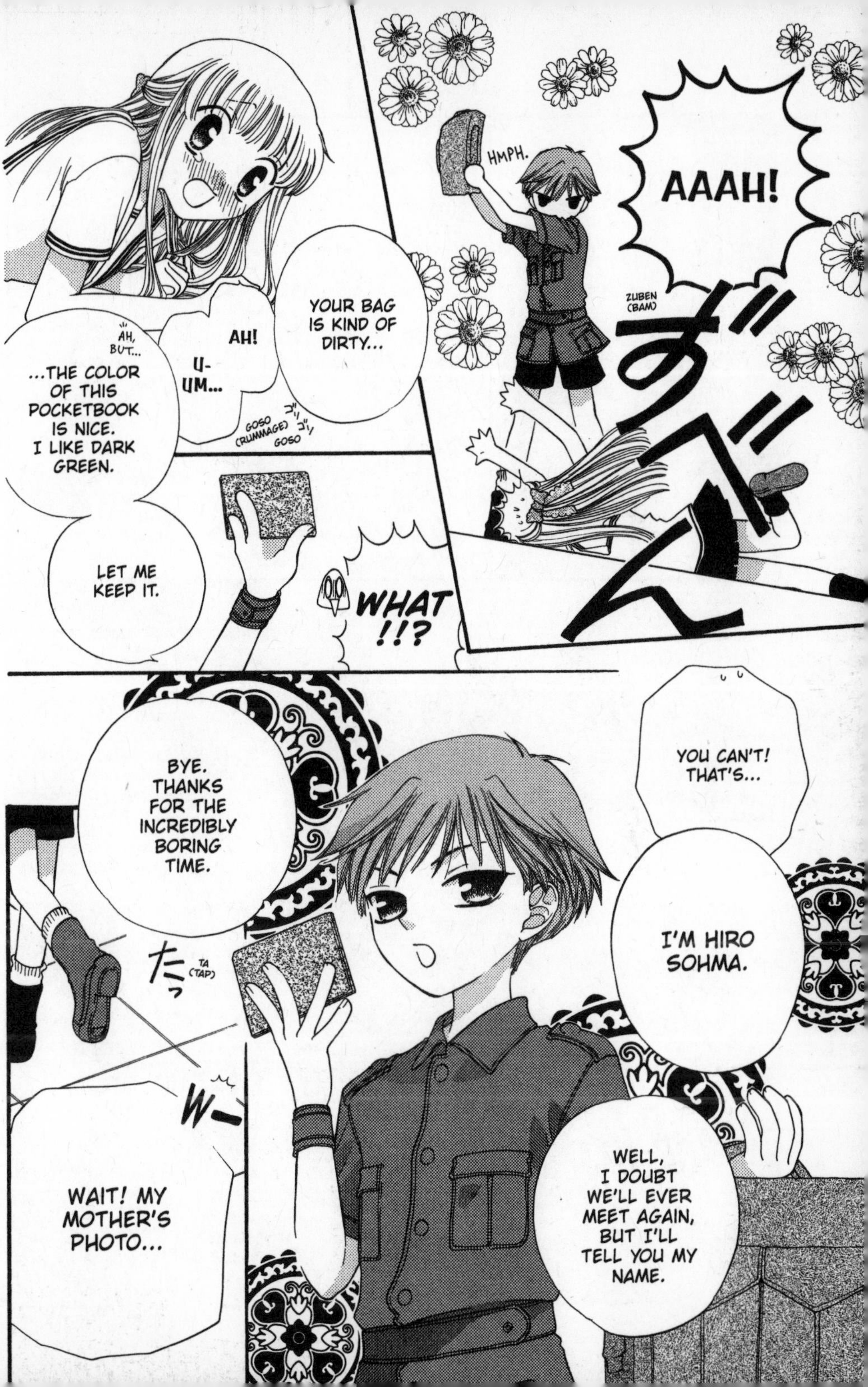

AAAH!
HMPH.
ZUBEN (BAM)
YOUR BAG IS KIND OF DIRTY...
AH!
U-UM...
GOSO (RUMMAGE) GOSO
AH, BUT...
...THE COLOR OF THIS POCKETBOOK IS NICE. I LIKE DARK GREEN.
WHAT !!?
LET ME KEEP IT.
YOU CAN'T! THAT'S...
I'M HIRO SOHMA.
WELL, I DOUBT WE'LL EVER MEET AGAIN, BUT I'LL TELL YOU MY NAME.
BYE. THANKS FOR THE INCREDIBLY BORING TIME.
TA (TAP)
W-
WAIT! MY MOTHER'S PHOTO...

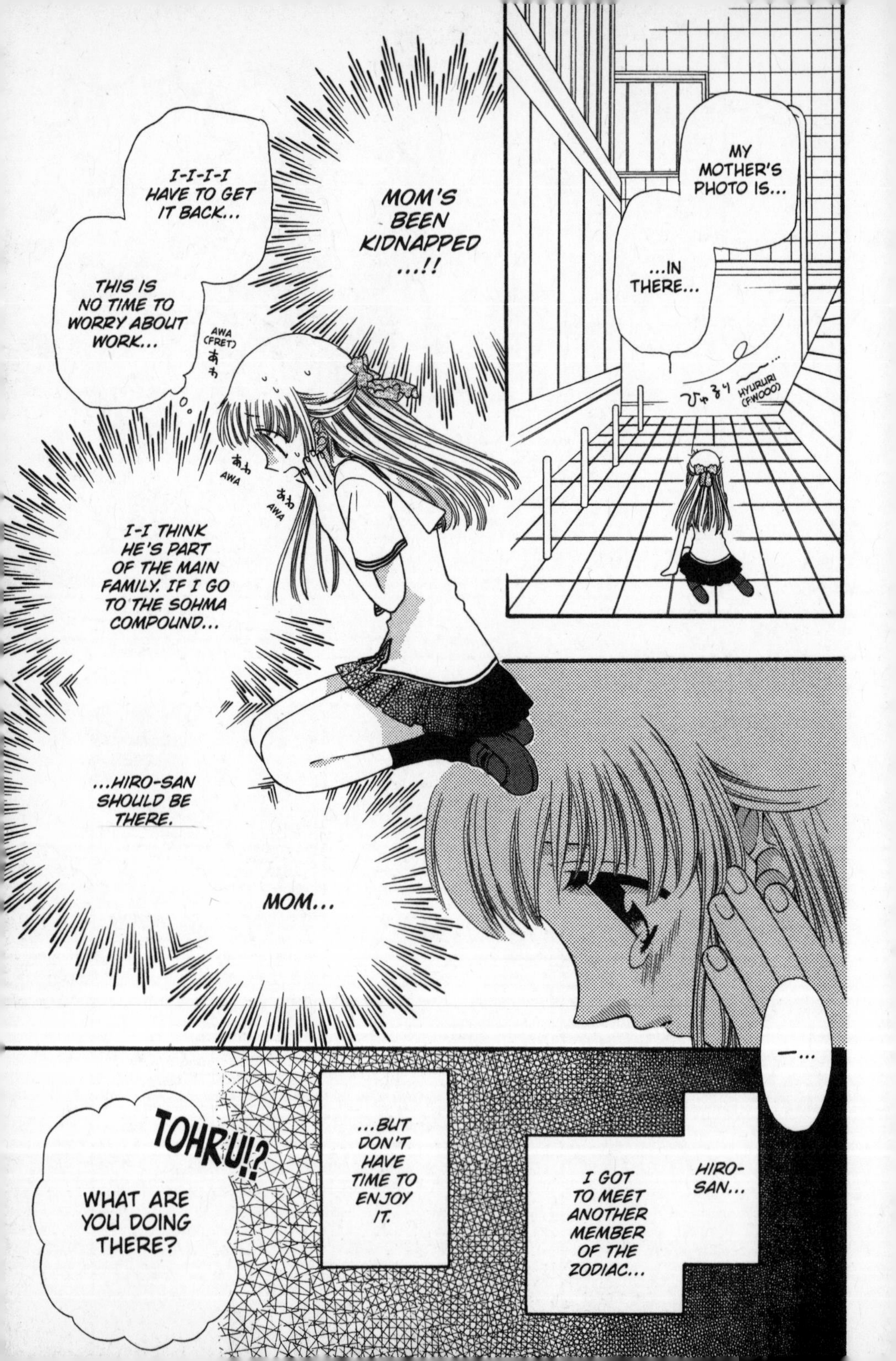
MY MOTHER'S PHOTO IS...
...IN THERE...
ぴゅるり HYURURI (FWOOO)
MOM'S BEEN KIDNAPPED ...!!
I-I-I-I HAVE TO GET IT BACK...
THIS IS NO TIME TO WORRY ABOUT WORK...
AWA (FRET) あわ
あわ AWA
あわ AWA
I-I THINK HE'S PART OF THE MAIN FAMILY. IF I GO TO THE SOHMA COMPOUND...
...HIRO-SAN SHOULD BE THERE.
MOM...
—...
HIRO-SAN...
I GOT TO MEET ANOTHER MEMBER OF THE ZODIAC...
...BUT DON'T HAVE TIME TO ENJOY IT.
TOHRU!?
WHAT ARE YOU DOING THERE?

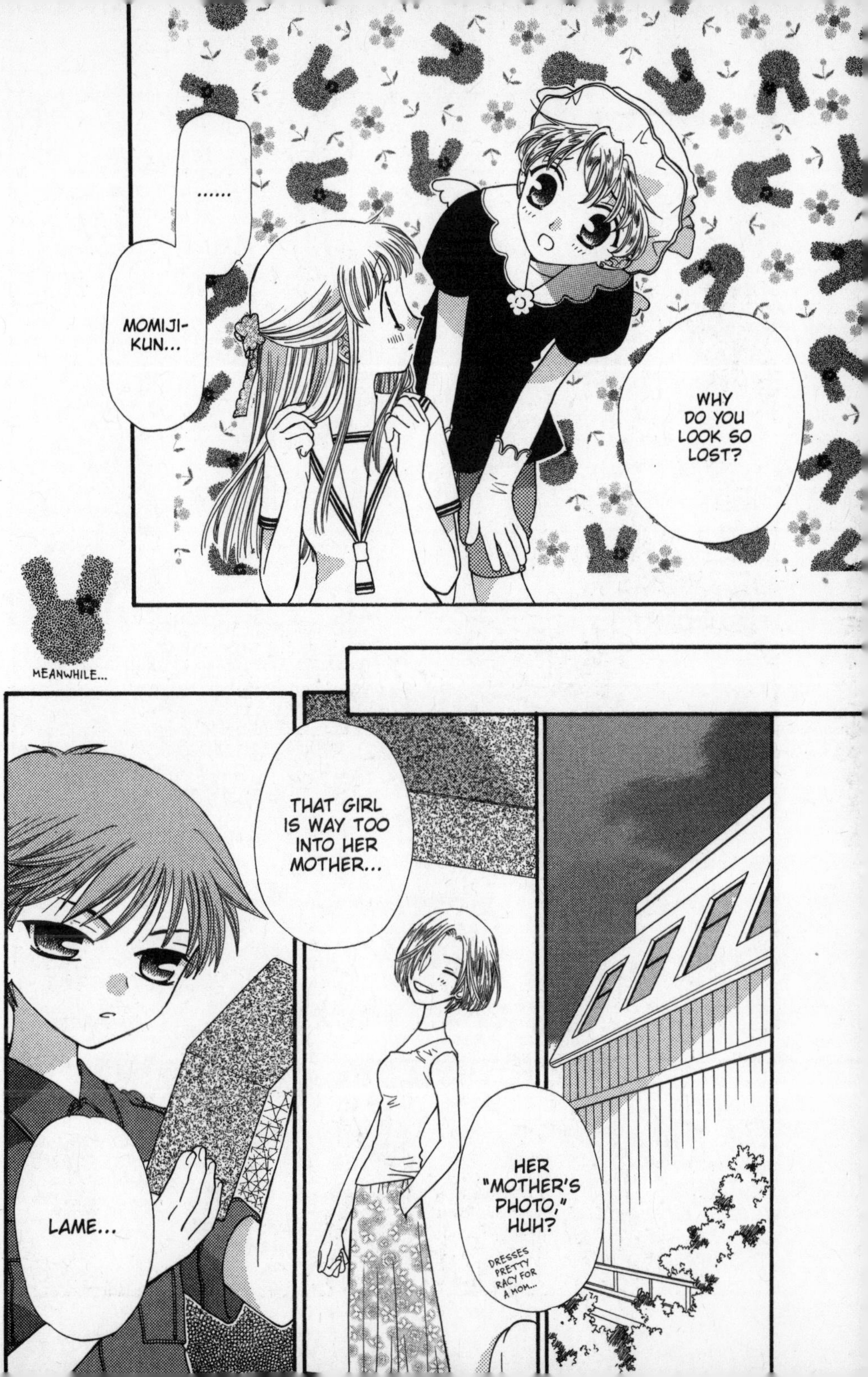
WHY DO YOU LOOK SO LOST?
......
MOMIJI-KUN...
MEANWHILE...
THAT GIRL IS WAY TOO INTO HER MOTHER...
HER "MOTHER'S PHOTO," HUH?
DRESSES PRETTY RACY FOR A MOM...
LAME...

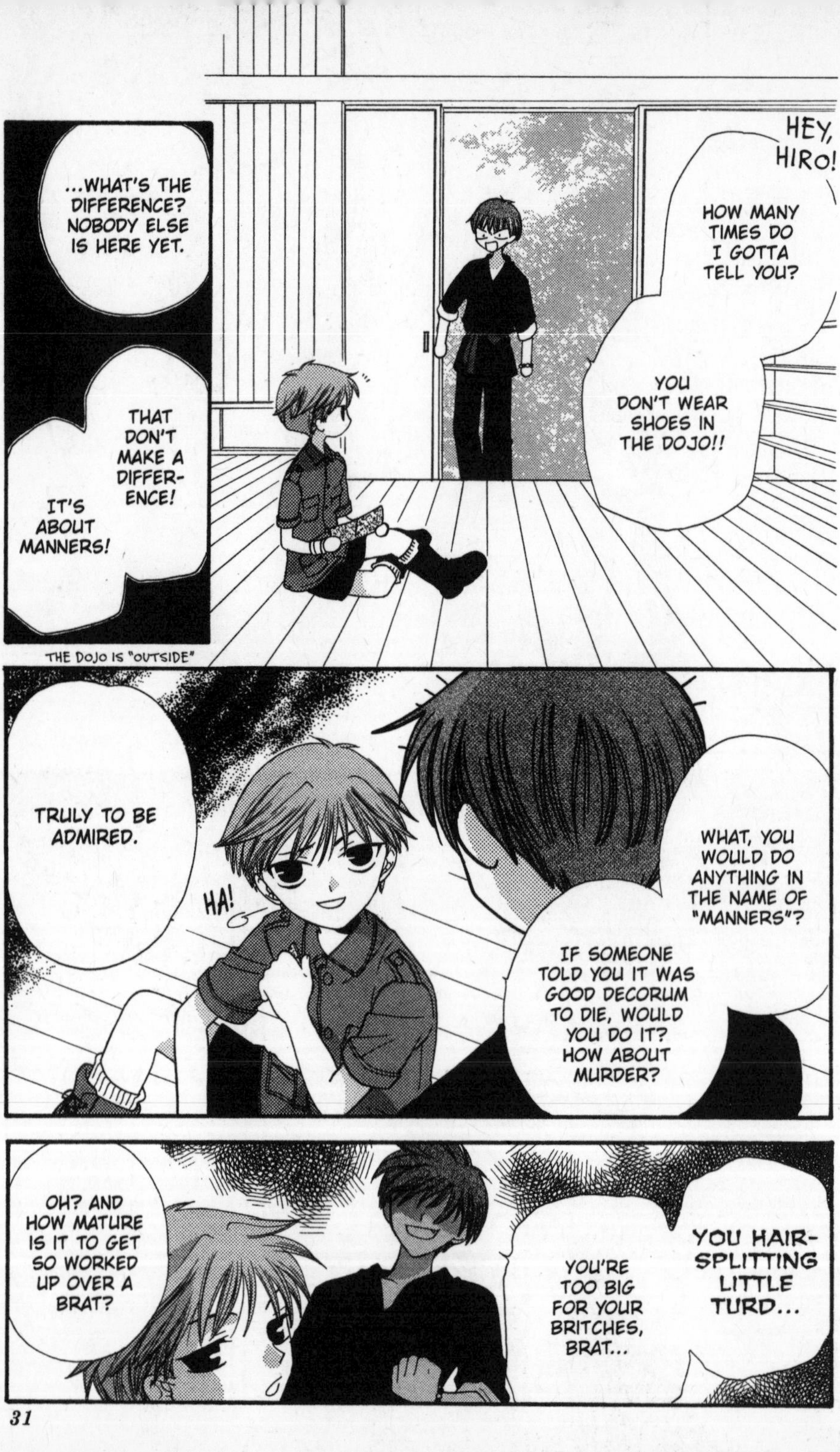
HEY, HIRO!
HOW MANY TIMES DO I GOTTA TELL YOU?
YOU DON'T WEAR SHOES IN THE DOJO!!
...WHAT'S THE DIFFERENCE? NOBODY ELSE IS HERE YET.
THAT DON'T MAKE A DIFFER-ENCE!
IT'S ABOUT MANNERS!
THE DOJO IS "OUTSIDE"
WHAT, YOU WOULD DO ANYTHING IN THE NAME OF "MANNERS"?
IF SOMEONE TOLD YOU IT WAS GOOD DECORUM TO DIE, WOULD YOU DO IT? HOW ABOUT MURDER?
HA!
TRULY TO BE ADMIRED.
YOU HAIR-SPLITTING LITTLE TURD...
YOU'RE TOO BIG FOR YOUR BRITCHES, BRAT...
OH? AND HOW MATURE IS IT TO GET SO WORKED UP OVER A BRAT?

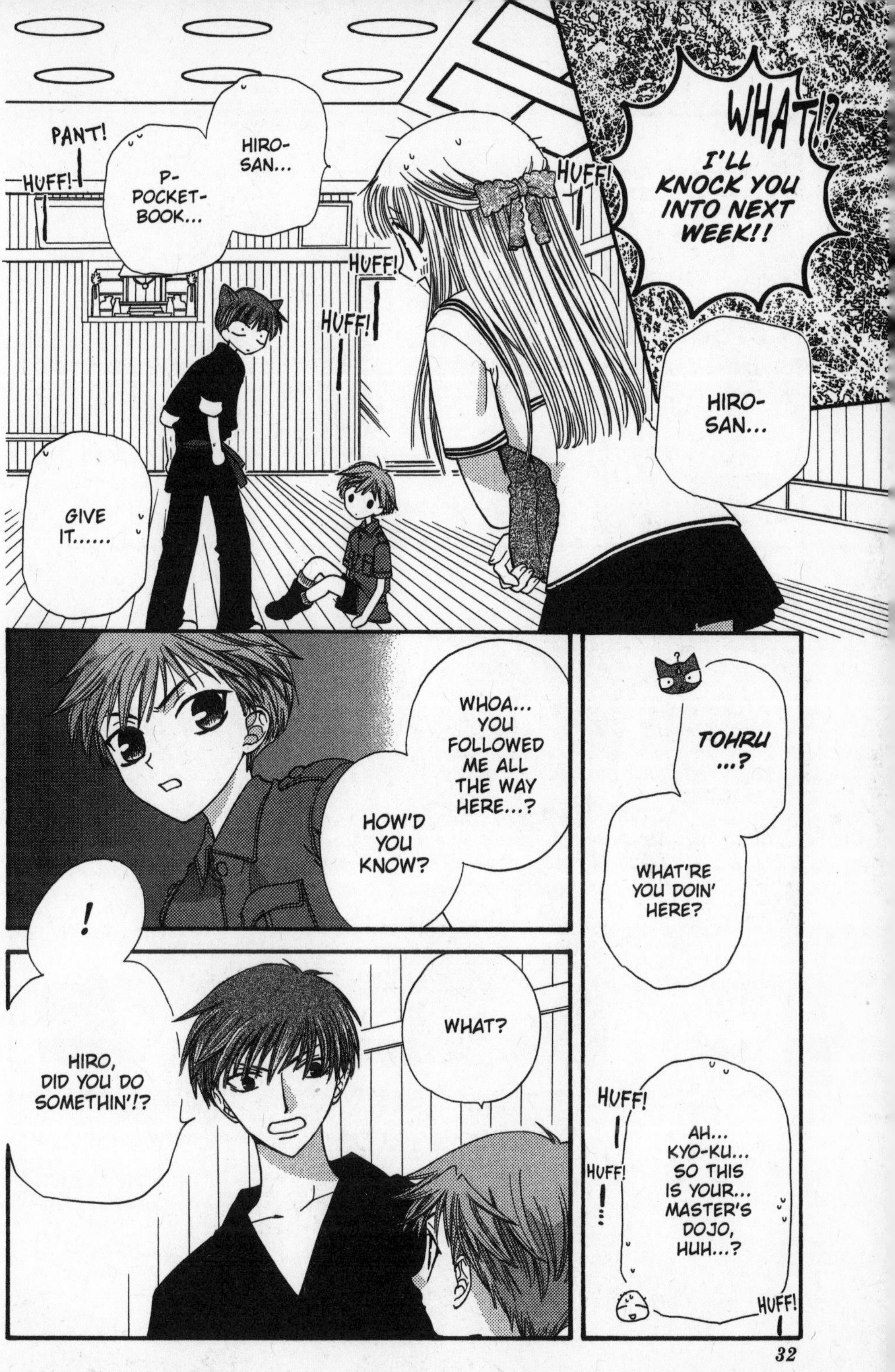
WHAT!?
I'LL KNOCK YOU INTO NEXT WEEK!!
HIRO-SAN...
HUFF!
HUFF!
HUFF!
HUFF!
HIRO-SAN...
P-POCKET-BOOK...
PANT!
HUFF!
GIVE IT......
TOHRU ...?
WHAT'RE YOU DOIN' HERE?
HUFF!
HUFF!
AH... KYO-KU... SO THIS IS YOUR... MASTER'S DOJO, HUH...?
HUFF!
WHOA... YOU FOLLOWED ME ALL THE WAY HERE...?
HOW'D YOU KNOW?
!
WHAT?
HIRO, DID YOU DO SOMETHIN'!?

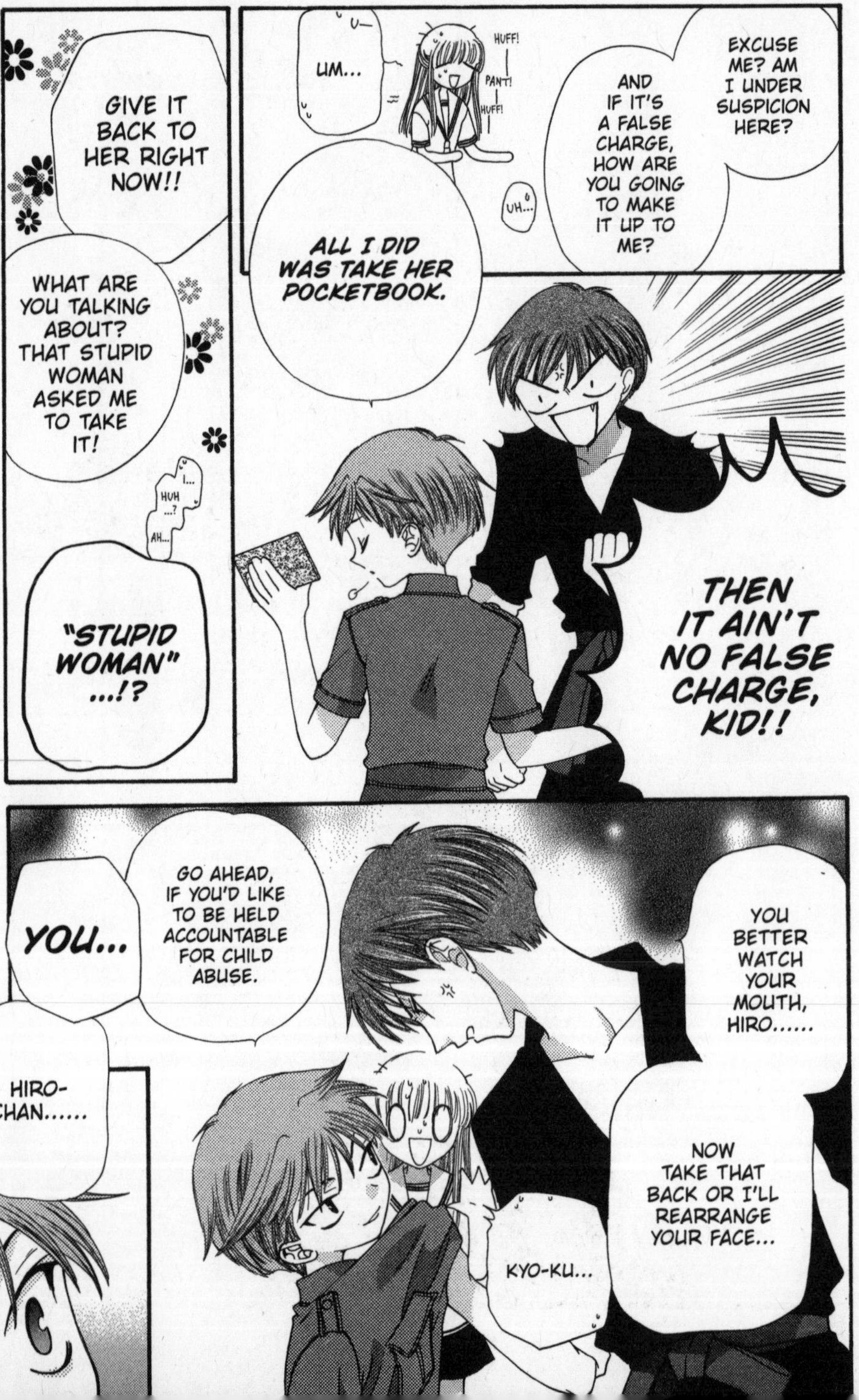
EXCUSE ME? AM I UNDER SUSPICION HERE?
AND IF IT'S A FALSE CHARGE, HOW ARE YOU GOING TO MAKE IT UP TO ME?
UH...
HUFF! PANT! HUFF!
UM...
THEN IT AIN'T NO FALSE CHARGE, KID!!
ALL I DID WAS TAKE HER POCKETBOOK.
GIVE IT BACK TO HER RIGHT NOW!!
WHAT ARE YOU TALKING ABOUT? THAT STUPID WOMAN ASKED ME TO TAKE IT!
I... HUH...? AH...
"STUPID WOMAN"...!?
YOU BETTER WATCH YOUR MOUTH, HIRO......
NOW TAKE THAT BACK OR I'LL REARRANGE YOUR FACE...
GO AHEAD, IF YOU'D LIKE TO BE HELD ACCOUNTABLE FOR CHILD ABUSE.
YOU...
KYO-KU...
HIRO-CHAN......

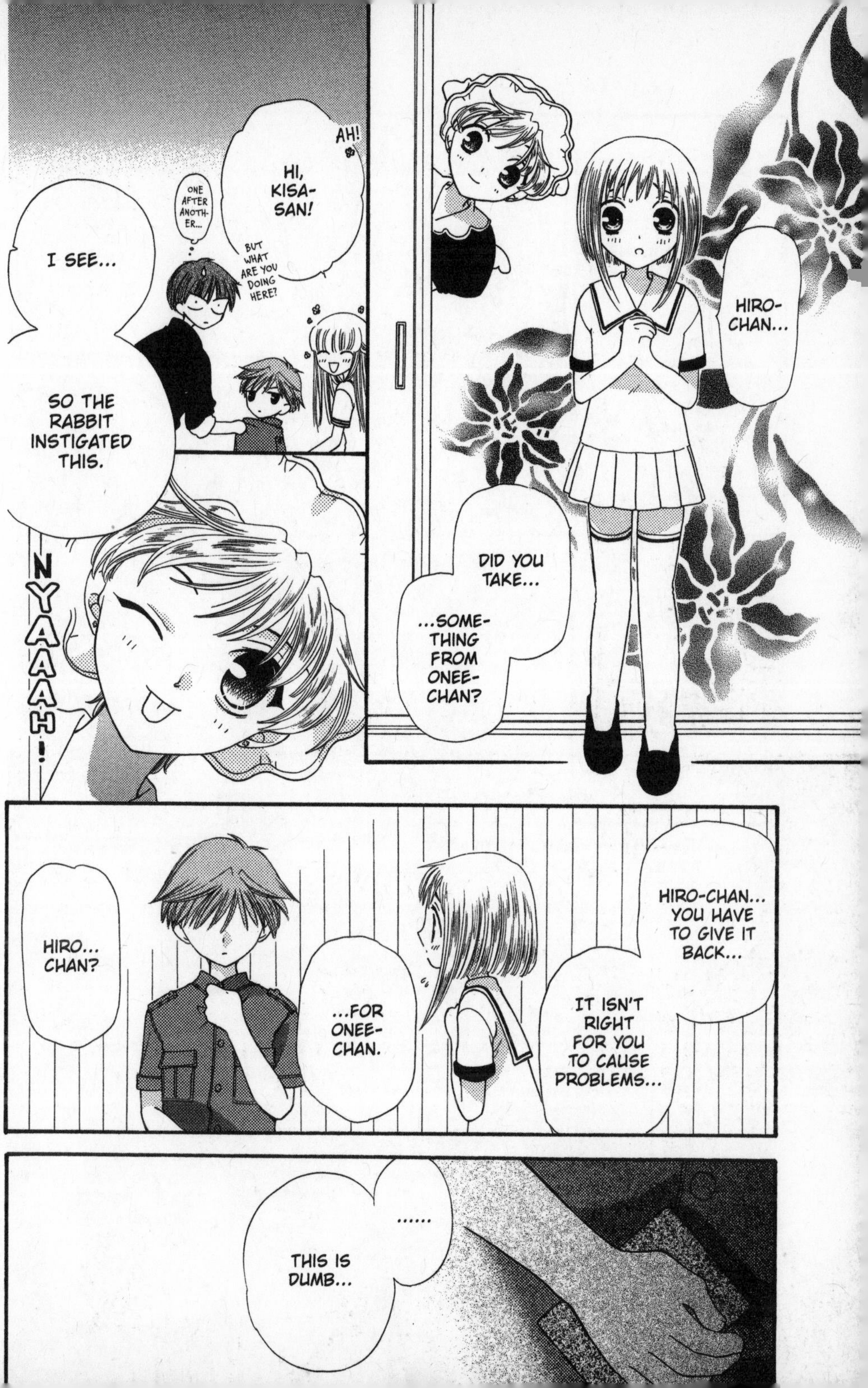

HIRO-CHAN...
DID YOU TAKE...
...SOMETHING FROM ONEE-CHAN?
AH!
HI, KISA-SAN!
BUT WHAT ARE YOU DOING HERE?
ONE AFTER ANOTHER...
I SEE...
SO THE RABBIT INSTIGATED THIS.
NYAAAAH!
HIRO-CHAN... YOU HAVE TO GIVE IT BACK...
IT ISN'T RIGHT FOR YOU TO CAUSE PROBLEMS...
...FOR ONEE-CHAN.
HIRO... CHAN?
......
THIS IS DUMB...

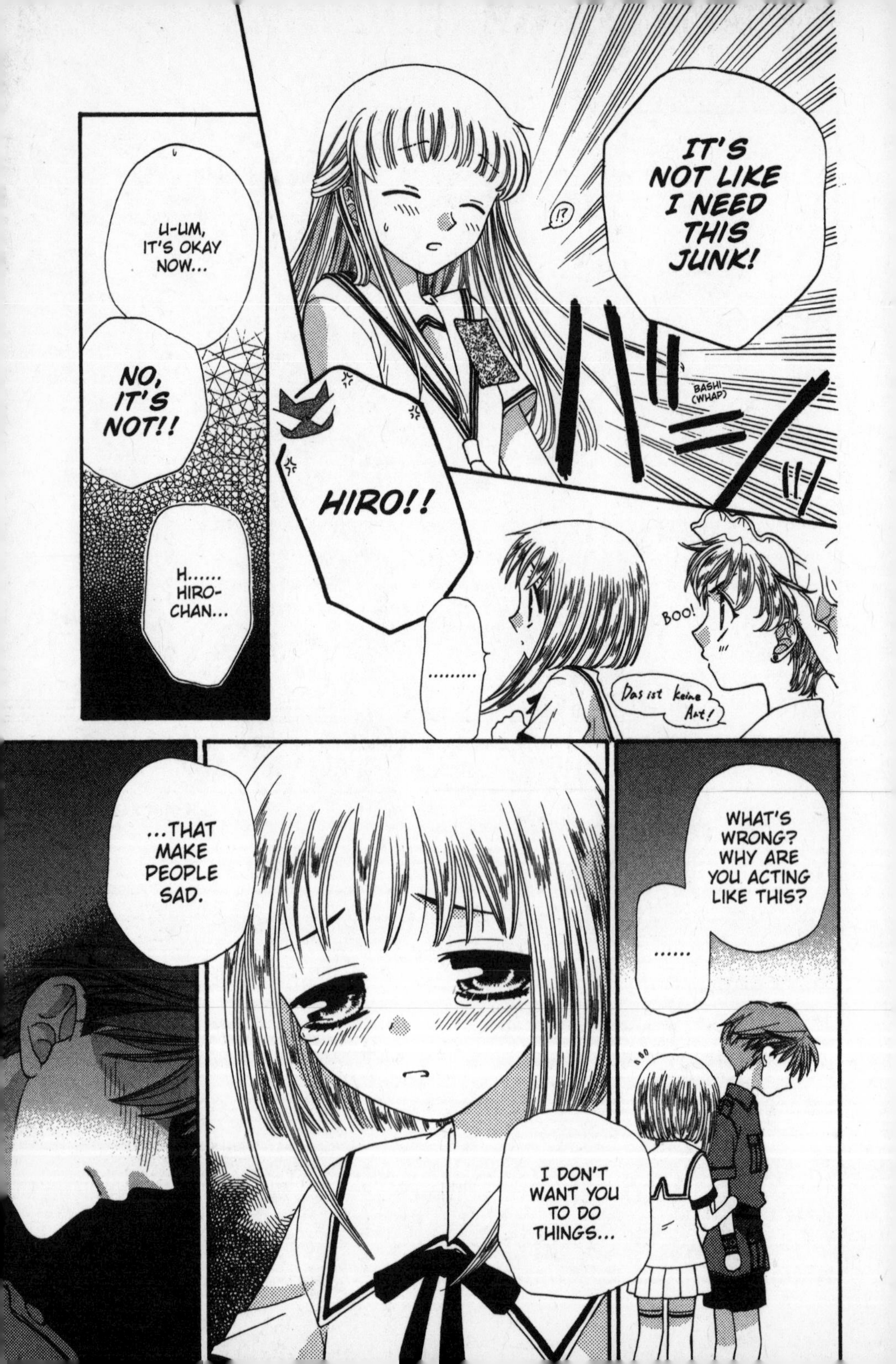
IT'S NOT LIKE I NEED THIS JUNK!
!?
BASHI (WHAP)
HIRO!!
....
BOO!
Das ist keine Art!
U-UM, IT'S OKAY NOW...
NO, IT'S NOT!!
H...... HIRO-CHAN...
WHAT'S WRONG? WHY ARE YOU ACTING LIKE THIS?
......
I DON'T WANT YOU TO DO THINGS...
...THAT MAKE PEOPLE SAD.

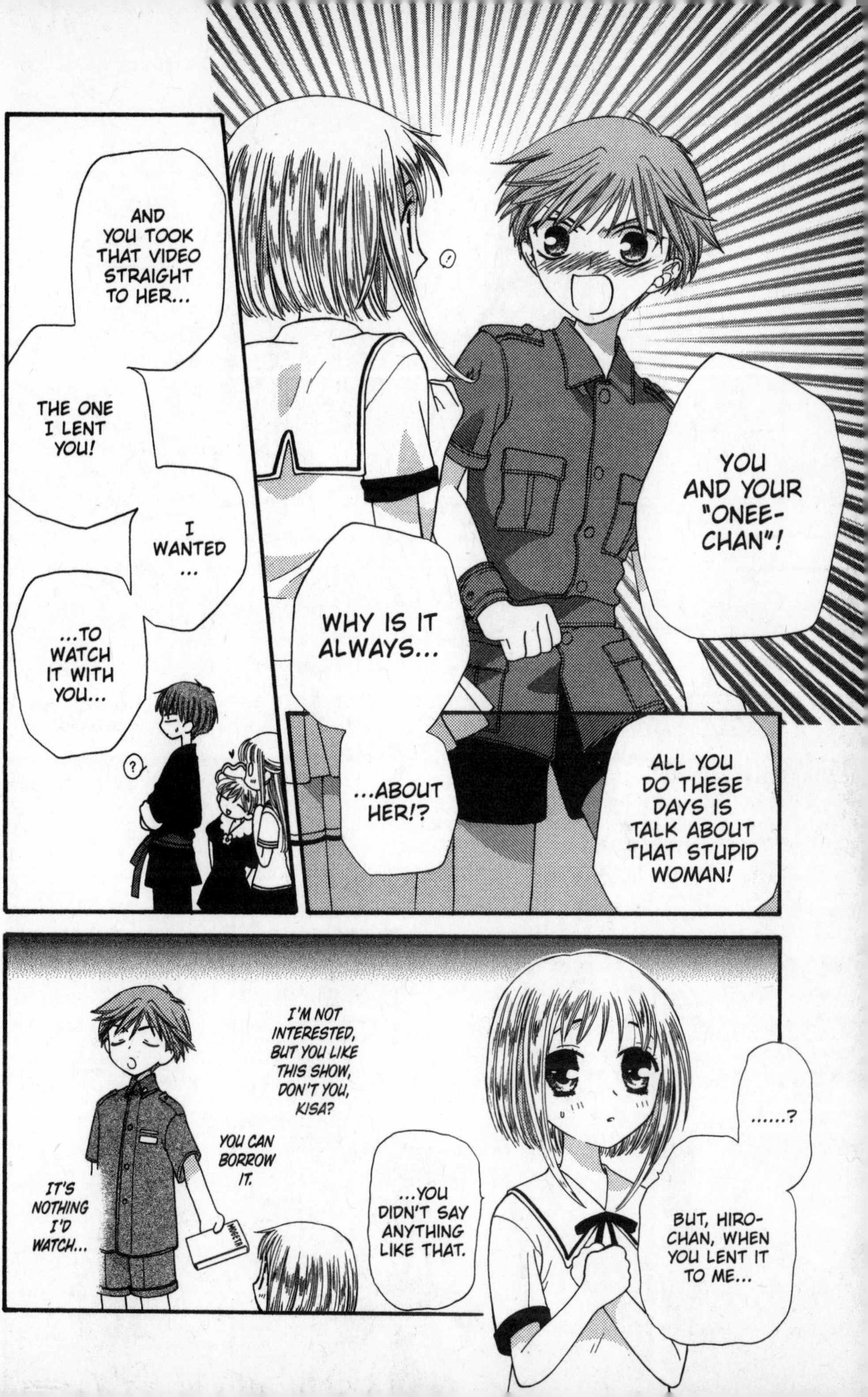
YOU AND YOUR "ONEE-CHAN"!
ALL YOU DO THESE DAYS IS TALK ABOUT THAT STUPID WOMAN!
WHY IS IT ALWAYS...
...ABOUT HER!?
!
AND YOU TOOK THAT VIDEO STRAIGHT TO HER...
THE ONE I LENT YOU!
I WANTED ...
...TO WATCH IT WITH YOU...
?
......?
BUT, HIRO-CHAN, WHEN YOU LENT IT TO ME...
...YOU DIDN'T SAY ANYTHING LIKE THAT.
I'M NOT INTERESTED, BUT YOU LIKE THIS SHOW, DON'T YOU, KISA?
YOU CAN BORROW IT.
IT'S NOTHING I'D WATCH...

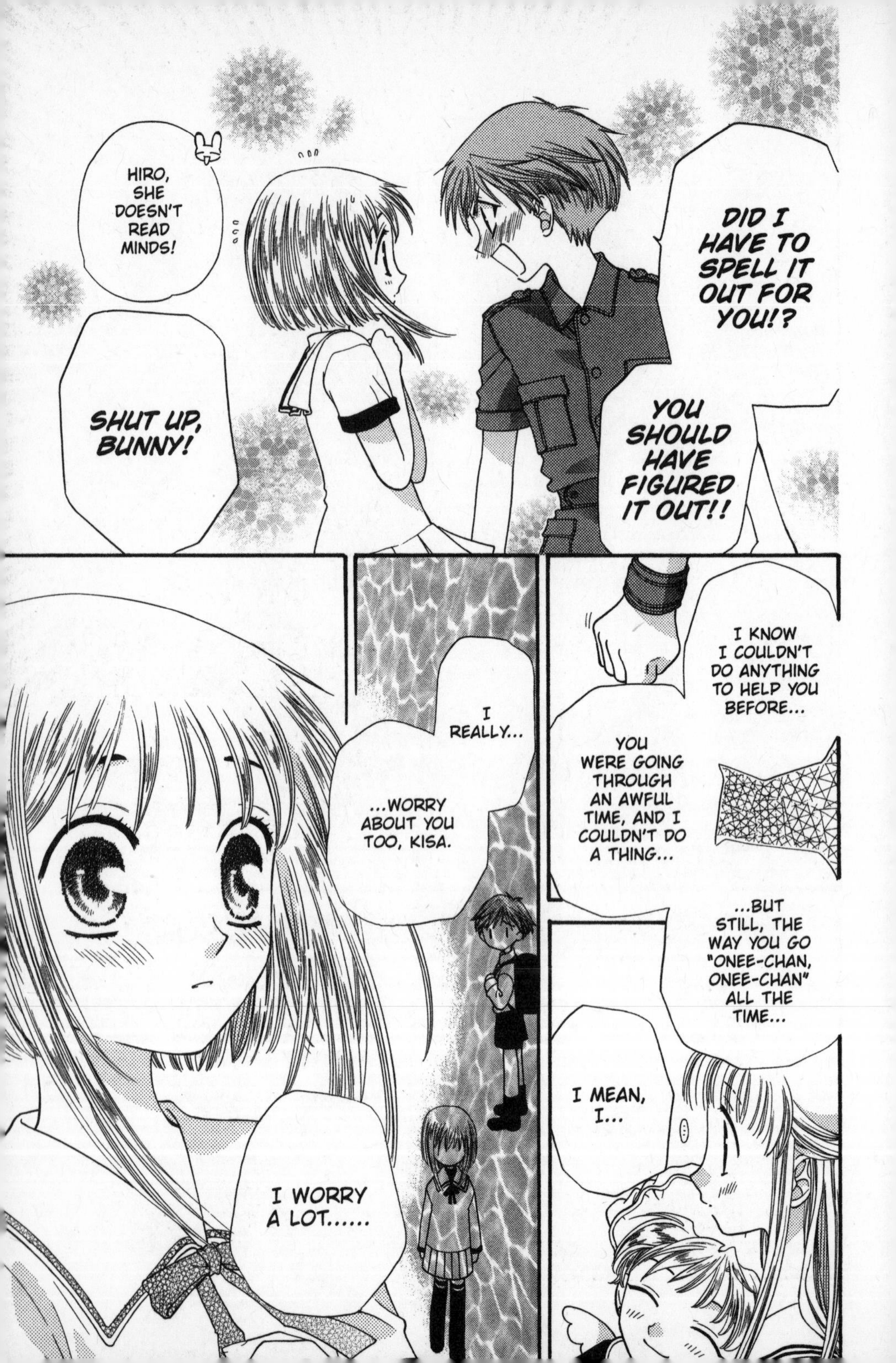
DID I HAVE TO SPELL IT OUT FOR YOU!?
YOU SHOULD HAVE FIGURED IT OUT!!
HIRO, SHE DOESN'T READ MINDS!
SHUT UP, BUNNY!
I KNOW I COULDN'T DO ANYTHING TO HELP YOU BEFORE...
YOU WERE GOING THROUGH AN AWFUL TIME, AND I COULDN'T DO A THING...
...BUT STILL, THE WAY YOU GO "ONEE-CHAN, ONEE-CHAN" ALL THE TIME...
I MEAN, I...
I REALLY...
...WORRY ABOUT YOU TOO, KISA.
I WORRY A LOT......

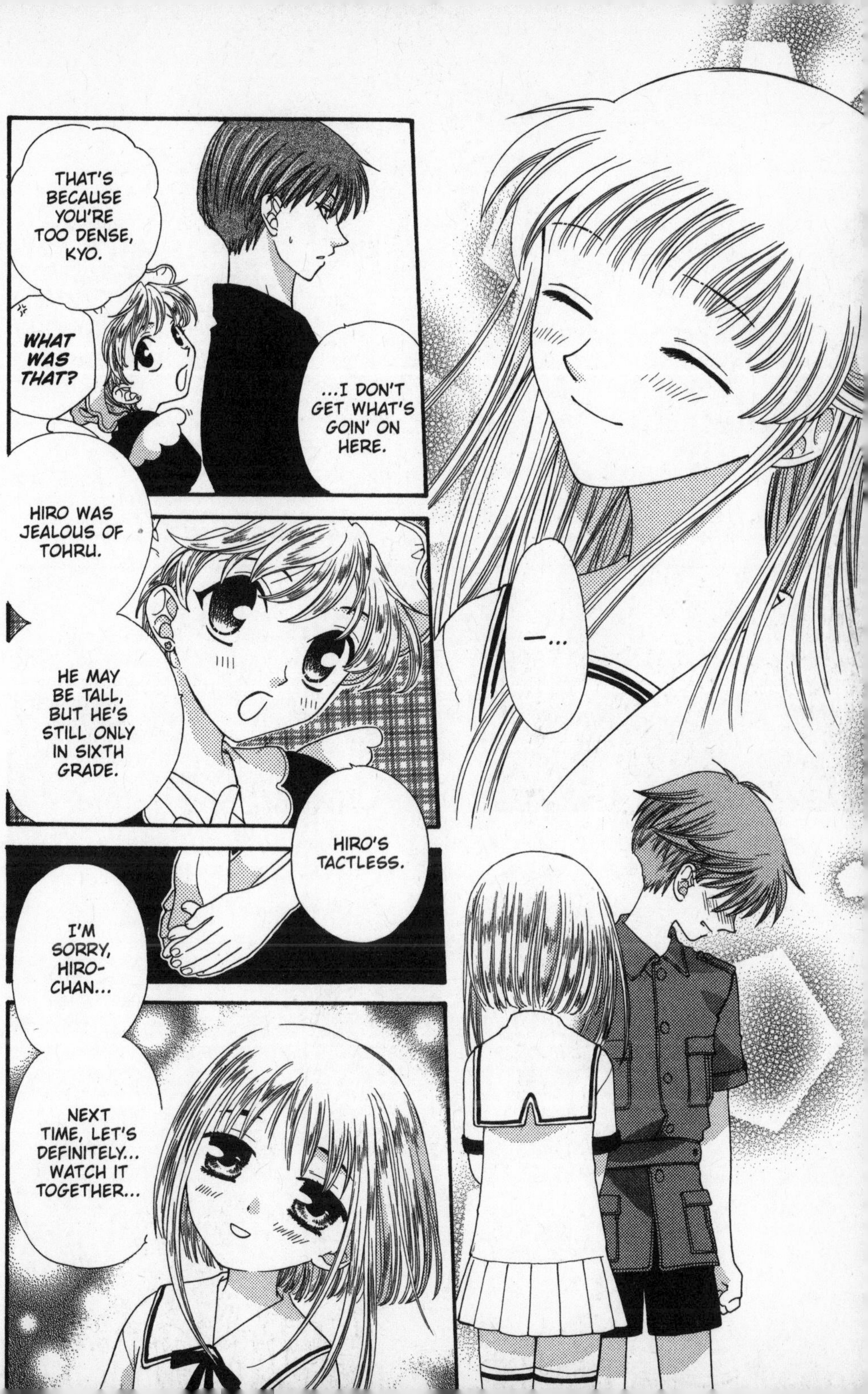
—...
...I DON'T GET WHAT'S GOIN' ON HERE.
THAT'S BECAUSE YOU'RE TOO DENSE, KYO.
WHAT WAS THAT?
HIRO WAS JEALOUS OF TOHRU.
HE MAY BE TALL, BUT HE'S STILL ONLY IN SIXTH GRADE.
HIRO'S TACTLESS.
I'M SORRY, HIRO-CHAN...
NEXT TIME, LET'S DEFINITELY... WATCH IT TOGETHER...

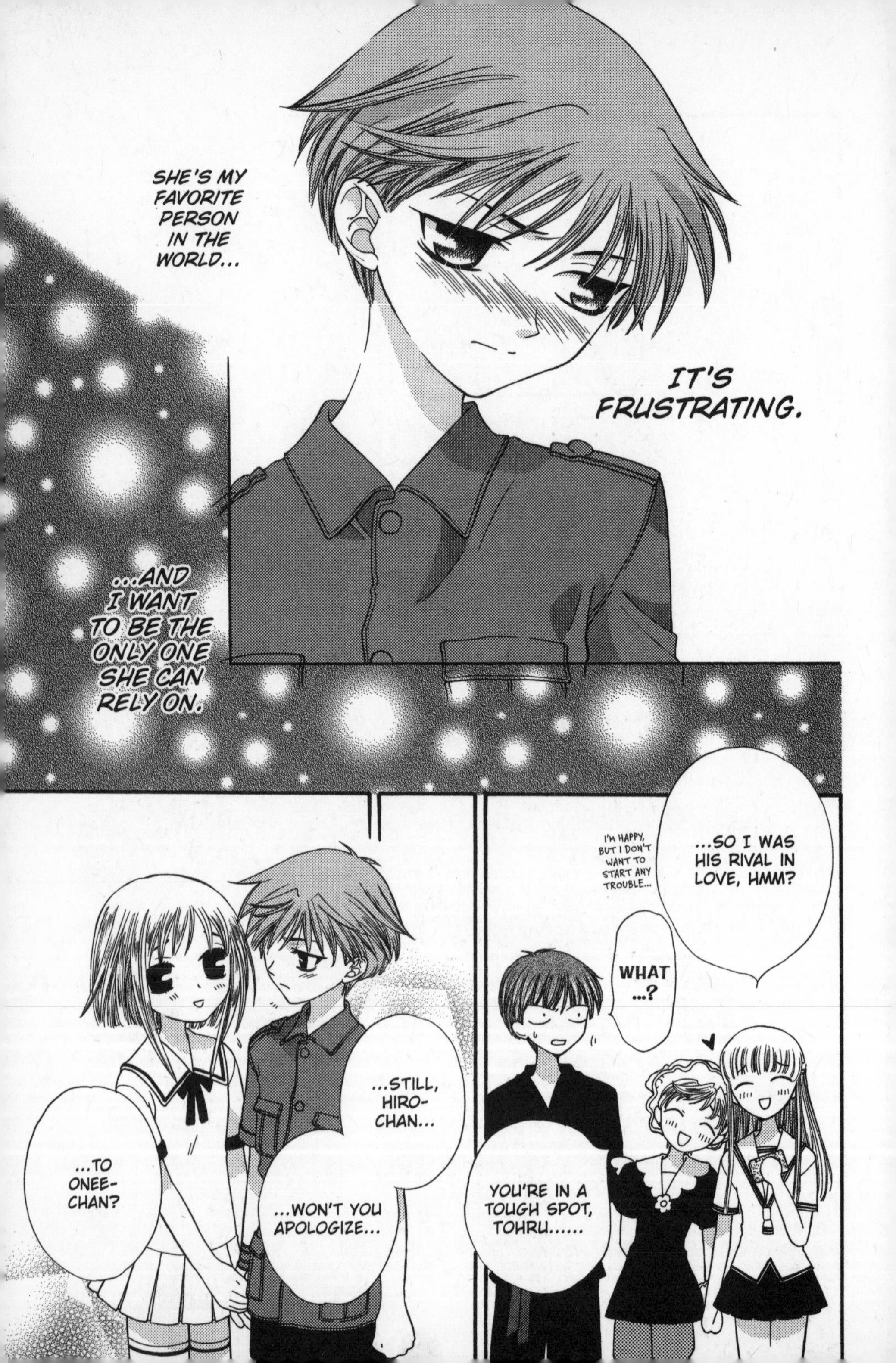
SHE'S MY FAVORITE PERSON IN THE WORLD...
IT'S FRUSTRATING.
...AND I WANT TO BE THE ONLY ONE SHE CAN RELY ON.
...SO I WAS HIS RIVAL IN LOVE, HMM?
I'M HAPPY, BUT I DON'T WANT TO START ANY TROUBLE...
WHAT ...?
YOU'RE IN A TOUGH SPOT, TOHRU......
...STILL, HIRO-CHAN...
...WON'T YOU APOLOGIZE...
...TO ONEE-CHAN?

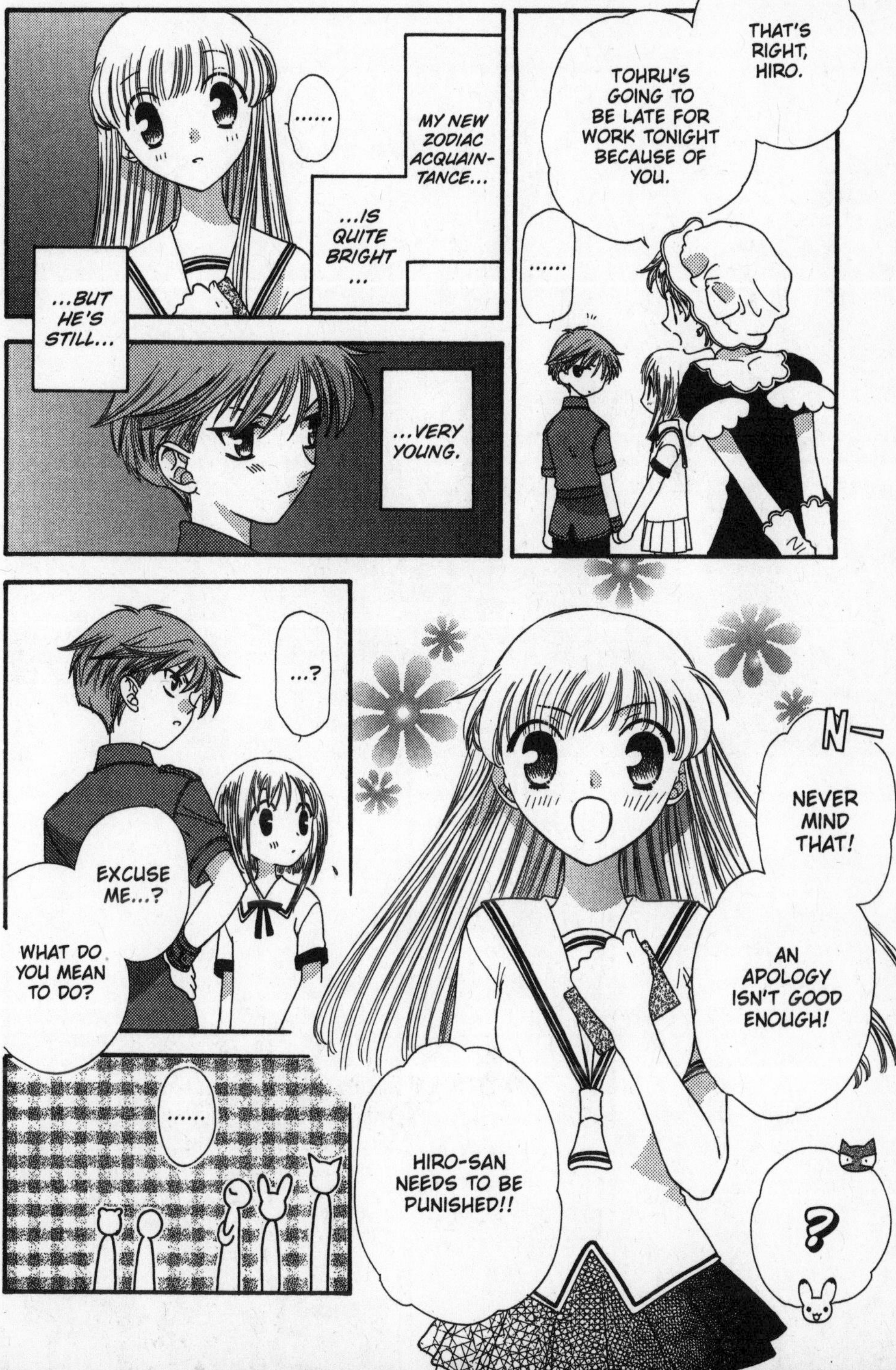
THAT'S RIGHT, HIRO.
TOHRU'S GOING TO BE LATE FOR WORK TONIGHT BECAUSE OF YOU.
......
......
MY NEW ZODIAC ACQUAINTANCE...
...IS QUITE BRIGHT ...
...BUT HE'S STILL...
...VERY YOUNG.
N—
NEVER MIND THAT!
AN APOLOGY ISN'T GOOD ENOUGH!
HIRO-SAN NEEDS TO BE PUNISHED!!
?
...?
EXCUSE ME...?
WHAT DO YOU MEAN TO DO?
......

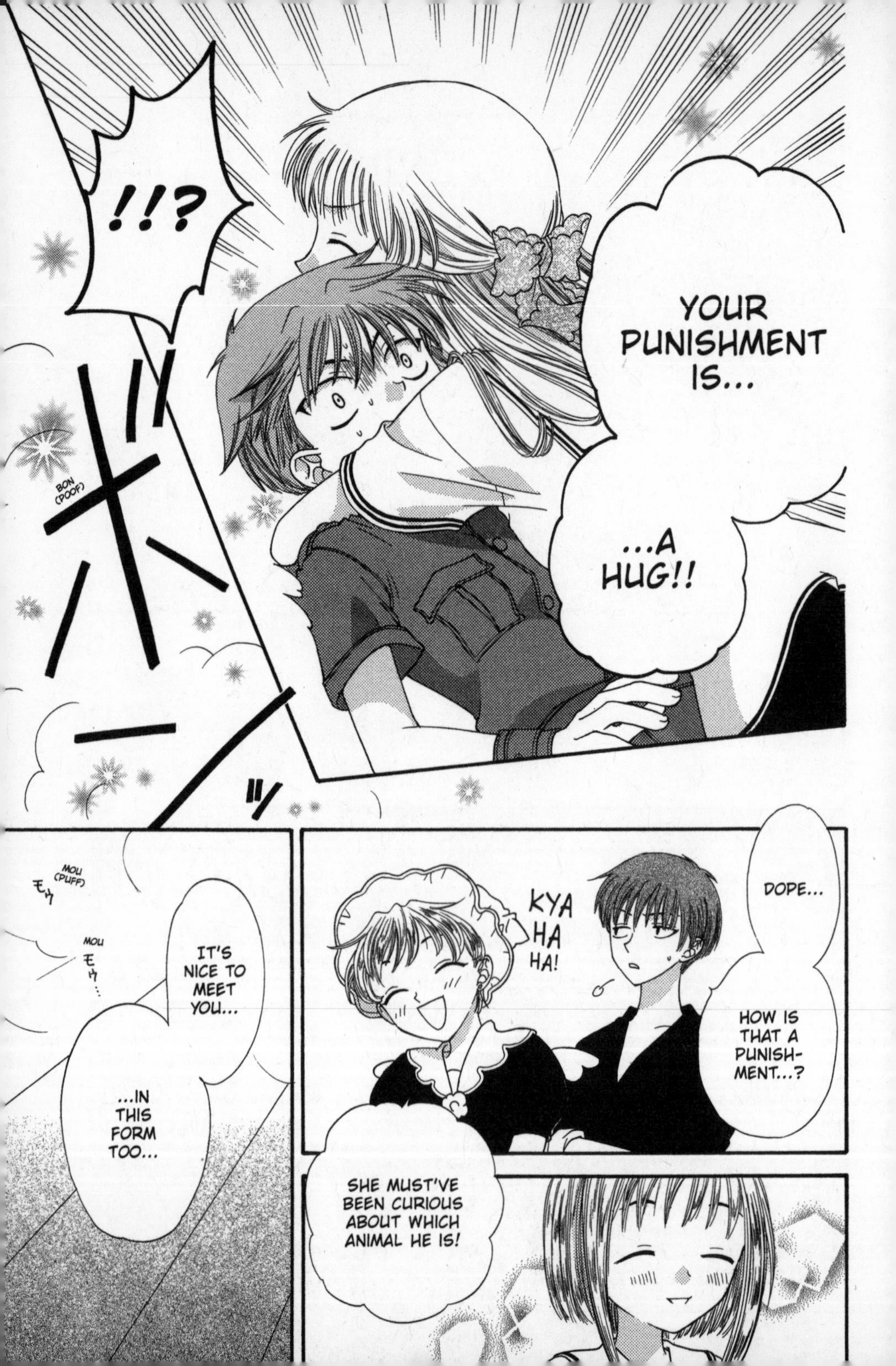
YOUR PUNISHMENT IS...
...A HUG!!
!!?
BON (POOF)
DOPE...
KYA HA HA!
HOW IS THAT A PUNISH-MENT...?
SHE MUST'VE BEEN CURIOUS ABOUT WHICH ANIMAL HE IS!
MOU (PUFF)
MOU
IT'S NICE TO MEET YOU...
...IN THIS FORM TOO...

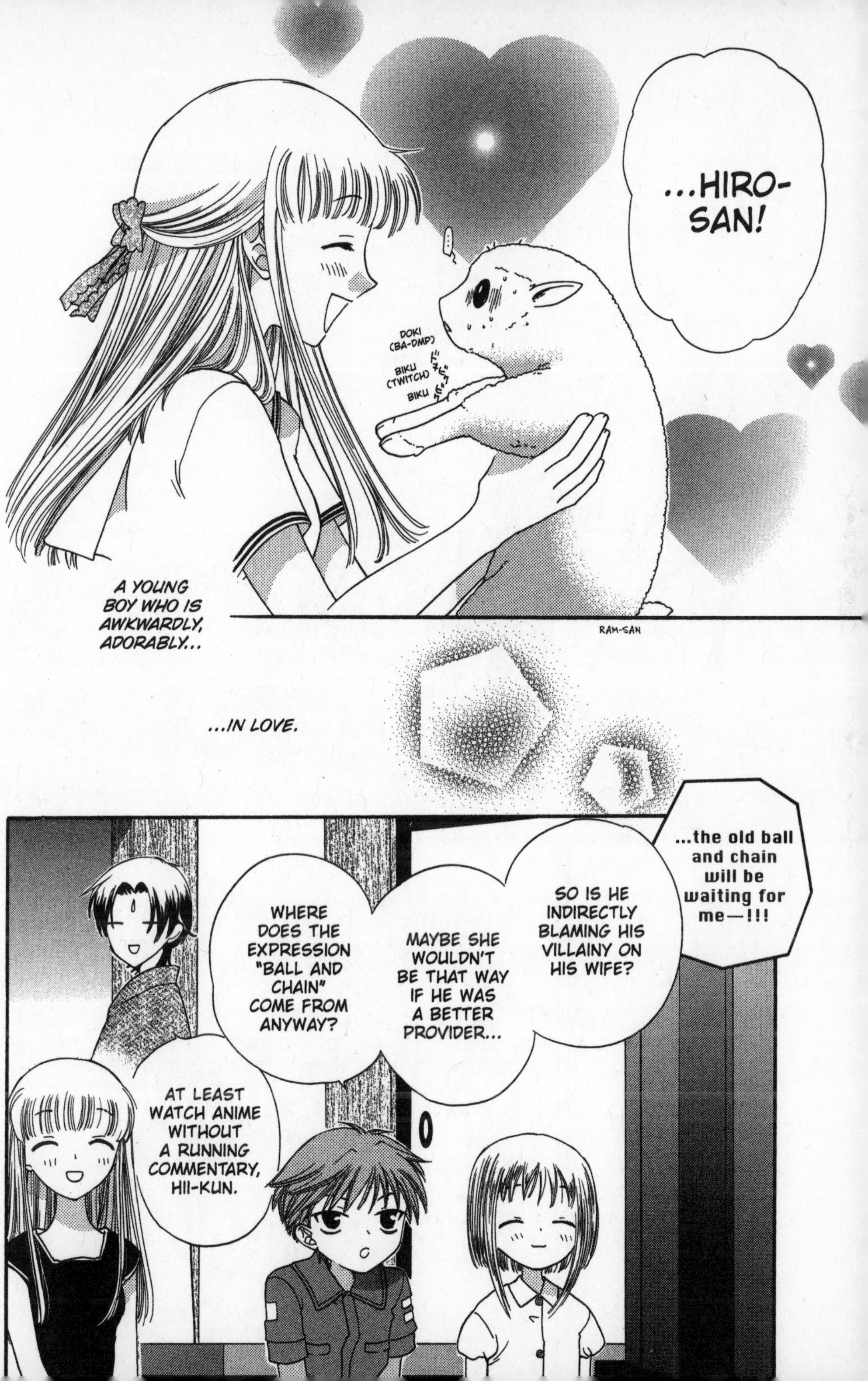
...HIRO-SAN!
DOKI (BA-DMP)
BIKU (TWITCH) BIKU
RAM-SAN
A YOUNG BOY WHO IS AWKWARDLY, ADORABLY...
...IN LOVE.
...the old ball and chain will be waiting for me—!!!
SO IS HE INDIRECTLY BLAMING HIS VILLAINY ON HIS WIFE?
MAYBE SHE WOULDN'T BE THAT WAY IF HE WAS A BETTER PROVIDER...
WHERE DOES THE EXPRESSION "BALL AND CHAIN" COME FROM ANYWAY?
AT LEAST WATCH ANIME WITHOUT A RUNNING COMMENTARY, HII-KUN.

Chapter 38

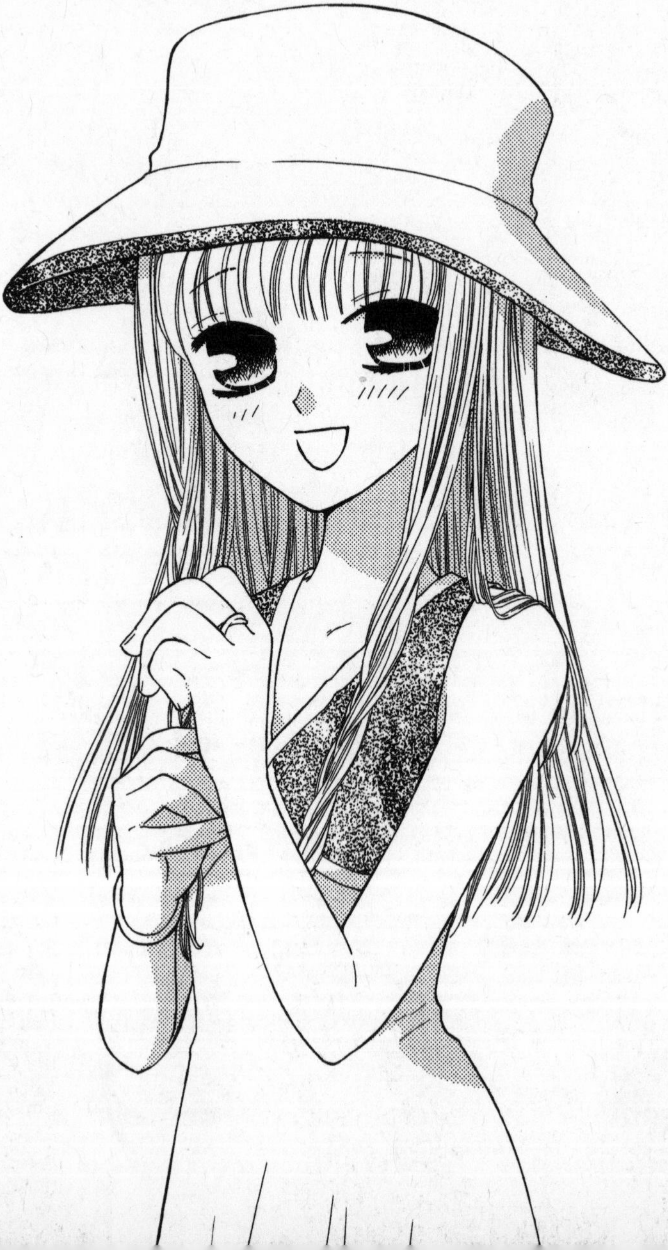

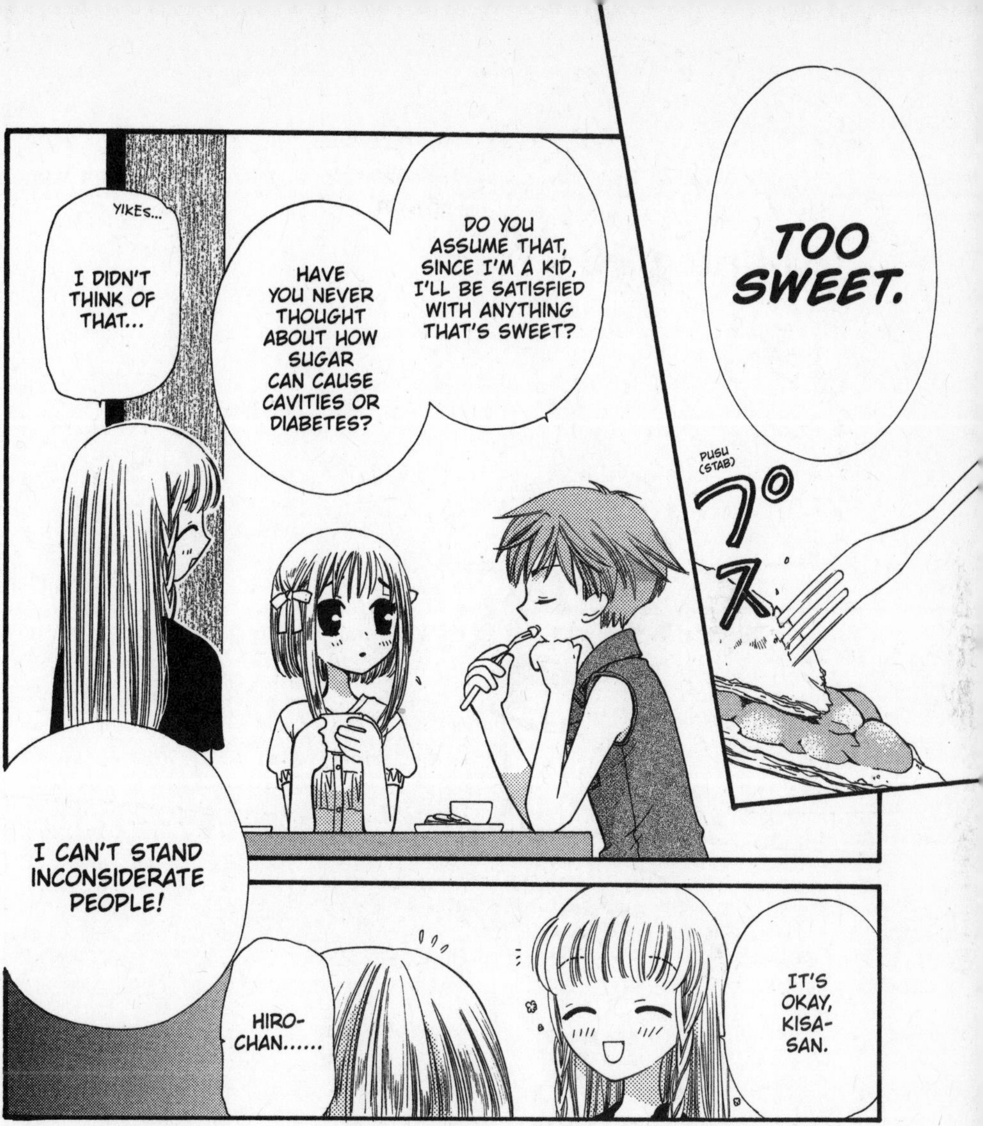
TOO SWEET.
PUSU (STAB)
プス
DO YOU ASSUME THAT, SINCE I'M A KID, I'LL BE SATISFIED WITH ANYTHING THAT'S SWEET?
HAVE YOU NEVER THOUGHT ABOUT HOW SUGAR CAN CAUSE CAVITIES OR DIABETES?
YIKES...
I DIDN'T THINK OF THAT...
I CAN'T STAND INCONSIDERATE PEOPLE!
IT'S OKAY, KISA-SAN.
HIRO-CHAN......

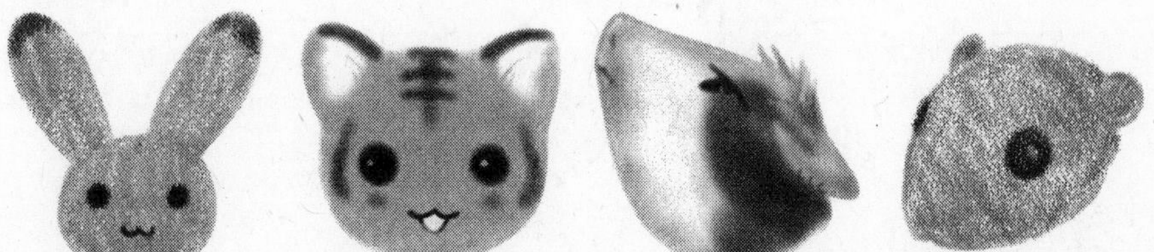

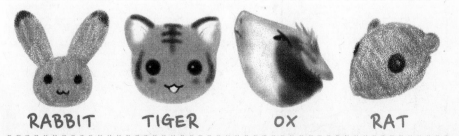

RABBIT TIGER OX RAT

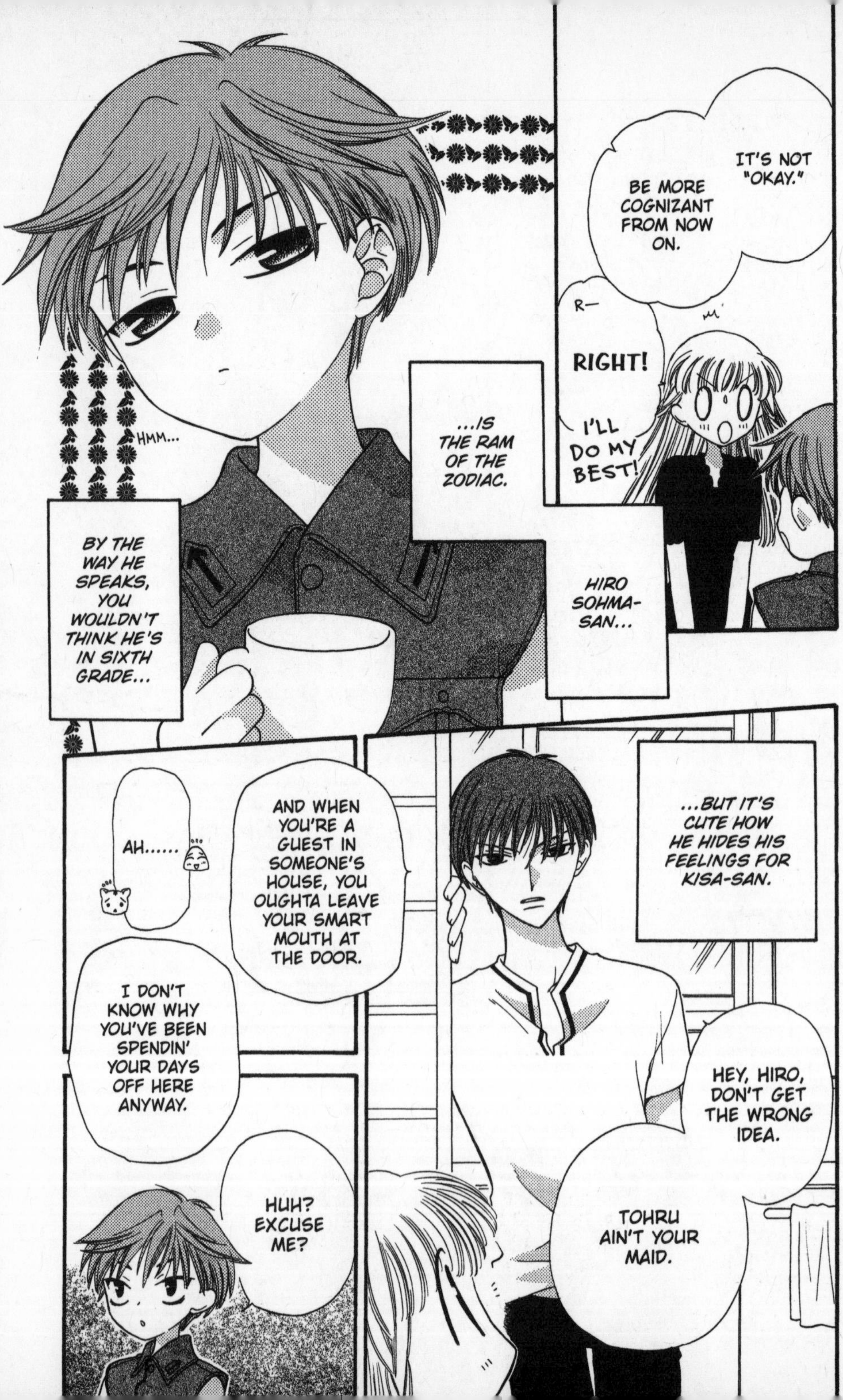

IT'S NOT "OKAY."
BE MORE COGNIZANT FROM NOW ON.
R—
RIGHT!
I'LL DO MY BEST!
HIRO SOHMA-SAN...
...IS THE RAM OF THE ZODIAC.
HMM...
BY THE WAY HE SPEAKS, YOU WOULDN'T THINK HE'S IN SIXTH GRADE...
...BUT IT'S CUTE HOW HE HIDES HIS FEELINGS FOR KISA-SAN.
HEY, HIRO, DON'T GET THE WRONG IDEA.
TOHRU AIN'T YOUR MAID.
AND WHEN YOU'RE A GUEST IN SOMEONE'S HOUSE, YOU OUGHTA LEAVE YOUR SMART MOUTH AT THE DOOR.
AH......
I DON'T KNOW WHY YOU'VE BEEN SPENDIN' YOUR DAYS OFF HERE ANYWAY.
HUH? EXCUSE ME?

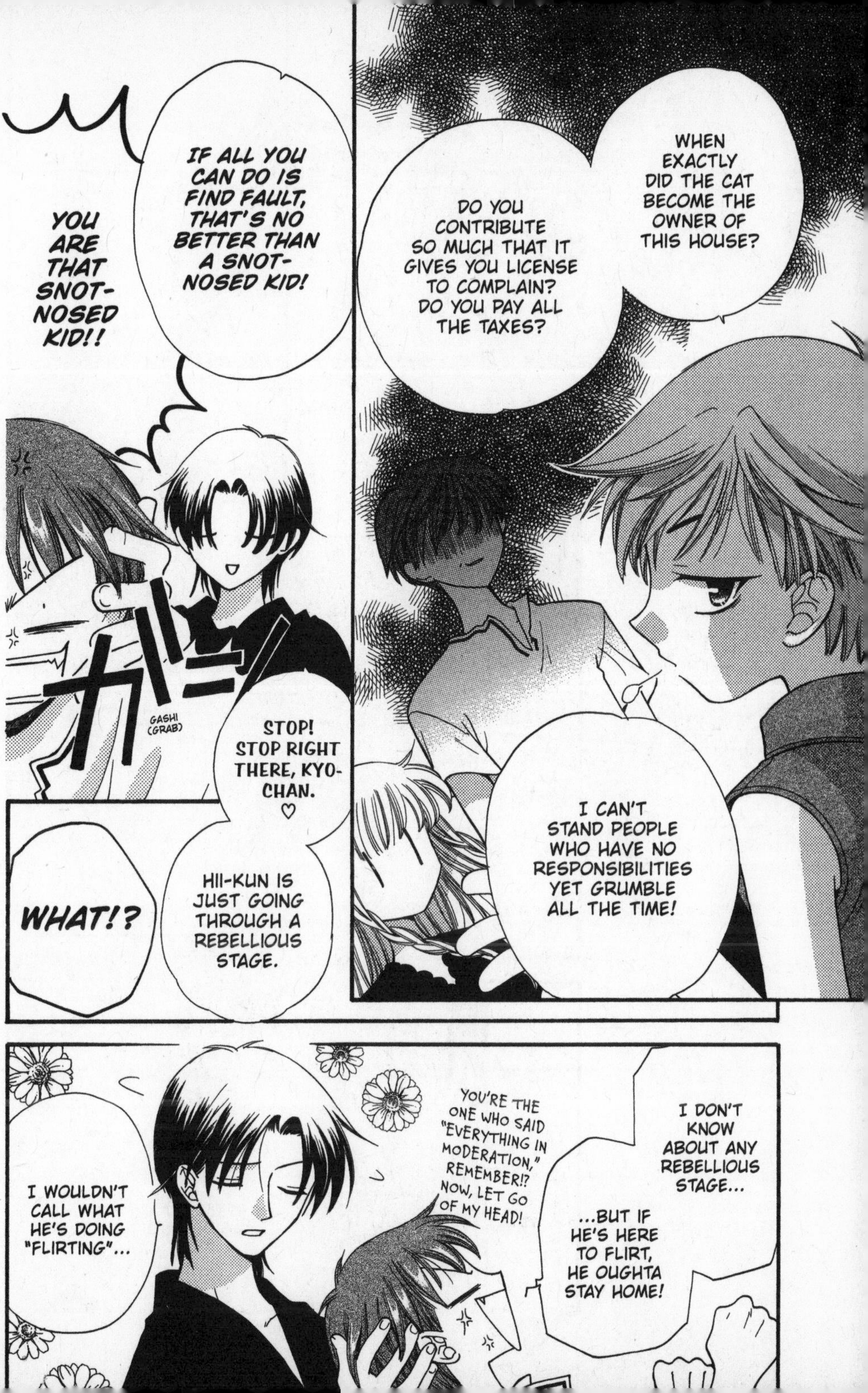

WHEN EXACTLY DID THE CAT BECOME THE OWNER OF THIS HOUSE?
DO YOU CONTRIBUTE SO MUCH THAT IT GIVES YOU LICENSE TO COMPLAIN? DO YOU PAY ALL THE TAXES?
I CAN'T STAND PEOPLE WHO HAVE NO RESPONSIBILITIES YET GRUMBLE ALL THE TIME!
IF ALL YOU CAN DO IS FIND FAULT, THAT'S NO BETTER THAN A SNOT-NOSED KID!
YOU ARE THAT SNOT-NOSED KID!!
GASHI (GRAB)
STOP! STOP RIGHT THERE, KYO-CHAN. ♡
HII-KUN IS JUST GOING THROUGH A REBELLIOUS STAGE.
WHAT!?
I DON'T KNOW ABOUT ANY REBELLIOUS STAGE...
...BUT IF HE'S HERE TO FLIRT, HE OUGHTA STAY HOME!
YOU'RE THE ONE WHO SAID "EVERYTHING IN MODERATION," REMEMBER!? NOW, LET GO OF MY HEAD!
I WOULDN'T CALL WHAT HE'S DOING "FLIRTING"...

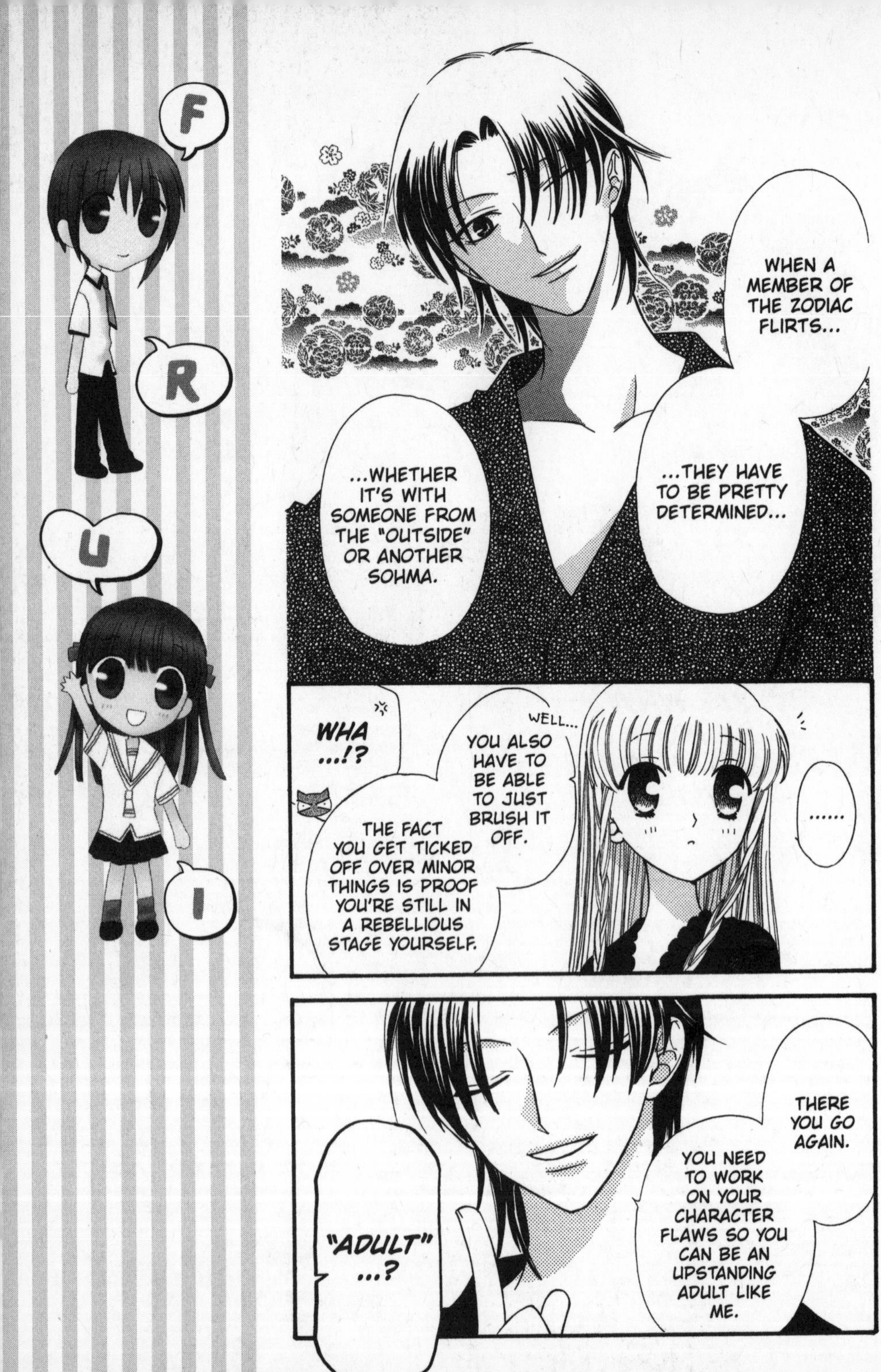
WHEN A MEMBER OF THE ZODIAC FLIRTS...
...THEY HAVE TO BE PRETTY DETERMINED...
...WHETHER IT'S WITH SOMEONE FROM THE "OUTSIDE" OR ANOTHER SOHMA.
......
WELL...
YOU ALSO HAVE TO BE ABLE TO JUST BRUSH IT OFF.
THE FACT YOU GET TICKED OFF OVER MINOR THINGS IS PROOF YOU'RE STILL IN A REBELLIOUS STAGE YOURSELF.
WHA ...!?
THERE YOU GO AGAIN.
YOU NEED TO WORK ON YOUR CHARACTER FLAWS SO YOU CAN BE AN UPSTANDING ADULT LIKE ME.
"ADULT" ...?
F
R
U
I

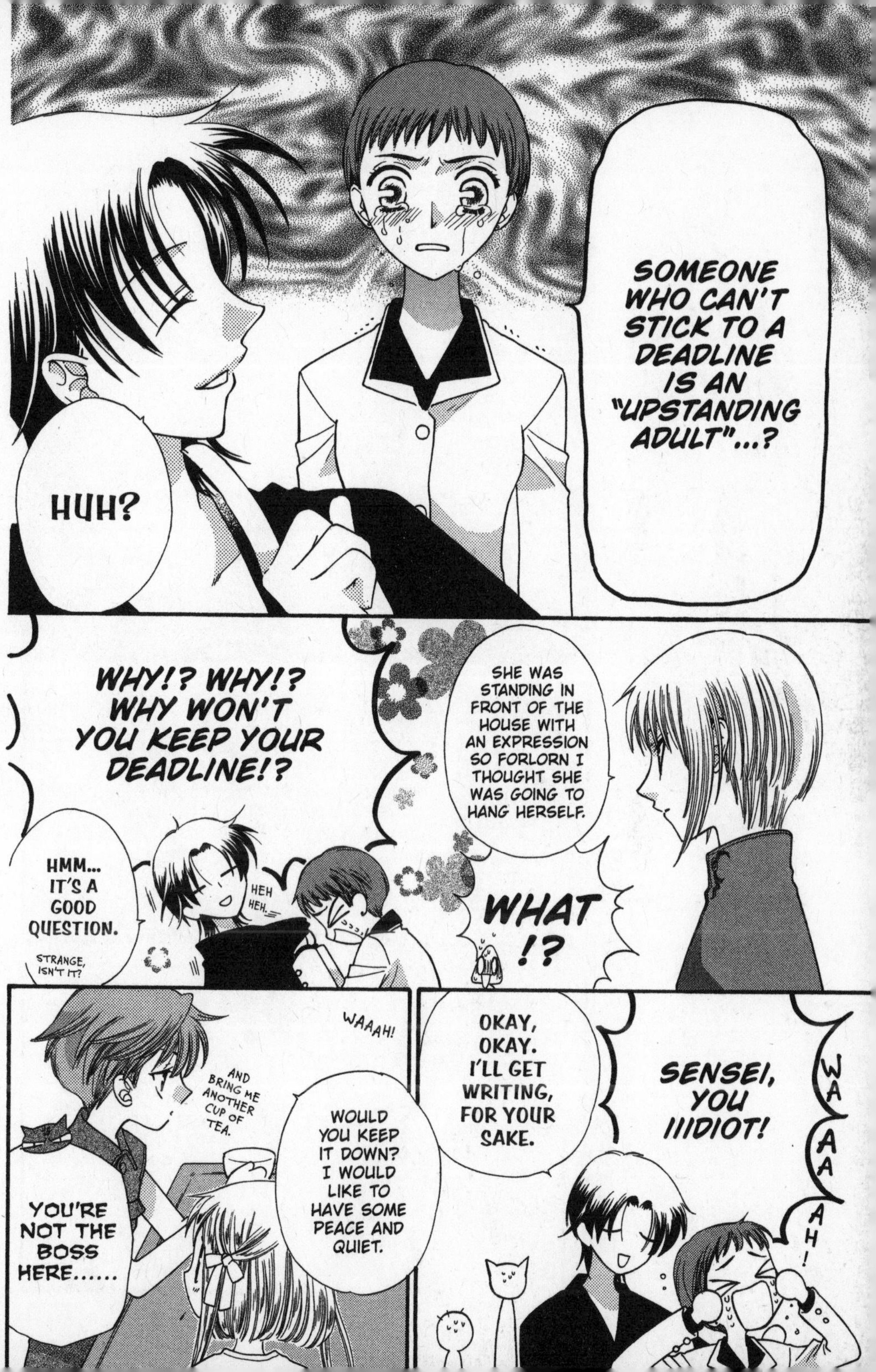
SOMEONE WHO CAN'T STICK TO A DEADLINE IS AN "UPSTANDING ADULT"...?
HUH?
SHE WAS STANDING IN FRONT OF THE HOUSE WITH AN EXPRESSION SO FORLORN I THOUGHT SHE WAS GOING TO HANG HERSELF.
WHAT!?
WHY!? WHY!? WHY WON'T YOU KEEP YOUR DEADLINE!?
HEH HEH.
HMM... IT'S A GOOD QUESTION.
STRANGE, ISN'T IT?
WAAAAH!
SENSEI, YOU IIIDIOT!
OKAY, OKAY. I'LL GET WRITING, FOR YOUR SAKE.
WAAAH!
WOULD YOU KEEP IT DOWN? I WOULD LIKE TO HAVE SOME PEACE AND QUIET.
AND BRING ME ANOTHER CUP OF TEA.
YOU'RE NOT THE BOSS HERE......

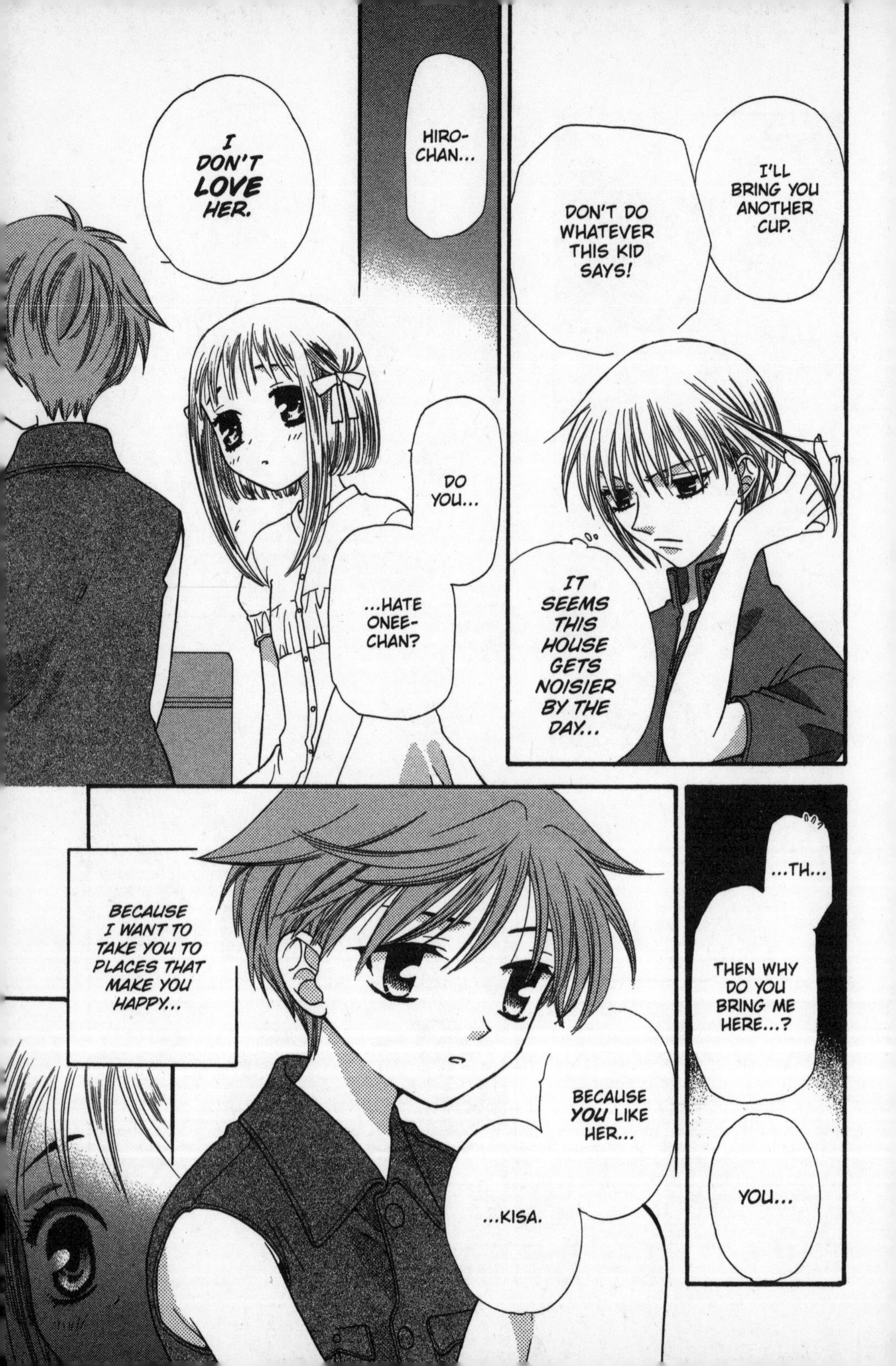
I'LL BRING YOU ANOTHER CUP.
DON'T DO WHATEVER THIS KID SAYS!
IT SEEMS THIS HOUSE GETS NOISIER BY THE DAY...
HIRO-CHAN...
I DON'T LOVE HER.
DO YOU...
...HATE ONEE-CHAN?
...TH...
THEN WHY DO YOU BRING ME HERE...?
YOU...
BECAUSE YOU LIKE HER...
...KISA.
BECAUSE I WANT TO TAKE YOU TO PLACES THAT MAKE YOU HAPPY...

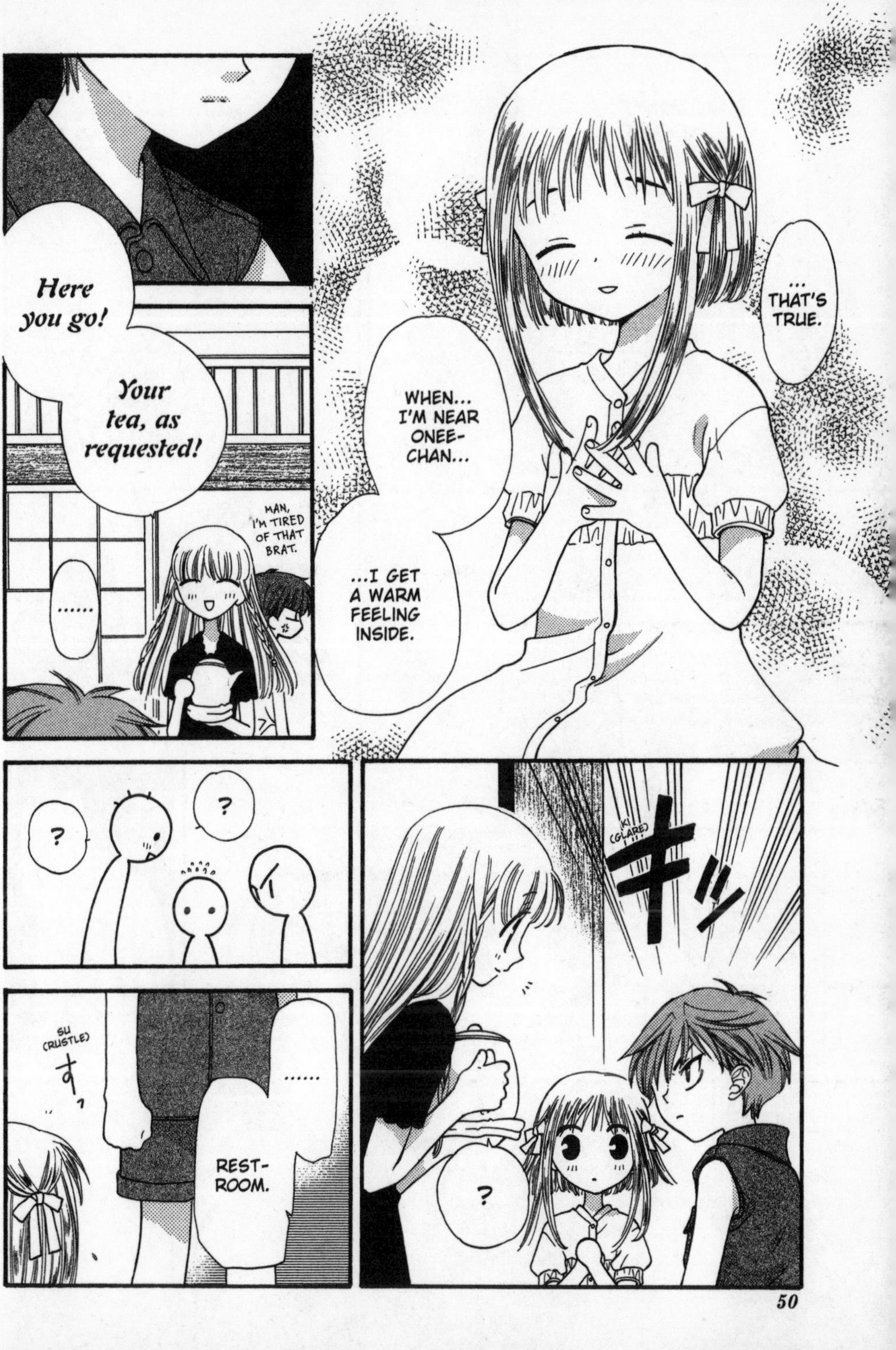

...THAT'S TRUE.
WHEN... I'M NEAR ONEE-CHAN...
...I GET A WARM FEELING INSIDE.
Here you go!
Your tea, as requested!
MAN, I'M TIRED OF THAT BRAT.
......
KI (GLARE)
?
?
?
......
SU (RUSTLE)
REST-ROOM.

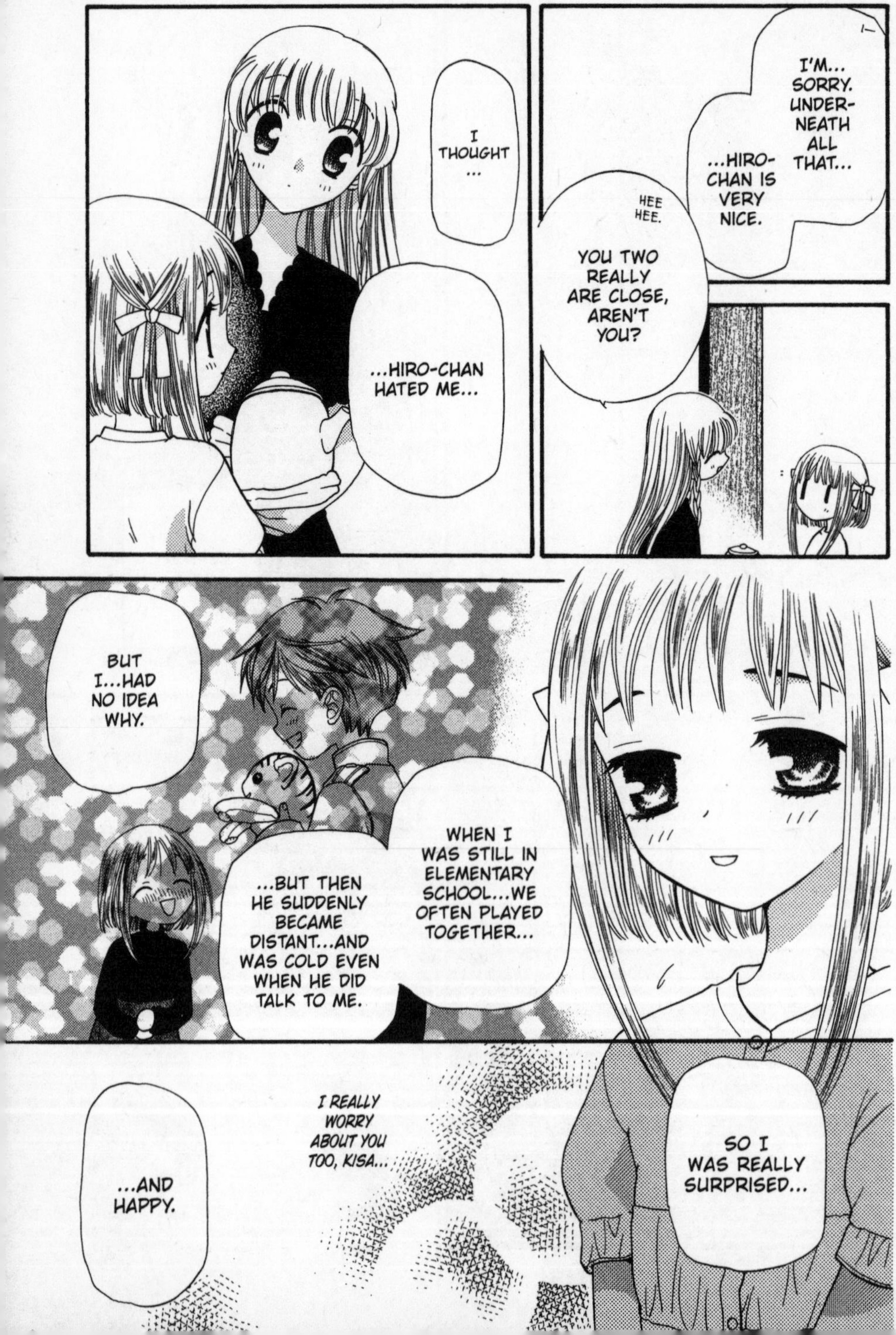
I–
I'M... SORRY. UNDER-NEATH ALL THAT...
...HIRO-CHAN IS VERY NICE.
HEE HEE.
YOU TWO REALLY ARE CLOSE, AREN'T YOU?
I THOUGHT...
...HIRO-CHAN HATED ME...
WHEN I WAS STILL IN ELEMENTARY SCHOOL...WE OFTEN PLAYED TOGETHER...
...BUT THEN HE SUDDENLY BECAME DISTANT...AND WAS COLD EVEN WHEN HE DID TALK TO ME.
BUT I...HAD NO IDEA WHY.
SO I WAS REALLY SURPRISED...
I REALLY WORRY ABOUT YOU TOO, KISA...
...AND HAPPY.

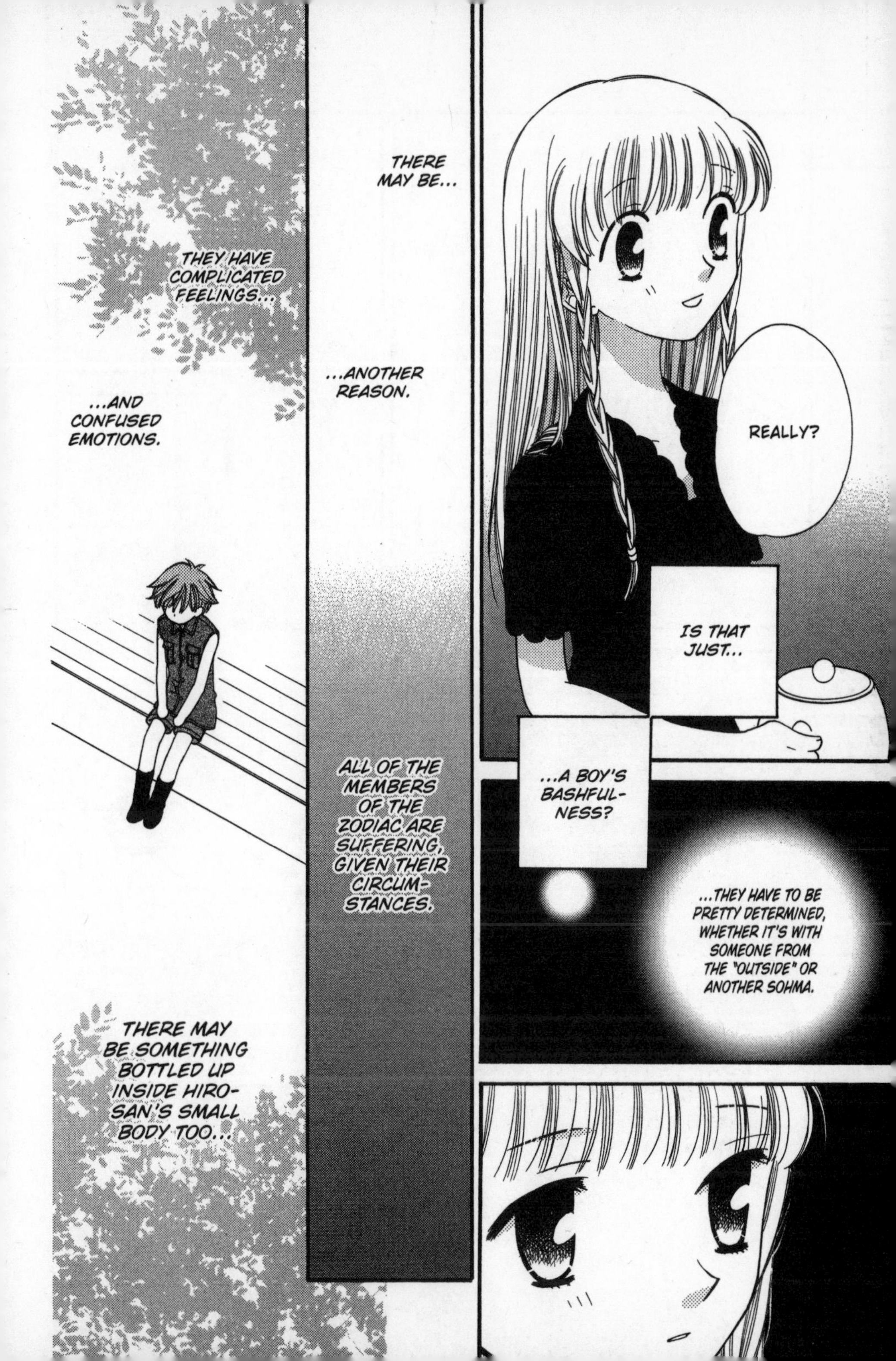

REALLY?
IS THAT JUST...
...A BOY'S BASHFUL-NESS?
...THEY HAVE TO BE PRETTY DETERMINED, WHETHER IT'S WITH SOMEONE FROM THE "OUTSIDE" OR ANOTHER SOHMA.
THERE MAY BE...
...ANOTHER REASON.
ALL OF THE MEMBERS OF THE ZODIAC ARE SUFFERING, GIVEN THEIR CIRCUM-STANCES.
THEY HAVE COMPLICATED FEELINGS...
...AND CONFUSED EMOTIONS.
THERE MAY BE SOMETHING BOTTLED UP INSIDE HIRO-SAN'S SMALL BODY TOO...

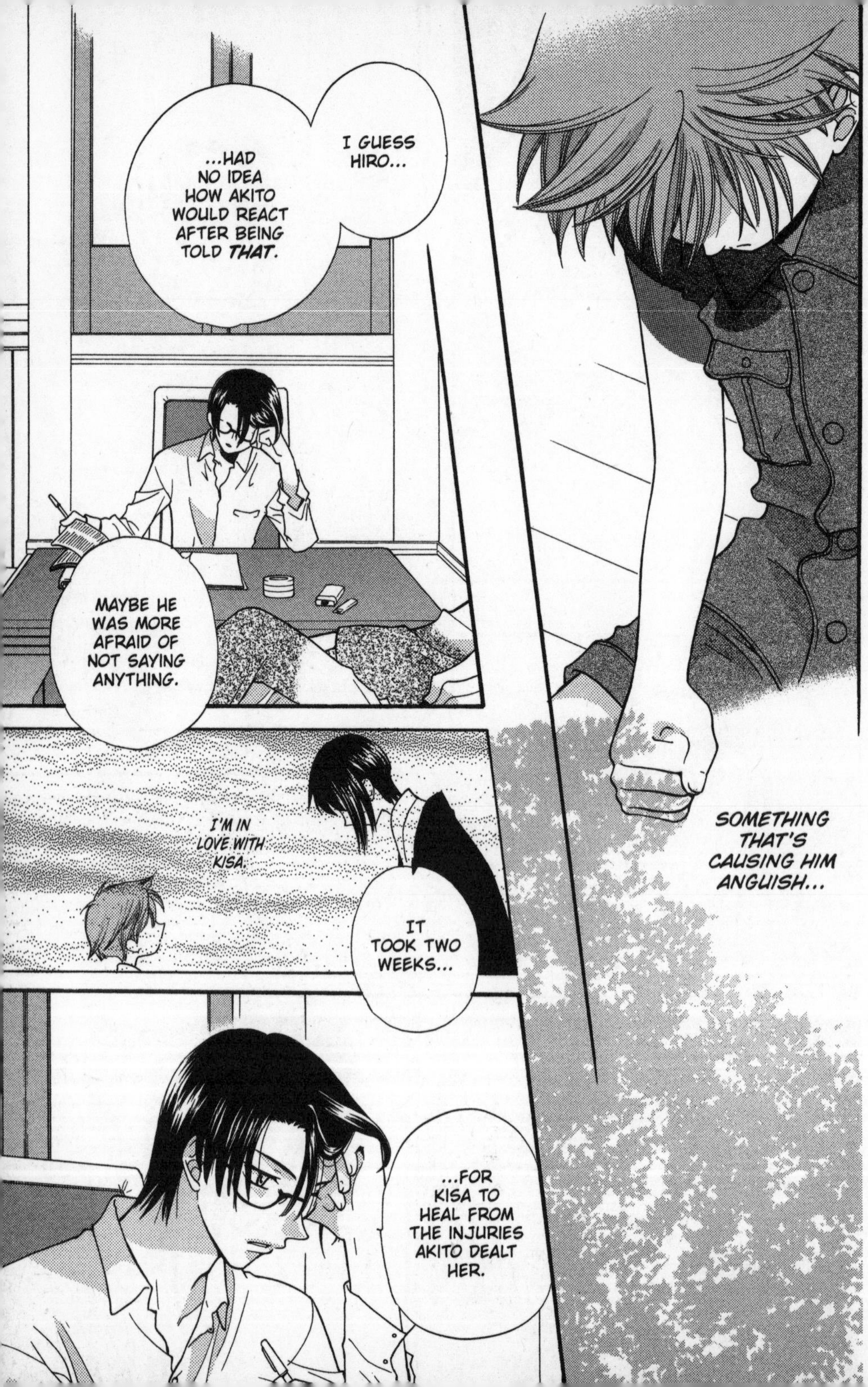
SOMETHING THAT'S CAUSING HIM ANGUISH...
I GUESS HIRO...
...HAD NO IDEA HOW AKITO WOULD REACT AFTER BEING TOLD *THAT*.
MAYBE HE WAS MORE AFRAID OF NOT SAYING ANYTHING.
I'M IN LOVE WITH KISA.
IT TOOK TWO WEEKS...
...FOR KISA TO HEAL FROM THE INJURIES AKITO DEALT HER.

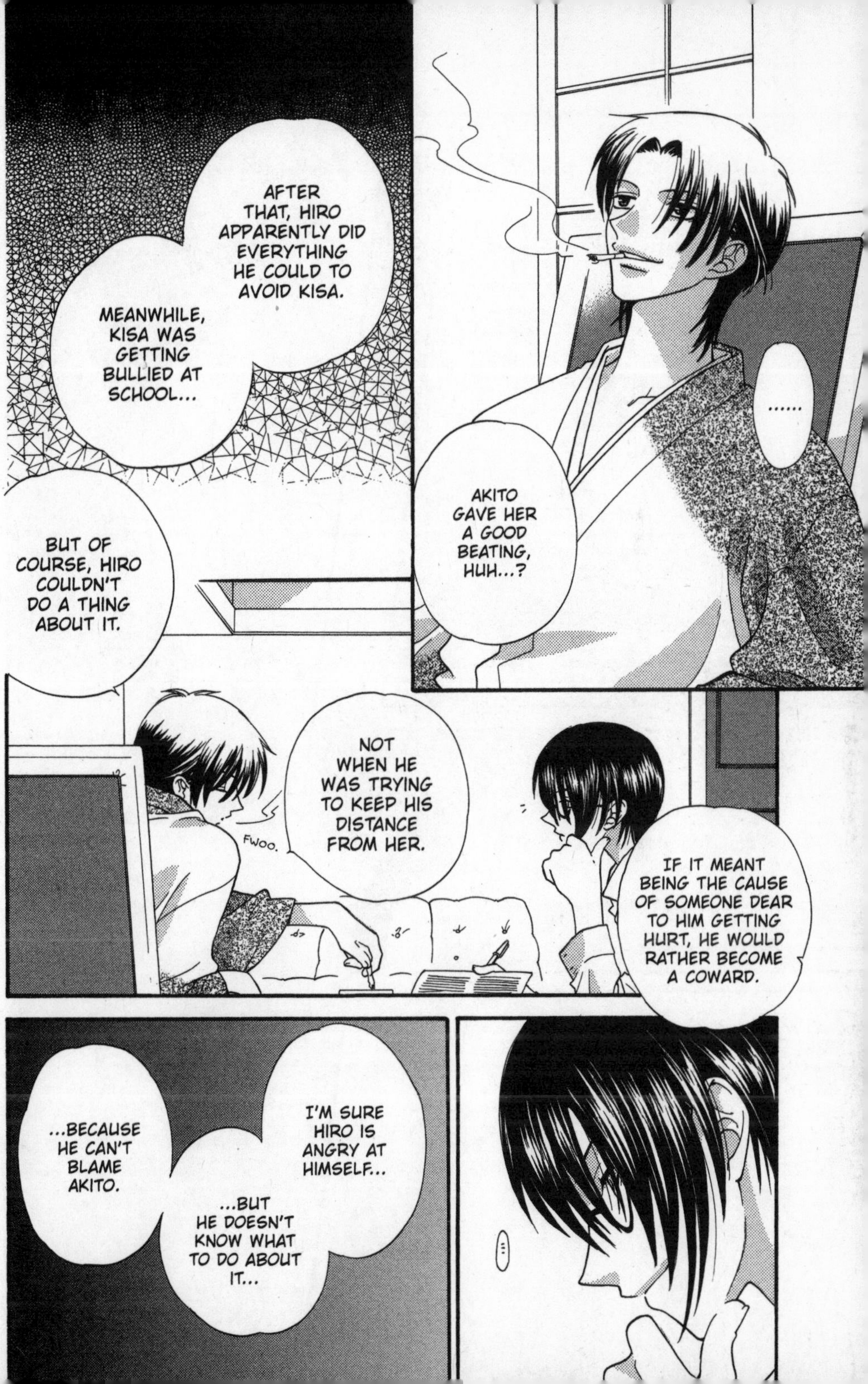
......
AKITO GAVE HER A GOOD BEATING, HUH...?
AFTER THAT, HIRO APPARENTLY DID EVERYTHING HE COULD TO AVOID KISA.
MEANWHILE, KISA WAS GETTING BULLIED AT SCHOOL...
BUT OF COURSE, HIRO COULDN'T DO A THING ABOUT IT.
NOT WHEN HE WAS TRYING TO KEEP HIS DISTANCE FROM HER.
FWOO.
IF IT MEANT BEING THE CAUSE OF SOMEONE DEAR TO HIM GETTING HURT, HE WOULD RATHER BECOME A COWARD.
...
I'M SURE HIRO IS ANGRY AT HIMSELF...
...BUT HE DOESN'T KNOW WHAT TO DO ABOUT IT...
...BECAUSE HE CAN'T BLAME AKITO.

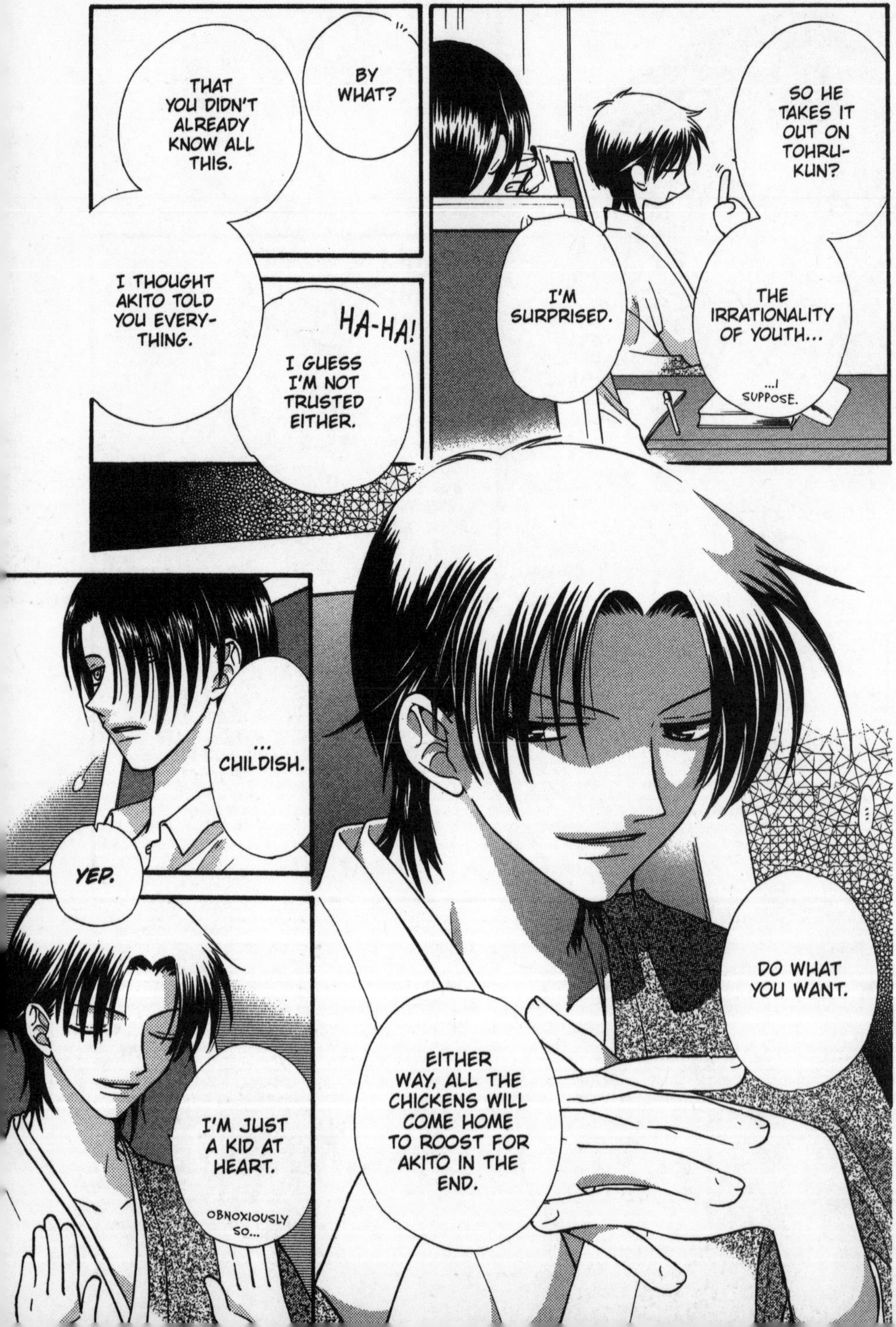
SO HE TAKES IT OUT ON TOHRU-KUN?
THE IRRATIONALITY OF YOUTH...
...I SUPPOSE.
I'M SURPRISED.
BY WHAT?
THAT YOU DIDN'T ALREADY KNOW ALL THIS.
I THOUGHT AKITO TOLD YOU EVERY-THING.
HA-HA!
I GUESS I'M NOT TRUSTED EITHER.
...
DO WHAT YOU WANT.
EITHER WAY, ALL THE CHICKENS WILL COME HOME TO ROOST FOR AKITO IN THE END.
... CHILDISH.
YEP.
I'M JUST A KID AT HEART.
OBNOXIOUSLY SO...

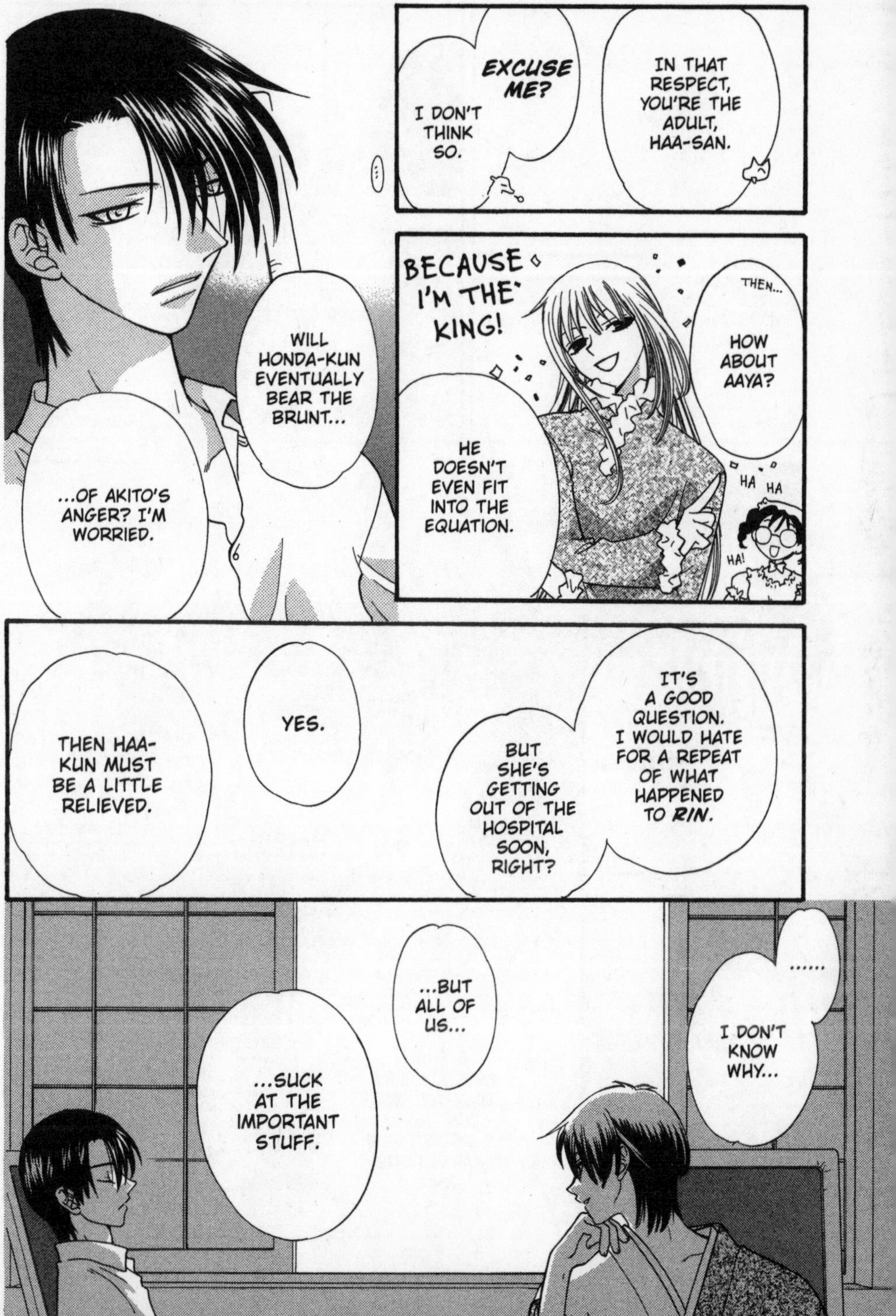
IN THAT RESPECT, YOU'RE THE ADULT, HAA-SAN.
EXCUSE ME?
I DON'T THINK SO.
THEN... HOW ABOUT AAYA?
HA HA HA!
BECAUSE I'M THE KING!
HE DOESN'T EVEN FIT INTO THE EQUATION.
...
WILL HONDA-KUN EVENTUALLY BEAR THE BRUNT...
...OF AKITO'S ANGER? I'M WORRIED.
IT'S A GOOD QUESTION. I WOULD HATE FOR A REPEAT OF WHAT HAPPENED TO *RIN*.
BUT SHE'S GETTING OUT OF THE HOSPITAL SOON, RIGHT?
YES.
THEN HAA-KUN MUST BE A LITTLE RELIEVED.
......
I DON'T KNOW WHY...
...BUT ALL OF US...
...SUCK AT THE IMPORTANT STUFF.

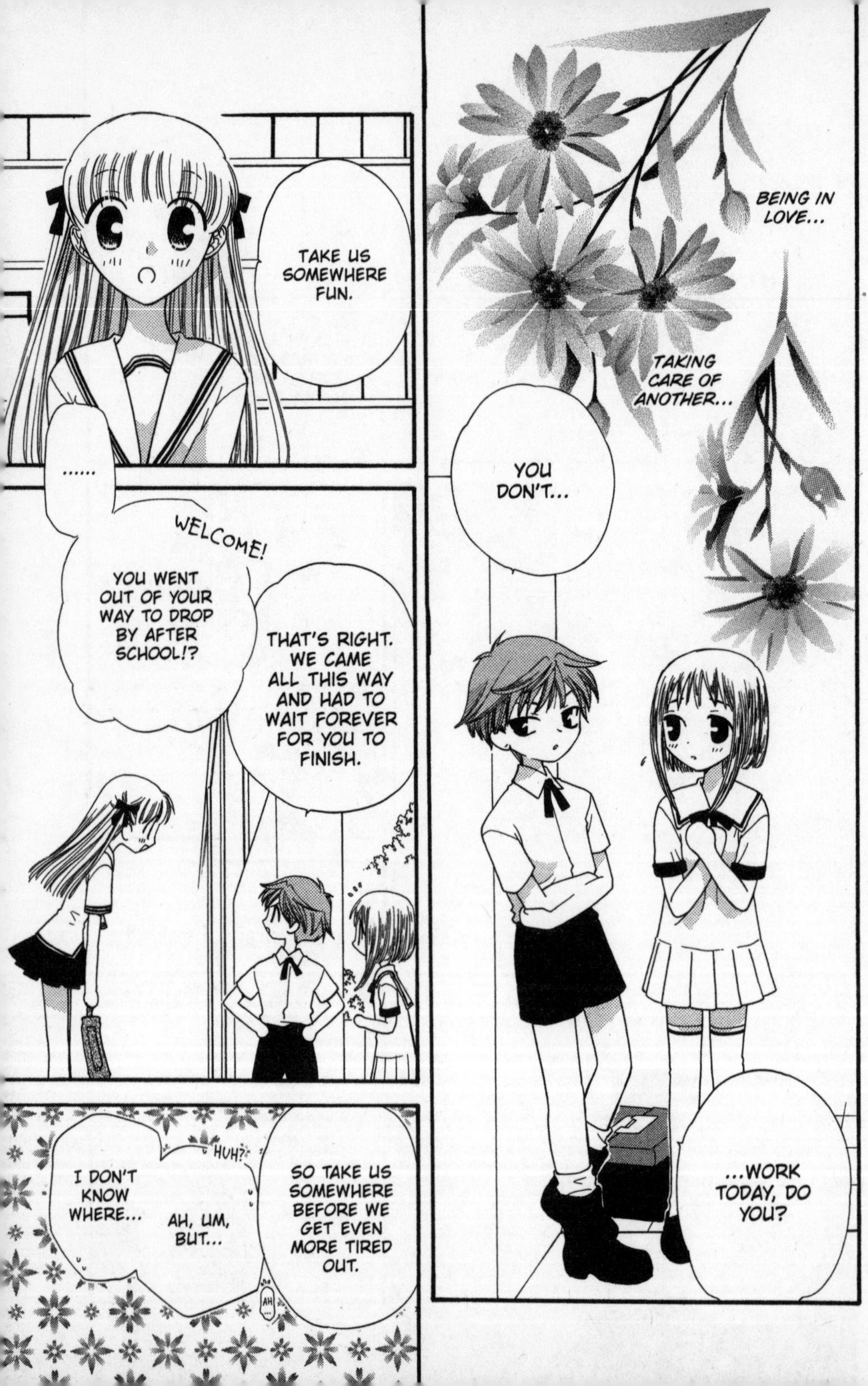
BEING IN LOVE...
TAKING CARE OF ANOTHER...
YOU DON'T...
...WORK TODAY, DO YOU?
TAKE US SOMEWHERE FUN.
......
WELCOME!
YOU WENT OUT OF YOUR WAY TO DROP BY AFTER SCHOOL!?
THAT'S RIGHT. WE CAME ALL THIS WAY AND HAD TO WAIT FOREVER FOR YOU TO FINISH.
SO TAKE US SOMEWHERE BEFORE WE GET EVEN MORE TIRED OUT.
HUH?
AH, UM, BUT...
I DON'T KNOW WHERE...
AH

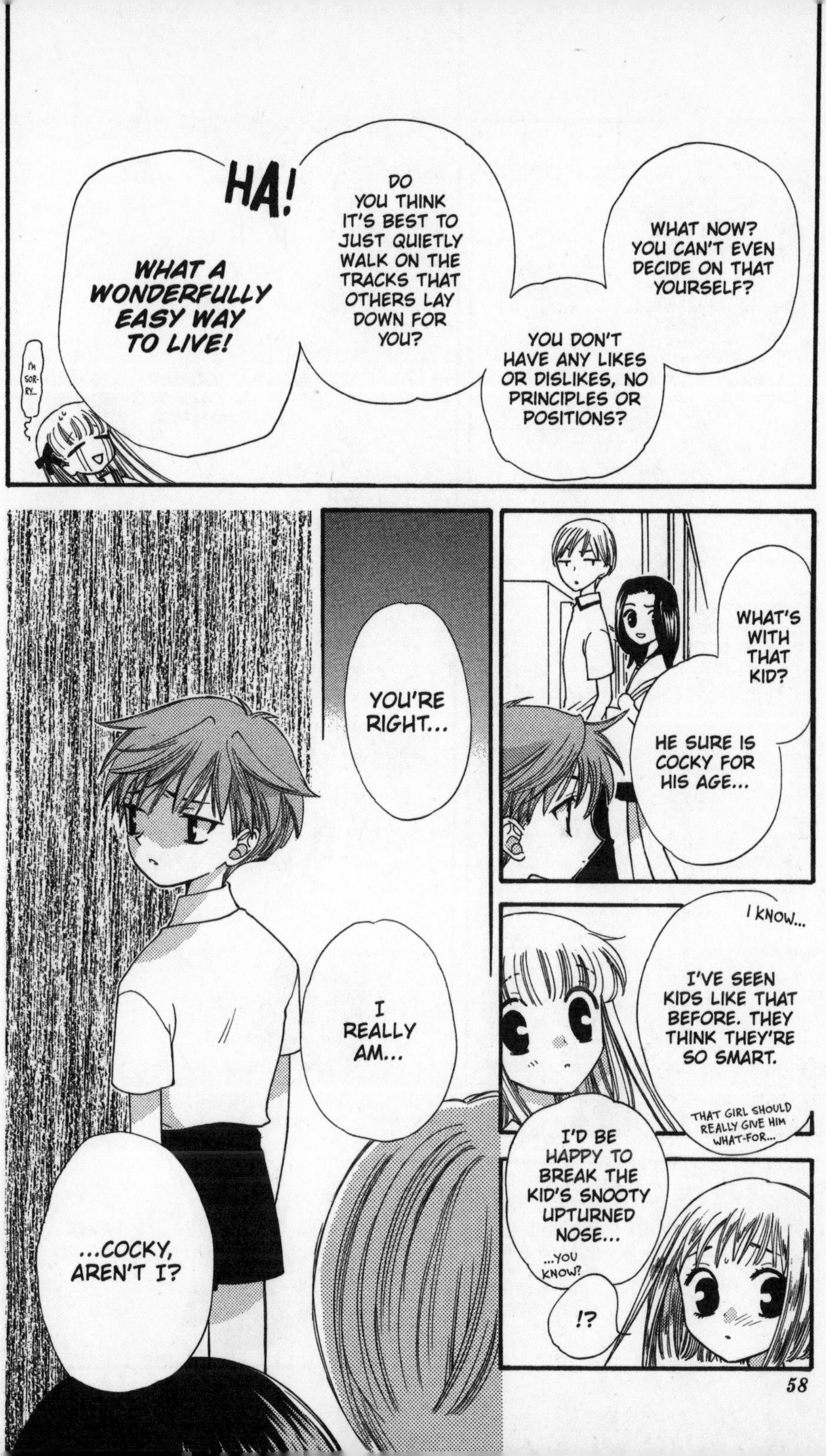
WHAT NOW? YOU CAN'T EVEN DECIDE ON THAT YOURSELF?
YOU DON'T HAVE ANY LIKES OR DISLIKES, NO PRINCIPLES OR POSITIONS?
DO YOU THINK IT'S BEST TO JUST QUIETLY WALK ON THE TRACKS THAT OTHERS LAY DOWN FOR YOU?
HA!
WHAT A WONDERFULLY EASY WAY TO LIVE!
I'M SORRY...
WHAT'S WITH THAT KID?
HE SURE IS COCKY FOR HIS AGE...
I KNOW...
I'VE SEEN KIDS LIKE THAT BEFORE. THEY THINK THEY'RE SO SMART.
THAT GIRL SHOULD REALLY GIVE HIM WHAT-FOR...
I'D BE HAPPY TO BREAK THE KID'S SNOOTY UPTURNED NOSE...
...YOU KNOW?
!?
YOU'RE RIGHT...
I REALLY AM...
...COCKY, AREN'T I?

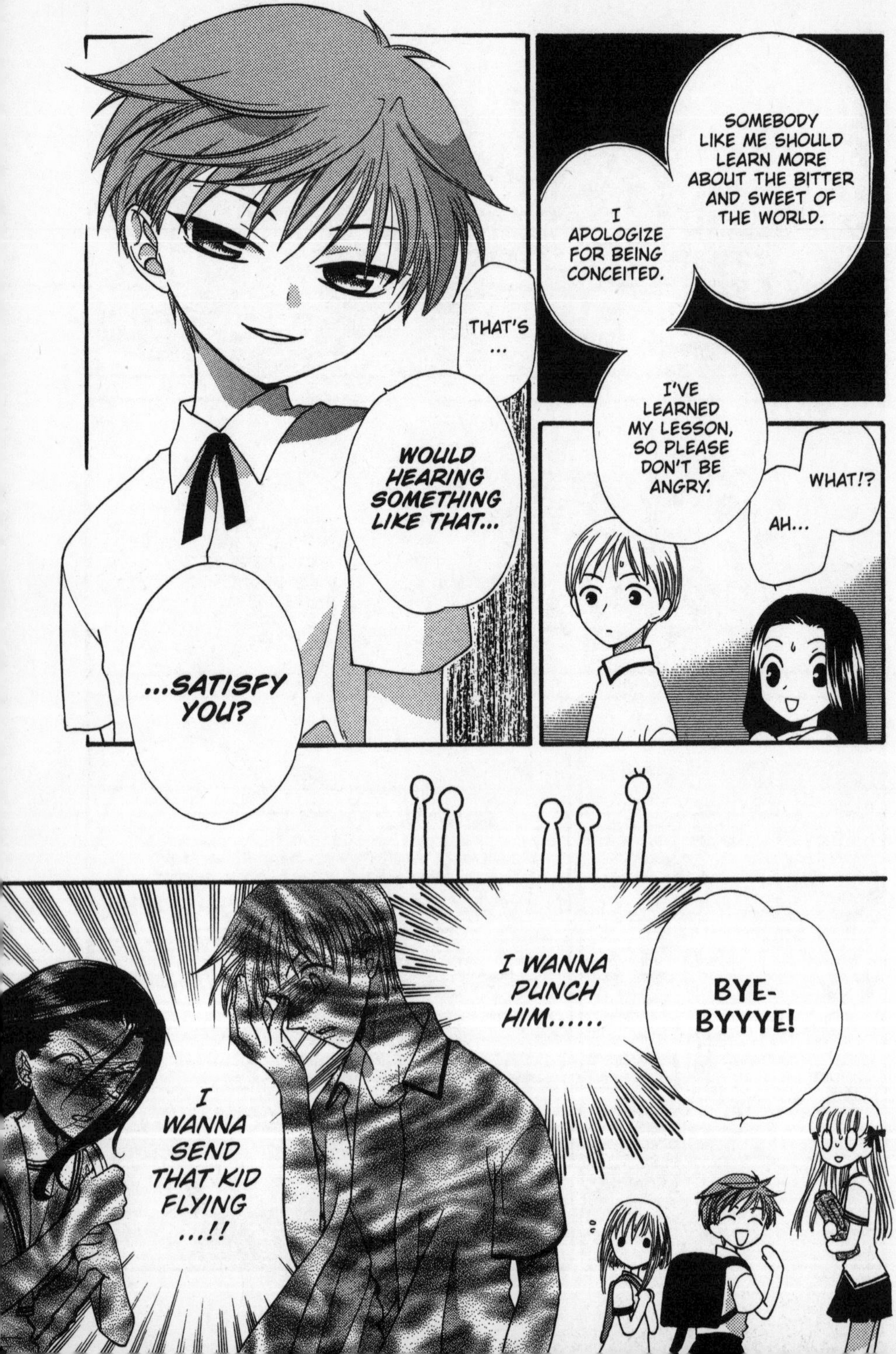
SOMEBODY LIKE ME SHOULD LEARN MORE ABOUT THE BITTER AND SWEET OF THE WORLD.
I APOLOGIZE FOR BEING CONCEITED.
I'VE LEARNED MY LESSON, SO PLEASE DON'T BE ANGRY.
WHAT!?
AH...
THAT'S ...
WOULD HEARING SOMETHING LIKE THAT...
...SATISFY YOU?
BYE-BYYYE!
I WANNA PUNCH HIM......
I WANNA SEND THAT KID FLYING ...!!

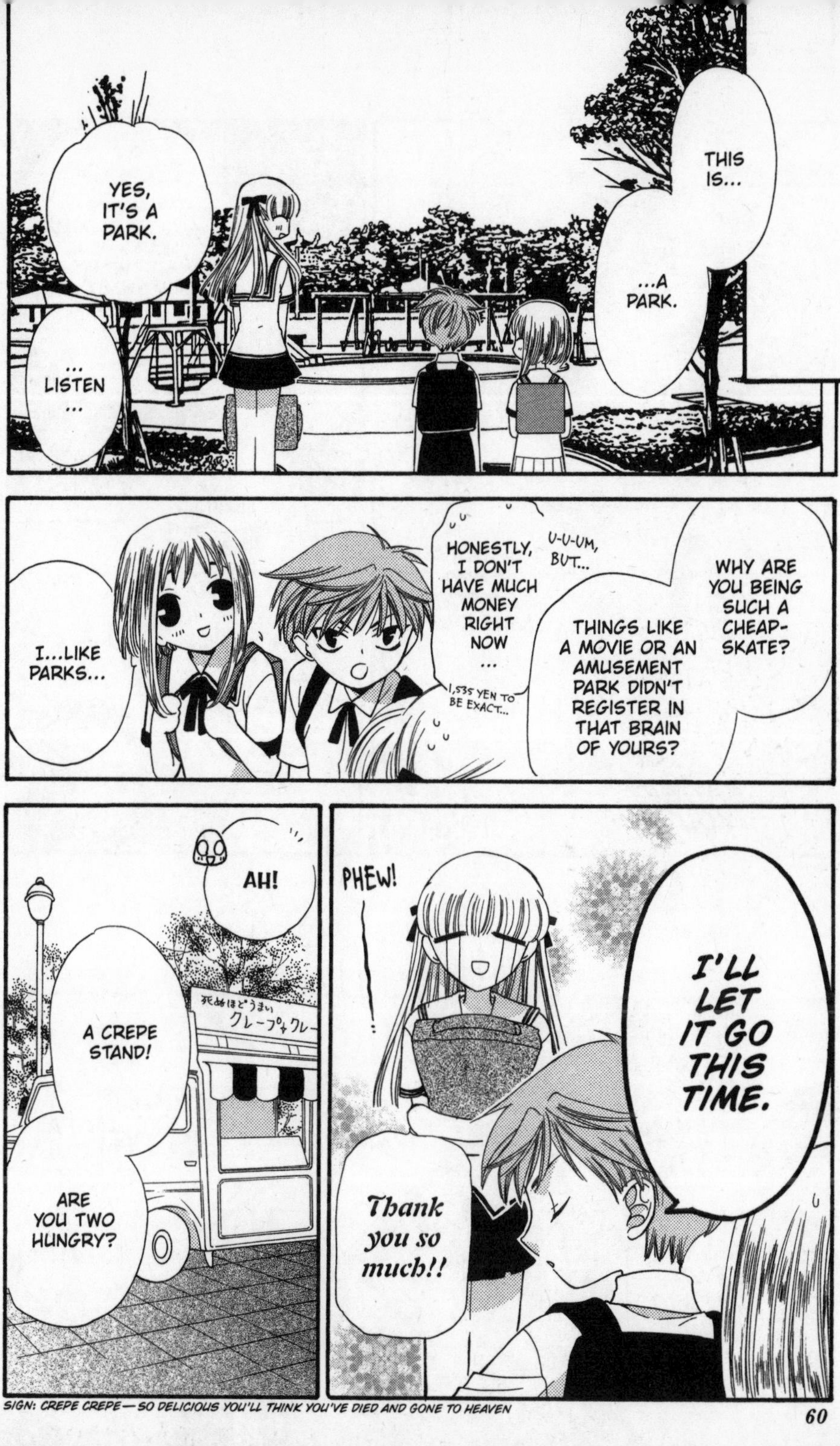
THIS IS...
...A PARK.
YES, IT'S A PARK.
...LISTEN...
WHY ARE YOU BEING SUCH A CHEAPSKATE?
THINGS LIKE A MOVIE OR AN AMUSEMENT PARK DIDN'T REGISTER IN THAT BRAIN OF YOURS?
U-U-UM, BUT...
HONESTLY, I DON'T HAVE MUCH MONEY RIGHT NOW...
1,535 YEN TO BE EXACT...
I...LIKE PARKS...
I'LL LET IT GO THIS TIME.
Thank you so much!!
PHEW!
AH!
死ぬほどうまい
A CREPE STAND!
ARE YOU TWO HUNGRY?
SIGN: CREPE CREPE—SO DELICIOUS YOU'LL THINK YOU'VE DIED AND GONE TO HEAVEN

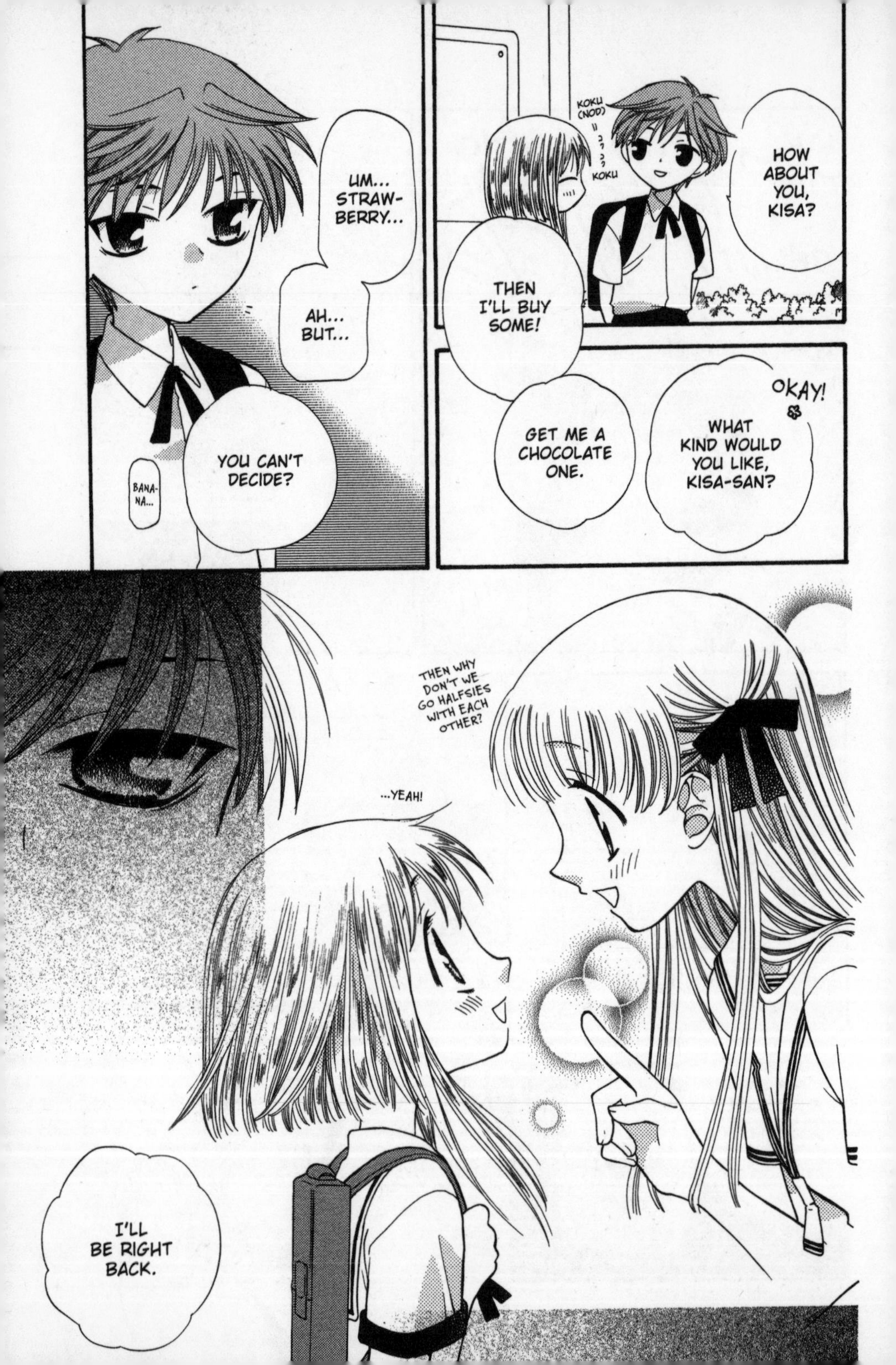
HOW ABOUT YOU, KISA?
KOKU (NOD)
KOKU
THEN I'LL BUY SOME!
OKAY!
WHAT KIND WOULD YOU LIKE, KISA-SAN?
GET ME A CHOCOLATE ONE.
UM... STRAWBERRY...
AH... BUT...
YOU CAN'T DECIDE?
BANANA...
THEN WHY DON'T WE GO HALFSIES WITH EACH OTHER?
...YEAH!
I'LL BE RIGHT BACK.

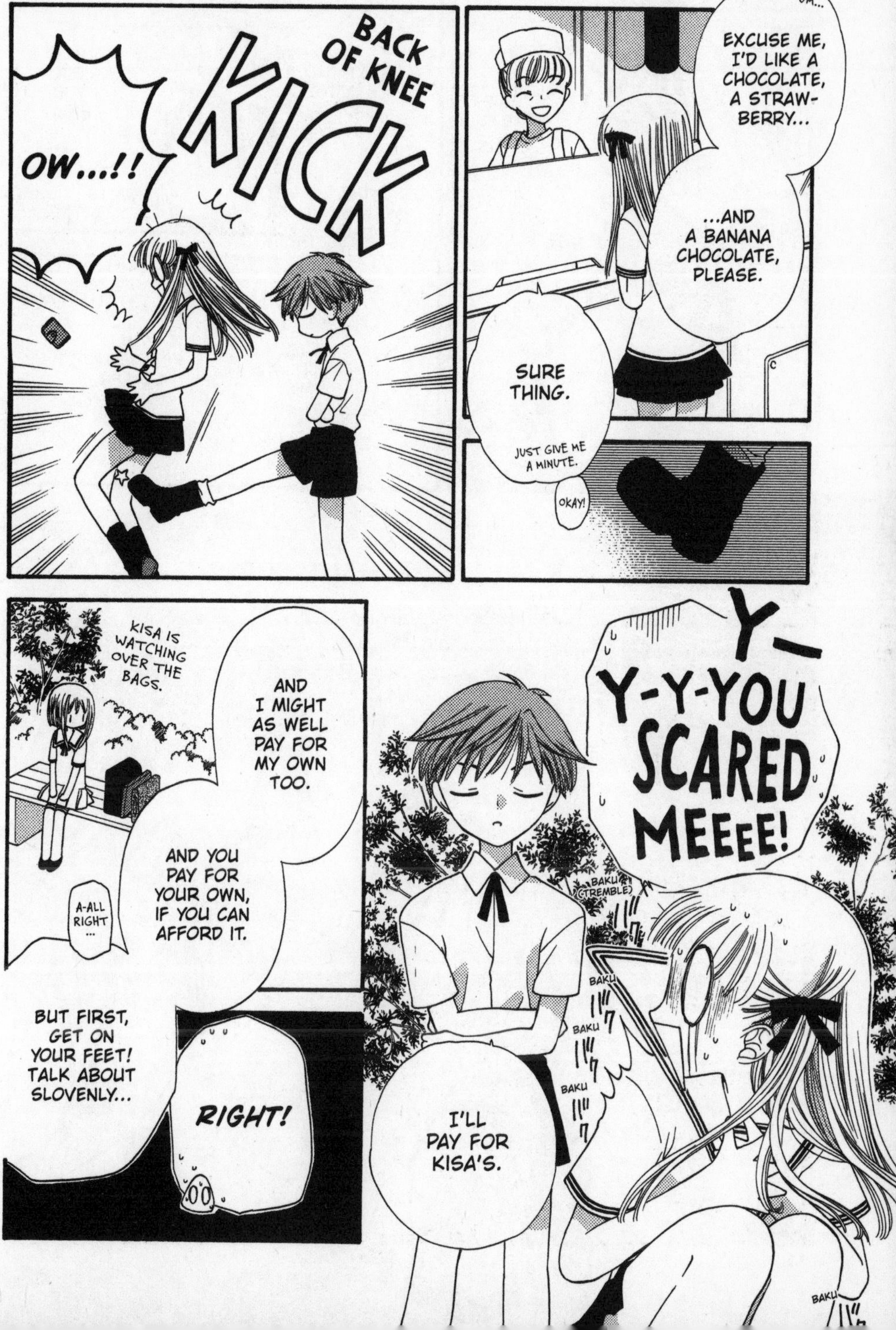
UM...
EXCUSE ME, I'D LIKE A CHOCOLATE, A STRAW-BERRY...
...AND A BANANA CHOCOLATE, PLEASE.
SURE THING.
JUST GIVE ME A MINUTE.
OKAY!
BACK OF KNEE KICK
OW...!!
Y-Y-Y-YOU SCARED MEEEEE!
BAKU (TREMBLE)
BAKU
BAKU
BAKU
I'LL PAY FOR KISA'S.
BAKU
KISA IS WATCHING OVER THE BAGS.
AND I MIGHT AS WELL PAY FOR MY OWN TOO.
AND YOU PAY FOR YOUR OWN, IF YOU CAN AFFORD IT.
A-ALL RIGHT ...
BUT FIRST, GET ON YOUR FEET! TALK ABOUT SLOVENLY...
RIGHT!

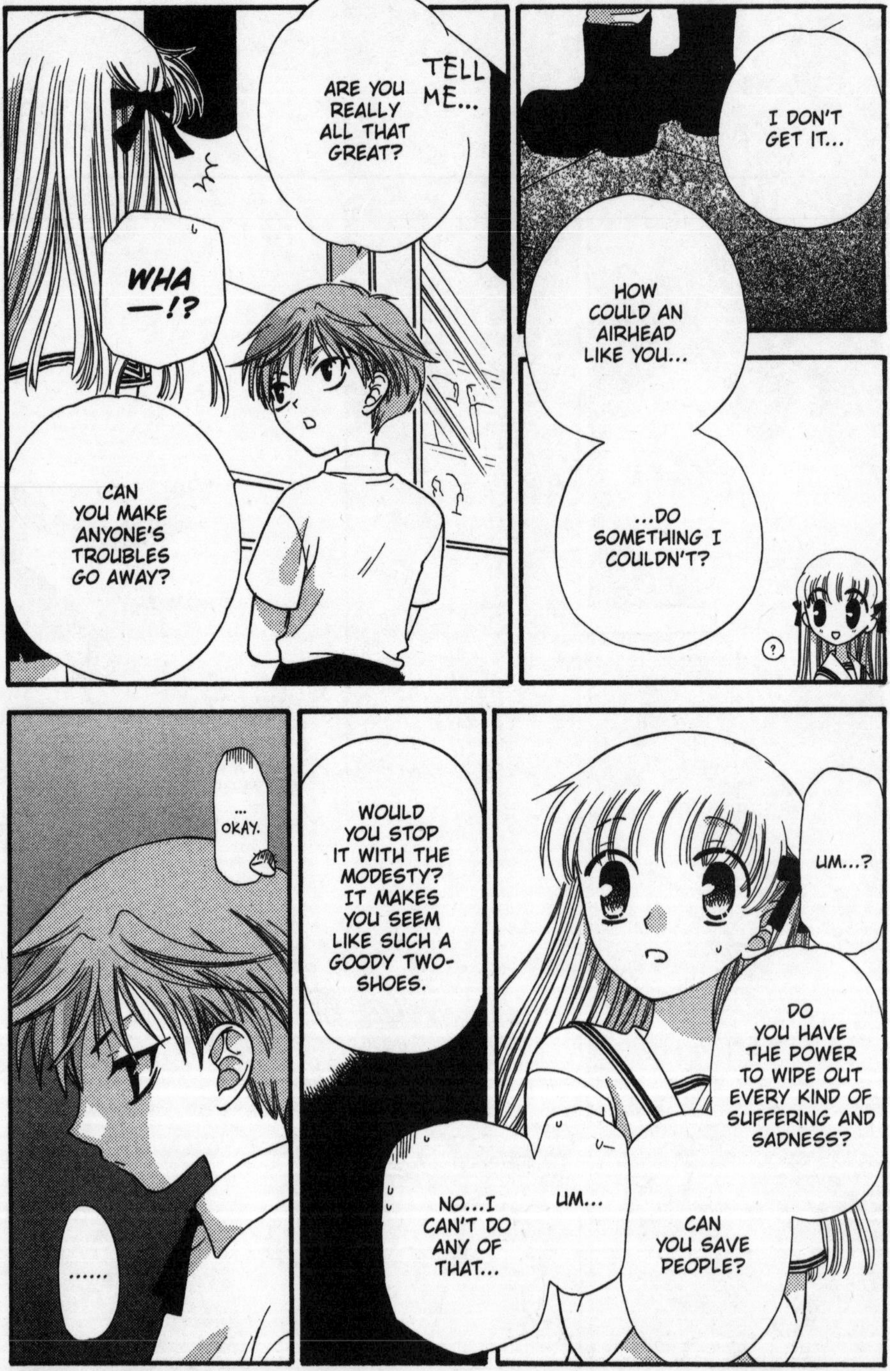
I DON'T GET IT...
HOW COULD AN AIRHEAD LIKE YOU...
...DO SOMETHING I COULDN'T?
?
TELL ME...
ARE YOU REALLY ALL THAT GREAT?
WHA—!?
CAN YOU MAKE ANYONE'S TROUBLES GO AWAY?
UM...?
DO YOU HAVE THE POWER TO WIPE OUT EVERY KIND OF SUFFERING AND SADNESS?
CAN YOU SAVE PEOPLE?
UM...
NO...I CAN'T DO ANY OF THAT...
WOULD YOU STOP IT WITH THE MODESTY? IT MAKES YOU SEEM LIKE SUCH A GOODY TWO-SHOES.
...OKAY.
......

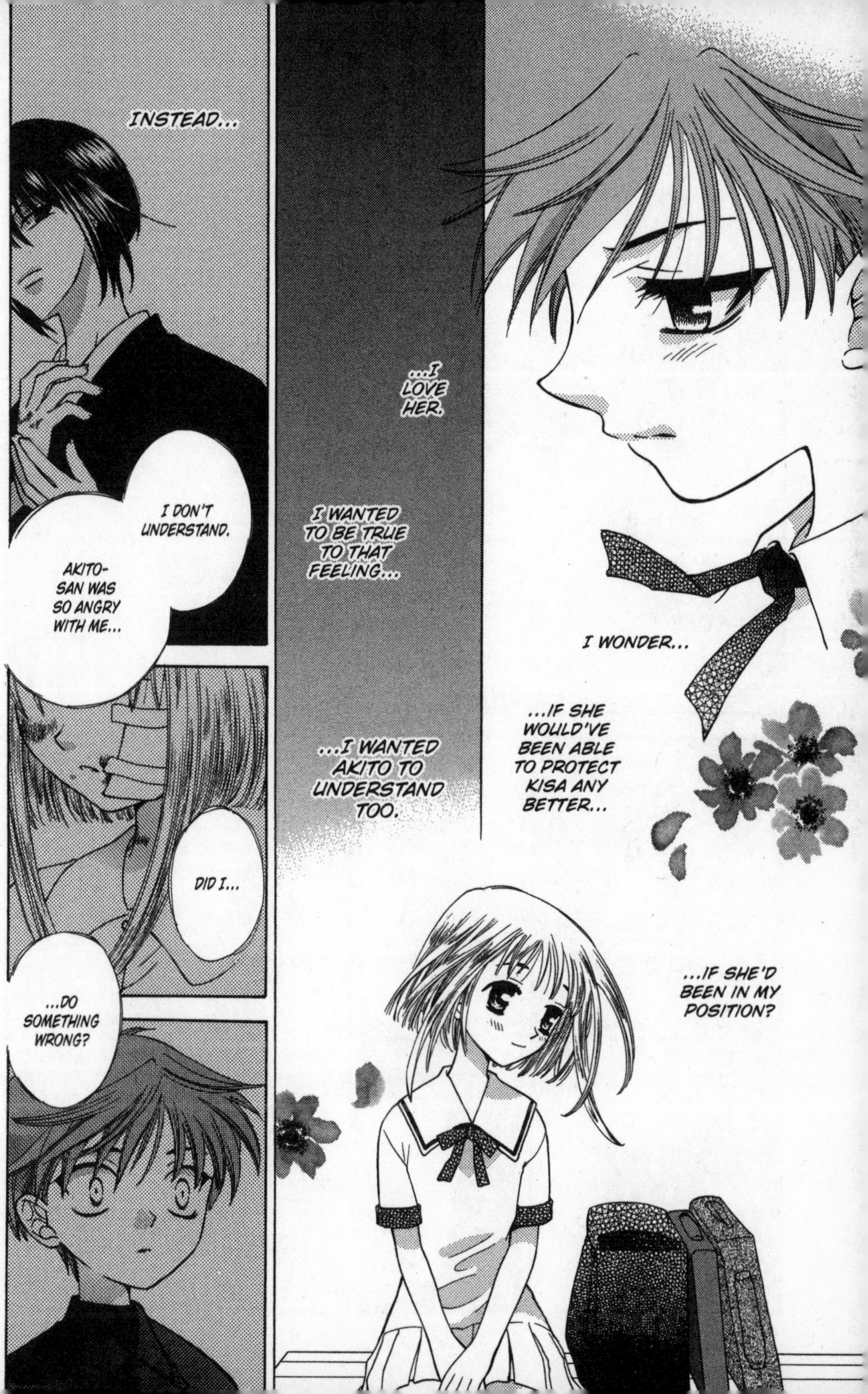
I WONDER...
...IF SHE WOULD'VE BEEN ABLE TO PROTECT KISA ANY BETTER...
...IF SHE'D BEEN IN MY POSITION?
...I LOVE HER.
I WANTED TO BE TRUE TO THAT FEELING...
...I WANTED AKITO TO UNDERSTAND TOO.
INSTEAD...
I DON'T UNDERSTAND.
AKITO-SAN WAS SO ANGRY WITH ME...
DID I...
...DO SOMETHING WRONG?

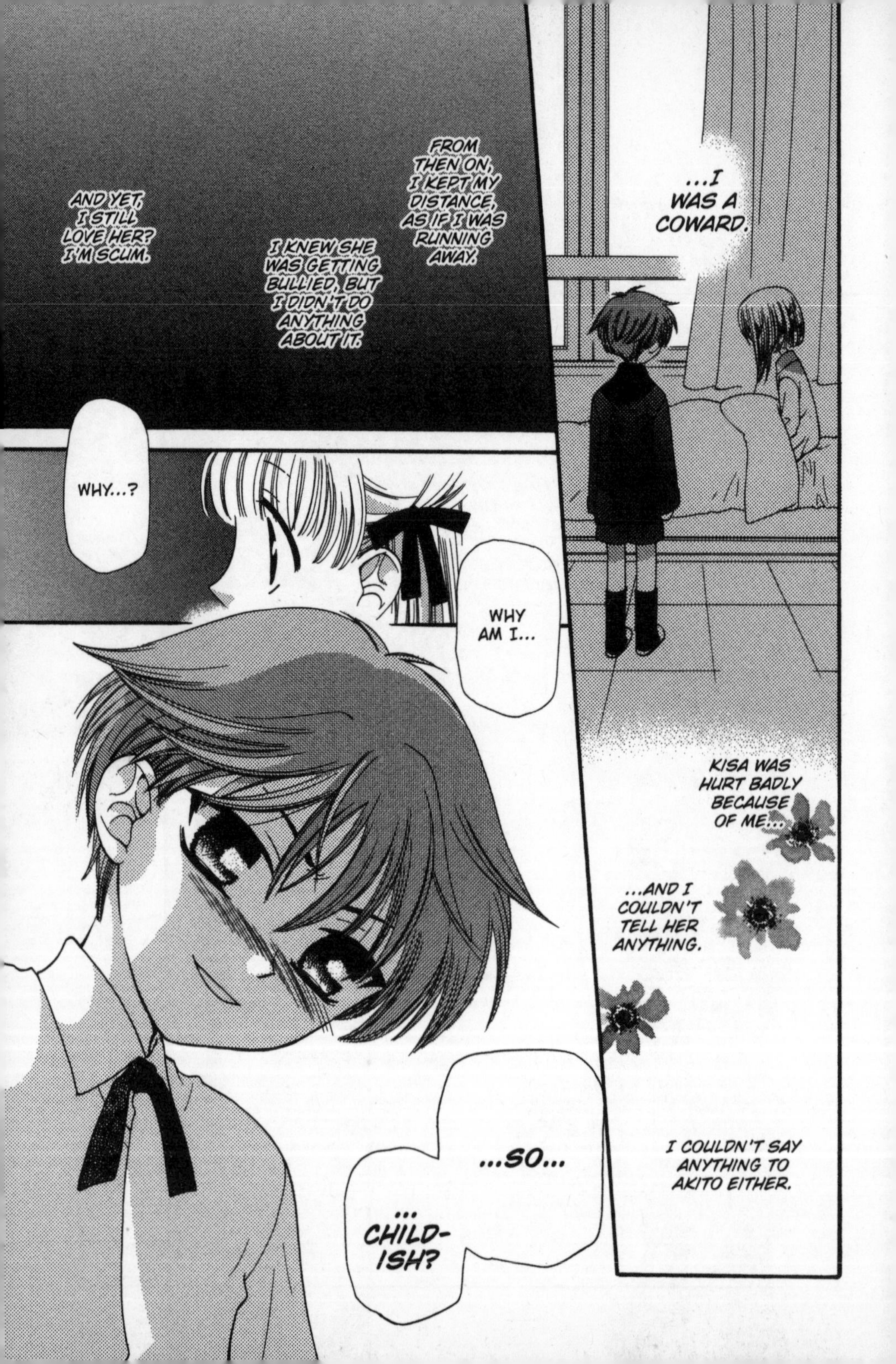
...I WAS A COWARD.
KISA WAS HURT BADLY BECAUSE OF ME...
...AND I COULDN'T TELL HER ANYTHING.
I COULDN'T SAY ANYTHING TO AKITO EITHER.
FROM THEN ON, I KEPT MY DISTANCE, AS IF I WAS RUNNING AWAY.
I KNEW SHE WAS GETTING BULLIED, BUT I DIDN'T DO ANYTHING ABOUT IT.
AND YET, I STILL LOVE HER? I'M SCUM.
WHY...?
WHY AM I...
...SO...
...CHILD-ISH?

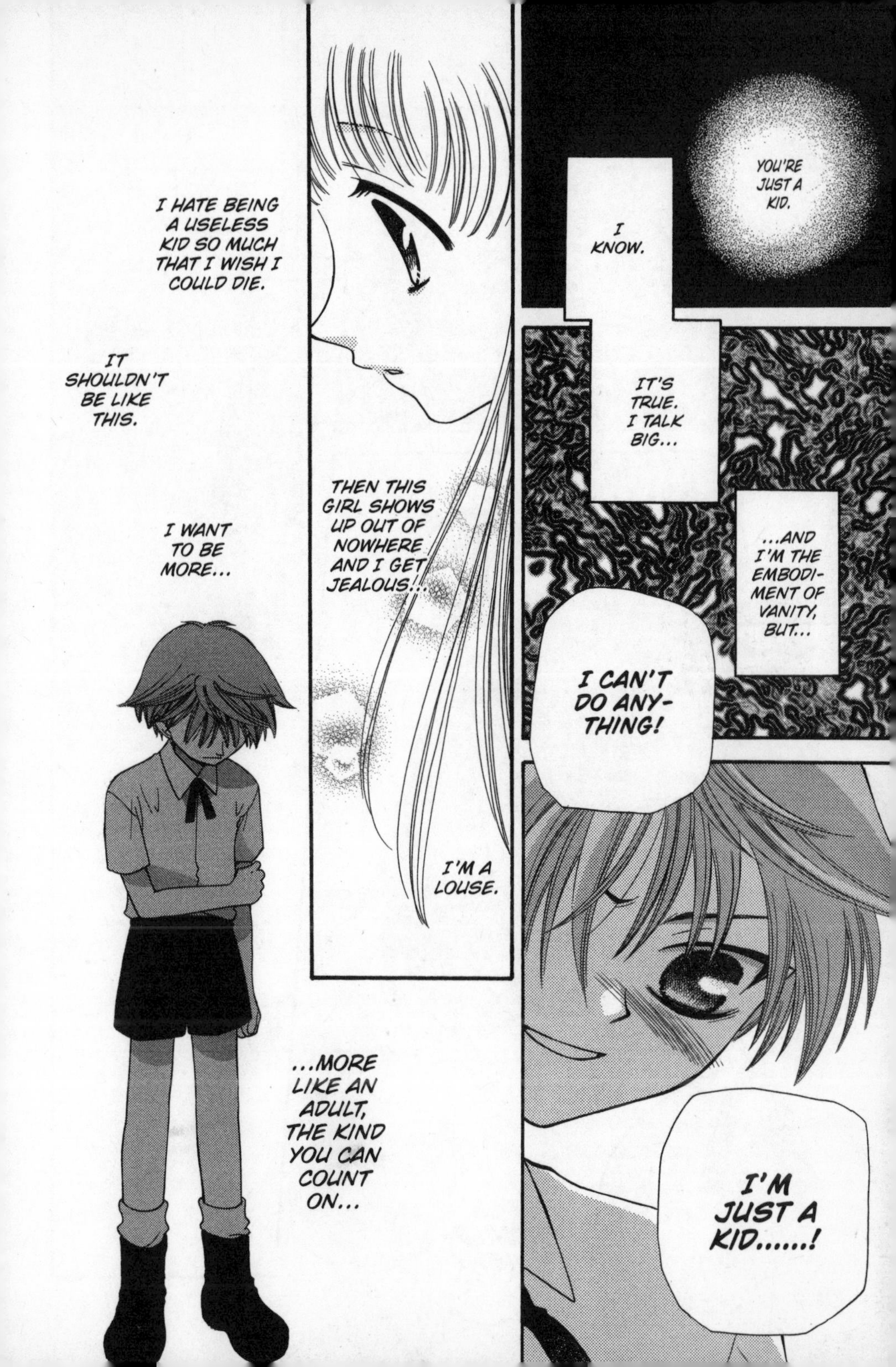
YOU'RE JUST A KID.
I KNOW.
IT'S TRUE. I TALK BIG...
...AND I'M THE EMBODIMENT OF VANITY, BUT...
I CAN'T DO ANYTHING!
I'M JUST A KID......!
THEN THIS GIRL SHOWS UP OUT OF NOWHERE AND I GET JEALOUS...
I'M A LOUSE.
I HATE BEING A USELESS KID SO MUCH THAT I WISH I COULD DIE.
IT SHOULDN'T BE LIKE THIS.
I WANT TO BE MORE...
...MORE LIKE AN ADULT, THE KIND YOU CAN COUNT ON...

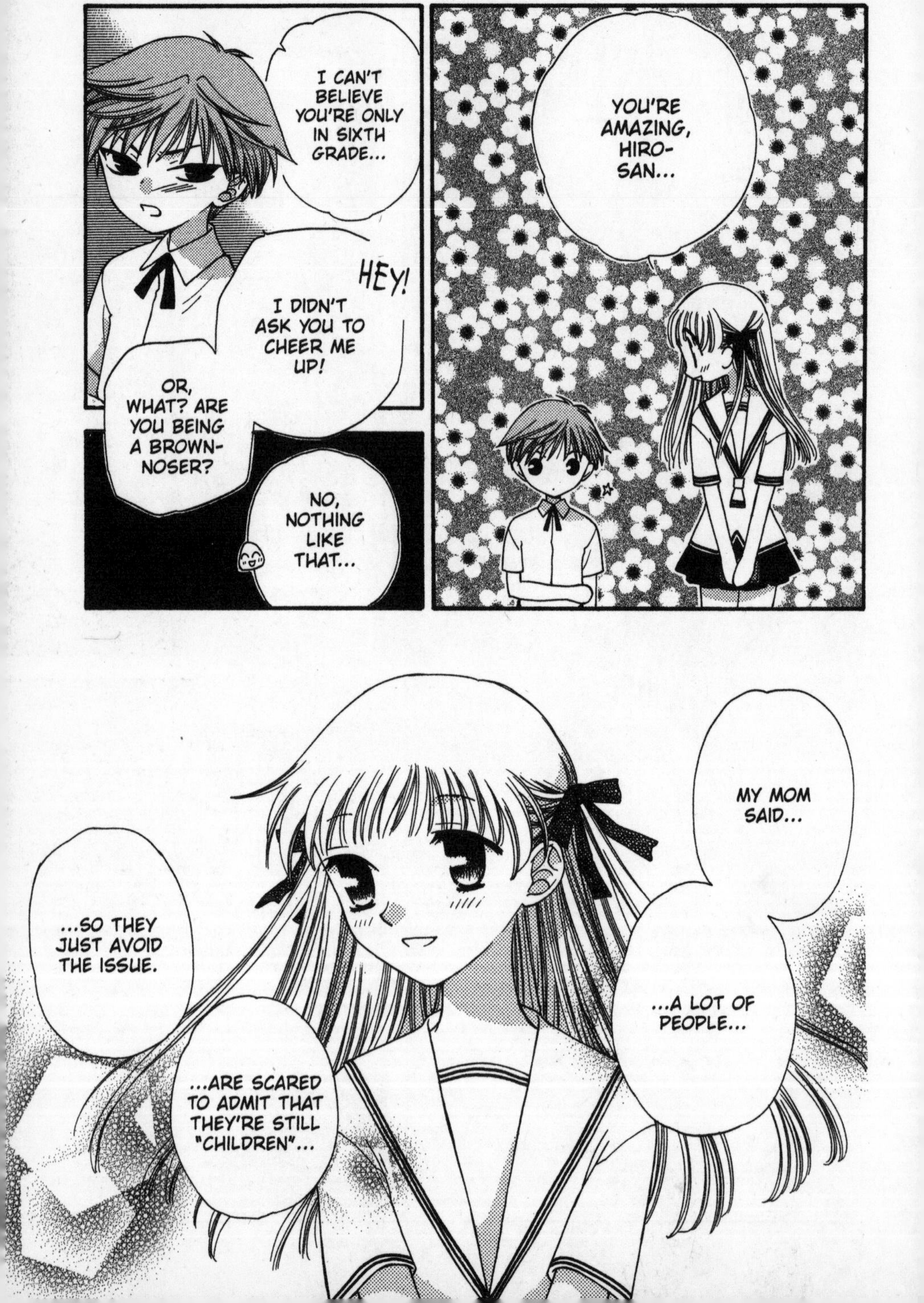
YOU'RE AMAZING, HIRO-SAN...
I CAN'T BELIEVE YOU'RE ONLY IN SIXTH GRADE...
HEY!
I DIDN'T ASK YOU TO CHEER ME UP!
OR, WHAT? ARE YOU BEING A BROWN-NOSER?
NO, NOTHING LIKE THAT...
MY MOM SAID...
...A LOT OF PEOPLE...
...ARE SCARED TO ADMIT THAT THEY'RE STILL "CHILDREN"...
...SO THEY JUST AVOID THE ISSUE.

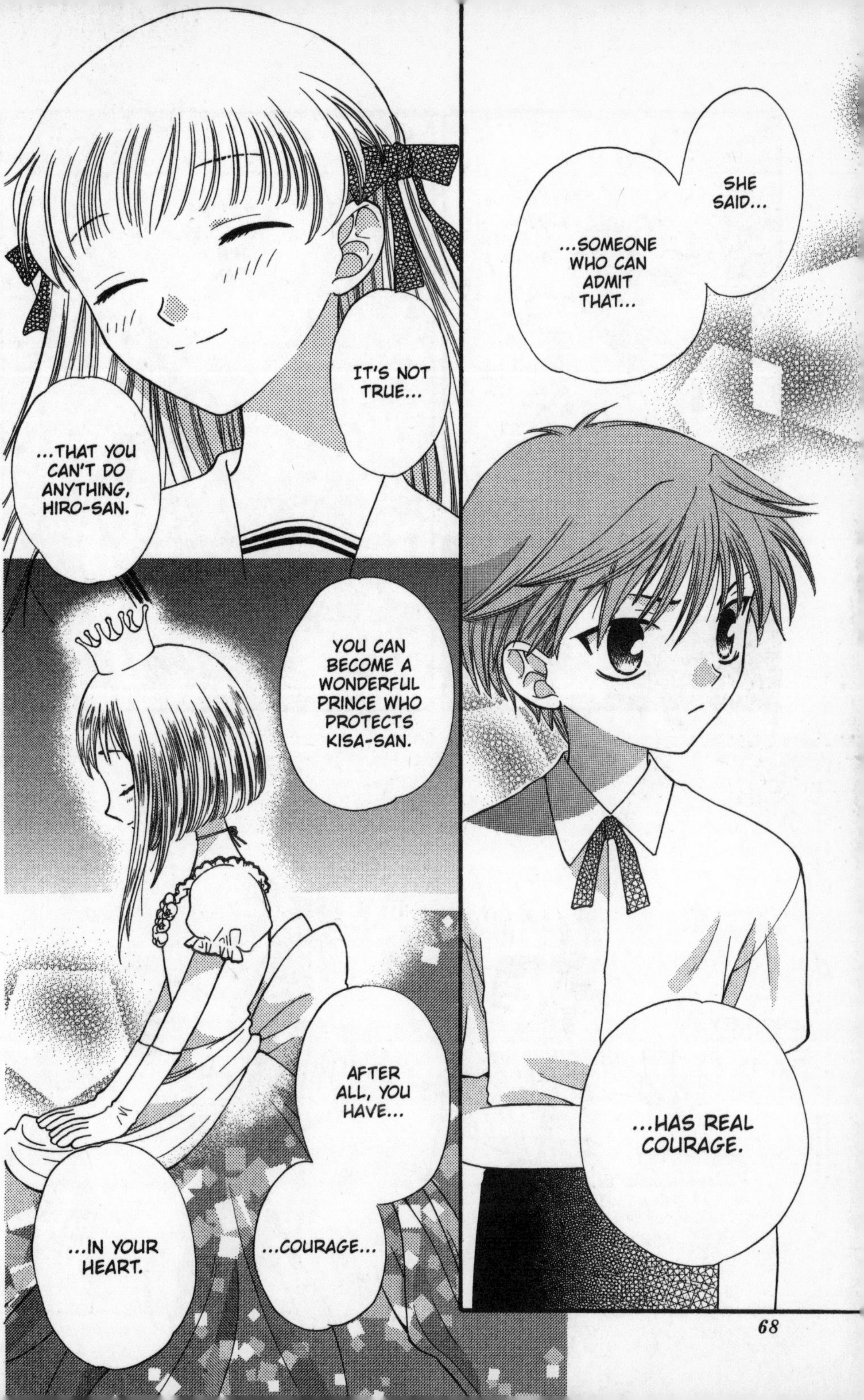
SHE SAID...
...SOMEONE WHO CAN ADMIT THAT...
...HAS REAL COURAGE.
IT'S NOT TRUE...
...THAT YOU CAN'T DO ANYTHING, HIRO-SAN.
YOU CAN BECOME A WONDERFUL PRINCE WHO PROTECTS KISA-SAN.
AFTER ALL, YOU HAVE...
...COURAGE...
...IN YOUR HEART.

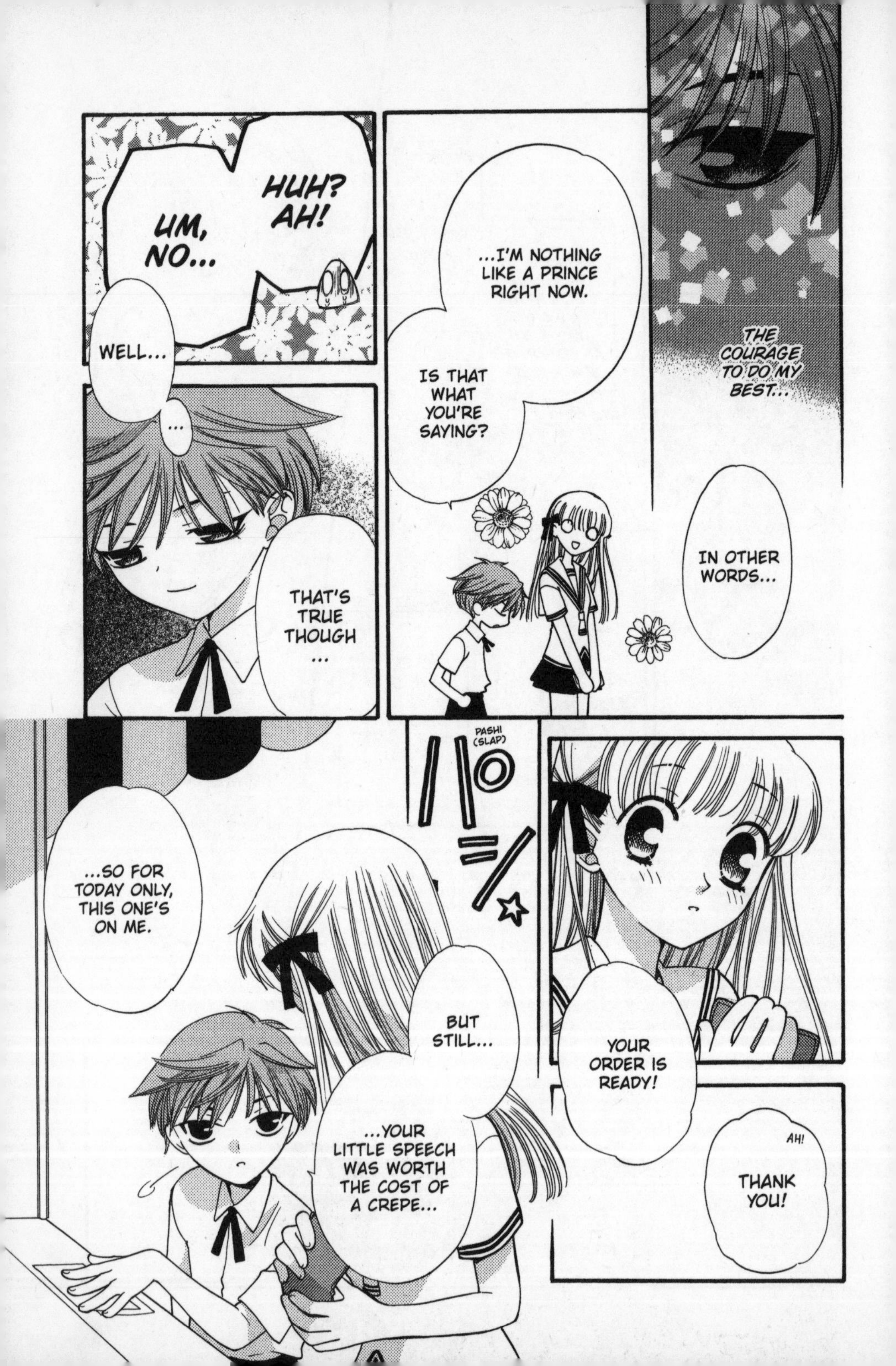
THE COURAGE TO DO MY BEST...
IN OTHER WORDS...
...I'M NOTHING LIKE A PRINCE RIGHT NOW.
IS THAT WHAT YOU'RE SAYING?
HUH? AH!
UM, NO...
WELL...
...
THAT'S TRUE THOUGH ...
PASHI (SLAP)
YOUR ORDER IS READY!
AH!
THANK YOU!
BUT STILL...
...YOUR LITTLE SPEECH WAS WORTH THE COST OF A CREPE...
...SO FOR TODAY ONLY, THIS ONE'S ON ME.

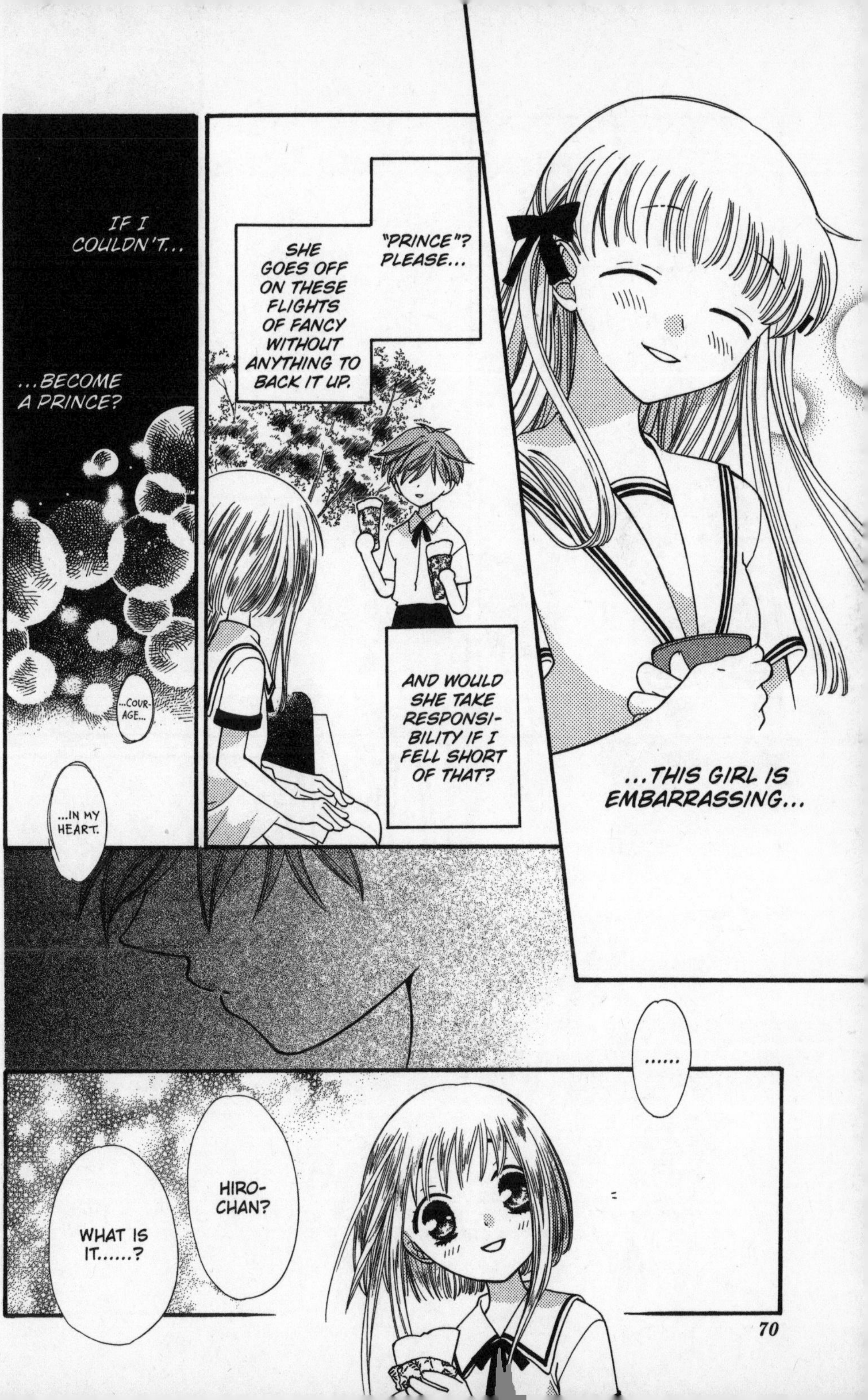
...THIS GIRL IS EMBARRASSING...
"PRINCE"? PLEASE...
SHE GOES OFF ON THESE FLIGHTS OF FANCY WITHOUT ANYTHING TO BACK IT UP.
AND WOULD SHE TAKE RESPONSIBILITY IF I FELL SHORT OF THAT?
IF I COULDN'T...
...BECOME A PRINCE?
...COURAGE...
...IN MY HEART.
......
HIRO-CHAN?
WHAT IS IT......?

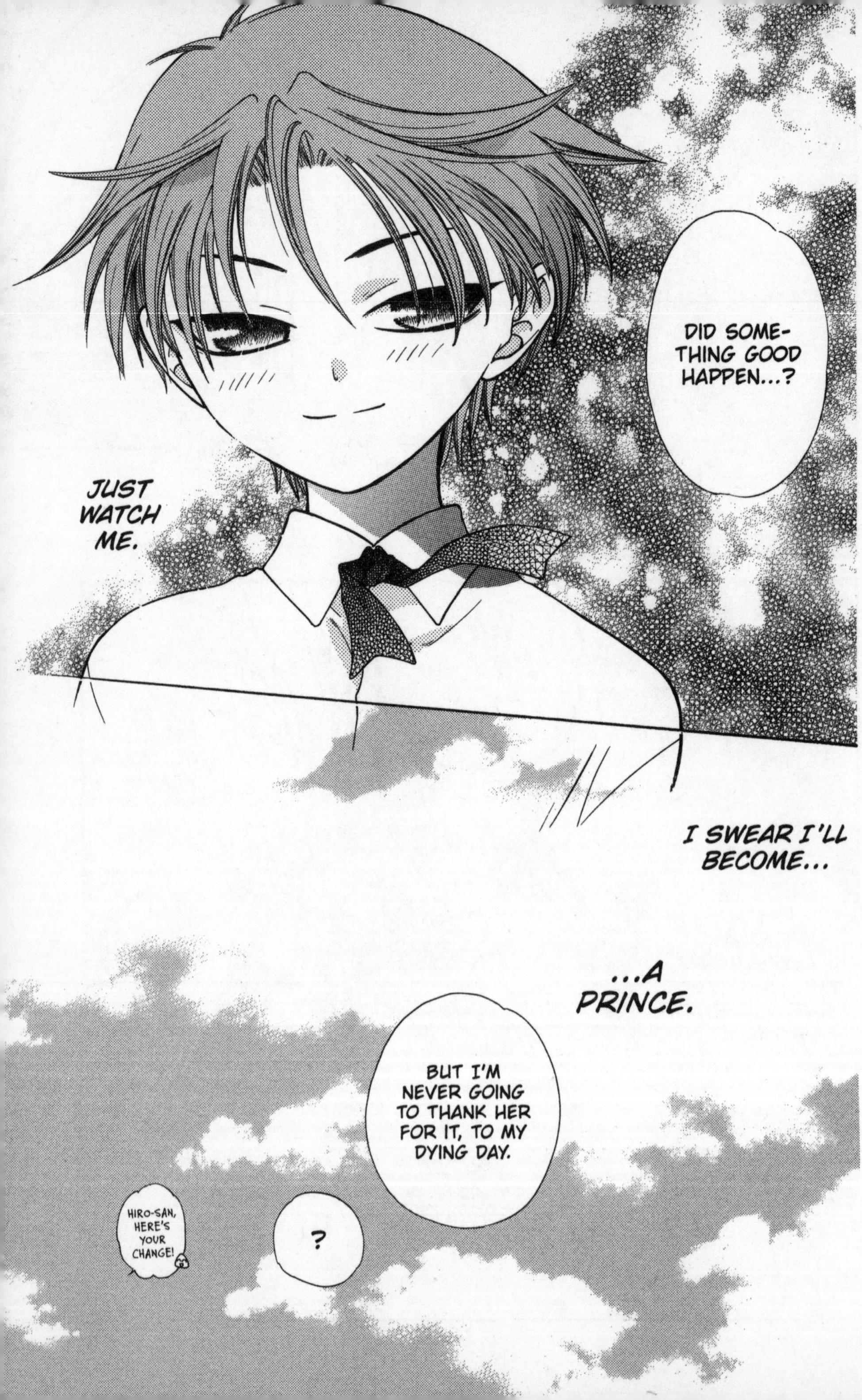
DID SOME-
THING GOOD
HAPPEN...?
JUST
WATCH
ME.
I SWEAR I'LL
BECOME...
...A
PRINCE.
BUT I'M
NEVER GOING
TO THANK HER
FOR IT, TO MY
DYING DAY.
?
HIRO-SAN,
HERE'S
YOUR
CHANGE!

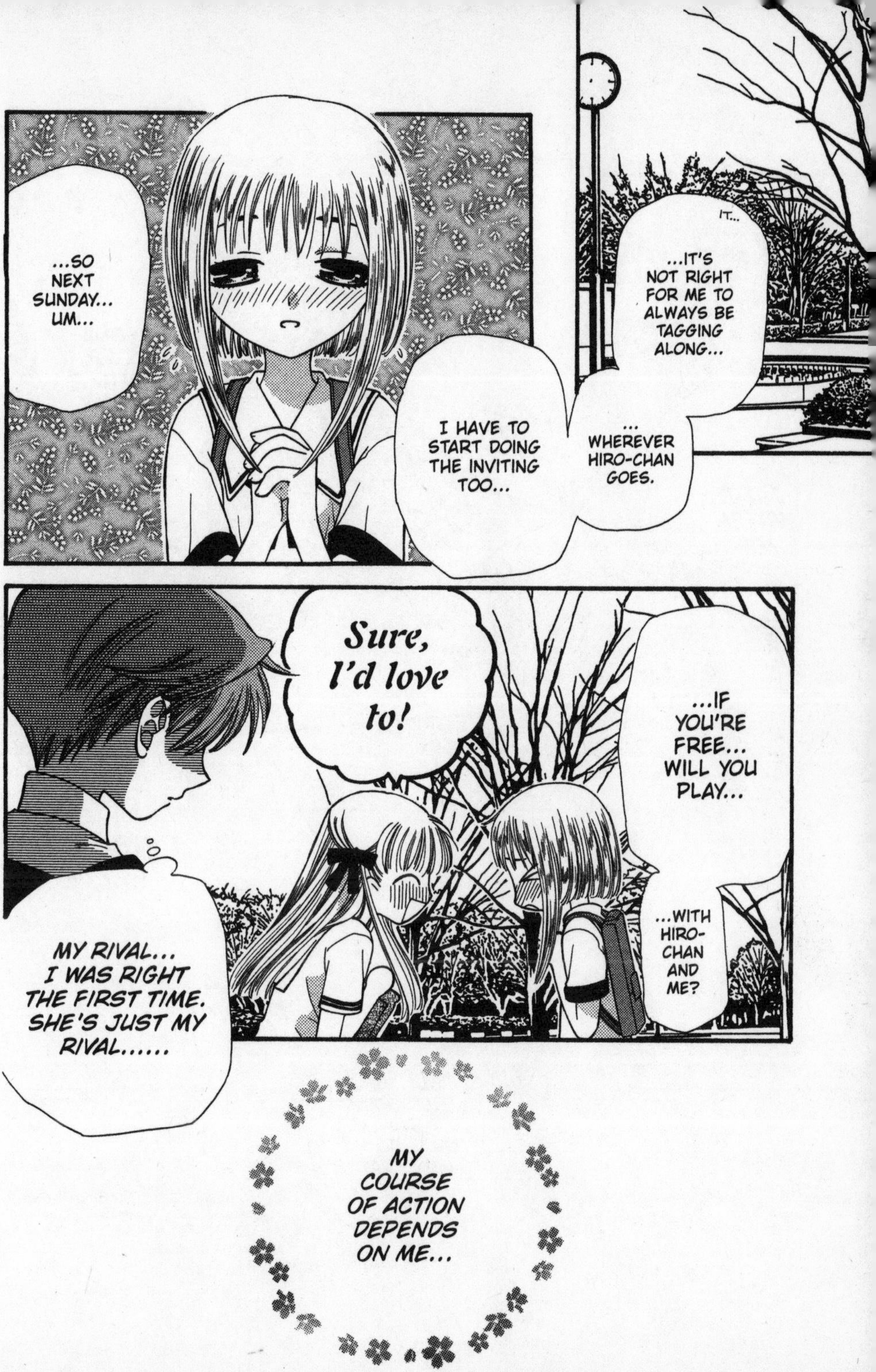
IT...
...IT'S NOT RIGHT FOR ME TO ALWAYS BE TAGGING ALONG...
...WHEREVER HIRO-CHAN GOES.
I HAVE TO START DOING THE INVITING TOO...
...SO NEXT SUNDAY... UM...
...IF YOU'RE FREE... WILL YOU PLAY...
...WITH HIRO-CHAN AND ME?
Sure, I'd love to!
MY RIVAL... I WAS RIGHT THE FIRST TIME. SHE'S JUST MY RIVAL......
MY COURSE OF ACTION DEPENDS ON ME...

COLLECTOR'S EDITION

Fruits Basket

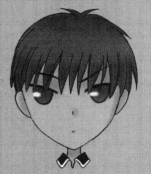

COLLECTOR'S EDITION

Fruits
Basket

Chapter 39

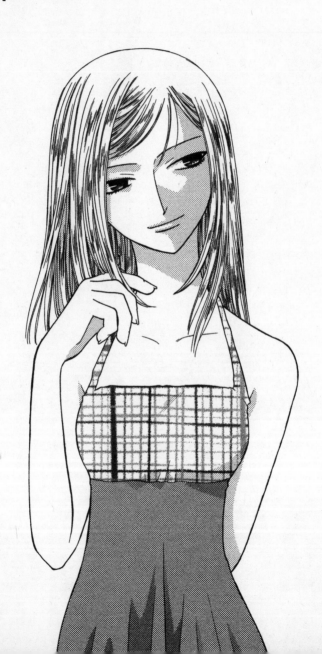

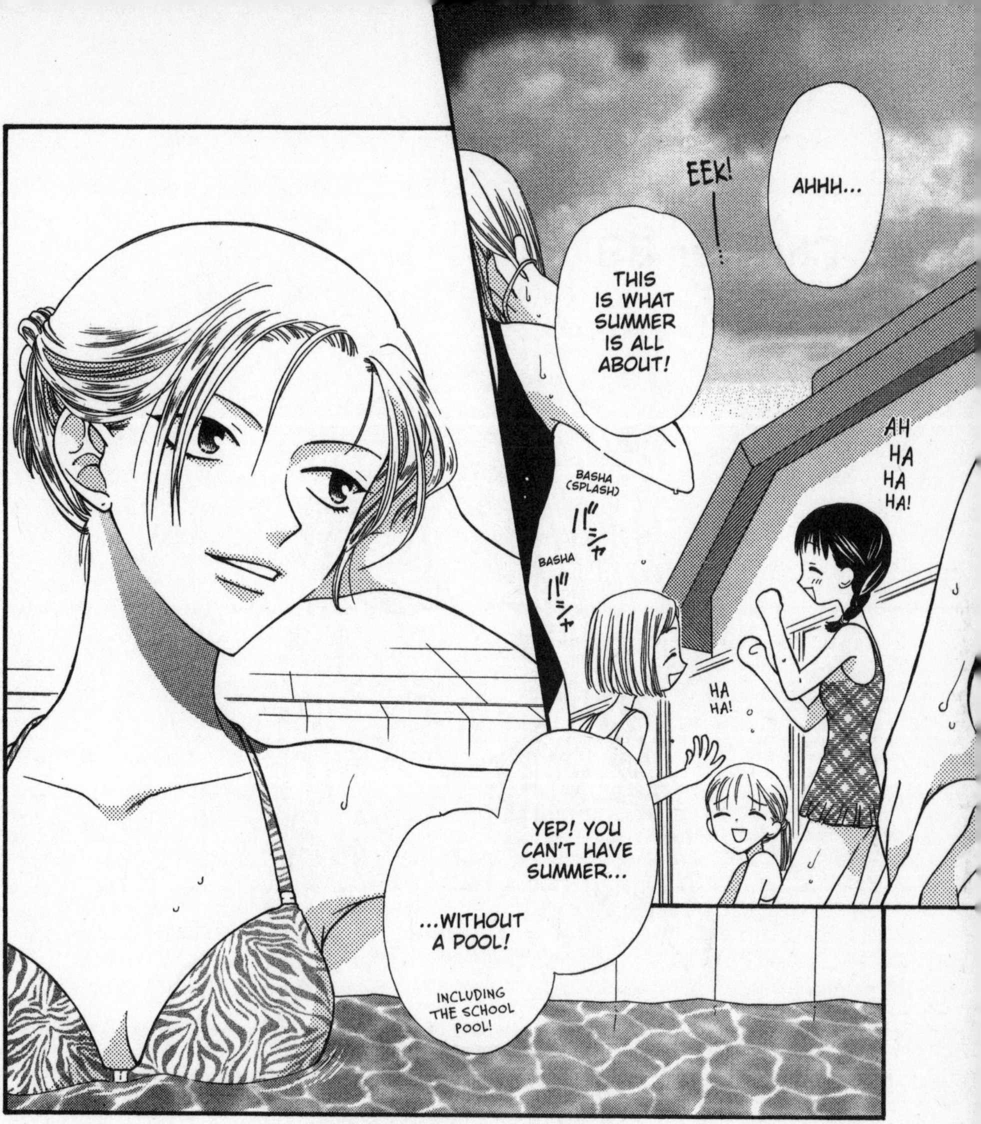
AHHH...
EEK!
THIS IS WHAT SUMMER IS ALL ABOUT!
AH HA HA HA!
BASHA (SPLASH)
BASHA
HA HA!
YEP! YOU CAN'T HAVE SUMMER...
...WITHOUT A POOL!
INCLUDING THE SCHOOL POOL!

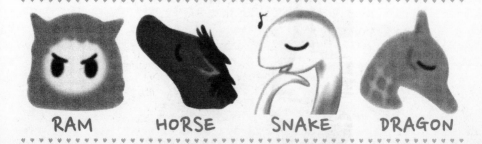

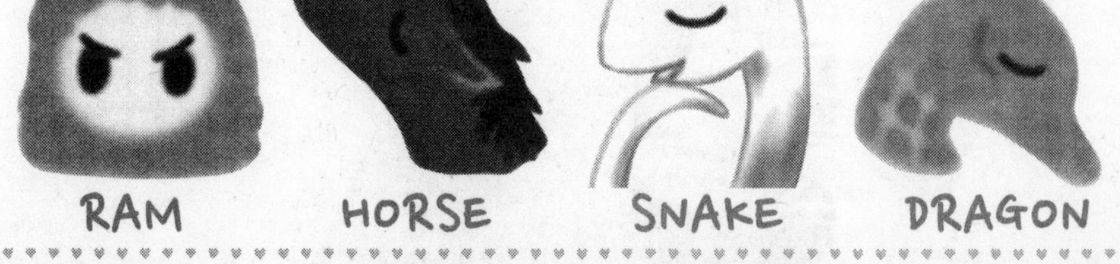
RAM
HORSE
SNAKE
DRAGON

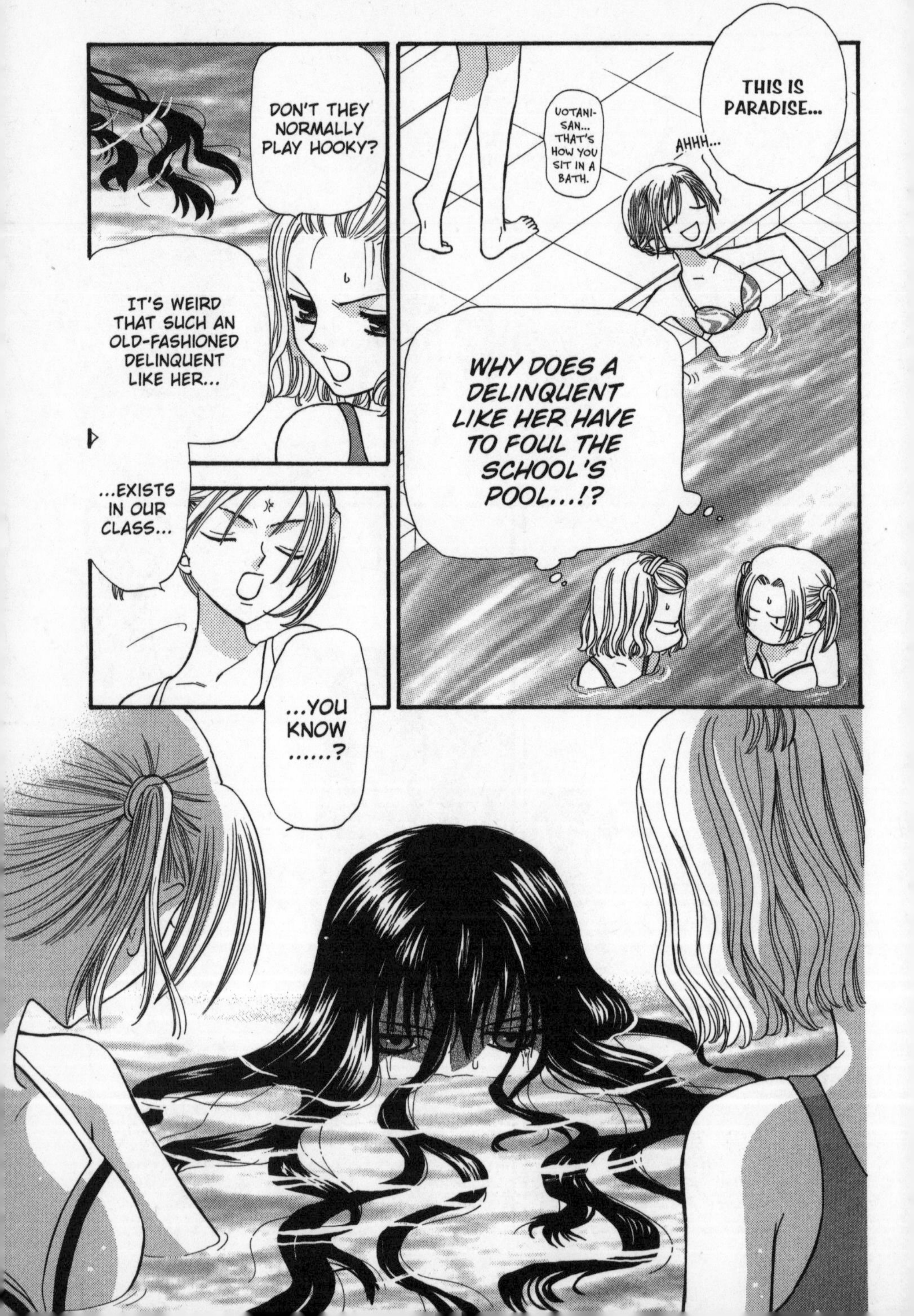
THIS IS PARADISE...
AHHH...
UOTANI-SAN... THAT'S HOW YOU SIT IN A BATH.
WHY DOES A DELINQUENT LIKE HER HAVE TO FOUL THE SCHOOL'S POOL...!?
DON'T THEY NORMALLY PLAY HOOKY?
IT'S WEIRD THAT SUCH AN OLD-FASHIONED DELINQUENT LIKE HER...
...EXISTS IN OUR CLASS...
...YOU KNOW ......?

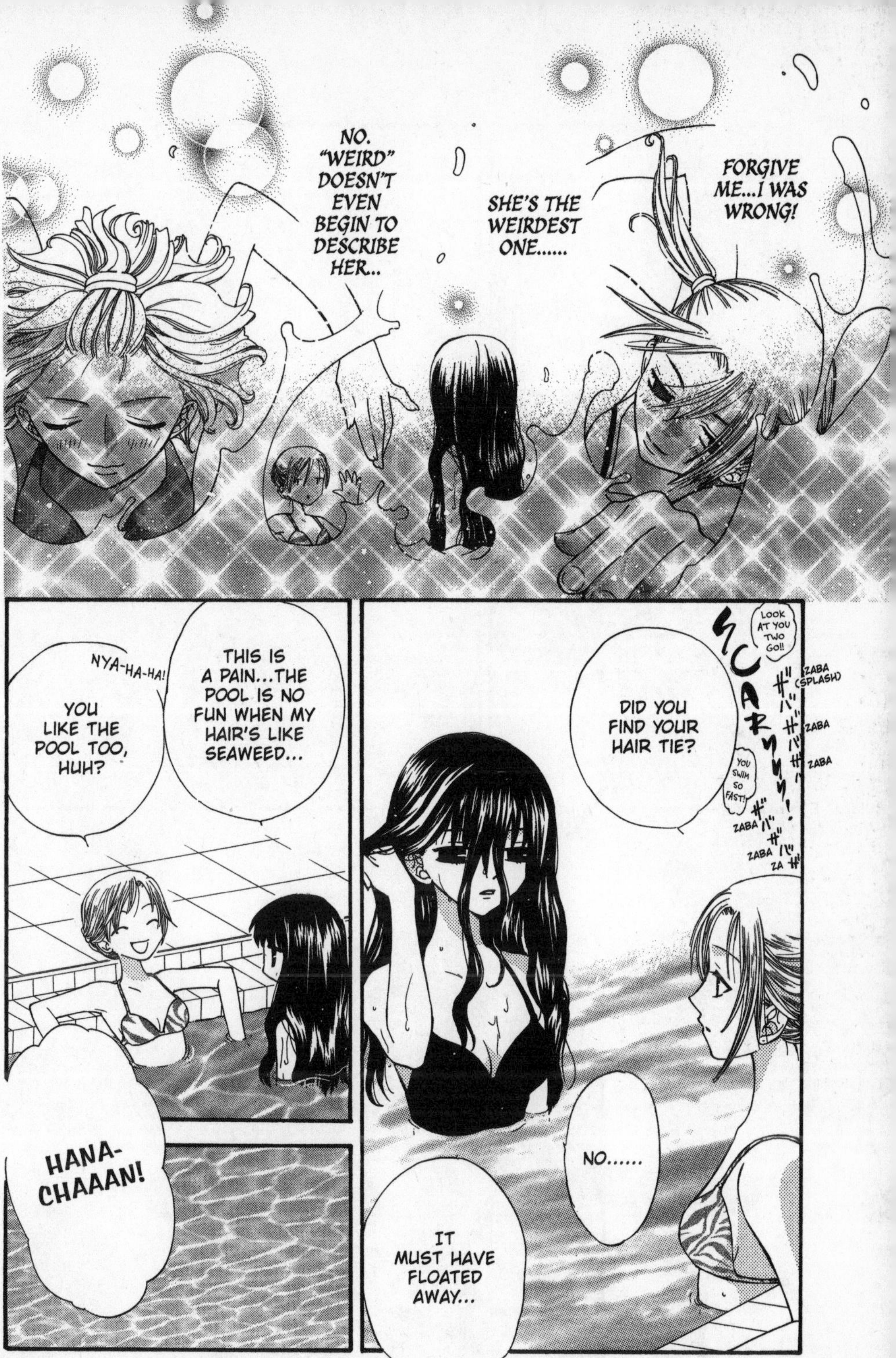
FORGIVE ME...I WAS WRONG!
SHE'S THE WEIRDEST ONE......
NO. "WEIRD" DOESN'T EVEN BEGIN TO DESCRIBE HER...
LOOK AT YOU TWO GO!!
SCARY!
YOU SWIM SO FAST!!
ZABA (SPLASH)
ZABA
ZABA
ZABA
ZABA
ZA
DID YOU FIND YOUR HAIR TIE?
NO......
IT MUST HAVE FLOATED AWAY...
THIS IS A PAIN...THE POOL IS NO FUN WHEN MY HAIR'S LIKE SEAWEED...
NYA-HA-HA!
YOU LIKE THE POOL TOO, HUH?
HANA-CHAAAN!

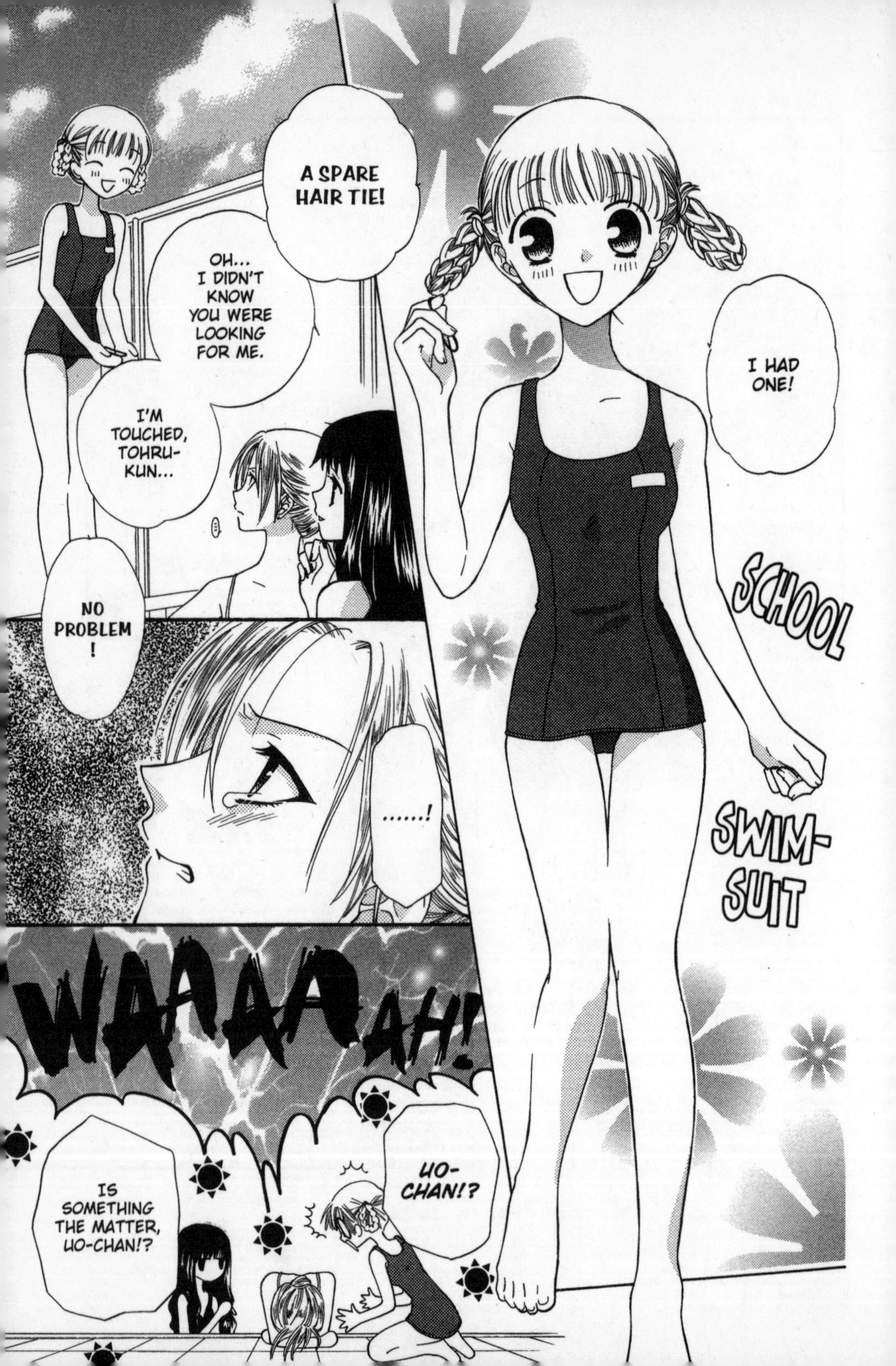
A SPARE HAIR TIE!
I HAD ONE!
SCHOOL SWIMSUIT
OH... I DIDN'T KNOW YOU WERE LOOKING FOR ME.
I'M TOUCHED, TOHRU-KUN...
NO PROBLEM!
......!
WAAAAAH!
UO-CHAN!?
IS SOMETHING THE MATTER, UO-CHAN!?

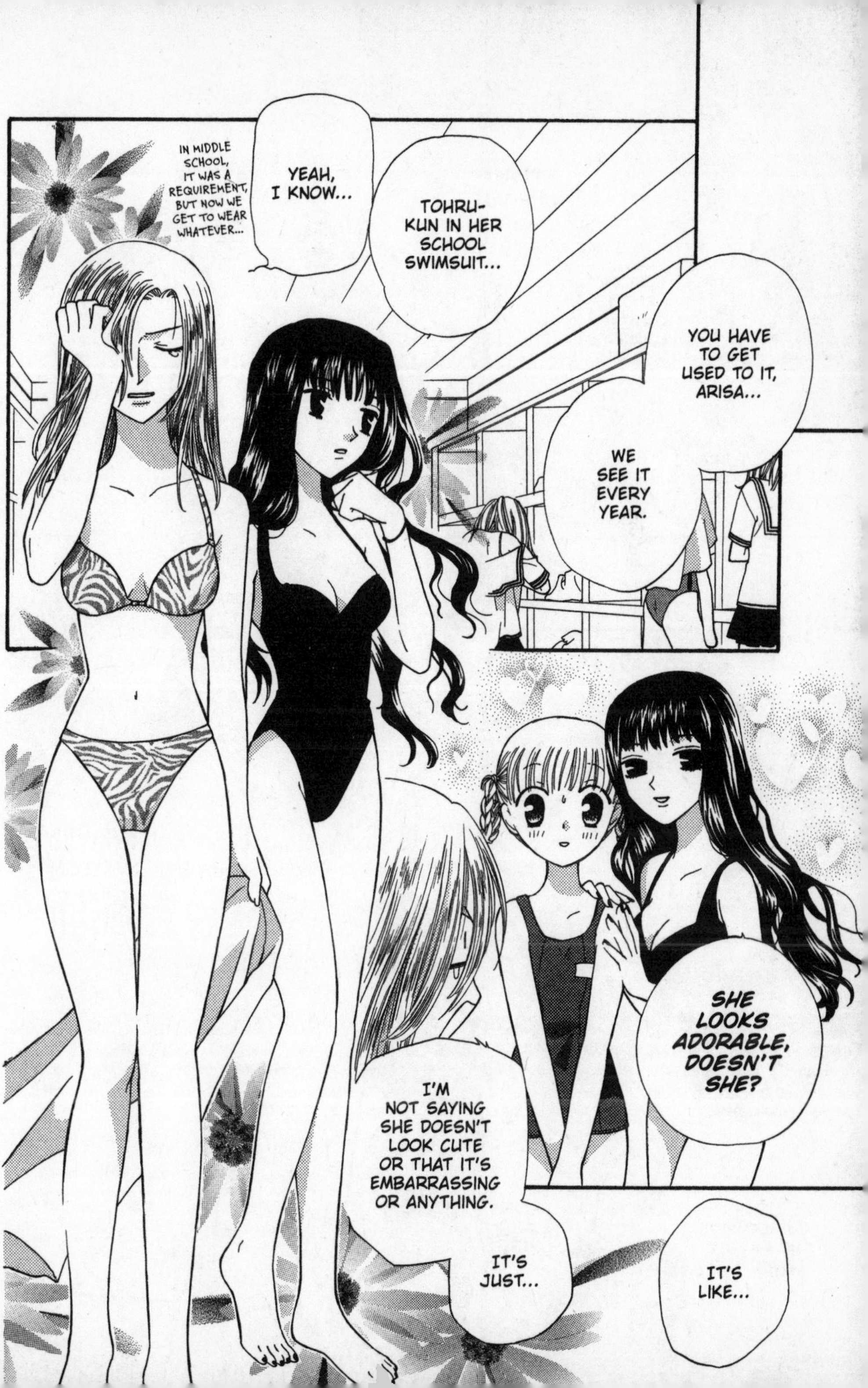
TOHRU-KUN IN HER SCHOOL SWIMSUIT...
YEAH, I KNOW...
IN MIDDLE SCHOOL, IT WAS A REQUIREMENT, BUT NOW WE GET TO WEAR WHATEVER...
YOU HAVE TO GET USED TO IT, ARISA...
WE SEE IT EVERY YEAR.
SHE LOOKS ADORABLE, DOESN'T SHE?
I'M NOT SAYING SHE DOESN'T LOOK CUTE OR THAT IT'S EMBARRASSING OR ANYTHING.
IT'S JUST...
IT'S LIKE...

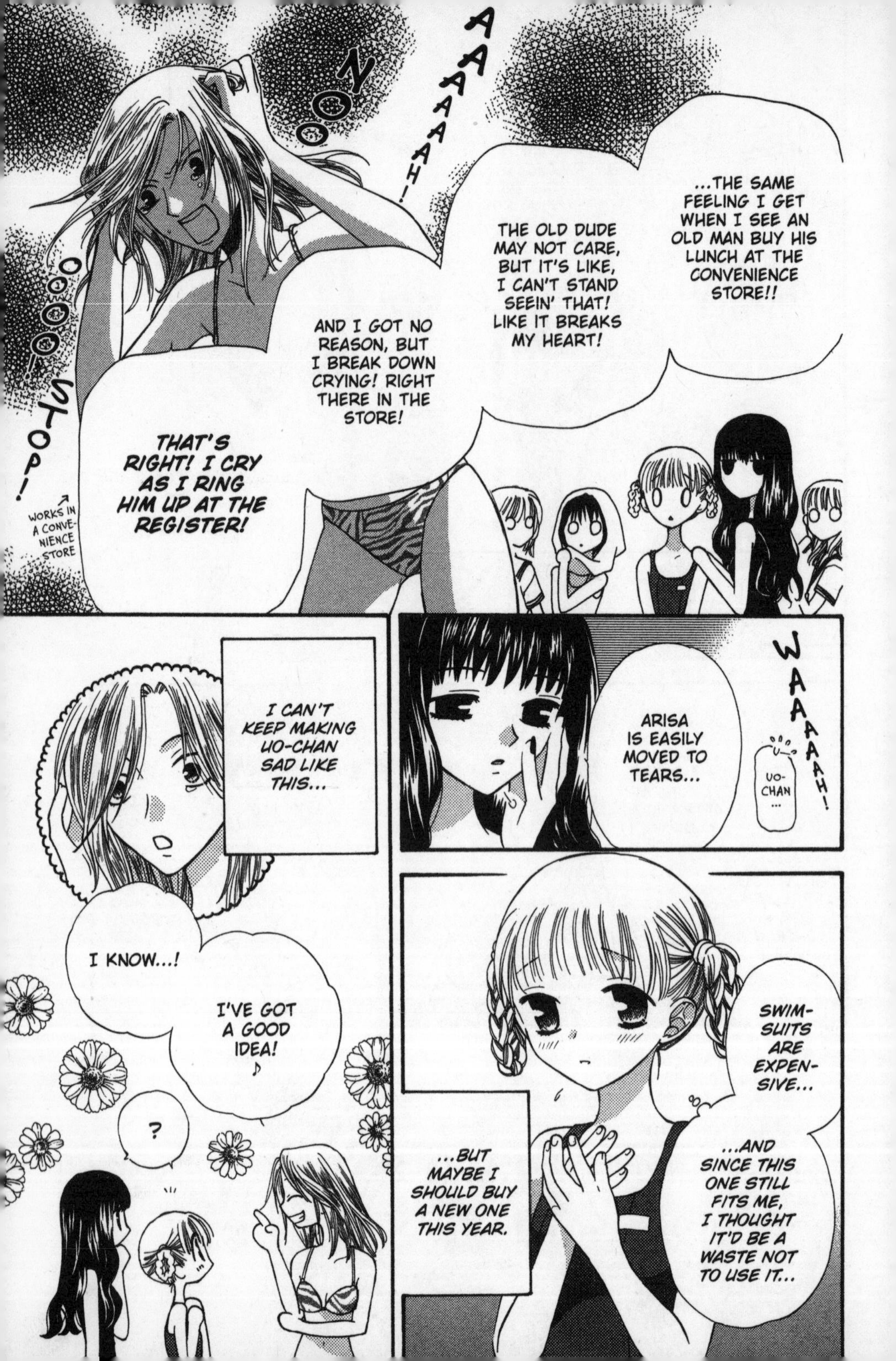
AAAAAAAH!
NOOOO
...THE SAME FEELING I GET WHEN I SEE AN OLD MAN BUY HIS LUNCH AT THE CONVENIENCE STORE!!
THE OLD DUDE MAY NOT CARE, BUT IT'S LIKE, I CAN'T STAND SEEIN' THAT! LIKE IT BREAKS MY HEART!
AND I GOT NO REASON, BUT I BREAK DOWN CRYING! RIGHT THERE IN THE STORE!
THAT'S RIGHT! I CRY AS I RING HIM UP AT THE REGISTER!
OOOOO-STOP!
WORKS IN A CONVE-NIENCE STORE
WAAAAAAH!
UO-CHAN ...
ARISA IS EASILY MOVED TO TEARS...
SWIM-SUITS ARE EXPEN-SIVE...
...AND SINCE THIS ONE STILL FITS ME, I THOUGHT IT'D BE A WASTE NOT TO USE IT...
...BUT MAYBE I SHOULD BUY A NEW ONE THIS YEAR.
I CAN'T KEEP MAKING UO-CHAN SAD LIKE THIS...
I KNOW...!
I'VE GOT A GOOD IDEA! ♪
?

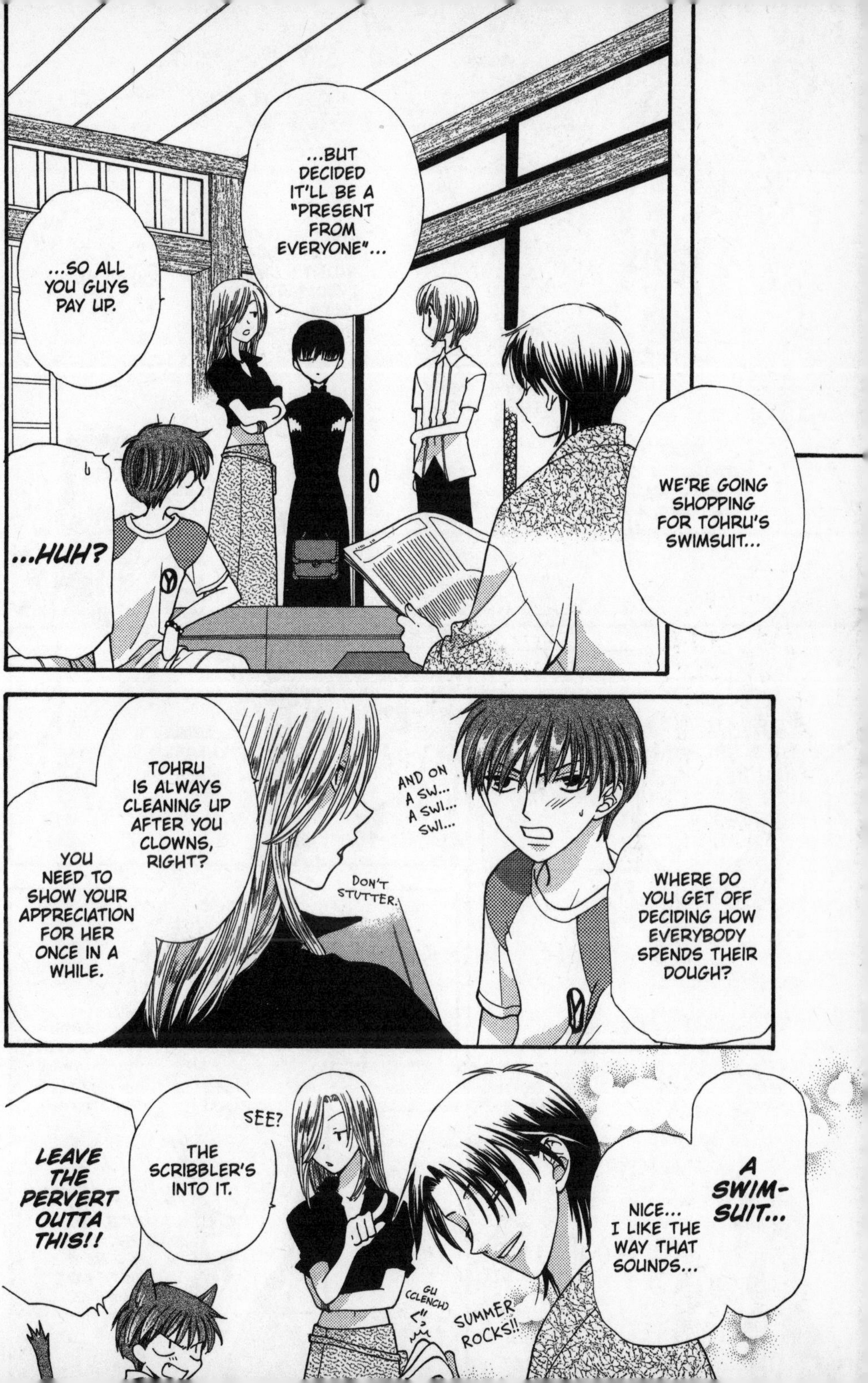
WE'RE GOING SHOPPING FOR TOHRU'S SWIMSUIT...
...BUT DECIDED IT'LL BE A "PRESENT FROM EVERYONE"...
...SO ALL YOU GUYS PAY UP.
...HUH?
WHERE DO YOU GET OFF DECIDING HOW EVERYBODY SPENDS THEIR DOUGH?
AND ON A SW... A SWI... SWI...
DON'T STUTTER.
TOHRU IS ALWAYS CLEANING UP AFTER YOU CLOWNS, RIGHT?
YOU NEED TO SHOW YOUR APPRECIATION FOR HER ONCE IN A WHILE.
A SWIM-SUIT...
NICE... I LIKE THE WAY THAT SOUNDS...
SUMMER ROCKS!!
GU (CLENCH)
SEE?
THE SCRIBBLER'S INTO IT.
LEAVE THE PERVERT OUTTA THIS!!

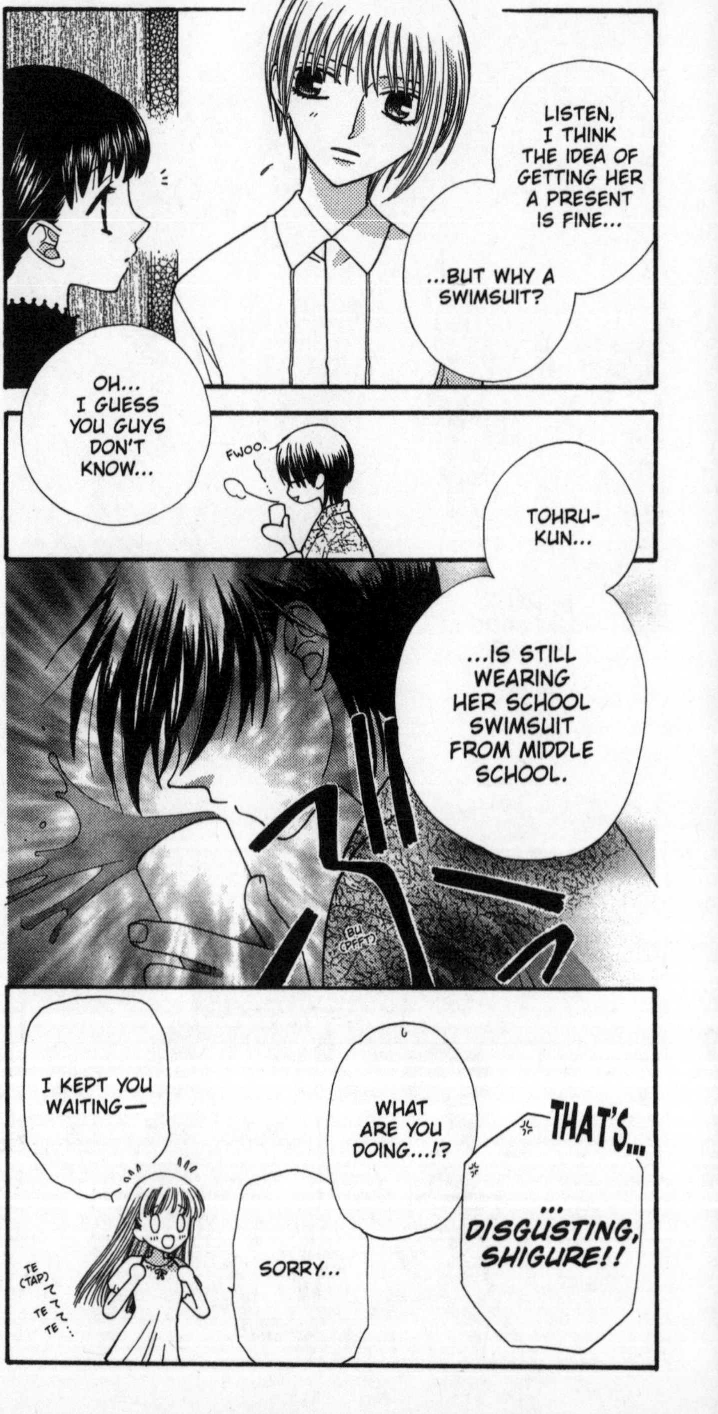
LISTEN, I THINK THE IDEA OF GETTING HER A PRESENT IS FINE...
...BUT WHY A SWIMSUIT?
OH... I GUESS YOU GUYS DON'T KNOW...
FWOO.
TOHRU-KUN...
...IS STILL WEARING HER SCHOOL SWIMSUIT FROM MIDDLE SCHOOL.
BU (PFFT)
THAT'S...
... DISGUSTING, SHIGURE!!
WHAT ARE YOU DOING...!?
SORRY...
I KEPT YOU WAITING—
TE (TAP) TE TE TE...

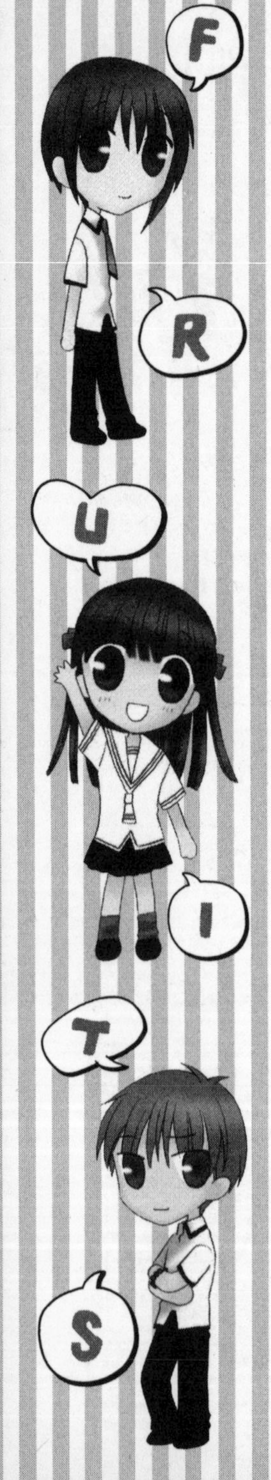
F
R
U
I
T
S

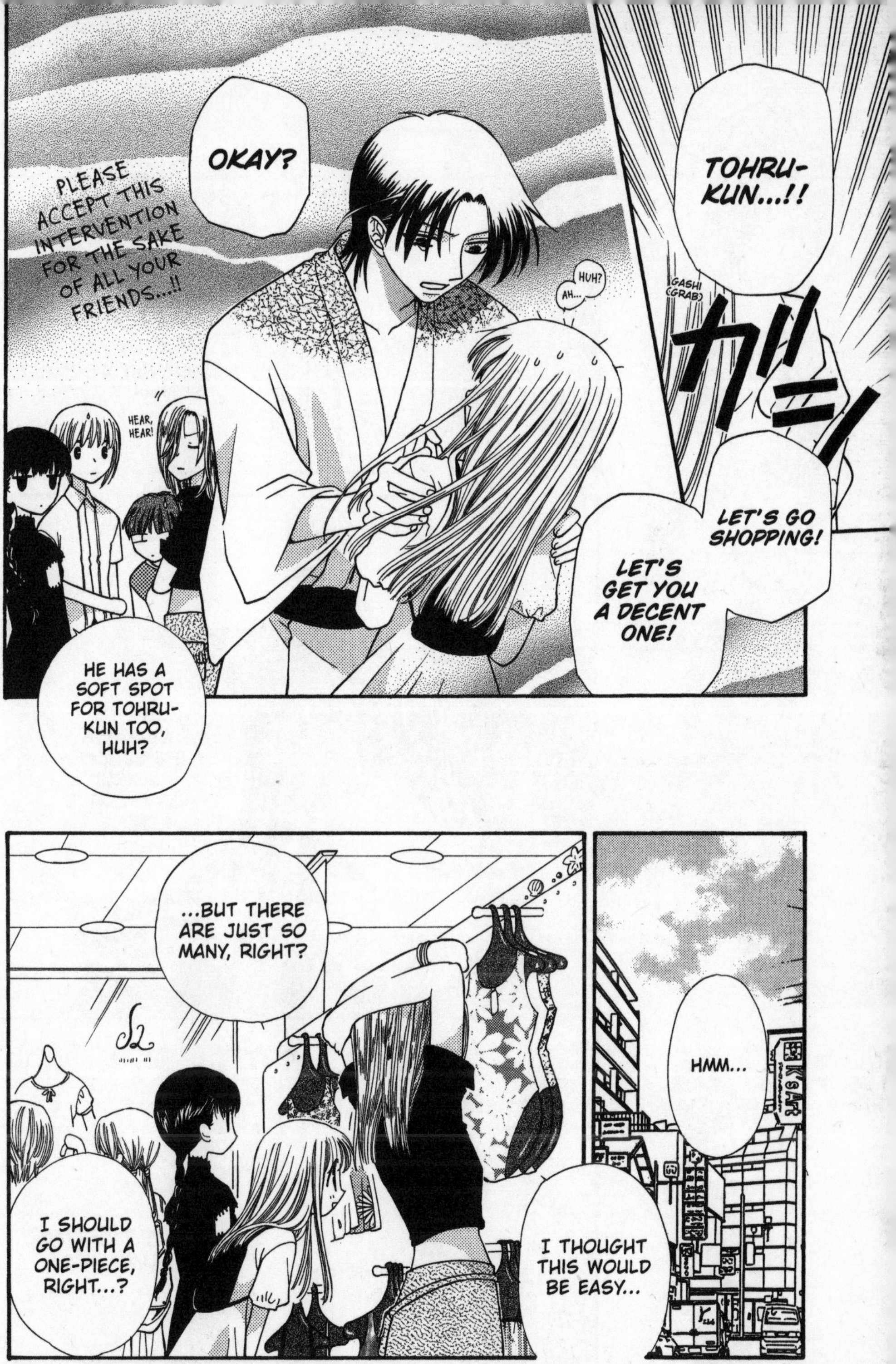
TOHRU-KUN...!!
OKAY?
PLEASE ACCEPT THIS INTERVENTION FOR THE SAKE OF ALL YOUR FRIENDS...!!
HUH? AH...
GASHI (GRAB)
LET'S GO SHOPPING!
LET'S GET YOU A DECENT ONE!
HEAR, HEAR!
HE HAS A SOFT SPOT FOR TOHRU-KUN TOO, HUH?
HMM...
I THOUGHT THIS WOULD BE EASY...
...BUT THERE ARE JUST SO MANY, RIGHT?
I SHOULD GO WITH A ONE-PIECE, RIGHT...?

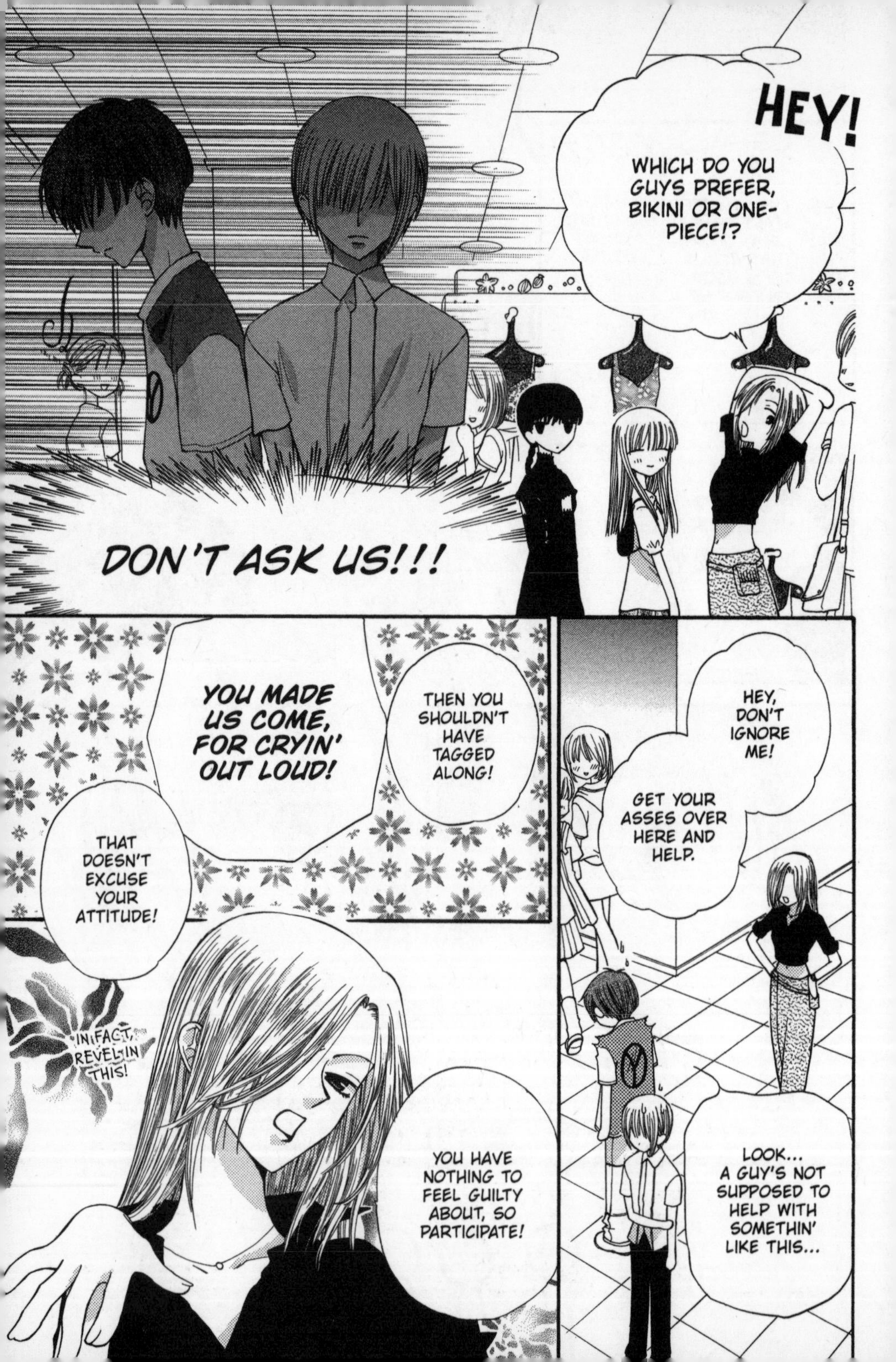
HEY!
WHICH DO YOU GUYS PREFER, BIKINI OR ONE-PIECE!?
DON'T ASK US!!!
HEY, DON'T IGNORE ME!
GET YOUR ASSES OVER HERE AND HELP.
LOOK... A GUY'S NOT SUPPOSED TO HELP WITH SOMETHIN' LIKE THIS...
THEN YOU SHOULDN'T HAVE TAGGED ALONG!
YOU MADE US COME, FOR CRYIN' OUT LOUD!
THAT DOESN'T EXCUSE YOUR ATTITUDE!
YOU HAVE NOTHING TO FEEL GUILTY ABOUT, SO PARTICIPATE!
IN FACT, REVEL IN THIS!

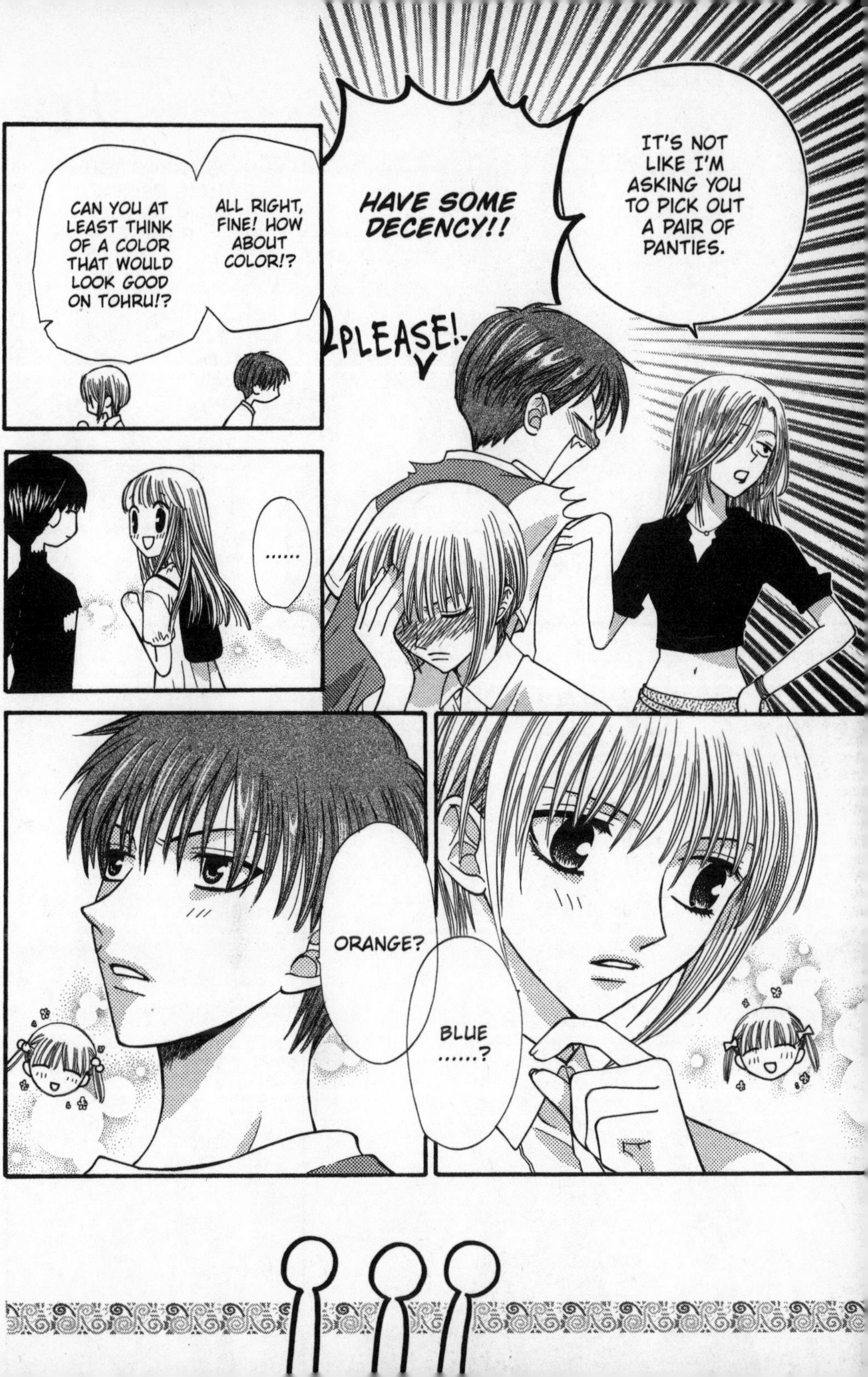
IT'S NOT LIKE I'M ASKING YOU TO PICK OUT A PAIR OF PANTIES.
HAVE SOME DECENCY!!
PLEASE!
ALL RIGHT, FINE! HOW ABOUT COLOR!?
CAN YOU AT LEAST THINK OF A COLOR THAT WOULD LOOK GOOD ON TOHRU!?
......
BLUE ......?
ORANGE?

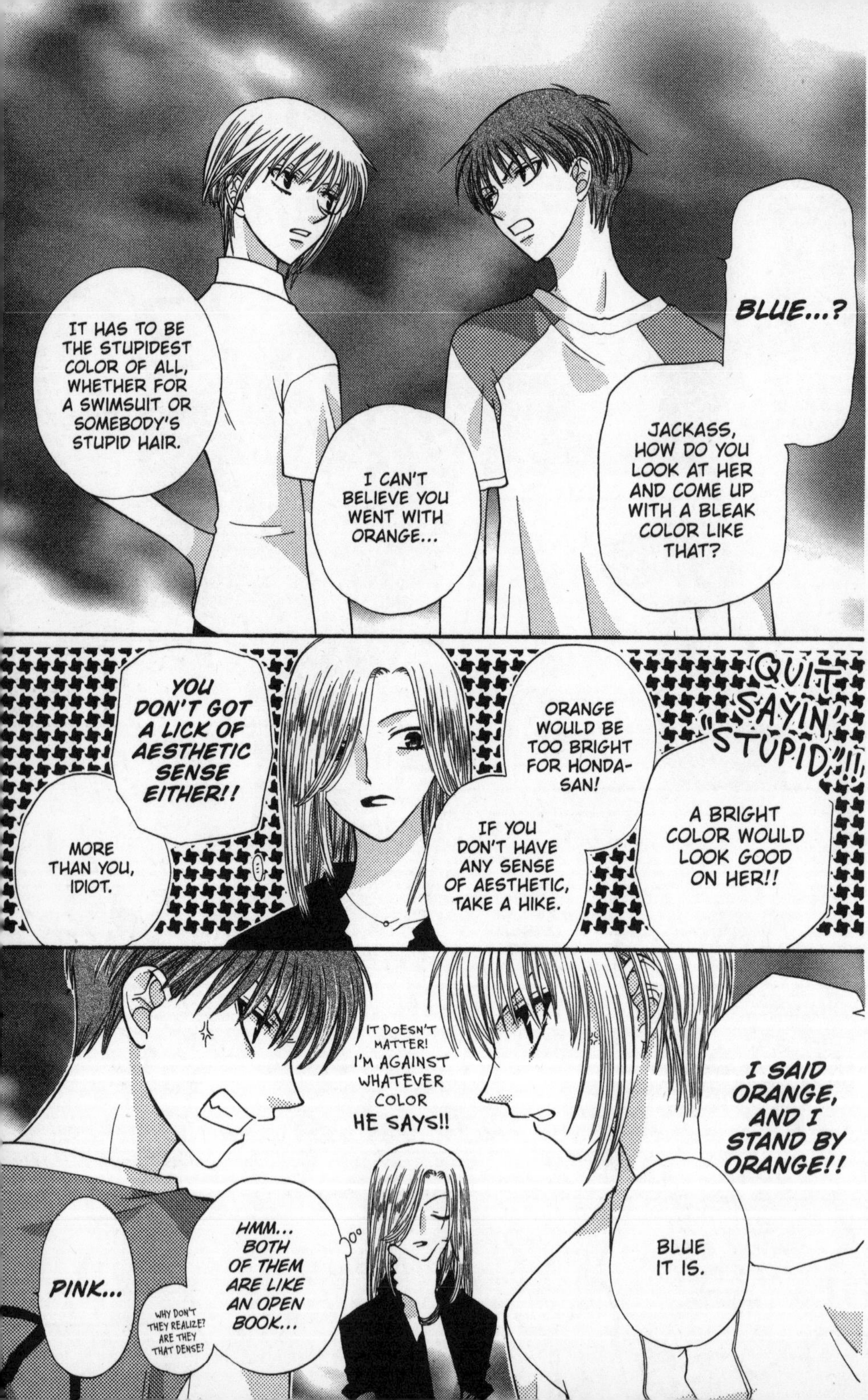
BLUE...?
JACKASS, HOW DO YOU LOOK AT HER AND COME UP WITH A BLEAK COLOR LIKE THAT?
I CAN'T BELIEVE YOU WENT WITH ORANGE...
IT HAS TO BE THE STUPIDEST COLOR OF ALL, WHETHER FOR A SWIMSUIT OR SOMEBODY'S STUPID HAIR.
QUIT SAYIN' "STUPID"!!
A BRIGHT COLOR WOULD LOOK GOOD ON HER!!
ORANGE WOULD BE TOO BRIGHT FOR HONDA-SAN!
IF YOU DON'T HAVE ANY SENSE OF AESTHETIC, TAKE A HIKE.
YOU DON'T GOT A LICK OF AESTHETIC SENSE EITHER!!
MORE THAN YOU, IDIOT.
I SAID ORANGE, AND I STAND BY ORANGE!!
IT DOESN'T MATTER! I'M AGAINST WHATEVER COLOR HE SAYS!!
BLUE IT IS.
HMM... BOTH OF THEM ARE LIKE AN OPEN BOOK...
WHY DON'T THEY REALIZE? ARE THEY THAT DENSE?
PINK...

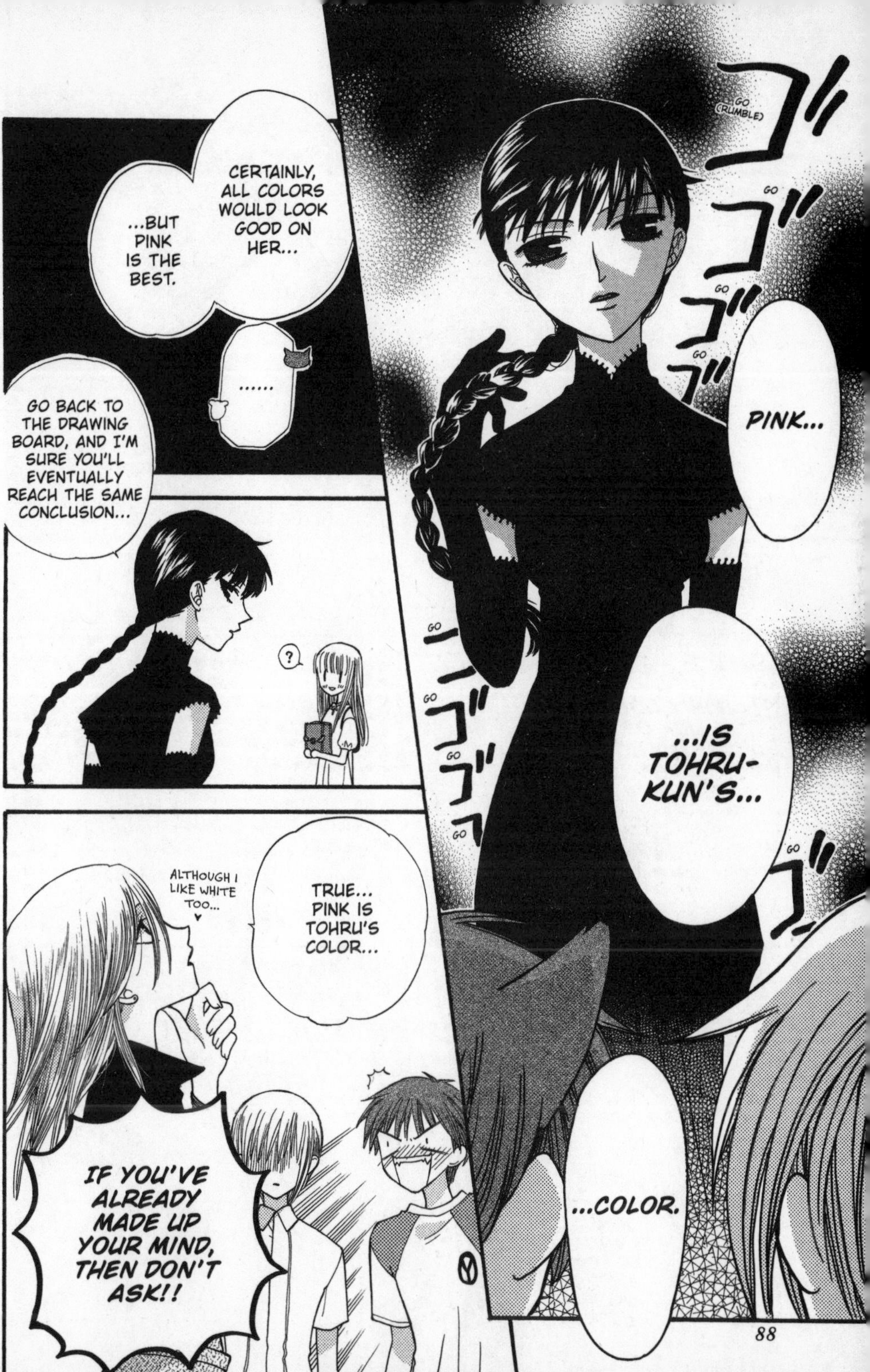
GO (RUMBLE)
GO
GO
GO
PINK...
GO
GO
GO
GO
...IS TOHRU-KUN'S...
GO
...COLOR.
CERTAINLY, ALL COLORS WOULD LOOK GOOD ON HER...
...BUT PINK IS THE BEST.
......
GO BACK TO THE DRAWING BOARD, AND I'M SURE YOU'LL EVENTUALLY REACH THE SAME CONCLUSION...
?
TRUE... PINK IS TOHRU'S COLOR...
ALTHOUGH I LIKE WHITE TOO...
IF YOU'VE ALREADY MADE UP YOUR MIND, THEN DON'T ASK!!

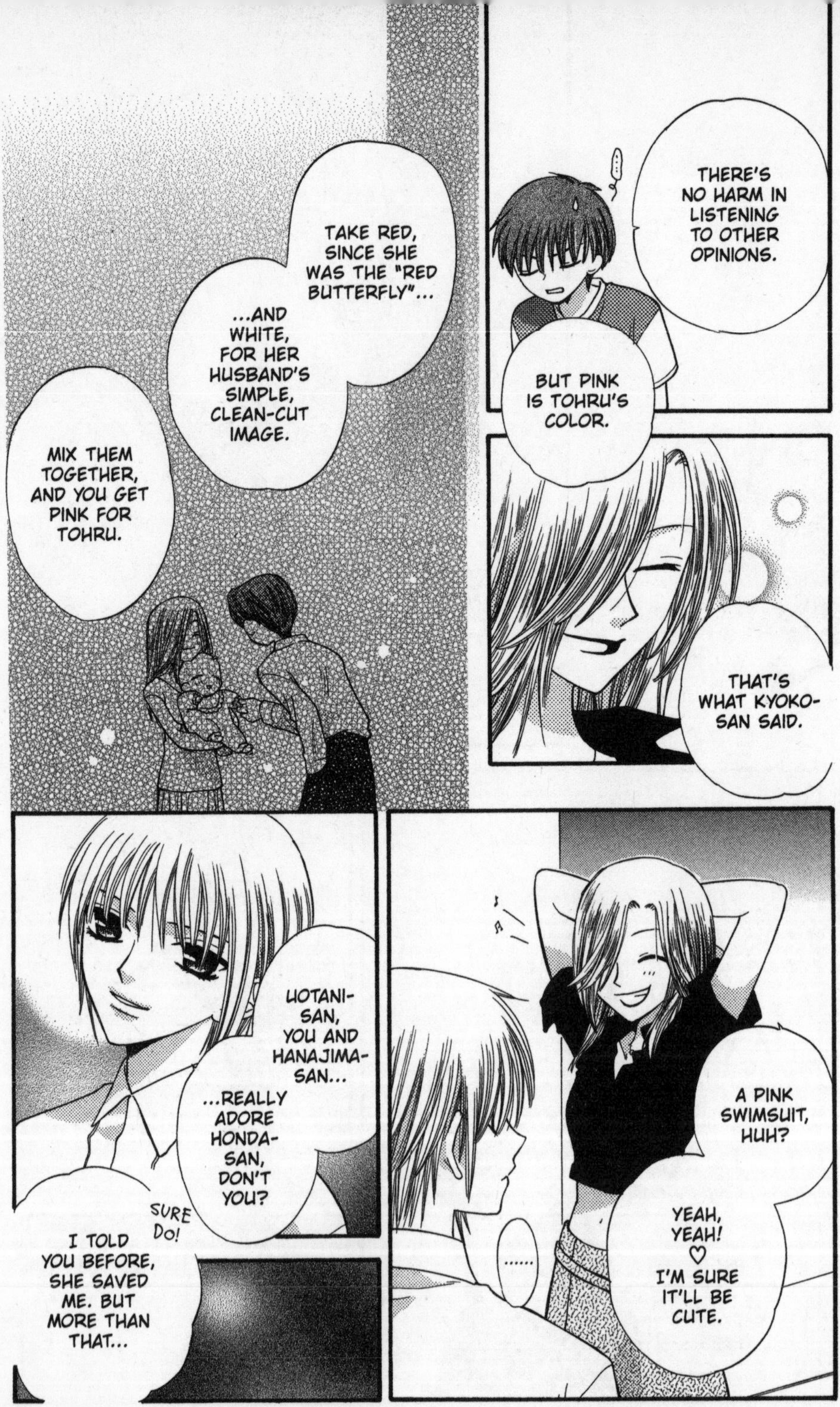
THERE'S NO HARM IN LISTENING TO OTHER OPINIONS.
BUT PINK IS TOHRU'S COLOR.
THAT'S WHAT KYOKO-SAN SAID.
TAKE RED, SINCE SHE WAS THE "RED BUTTERFLY"...
...AND WHITE, FOR HER HUSBAND'S SIMPLE, CLEAN-CUT IMAGE.
MIX THEM TOGETHER, AND YOU GET PINK FOR TOHRU.
A PINK SWIMSUIT, HUH?
YEAH, YEAH! ♡ I'M SURE IT'LL BE CUTE.
......
UOTANI-SAN, YOU AND HANAJIMA-SAN...
...REALLY ADORE HONDA-SAN, DON'T YOU?
SURE DO!
I TOLD YOU BEFORE, SHE SAVED ME. BUT MORE THAN THAT...

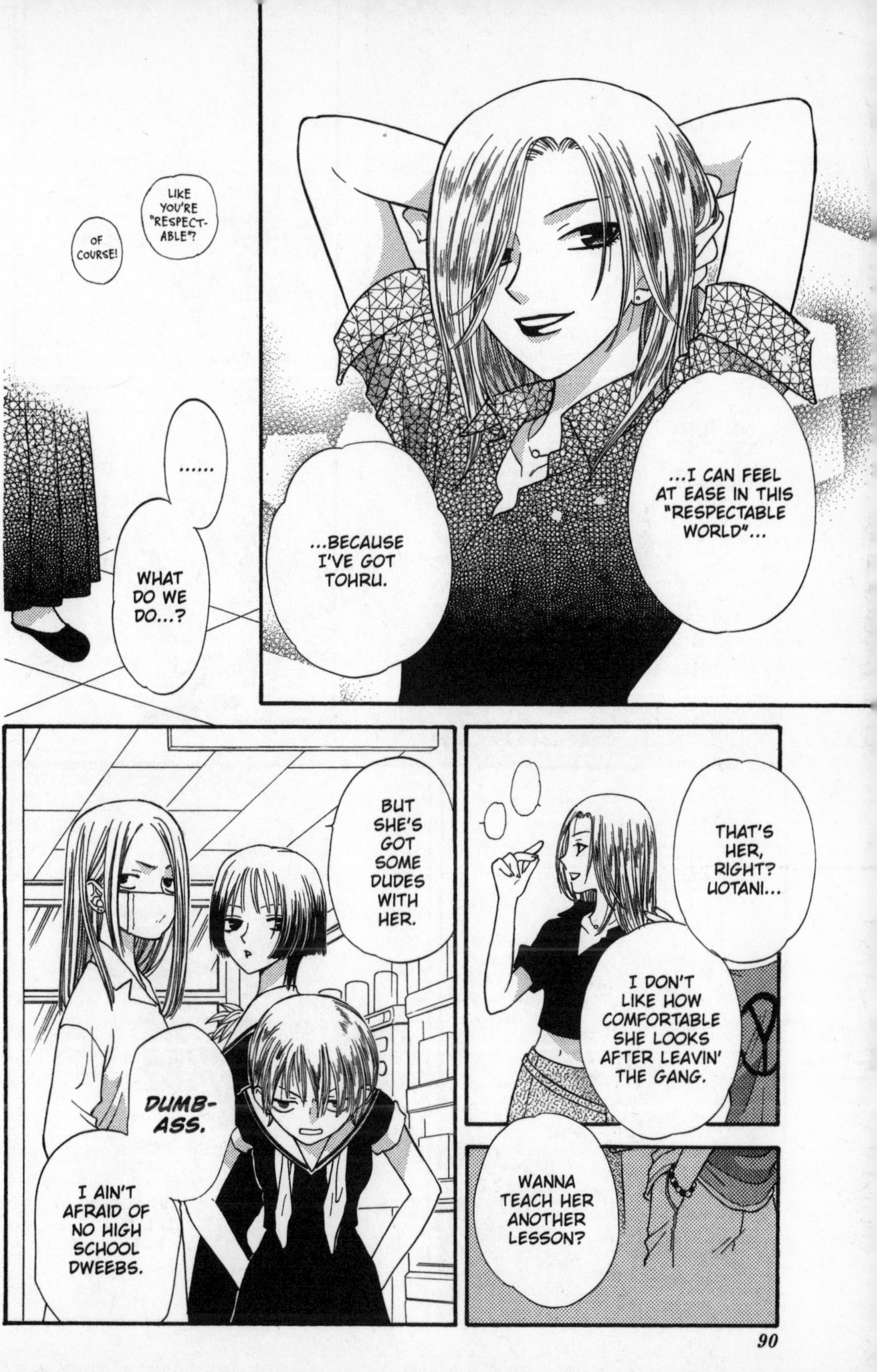
...I CAN FEEL AT EASE IN THIS "RESPECTABLE WORLD"...
...BECAUSE I'VE GOT TOHRU.
LIKE YOU'RE "RESPECT-ABLE"?
OF COURSE!
......
WHAT DO WE DO...?
THAT'S HER, RIGHT? UOTANI...
I DON'T LIKE HOW COMFORTABLE SHE LOOKS AFTER LEAVIN' THE GANG.
WANNA TEACH HER ANOTHER LESSON?
BUT SHE'S GOT SOME DUDES WITH HER.
DUMB-ASS.
I AIN'T AFRAID OF NO HIGH SCHOOL DWEEBS.

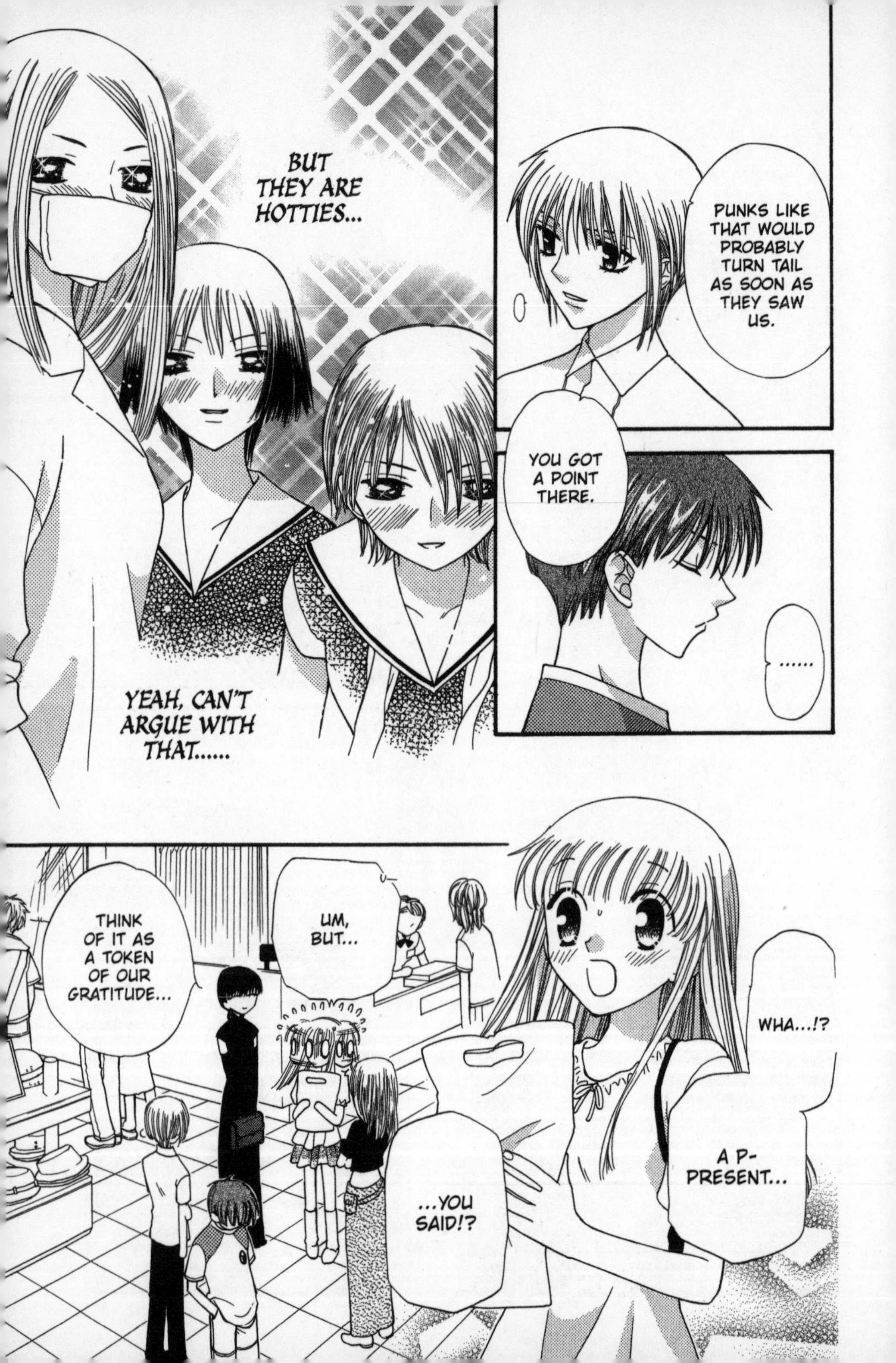
PUNKS LIKE THAT WOULD PROBABLY TURN TAIL AS SOON AS THEY SAW US.
YOU GOT A POINT THERE.
......
BUT THEY ARE HOTTIES...
YEAH, CAN'T ARGUE WITH THAT......
WHA...!?
A P-PRESENT...
...YOU SAID!?
UM, BUT...
THINK OF IT AS A TOKEN OF OUR GRATITUDE...

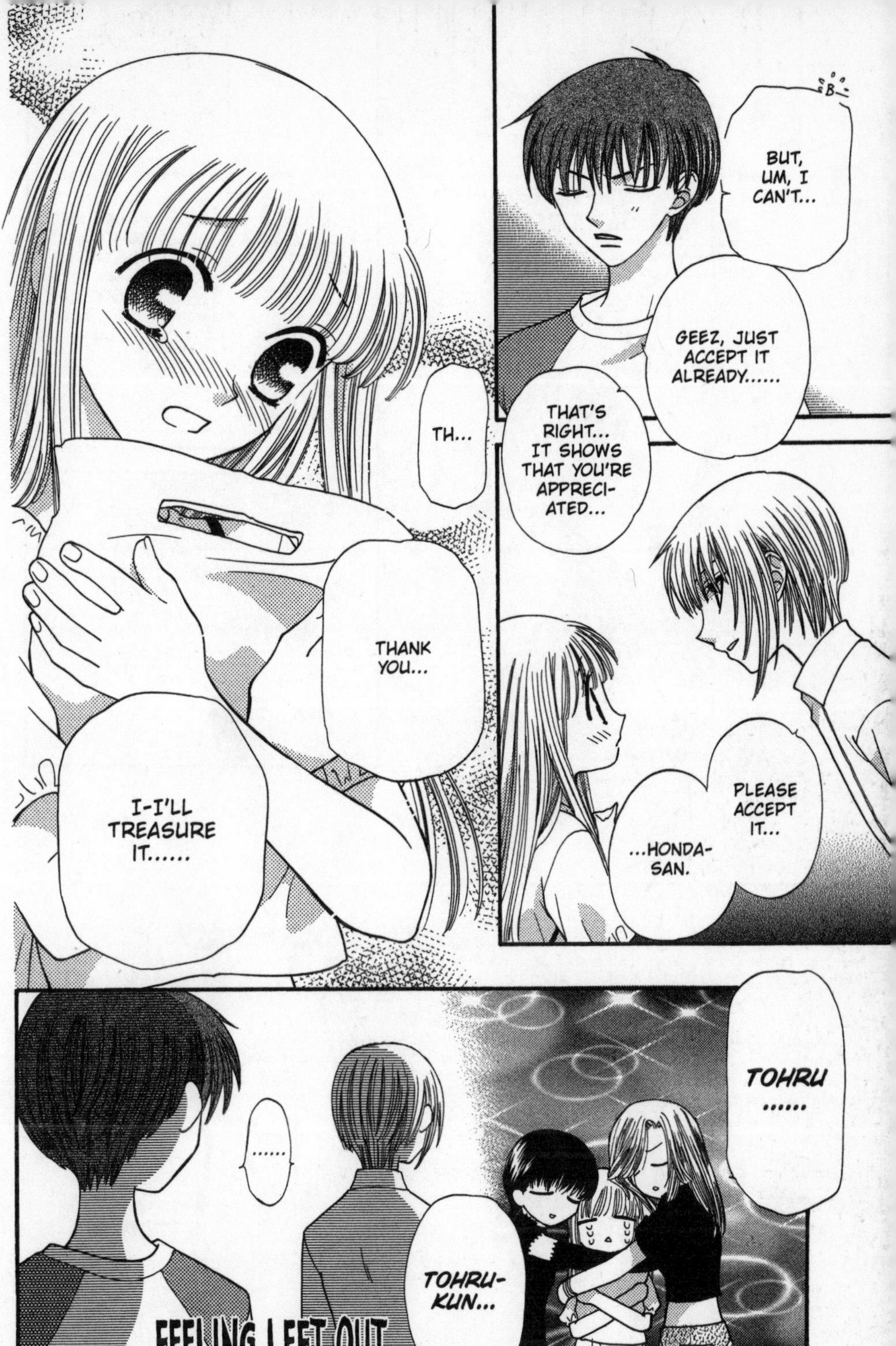
B
BUT, UM, I CAN'T...
GEEZ, JUST ACCEPT IT ALREADY......
THAT'S RIGHT... IT SHOWS THAT YOU'RE APPRECIATED...
PLEASE ACCEPT IT...
...HONDA-SAN.
TH...
THANK YOU...
I-I'LL TREASURE IT......
TOHRU ......
TOHRU-KUN...
......
FEELING LEFT OUT

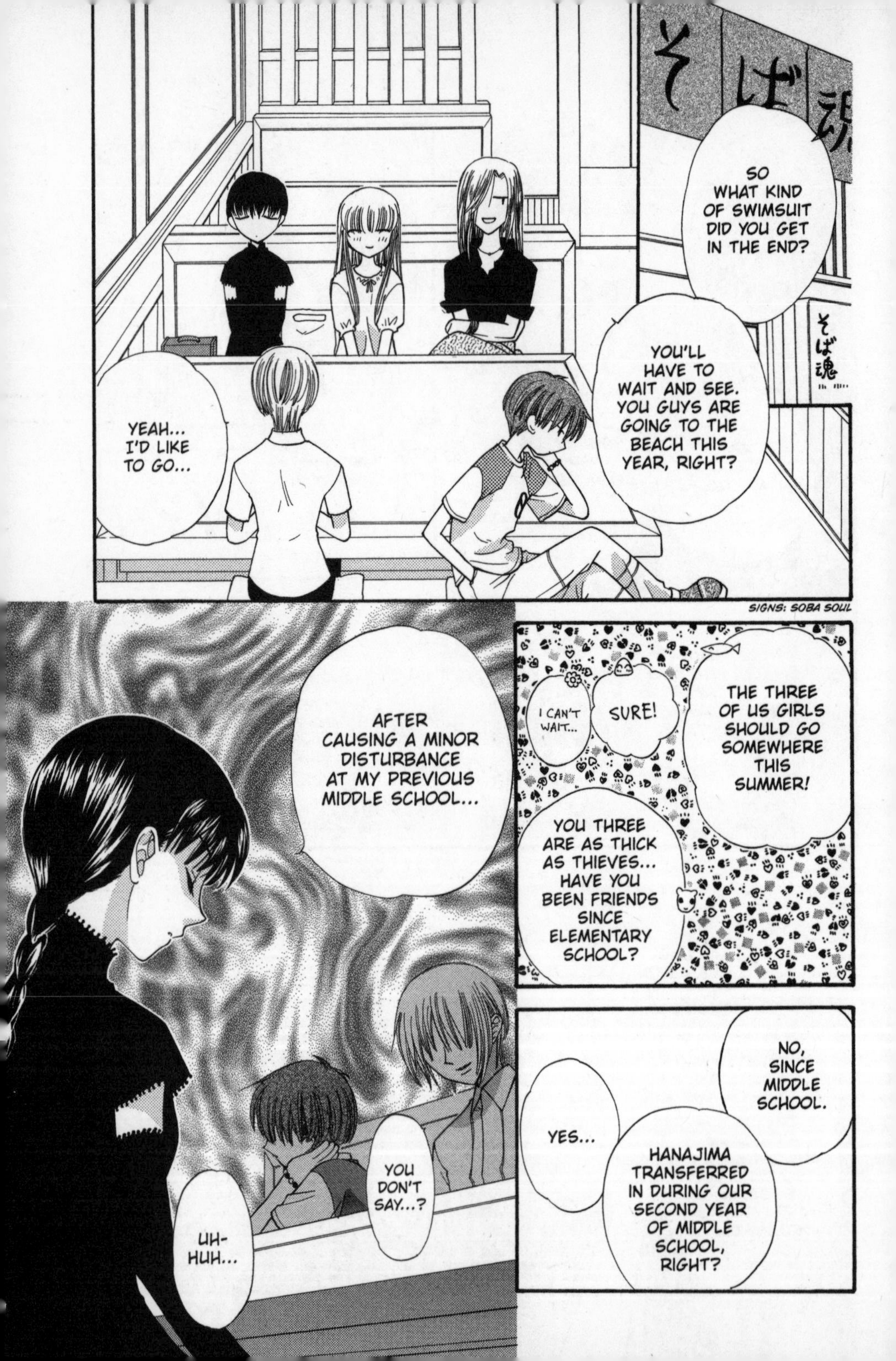
そば魂
SO WHAT KIND OF SWIMSUIT DID YOU GET IN THE END?
YOU'LL HAVE TO WAIT AND SEE. YOU GUYS ARE GOING TO THE BEACH THIS YEAR, RIGHT?
YEAH... I'D LIKE TO GO...
SIGNS: SOBA SOUL
THE THREE OF US GIRLS SHOULD GO SOMEWHERE THIS SUMMER!
SURE!
I CAN'T WAIT...
YOU THREE ARE AS THICK AS THIEVES... HAVE YOU BEEN FRIENDS SINCE ELEMENTARY SCHOOL?
NO, SINCE MIDDLE SCHOOL.
YES...
HANAJIMA TRANSFERRED IN DURING OUR SECOND YEAR OF MIDDLE SCHOOL, RIGHT?
AFTER CAUSING A MINOR DISTURBANCE AT MY PREVIOUS MIDDLE SCHOOL...
YOU DON'T SAY...?
UH-HUH...

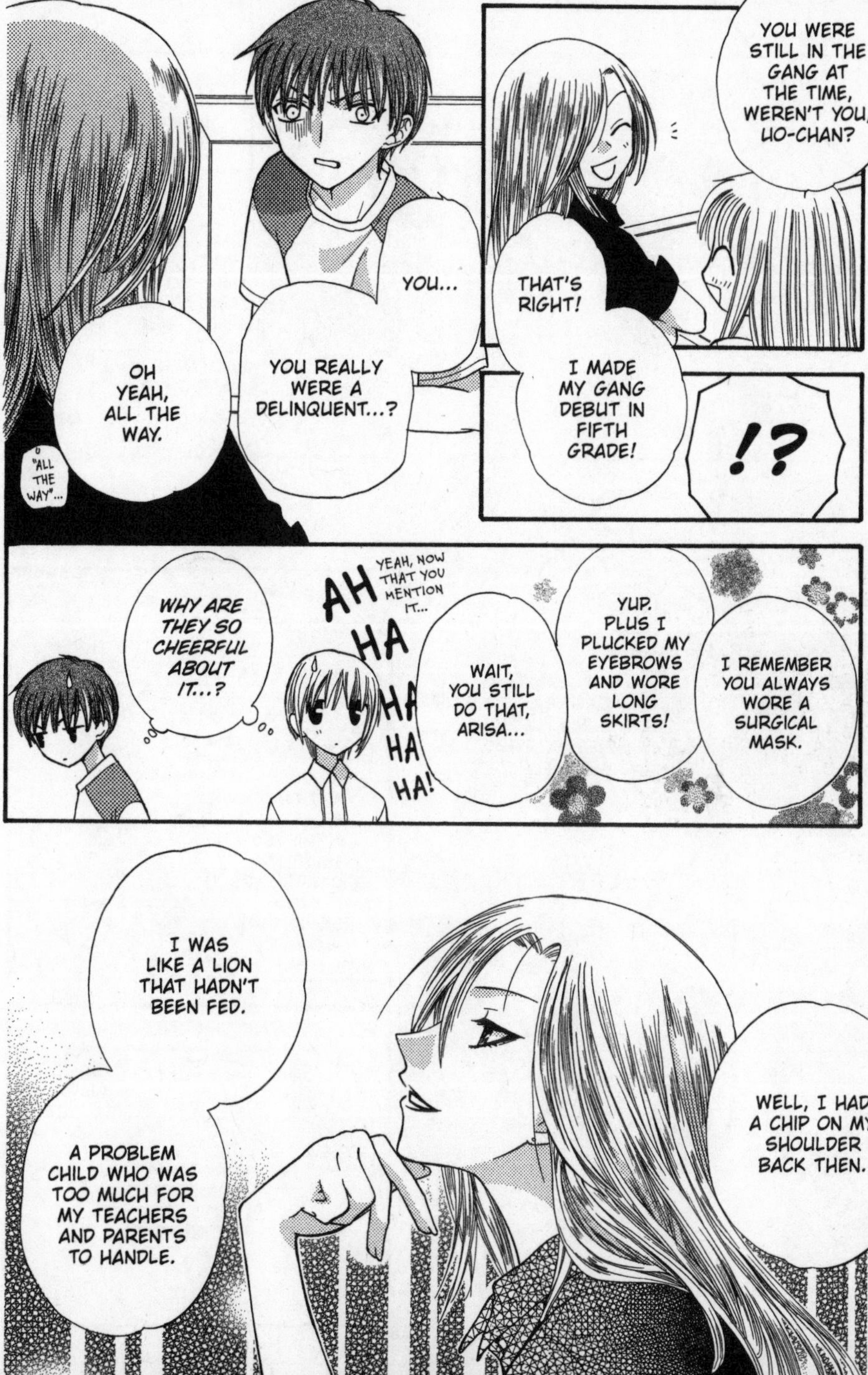
YOU WERE STILL IN THE GANG AT THE TIME, WEREN'T YOU, UO-CHAN?
THAT'S RIGHT!
I MADE MY GANG DEBUT IN FIFTH GRADE!
!?
YOU...
YOU REALLY WERE A DELINQUENT...?
OH YEAH, ALL THE WAY.
"ALL THE WAY"...
I REMEMBER YOU ALWAYS WORE A SURGICAL MASK.
YUP. PLUS I PLUCKED MY EYEBROWS AND WORE LONG SKIRTS!
WAIT, YOU STILL DO THAT, ARISA...
YEAH, NOW THAT YOU MENTION IT...
AH HA HA HA HA!
WHY ARE THEY SO CHEERFUL ABOUT IT...?
WELL, I HAD A CHIP ON MY SHOULDER BACK THEN.
I WAS LIKE A LION THAT HADN'T BEEN FED.
A PROBLEM CHILD WHO WAS TOO MUCH FOR MY TEACHERS AND PARENTS TO HANDLE.

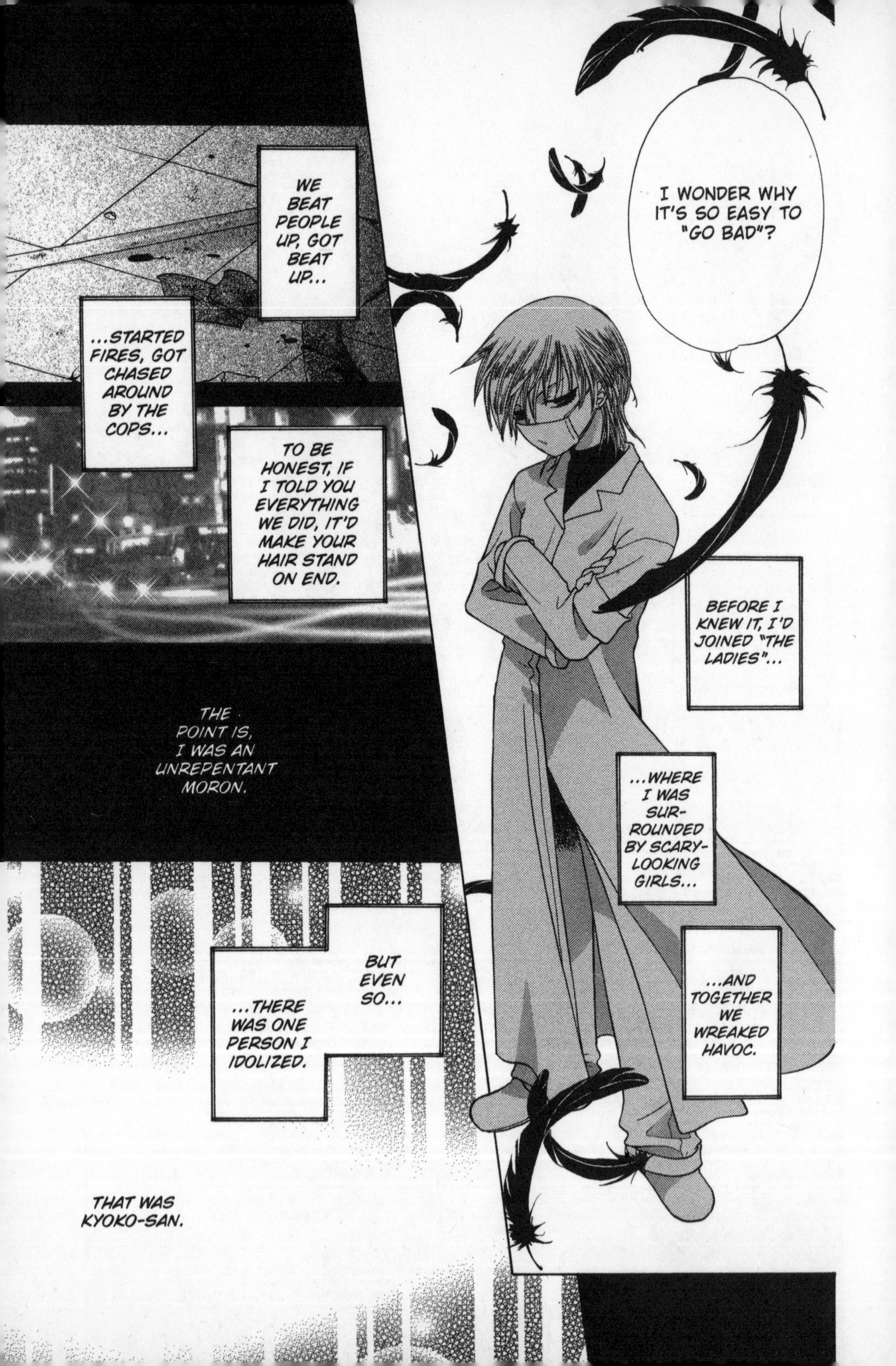
I WONDER WHY IT'S SO EASY TO "GO BAD"?
BEFORE I KNEW IT, I'D JOINED "THE LADIES"...
...WHERE I WAS SUR-ROUNDED BY SCARY-LOOKING GIRLS...
...AND TOGETHER WE WREAKED HAVOC.
WE BEAT PEOPLE UP, GOT BEAT UP...
...STARTED FIRES, GOT CHASED AROUND BY THE COPS...
TO BE HONEST, IF I TOLD YOU EVERYTHING WE DID, IT'D MAKE YOUR HAIR STAND ON END.
THE POINT IS, I WAS AN UNREPENTANT MORON.
BUT EVEN SO...
...THERE WAS ONE PERSON I IDOLIZED.
THAT WAS KYOKO-SAN.

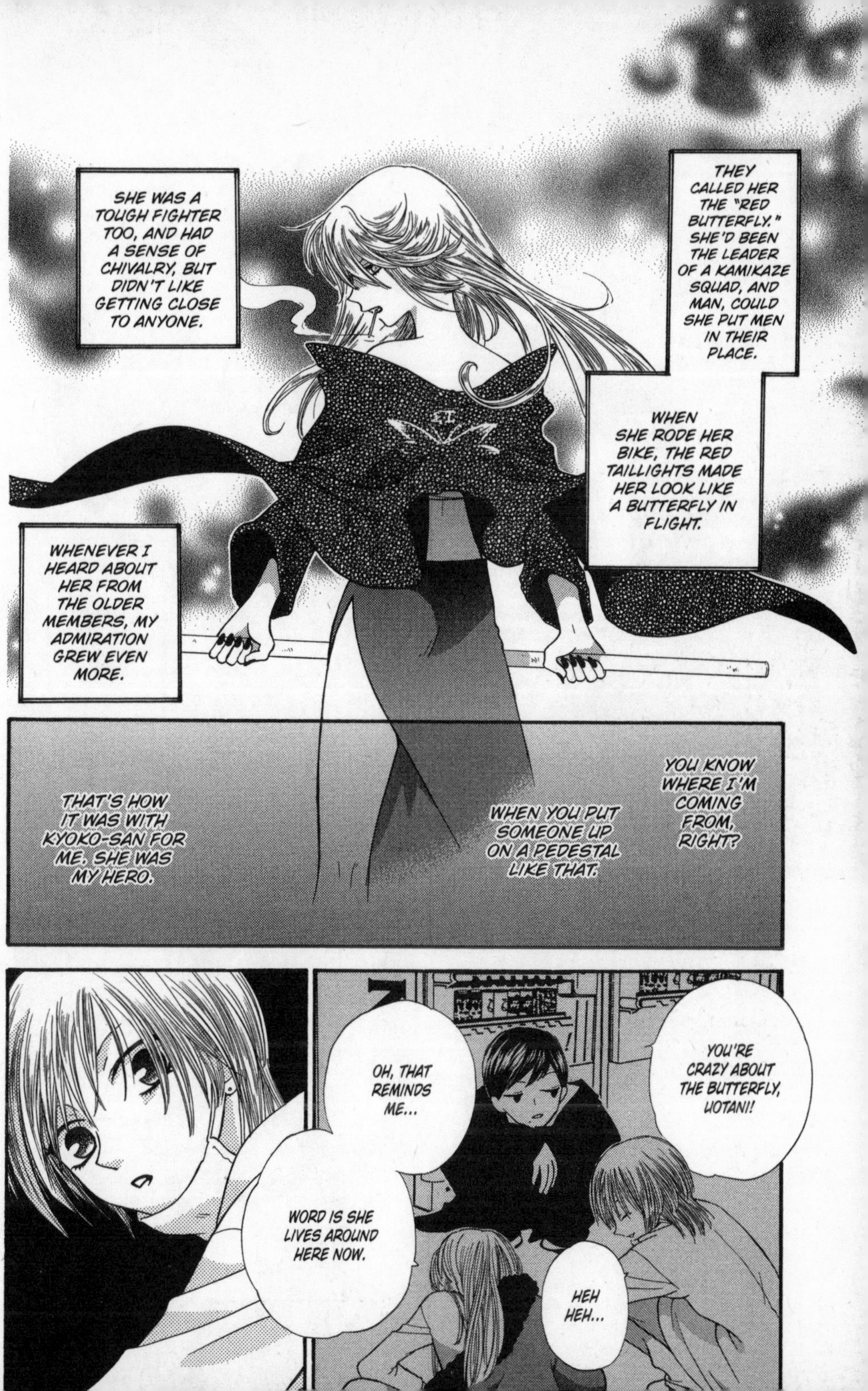
THEY CALLED HER THE "RED BUTTERFLY." SHE'D BEEN THE LEADER OF A KAMIKAZE SQUAD, AND MAN, COULD SHE PUT MEN IN THEIR PLACE.
WHEN SHE RODE HER BIKE, THE RED TAILLIGHTS MADE HER LOOK LIKE A BUTTERFLY IN FLIGHT.
SHE WAS A TOUGH FIGHTER TOO, AND HAD A SENSE OF CHIVALRY, BUT DIDN'T LIKE GETTING CLOSE TO ANYONE.
WHENEVER I HEARD ABOUT HER FROM THE OLDER MEMBERS, MY ADMIRATION GREW EVEN MORE.
YOU KNOW WHERE I'M COMING FROM, RIGHT?
WHEN YOU PUT SOMEONE UP ON A PEDESTAL LIKE THAT.
THAT'S HOW IT WAS WITH KYOKO-SAN FOR ME. SHE WAS MY HERO.
YOU'RE CRAZY ABOUT THE BUTTERFLY, UOTANI!
HEH HEH...
OH, THAT REMINDS ME...
WORD IS SHE LIVES AROUND HERE NOW.

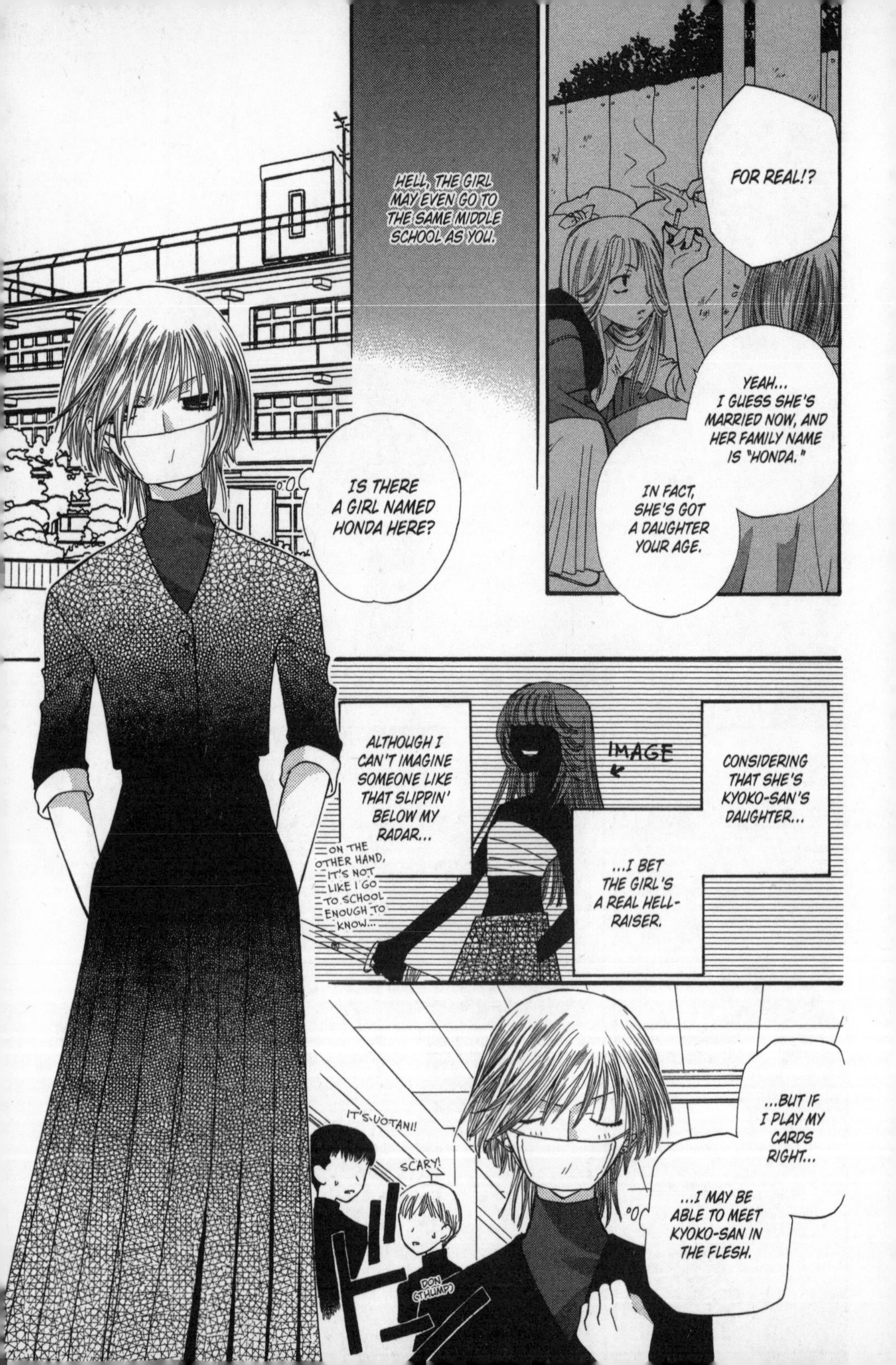
FOR REAL!?
YEAH... I GUESS SHE'S MARRIED NOW, AND HER FAMILY NAME IS "HONDA."
IN FACT, SHE'S GOT A DAUGHTER YOUR AGE.
HELL, THE GIRL MAY EVEN GO TO THE SAME MIDDLE SCHOOL AS YOU.
CONSIDERING THAT SHE'S KYOKO-SAN'S DAUGHTER...
...I BET THE GIRL'S A REAL HELL-RAISER.
IMAGE
ALTHOUGH I CAN'T IMAGINE SOMEONE LIKE THAT SLIPPIN' BELOW MY RADAR...
ON THE OTHER HAND, IT'S NOT LIKE I GO TO SCHOOL ENOUGH TO KNOW...
...BUT IF I PLAY MY CARDS RIGHT...
...I MAY BE ABLE TO MEET KYOKO-SAN IN THE FLESH.
SCARY!
IT'S UOTANI!
DON (THUMP)
IS THERE A GIRL NAMED HONDA HERE?

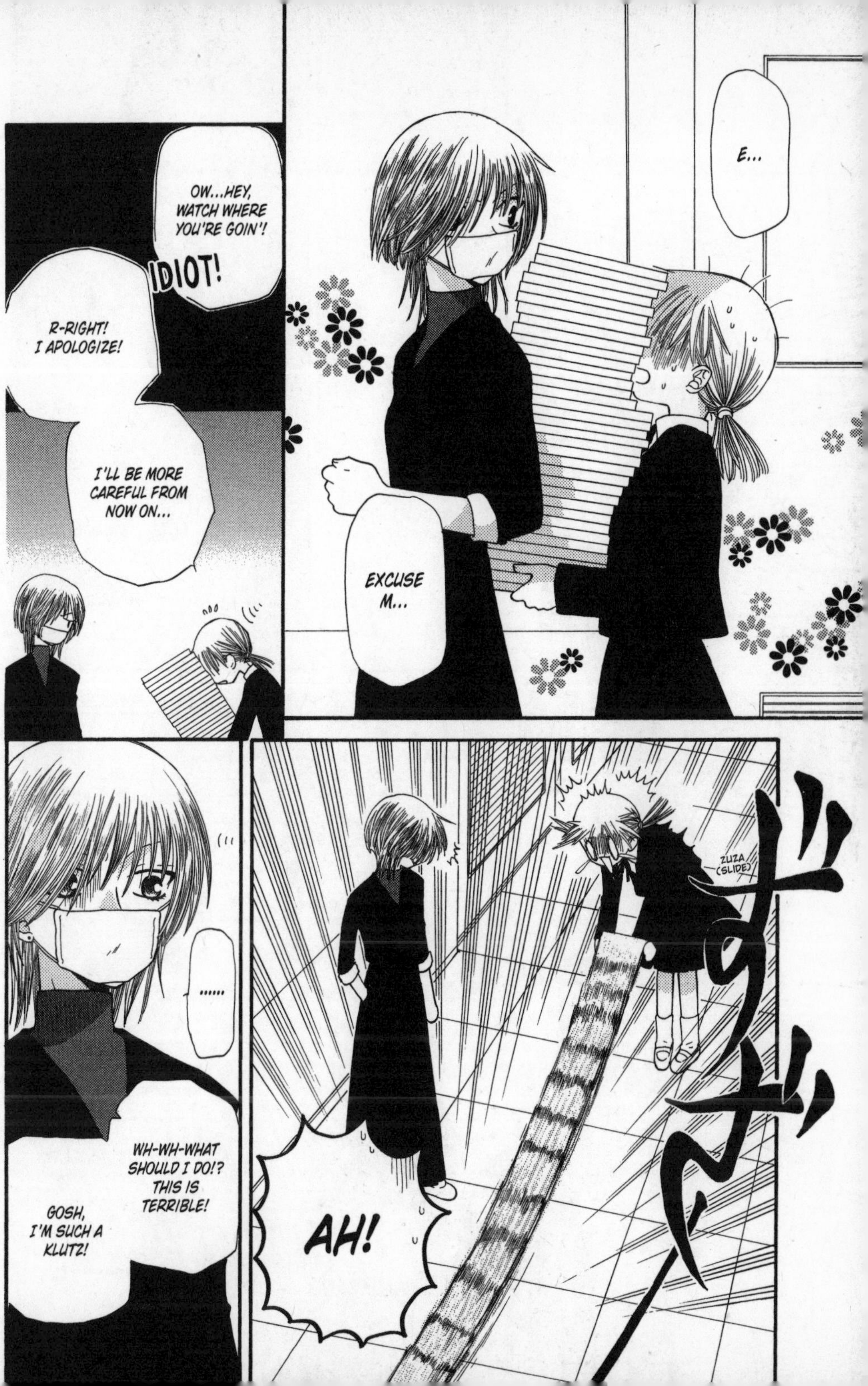
E...
EXCUSE M...
OW...HEY, WATCH WHERE YOU'RE GOIN'!
IDIOT!
R-RIGHT! I APOLOGIZE!
I'LL BE MORE CAREFUL FROM NOW ON...
ZUZA (SLIDE)
AH!
......
WH-WH-WHAT SHOULD I DO!? THIS IS TERRIBLE!
GOSH, I'M SUCH A KLUTZ!

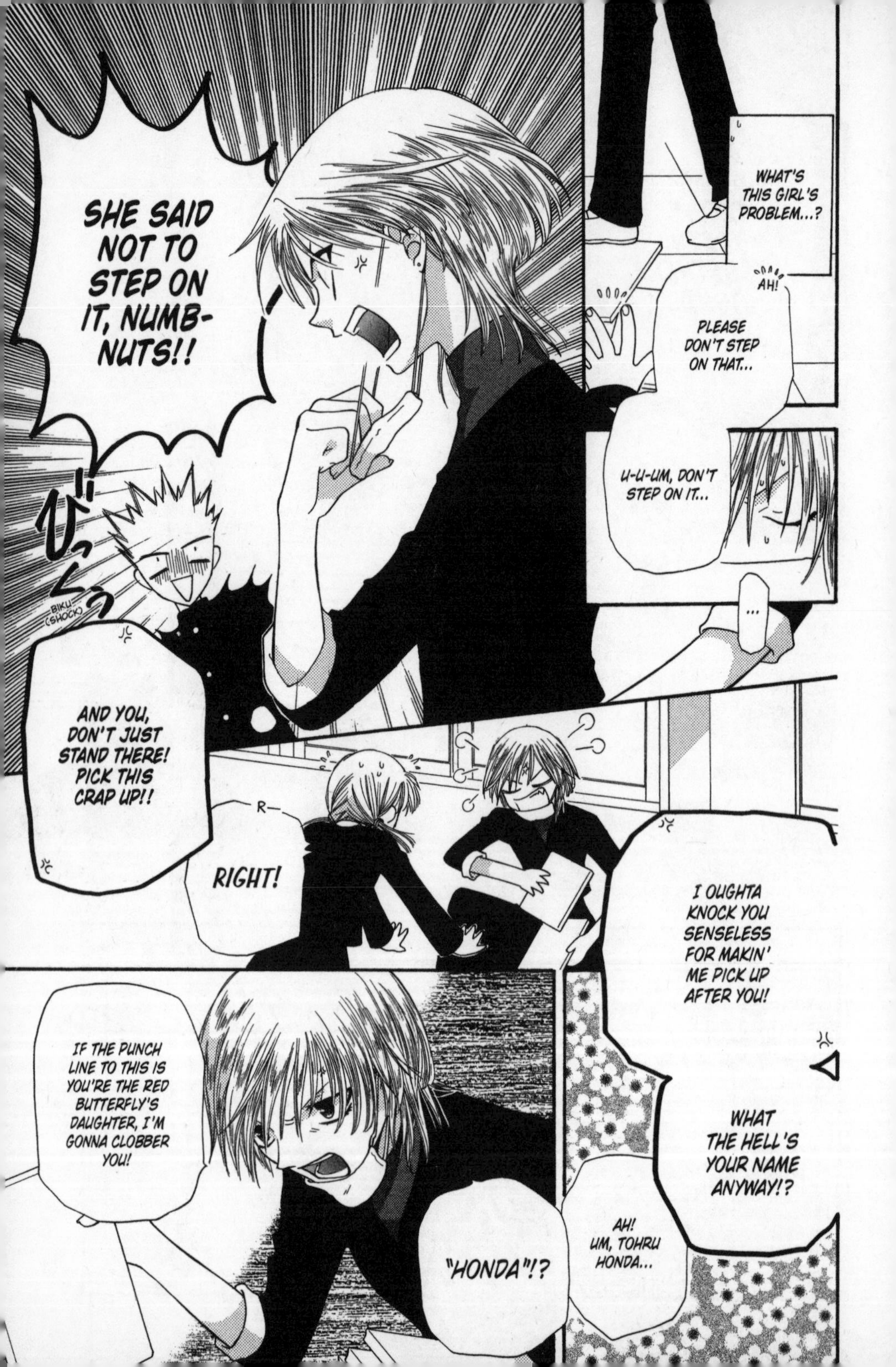
WHAT'S THIS GIRL'S PROBLEM...?
AH!
PLEASE DON'T STEP ON THAT...
U-U-UM, DON'T STEP ON IT...
...
SHE SAID NOT TO STEP ON IT, NUMB-NUTS!!
BIKU (SHOCK)
AND YOU, DON'T JUST STAND THERE! PICK THIS CRAP UP!!
I OUGHTA KNOCK YOU SENSELESS FOR MAKIN' ME PICK UP AFTER YOU!
R— RIGHT!
WHAT THE HELL'S YOUR NAME ANYWAY!?
AH! UM, TOHRU HONDA...
"HONDA"!?
IF THE PUNCH LINE TO THIS IS YOU'RE THE RED BUTTERFLY'S DAUGHTER, I'M GONNA CLOBBER YOU!

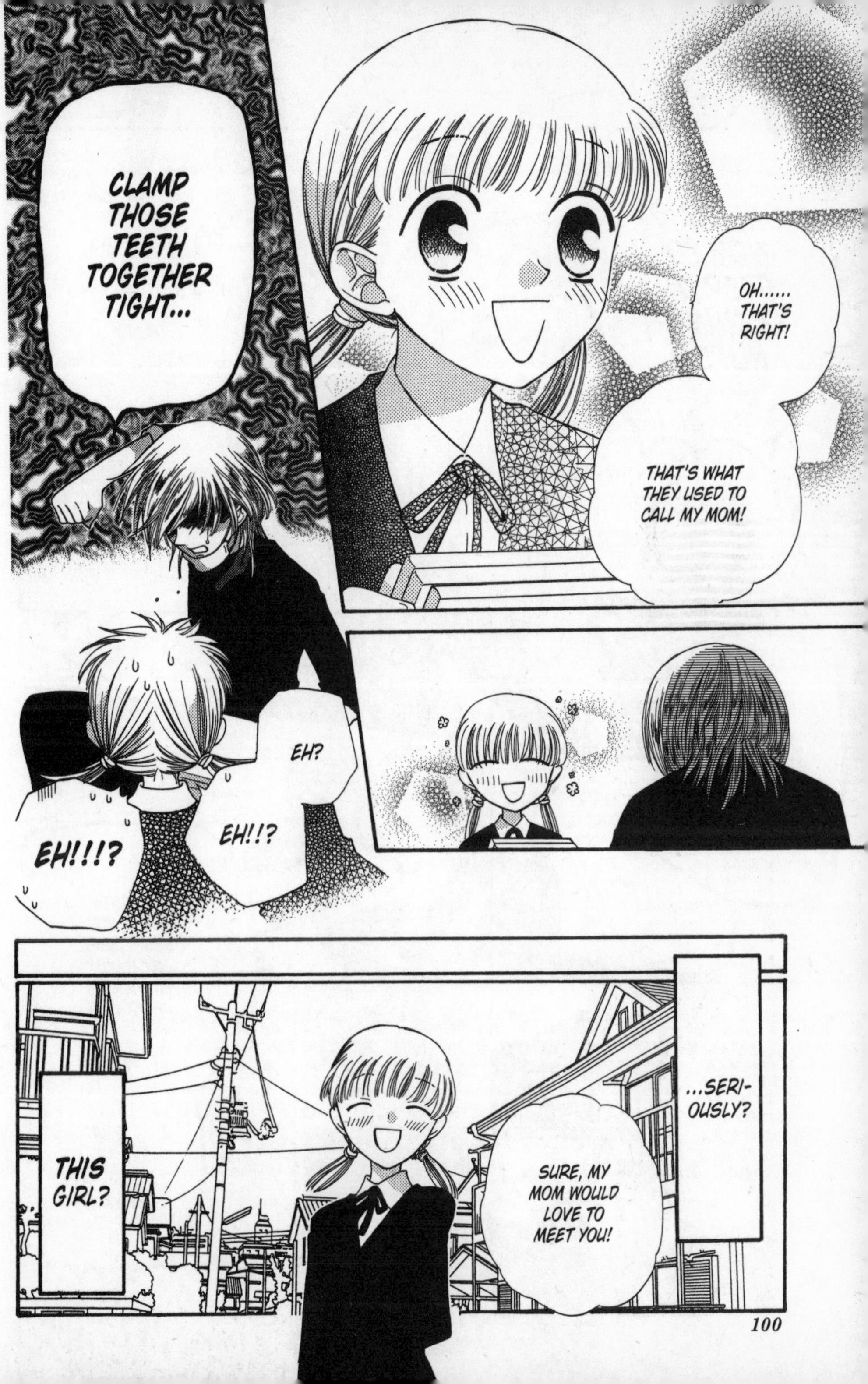
OH...... THAT'S RIGHT!
THAT'S WHAT THEY USED TO CALL MY MOM!
CLAMP THOSE TEETH TOGETHER TIGHT...
EH?
EH!!?
EH!!!?
...SERI-OUSLY?
SURE, MY MOM WOULD LOVE TO MEET YOU!
THIS GIRL?

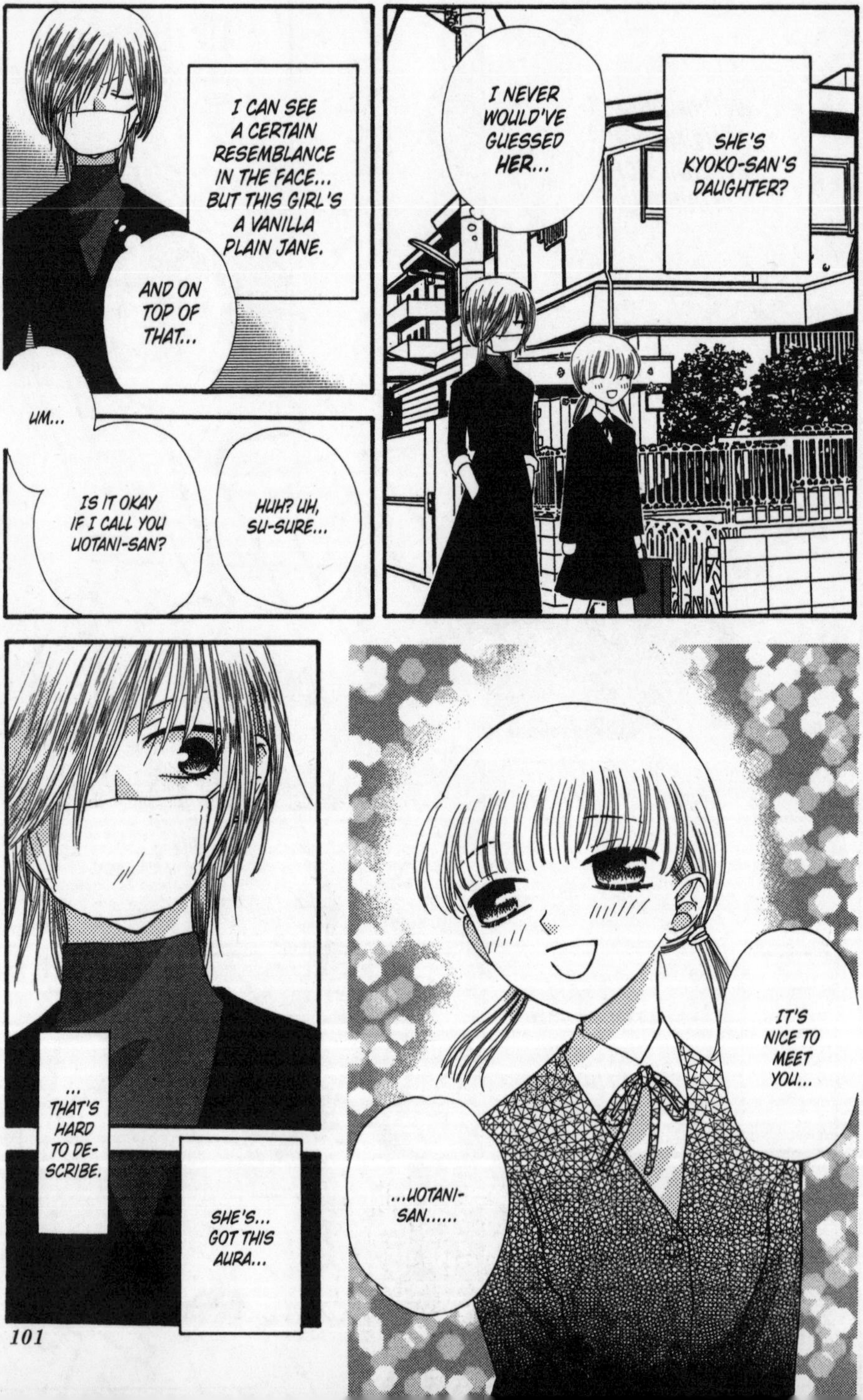
SHE'S KYOKO-SAN'S DAUGHTER?
I NEVER WOULD'VE GUESSED HER...
I CAN SEE A CERTAIN RESEMBLANCE IN THE FACE... BUT THIS GIRL'S A VANILLA PLAIN JANE.
AND ON TOP OF THAT...
UM...
IS IT OKAY IF I CALL YOU UOTANI-SAN?
HUH? UH, SU-SURE...
IT'S NICE TO MEET YOU...
...UOTANI-SAN......
SHE'S... GOT THIS AURA...
... THAT'S HARD TO DE-SCRIBE.

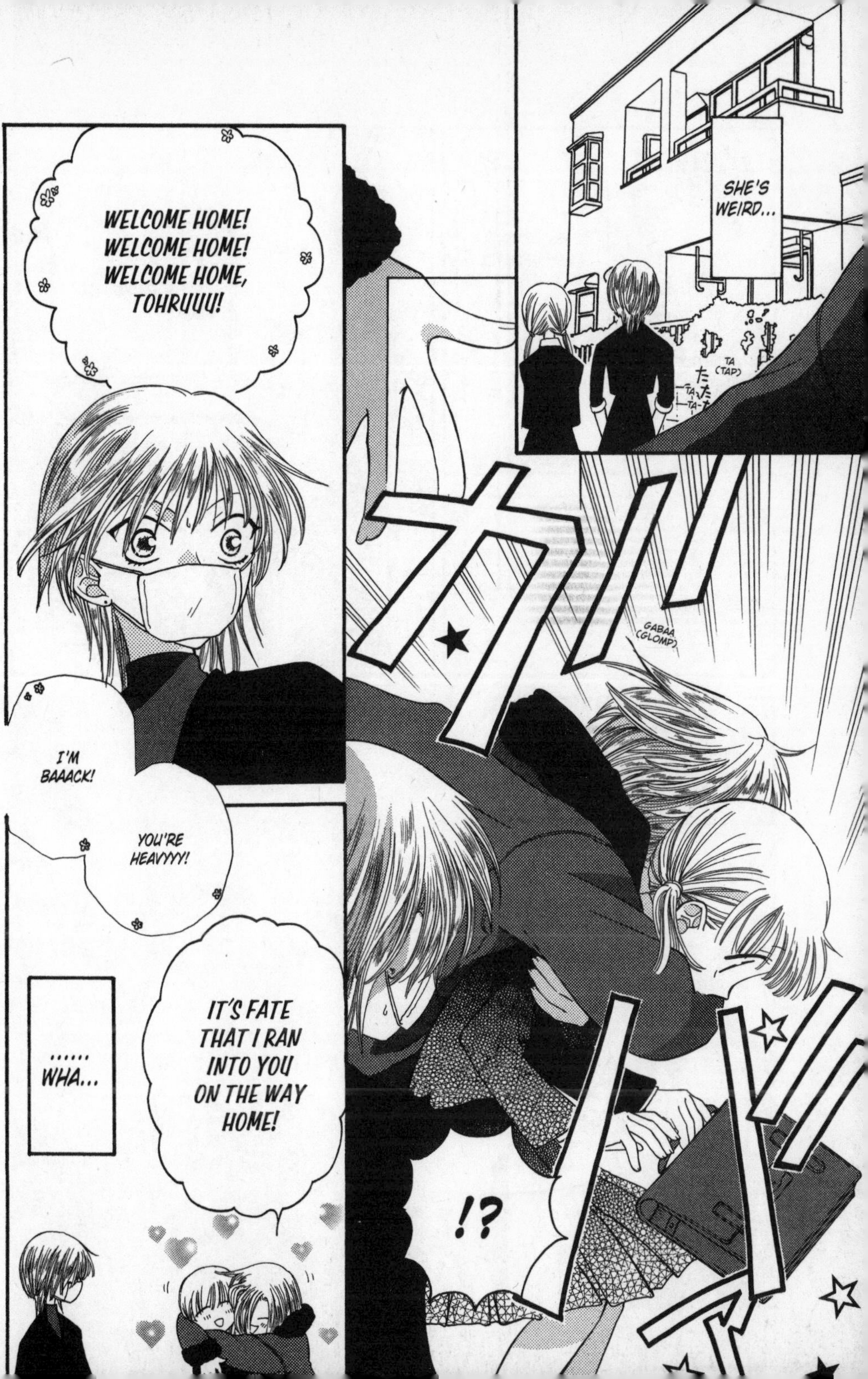
SHE'S WEIRD...
TA (TAP)
TA- TA-
GABAA (GLOMP)
!?
WELCOME HOME! WELCOME HOME! WELCOME HOME, TOHRUUU!
I'M BAAACK!
YOU'RE HEAVYYY!
IT'S FATE THAT I RAN INTO YOU ON THE WAY HOME!
...... WHA...

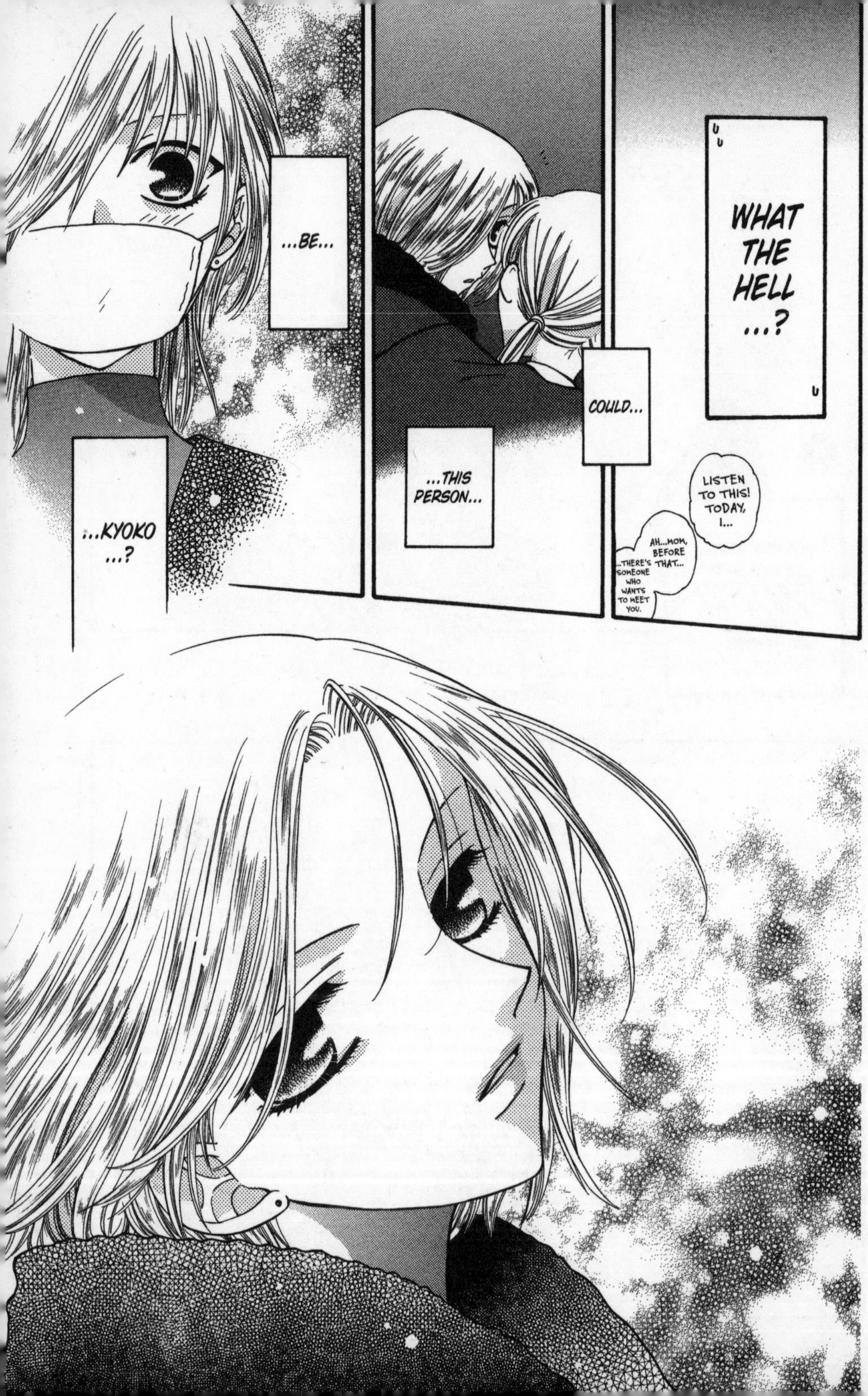

WHAT THE HELL ...?
LISTEN TO THIS! TODAY, I...
AH...MOM, BEFORE THAT...
...THERE'S SOMEONE WHO WANTS TO MEET YOU.
COULD...
...THIS PERSON...
...BE...
...KYOKO ...?

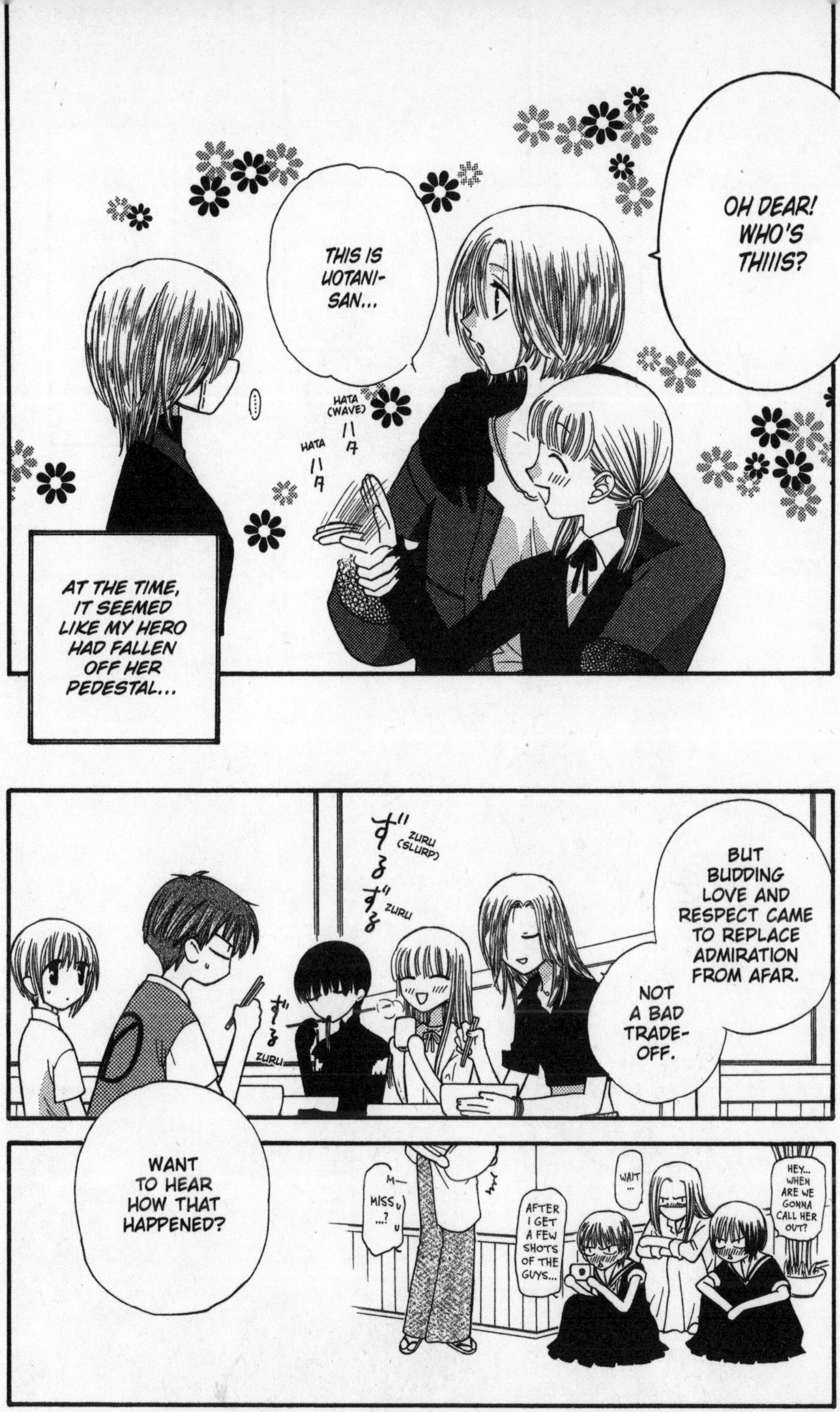
OH DEAR! WHO'S THIIIS?
THIS IS UOTANI-SAN...
HATA (WAVE) ハタ
HATA ハタ
......
AT THE TIME, IT SEEMED LIKE MY HERO HAD FALLEN OFF HER PEDESTAL...
BUT BUDDING LOVE AND RESPECT CAME TO REPLACE ADMIRATION FROM AFAR.
NOT A BAD TRADE-OFF.
ずる ZURU (SLURP)
ずる ZURU
ずる ZURU
HEY... WHEN ARE WE GONNA CALL HER OUT?
WAIT...
AFTER I GET A FEW SHOTS OF THE GUYS...
M— MISS...?
WANT TO HEAR HOW THAT HAPPENED?

Chapter 40

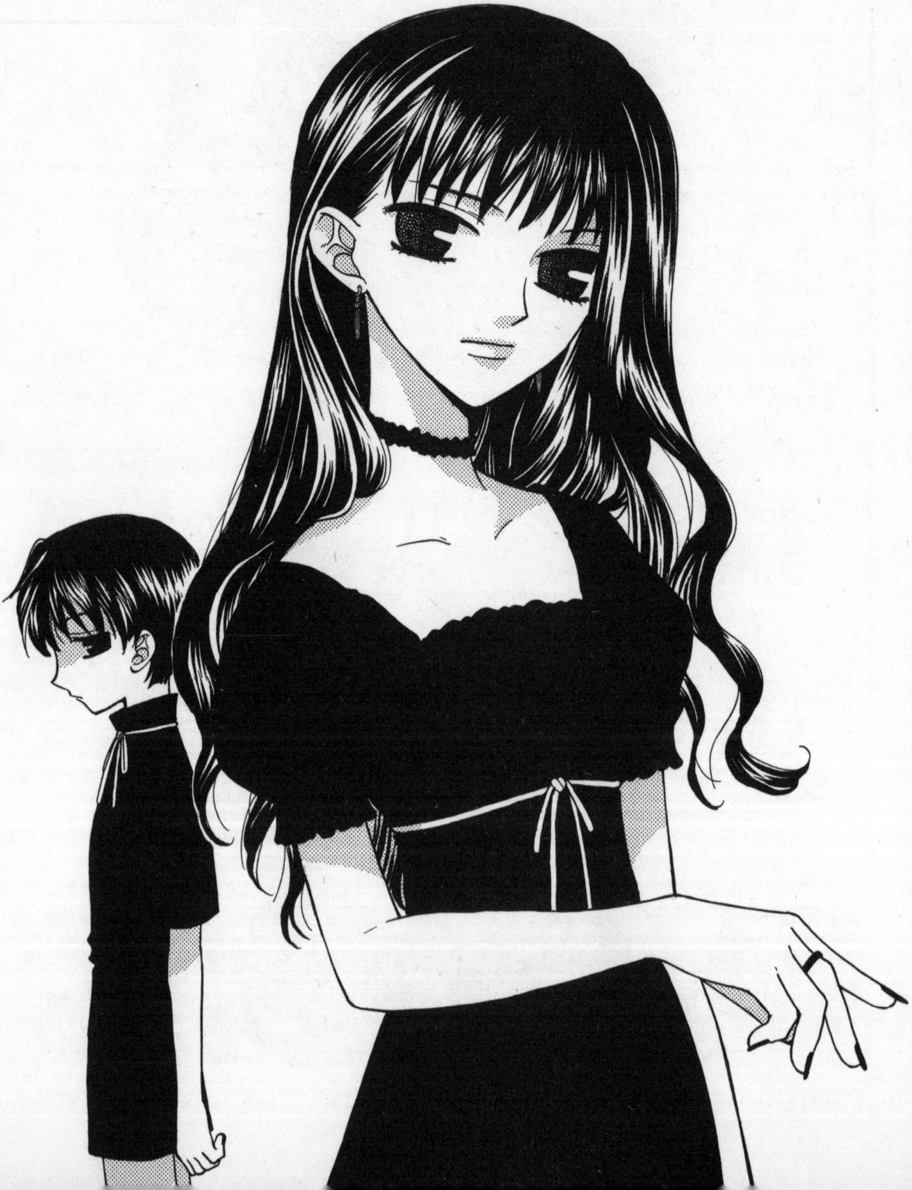

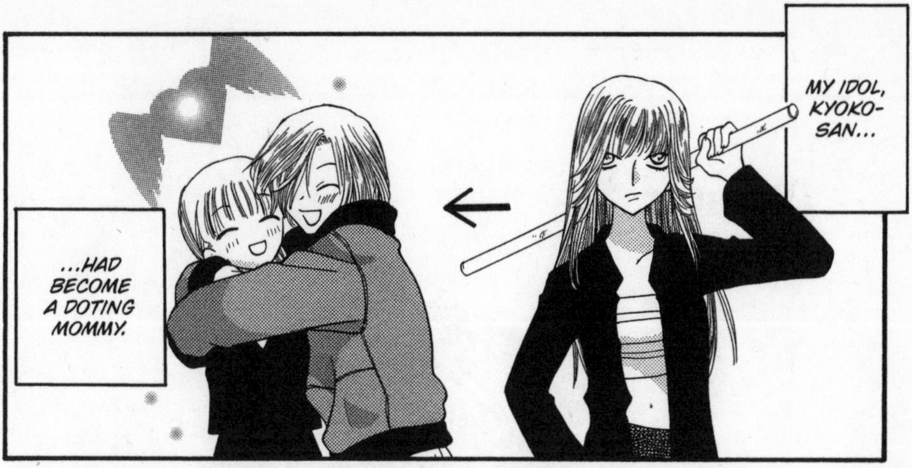
MY IDOL, KYOKO-SAN...
...HAD BECOME A DOTING MOMMY.

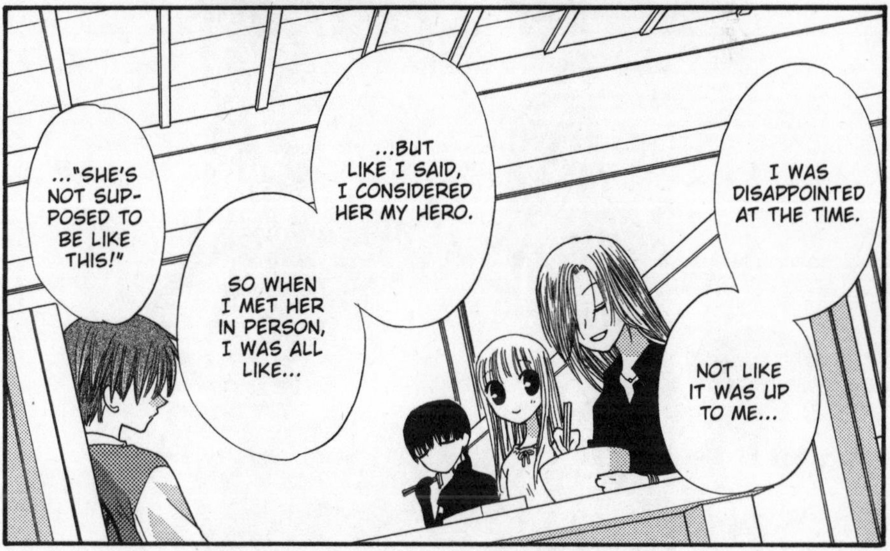
I WAS DISAPPOINTED AT THE TIME.
NOT LIKE IT WAS UP TO ME...
...BUT LIKE I SAID, I CONSIDERED HER MY HERO.
SO WHEN I MET HER IN PERSON, I WAS ALL LIKE...
..."SHE'S NOT SUP-POSED TO BE LIKE THIS!"

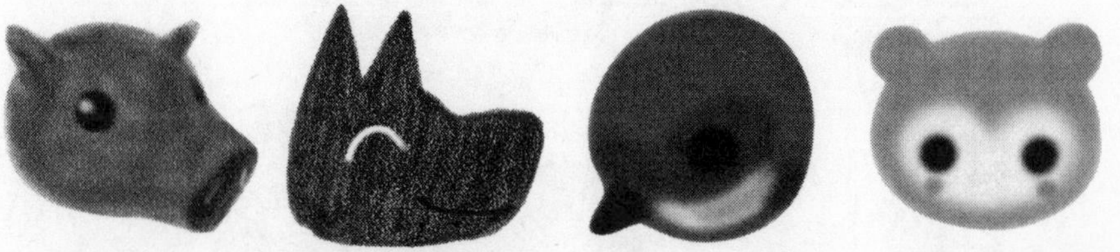

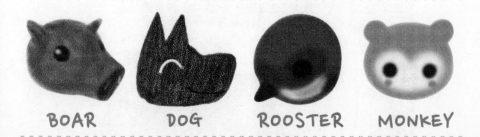

BOAR DOG ROOSTER MONKEY

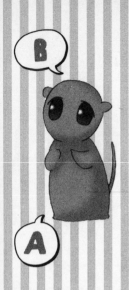

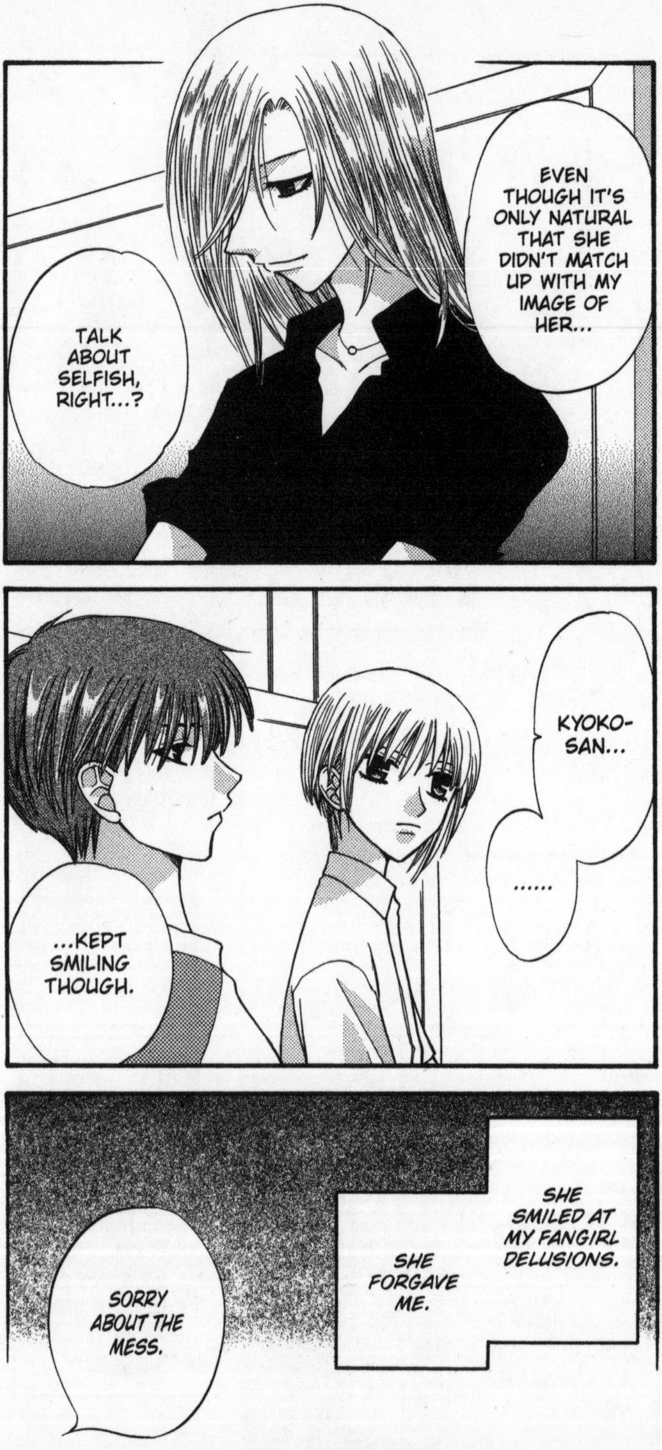
EVEN THOUGH IT'S ONLY NATURAL THAT SHE DIDN'T MATCH UP WITH MY IMAGE OF HER...
TALK ABOUT SELFISH, RIGHT...?
KYOKO-SAN...
......
...KEPT SMILING THOUGH.
SHE SMILED AT MY FANGIRL DELUSIONS.
SHE FORGAVE ME.
SORRY ABOUT THE MESS.
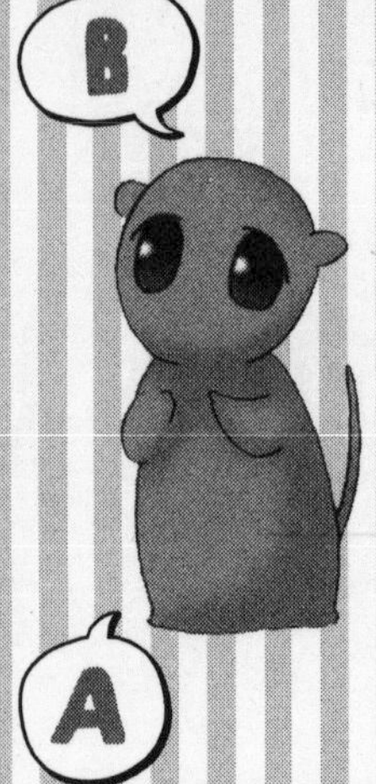
B
A

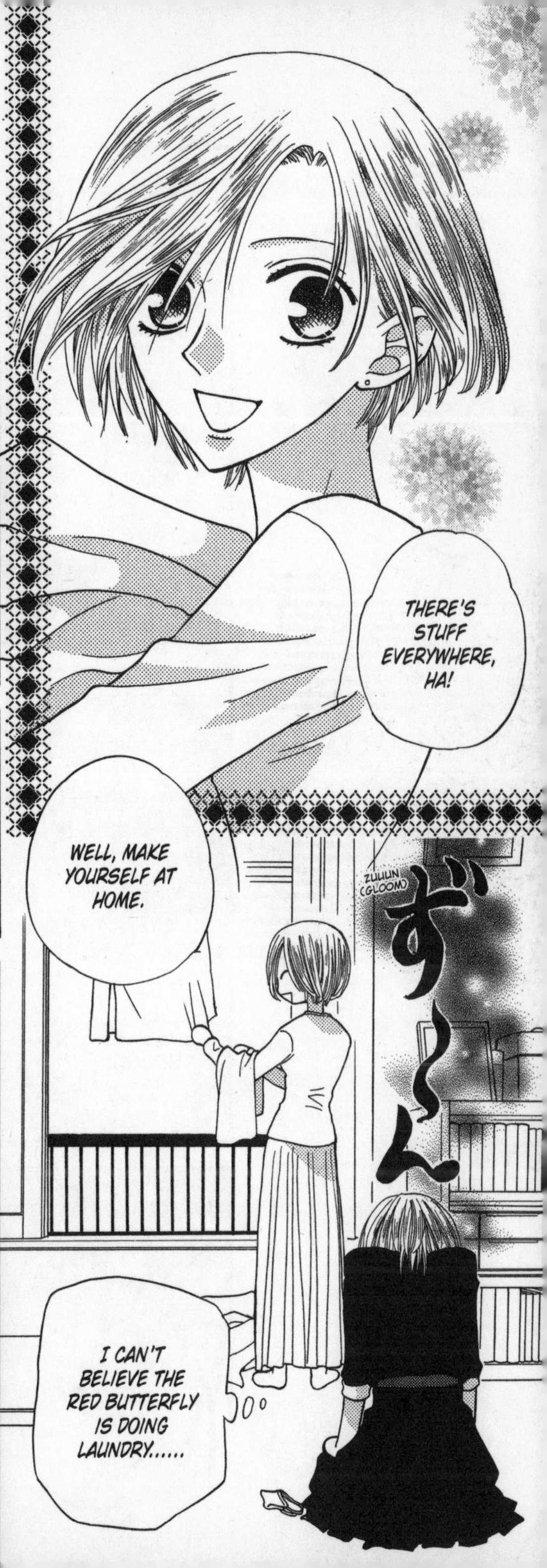
THERE'S STUFF EVERYWHERE, HA!
WELL, MAKE YOURSELF AT HOME.
ZUUUN (GLOOM)
I CAN'T BELIEVE THE RED BUTTERFLY IS DOING LAUNDRY......
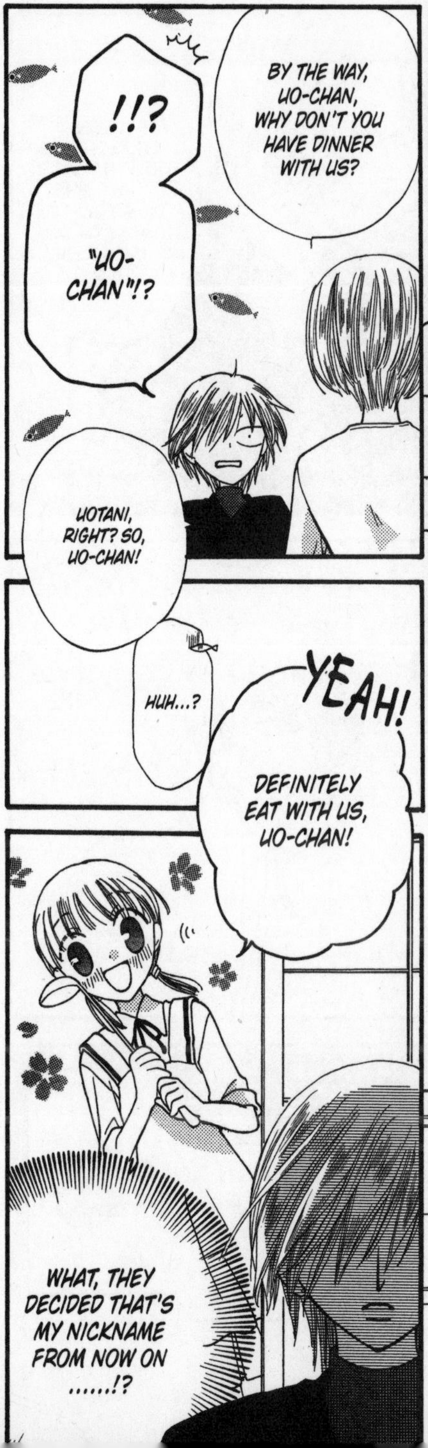
BY THE WAY, UO-CHAN, WHY DON'T YOU HAVE DINNER WITH US?
!!?
"UO-CHAN"!?
UOTANI, RIGHT? SO, UO-CHAN!
HUH...?
YEAH!
DEFINITELY EAT WITH US, UO-CHAN!
WHAT, THEY DECIDED THAT'S MY NICKNAME FROM NOW ON ......!?

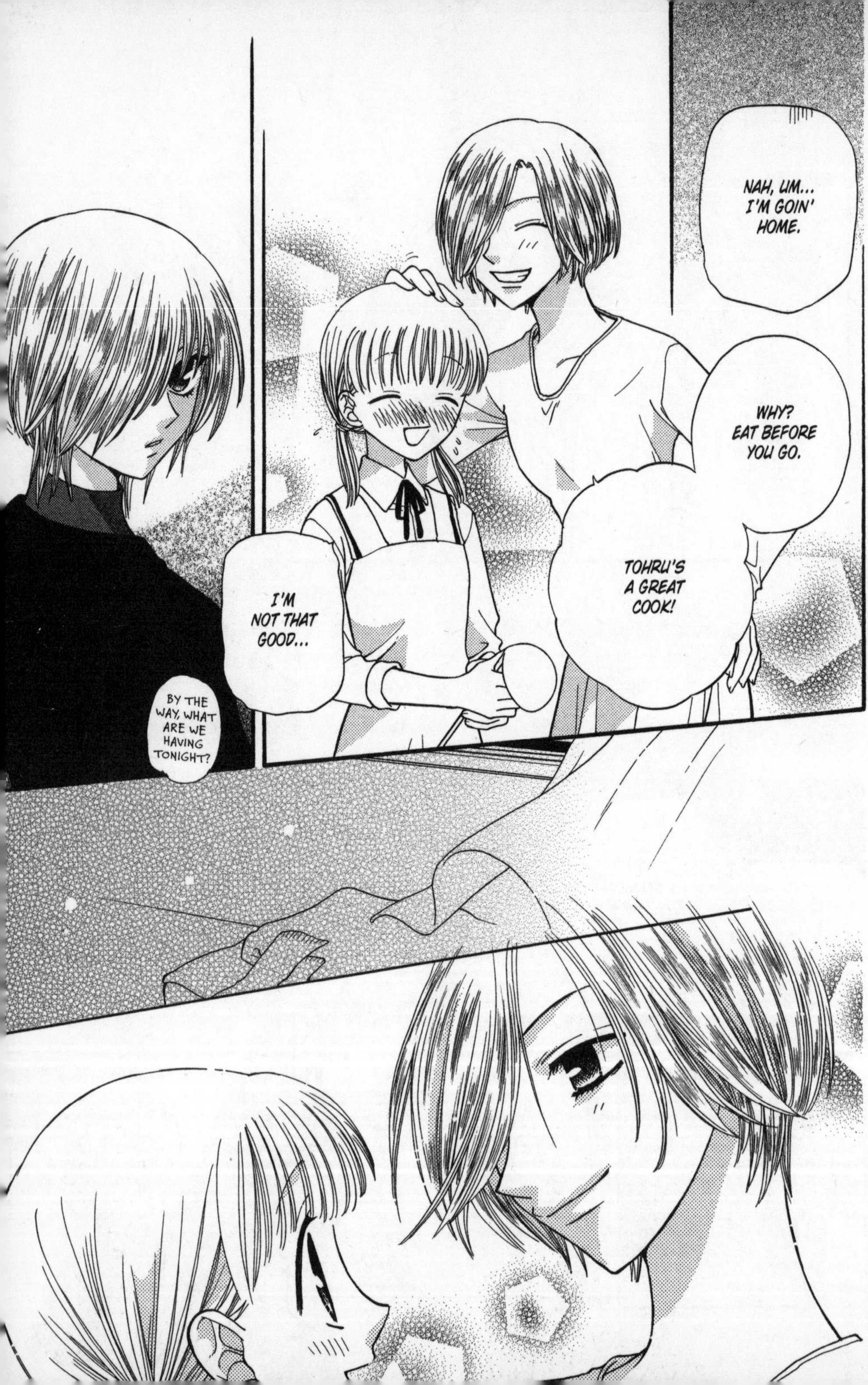
NAH, UM... I'M GOIN' HOME.
WHY? EAT BEFORE YOU GO.
TOHRU'S A GREAT COOK!
I'M NOT THAT GOOD...
BY THE WAY, WHAT ARE WE HAVING TONIGHT?

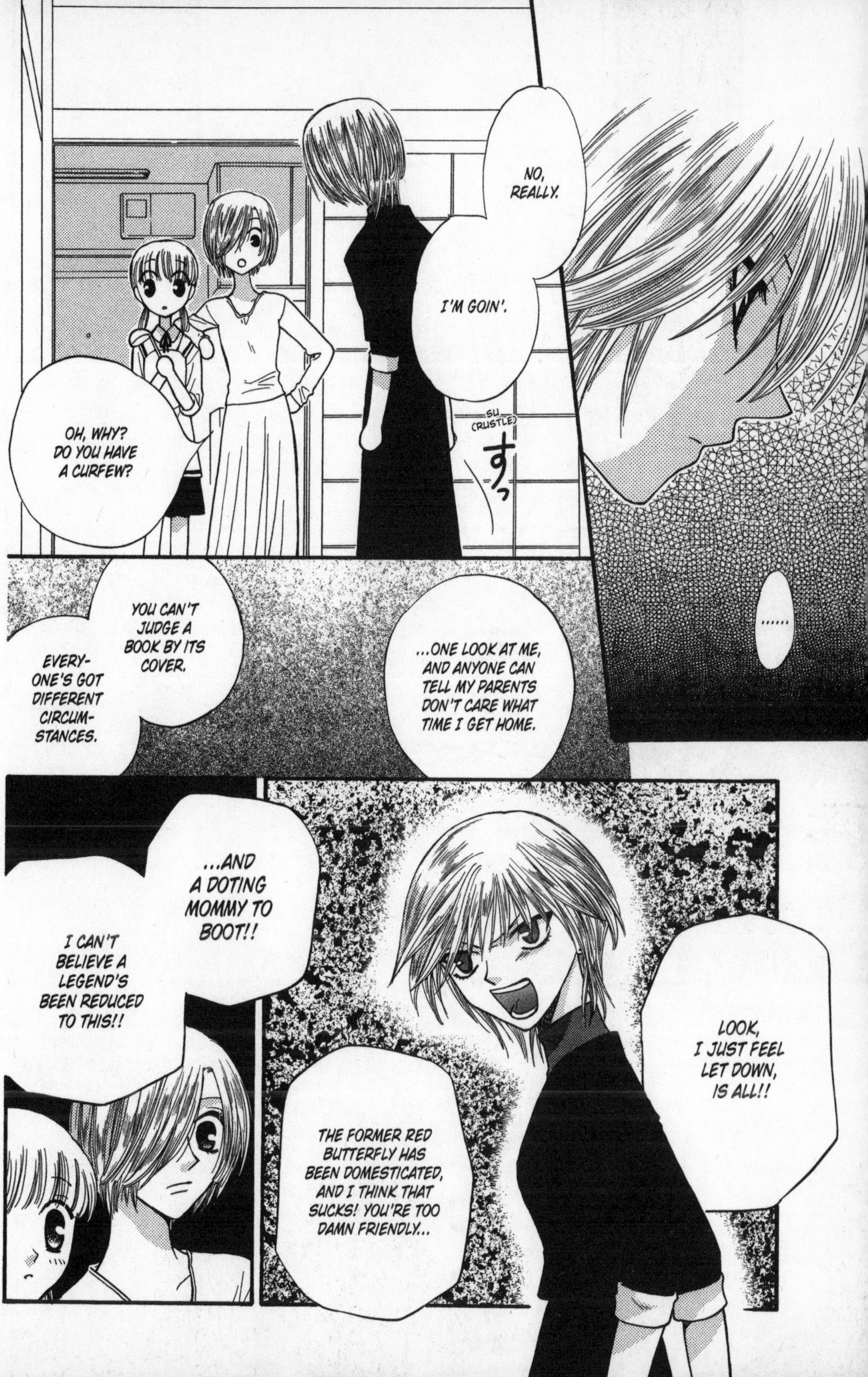
......
NO, REALLY.
I'M GOIN'.
SU (RUSTLE)
すっ
OH, WHY? DO YOU HAVE A CURFEW?
...ONE LOOK AT ME, AND ANYONE CAN TELL MY PARENTS DON'T CARE WHAT TIME I GET HOME.
YOU CAN'T JUDGE A BOOK BY ITS COVER.
EVERY-ONE'S GOT DIFFERENT CIRCUM-STANCES.
LOOK, I JUST FEEL LET DOWN, IS ALL!!
THE FORMER RED BUTTERFLY HAS BEEN DOMESTICATED, AND I THINK THAT SUCKS! YOU'RE TOO DAMN FRIENDLY...
...AND A DOTING MOMMY TO BOOT!!
I CAN'T BELIEVE A LEGEND'S BEEN REDUCED TO THIS!!

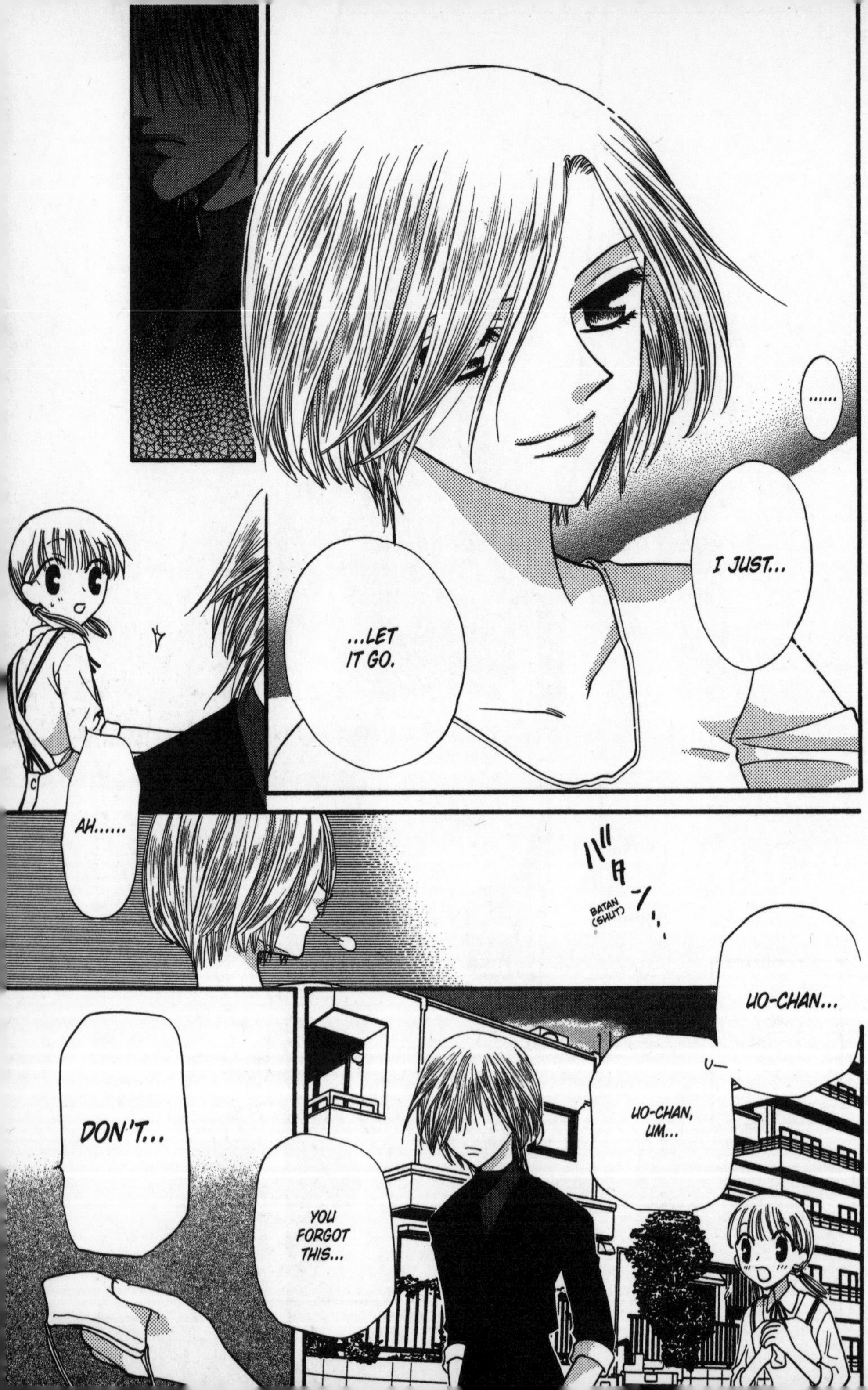
......
I JUST...
...LET IT GO.
バタン
BATAN (SHUT)
AH......
UO-CHAN...
U—
UO-CHAN, UM...
YOU FORGOT THIS...
DON'T...

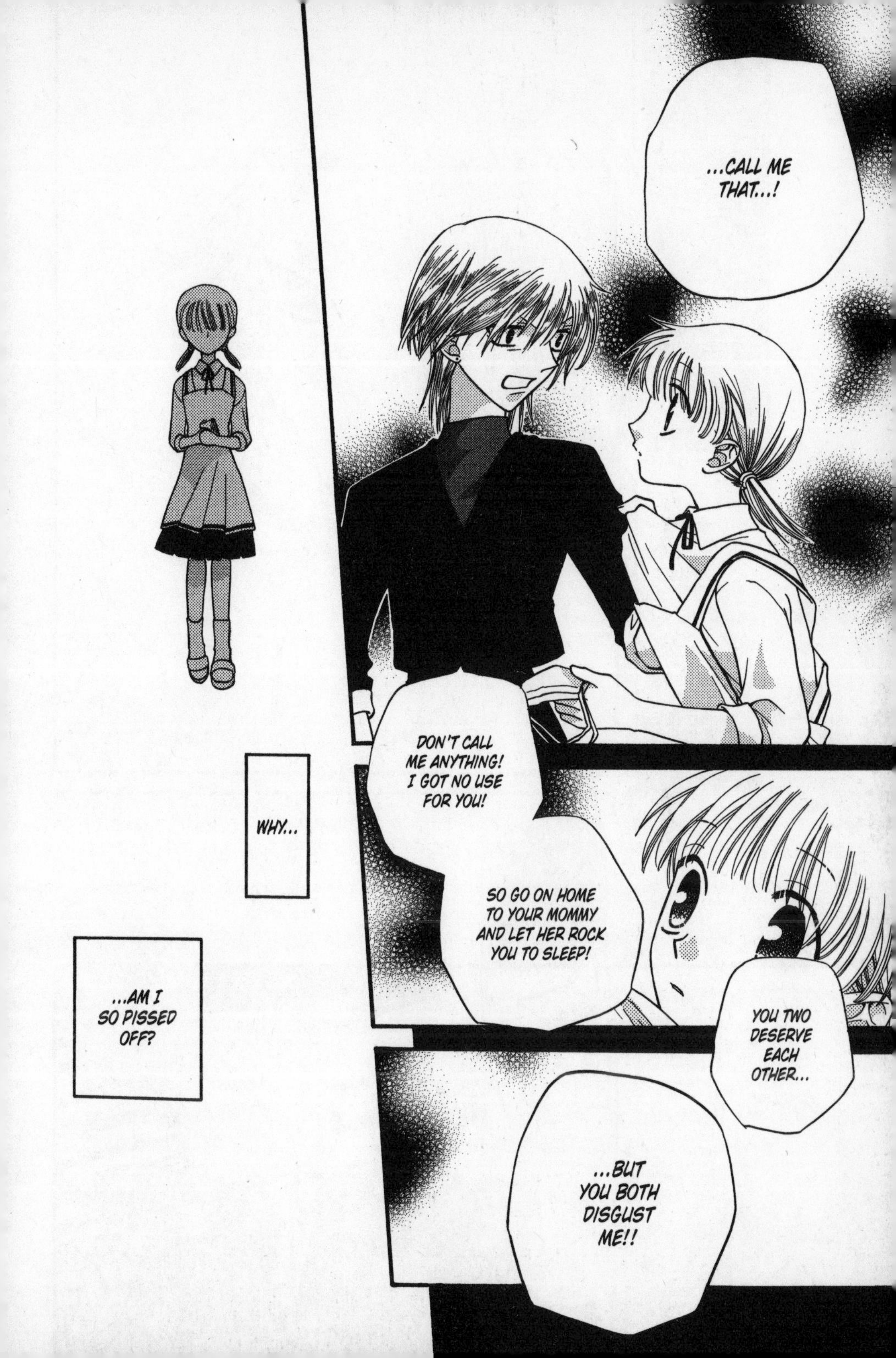
...CALL ME THAT...!
DON'T CALL ME ANYTHING! I GOT NO USE FOR YOU!
SO GO ON HOME TO YOUR MOMMY AND LET HER ROCK YOU TO SLEEP!
YOU TWO DESERVE EACH OTHER...
...BUT YOU BOTH DISGUST ME!!
WHY...
...AM I SO PISSED OFF?

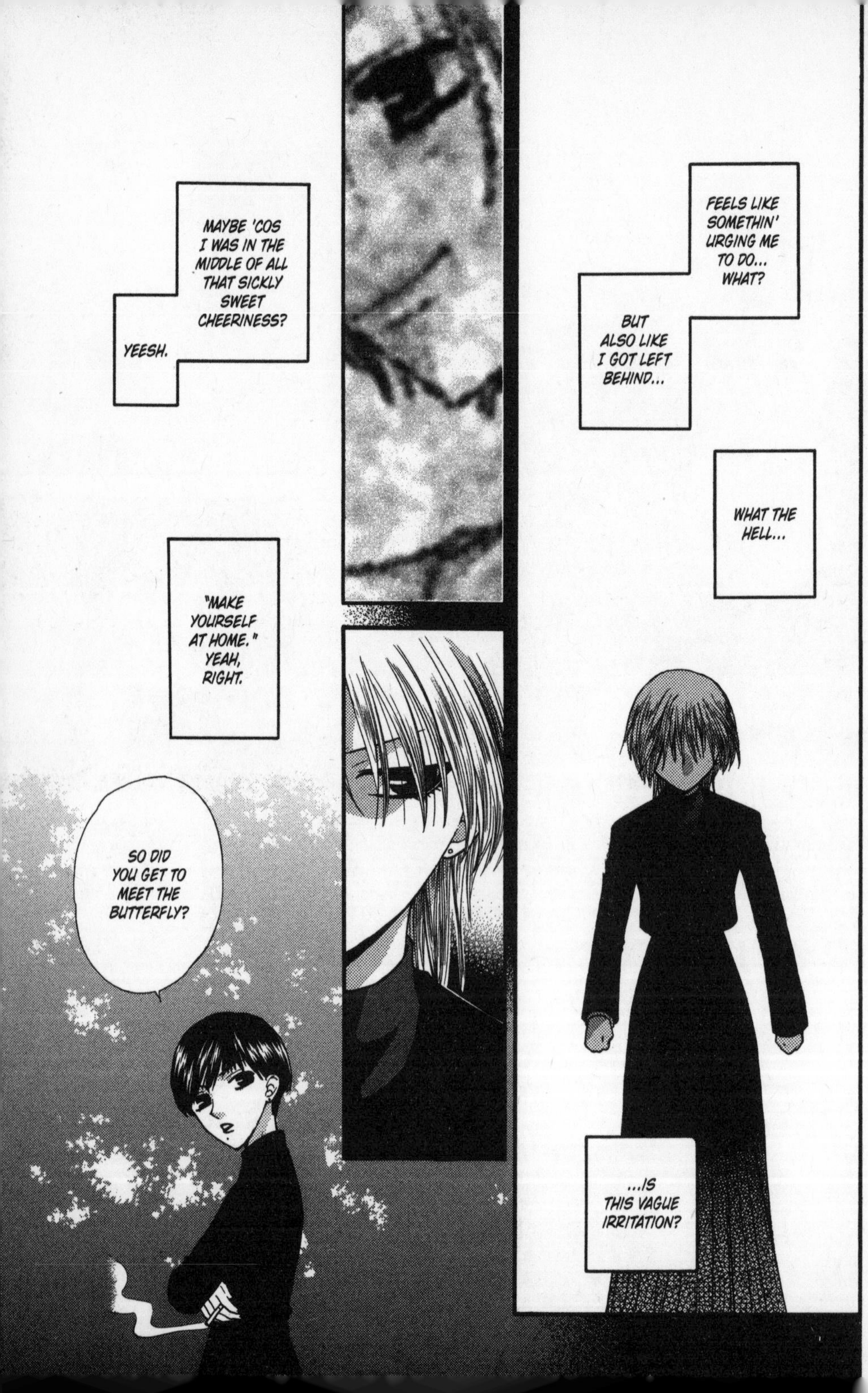
FEELS LIKE SOMETHIN' URGING ME TO DO... WHAT?
BUT ALSO LIKE I GOT LEFT BEHIND...
WHAT THE HELL...
...IS THIS VAGUE IRRITATION?
MAYBE 'COS I WAS IN THE MIDDLE OF ALL THAT SICKLY SWEET CHEERINESS?
YEESH.
"MAKE YOURSELF AT HOME." YEAH, RIGHT.
SO DID YOU GET TO MEET THE BUTTERFLY?

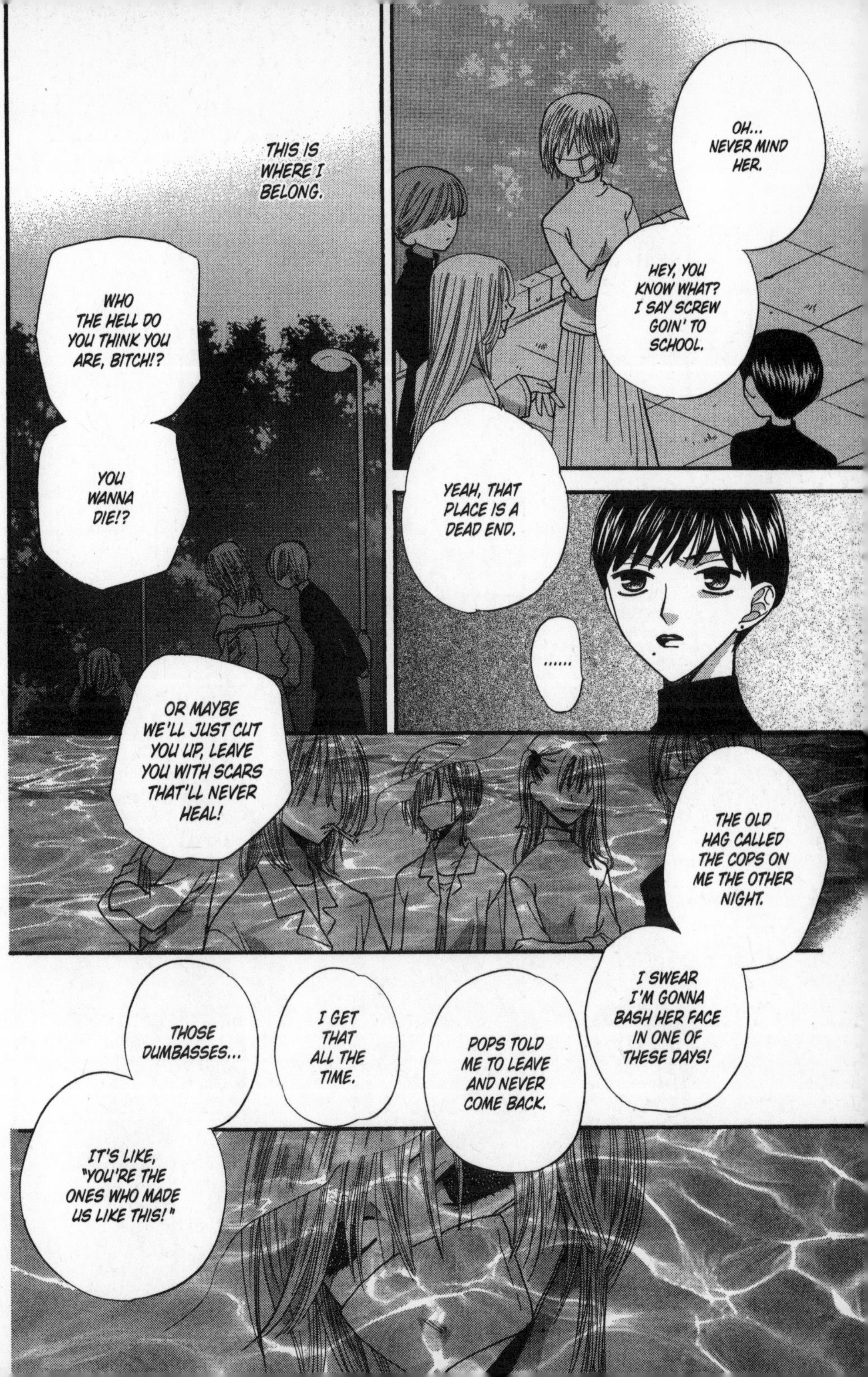
OH... NEVER MIND HER.
HEY, YOU KNOW WHAT? I SAY SCREW GOIN' TO SCHOOL.
YEAH, THAT PLACE IS A DEAD END.
......
THIS IS WHERE I BELONG.
WHO THE HELL DO YOU THINK YOU ARE, BITCH!?
YOU WANNA DIE!?
OR MAYBE WE'LL JUST CUT YOU UP, LEAVE YOU WITH SCARS THAT'LL NEVER HEAL!
THE OLD HAG CALLED THE COPS ON ME THE OTHER NIGHT.
I SWEAR I'M GONNA BASH HER FACE IN ONE OF THESE DAYS!
POPS TOLD ME TO LEAVE AND NEVER COME BACK.
I GET THAT ALL THE TIME.
THOSE DUMBASSES...
IT'S LIKE, "YOU'RE THE ONES WHO MADE US LIKE THIS!"

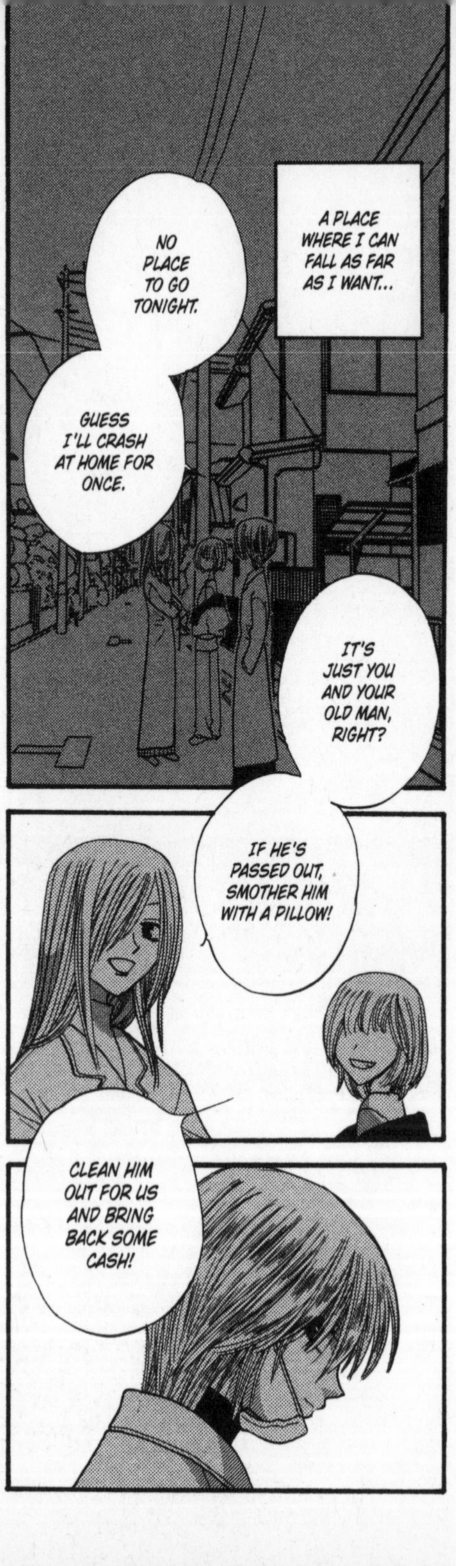
A PLACE WHERE I CAN FALL AS FAR AS I WANT...
NO PLACE TO GO TONIGHT.
GUESS I'LL CRASH AT HOME FOR ONCE.
IT'S JUST YOU AND YOUR OLD MAN, RIGHT?
IF HE'S PASSED OUT, SMOTHER HIM WITH A PILLOW!
CLEAN HIM OUT FOR US AND BRING BACK SOME CASH!
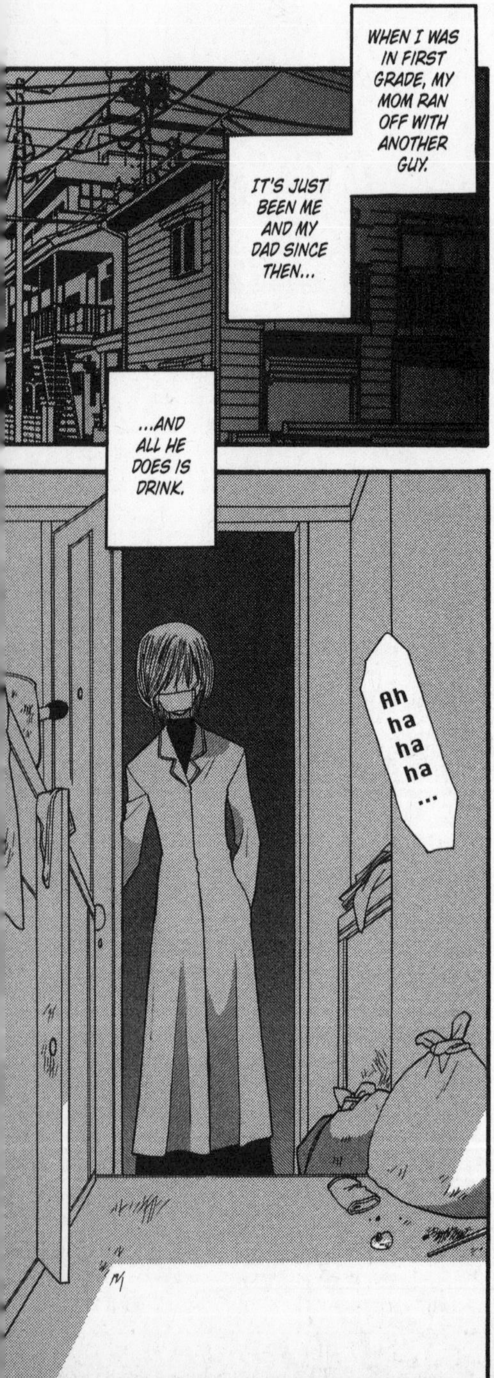
WHEN I WAS IN FIRST GRADE, MY MOM RAN OFF WITH ANOTHER GUY.
IT'S JUST BEEN ME AND MY DAD SINCE THEN...
...AND ALL HE DOES IS DRINK.
Ah ha ha ha...

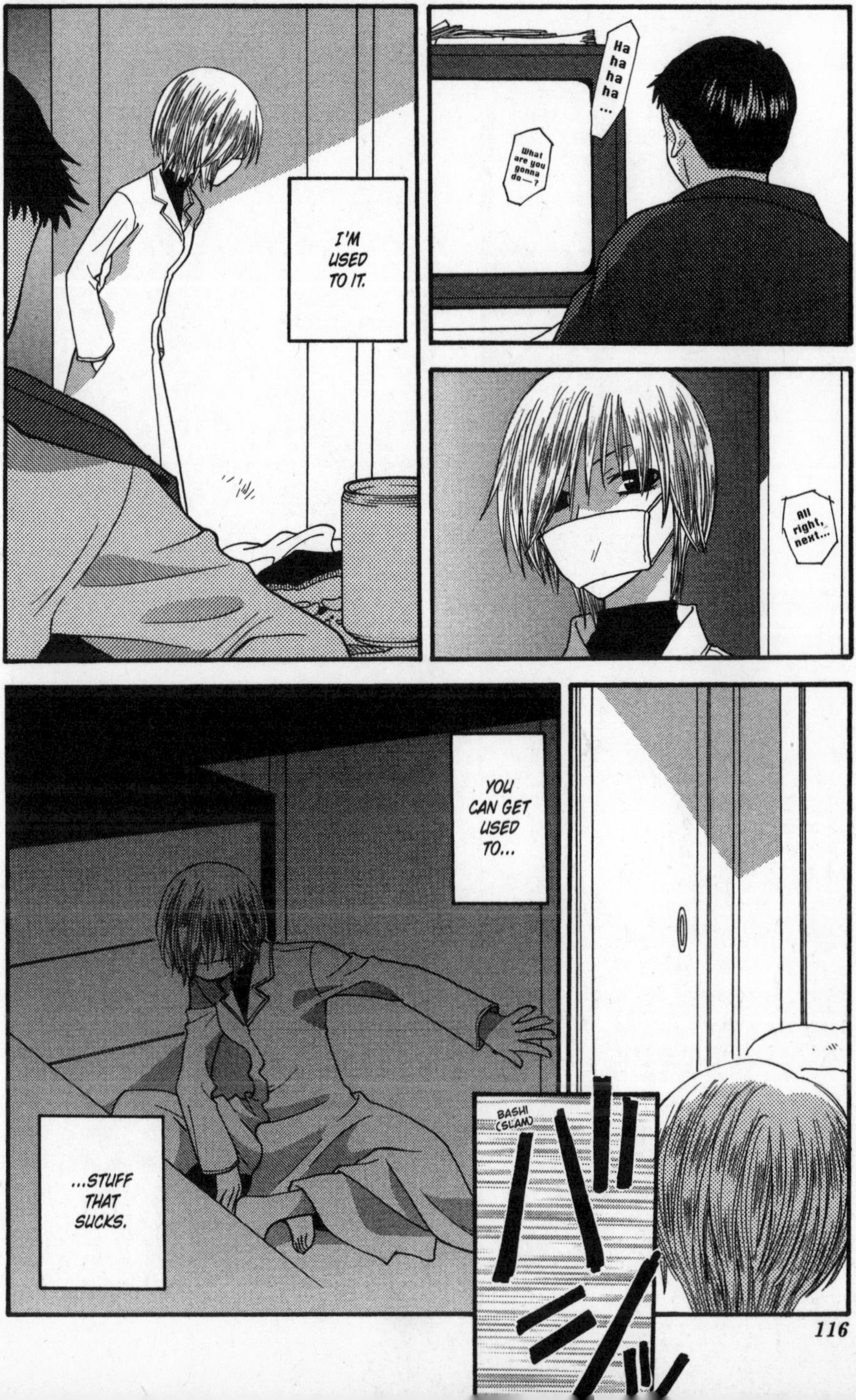
Ha ha ha ha...
What are you gonna do—?
All right, next...
I'M USED TO IT.
BASHI (SLAM)
YOU CAN GET USED TO...
...STUFF THAT SUCKS.

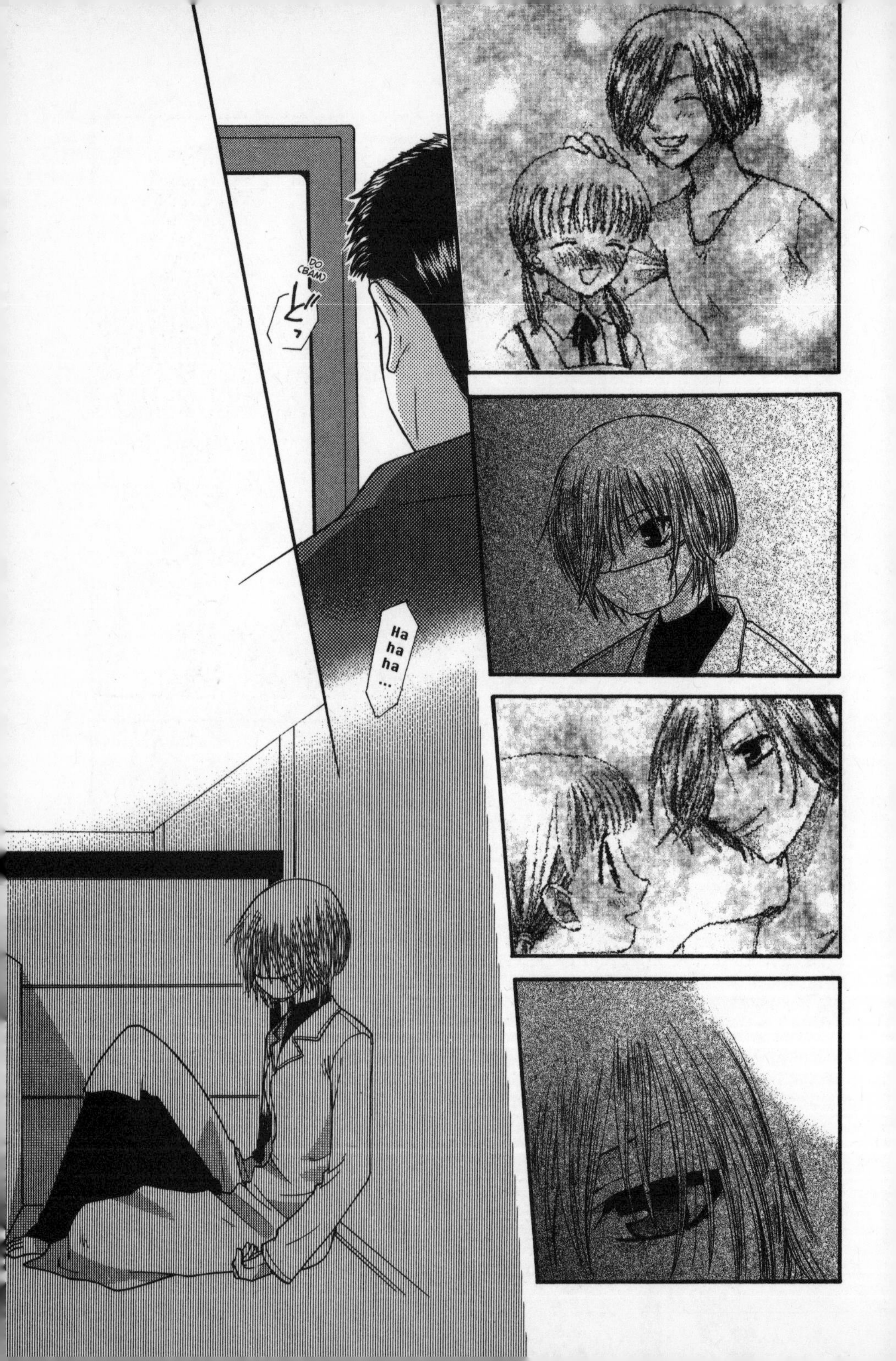
DO (BAM)
どっ
Ha ha ha ...

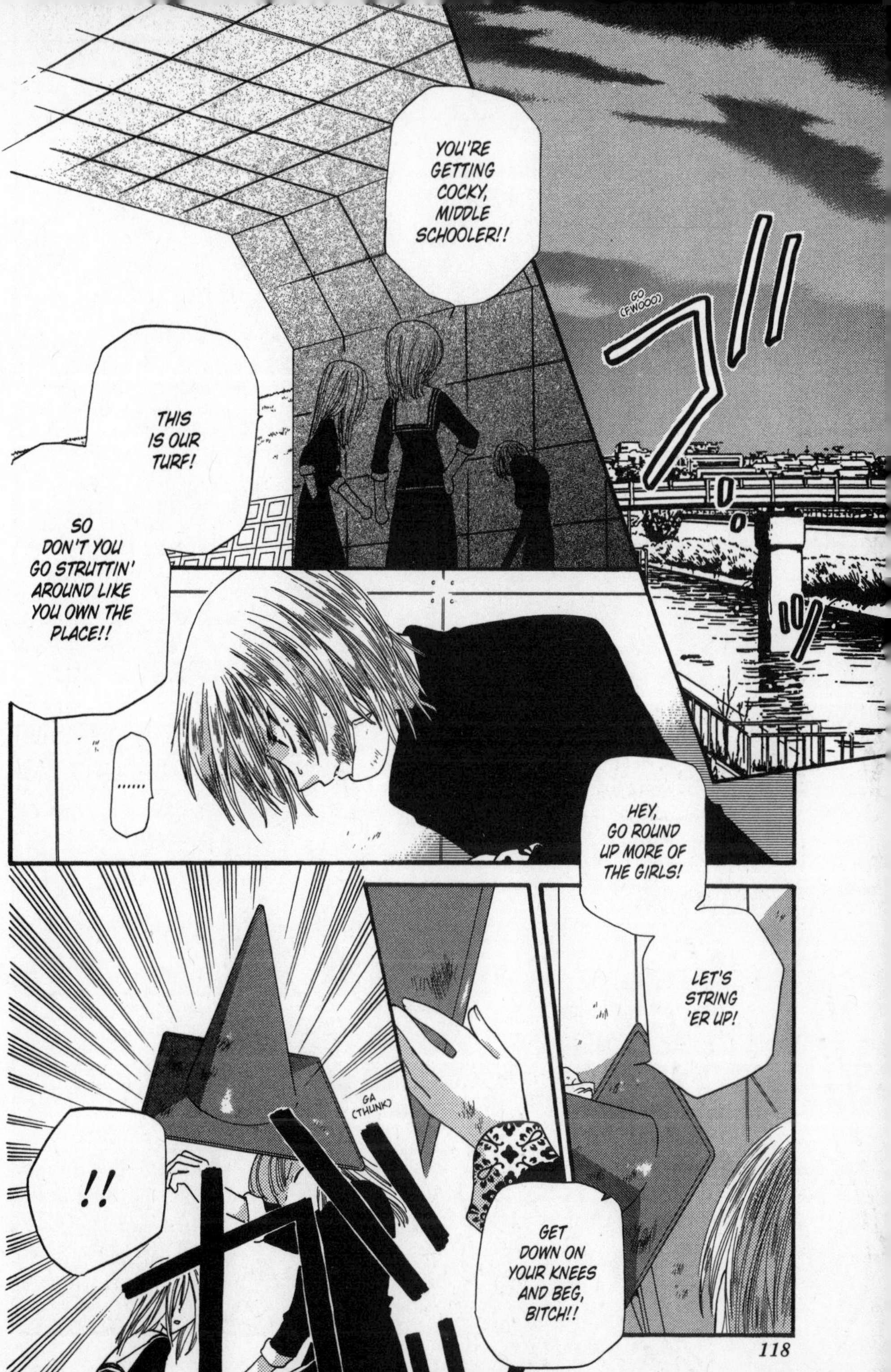
GO (FWOOO)
YOU'RE GETTING COCKY, MIDDLE SCHOOLER!!
THIS IS OUR TURF!
SO DON'T YOU GO STRUTTIN' AROUND LIKE YOU OWN THE PLACE!!
......
HEY, GO ROUND UP MORE OF THE GIRLS!
LET'S STRING 'ER UP!
GET DOWN ON YOUR KNEES AND BEG, BITCH!!
GA (THUNK)
!!

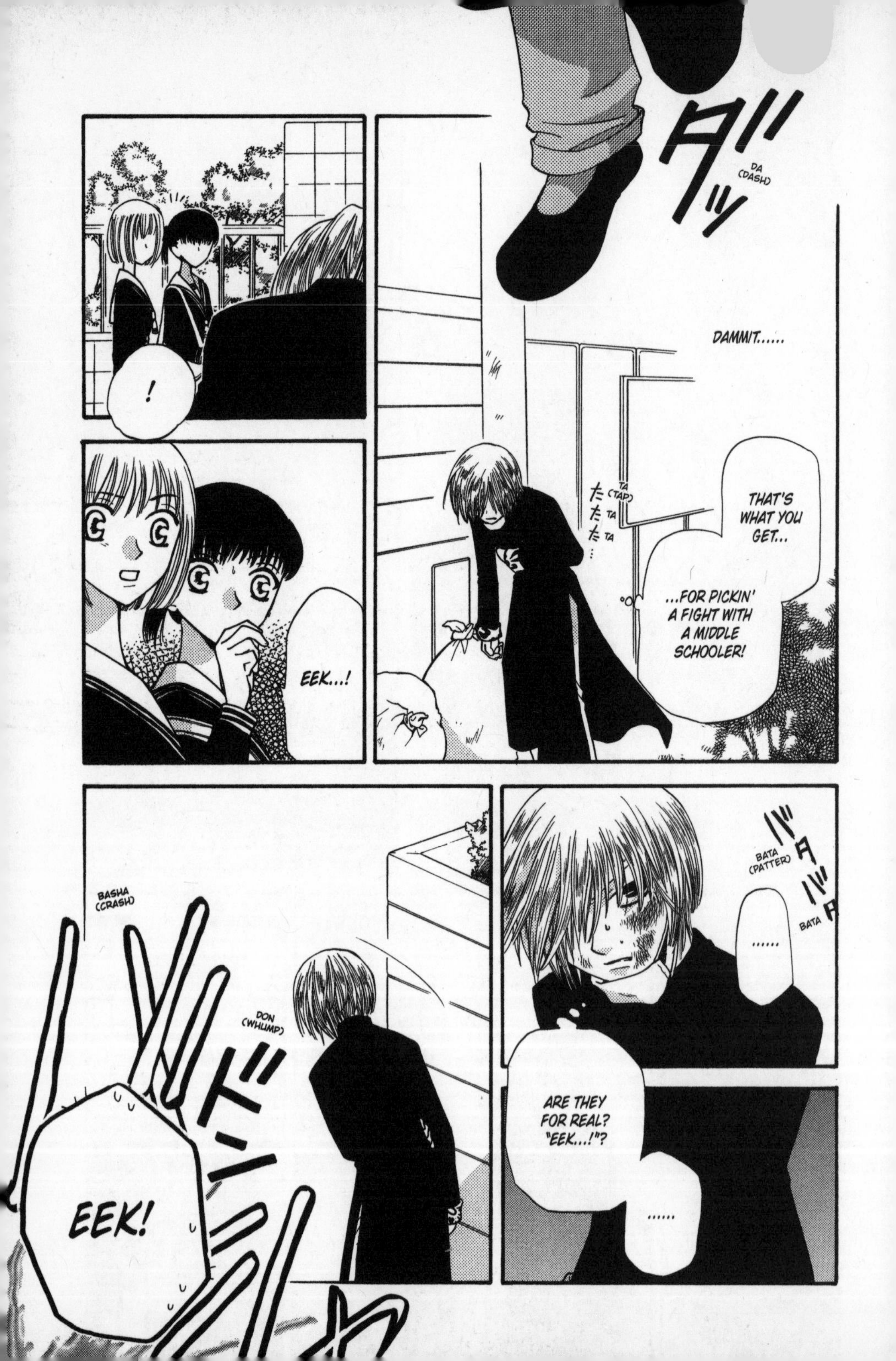
DA (DASH)
DAMMIT......
TA (TAP) TA TA
THAT'S WHAT YOU GET...
...FOR PICKIN' A FIGHT WITH A MIDDLE SCHOOLER!
!
EEK...!
BATA (PATTER) BATA
......
ARE THEY FOR REAL? "EEK...!"?
......
BASHA (CRASH)
DON (WHUMP)
EEK!

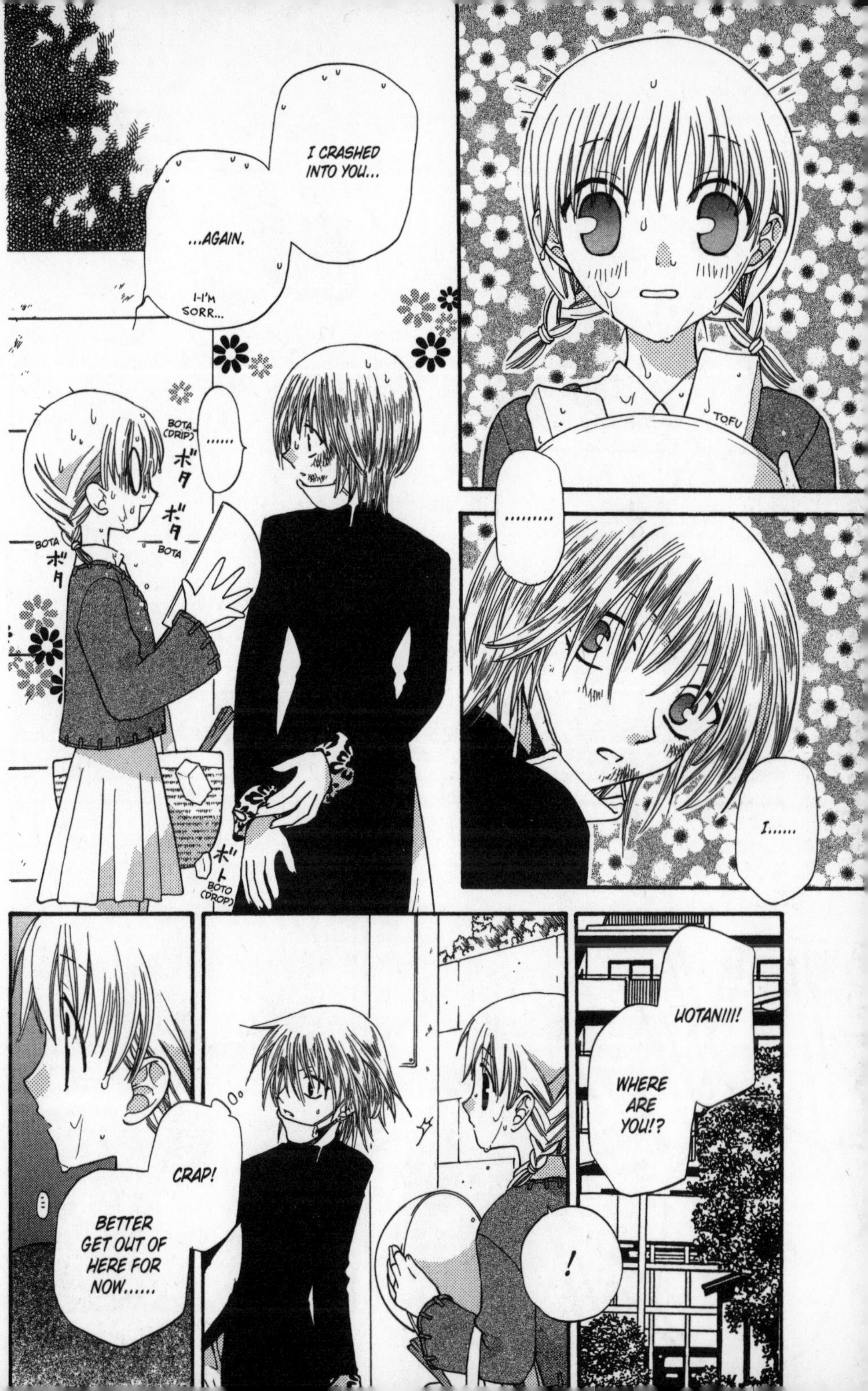

TOFU
....
I......
I CRASHED INTO YOU...
...AGAIN.
I-I'M SORR...
......
ボタ
BOTA (DRIP)
ボタ
BOTA
ボタ
BOTA
ボト
BOTO (DROP)
UOTANIII!
WHERE ARE YOU!?
!
CRAP!
...
BETTER GET OUT OF HERE FOR NOW......

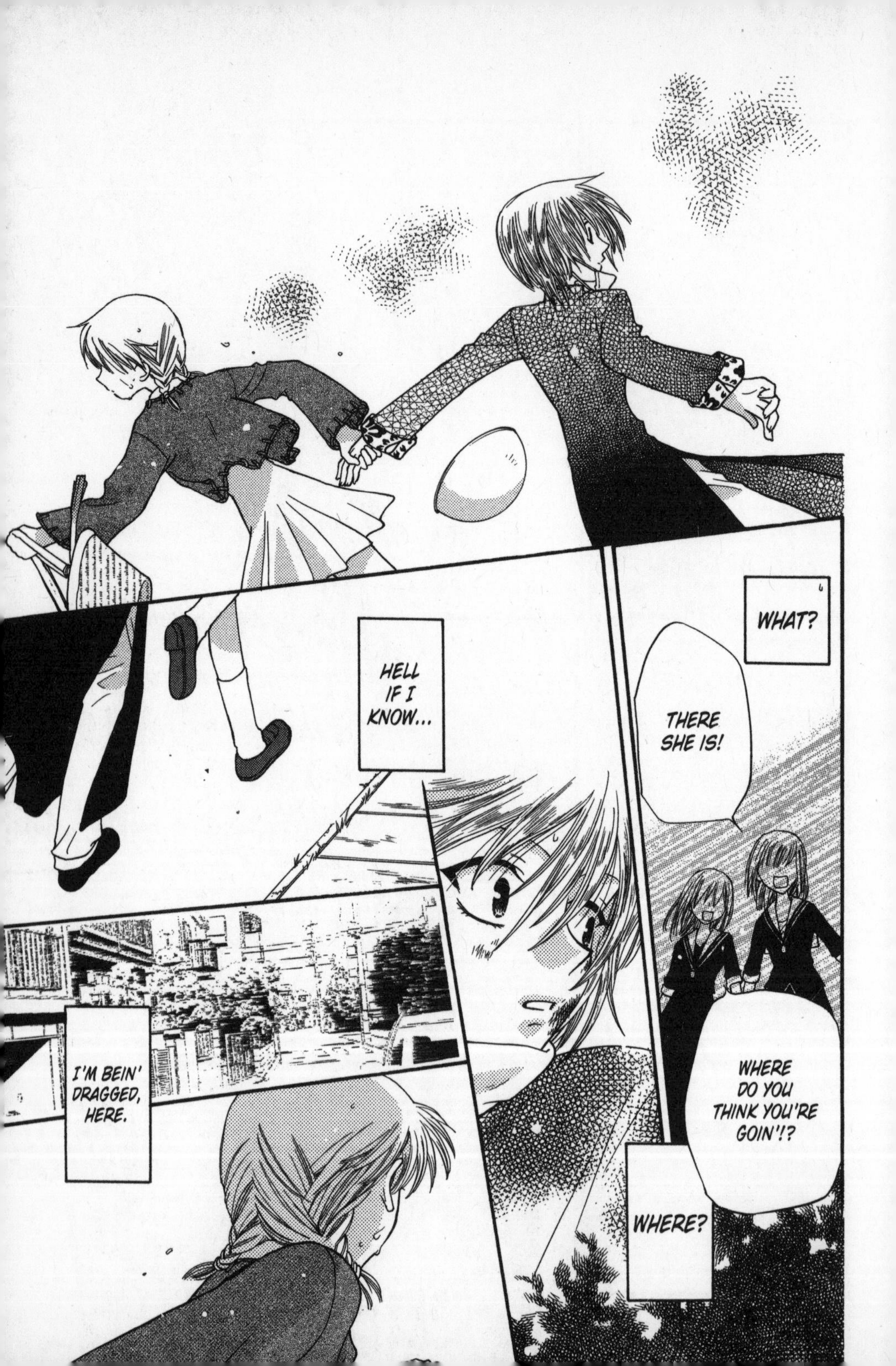
WHAT?
THERE SHE IS!
WHERE DO YOU THINK YOU'RE GOIN'!?
WHERE?
HELL IF I KNOW...
I'M BEIN' DRAGGED, HERE.

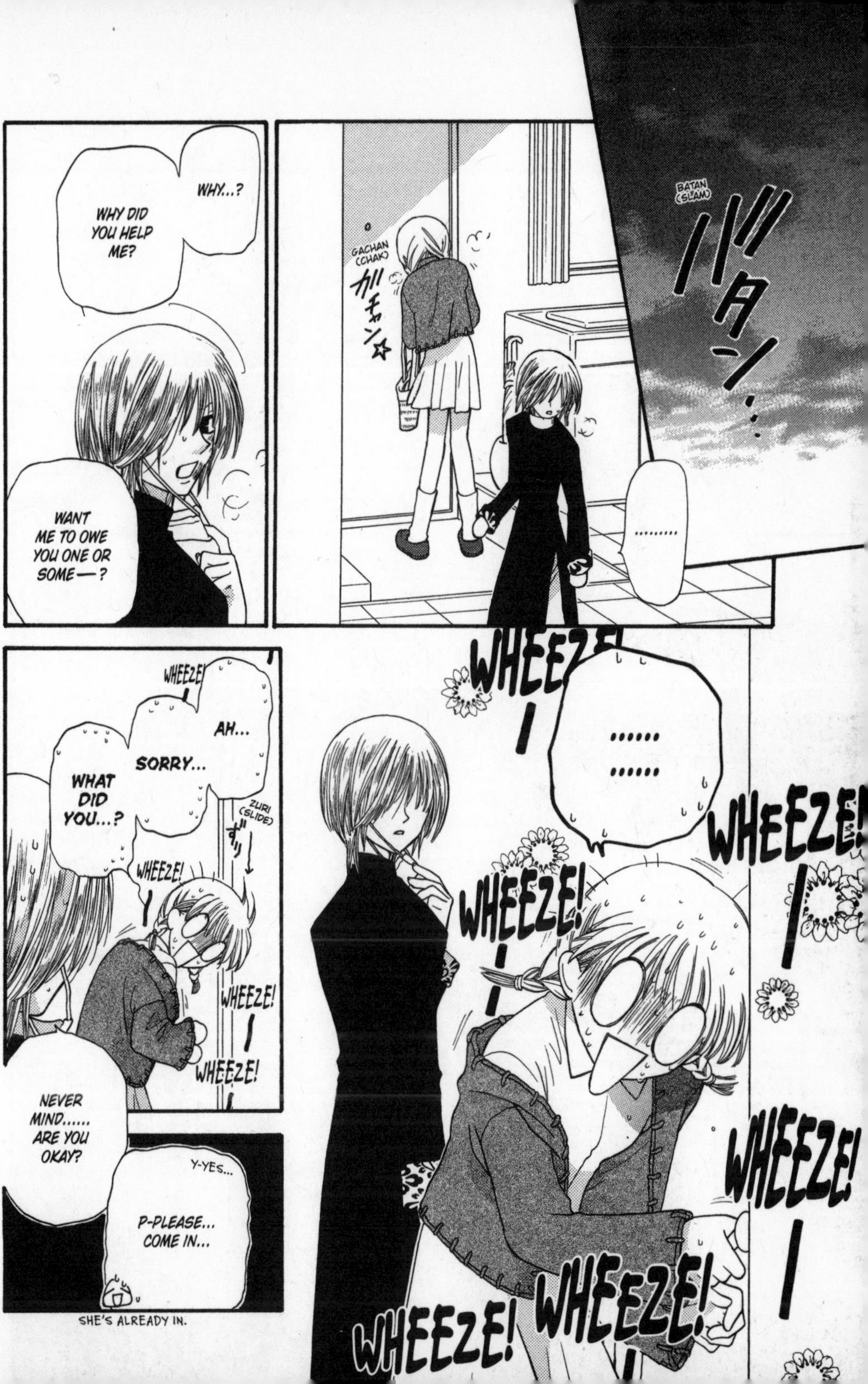

BATAN (SLAM)
....
GACHAN (CHAK)
WHY...?
WHY DID YOU HELP ME?
WANT ME TO OWE YOU ONE OR SOME—?
WHEEZE!
......
......
WHEEZE!
WHEEZE!
WHEEZE!
WHEEZE!
WHEEZE!
WHEEZE!
AH...
SORRY...
WHAT DID YOU...?
ZURI (SLIDE)
WHEEZE!
WHEEZE!
WHEEZE!
NEVER MIND...... ARE YOU OKAY?
Y-YES...
P-PLEASE... COME IN...
SHE'S ALREADY IN.

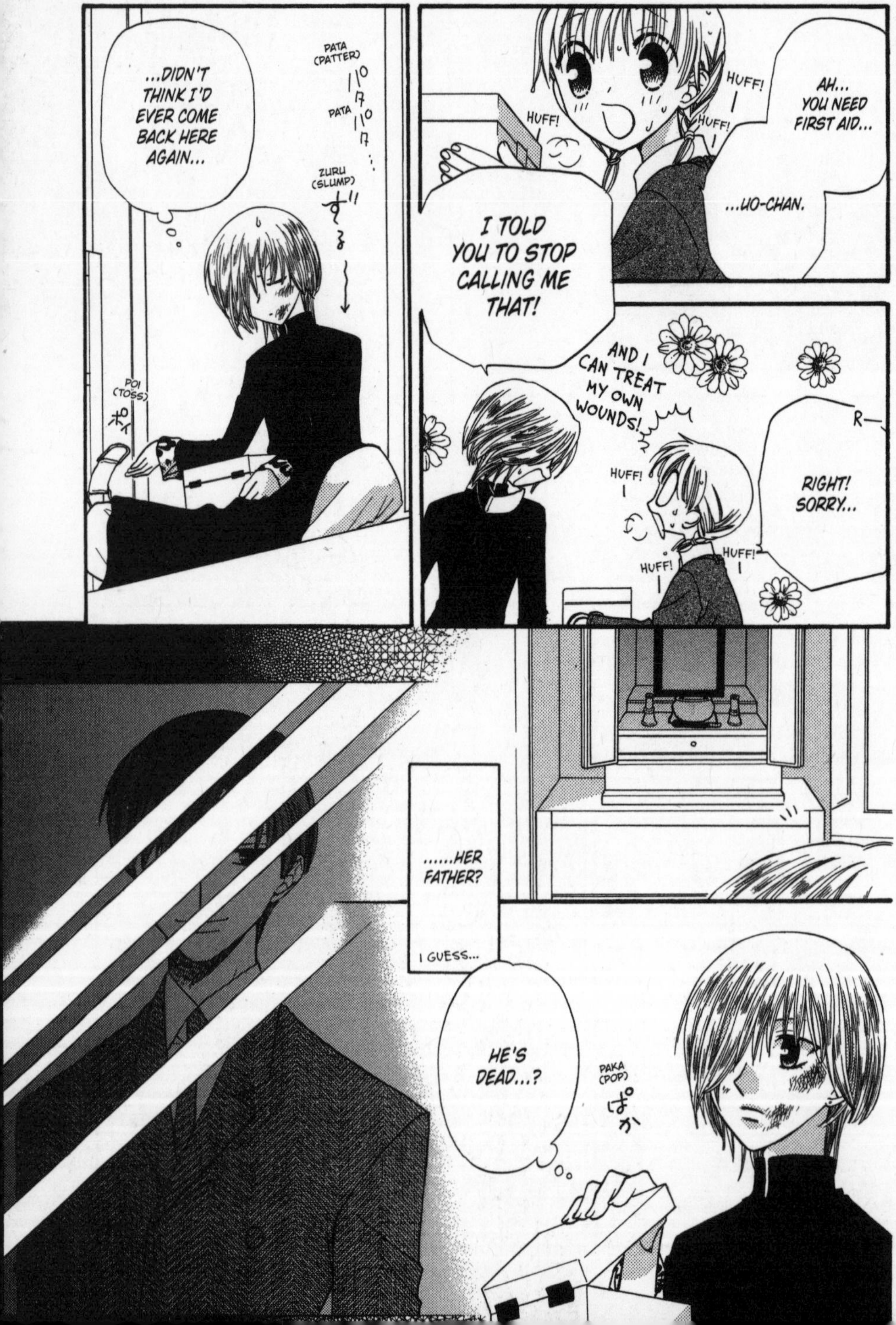
AH... YOU NEED FIRST AID...
HUFF! HUFF!
HUFF!
...UO-CHAN.
I TOLD YOU TO STOP CALLING ME THAT!
R— RIGHT! SORRY...
AND I CAN TREAT MY OWN WOUNDS!
HUFF! HUFF! HUFF!
PATA (PATTER) PATA
...DIDN'T THINK I'D EVER COME BACK HERE AGAIN...
ZURU (SLUMP)
POI (TOSS)
......HER FATHER?
I GUESS...
PAKA (POP)
HE'S DEAD...?

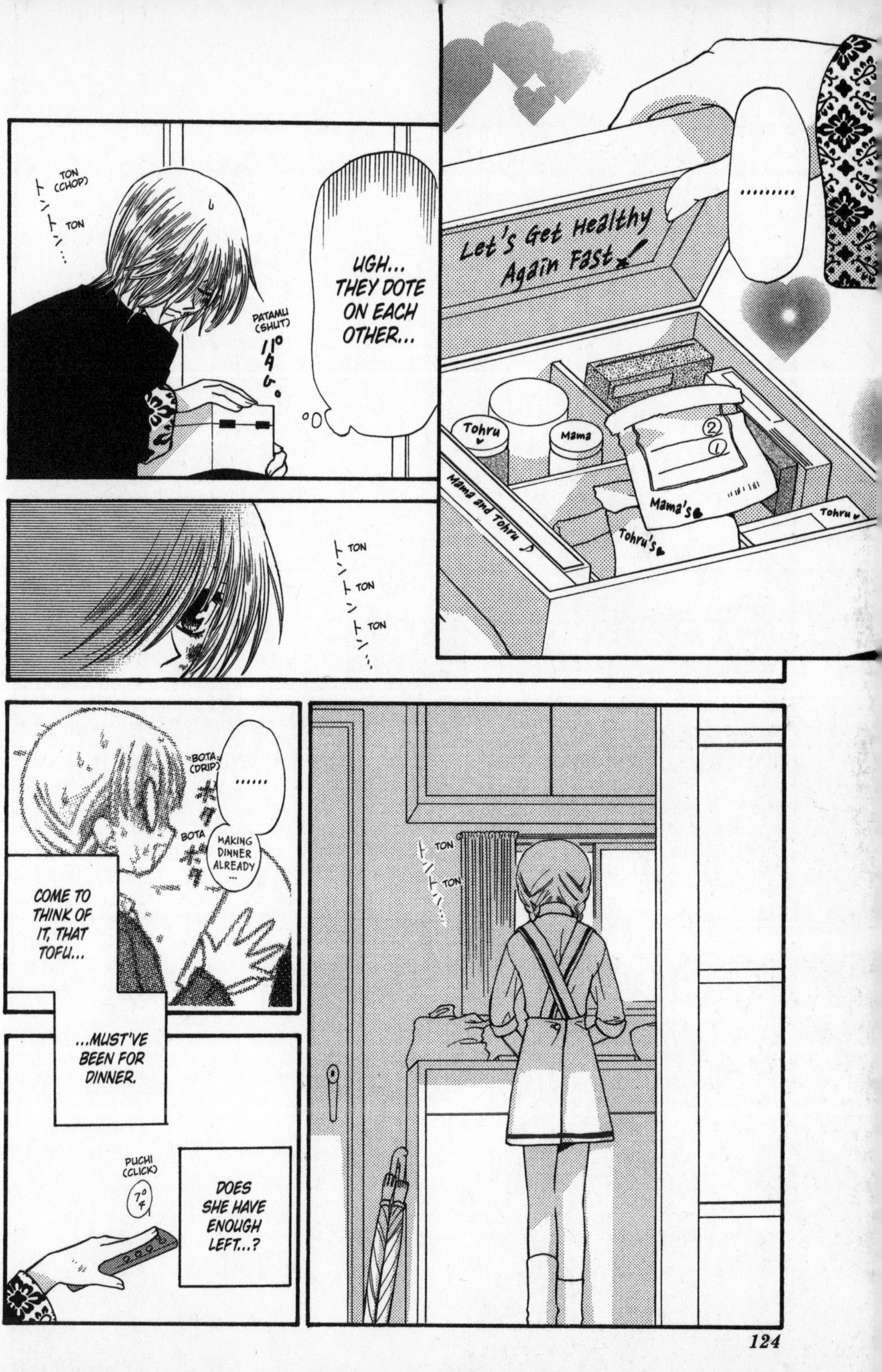

....
Let's Get Healthy Again Fast
Tohru
Mama
Mama and Tohru
Mama's
Tohru's
Tohru
UGH... THEY DOTE ON EACH OTHER...
PATAMU (SHUT)
TON (CHOP)
TON
TON
TON
TON
TON
TON
......
MAKING DINNER ALREADY ...
BOTA (DRIP)
BOTA
COME TO THINK OF IT, THAT TOFU...
...MUST'VE BEEN FOR DINNER.
DOES SHE HAVE ENOUGH LEFT...?
PUCHI (CLICK)

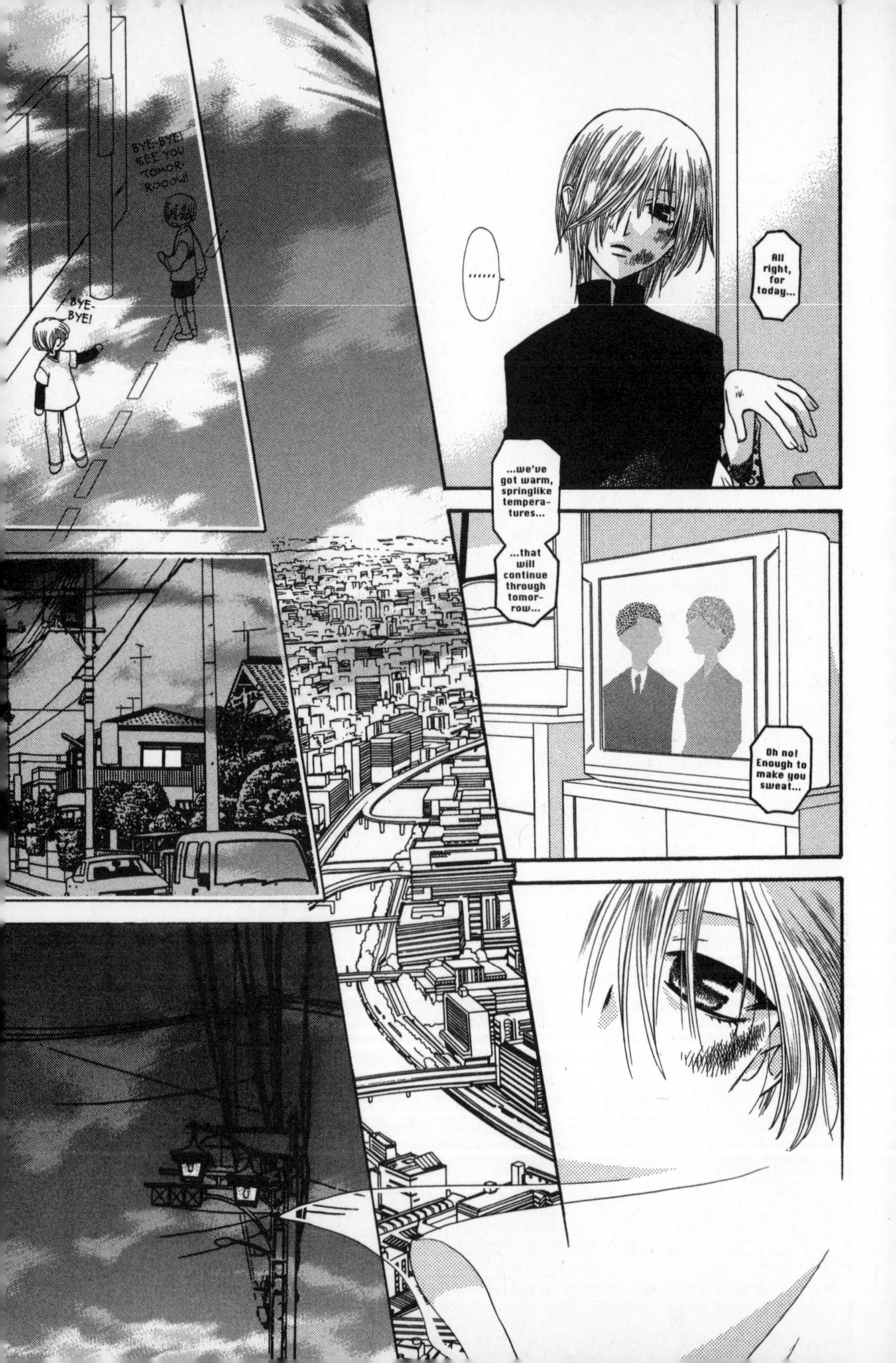
All right, for today...
......
...we've got warm, springlike tempera-tures...
...that will continue through tomor-row...
Oh no! Enough to make you sweat...
BYE-BYE! SEE YOU TOMOR-ROOOW!
BYE-BYE!

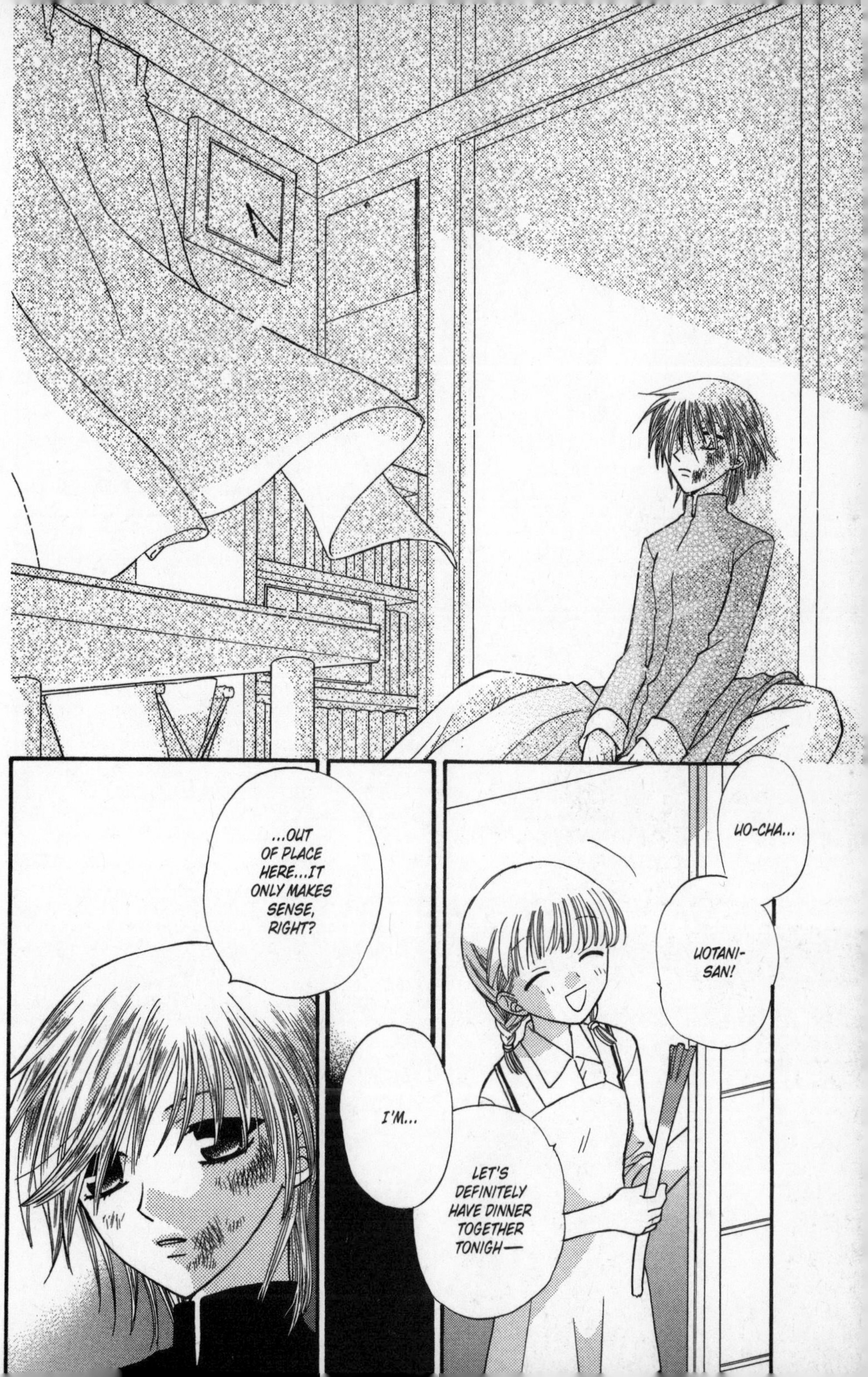
UO-CHA...
UOTANI-SAN!
LET'S DEFINITELY HAVE DINNER TOGETHER TONIGH—
I'M...
...OUT OF PLACE HERE...IT ONLY MAKES SENSE, RIGHT?

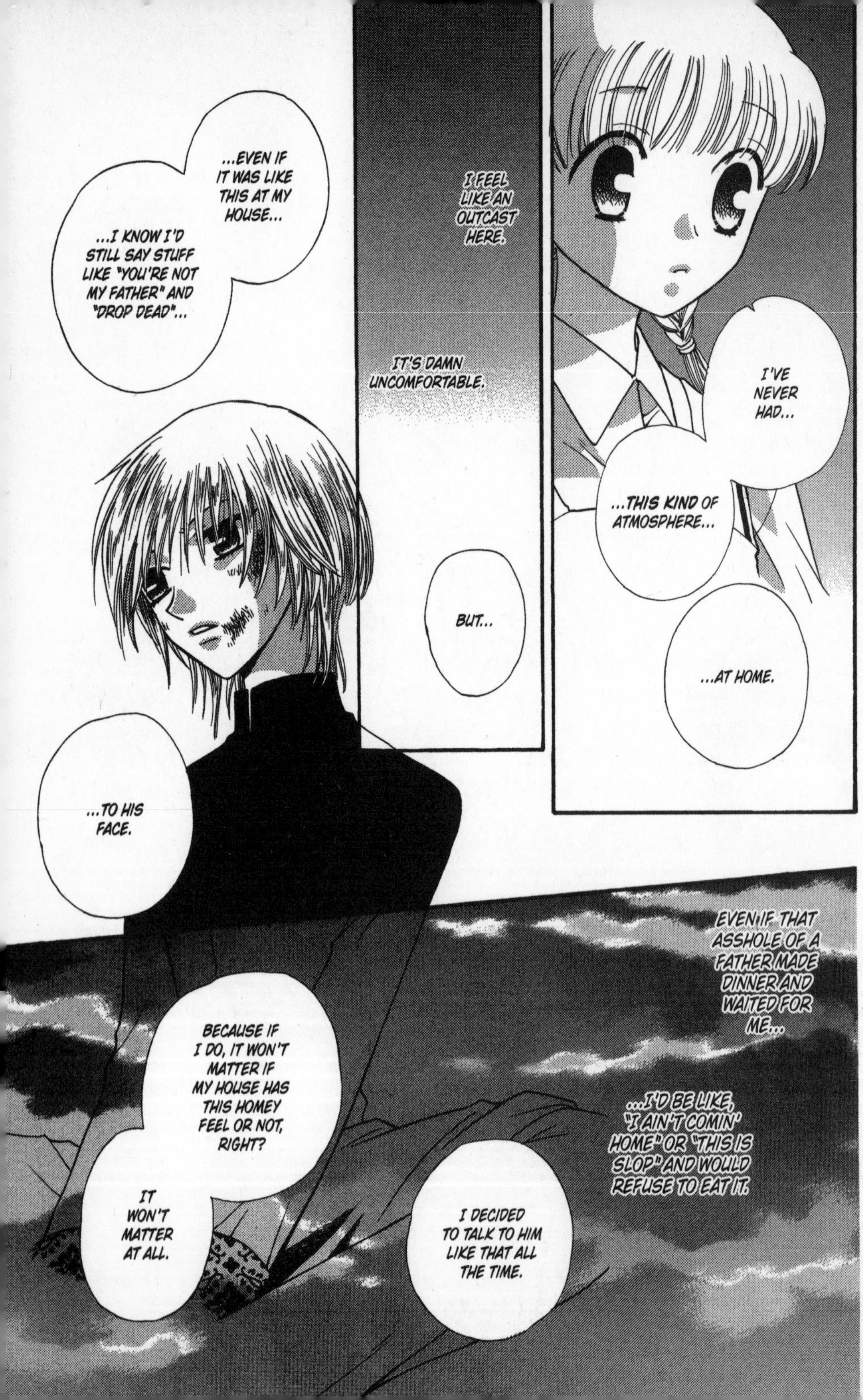
I'VE NEVER HAD...
...THIS KIND OF ATMOSPHERE...
...AT HOME.
I FEEL LIKE AN OUTCAST HERE.
IT'S DAMN UNCOMFORTABLE.
BUT...
...EVEN IF IT WAS LIKE THIS AT MY HOUSE...
...I KNOW I'D STILL SAY STUFF LIKE "YOU'RE NOT MY FATHER" AND "DROP DEAD"...
...TO HIS FACE.
EVEN IF THAT ASSHOLE OF A FATHER MADE DINNER AND WAITED FOR ME...
...I'D BE LIKE, "I AIN'T COMIN' HOME" OR "THIS IS SLOP" AND WOULD REFUSE TO EAT IT.
I DECIDED TO TALK TO HIM LIKE THAT ALL THE TIME.
BECAUSE IF I DO, IT WON'T MATTER IF MY HOUSE HAS THIS HOMEY FEEL OR NOT, RIGHT?
IT WON'T MATTER AT ALL.

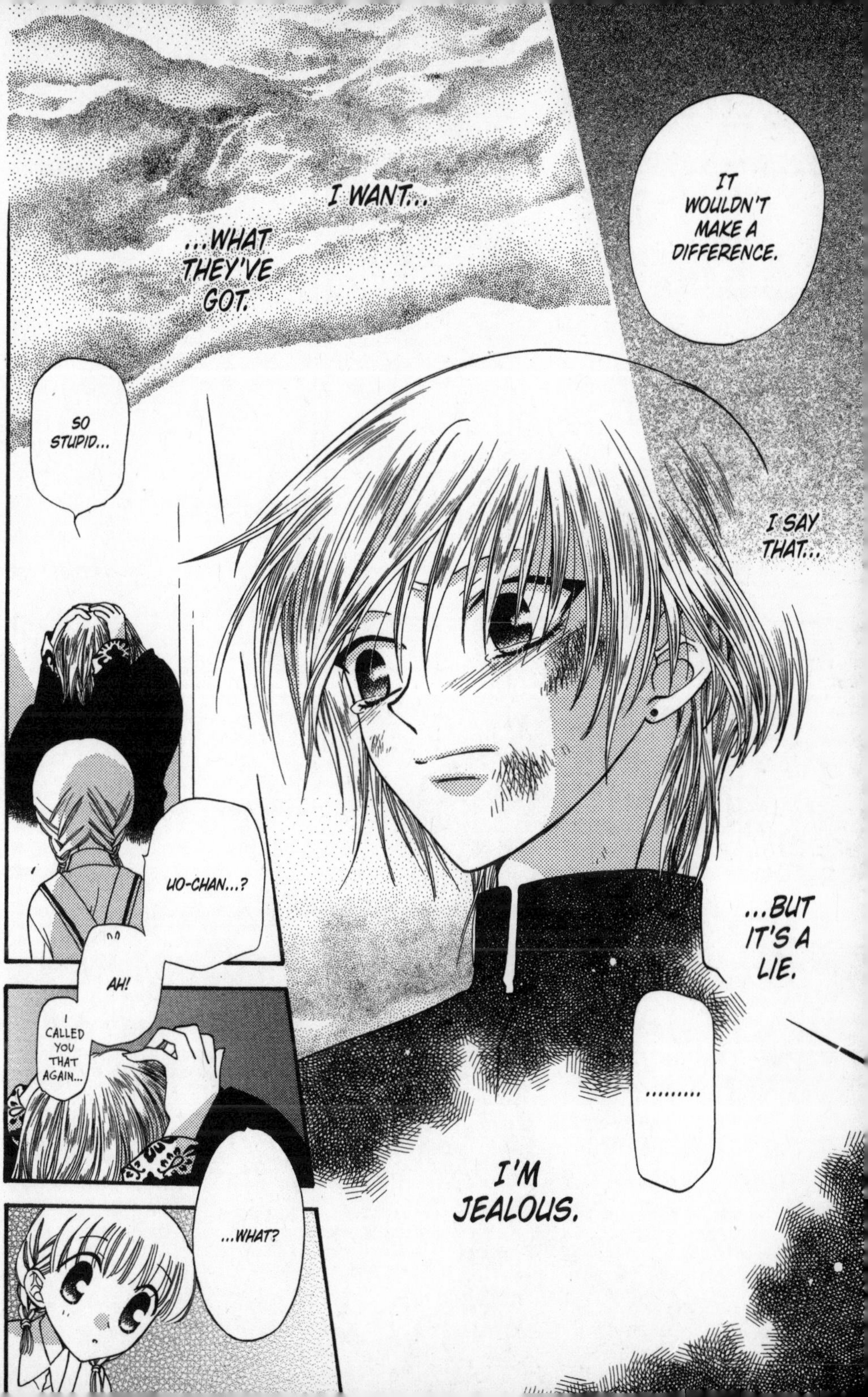
IT WOULDN'T MAKE A DIFFERENCE.
I SAY THAT...
...BUT IT'S A LIE.
I WANT...
...WHAT THEY'VE GOT.
SO STUPID...
....
I'M JEALOUS.
UO-CHAN...?
AH!
I CALLED YOU THAT AGAIN...
...WHAT?

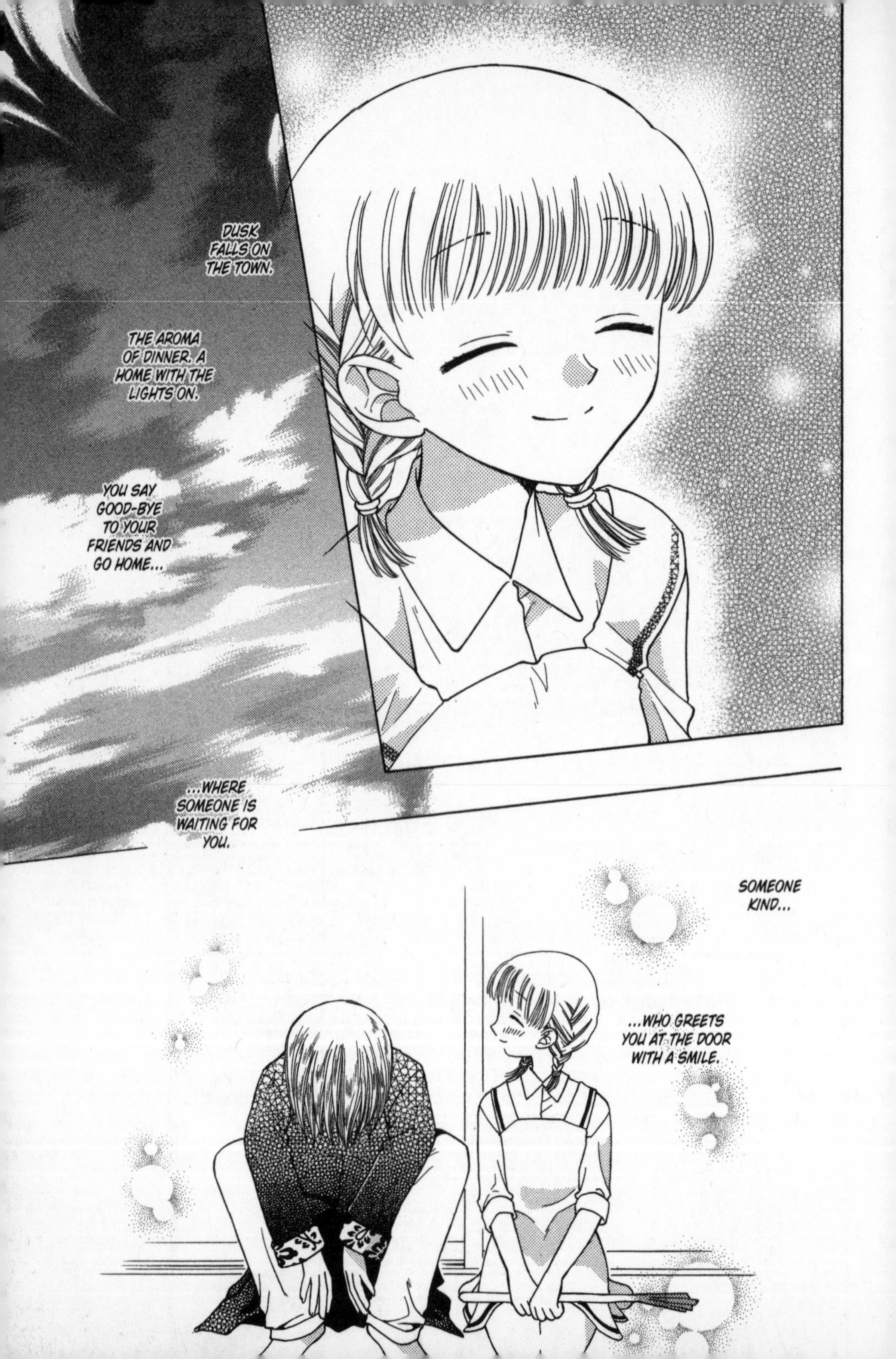
DUSK FALLS ON THE TOWN.
THE AROMA OF DINNER. A HOME WITH THE LIGHTS ON.
YOU SAY GOOD-BYE TO YOUR FRIENDS AND GO HOME...
...WHERE SOMEONE IS WAITING FOR YOU.
SOMEONE KIND...
...WHO GREETS YOU AT THE DOOR WITH A SMILE.

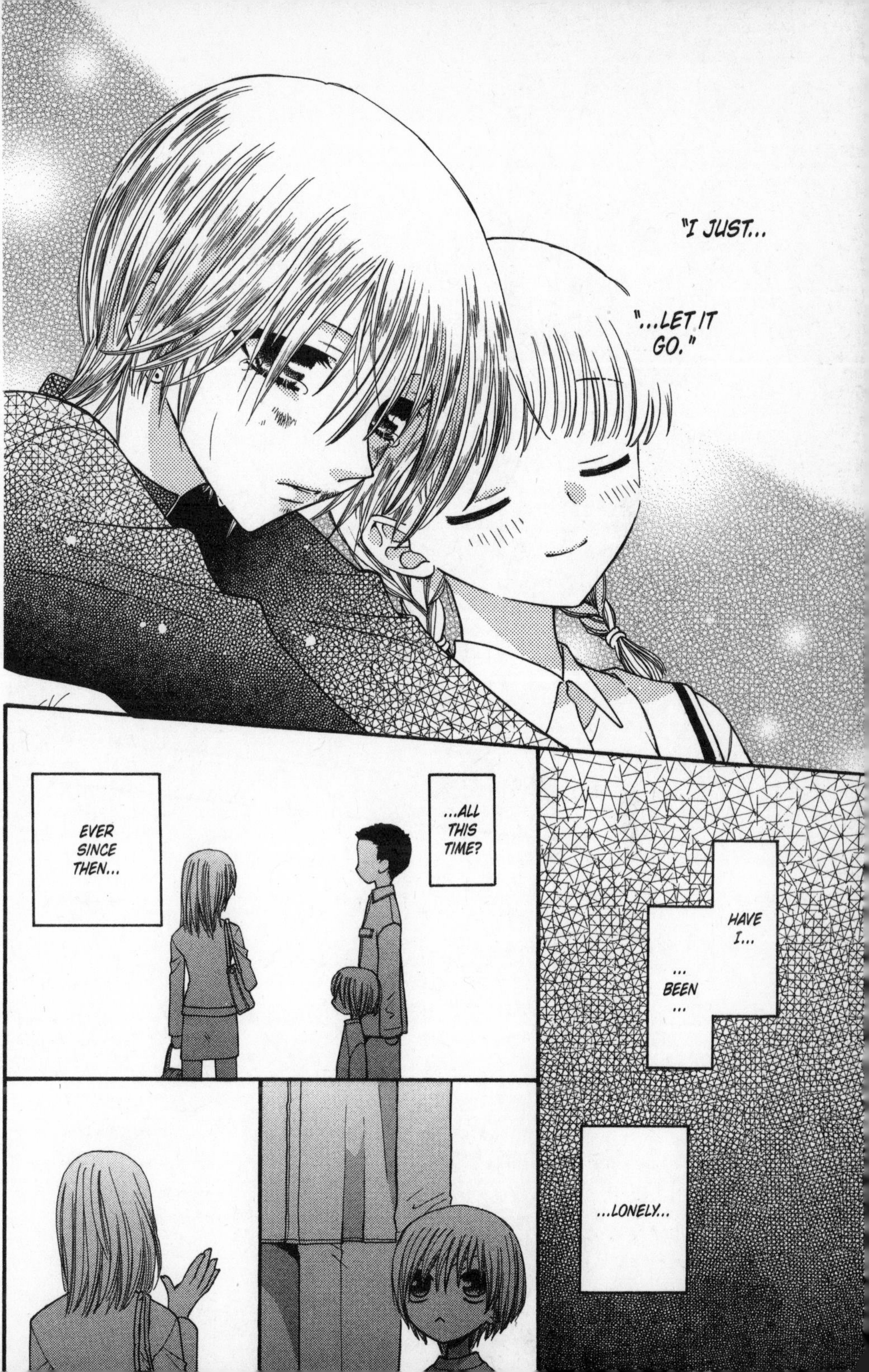
"I JUST...
"...LET IT GO."
HAVE I...
...BEEN...
...LONELY...
...ALL THIS TIME?
EVER SINCE THEN...

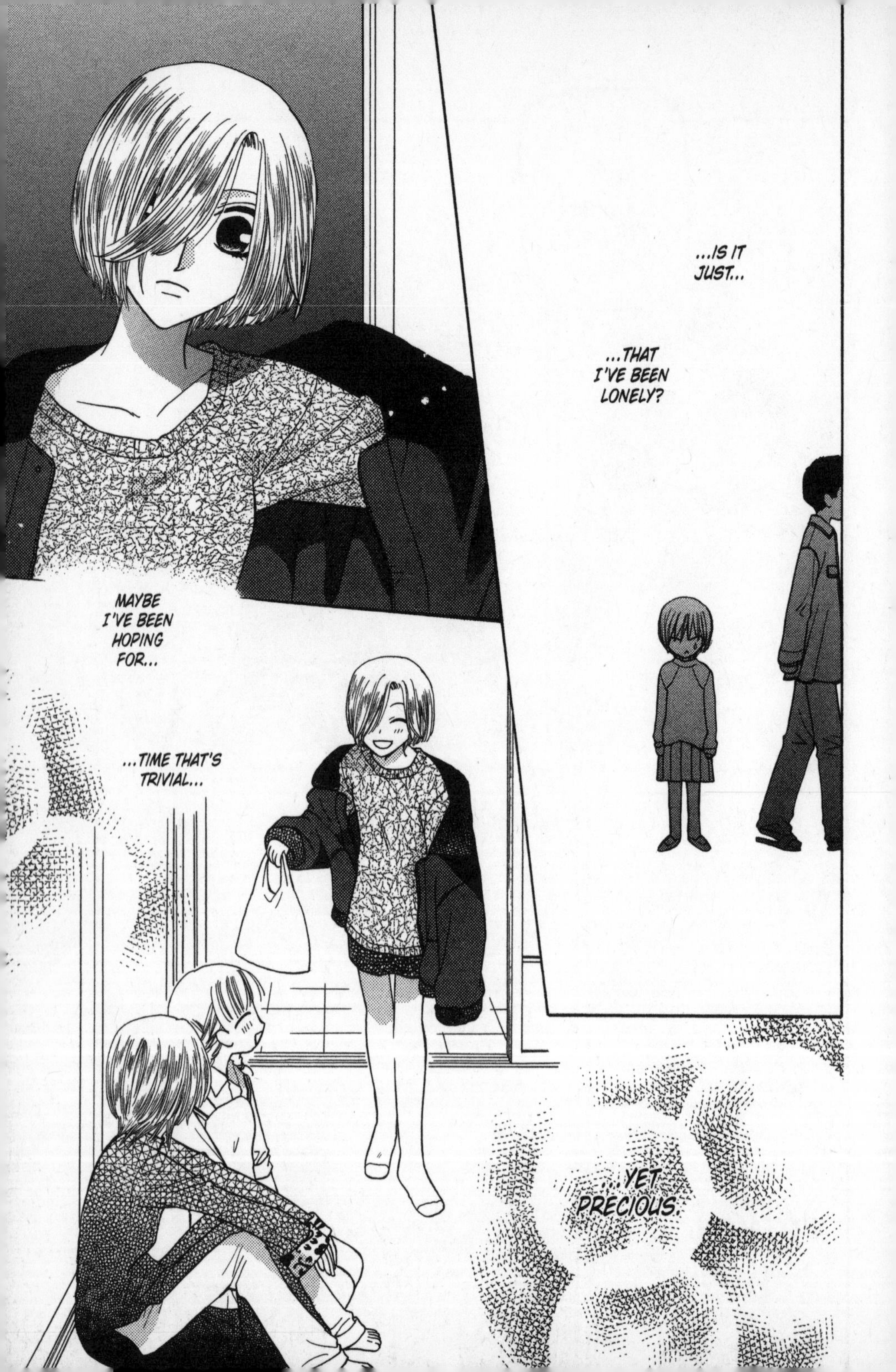
...IS IT JUST...
...THAT I'VE BEEN LONELY?
MAYBE I'VE BEEN HOPING FOR...
...TIME THAT'S TRIVIAL...
...YET PRECIOUS.

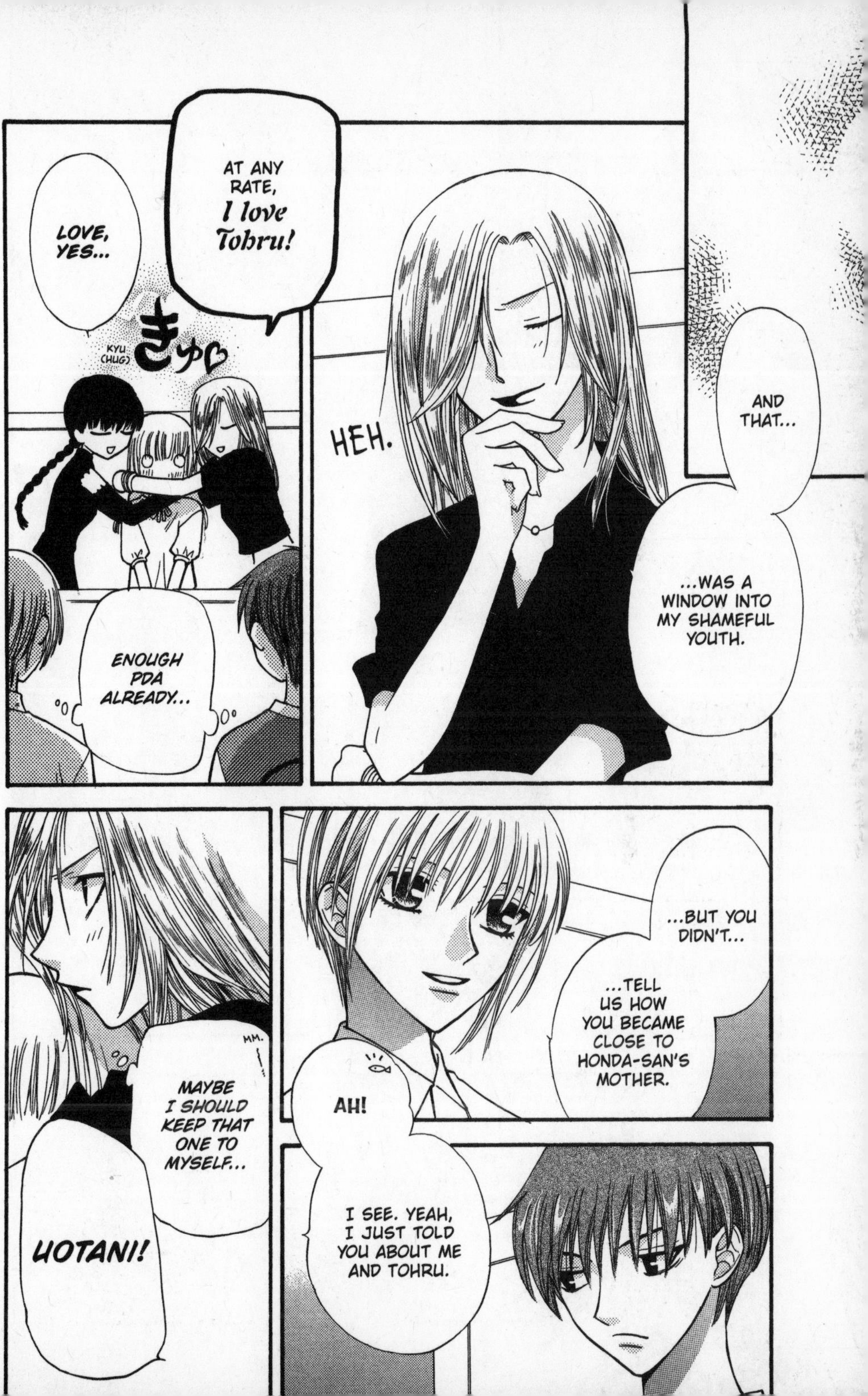
AND THAT...
...WAS A WINDOW INTO MY SHAMEFUL YOUTH.
HEH.
AT ANY RATE, I love Tohru!
LOVE, YES...
KYU (HUG)
ENOUGH PDA ALREADY...
...BUT YOU DIDN'T...
...TELL US HOW YOU BECAME CLOSE TO HONDA-SAN'S MOTHER.
AH!
I SEE. YEAH, I JUST TOLD YOU ABOUT ME AND TOHRU.
MM.
MAYBE I SHOULD KEEP THAT ONE TO MYSELF...
UOTANI!

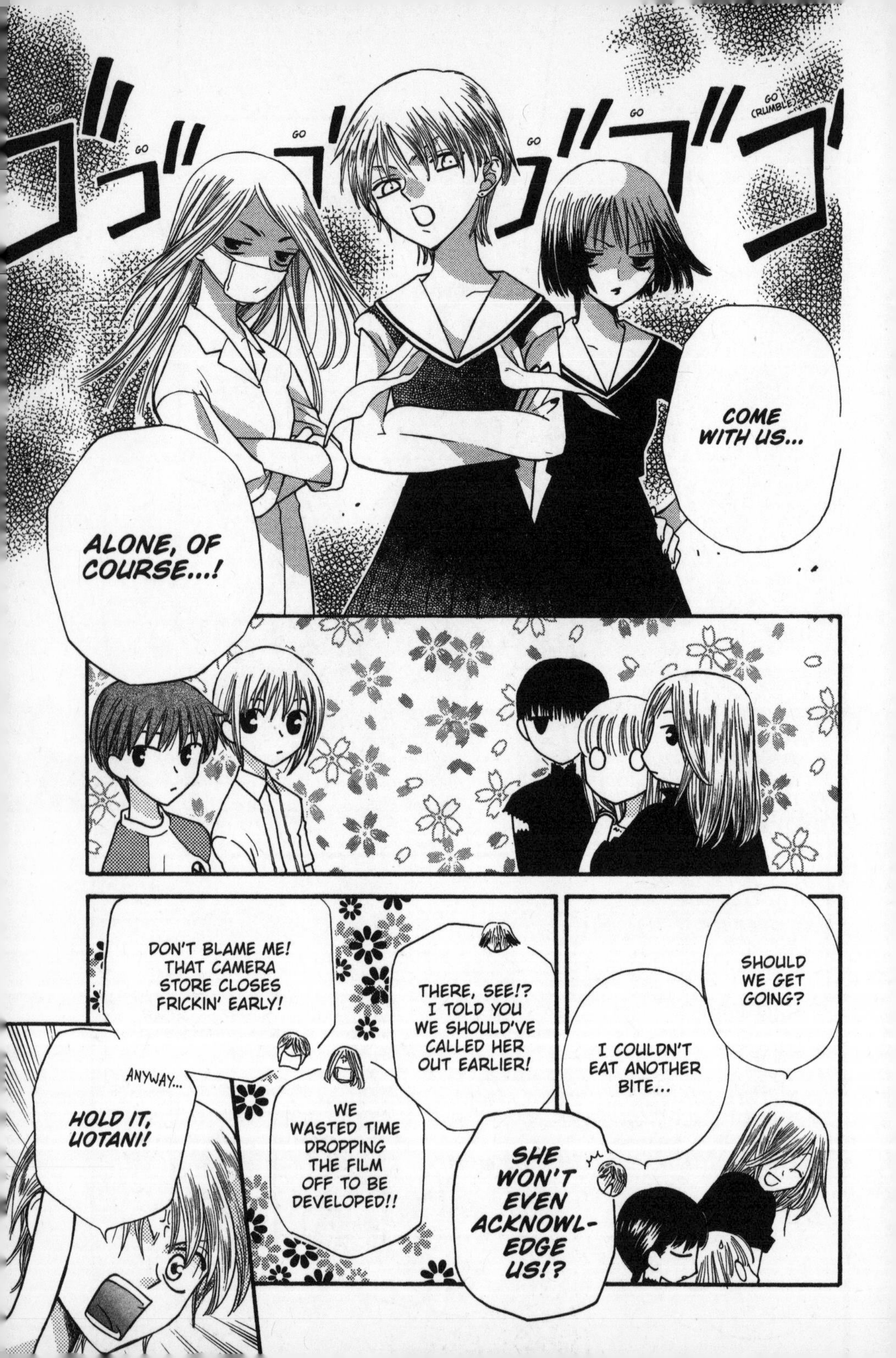
GO (RUMBLE)
GO
GO
GO
GO
GO
COME WITH US...
ALONE, OF COURSE...!
SHOULD WE GET GOING?
I COULDN'T EAT ANOTHER BITE...
SHE WON'T EVEN ACKNOWLEDGE US!?
THERE, SEE!? I TOLD YOU WE SHOULD'VE CALLED HER OUT EARLIER!
DON'T BLAME ME! THAT CAMERA STORE CLOSES FRICKIN' EARLY!
WE WASTED TIME DROPPING THE FILM OFF TO BE DEVELOPED!!
ANYWAY...
HOLD IT, UOTANI!

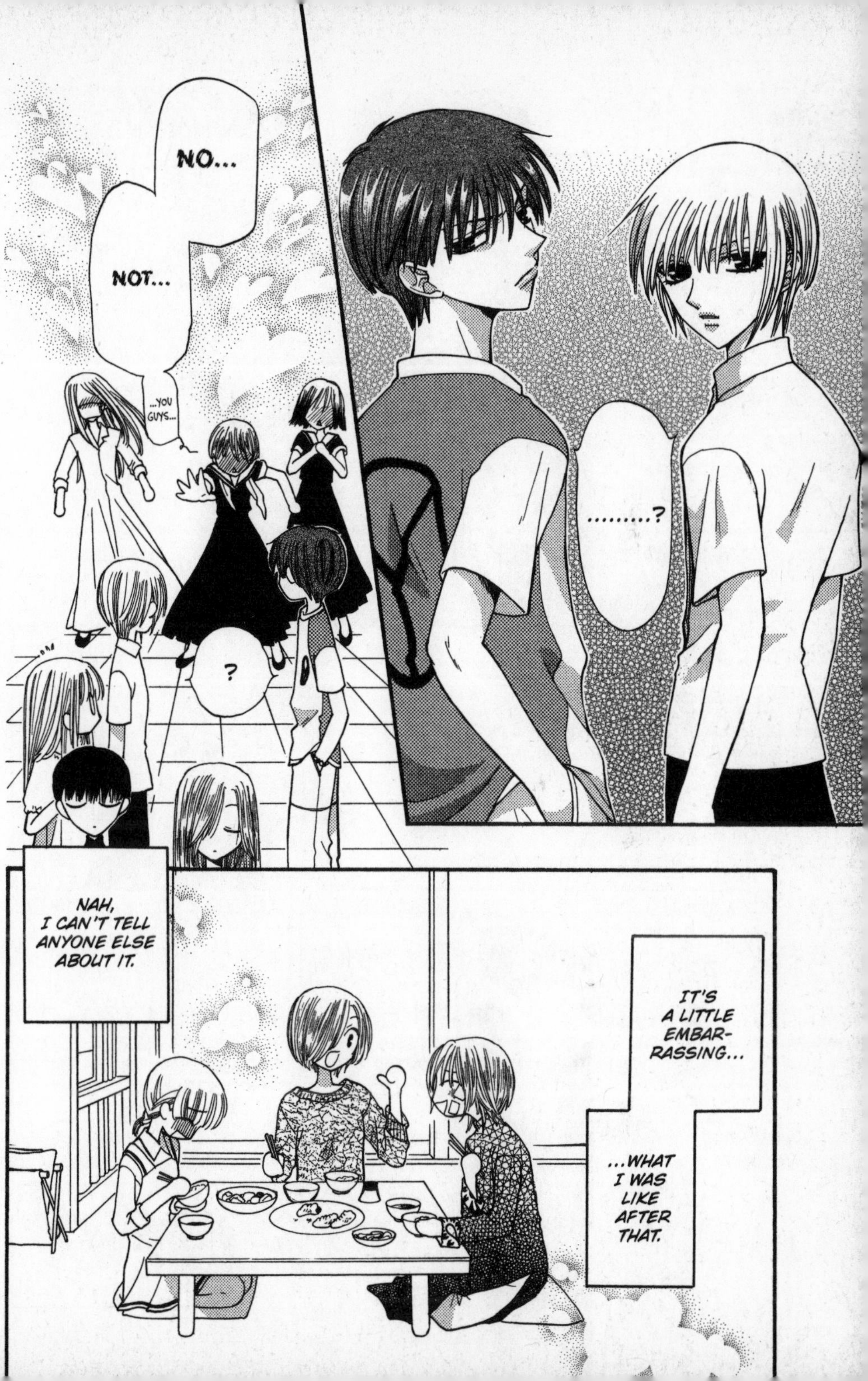
........?
NO...
NOT...
...YOU GUYS...
?
NAH, I CAN'T TELL ANYONE ELSE ABOUT IT.
IT'S A LITTLE EMBARRASSING...
...WHAT I WAS LIKE AFTER THAT.

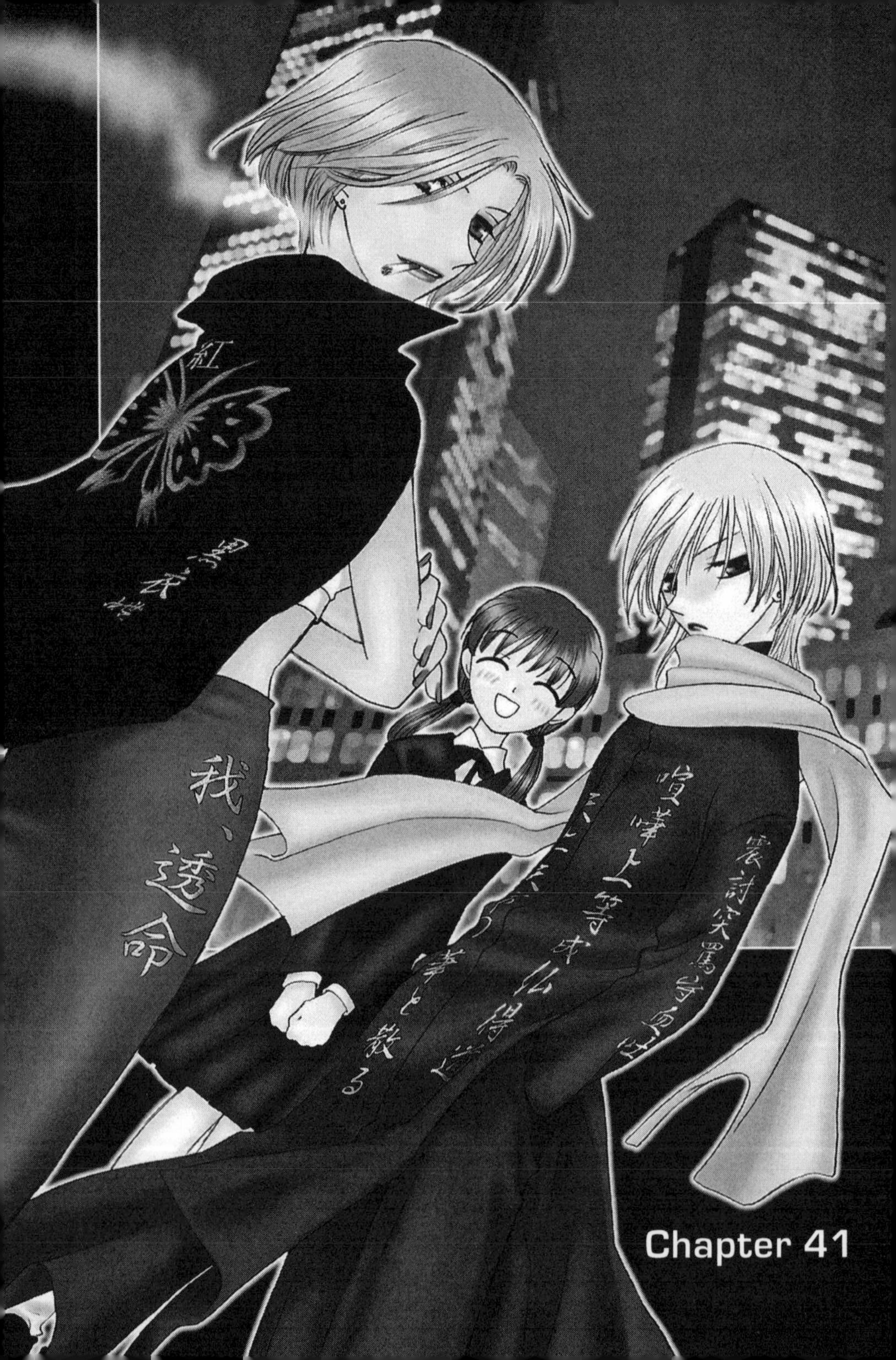
Chapter 41

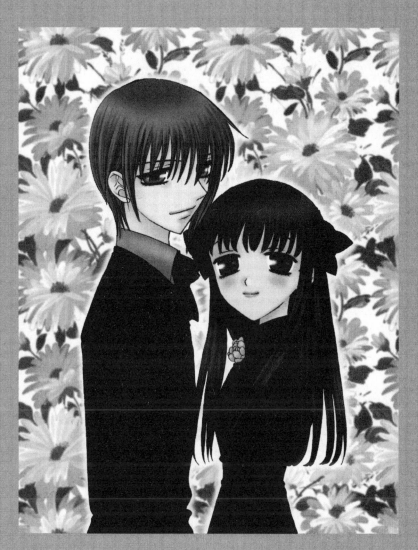

COLLECTOR'S EDITION
Fruits Basket

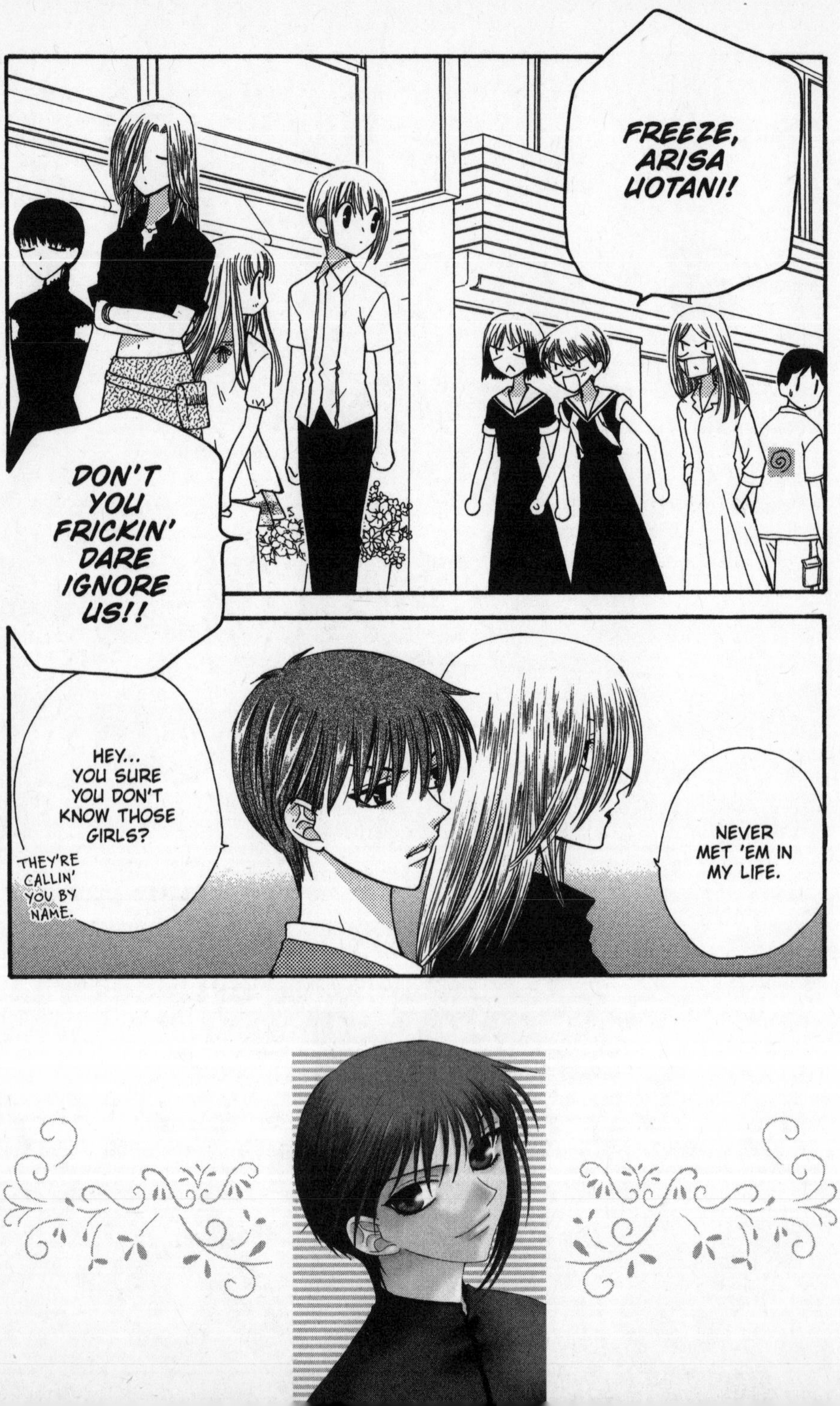
FREEZE, ARISA UOTANI!
DON'T YOU FRICKIN' DARE IGNORE US!!
HEY... YOU SURE YOU DON'T KNOW THOSE GIRLS?
THEY'RE CALLIN' YOU BY NAME.
NEVER MET 'EM IN MY LIFE.

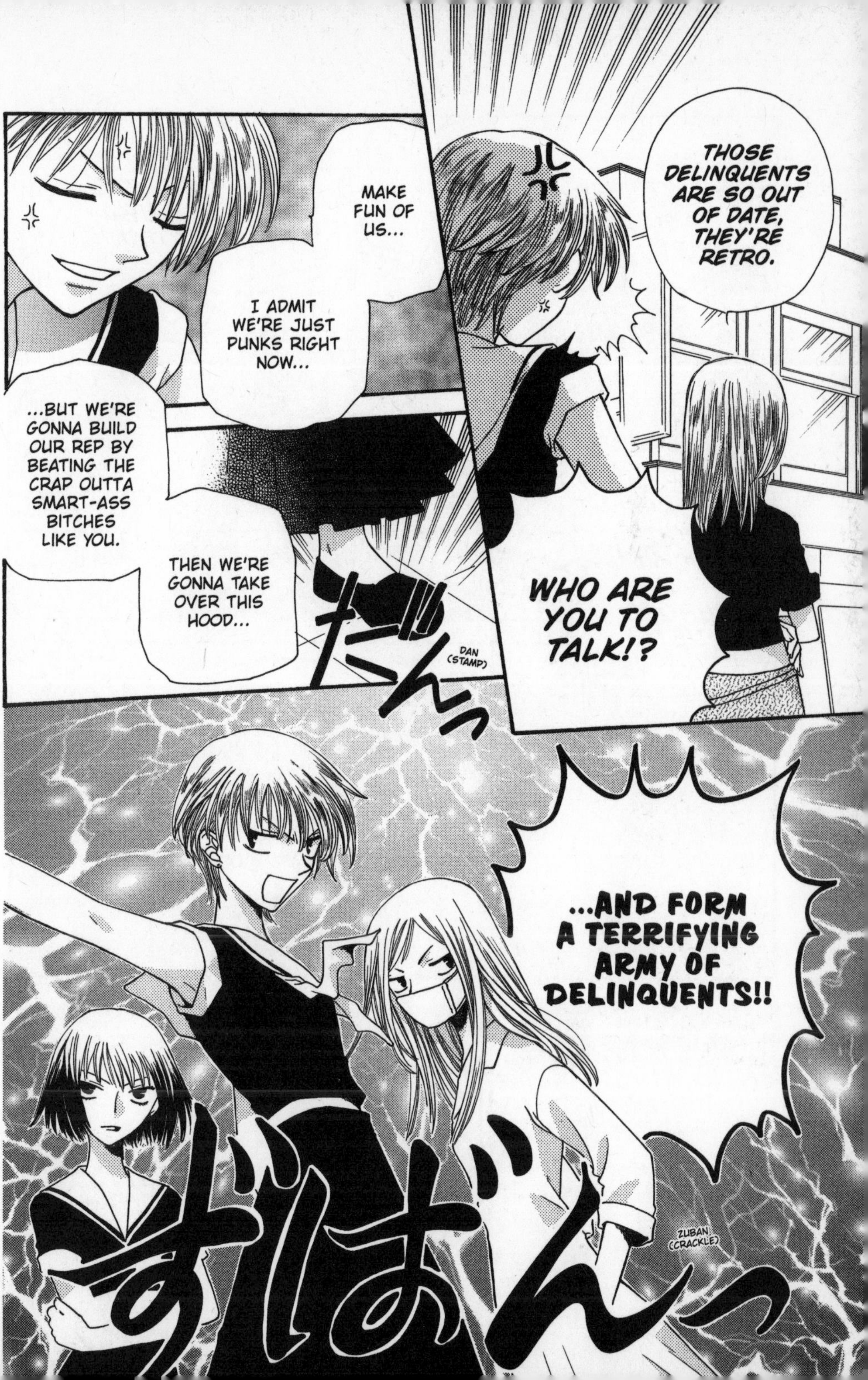

THOSE DELINQUENTS ARE SO OUT OF DATE, THEY'RE RETRO.
WHO ARE YOU TO TALK!?
MAKE FUN OF US...
I ADMIT WE'RE JUST PUNKS RIGHT NOW...
...BUT WE'RE GONNA BUILD OUR REP BY BEATING THE CRAP OUTTA SMART-ASS BITCHES LIKE YOU.
THEN WE'RE GONNA TAKE OVER THIS HOOD...
だんっ
DAN (STAMP)
...AND FORM A TERRIFYING ARMY OF DELINQUENTS!!
ずばんっ
ZUBAN (CRACKLE)

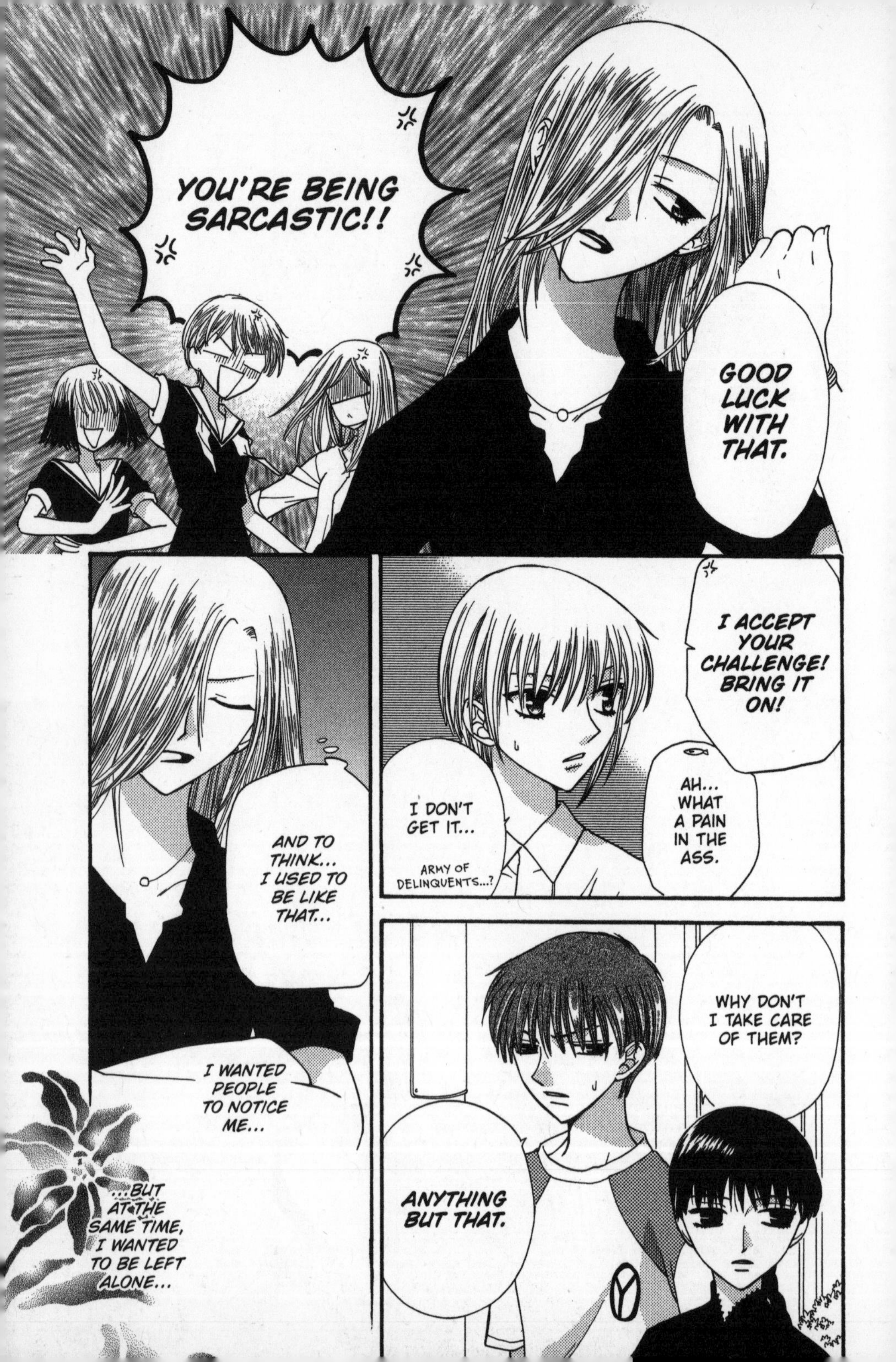
GOOD LUCK WITH THAT.
YOU'RE BEING SARCASTIC!!
I ACCEPT YOUR CHALLENGE! BRING IT ON!
AH... WHAT A PAIN IN THE ASS.
I DON'T GET IT...
ARMY OF DELINQUENTS...?
WHY DON'T I TAKE CARE OF THEM?
ANYTHING BUT THAT.
AND TO THINK... I USED TO BE LIKE THAT...
I WANTED PEOPLE TO NOTICE ME...
...BUT AT THE SAME TIME, I WANTED TO BE LEFT ALONE...

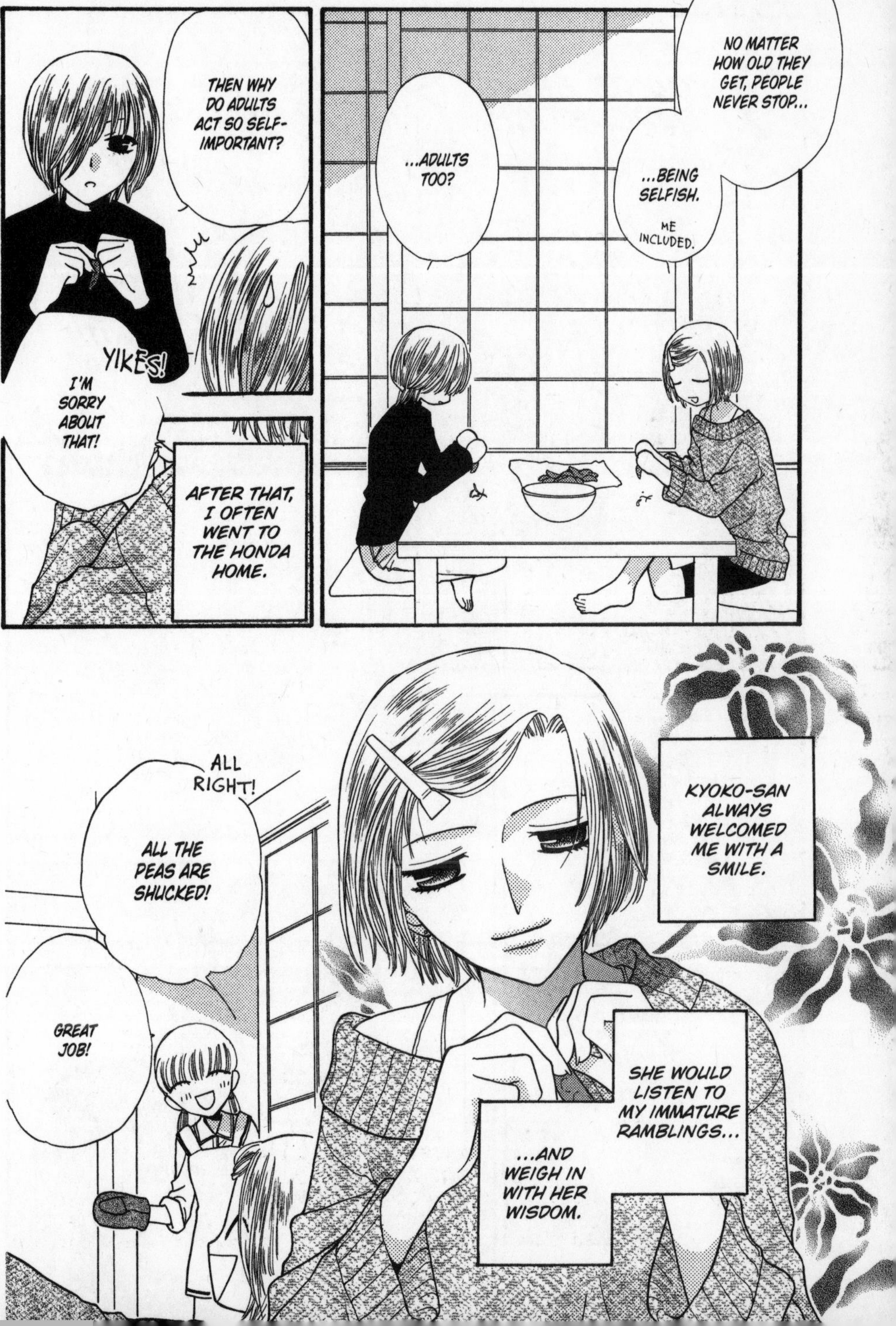
NO MATTER HOW OLD THEY GET, PEOPLE NEVER STOP...
...BEING SELFISH.
ME INCLUDED.
...ADULTS TOO?
THEN WHY DO ADULTS ACT SO SELF-IMPORTANT?
YIKES!
I'M SORRY ABOUT THAT!
AFTER THAT, I OFTEN WENT TO THE HONDA HOME.
KYOKO-SAN ALWAYS WELCOMED ME WITH A SMILE.
SHE WOULD LISTEN TO MY IMMATURE RAMBLINGS...
...AND WEIGH IN WITH HER WISDOM.
ALL RIGHT!
ALL THE PEAS ARE SHUCKED!
GREAT JOB!

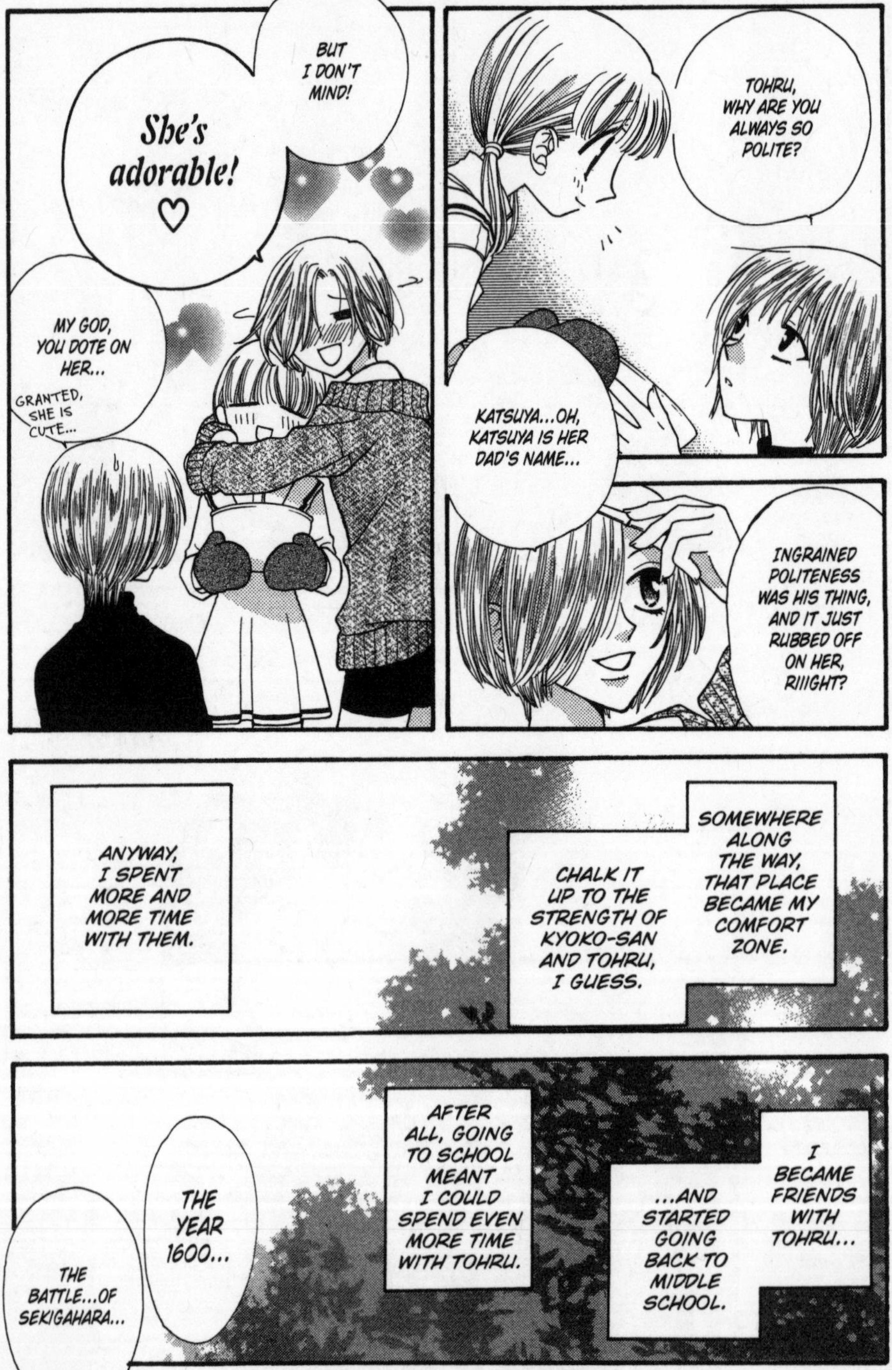
TOHRU, WHY ARE YOU ALWAYS SO POLITE?
KATSUYA...OH, KATSUYA IS HER DAD'S NAME...
INGRAINED POLITENESS WAS HIS THING, AND IT JUST RUBBED OFF ON HER, RIIIGHT?
BUT I DON'T MIND!
She's adorable! ♡
MY GOD, YOU DOTE ON HER...
GRANTED, SHE IS CUTE...
SOMEWHERE ALONG THE WAY, THAT PLACE BECAME MY COMFORT ZONE.
CHALK IT UP TO THE STRENGTH OF KYOKO-SAN AND TOHRU, I GUESS.
ANYWAY, I SPENT MORE AND MORE TIME WITH THEM.
I BECAME FRIENDS WITH TOHRU...
...AND STARTED GOING BACK TO MIDDLE SCHOOL.
AFTER ALL, GOING TO SCHOOL MEANT I COULD SPEND EVEN MORE TIME WITH TOHRU.
THE YEAR 1600...
THE BATTLE...OF SEKIGAHARA...

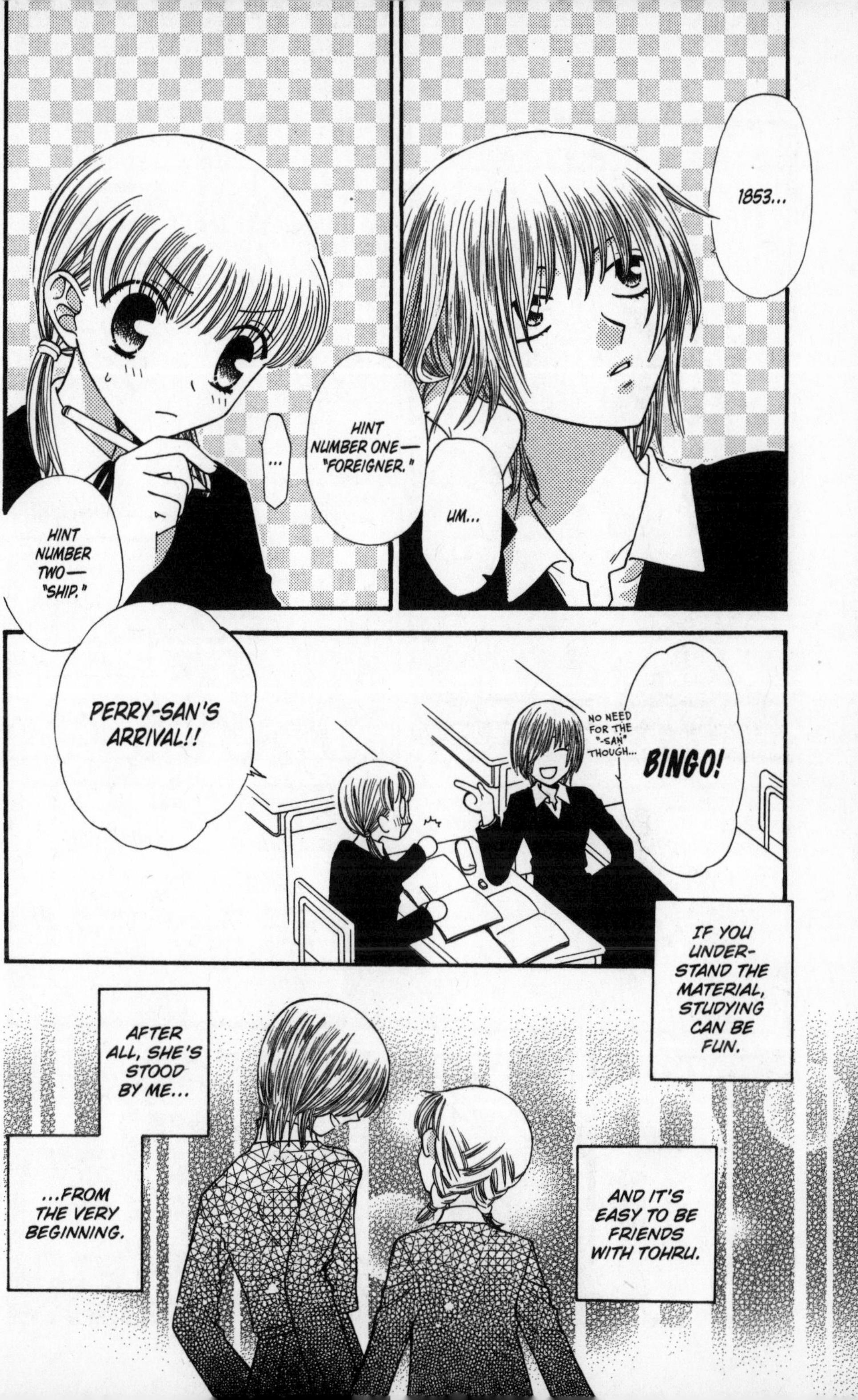
1853...
HINT NUMBER ONE— "FOREIGNER."
...
UM...
HINT NUMBER TWO— "SHIP."
PERRY-SAN'S ARRIVAL!!
BINGO!
NO NEED FOR THE "-SAN" THOUGH...
IF YOU UNDER-STAND THE MATERIAL, STUDYING CAN BE FUN.
AND IT'S EASY TO BE FRIENDS WITH TOHRU.
AFTER ALL, SHE'S STOOD BY ME...
...FROM THE VERY BEGINNING.

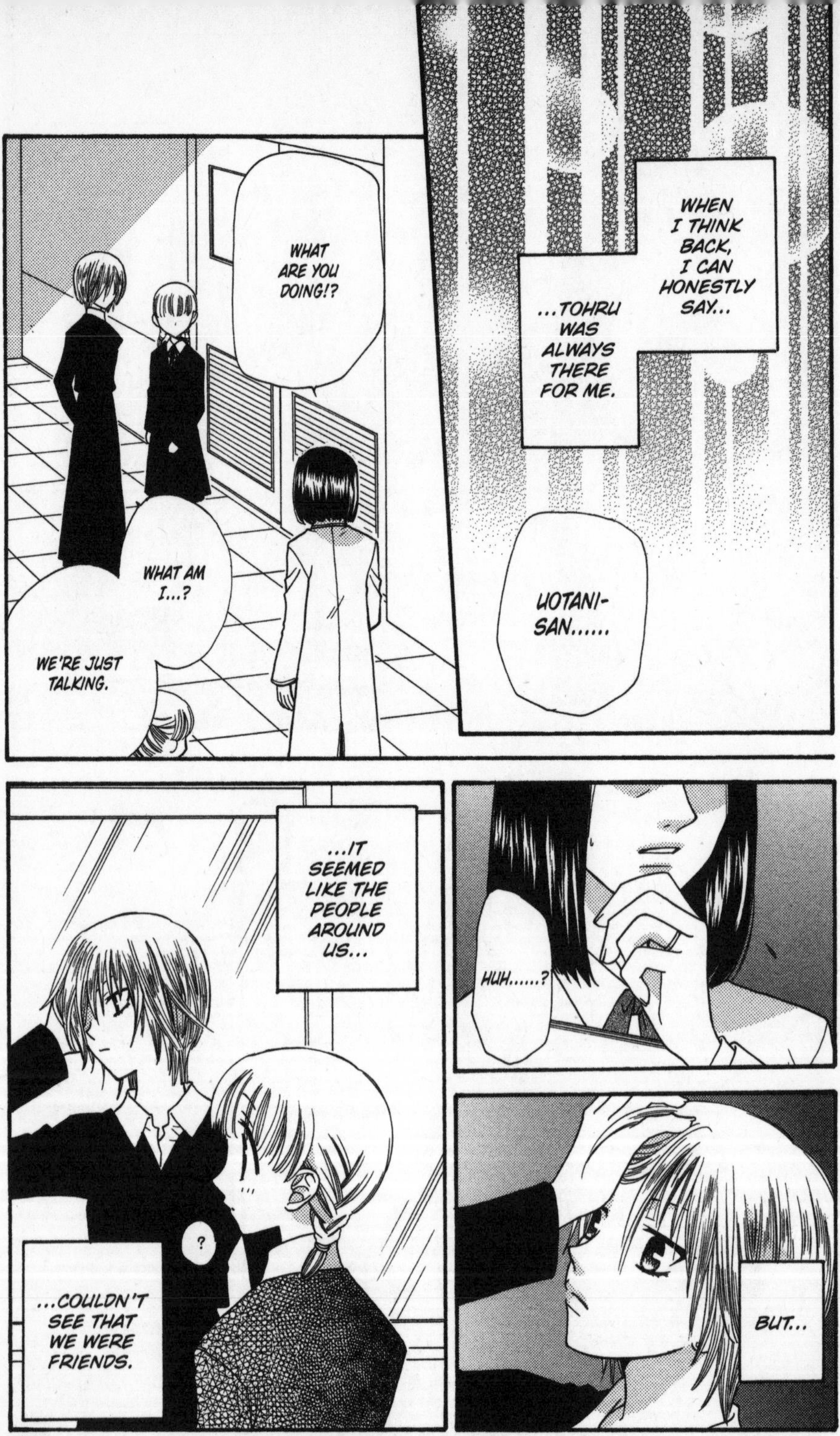
WHEN I THINK BACK, I CAN HONESTLY SAY...
...TOHRU WAS ALWAYS THERE FOR ME.
UOTANI-SAN......
WHAT ARE YOU DOING!?
WHAT AM I...?
WE'RE JUST TALKING.
HUH......?
BUT...
...IT SEEMED LIKE THE PEOPLE AROUND US...
...
?
...COULDN'T SEE THAT WE WERE FRIENDS.

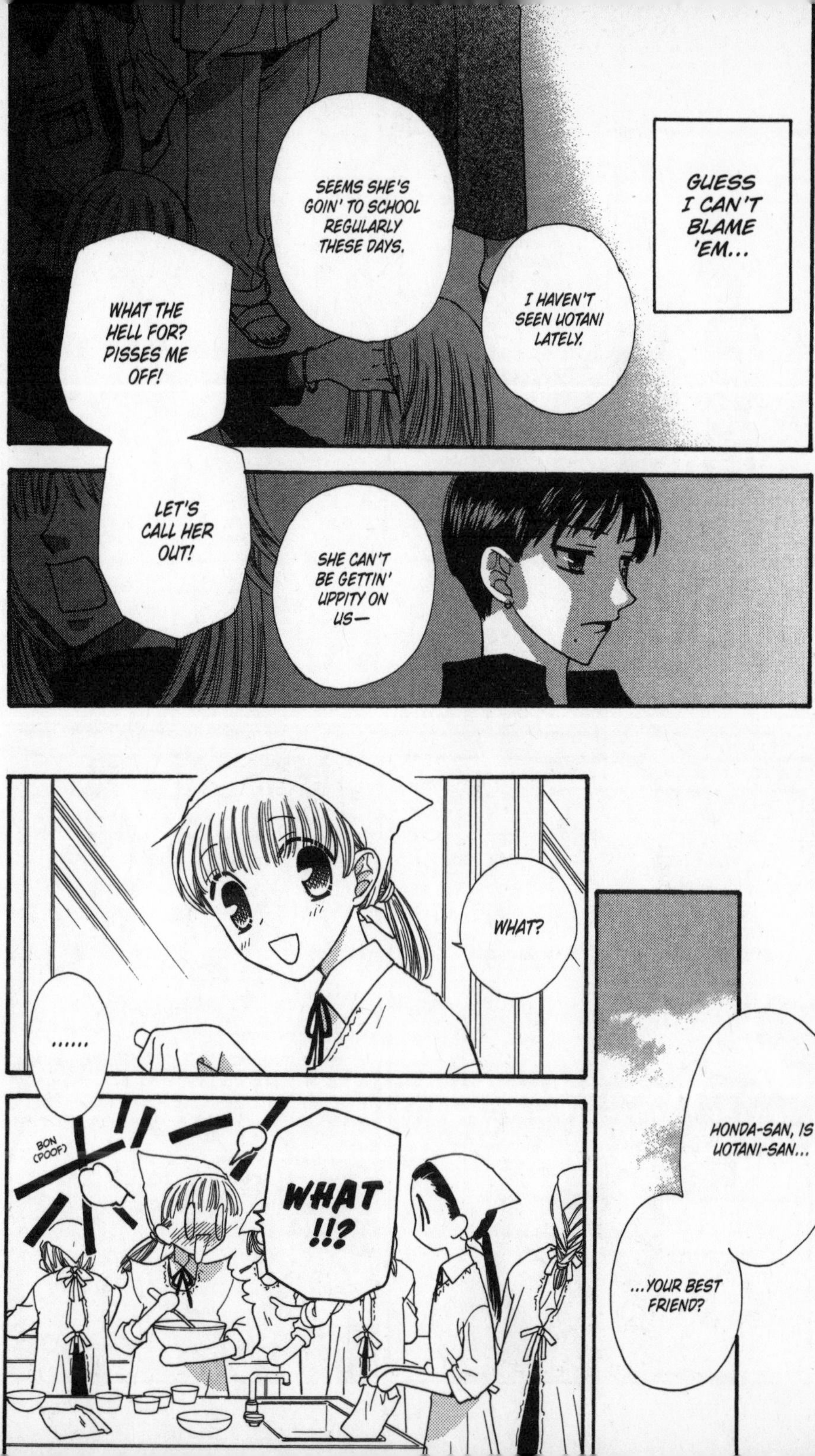

GUESS I CAN'T BLAME 'EM...
I HAVEN'T SEEN UOTANI LATELY.
SEEMS SHE'S GOIN' TO SCHOOL REGULARLY THESE DAYS.
WHAT THE HELL FOR? PISSES ME OFF!
SHE CAN'T BE GETTIN' UPPITY ON US—
LET'S CALL HER OUT!
HONDA-SAN, IS UOTANI-SAN...
...YOUR BEST FRIEND?
WHAT?
......
WHAT !!?
BON (POOF)

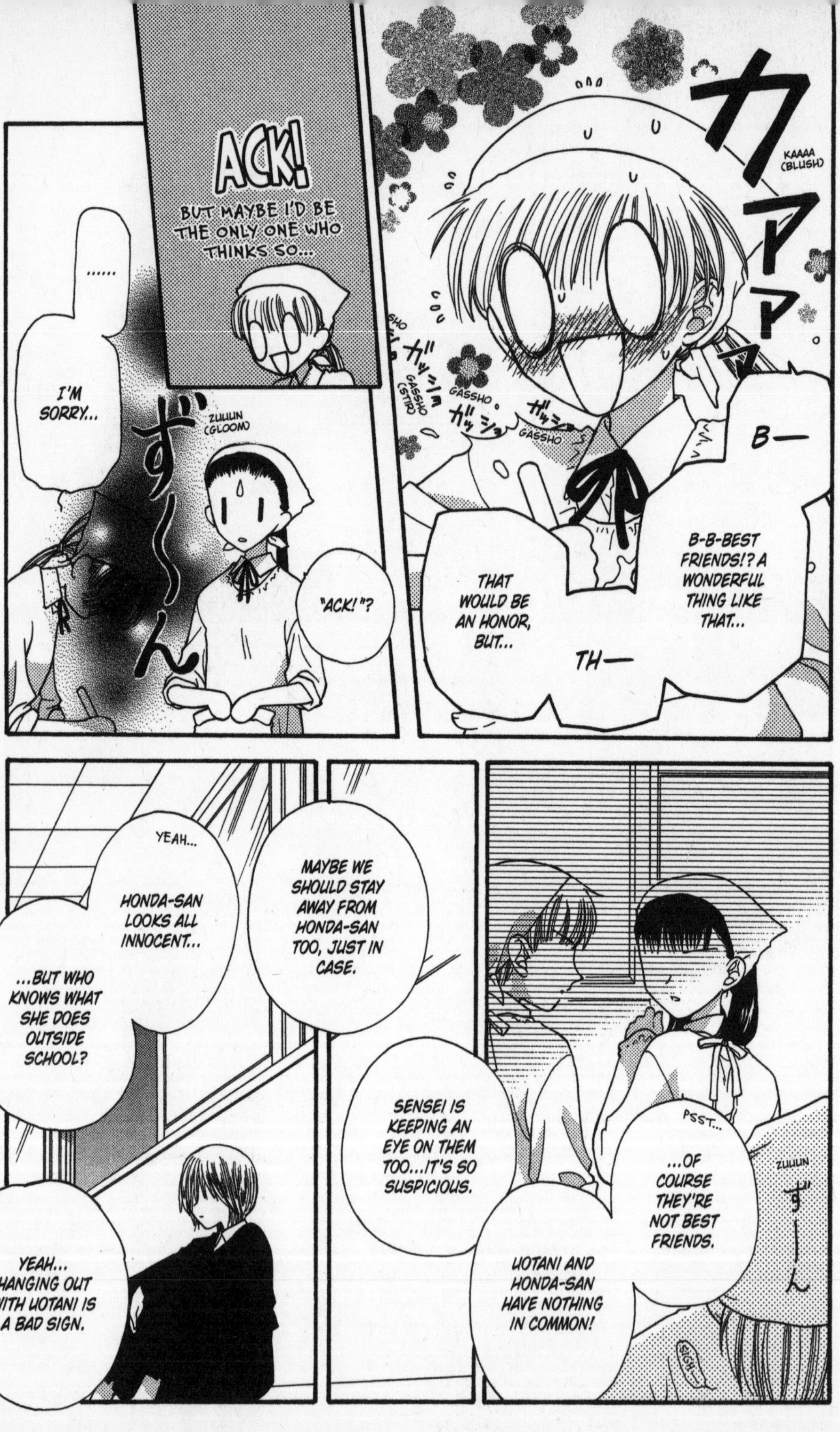
KAAAA (BLUSH)
B—
B-B-BEST FRIENDS!? A WONDERFUL THING LIKE THAT...
TH—
THAT WOULD BE AN HONOR, BUT...
SHO
GASSHO (STIR)
GASSHO
GASSHO
ACK!
BUT MAYBE I'D BE THE ONLY ONE WHO THINKS SO...
ZUUUN (GLOOM)
"ACK!"?
......
I'M SORRY...
PSST...
...OF COURSE THEY'RE NOT BEST FRIENDS.
ZUUUN
UOTANI AND HONDA-SAN HAVE NOTHING IN COMMON!
SIGH
SENSEI IS KEEPING AN EYE ON THEM TOO...IT'S SO SUSPICIOUS.
MAYBE WE SHOULD STAY AWAY FROM HONDA-SAN TOO, JUST IN CASE.
YEAH...
HONDA-SAN LOOKS ALL INNOCENT...
...BUT WHO KNOWS WHAT SHE DOES OUTSIDE SCHOOL?
YEAH... HANGING OUT WITH UOTANI IS A BAD SIGN.

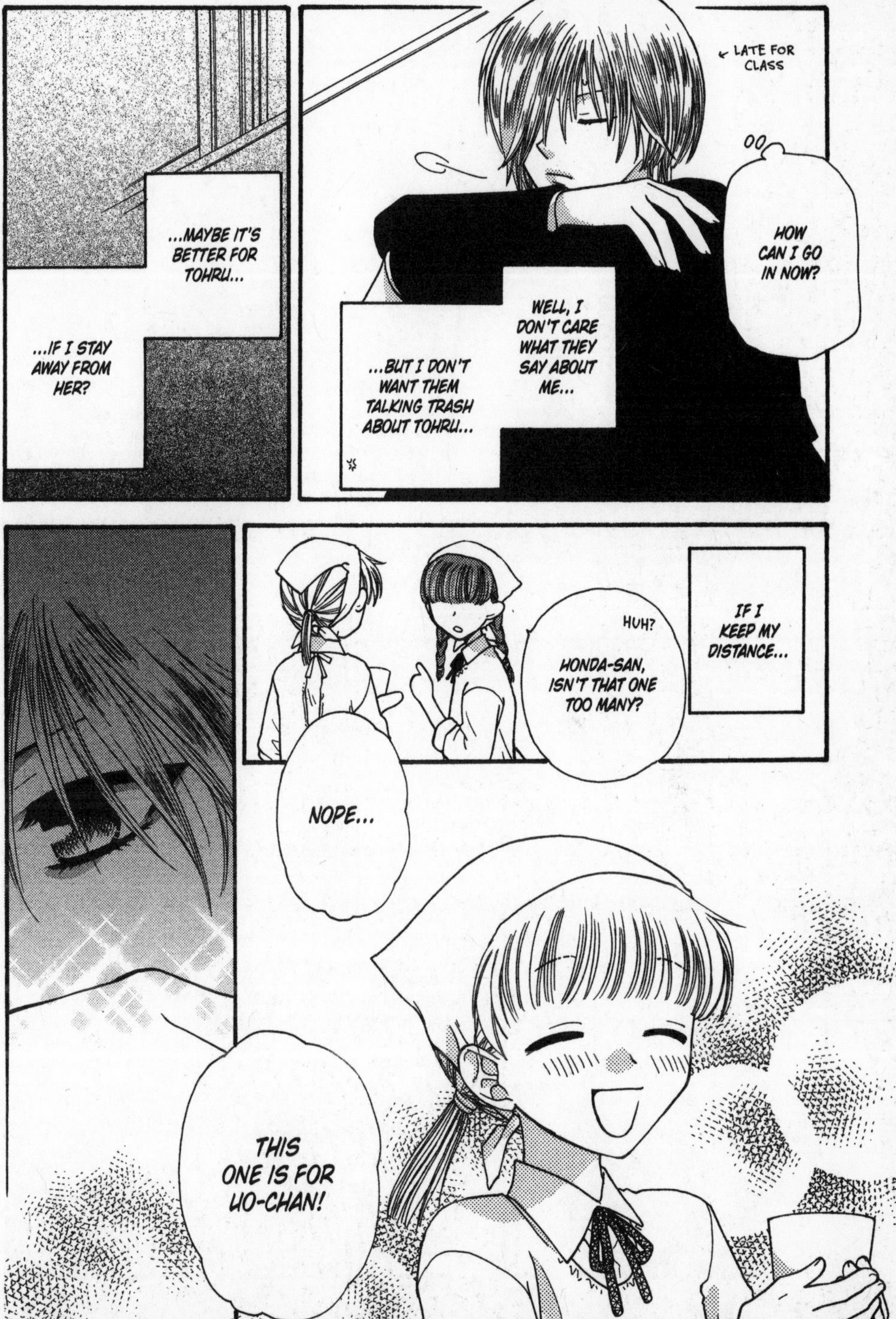
LATE FOR CLASS
HOW CAN I GO IN NOW?
WELL, I DON'T CARE WHAT THEY SAY ABOUT ME...
...BUT I DON'T WANT THEM TALKING TRASH ABOUT TOHRU...
...MAYBE IT'S BETTER FOR TOHRU...
...IF I STAY AWAY FROM HER?
IF I KEEP MY DISTANCE...
HUH?
HONDA-SAN, ISN'T THAT ONE TOO MANY?
NOPE...
THIS ONE IS FOR UO-CHAN!

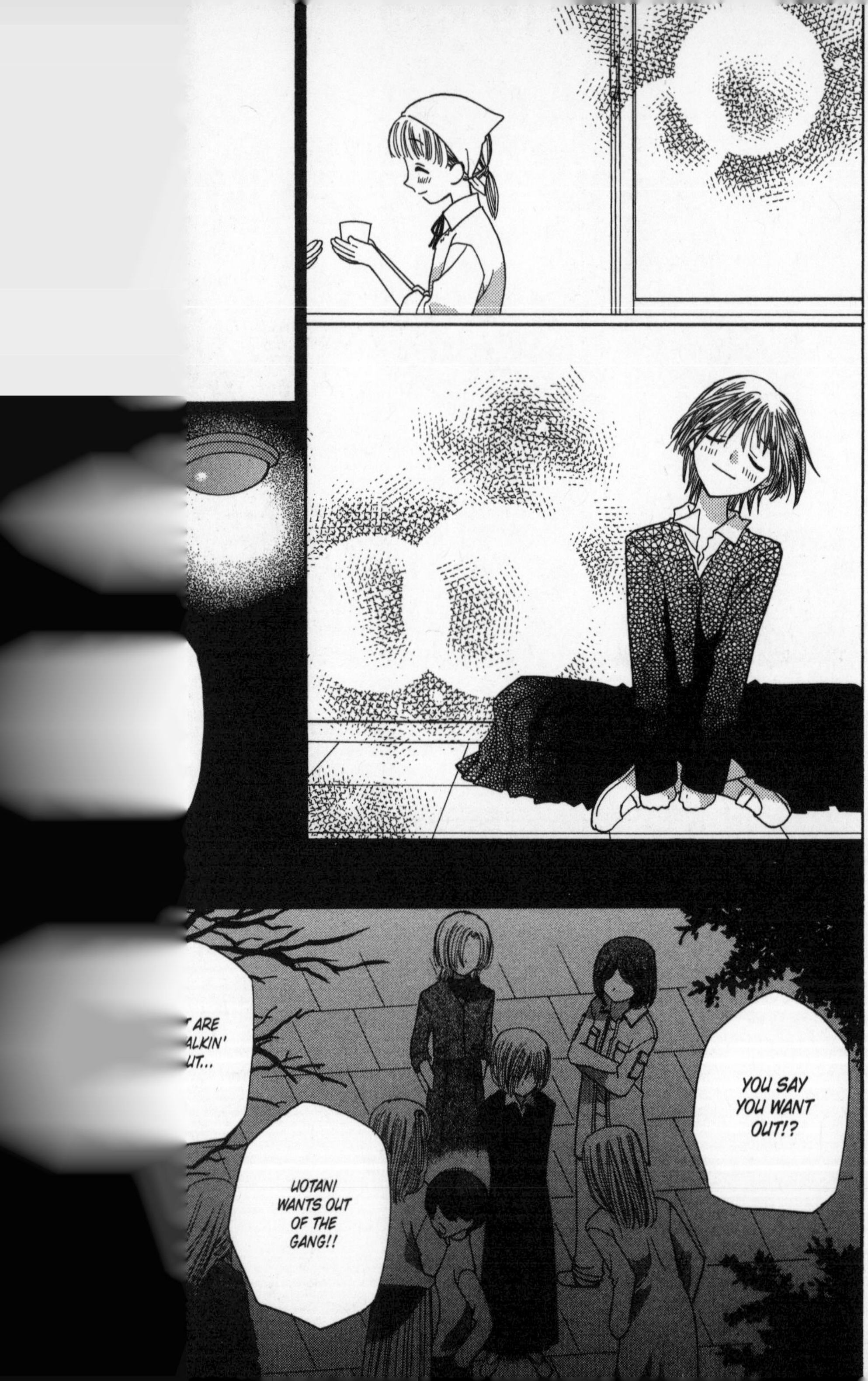
YOU SAY YOU WANT OUT!?
UOTANI WANTS OUT OF THE GANG!!

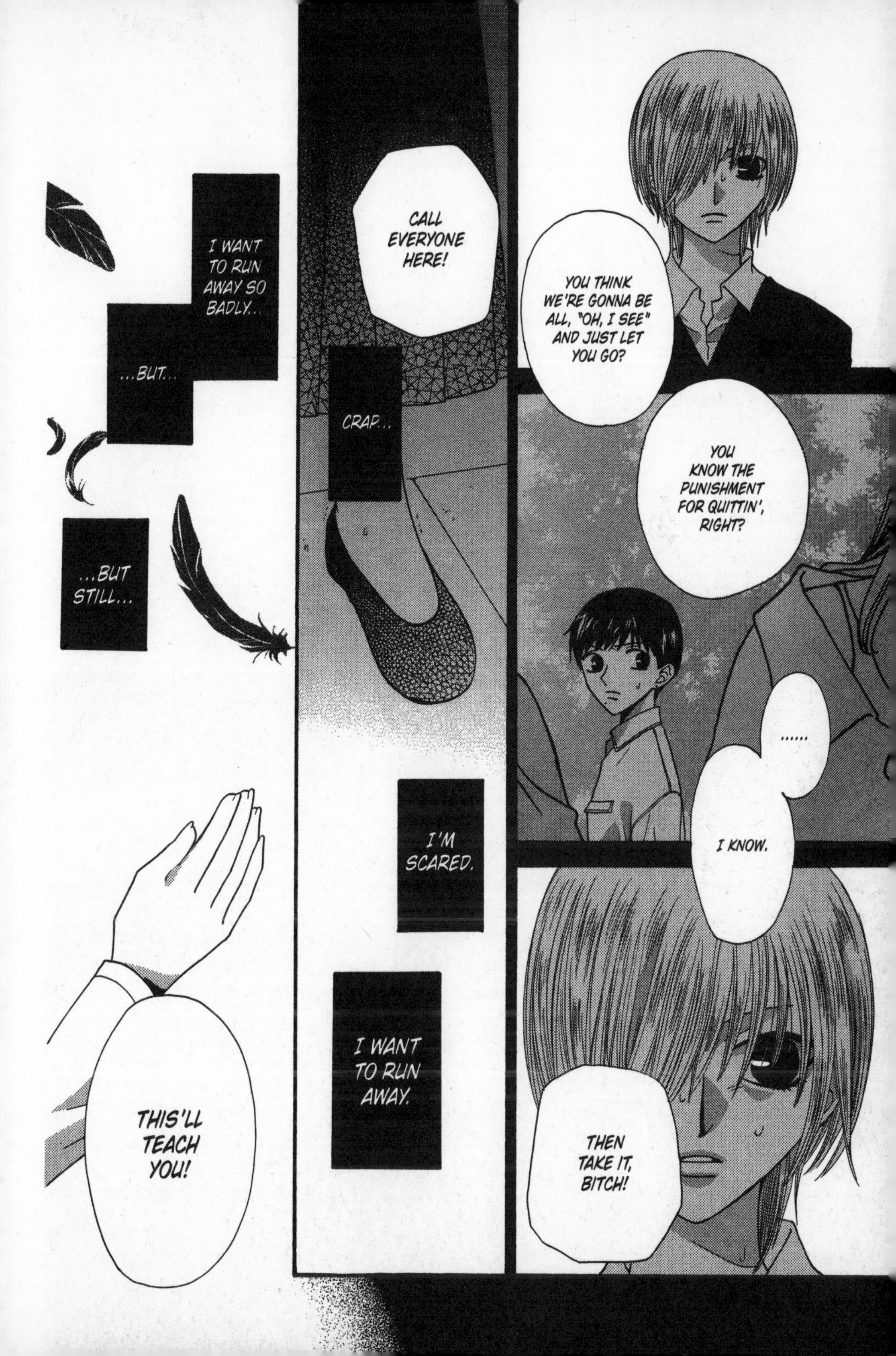
YOU THINK WE'RE GONNA BE ALL, "OH, I SEE" AND JUST LET YOU GO?
YOU KNOW THE PUNISHMENT FOR QUITTIN', RIGHT?
......
I KNOW.
THEN TAKE IT, BITCH!
CALL EVERYONE HERE!
CRAP...
I'M SCARED.
I WANT TO RUN AWAY.
I WANT TO RUN AWAY SO BADLY...
...BUT...
...BUT STILL...
THIS'LL TEACH YOU!

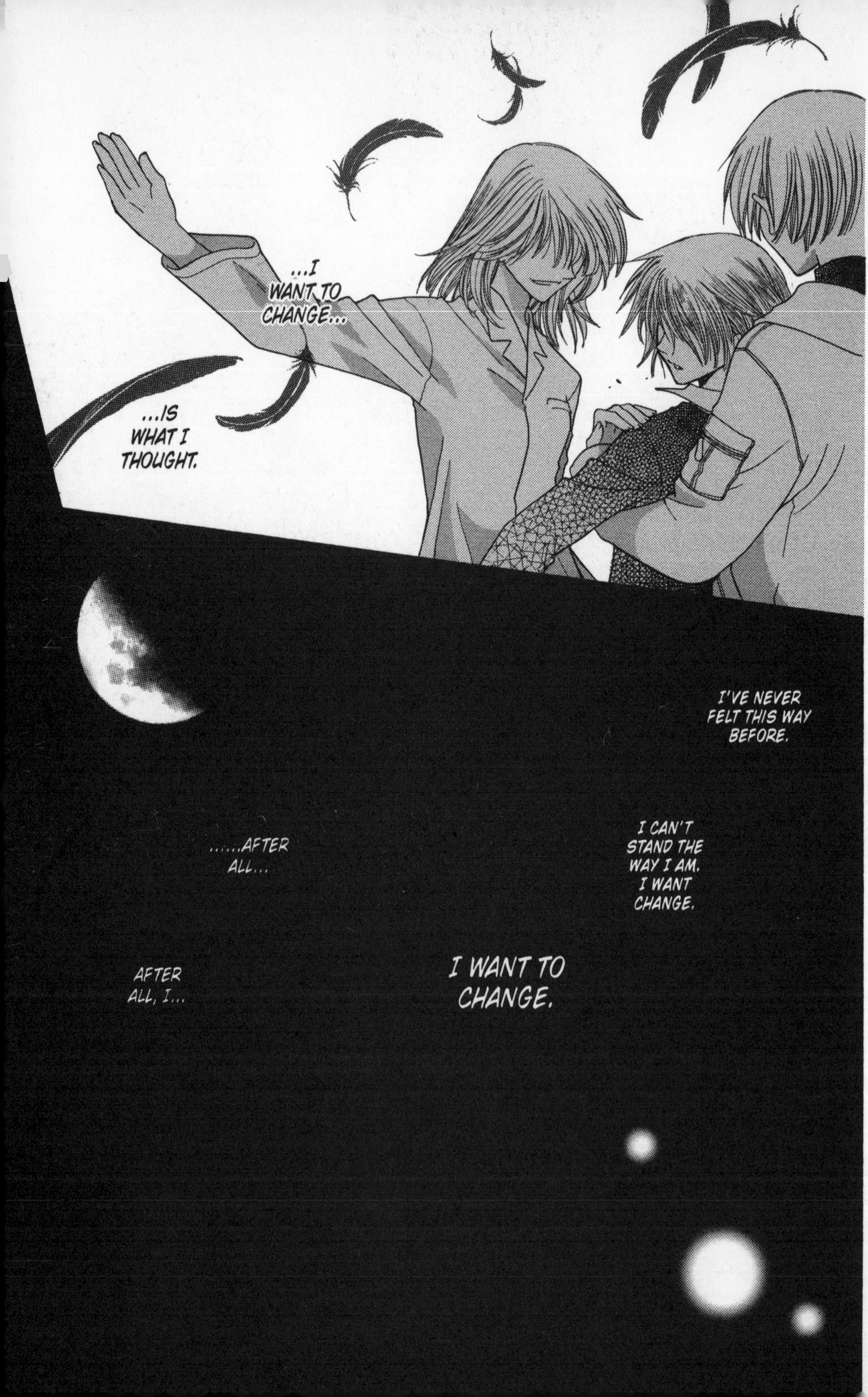
...I WANT TO CHANGE...
...IS WHAT I THOUGHT.
I'VE NEVER FELT THIS WAY BEFORE.
I CAN'T STAND THE WAY I AM. I WANT CHANGE.
......AFTER ALL...
I WANT TO CHANGE.
AFTER ALL, I...

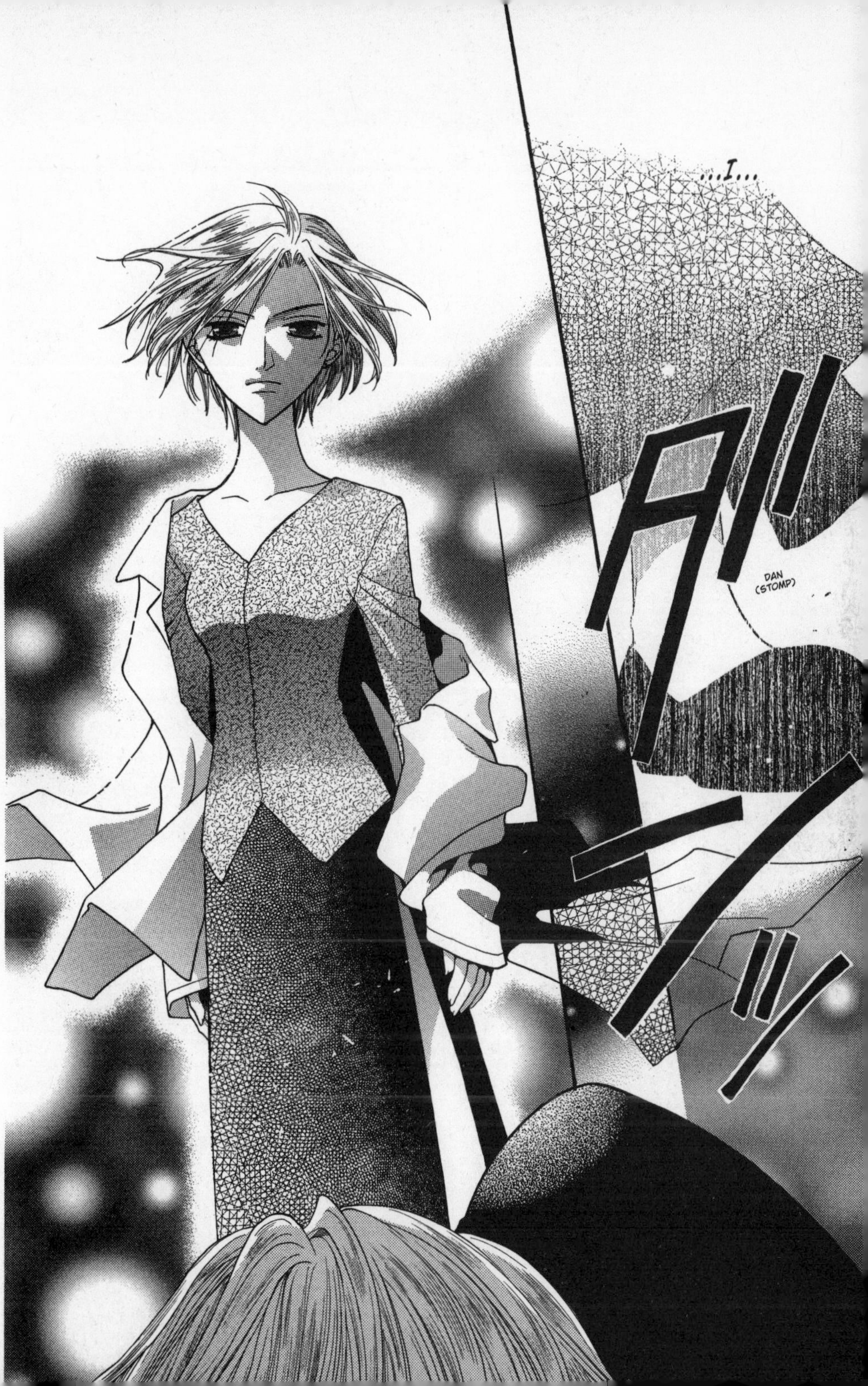
...I...
DAN
(STOMP)

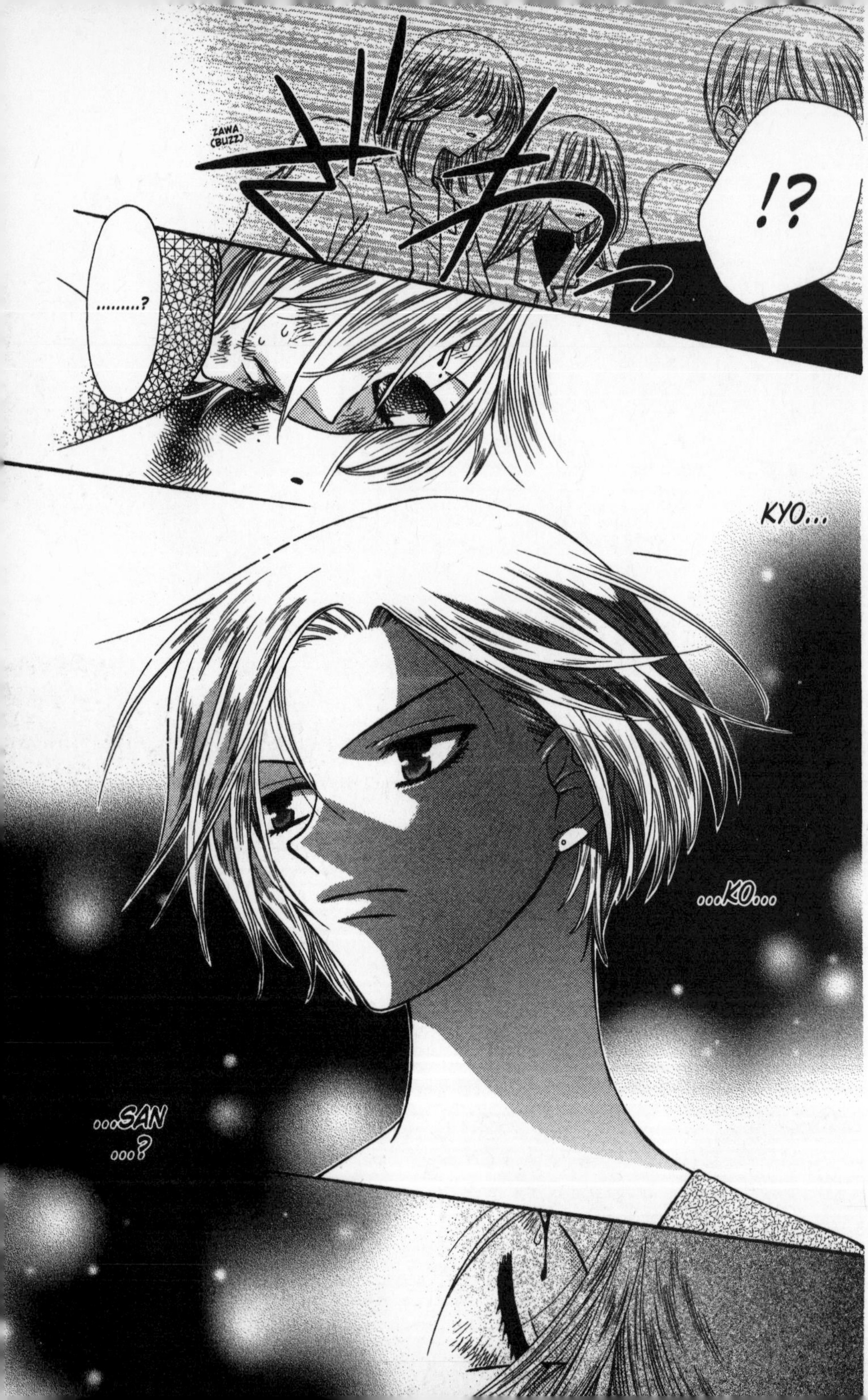
!?
ZAWA (BUZZ)
........?
KYO...
...KO...
...SAN ...?

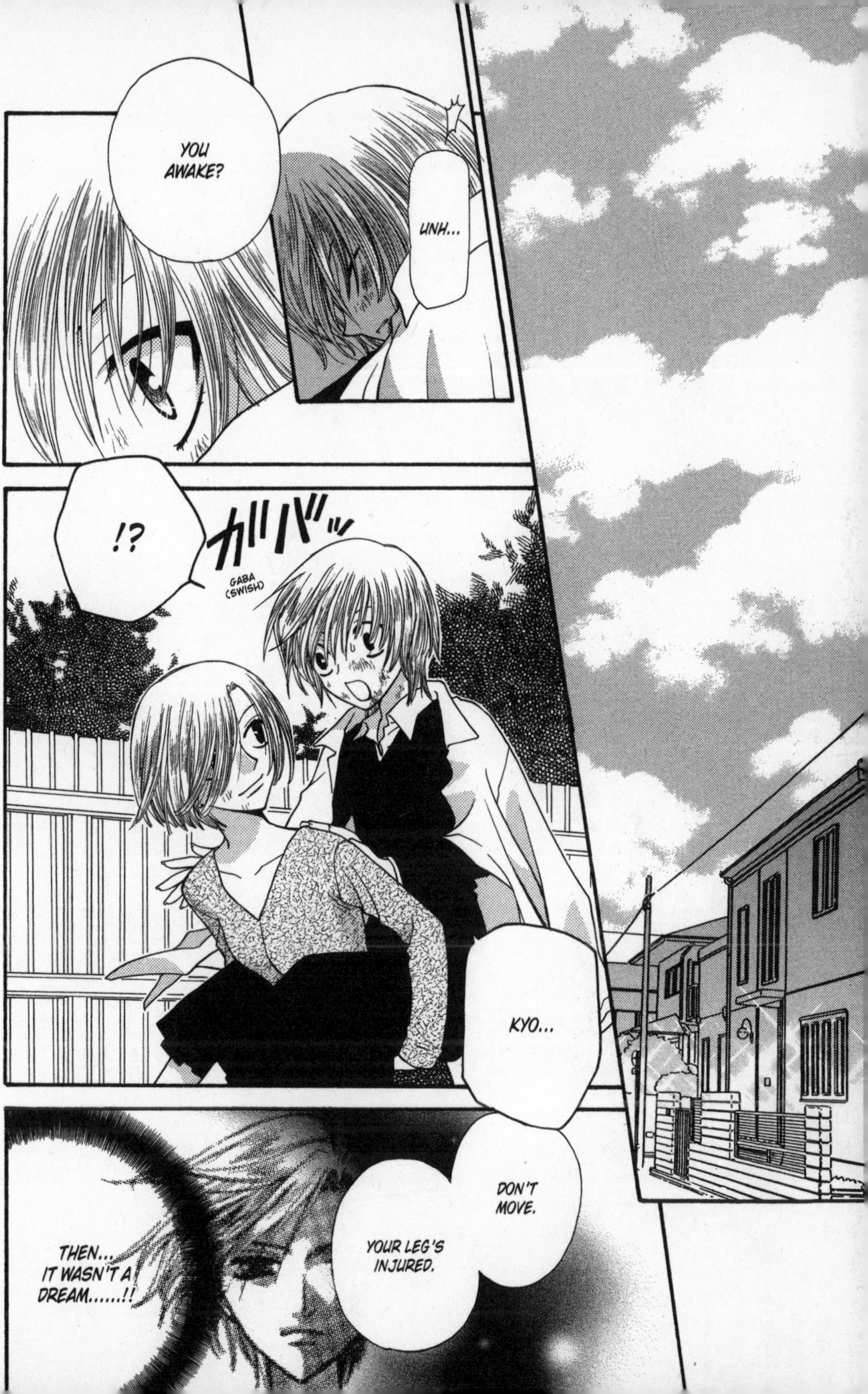
YOU AWAKE?
UNH...
!?
カバッ
GABA (SWISH)
KYO...
DON'T MOVE.
YOUR LEG'S INJURED.
THEN... IT WASN'T A DREAM......!!

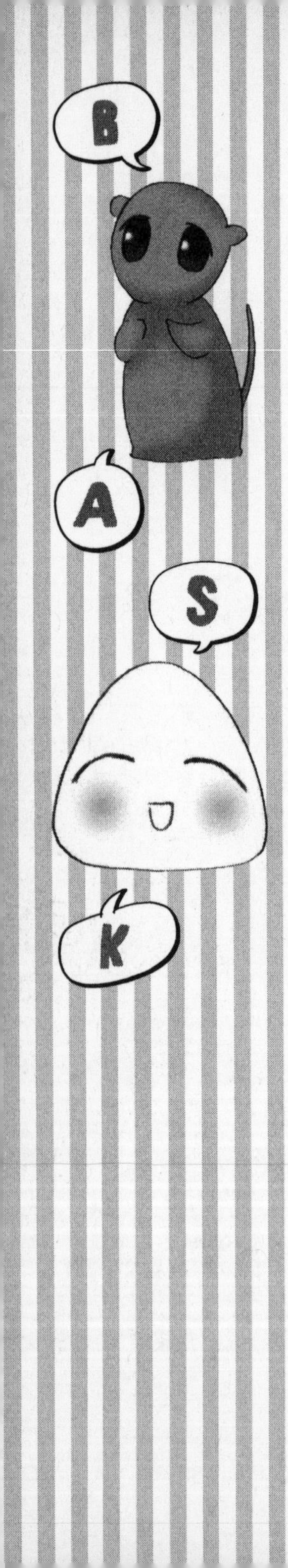
B
A
S
K

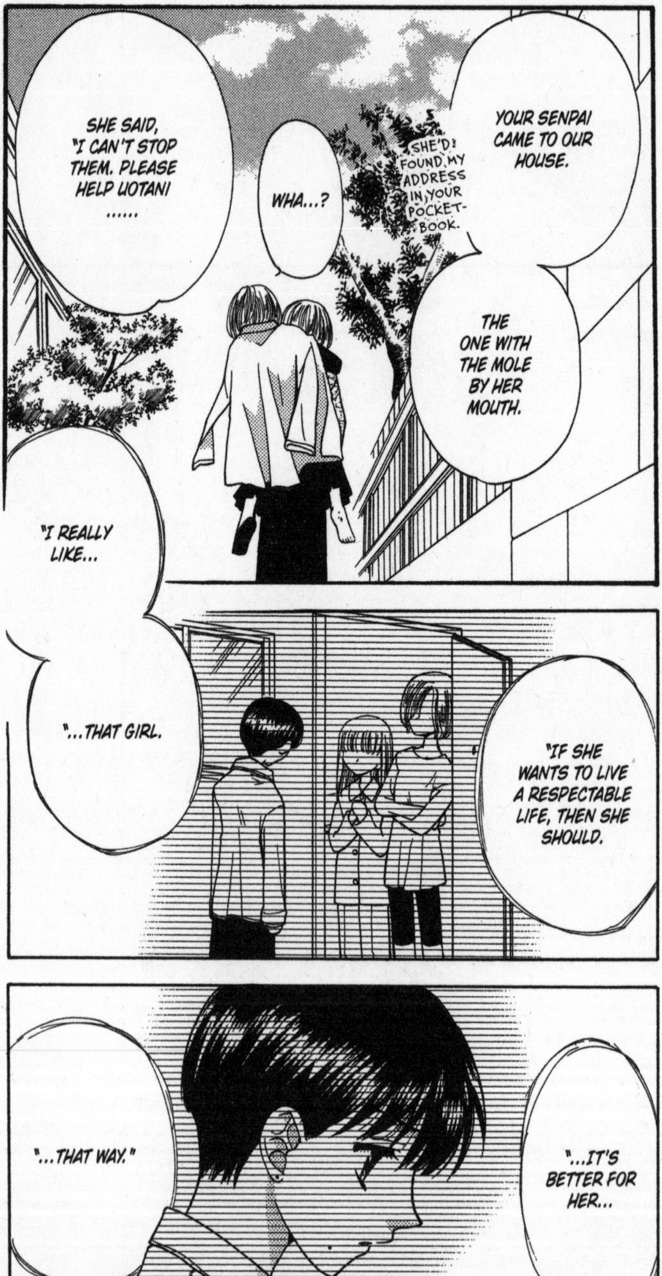
YOUR SENPAI CAME TO OUR HOUSE.
SHE'D FOUND MY ADDRESS IN YOUR POCKET-BOOK.
THE ONE WITH THE MOLE BY HER MOUTH.
WHA...?
SHE SAID, "I CAN'T STOP THEM. PLEASE HELP UOTANI ......
"I REALLY LIKE...
"...THAT GIRL.
"IF SHE WANTS TO LIVE A RESPECTABLE LIFE, THEN SHE SHOULD.
"...IT'S BETTER FOR HER...
"...THAT WAY."

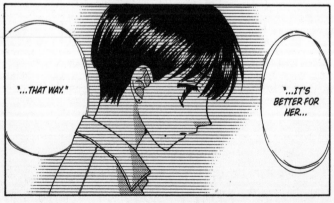

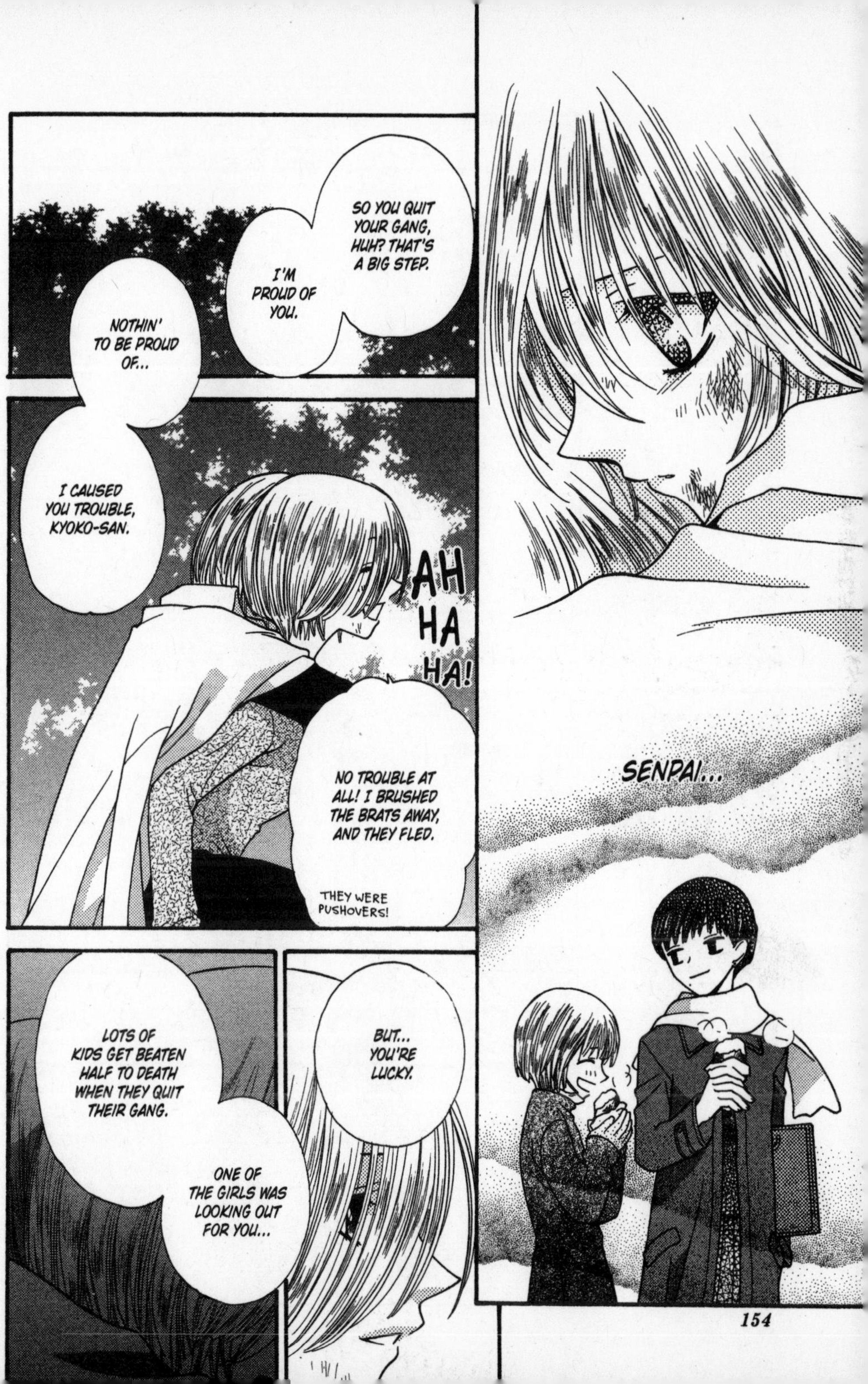
SENPAI...
SO YOU QUIT YOUR GANG, HUH? THAT'S A BIG STEP.
I'M PROUD OF YOU.
NOTHIN' TO BE PROUD OF...
I CAUSED YOU TROUBLE, KYOKO-SAN.
AH HA HA!
NO TROUBLE AT ALL! I BRUSHED THE BRATS AWAY, AND THEY FLED.
THEY WERE PUSHOVERS!
BUT... YOU'RE LUCKY.
LOTS OF KIDS GET BEATEN HALF TO DEATH WHEN THEY QUIT THEIR GANG.
ONE OF THE GIRLS WAS LOOKING OUT FOR YOU...

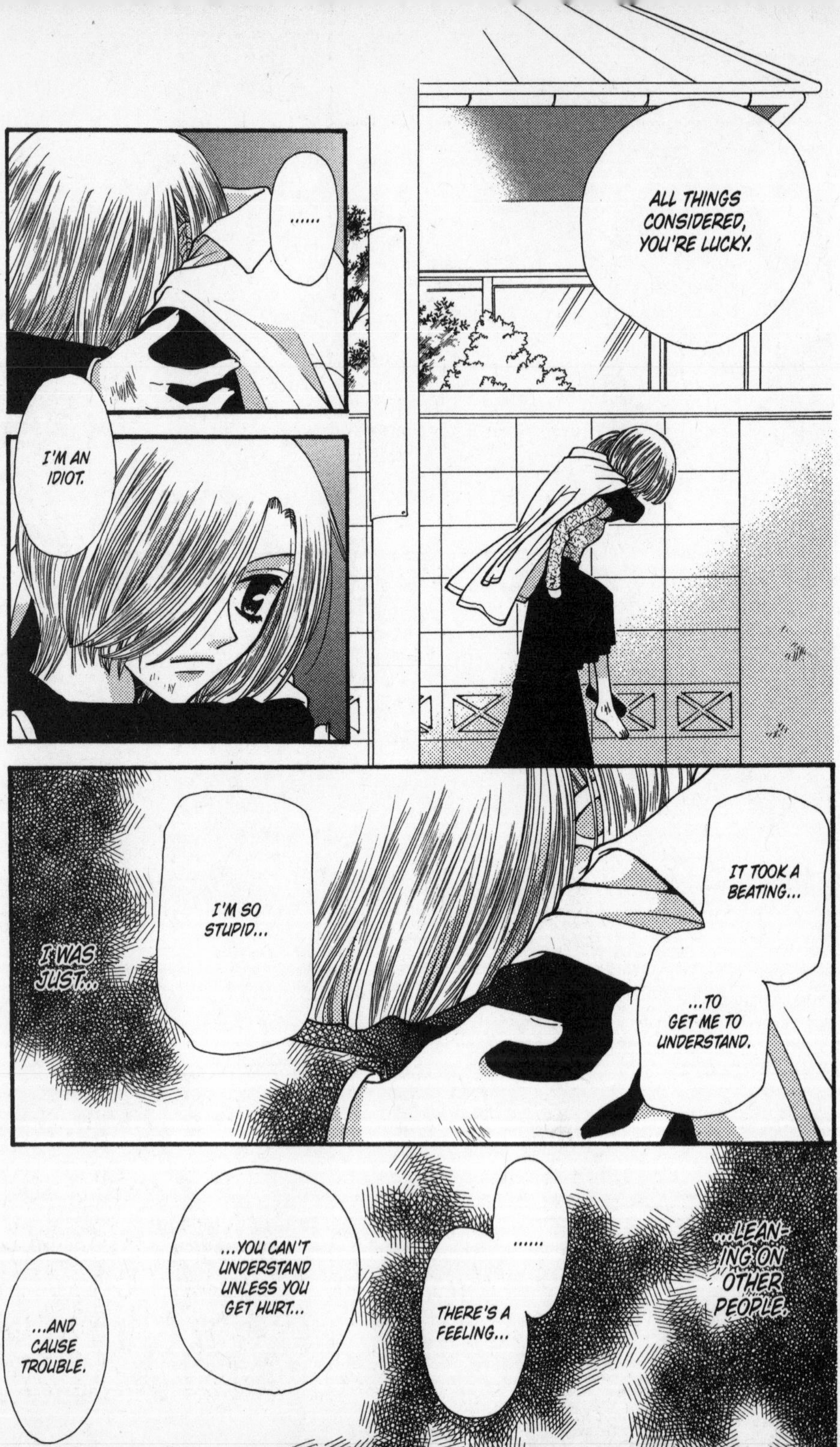
ALL THINGS CONSIDERED, YOU'RE LUCKY.
......
I'M AN IDIOT.
IT TOOK A BEATING...
...TO GET ME TO UNDERSTAND.
I'M SO STUPID...
I WAS JUST...
...LEANING ON OTHER PEOPLE.
......
THERE'S A FEELING...
...YOU CAN'T UNDERSTAND UNLESS YOU GET HURT...
...AND CAUSE TROUBLE.

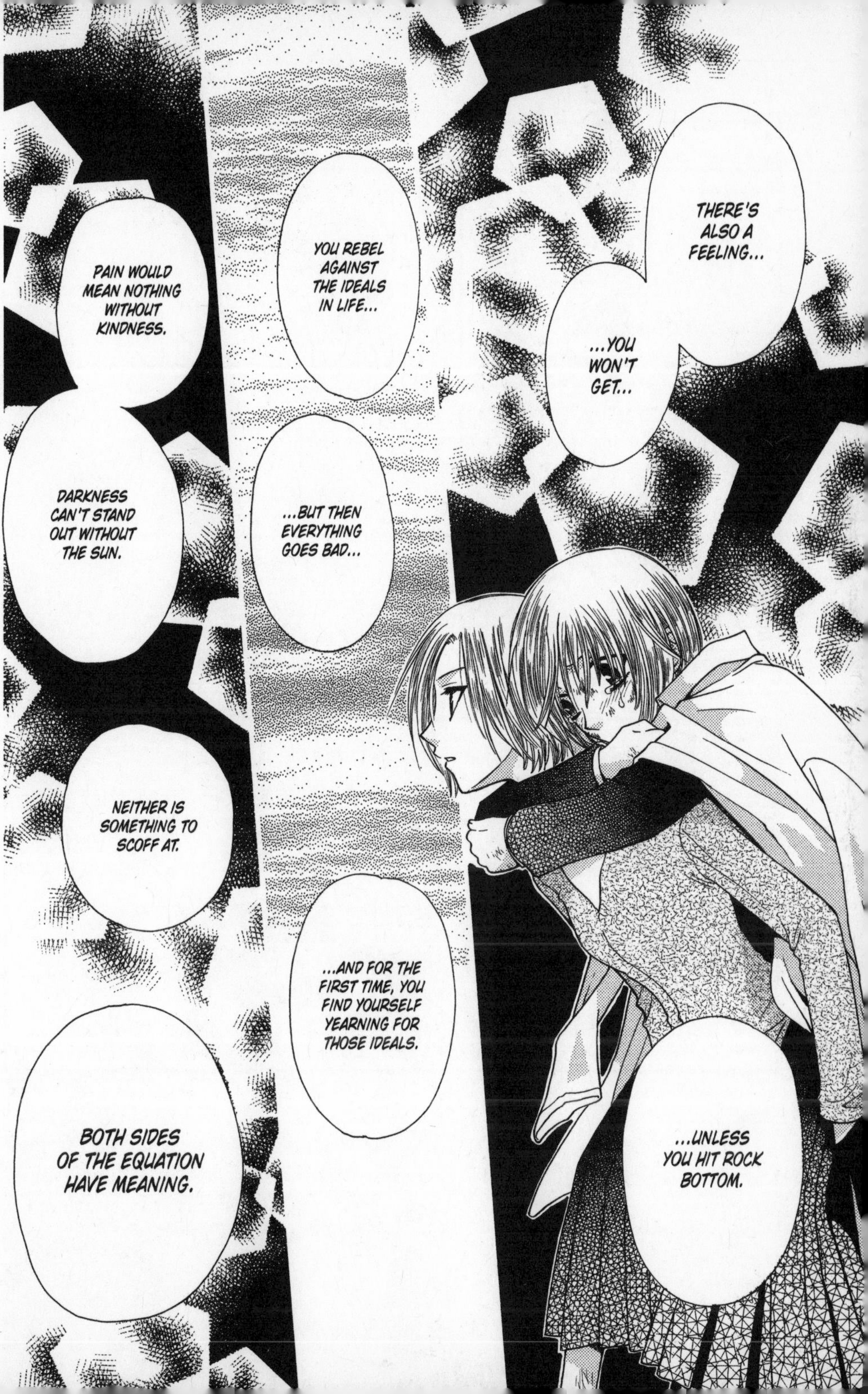
THERE'S ALSO A FEELING...
...YOU WON'T GET...
...UNLESS YOU HIT ROCK BOTTOM.
YOU REBEL AGAINST THE IDEALS IN LIFE...
...BUT THEN EVERYTHING GOES BAD...
...AND FOR THE FIRST TIME, YOU FIND YOURSELF YEARNING FOR THOSE IDEALS.
PAIN WOULD MEAN NOTHING WITHOUT KINDNESS.
DARKNESS CAN'T STAND OUT WITHOUT THE SUN.
NEITHER IS SOMETHING TO SCOFF AT.
BOTH SIDES OF THE EQUATION HAVE MEANING.

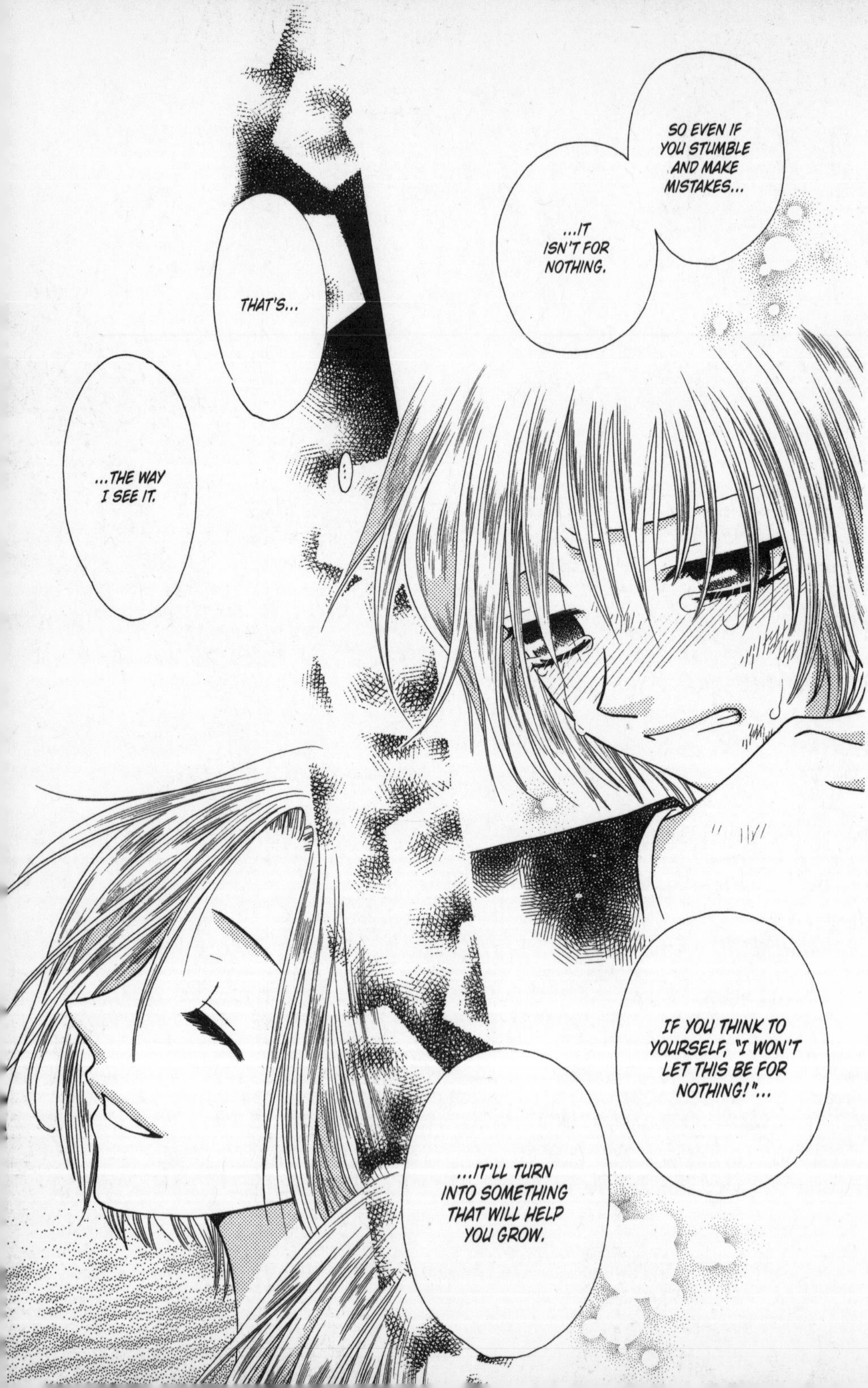
SO EVEN IF YOU STUMBLE AND MAKE MISTAKES...
...IT ISN'T FOR NOTHING.
THAT'S...
...THE WAY I SEE IT.
IF YOU THINK TO YOURSELF, "I WON'T LET THIS BE FOR NOTHING!"...
...IT'LL TURN INTO SOMETHING THAT WILL HELP YOU GROW.

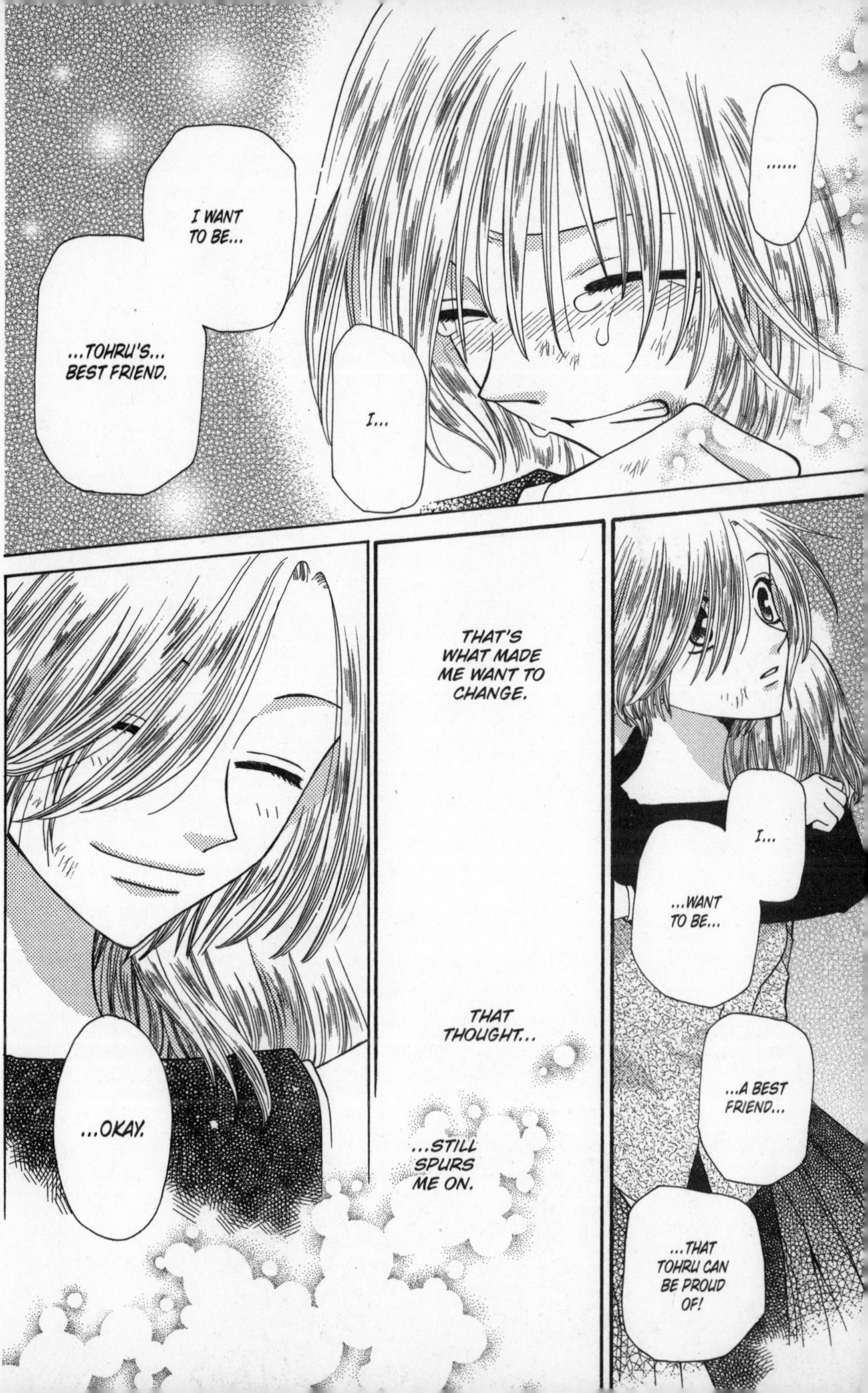
......
I...
I WANT TO BE...
...TOHRU'S... BEST FRIEND.
I...
...WANT TO BE...
...A BEST FRIEND...
...THAT TOHRU CAN BE PROUD OF!
THAT'S WHAT MADE ME WANT TO CHANGE.
THAT THOUGHT...
...STILL SPURS ME ON.
...OKAY.

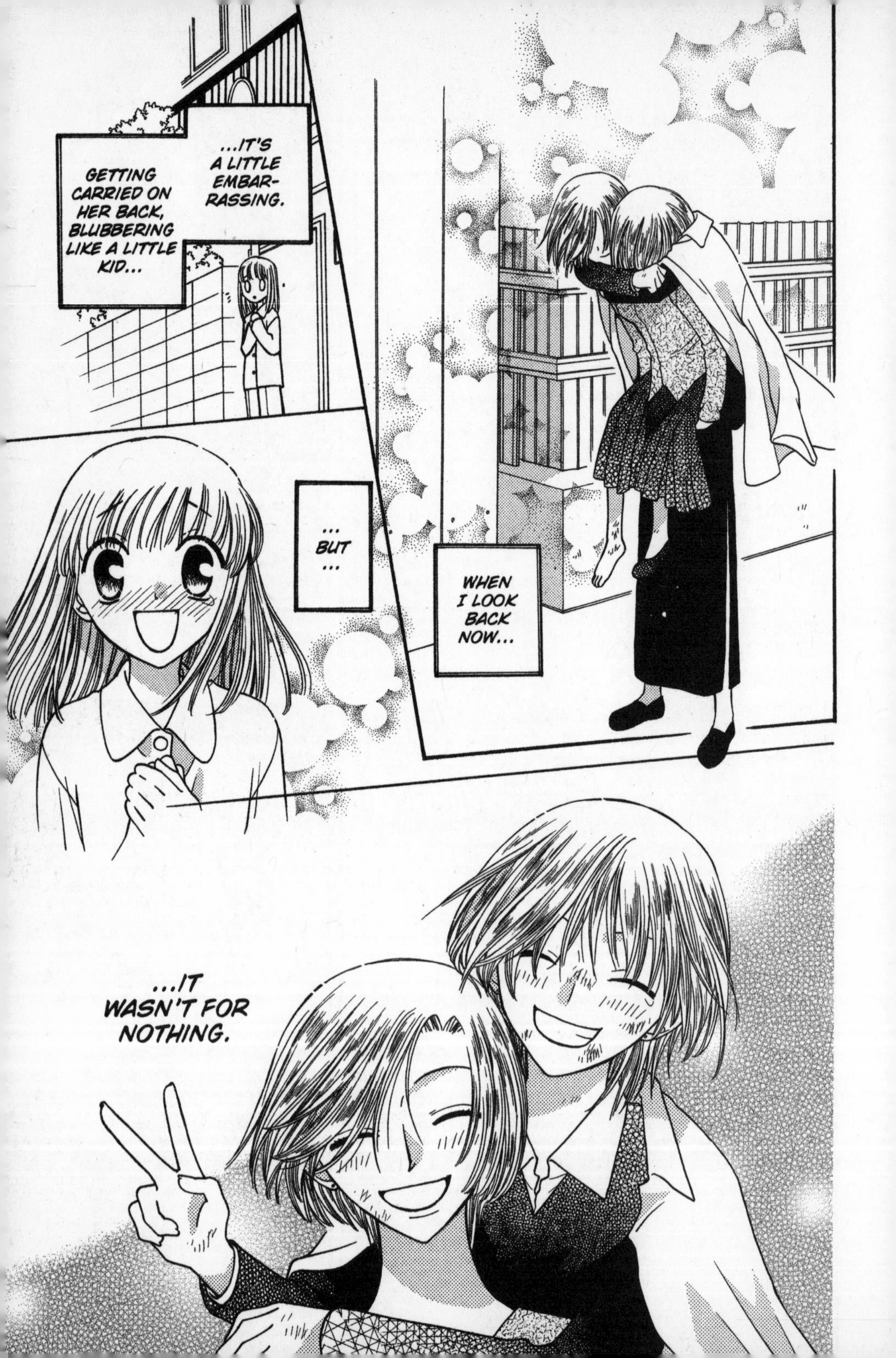

WHEN I LOOK BACK NOW...
GETTING CARRIED ON HER BACK, BLUBBERING LIKE A LITTLE KID...
...IT'S A LITTLE EMBARRASSING.
...BUT...
...IT WASN'T FOR NOTHING.

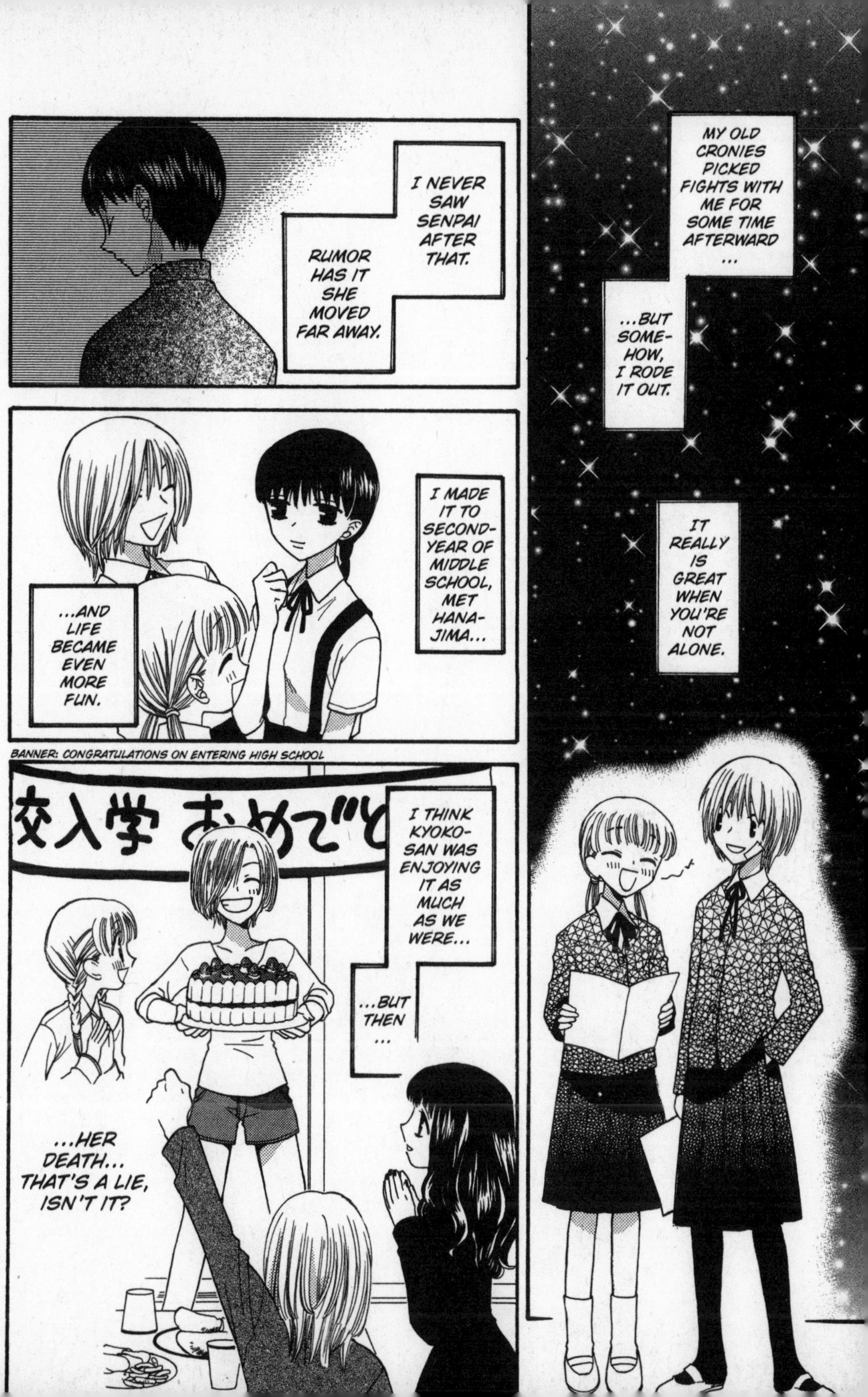
MY OLD CRONIES PICKED FIGHTS WITH ME FOR SOME TIME AFTERWARD ...
...BUT SOME-HOW, I RODE IT OUT.
IT REALLY IS GREAT WHEN YOU'RE NOT ALONE.
I NEVER SAW SENPAI AFTER THAT.
RUMOR HAS IT SHE MOVED FAR AWAY.
I MADE IT TO SECOND-YEAR OF MIDDLE SCHOOL, MET HANA-JIMA...
...AND LIFE BECAME EVEN MORE FUN.
BANNER: CONGRATULATIONS ON ENTERING HIGH SCHOOL
校入学 おめでと
I THINK KYOKO-SAN WAS ENJOYING IT AS MUCH AS WE WERE...
...BUT THEN ...
...HER DEATH... THAT'S A LIE, ISN'T IT?

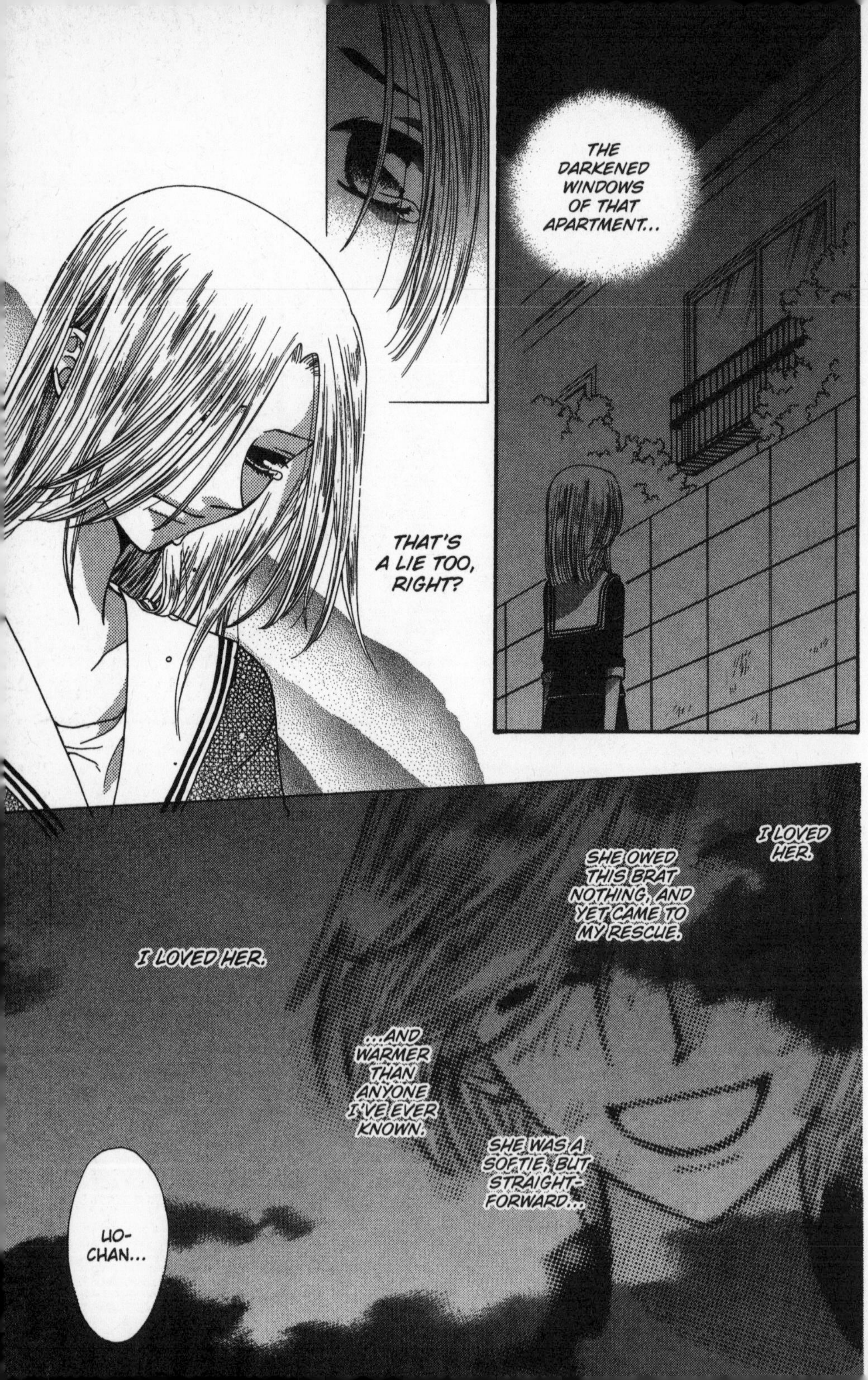
THE DARKENED WINDOWS OF THAT APARTMENT...
THAT'S A LIE TOO, RIGHT?
I LOVED HER.
SHE OWED THIS BRAT NOTHING, AND YET CAME TO MY RESCUE.
SHE WAS A SOFTIE, BUT STRAIGHT-FORWARD...
...AND WARMER THAN ANYONE I'VE EVER KNOWN.
I LOVED HER.
UO-CHAN...

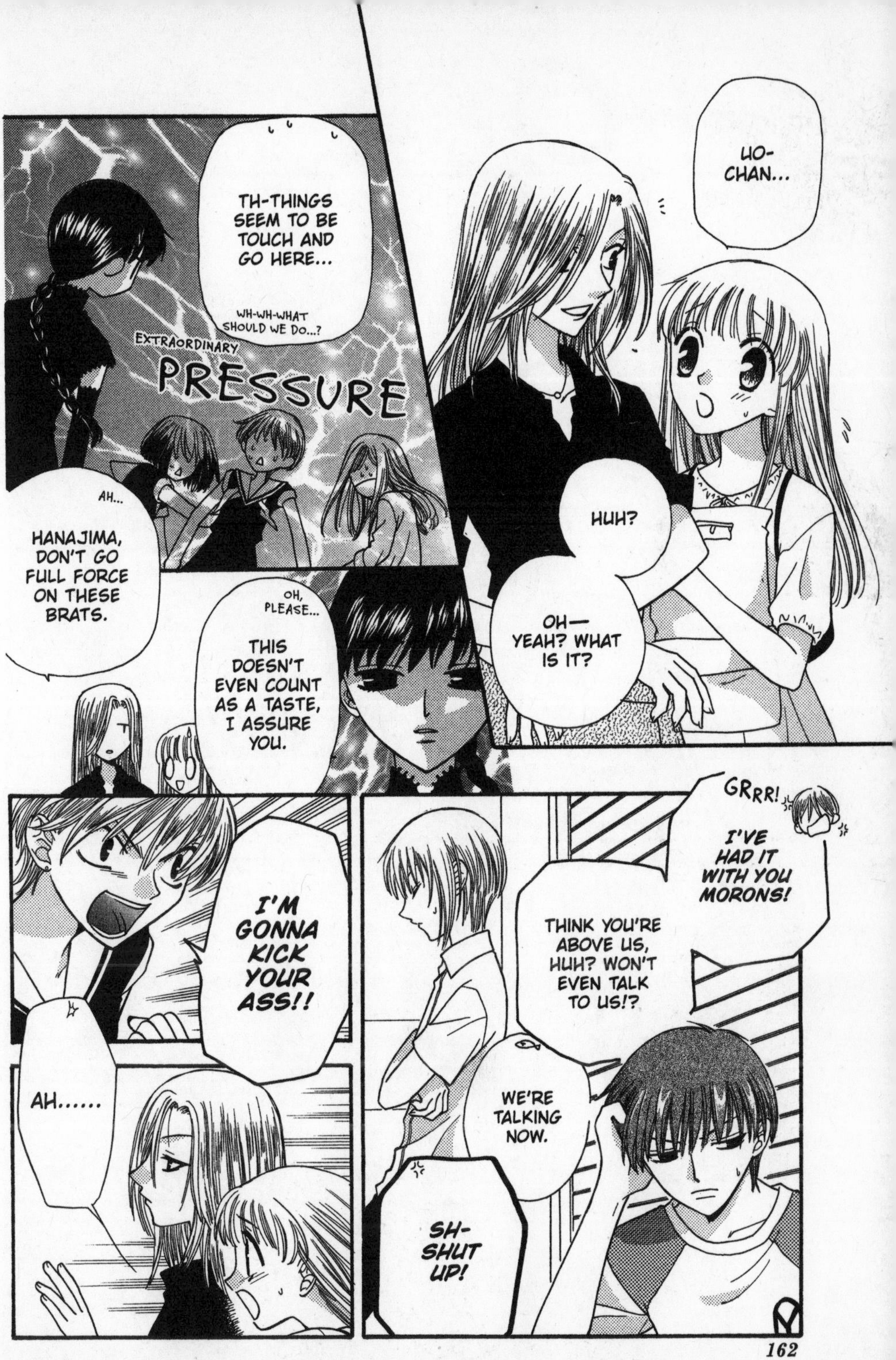
UO-CHAN...
HUH?
OH—YEAH? WHAT IS IT?
TH-THINGS SEEM TO BE TOUCH AND GO HERE...
WH-WH-WHAT SHOULD WE DO...?
EXTRAORDINARY
PRESSURE
AH...
HANAJIMA, DON'T GO FULL FORCE ON THESE BRATS.
OH, PLEASE...
THIS DOESN'T EVEN COUNT AS A TASTE, I ASSURE YOU.
GRRR!
I'VE HAD IT WITH YOU MORONS!
THINK YOU'RE ABOVE US, HUH? WON'T EVEN TALK TO US!?
WE'RE TALKING NOW.
SH-SHUT UP!
I'M GONNA KICK YOUR ASS!!
AH......

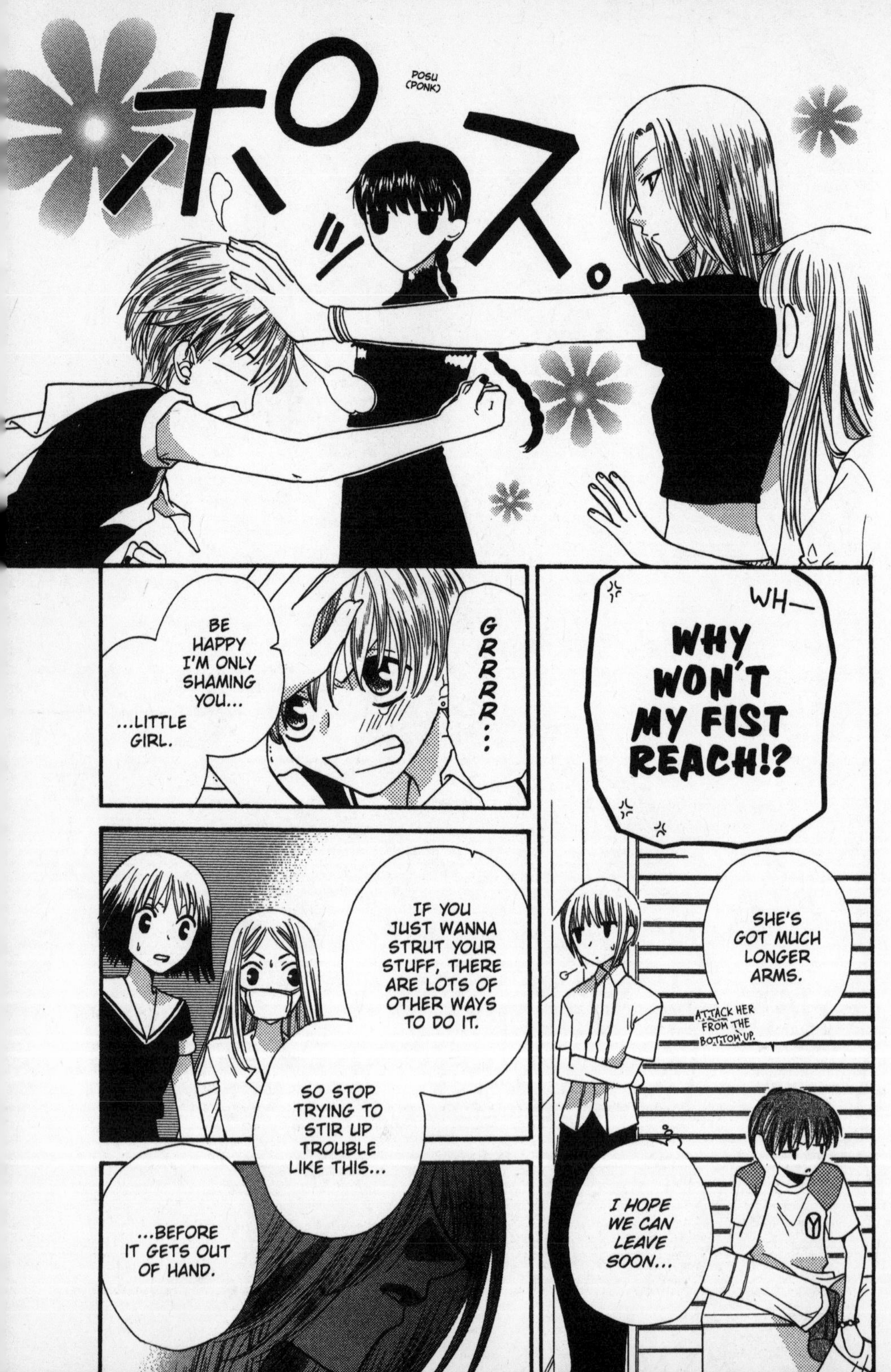
ポスッ。
POSU (PONK)
WH—
WHY WON'T MY FIST REACH!?
BE HAPPY I'M ONLY SHAMING YOU...
...LITTLE GIRL.
GRRRR...
IF YOU JUST WANNA STRUT YOUR STUFF, THERE ARE LOTS OF OTHER WAYS TO DO IT.
SO STOP TRYING TO STIR UP TROUBLE LIKE THIS...
...BEFORE IT GETS OUT OF HAND.
SHE'S GOT MUCH LONGER ARMS.
ATTACK HER FROM THE BOTTOM UP.
I HOPE WE CAN LEAVE SOON...

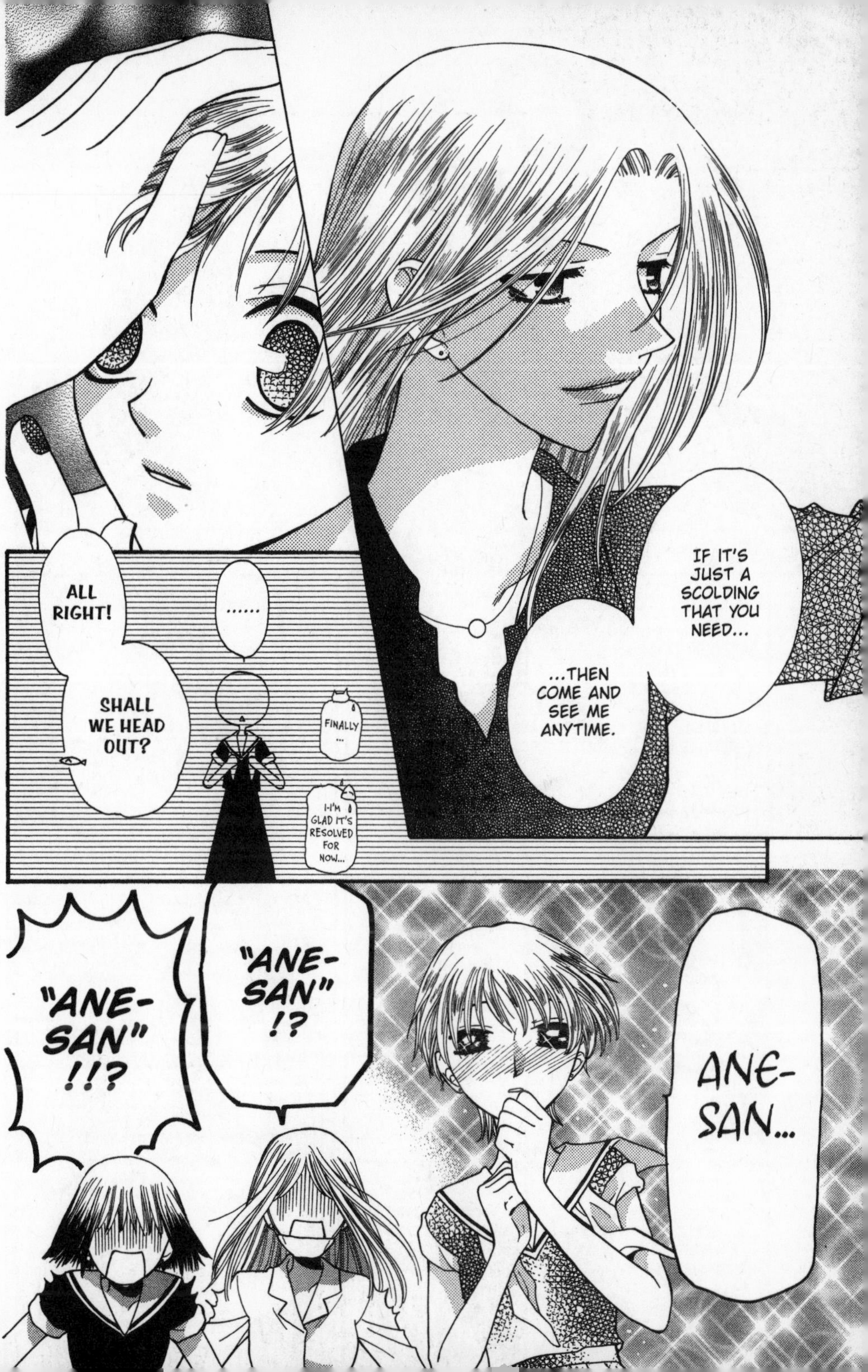
IF IT'S JUST A SCOLDING THAT YOU NEED...
...THEN COME AND SEE ME ANYTIME.
......
ALL RIGHT!
SHALL WE HEAD OUT?
FINALLY...
I-I'M GLAD IT'S RESOLVED FOR NOW...
ANE-SAN...
"ANE-SAN"!?
"ANE-SAN"!!?

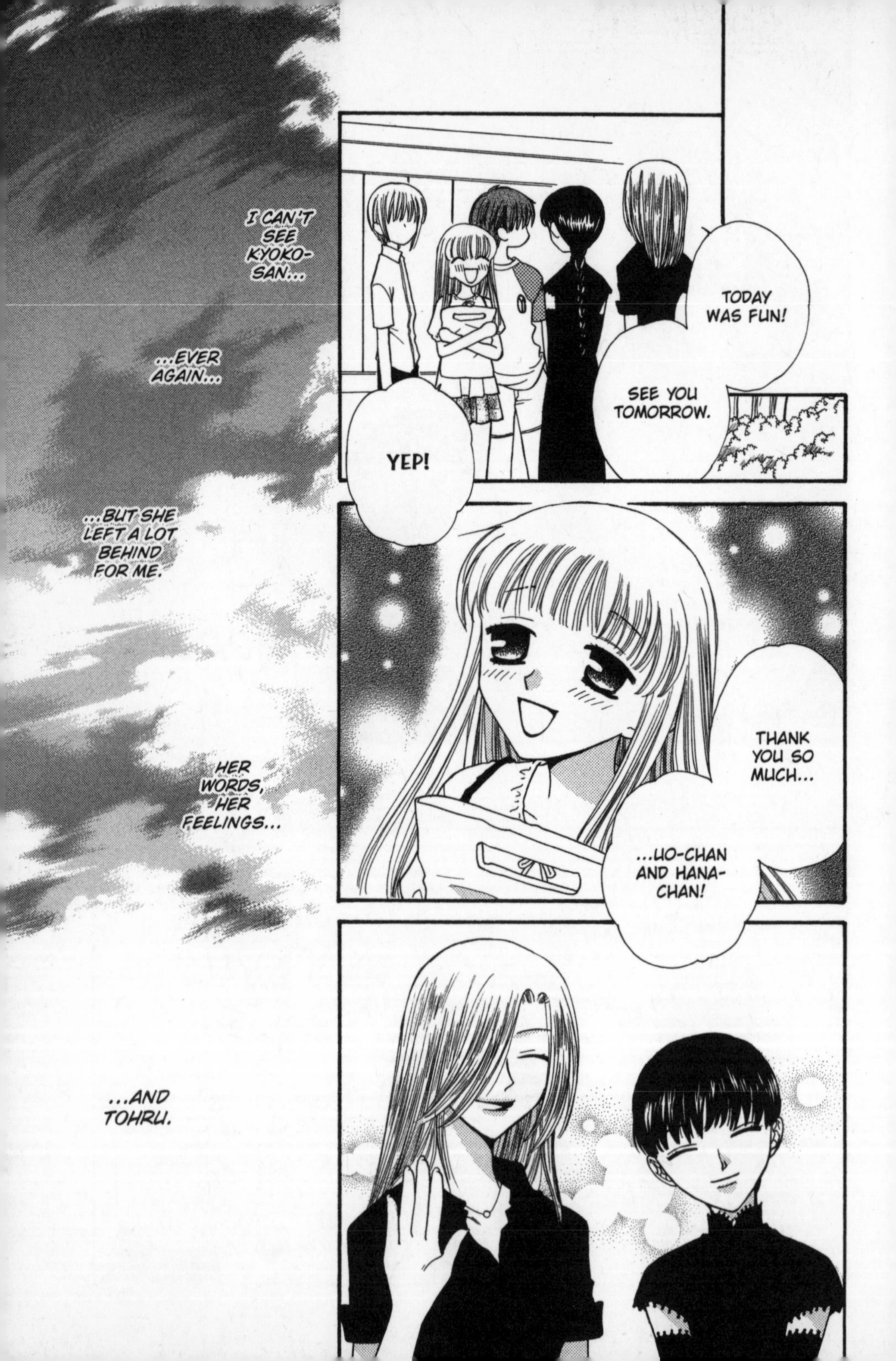
TODAY WAS FUN!
SEE YOU TOMORROW.
YEP!
THANK YOU SO MUCH...
...UO-CHAN AND HANA-CHAN!
I CAN'T SEE KYOKO-SAN...
...EVER AGAIN...
...BUT SHE LEFT A LOT BEHIND FOR ME.
HER WORDS, HER FEELINGS...
...AND TOHRU.

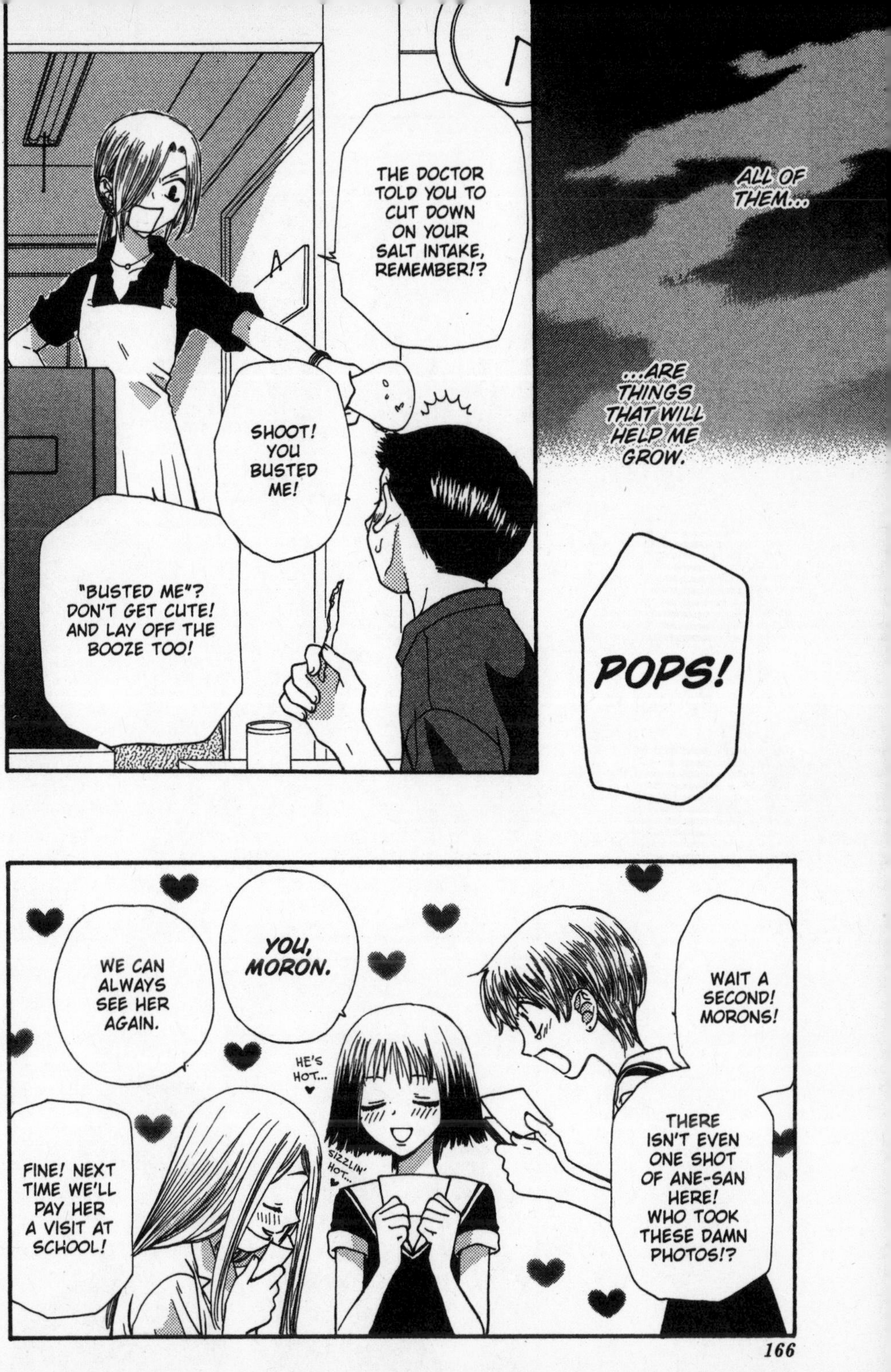
ALL OF THEM...
...ARE THINGS THAT WILL HELP ME GROW.
POPS!
THE DOCTOR TOLD YOU TO CUT DOWN ON YOUR SALT INTAKE, REMEMBER!?
SHOOT! YOU BUSTED ME!
"BUSTED ME"? DON'T GET CUTE! AND LAY OFF THE BOOZE TOO!
WAIT A SECOND! MORONS!
THERE ISN'T EVEN ONE SHOT OF ANE-SAN HERE! WHO TOOK THESE DAMN PHOTOS!?
HE'S HOT...
SIZZLIN' HOT...
YOU, MORON.
WE CAN ALWAYS SEE HER AGAIN.
FINE! NEXT TIME WE'LL PAY HER A VISIT AT SCHOOL!

COLLECTOR'S EDITION

Fruits Basket

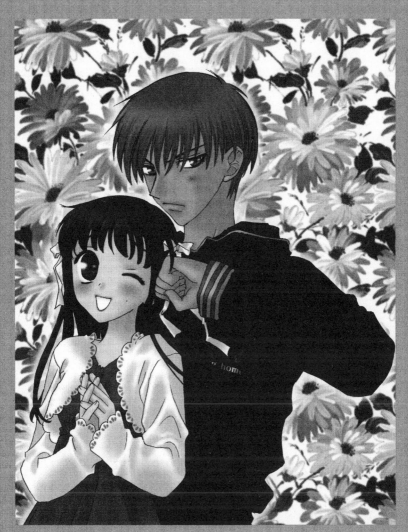

COLLECTOR'S EDITION
Fruits Basket

Chapter 42

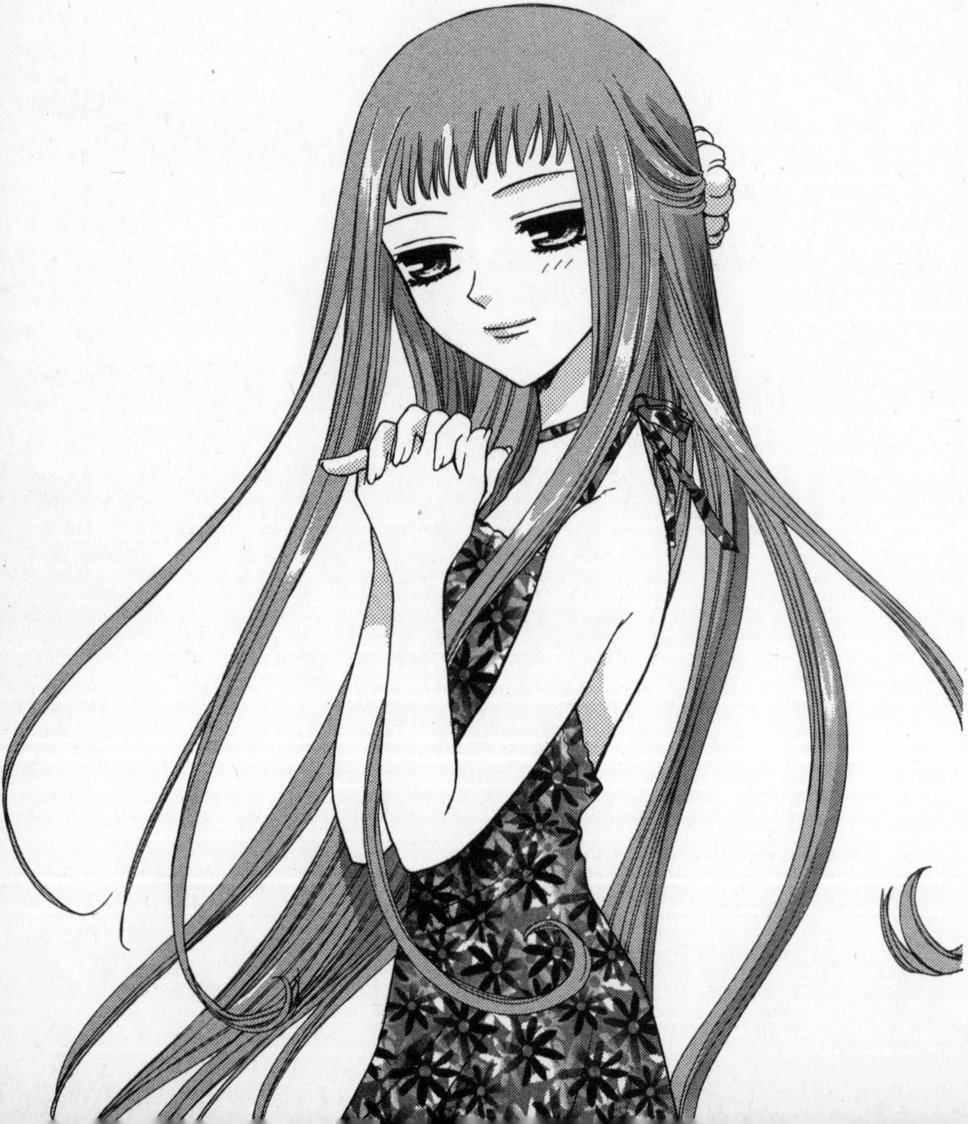

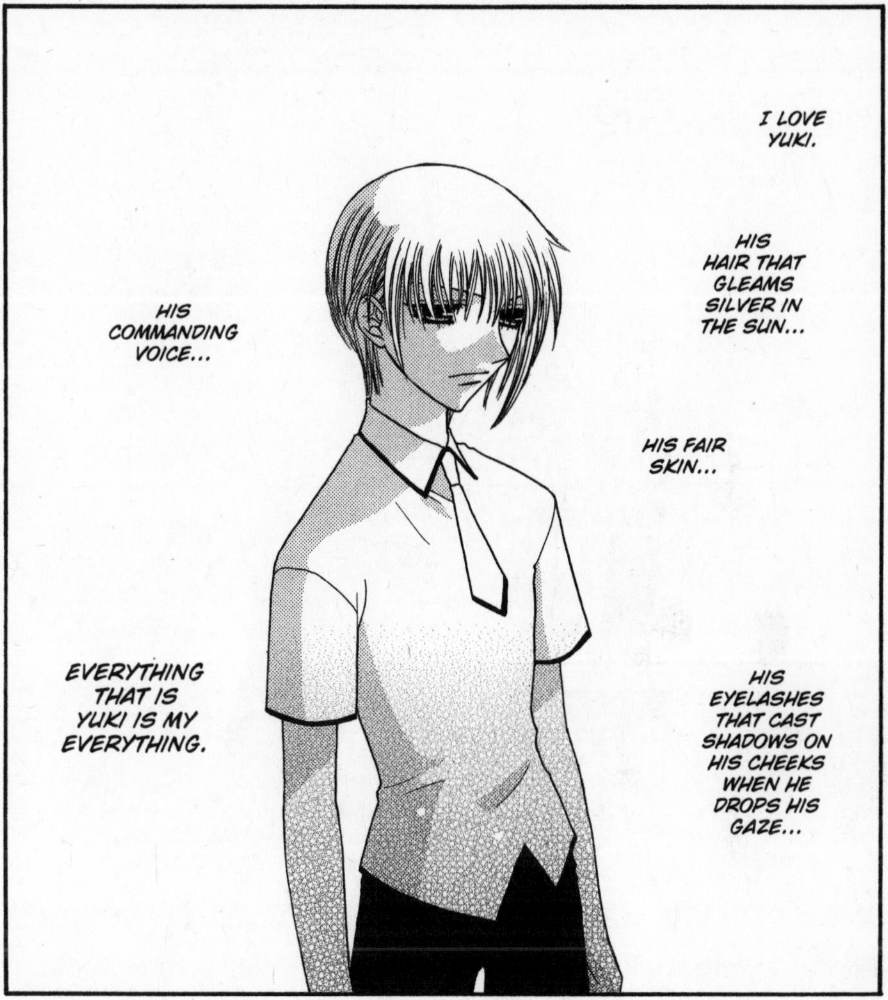
I LOVE YUKI.
HIS HAIR THAT GLEAMS SILVER IN THE SUN...
HIS COMMANDING VOICE...
HIS FAIR SKIN...
HIS EYELASHES THAT CAST SHADOWS ON HIS CHEEKS WHEN HE DROPS HIS GAZE...
EVERYTHING THAT IS YUKI IS MY EVERYTHING.

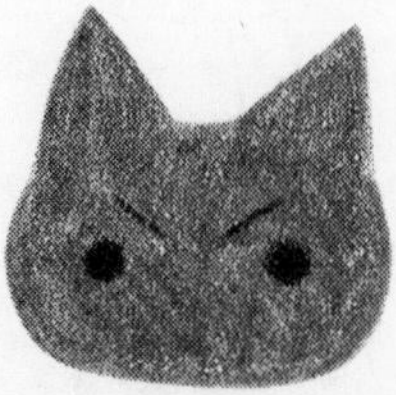

CAT

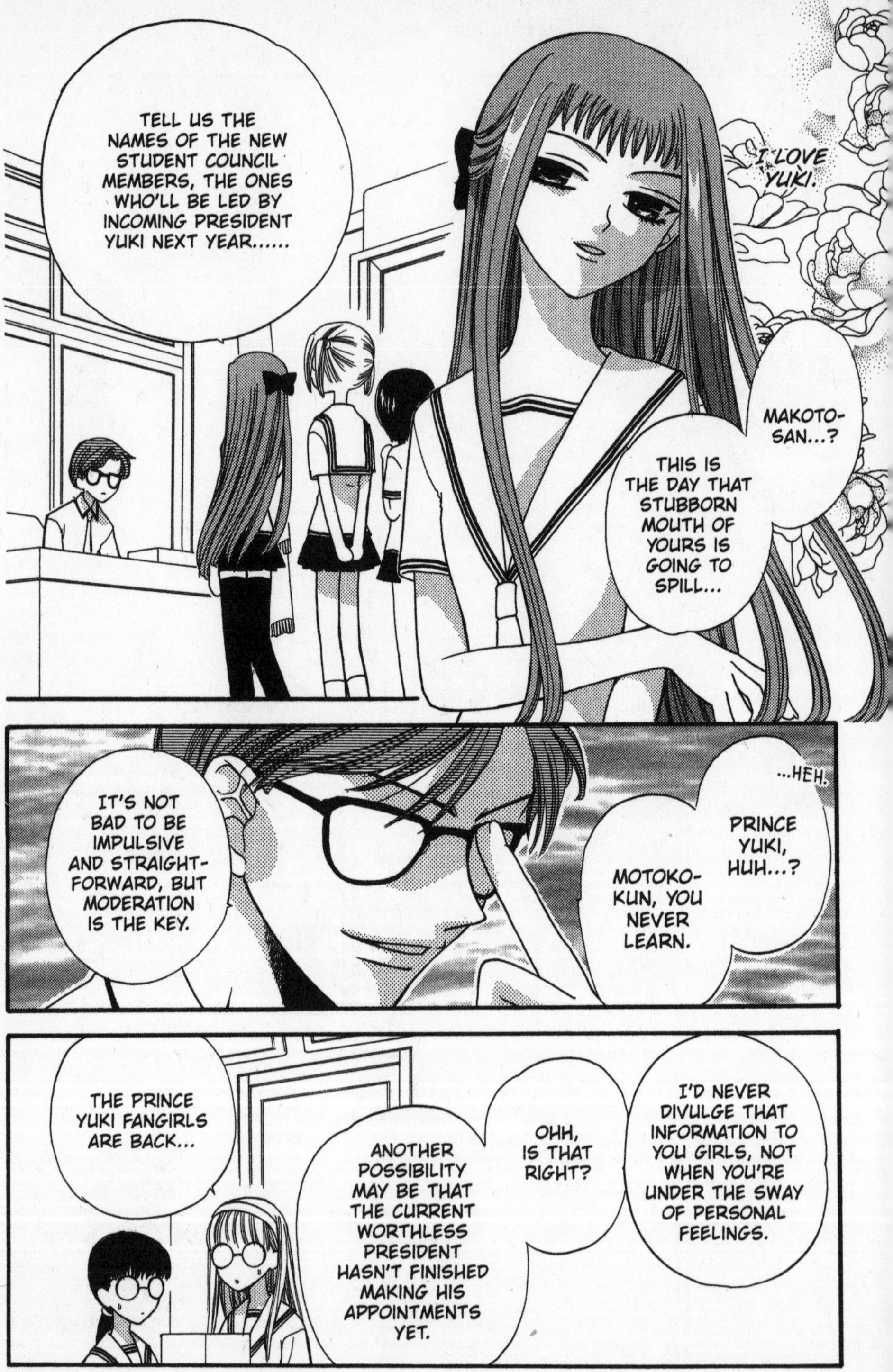
I LOVE YUKI.
TELL US THE NAMES OF THE NEW STUDENT COUNCIL MEMBERS, THE ONES WHO'LL BE LED BY INCOMING PRESIDENT YUKI NEXT YEAR......
MAKOTO-SAN...?
THIS IS THE DAY THAT STUBBORN MOUTH OF YOURS IS GOING TO SPILL...
...HEH.
PRINCE YUKI, HUH...?
MOTOKO-KUN, YOU NEVER LEARN.
IT'S NOT BAD TO BE IMPULSIVE AND STRAIGHT-FORWARD, BUT MODERATION IS THE KEY.
I'D NEVER DIVULGE THAT INFORMATION TO YOU GIRLS, NOT WHEN YOU'RE UNDER THE SWAY OF PERSONAL FEELINGS.
OHH, IS THAT RIGHT?
ANOTHER POSSIBILITY MAY BE THAT THE CURRENT WORTHLESS PRESIDENT HASN'T FINISHED MAKING HIS APPOINTMENTS YET.
THE PRINCE YUKI FANGIRLS ARE BACK...

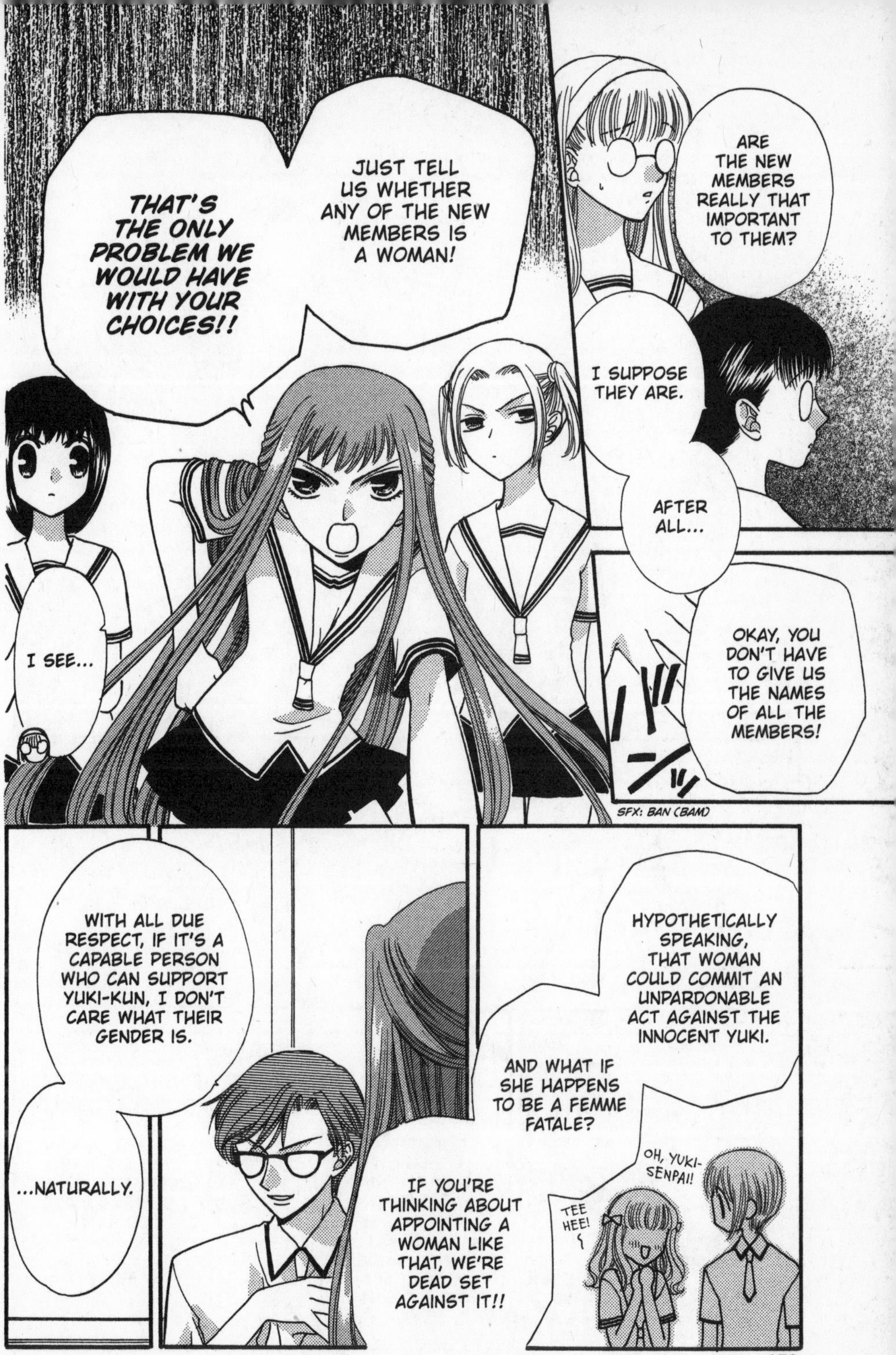
ARE THE NEW MEMBERS REALLY THAT IMPORTANT TO THEM?
I SUPPOSE THEY ARE.
AFTER ALL...
OKAY, YOU DON'T HAVE TO GIVE US THE NAMES OF ALL THE MEMBERS!
SFX: BAN (BAM)
JUST TELL US WHETHER ANY OF THE NEW MEMBERS IS A WOMAN!
THAT'S THE ONLY PROBLEM WE WOULD HAVE WITH YOUR CHOICES!!
I SEE...
HYPOTHETICALLY SPEAKING, THAT WOMAN COULD COMMIT AN UNPARDONABLE ACT AGAINST THE INNOCENT YUKI.
AND WHAT IF SHE HAPPENS TO BE A FEMME FATALE?
OH, YUKI-SENPAI!
TEE HEE!
IF YOU'RE THINKING ABOUT APPOINTING A WOMAN LIKE THAT, WE'RE DEAD SET AGAINST IT!!
WITH ALL DUE RESPECT, IF IT'S A CAPABLE PERSON WHO CAN SUPPORT YUKI-KUN, I DON'T CARE WHAT THEIR GENDER IS.
...NATURALLY.

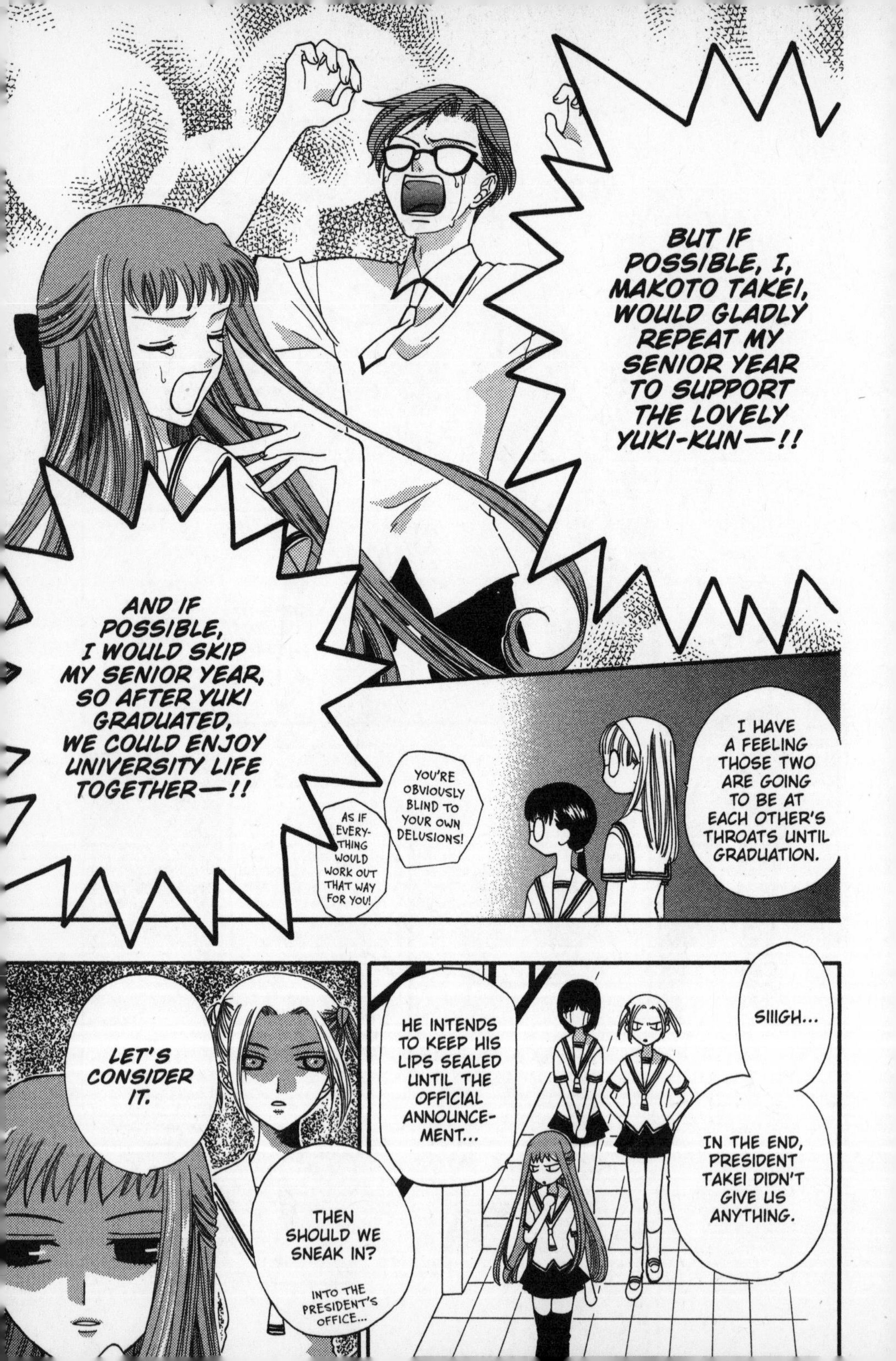
BUT IF POSSIBLE, I, MAKOTO TAKEI, WOULD GLADLY REPEAT MY SENIOR YEAR TO SUPPORT THE LOVELY YUKI-KUN—!!
AND IF POSSIBLE, I WOULD SKIP MY SENIOR YEAR, SO AFTER YUKI GRADUATED, WE COULD ENJOY UNIVERSITY LIFE TOGETHER—!!
I HAVE A FEELING THOSE TWO ARE GOING TO BE AT EACH OTHER'S THROATS UNTIL GRADUATION.
YOU'RE OBVIOUSLY BLIND TO YOUR OWN DELUSIONS!
AS IF EVERYTHING WOULD WORK OUT THAT WAY FOR YOU!
SIIIGH...
IN THE END, PRESIDENT TAKEI DIDN'T GIVE US ANYTHING.
HE INTENDS TO KEEP HIS LIPS SEALED UNTIL THE OFFICIAL ANNOUNCEMENT...
THEN SHOULD WE SNEAK IN?
INTO THE PRESIDENT'S OFFICE...
LET'S CONSIDER IT.

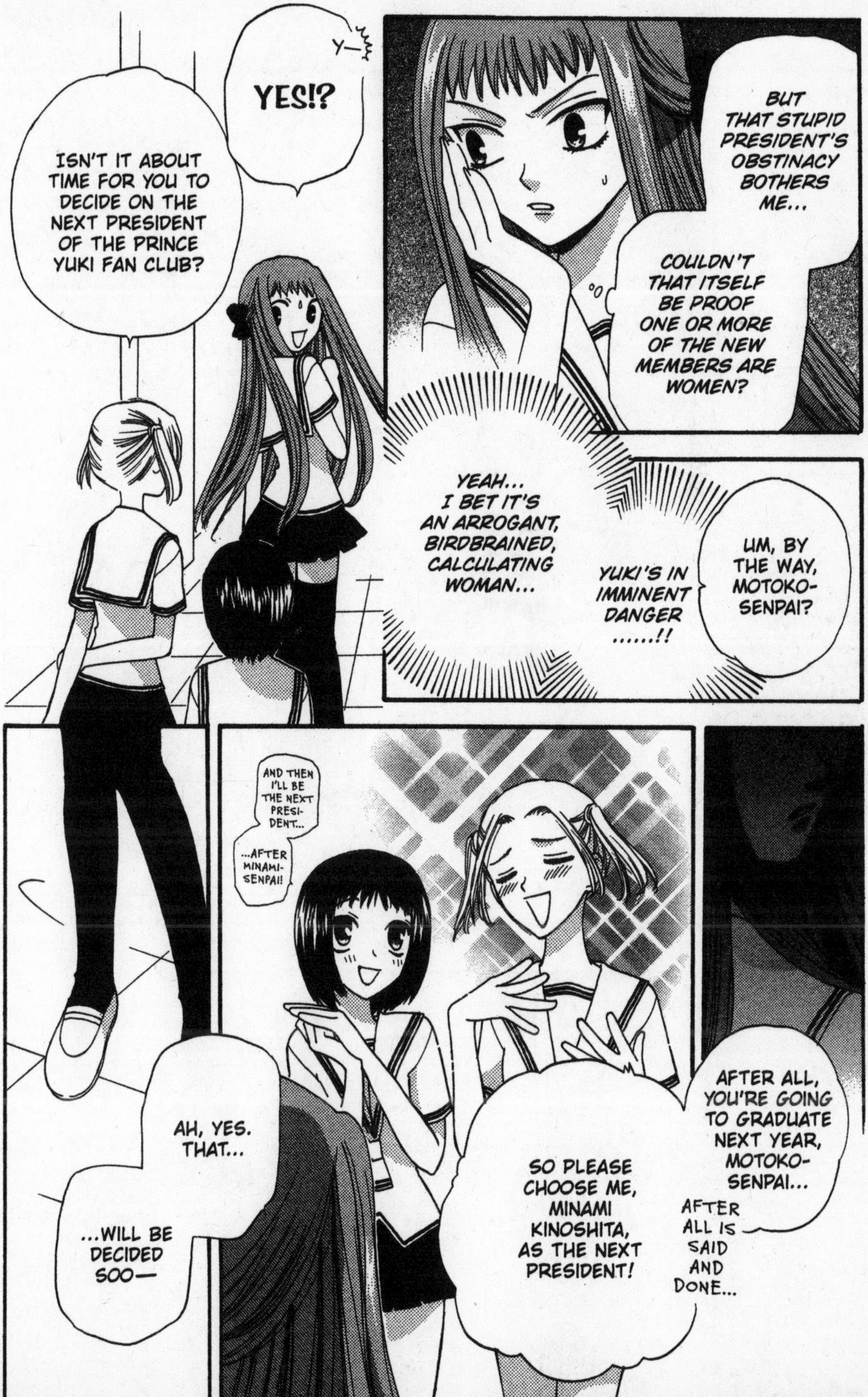
BUT THAT STUPID PRESIDENT'S OBSTINACY BOTHERS ME...
COULDN'T THAT ITSELF BE PROOF ONE OR MORE OF THE NEW MEMBERS ARE WOMEN?
YEAH... I BET IT'S AN ARROGANT, BIRDBRAINED, CALCULATING WOMAN...
YUKI'S IN IMMINENT DANGER ......!!
UM, BY THE WAY, MOTOKO-SENPAI?
Y—
YES!?
ISN'T IT ABOUT TIME FOR YOU TO DECIDE ON THE NEXT PRESIDENT OF THE PRINCE YUKI FAN CLUB?
AFTER ALL, YOU'RE GOING TO GRADUATE NEXT YEAR, MOTOKO-SENPAI...
AFTER ALL IS SAID AND DONE...
SO PLEASE CHOOSE ME, MINAMI KINOSHITA, AS THE NEXT PRESIDENT!
AND THEN I'LL BE THE NEXT PRESI-DENT...
...AFTER MINAMI-SENPAI!
AH, YES. THAT...
...WILL BE DECIDED SOO—

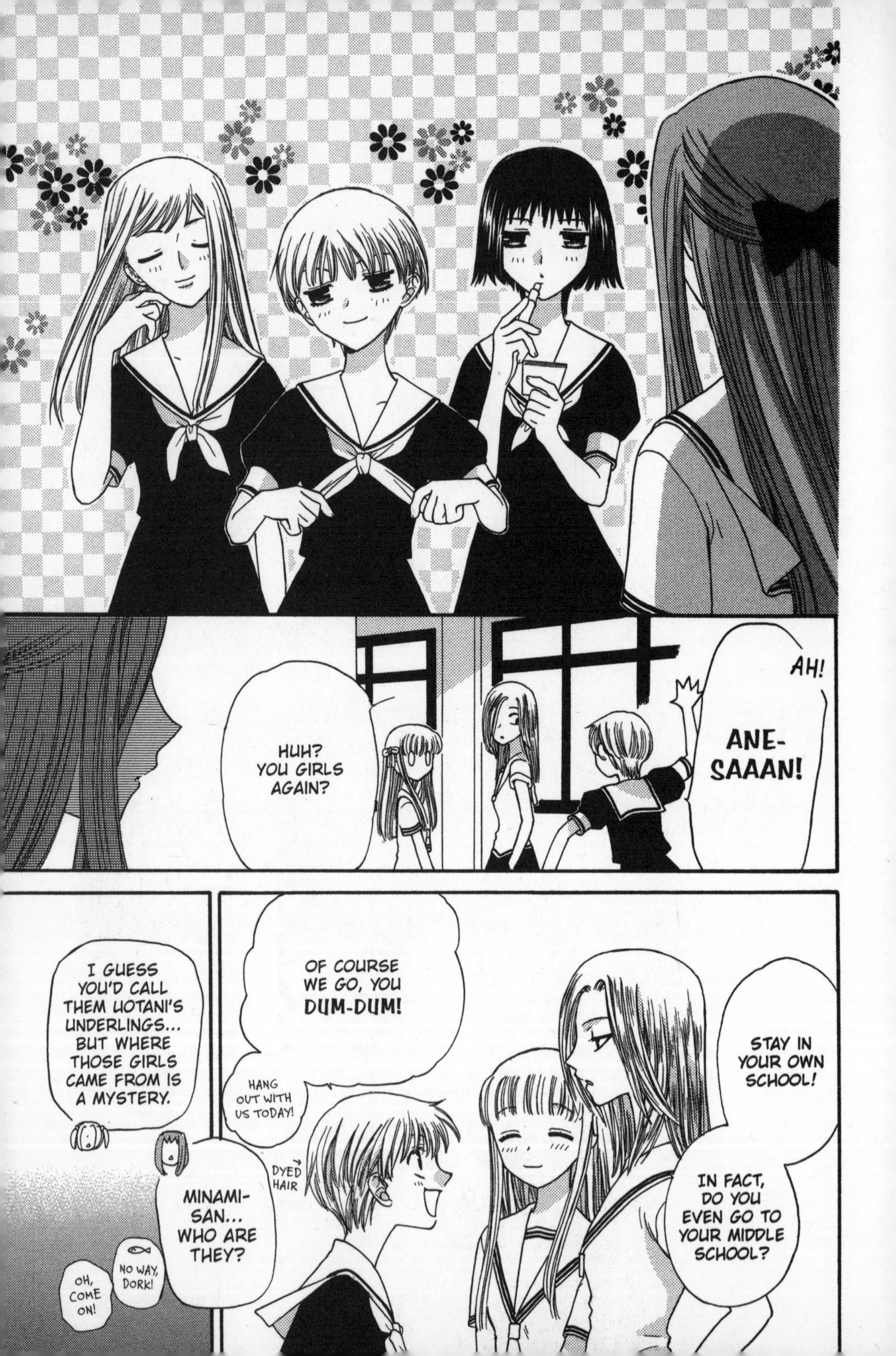

AH!
ANE-SAAAN!
HUH? YOU GIRLS AGAIN?
STAY IN YOUR OWN SCHOOL!
IN FACT, DO YOU EVEN GO TO YOUR MIDDLE SCHOOL?
OF COURSE WE GO, YOU **DUM-DUM!**
HANG OUT WITH US TODAY!
DYED HAIR
I GUESS YOU'D CALL THEM UOTANI'S UNDERLINGS... BUT WHERE THOSE GIRLS CAME FROM IS A MYSTERY.
MINAMI-SAN... WHO ARE THEY?
NO WAY, DORK!
OH, COME ON!

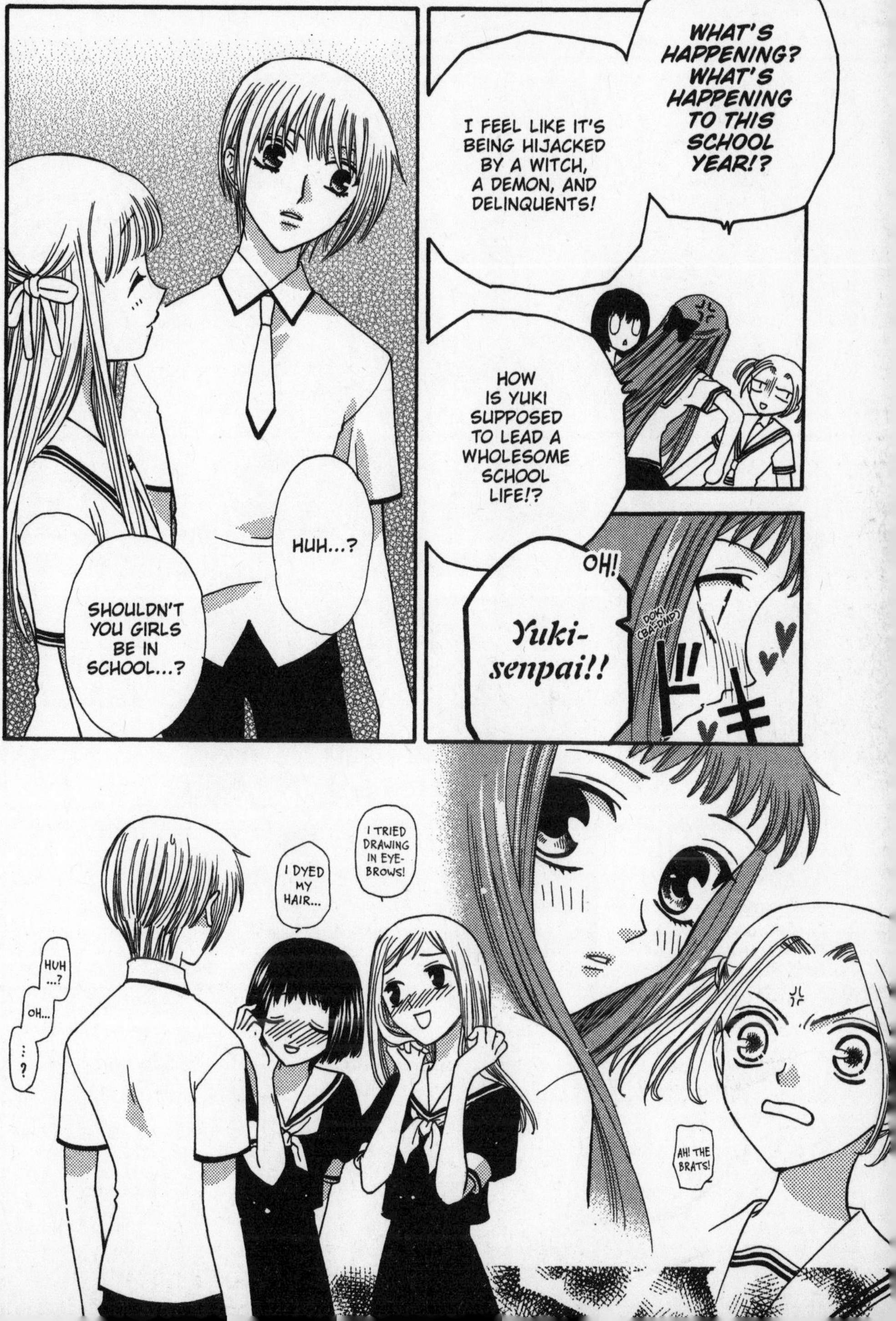
WHAT'S HAPPENING? WHAT'S HAPPENING TO THIS SCHOOL YEAR!?
I FEEL LIKE IT'S BEING HIJACKED BY A WITCH, A DEMON, AND DELINQUENTS!
HOW IS YUKI SUPPOSED TO LEAD A WHOLESOME SCHOOL LIFE!?
OH!
Yuki-senpai!!
DOKI (BA-DMP)
ドキ
HUH...?
SHOULDN'T YOU GIRLS BE IN SCHOOL...?
AH! THE BRATS!
I TRIED DRAWING IN EYE-BROWS!
I DYED MY HAIR...
HUH ...?
OH...
...?

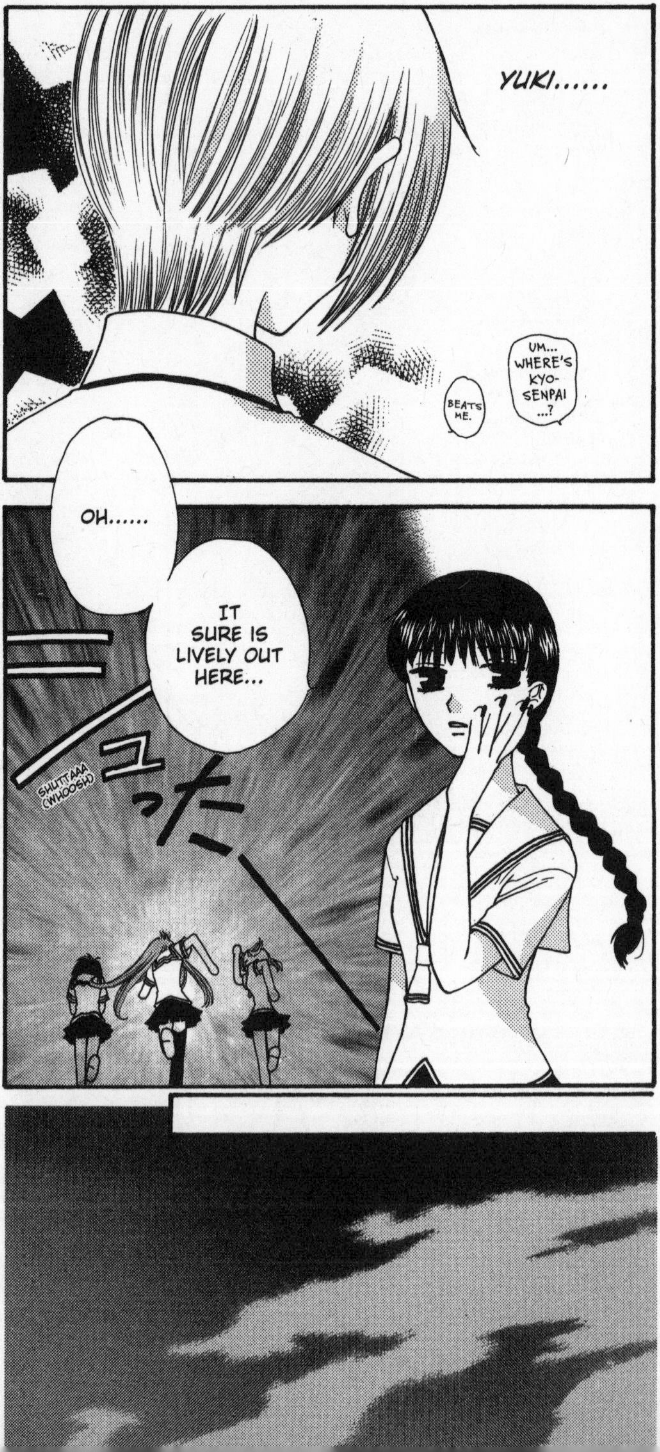
YUKI......
UM... WHERE'S KYO-SENPAI...?
BEATS ME.
OH......
IT SURE IS LIVELY OUT HERE...
SHUTTAAA (WHOOSH)
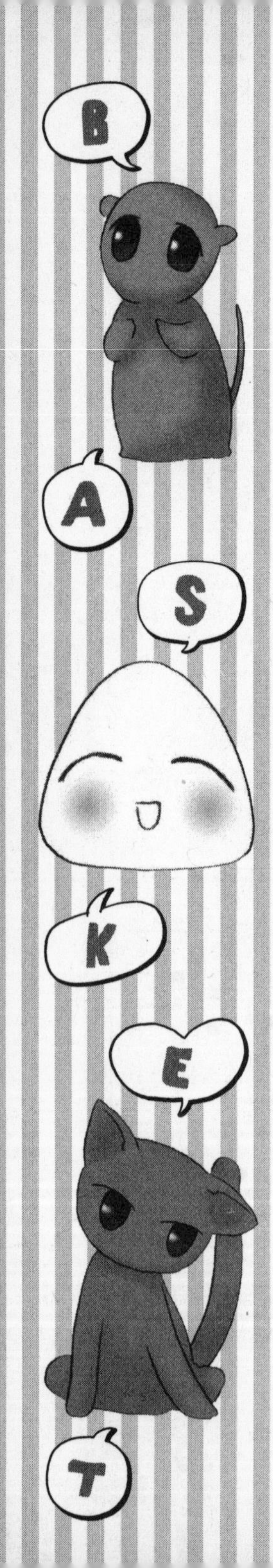
B
A
S
K
E
T

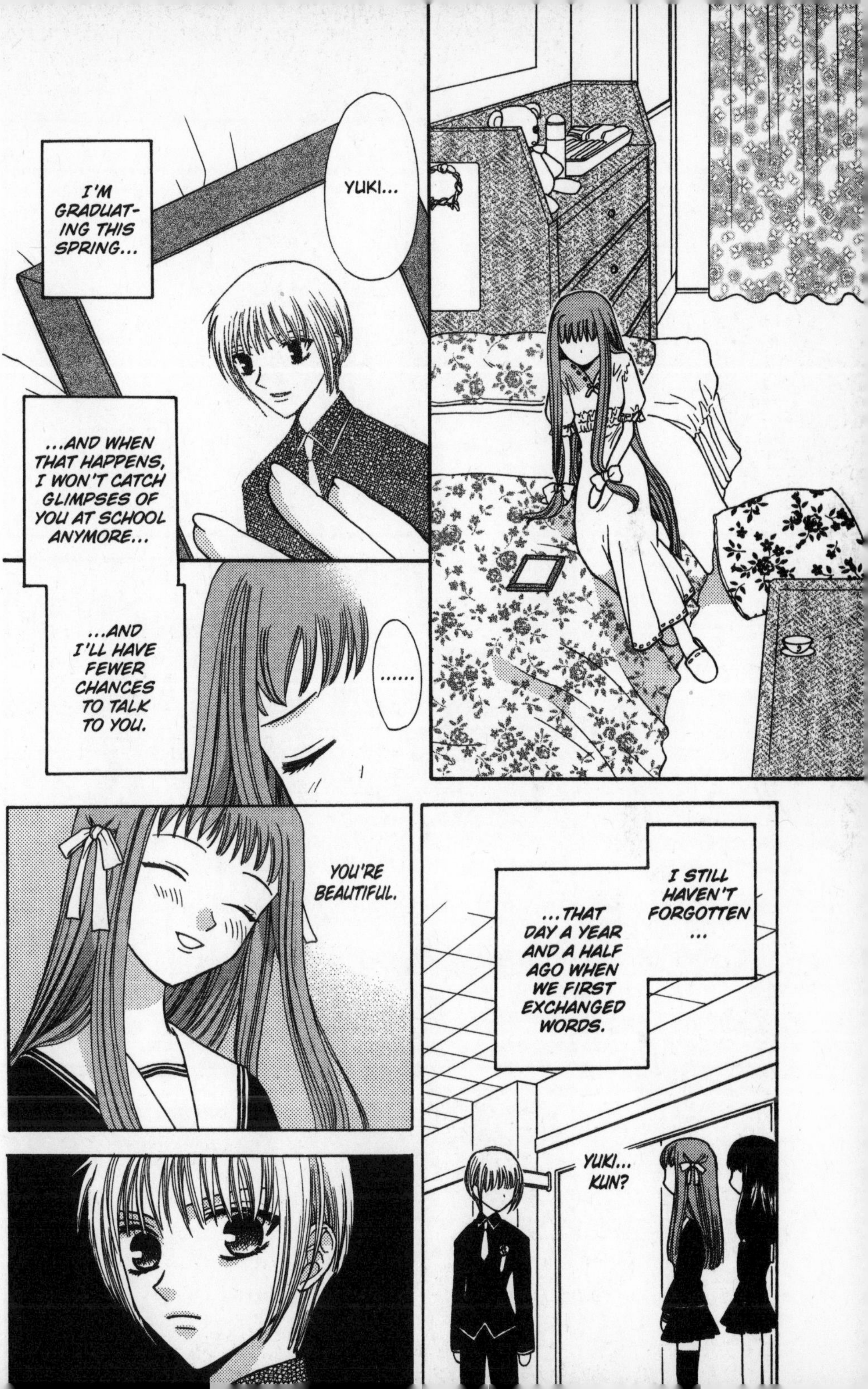
YUKI...
I'M GRADUAT-ING THIS SPRING...
...AND WHEN THAT HAPPENS, I WON'T CATCH GLIMPSES OF YOU AT SCHOOL ANYMORE...
......
...AND I'LL HAVE FEWER CHANCES TO TALK TO YOU.
I STILL HAVEN'T FORGOTTEN...
...THAT DAY A YEAR AND A HALF AGO WHEN WE FIRST EXCHANGED WORDS.
YUKI... KUN?
YOU'RE BEAUTIFUL.

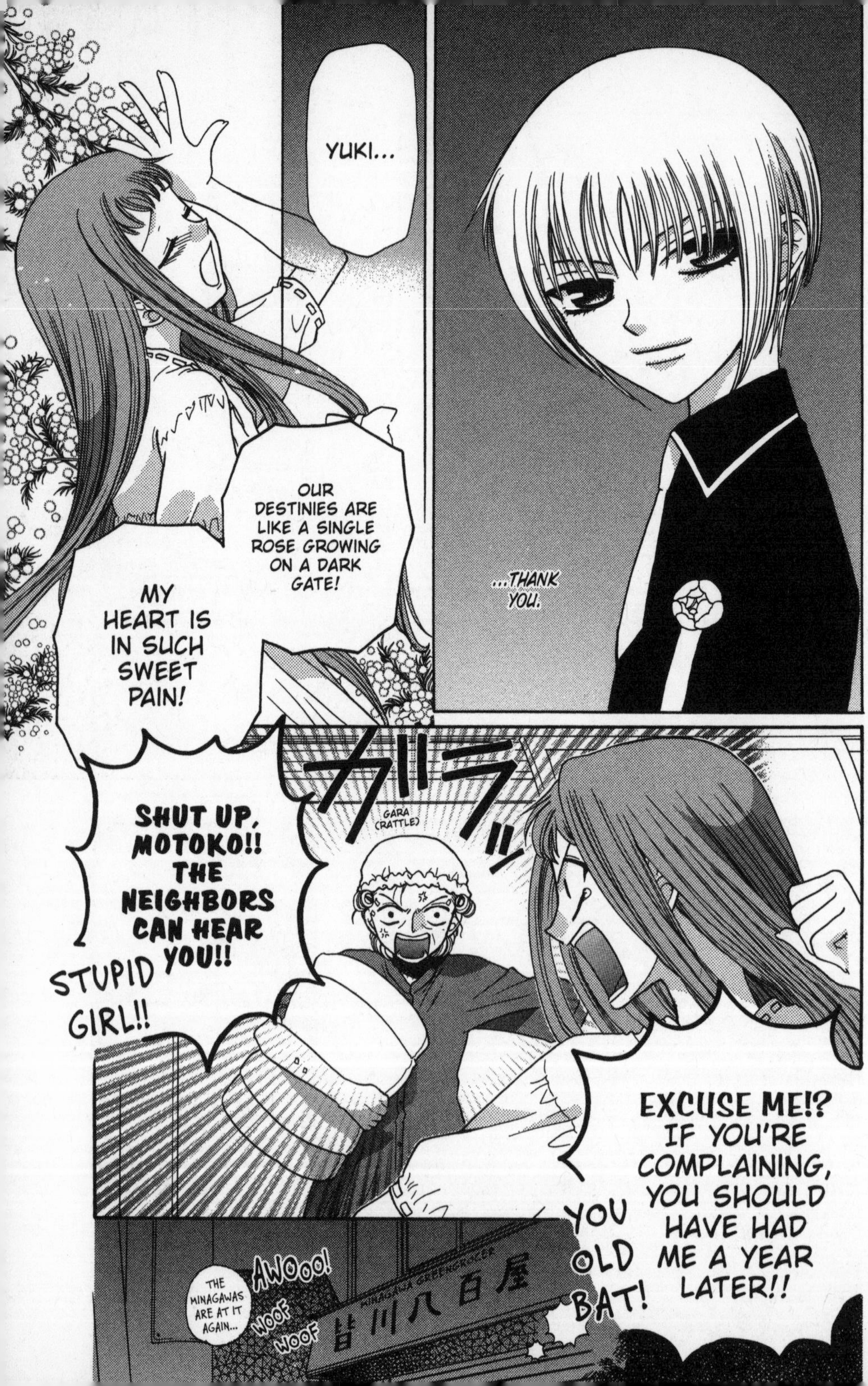
...THANK YOU.
YUKI...
OUR DESTINIES ARE LIKE A SINGLE ROSE GROWING ON A DARK GATE!
MY HEART IS IN SUCH SWEET PAIN!
ガラッ
GARA (RATTLE)
SHUT UP, MOTOKO!! THE NEIGHBORS CAN HEAR YOU!!
STUPID GIRL!!
EXCUSE ME!? IF YOU'RE COMPLAINING, YOU SHOULD HAVE HAD ME A YEAR LATER!!
YOU OLD BAT!
MINAGAWA GREENGROCER
皆川八百屋
AWOOO!
WOOF
WOOF
THE MINAGAWAS ARE AT IT AGAIN...

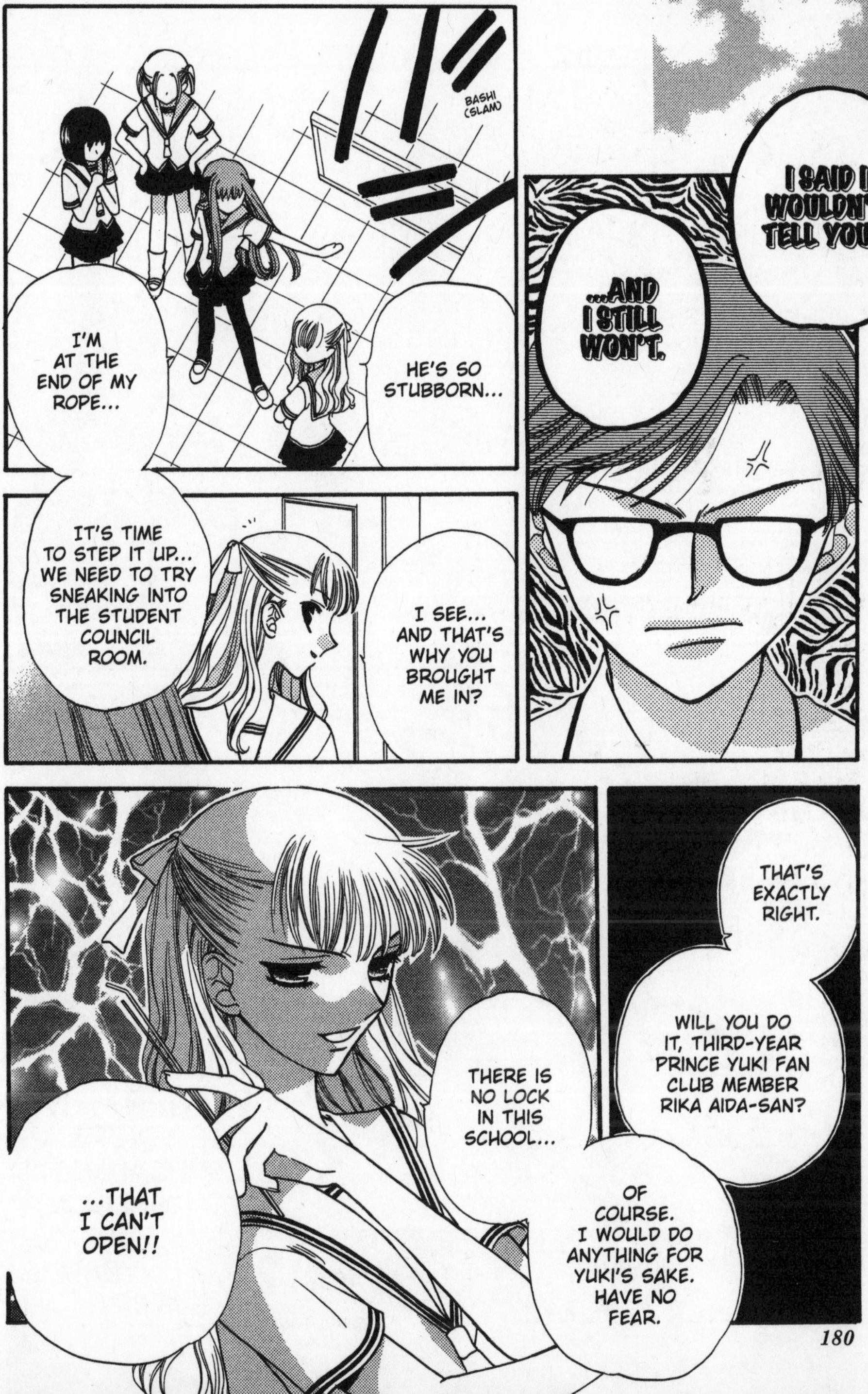
I SAID I WOULDN'T TELL YOU...
...AND I STILL WON'T.
BASHI (SLAM)
HE'S SO STUBBORN...
I'M AT THE END OF MY ROPE...
IT'S TIME TO STEP IT UP... WE NEED TO TRY SNEAKING INTO THE STUDENT COUNCIL ROOM.
I SEE... AND THAT'S WHY YOU BROUGHT ME IN?
THAT'S EXACTLY RIGHT.
WILL YOU DO IT, THIRD-YEAR PRINCE YUKI FAN CLUB MEMBER RIKA AIDA-SAN?
OF COURSE. I WOULD DO ANYTHING FOR YUKI'S SAKE. HAVE NO FEAR.
THERE IS NO LOCK IN THIS SCHOOL...
...THAT I CAN'T OPEN!!

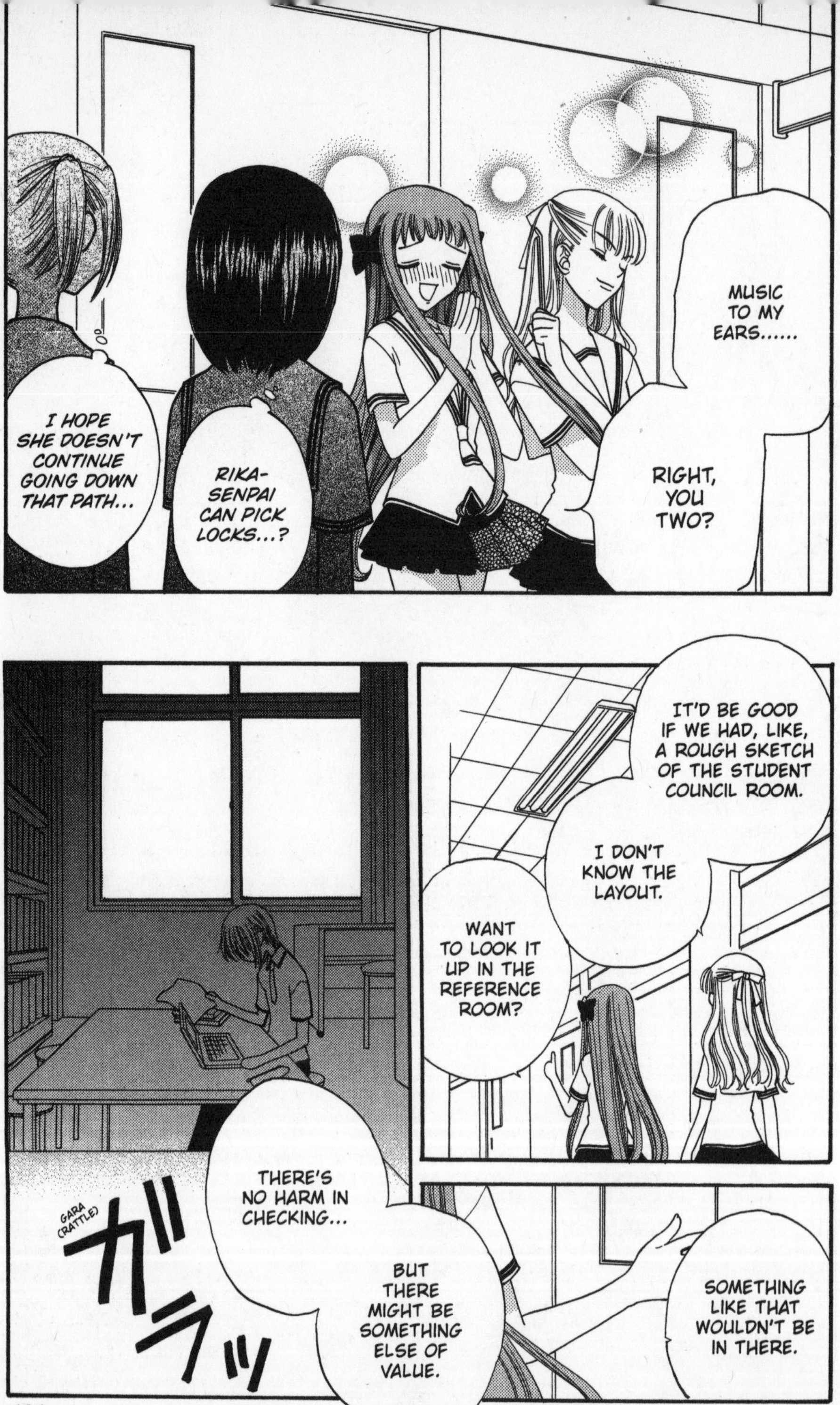
MUSIC TO MY EARS......
RIGHT, YOU TWO?
RIKA-SENPAI CAN PICK LOCKS...?
I HOPE SHE DOESN'T CONTINUE GOING DOWN THAT PATH...
IT'D BE GOOD IF WE HAD, LIKE, A ROUGH SKETCH OF THE STUDENT COUNCIL ROOM.
I DON'T KNOW THE LAYOUT.
WANT TO LOOK IT UP IN THE REFERENCE ROOM?
SOMETHING LIKE THAT WOULDN'T BE IN THERE.
BUT THERE MIGHT BE SOMETHING ELSE OF VALUE.
THERE'S NO HARM IN CHECKING...
GARA (RATTLE)
ガラッ

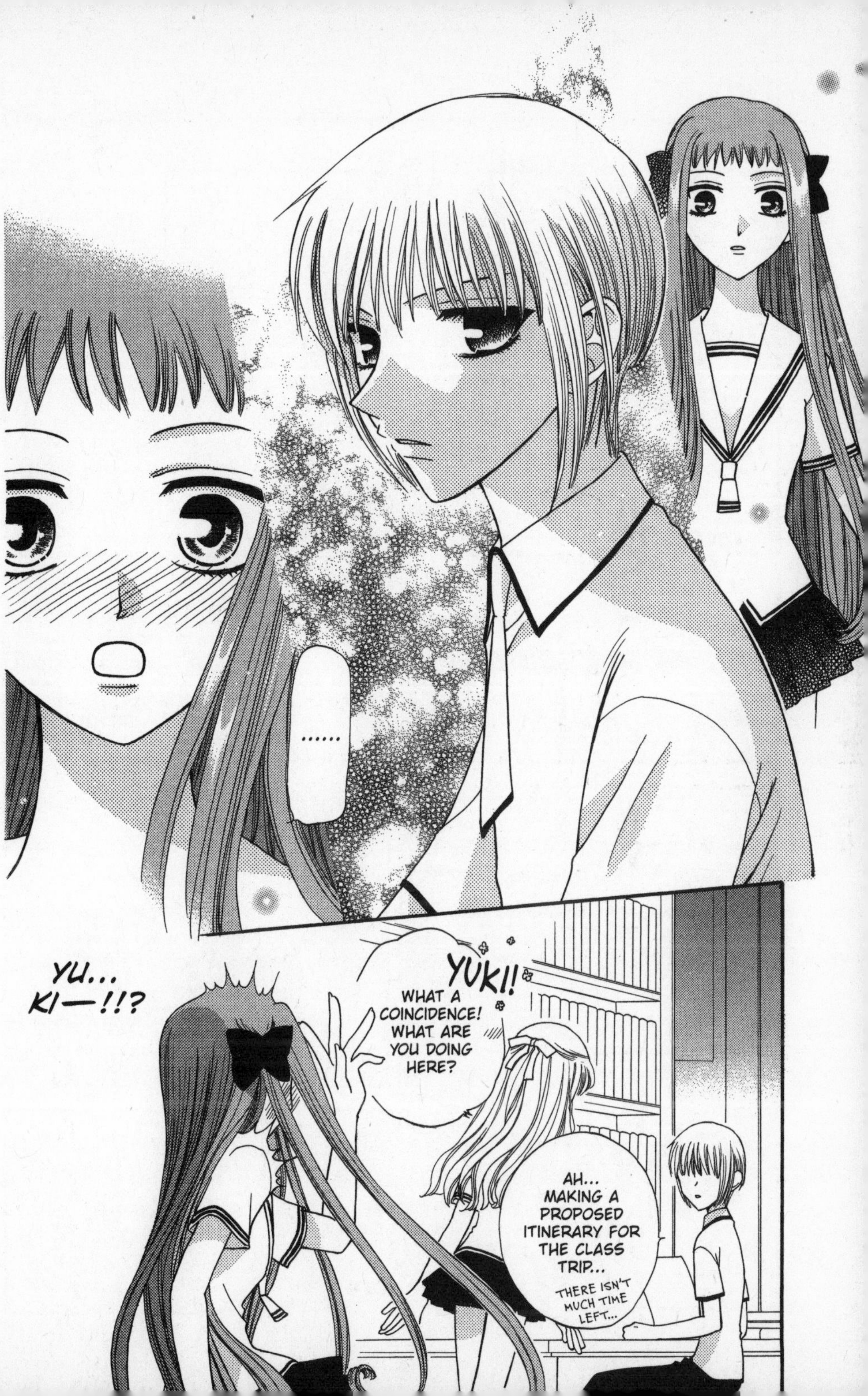
......
YUKI!
WHAT A COINCIDENCE! WHAT ARE YOU DOING HERE?
AH... MAKING A PROPOSED ITINERARY FOR THE CLASS TRIP...
THERE ISN'T MUCH TIME LEFT...
YU... KI—!!?

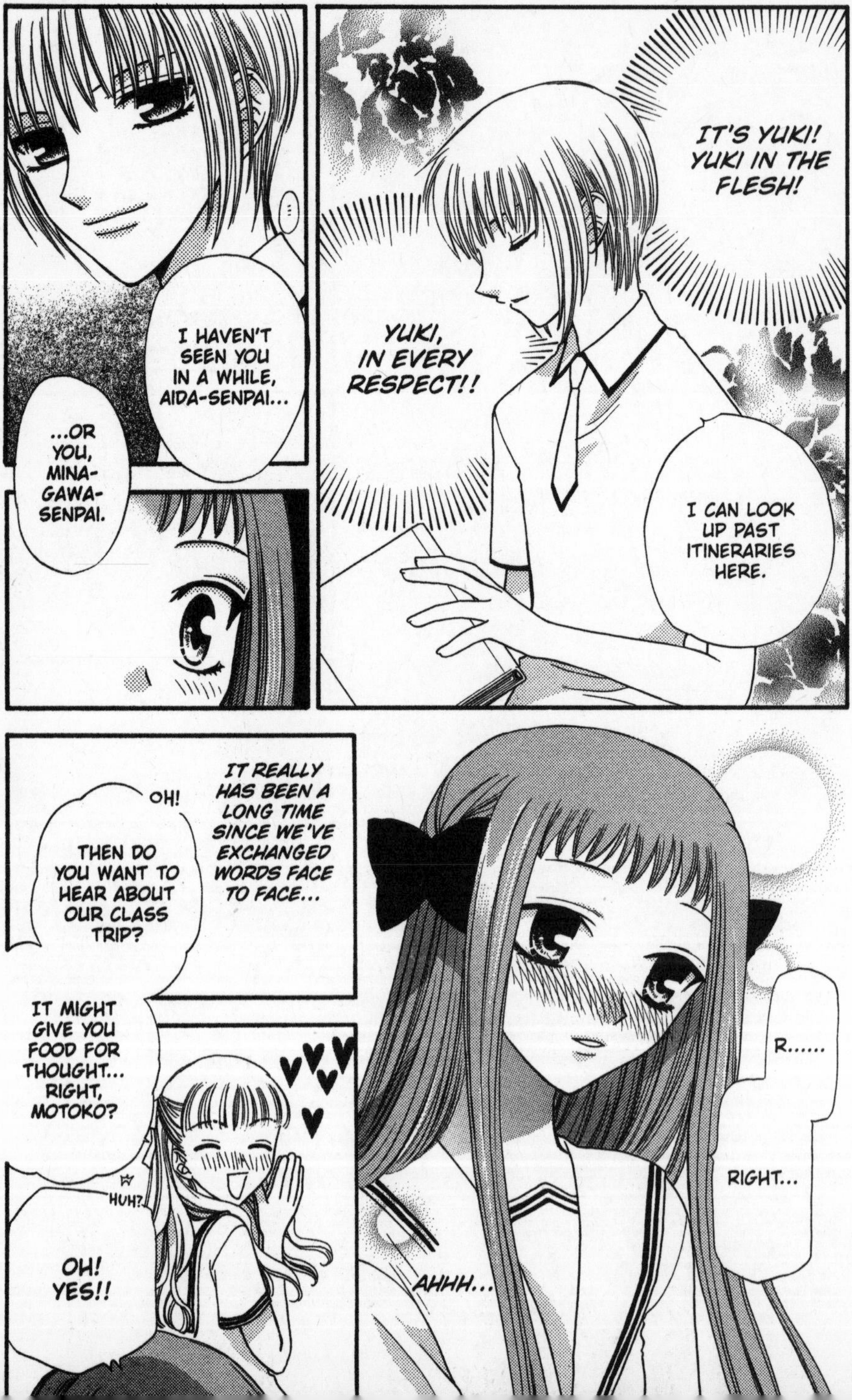
IT'S YUKI! YUKI IN THE FLESH!
YUKI, IN EVERY RESPECT!!
I CAN LOOK UP PAST ITINERARIES HERE.
I HAVEN'T SEEN YOU IN A WHILE, AIDA-SENPAI...
...OR YOU, MINA-GAWA-SENPAI.
R......
RIGHT...
AHHH...
IT REALLY HAS BEEN A LONG TIME SINCE WE'VE EXCHANGED WORDS FACE TO FACE...
OH!
THEN DO YOU WANT TO HEAR ABOUT OUR CLASS TRIP?
IT MIGHT GIVE YOU FOOD FOR THOUGHT... RIGHT, MOTOKO?
HUH?
OH! YES!!

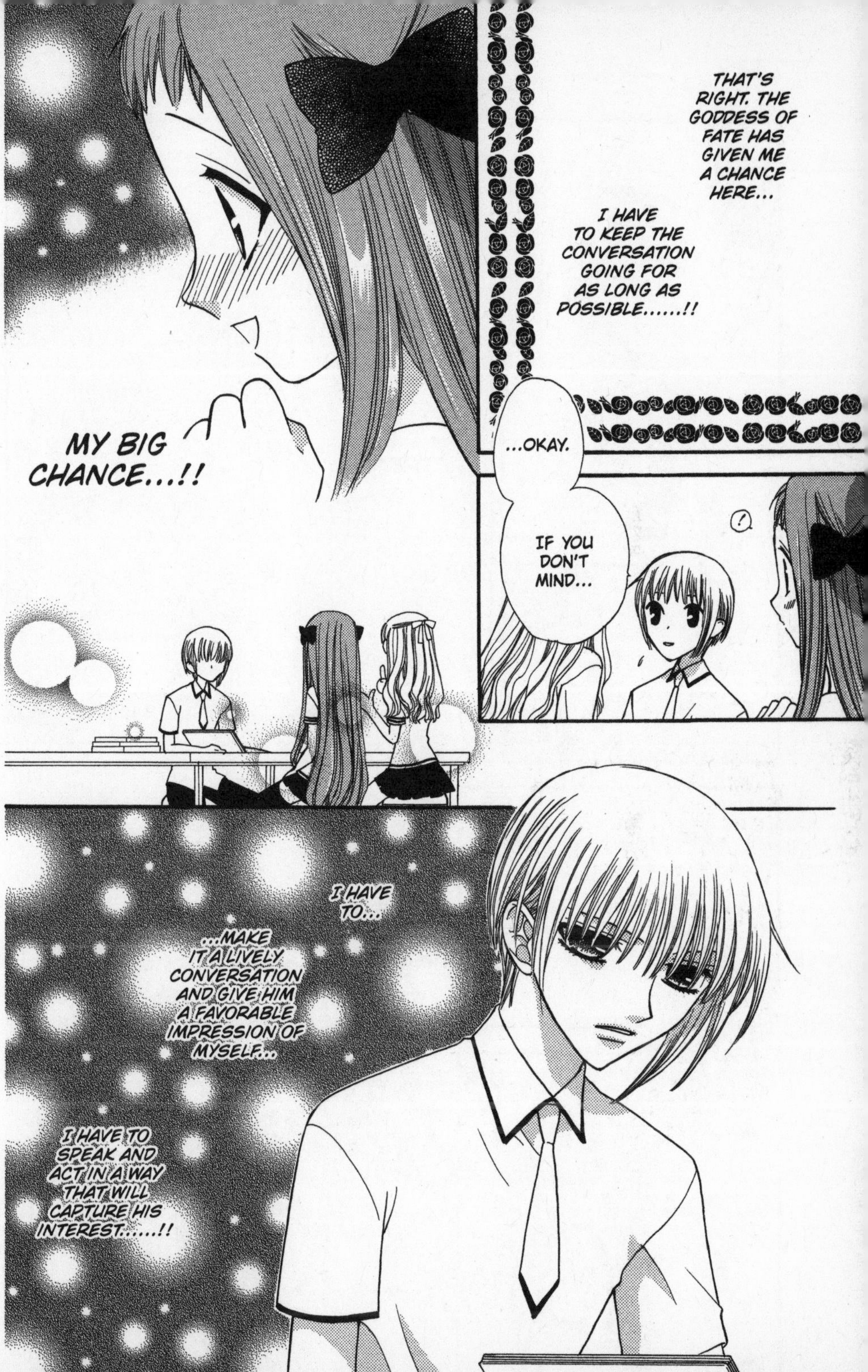
THAT'S RIGHT. THE GODDESS OF FATE HAS GIVEN ME A CHANCE HERE...
I HAVE TO KEEP THE CONVERSATION GOING FOR AS LONG AS POSSIBLE......!!
...OKAY.
IF YOU DON'T MIND...
!
MY BIG CHANCE...!!
I HAVE TO...
...MAKE IT A LIVELY CONVERSATION AND GIVE HIM A FAVORABLE IMPRESSION OF MYSELF...
I HAVE TO SPEAK AND ACT IN A WAY THAT WILL CAPTURE HIS INTEREST......!!

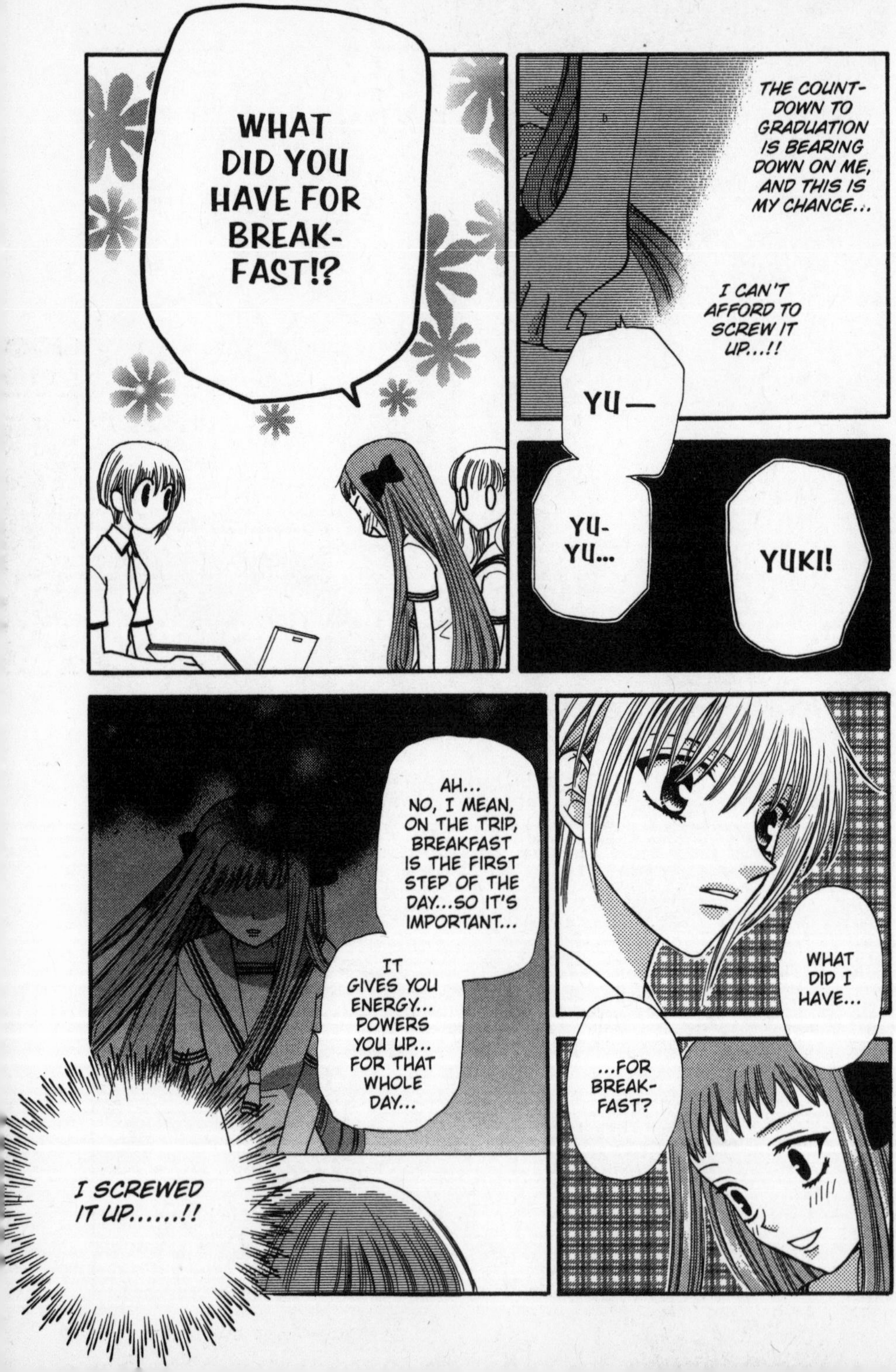
THE COUNT-DOWN TO GRADUATION IS BEARING DOWN ON ME, AND THIS IS MY CHANCE...
I CAN'T AFFORD TO SCREW IT UP...!!
YU—
YU-YU...
YUKI!
WHAT DID YOU HAVE FOR BREAK-FAST!?
WHAT DID I HAVE...
...FOR BREAK-FAST?
AH... NO, I MEAN, ON THE TRIP, BREAKFAST IS THE FIRST STEP OF THE DAY...SO IT'S IMPORTANT...
IT GIVES YOU ENERGY... POWERS YOU UP... FOR THAT WHOLE DAY...
I SCREWED IT UP......!!

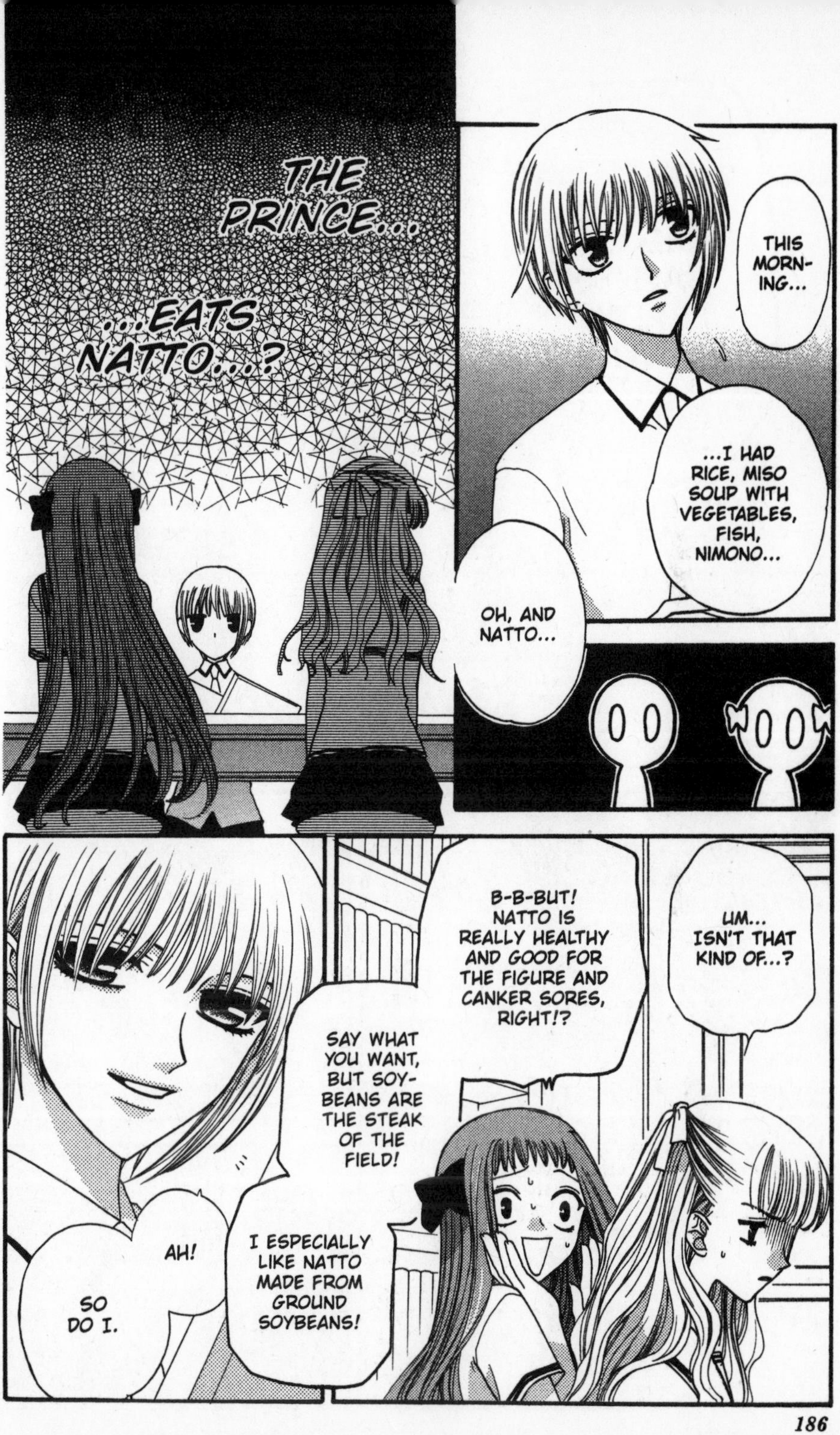
THIS MORNING-ING...
...I HAD RICE, MISO SOUP WITH VEGETABLES, FISH, NIMONO...
OH, AND NATTO...
THE PRINCE...
...EATS NATTO...?
UM... ISN'T THAT KIND OF...?
B-B-BUT! NATTO IS REALLY HEALTHY AND GOOD FOR THE FIGURE AND CANKER SORES, RIGHT!?
SAY WHAT YOU WANT, BUT SOY-BEANS ARE THE STEAK OF THE FIELD!
I ESPECIALLY LIKE NATTO MADE FROM GROUND SOYBEANS!
AH!
SO DO I.

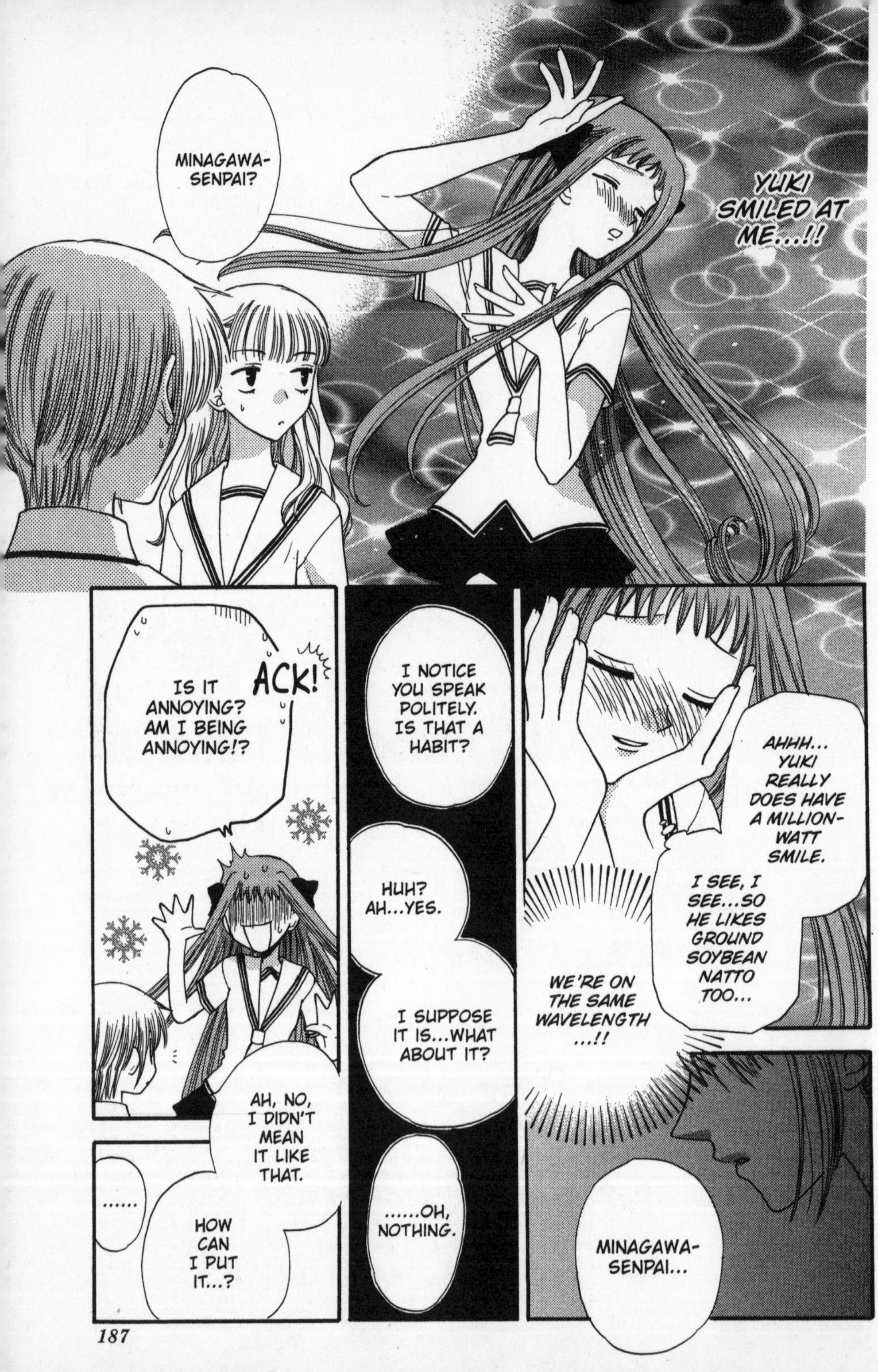

YUKI SMILED AT ME...!!
MINAGAWA-SENPAI?
AHHH... YUKI REALLY DOES HAVE A MILLION-WATT SMILE.
I SEE, I SEE...SO HE LIKES GROUND SOYBEAN NATTO TOO...
WE'RE ON THE SAME WAVELENGTH...!!
MINAGAWA-SENPAI...
I NOTICE YOU SPEAK POLITELY. IS THAT A HABIT?
HUH? AH...YES.
I SUPPOSE IT IS...WHAT ABOUT IT?
......OH, NOTHING.
ACK!
IS IT ANNOYING? AM I BEING ANNOYING!?
AH, NO, I DIDN'T MEAN IT LIKE THAT.
HOW CAN I PUT IT...?
......

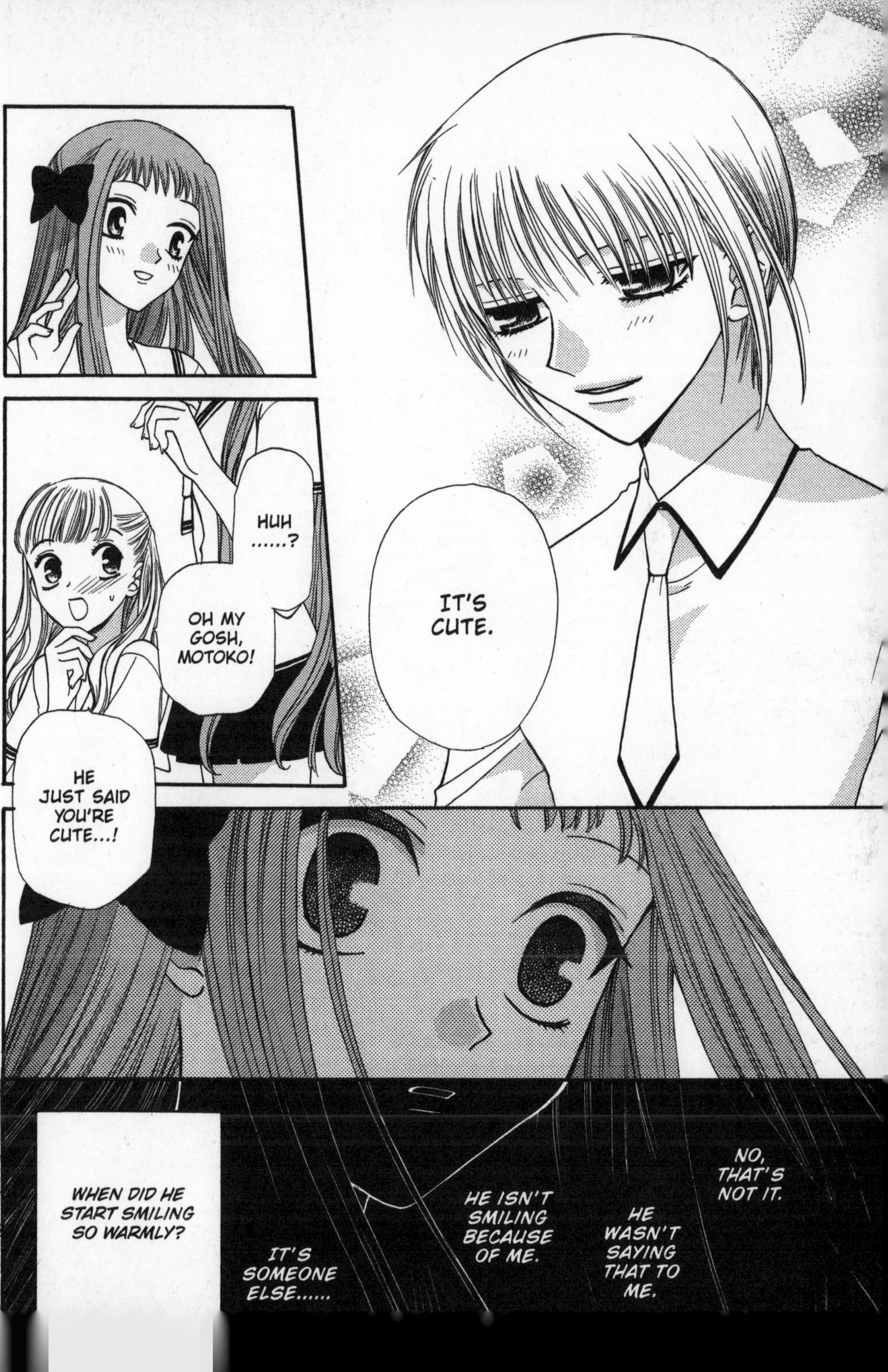
IT'S CUTE.
HUH ......?
OH MY GOSH, MOTOKO!
HE JUST SAID YOU'RE CUTE...!
NO, THAT'S NOT IT.
HE ISN'T SMILING BECAUSE OF ME.
HE WASN'T SAYING THAT TO ME.
IT'S SOMEONE ELSE......
WHEN DID HE START SMILING SO WARMLY?

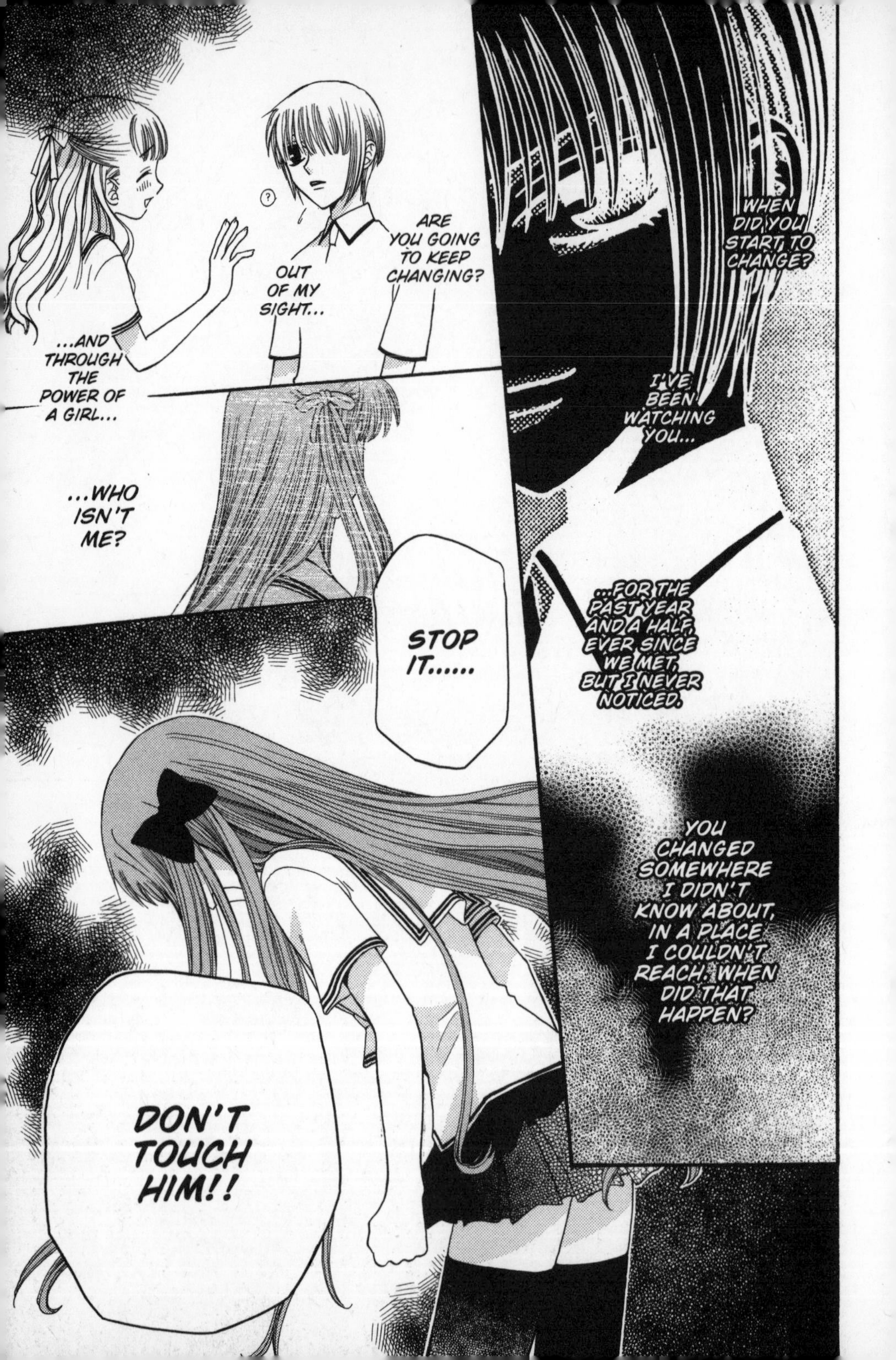
WHEN DID YOU START TO CHANGE?
I'VE BEEN WATCHING YOU...
...FOR THE PAST YEAR AND A HALF, EVER SINCE WE MET, BUT I NEVER NOTICED.
YOU CHANGED SOMEWHERE I DIDN'T KNOW ABOUT, IN A PLACE I COULDN'T REACH. WHEN DID THAT HAPPEN?
ARE YOU GOING TO KEEP CHANGING?
?
OUT OF MY SIGHT...
...AND THROUGH THE POWER OF A GIRL...
...WHO ISN'T ME?
STOP IT......
DON'T TOUCH HIM!!

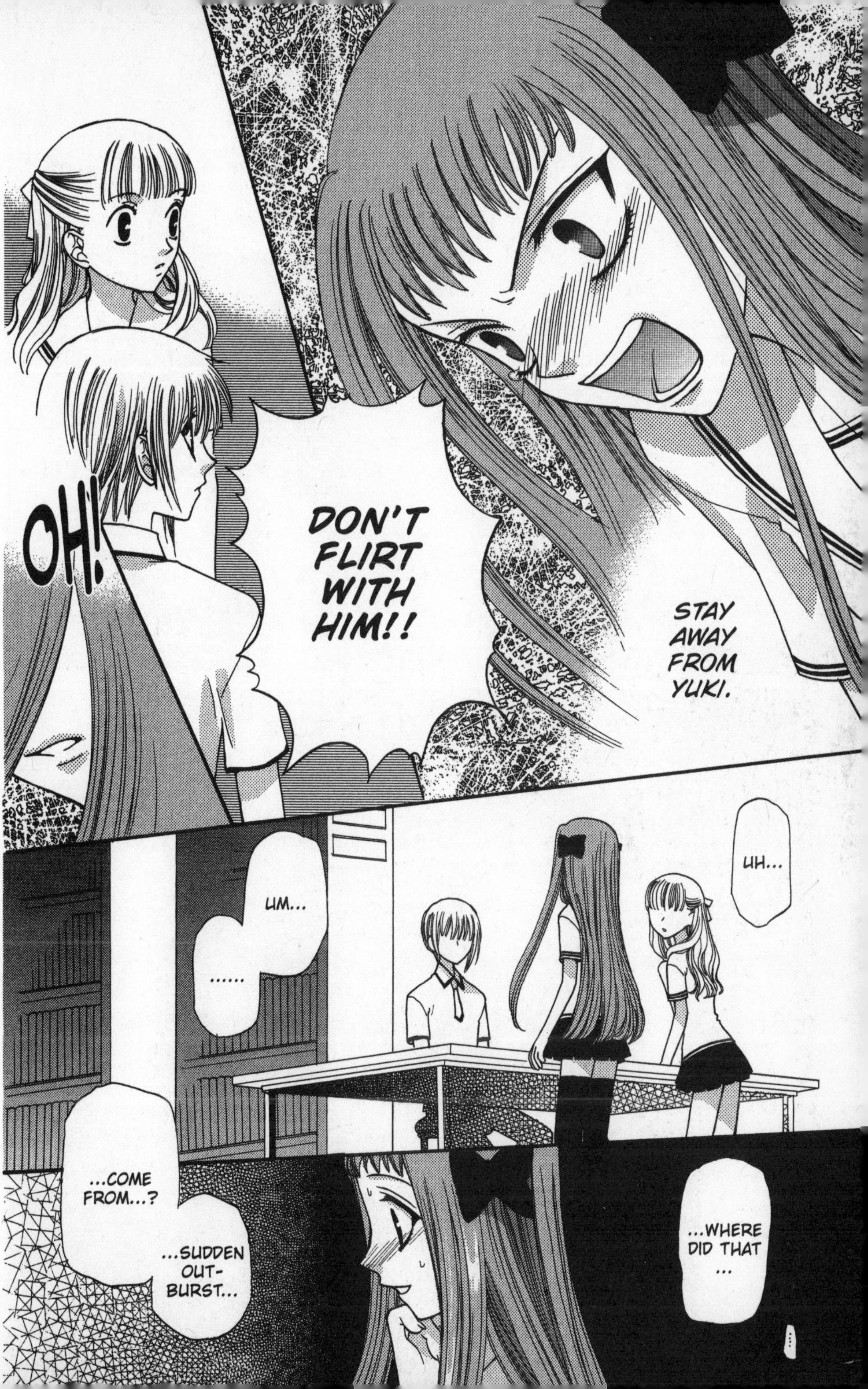
STAY AWAY FROM YUKI.
DON'T FLIRT WITH HIM!!
OH!
UH...
UM...
......
...WHERE DID THAT ...
...SUDDEN OUT-BURST...
...COME FROM...?
...

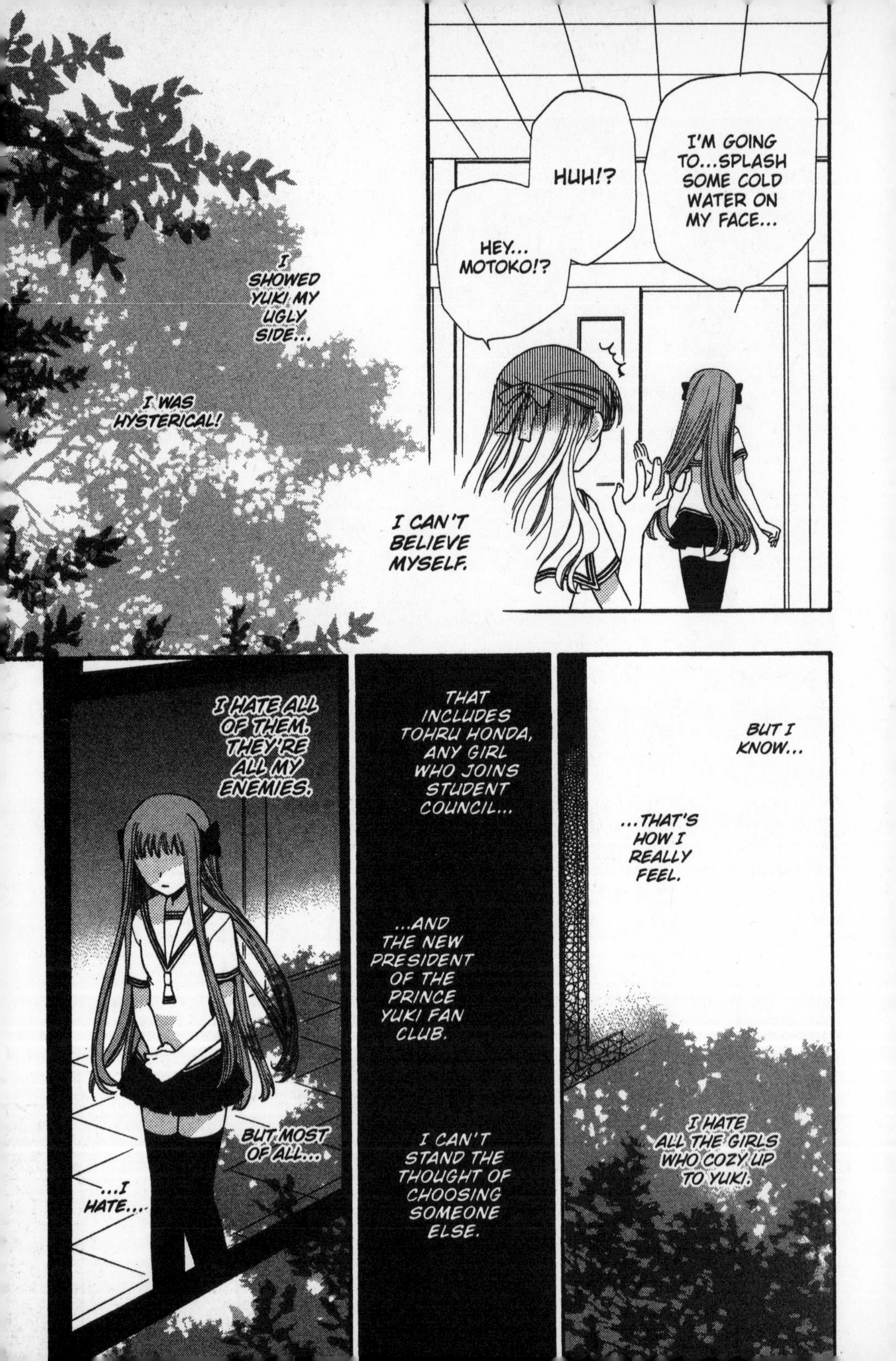
I'M GOING TO...SPLASH SOME COLD WATER ON MY FACE...
HUH!?
HEY... MOTOKO!?
I CAN'T BELIEVE MYSELF.
I SHOWED YUKI MY UGLY SIDE...
I WAS HYSTERICAL!
BUT I KNOW...
...THAT'S HOW I REALLY FEEL.
I HATE ALL THE GIRLS WHO COZY UP TO YUKI.
THAT INCLUDES TOHRU HONDA, ANY GIRL WHO JOINS STUDENT COUNCIL...
...AND THE NEW PRESIDENT OF THE PRINCE YUKI FAN CLUB.
I CAN'T STAND THE THOUGHT OF CHOOSING SOMEONE ELSE.
I HATE ALL OF THEM. THEY'RE ALL MY ENEMIES.
BUT MOST OF ALL...
...I HATE...

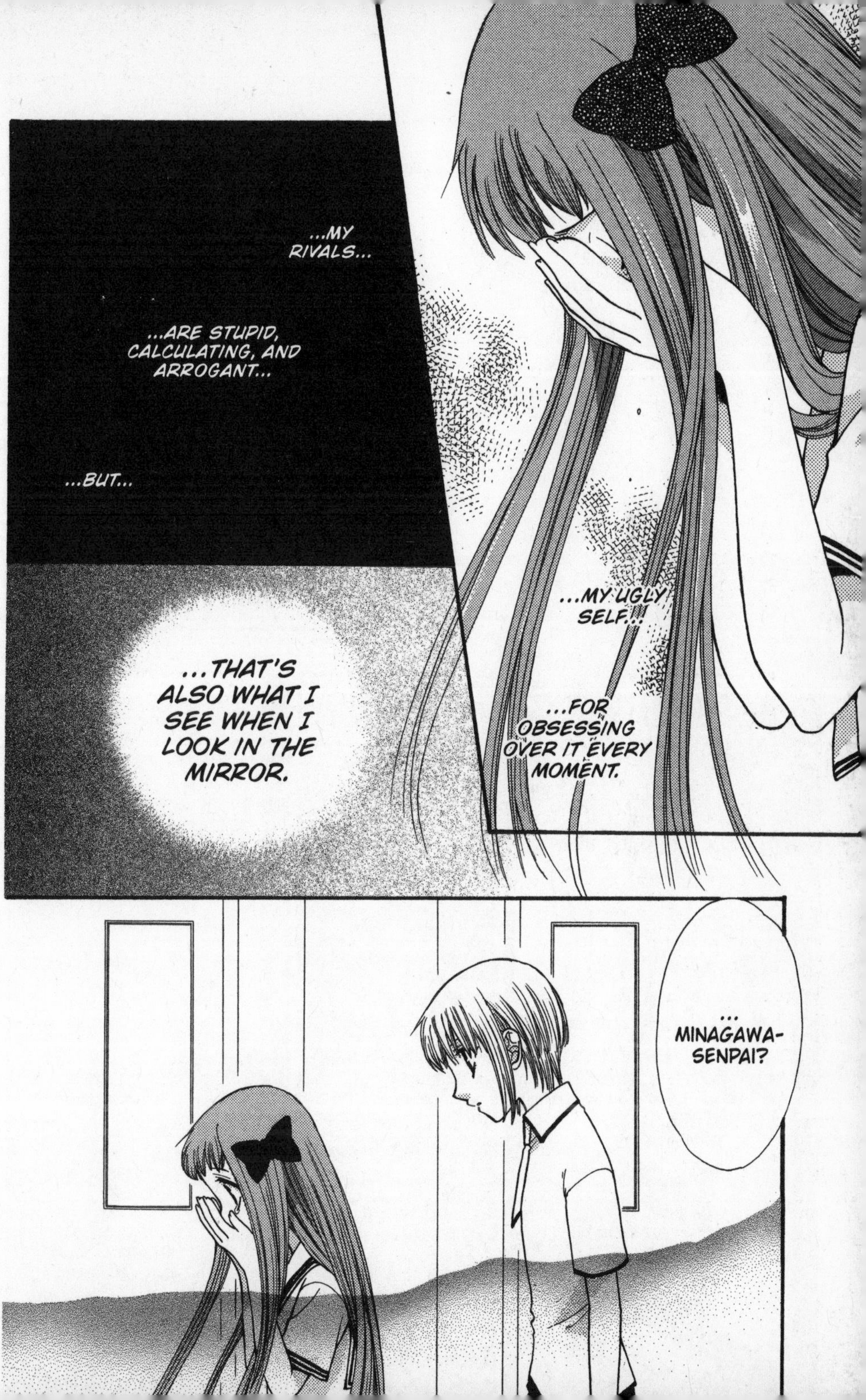
...MY UGLY SELF...
...FOR OBSESSING OVER IT EVERY MOMENT.
...MY RIVALS...
...ARE STUPID, CALCULATING, AND ARROGANT...
...BUT...
...THAT'S ALSO WHAT I SEE WHEN I LOOK IN THE MIRROR.
... MINAGAWA-SENPAI?

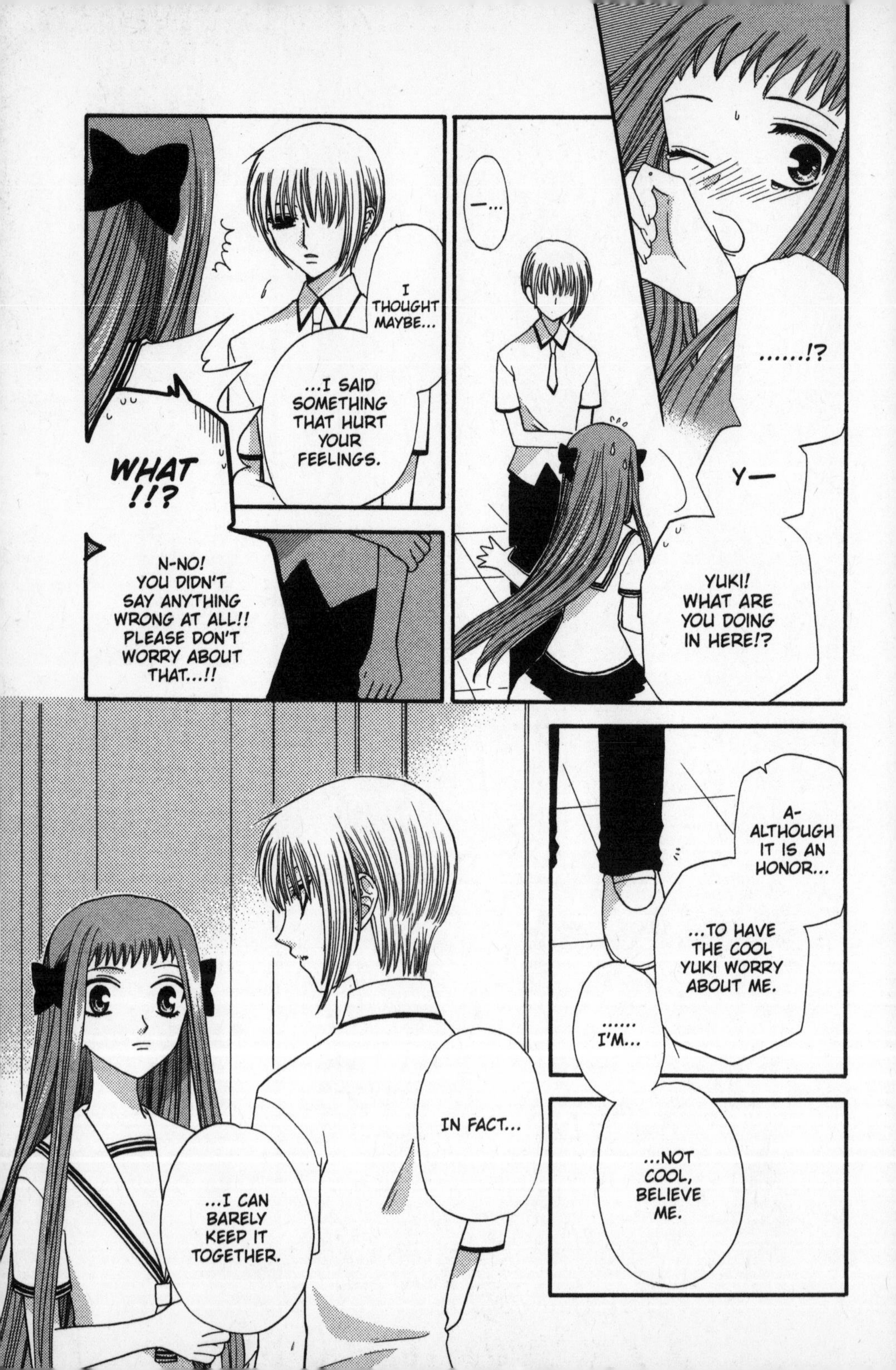
......!?
Y—
YUKI! WHAT ARE YOU DOING IN HERE!?
—...
I THOUGHT MAYBE...
...I SAID SOMETHING THAT HURT YOUR FEELINGS.
WHAT!!?
N-NO! YOU DIDN'T SAY ANYTHING WRONG AT ALL!! PLEASE DON'T WORRY ABOUT THAT...!!
A-ALTHOUGH IT IS AN HONOR...
...TO HAVE THE COOL YUKI WORRY ABOUT ME.
...... I'M...
...NOT COOL, BELIEVE ME.
IN FACT...
...I CAN BARELY KEEP IT TOGETHER.

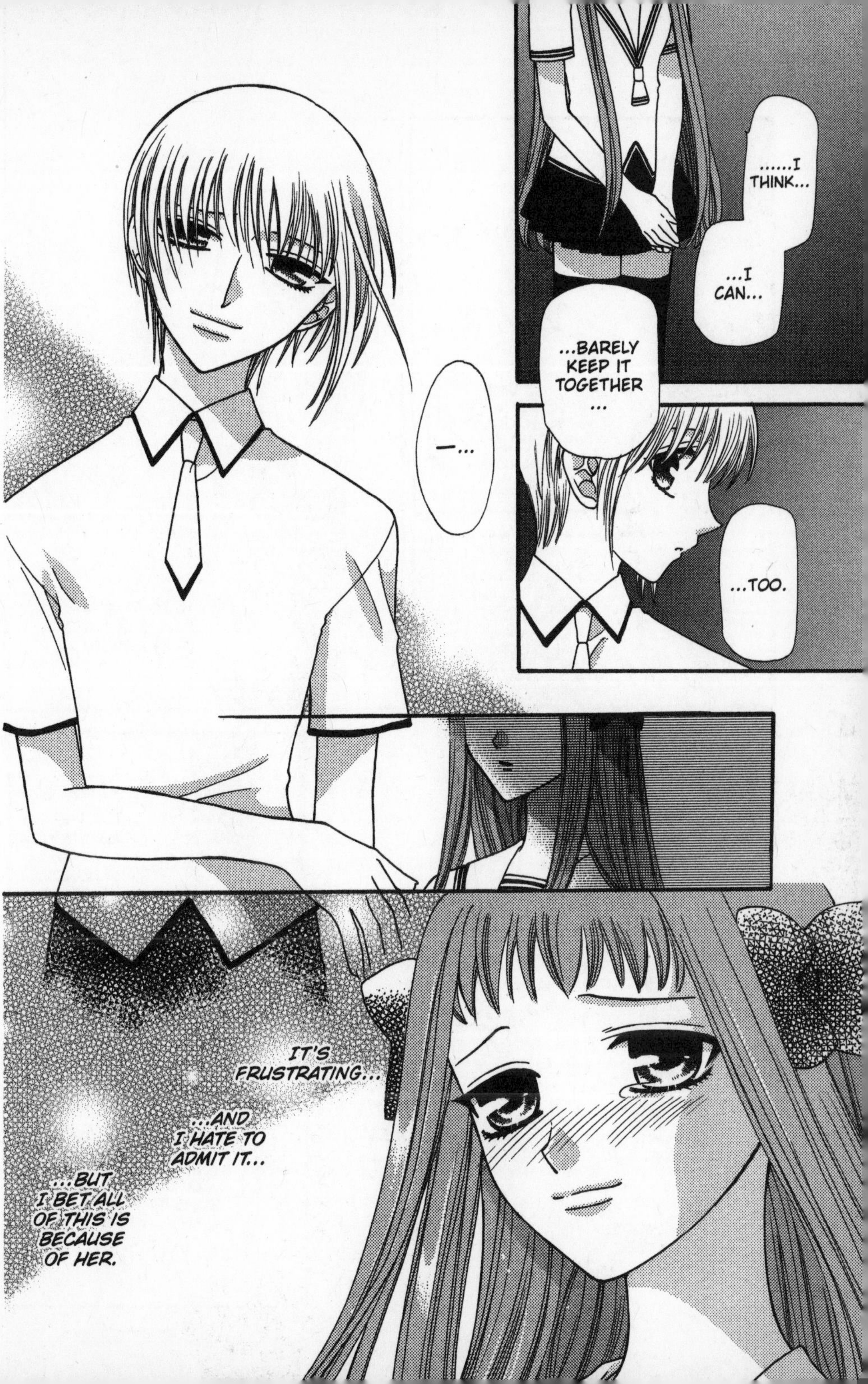
......I THINK...
...I CAN...
...BARELY KEEP IT TOGETHER ...
...TOO.
—...
IT'S FRUSTRATING...
...AND I HATE TO ADMIT IT...
...BUT I BET ALL OF THIS IS BECAUSE OF HER.

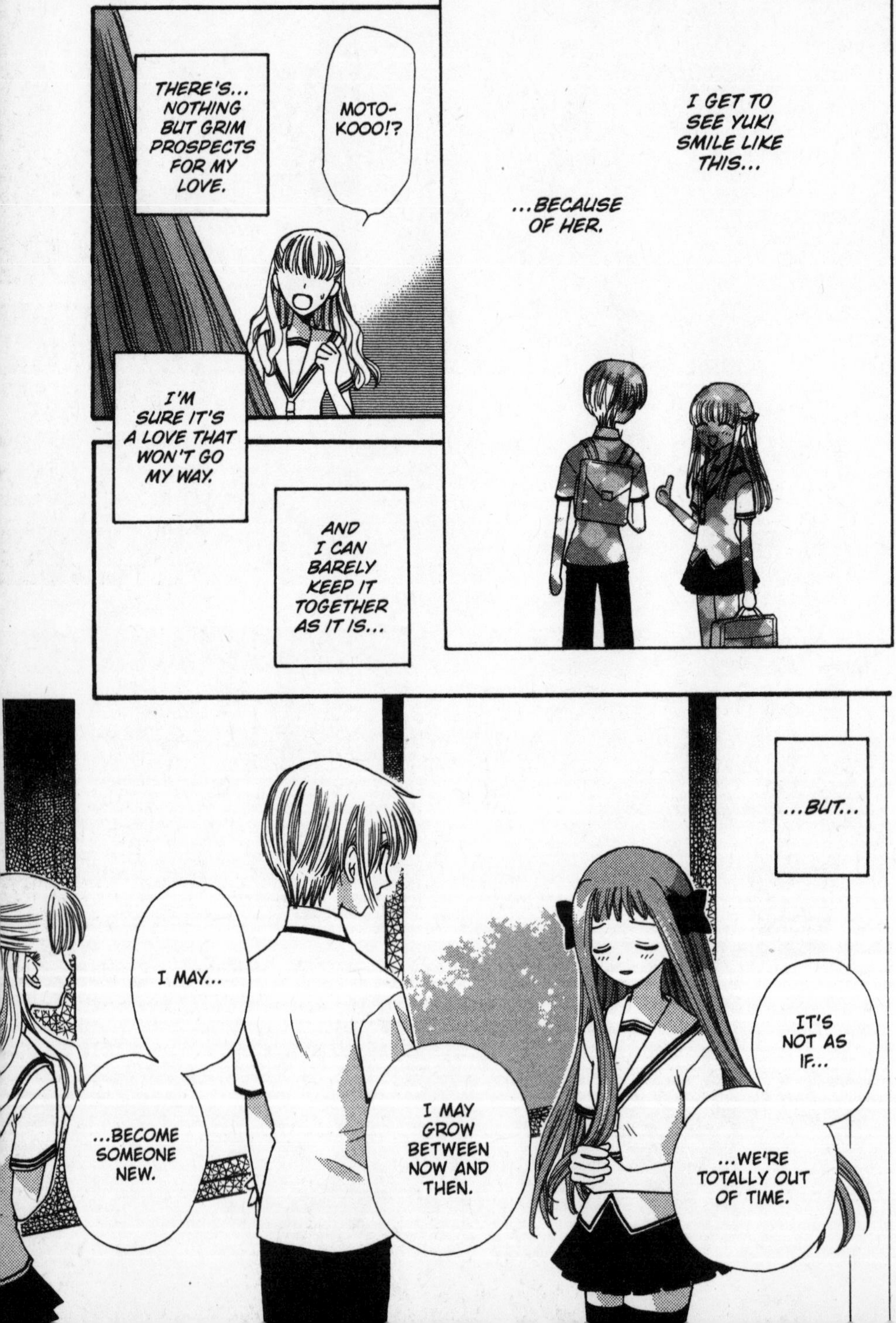
I GET TO SEE YUKI SMILE LIKE THIS...
...BECAUSE OF HER.
MOTO-KOOO!?
THERE'S... NOTHING BUT GRIM PROSPECTS FOR MY LOVE.
I'M SURE IT'S A LOVE THAT WON'T GO MY WAY.
AND I CAN BARELY KEEP IT TOGETHER AS IT IS...
...BUT...
IT'S NOT AS IF...
...WE'RE TOTALLY OUT OF TIME.
I MAY GROW BETWEEN NOW AND THEN.
I MAY...
...BECOME SOMEONE NEW.

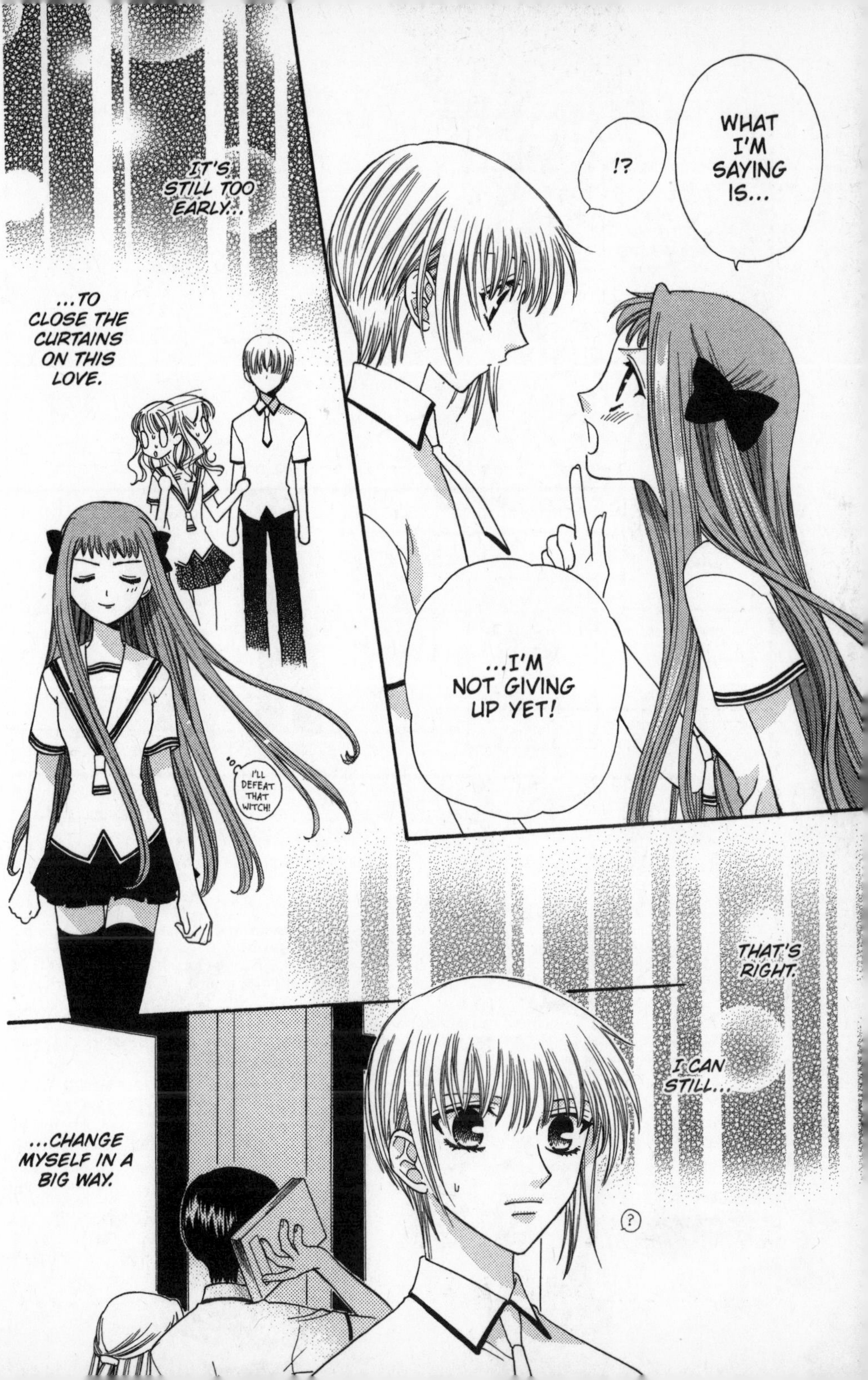

!?
WHAT I'M SAYING IS...
...I'M NOT GIVING UP YET!
IT'S STILL TOO EARLY...
...TO CLOSE THE CURTAINS ON THIS LOVE.
I'LL DEFEAT THAT WITCH!
THAT'S RIGHT.
I CAN STILL...
?
...CHANGE MYSELF IN A BIG WAY.

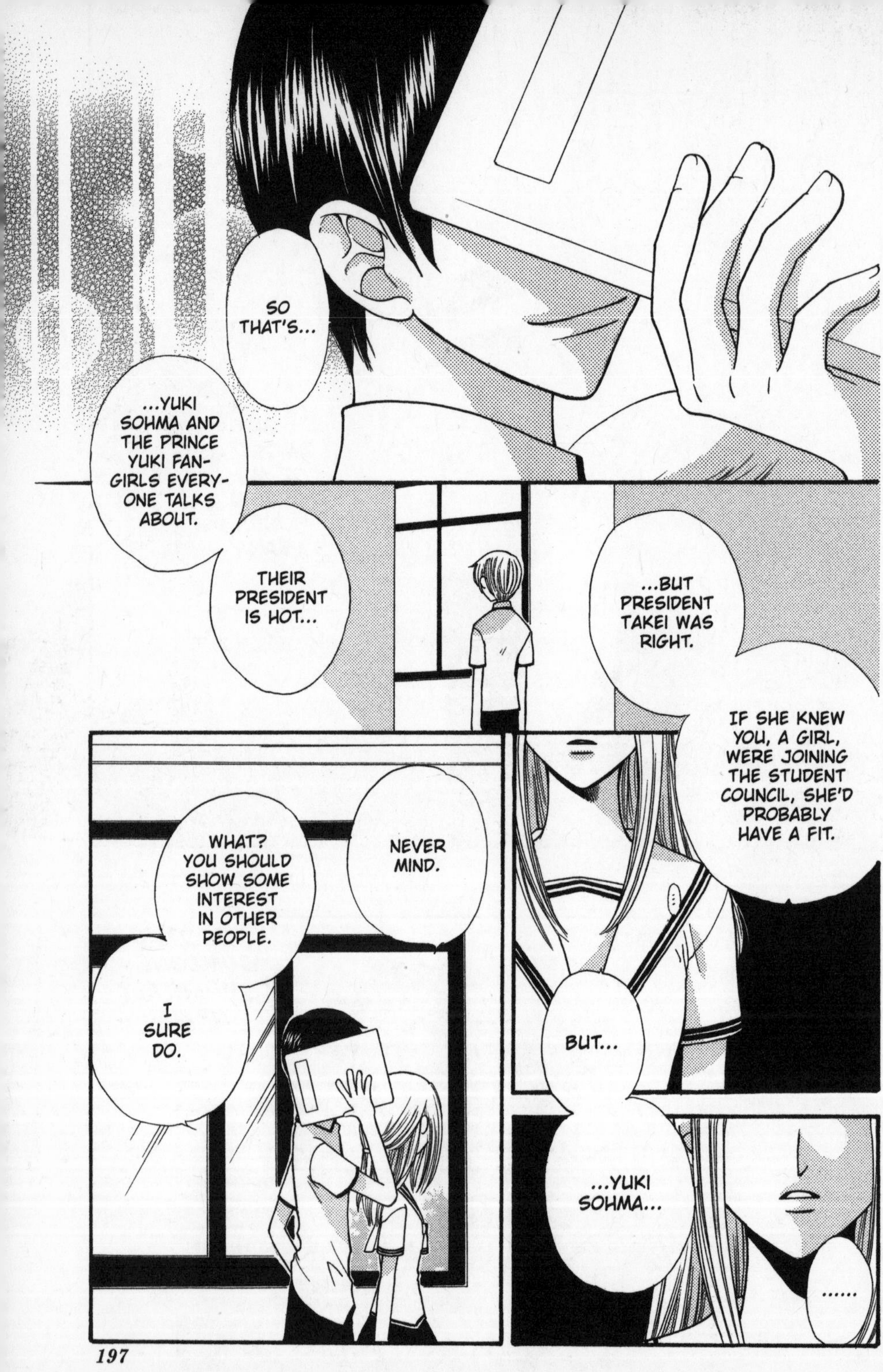
SO THAT'S...
...YUKI SOHMA AND THE PRINCE YUKI FAN-GIRLS EVERY-ONE TALKS ABOUT.
THEIR PRESIDENT IS HOT...
...BUT PRESIDENT TAKEI WAS RIGHT.
IF SHE KNEW YOU, A GIRL, WERE JOINING THE STUDENT COUNCIL, SHE'D PROBABLY HAVE A FIT.
BUT...
...YUKI SOHMA...
......
NEVER MIND.
WHAT? YOU SHOULD SHOW SOME INTEREST IN OTHER PEOPLE.
I SURE DO.

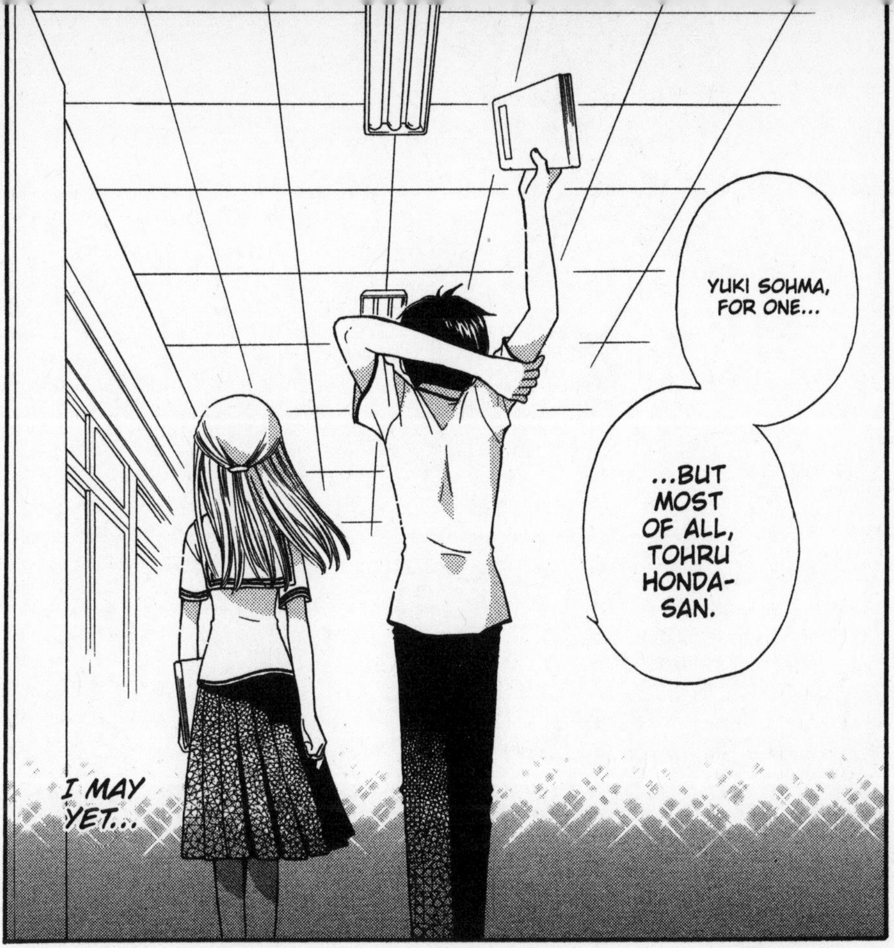
YUKI SOHMA, FOR ONE...
...BUT MOST OF ALL, TOHRU HONDA-SAN.
I MAY YET...

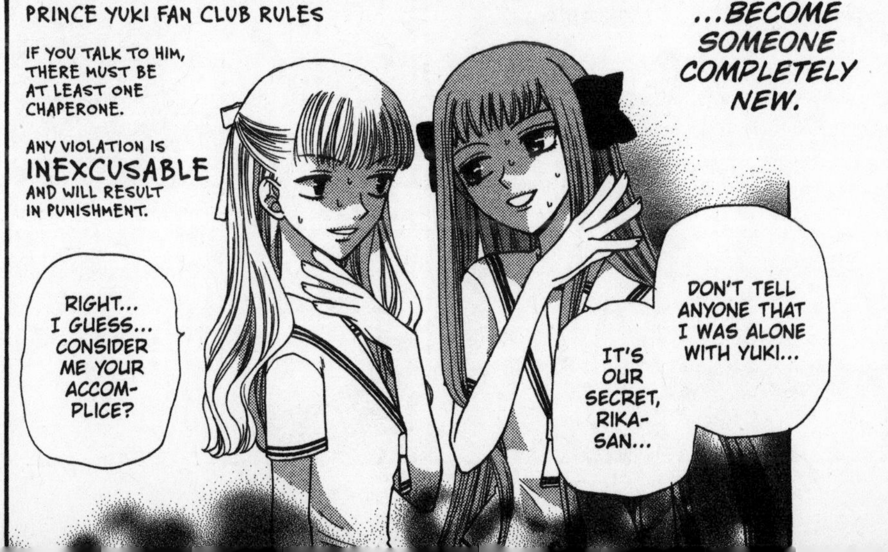
...BECOME SOMEONE COMPLETELY NEW.
PRINCE YUKI FAN CLUB RULES
IF YOU TALK TO HIM, THERE MUST BE AT LEAST ONE CHAPERONE.
ANY VIOLATION IS INEXCUSABLE AND WILL RESULT IN PUNISHMENT.
DON'T TELL ANYONE THAT I WAS ALONE WITH YUKI...
IT'S OUR SECRET, RIKA-SAN...
RIGHT... I GUESS... CONSIDER ME YOUR ACCOMPLICE?

COLLECTOR'S EDITION

Fruits Basket

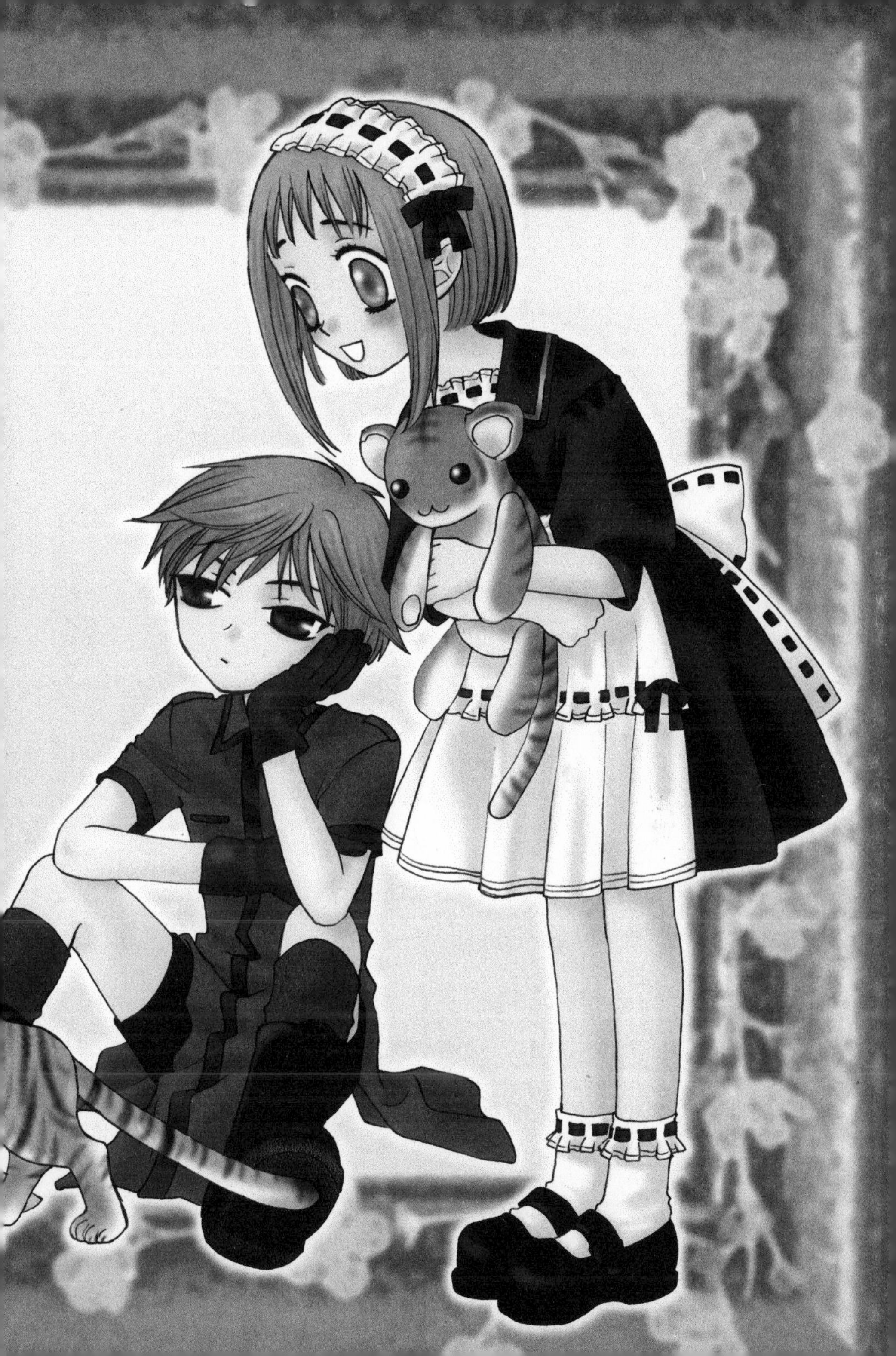

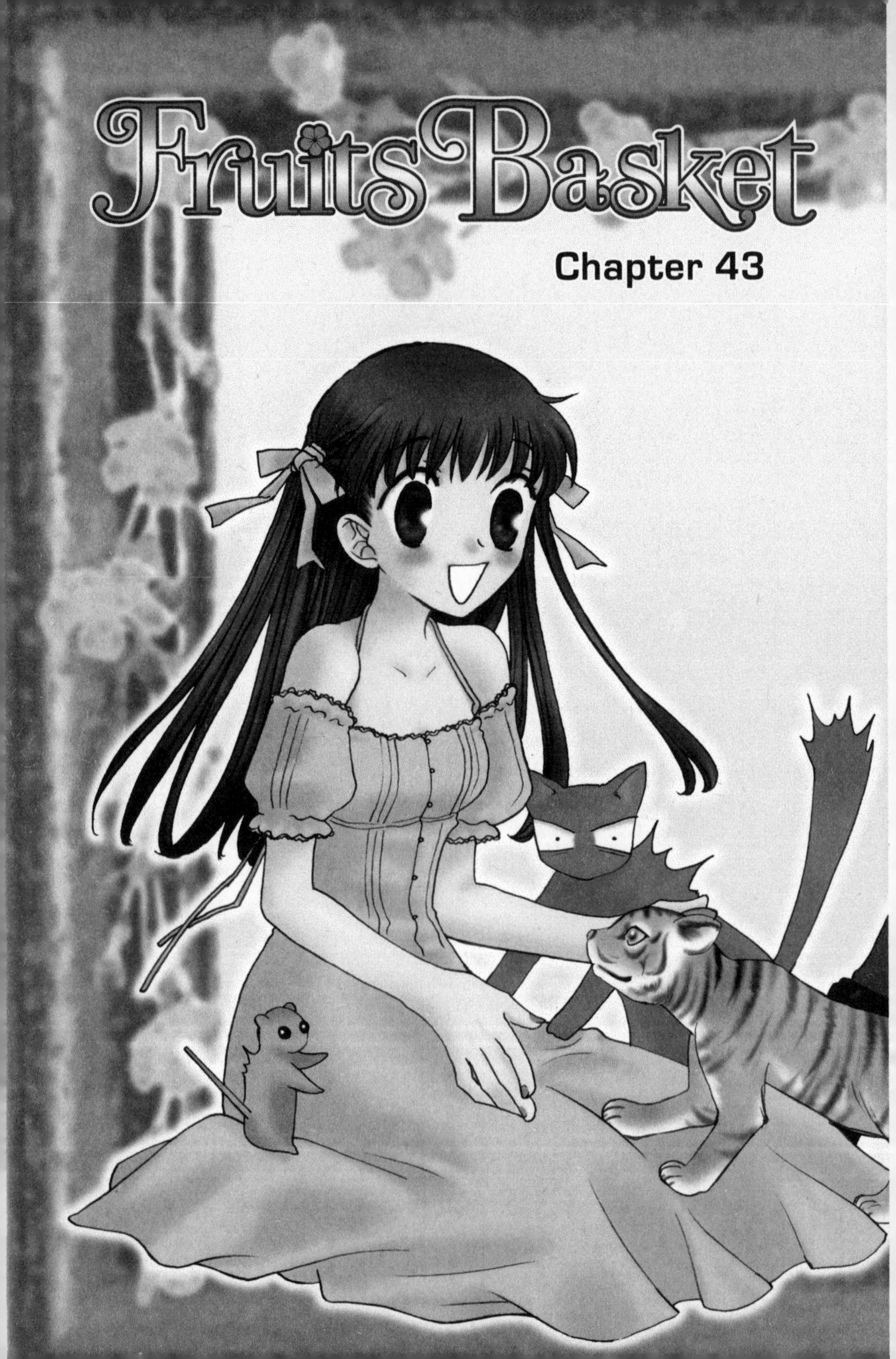
Fruits Basket
Chapter 43

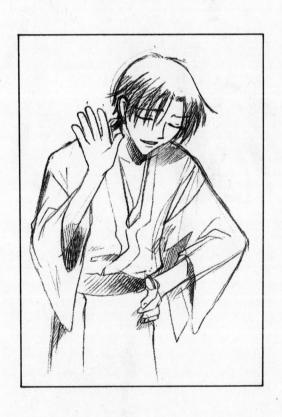

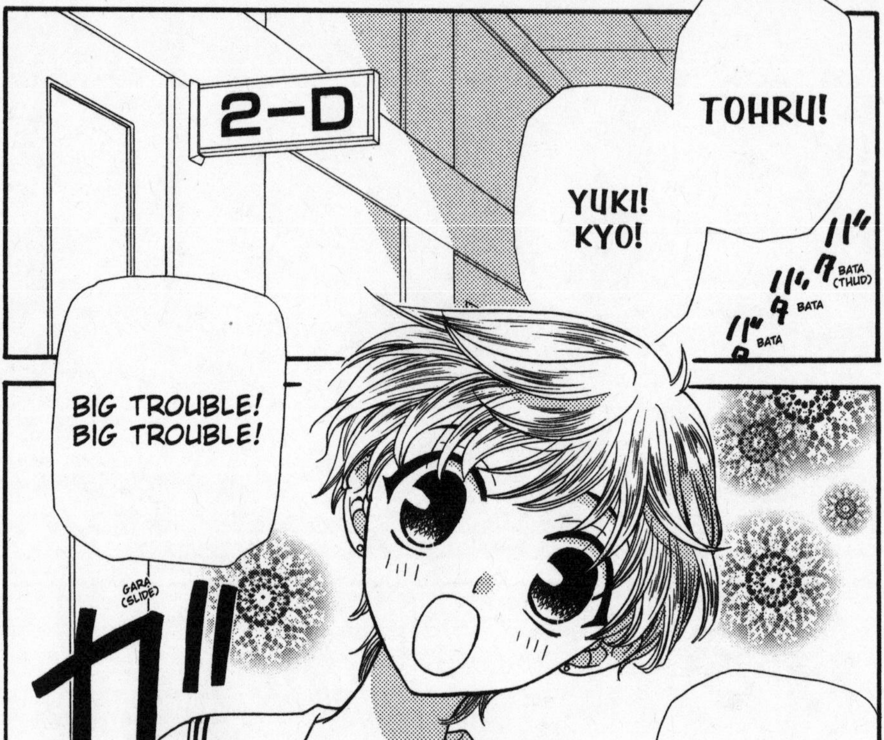
2-D
TOHRU!
YUKI! KYO!
BATA (THUD)
BATA
BATA
GARA (SLIDE)
BIG TROUBLE! BIG TROUBLE!
WE'VE GOT BIIIG TROUBLE!!

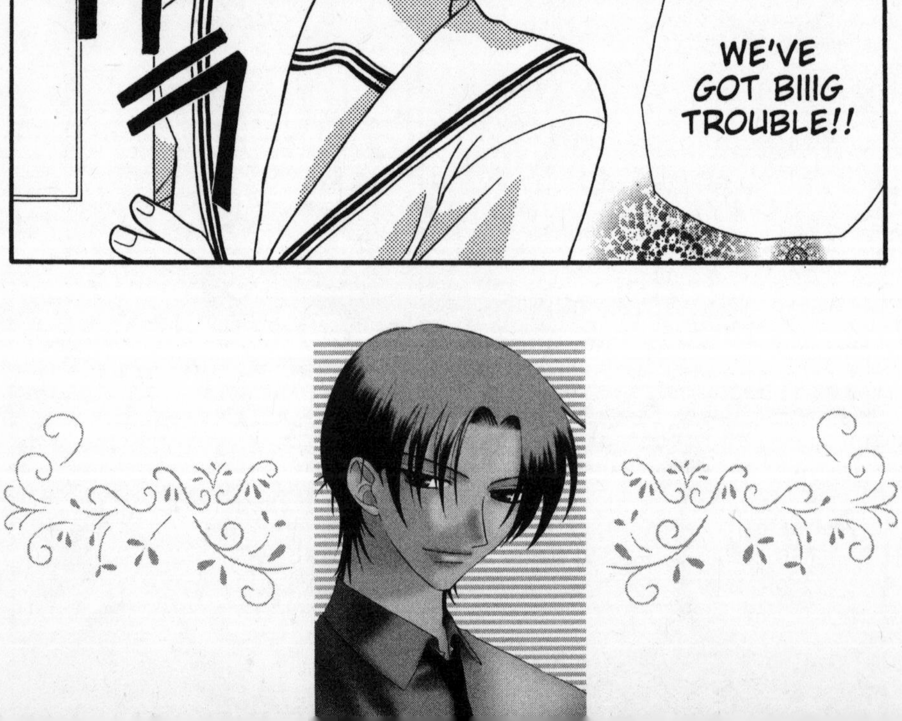

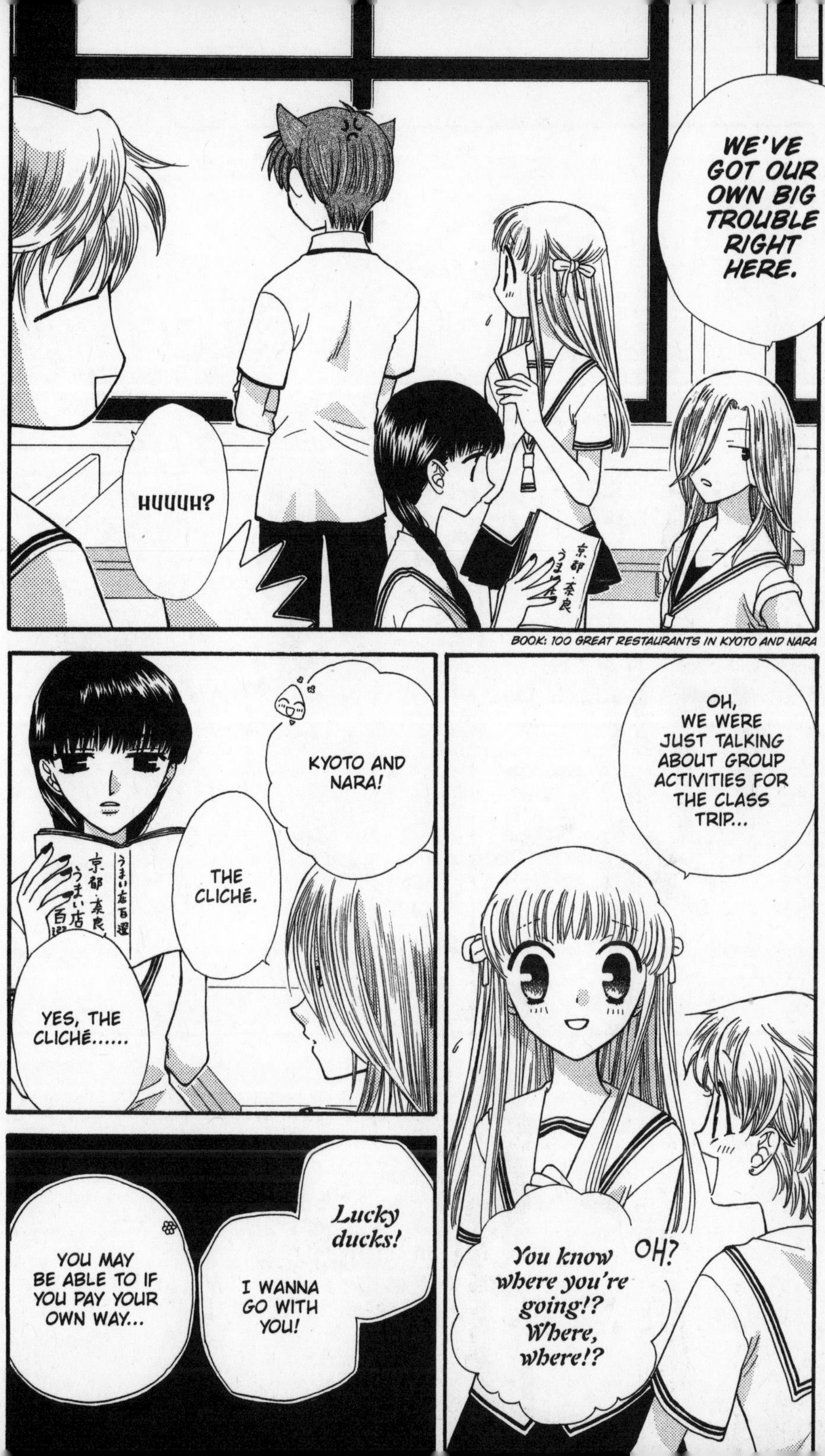
WE'VE GOT OUR OWN BIG TROUBLE RIGHT HERE.
HUUUH?
BOOK: 100 GREAT RESTAURANTS IN KYOTO AND NARA
OH, WE WERE JUST TALKING ABOUT GROUP ACTIVITIES FOR THE CLASS TRIP...
OH?
You know where you're going!? Where, where!?
KYOTO AND NARA!
THE CLICHÉ.
YES, THE CLICHÉ......
Lucky ducks!
I WANNA GO WITH YOU!
YOU MAY BE ABLE TO IF YOU PAY YOUR OWN WAY...

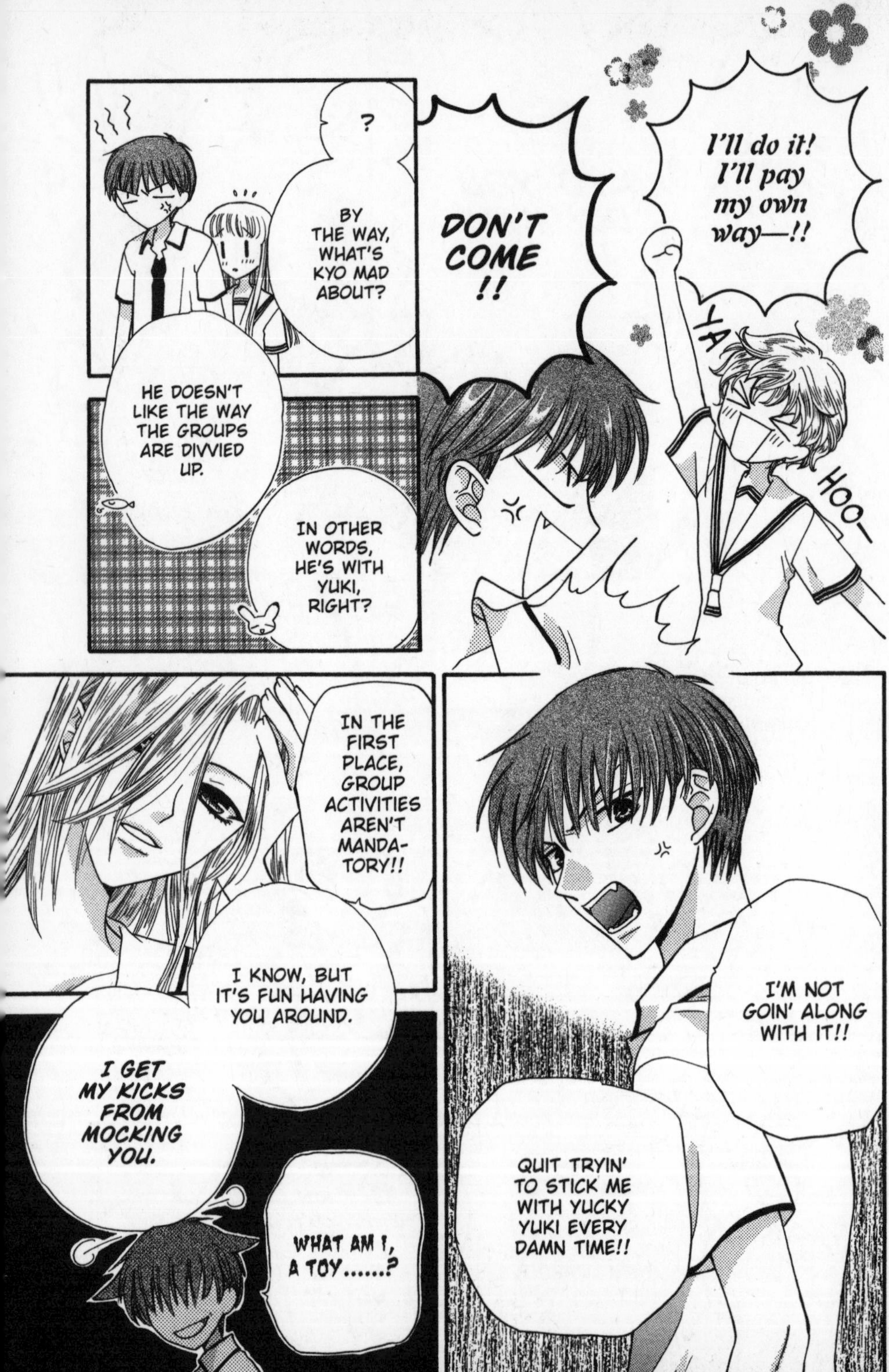
I'll do it! I'll pay my own way—!!
DON'T COME!!
YA
HOO-
?
BY THE WAY, WHAT'S KYO MAD ABOUT?
HE DOESN'T LIKE THE WAY THE GROUPS ARE DIVVIED UP.
IN OTHER WORDS, HE'S WITH YUKI, RIGHT?
I'M NOT GOIN' ALONG WITH IT!!
QUIT TRYIN' TO STICK ME WITH YUCKY YUKI EVERY DAMN TIME!!
IN THE FIRST PLACE, GROUP ACTIVITIES AREN'T MANDA-TORY!!
I KNOW, BUT IT'S FUN HAVING YOU AROUND.
I GET MY KICKS FROM MOCKING YOU.
WHAT AM I, A TOY......?

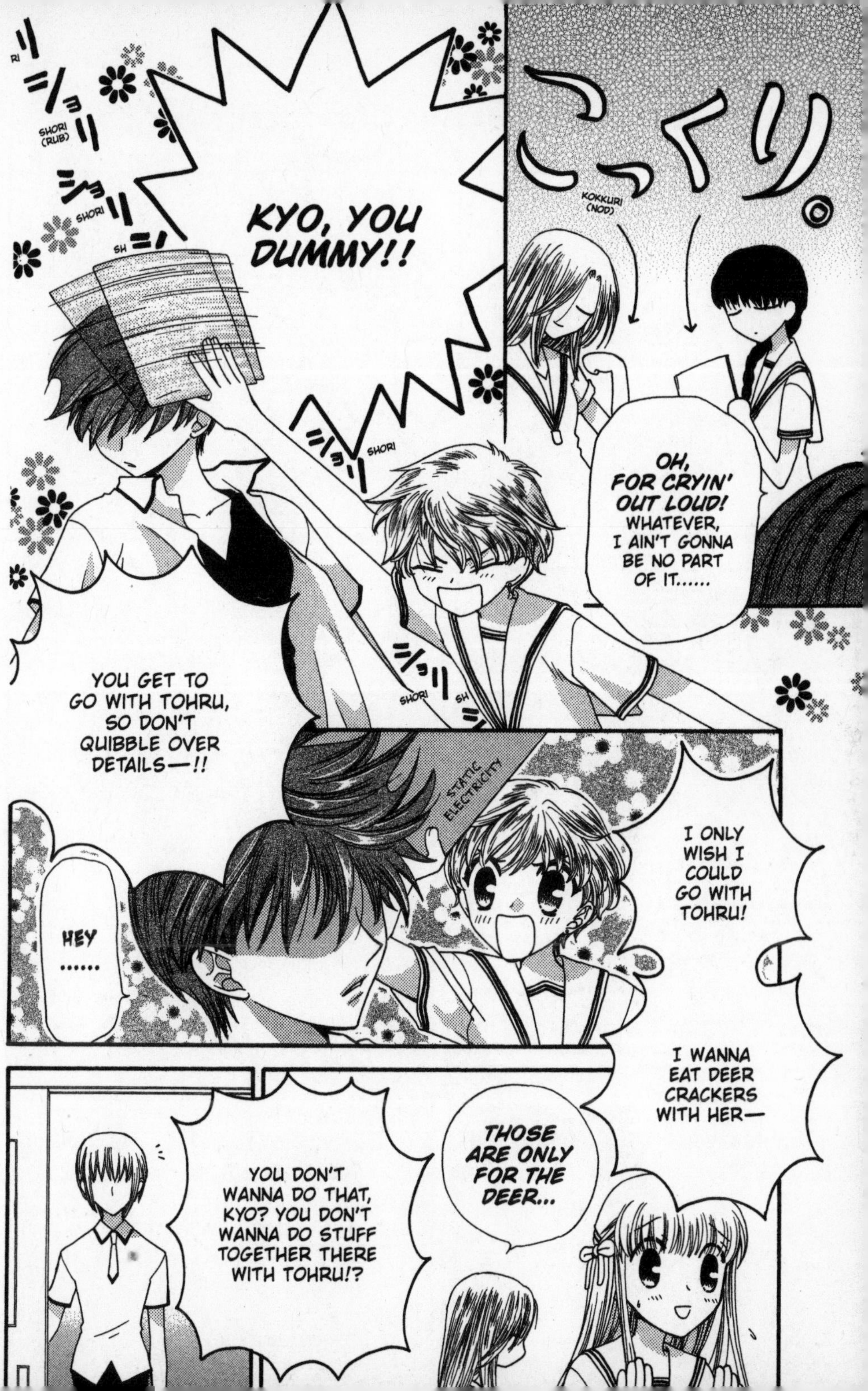
こっくり。
KOKKURI (NOD)
OH, FOR CRYIN' OUT LOUD! WHATEVER, I AIN'T GONNA BE NO PART OF IT......
リ
RI
ショリ
SHORI (RUB)
ショリ
SHORI
シ
SH
KYO, YOU DUMMY!!
ショリ
SHORI
ショリ
SHORI
シ
SH
YOU GET TO GO WITH TOHRU, SO DON'T QUIBBLE OVER DETAILS—!!
STATIC ELECTRICITY
I ONLY WISH I COULD GO WITH TOHRU!
HEY ....
I WANNA EAT DEER CRACKERS WITH HER—
THOSE ARE ONLY FOR THE DEER...
YOU DON'T WANNA DO THAT, KYO? YOU DON'T WANNA DO STUFF TOGETHER THERE WITH TOHRU!?

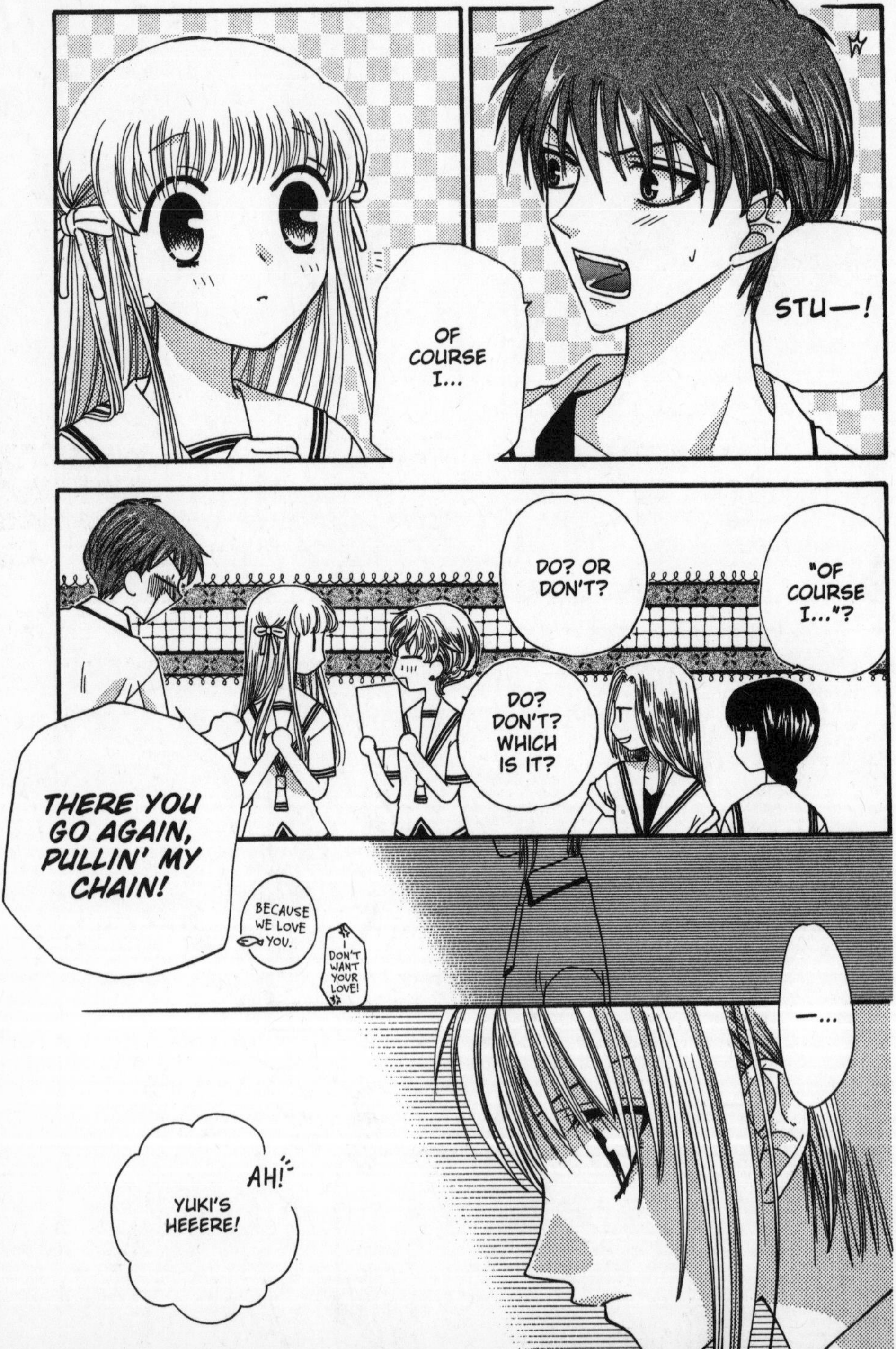
STU—!
OF COURSE I...
"OF COURSE I..."?
DO? OR DON'T?
DO? DON'T? WHICH IS IT?
THERE YOU GO AGAIN, PULLIN' MY CHAIN!
BECAUSE WE LOVE YOU.
I DON'T WANT YOUR LOVE!
—...
AH!
YUKI'S HEEERE!

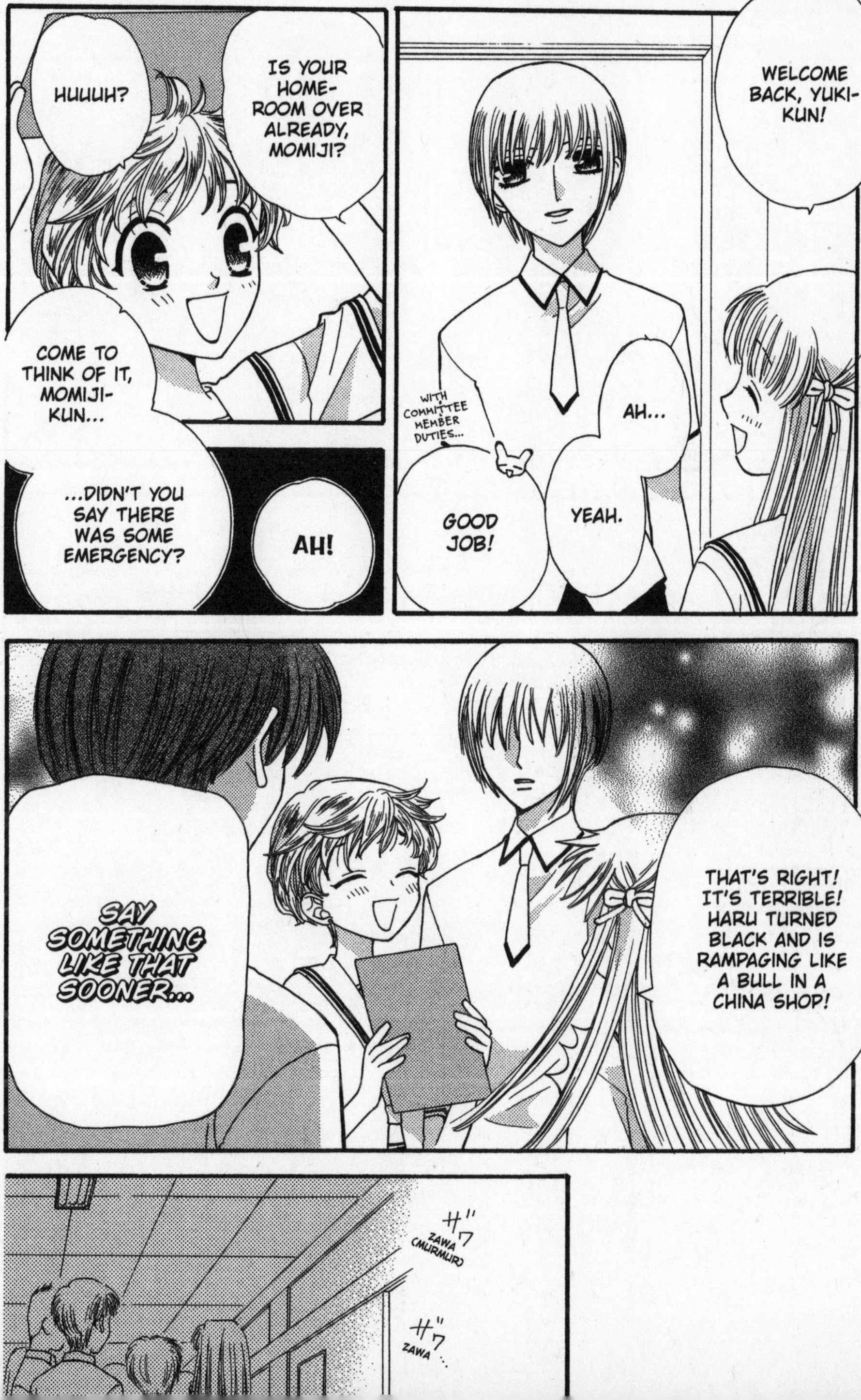
WELCOME BACK, YUKI-KUN!
AH... YEAH.
WITH COMMITTEE MEMBER DUTIES...
GOOD JOB!
IS YOUR HOME-ROOM OVER ALREADY, MOMIJI?
HUUUH?
COME TO THINK OF IT, MOMIJI-KUN...
...DIDN'T YOU SAY THERE WAS SOME EMERGENCY?
AH!
THAT'S RIGHT! IT'S TERRIBLE! HARU TURNED BLACK AND IS RAMPAGING LIKE A BULL IN A CHINA SHOP!
SAY SOMETHING LIKE THAT SOONER...
ザワ
ZAWA (MURMUR)
ザワ
ZAWA...

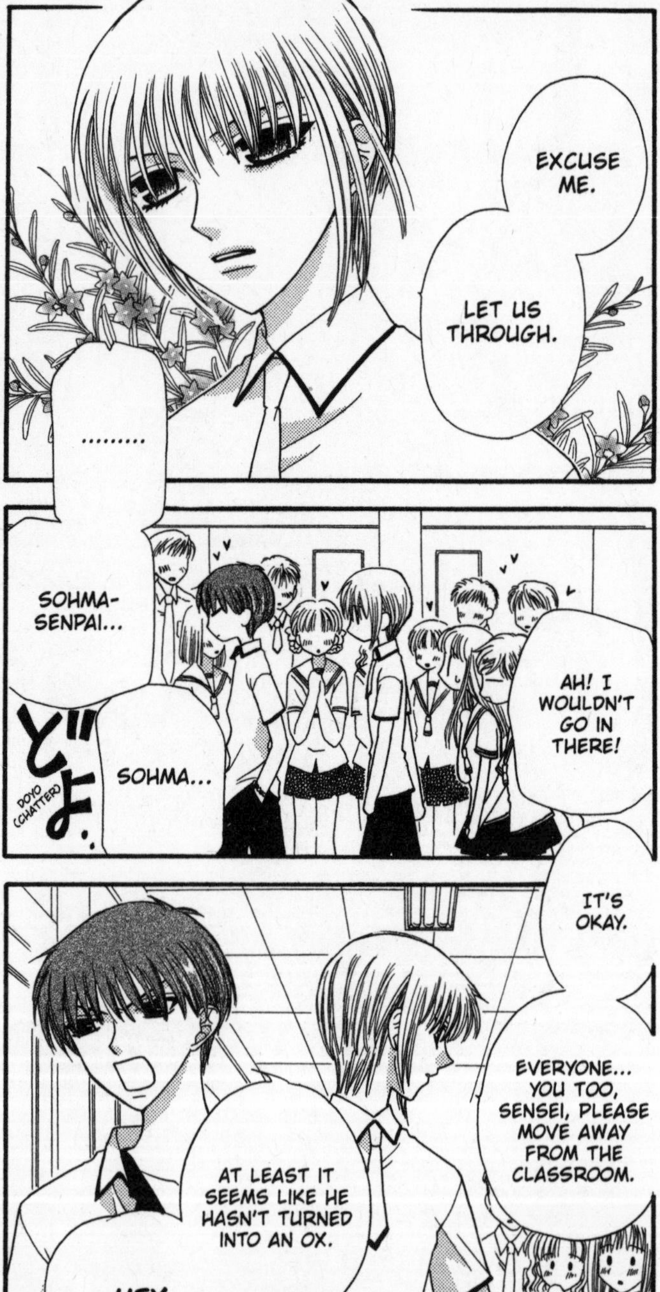
EXCUSE ME.
LET US THROUGH.
....
AH! I WOULDN'T GO IN THERE!
SOHMA-SENPAI...
SOHMA...
DOYO (CHATTER)
IT'S OKAY.
EVERYONE... YOU TOO, SENSEI, PLEASE MOVE AWAY FROM THE CLASSROOM.
AT LEAST IT SEEMS LIKE HE HASN'T TURNED INTO AN OX.
HEY, HARU!
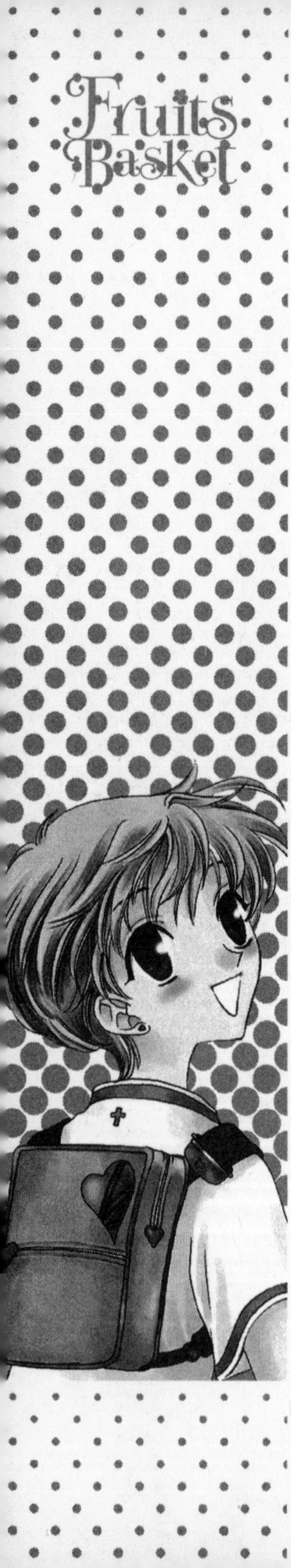
Fruits Basket

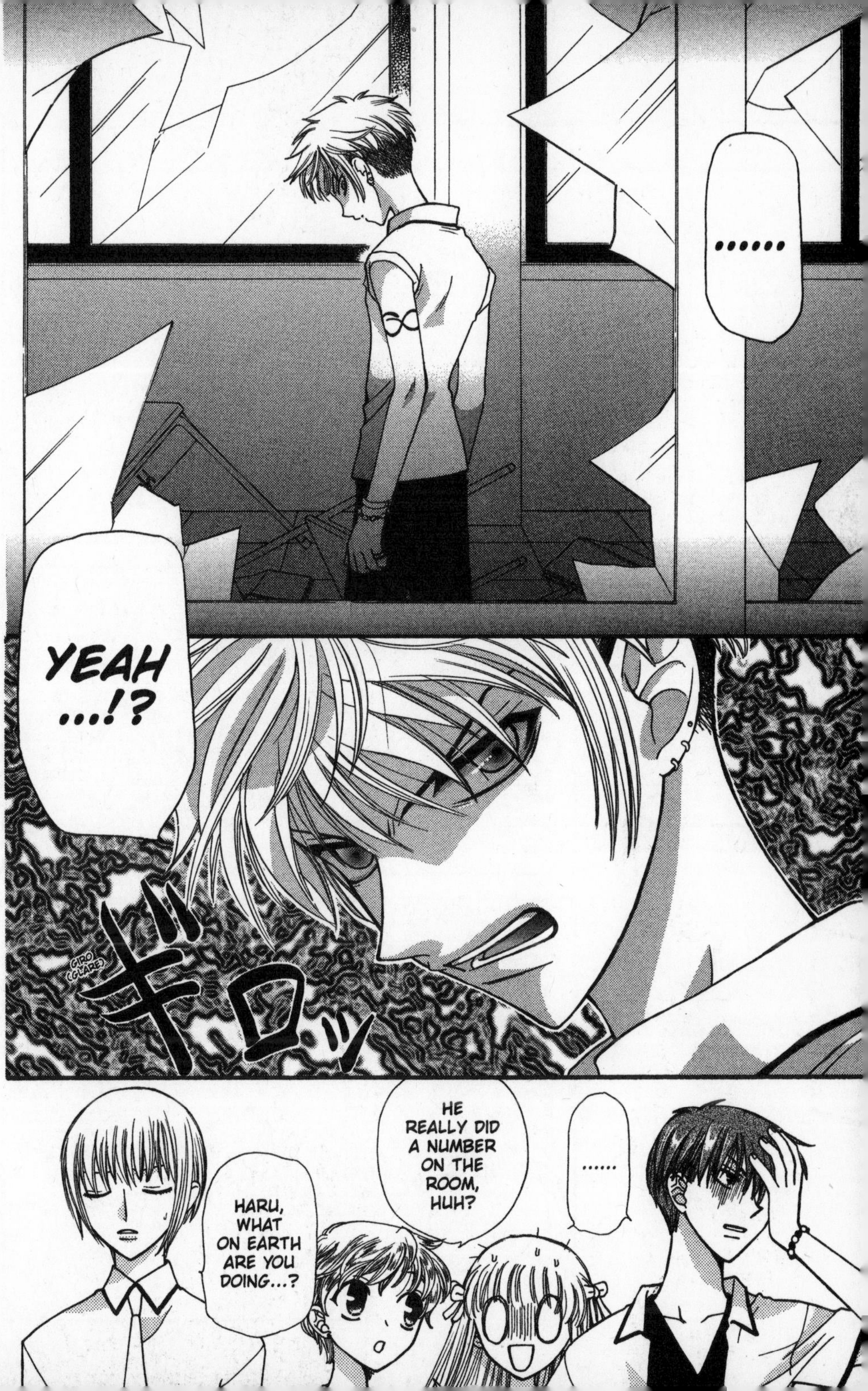
......
YEAH ...!?
GIRO (GLARE)
......
HE REALLY DID A NUMBER ON THE ROOM, HUH?
HARU, WHAT ON EARTH ARE YOU DOING...?

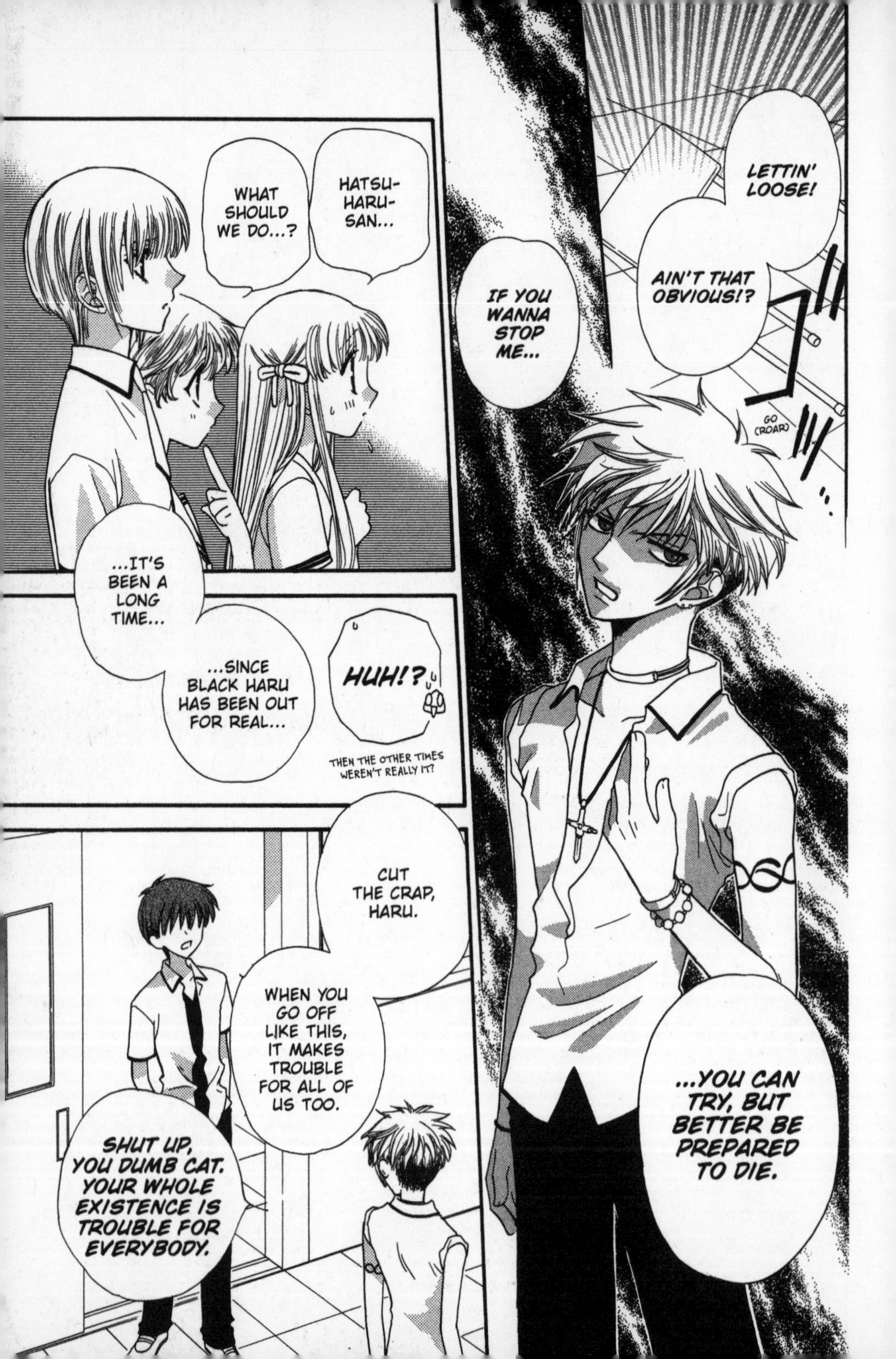
LETTIN' LOOSE!
AIN'T THAT OBVIOUS!?
GO (ROAR)
IF YOU WANNA STOP ME...
...YOU CAN TRY, BUT BETTER BE PREPARED TO DIE.
HATSU-HARU-SAN...
WHAT SHOULD WE DO...?
...IT'S BEEN A LONG TIME...
...SINCE BLACK HARU HAS BEEN OUT FOR REAL...
HUH!?
THEN THE OTHER TIMES WEREN'T REALLY IT?
CUT THE CRAP, HARU.
WHEN YOU GO OFF LIKE THIS, IT MAKES TROUBLE FOR ALL OF US TOO.
SHUT UP, YOU DUMB CAT. YOUR WHOLE EXISTENCE IS TROUBLE FOR EVERYBODY.

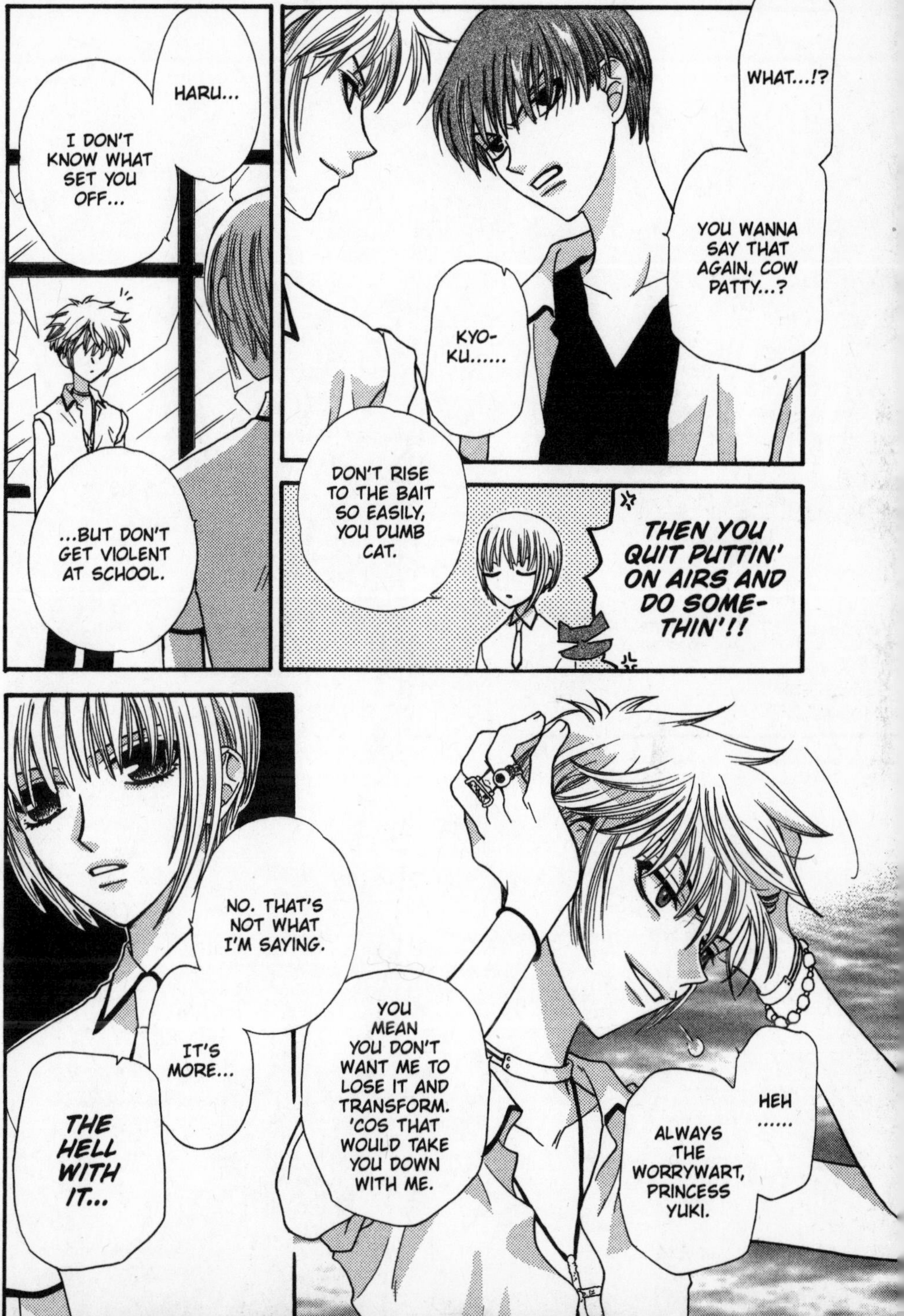
WHAT...!?
YOU WANNA SAY THAT AGAIN, COW PATTY...?
KYO-KU......
THEN YOU QUIT PUTTIN' ON AIRS AND DO SOME-THIN'!!
DON'T RISE TO THE BAIT SO EASILY, YOU DUMB CAT.
HARU...
I DON'T KNOW WHAT SET YOU OFF...
...BUT DON'T GET VIOLENT AT SCHOOL.
HEH ......
ALWAYS THE WORRYWART, PRINCESS YUKI.
YOU MEAN YOU DON'T WANT ME TO LOSE IT AND TRANSFORM. 'COS THAT WOULD TAKE YOU DOWN WITH ME.
NO. THAT'S NOT WHAT I'M SAYING.
IT'S MORE...
THE HELL WITH IT...

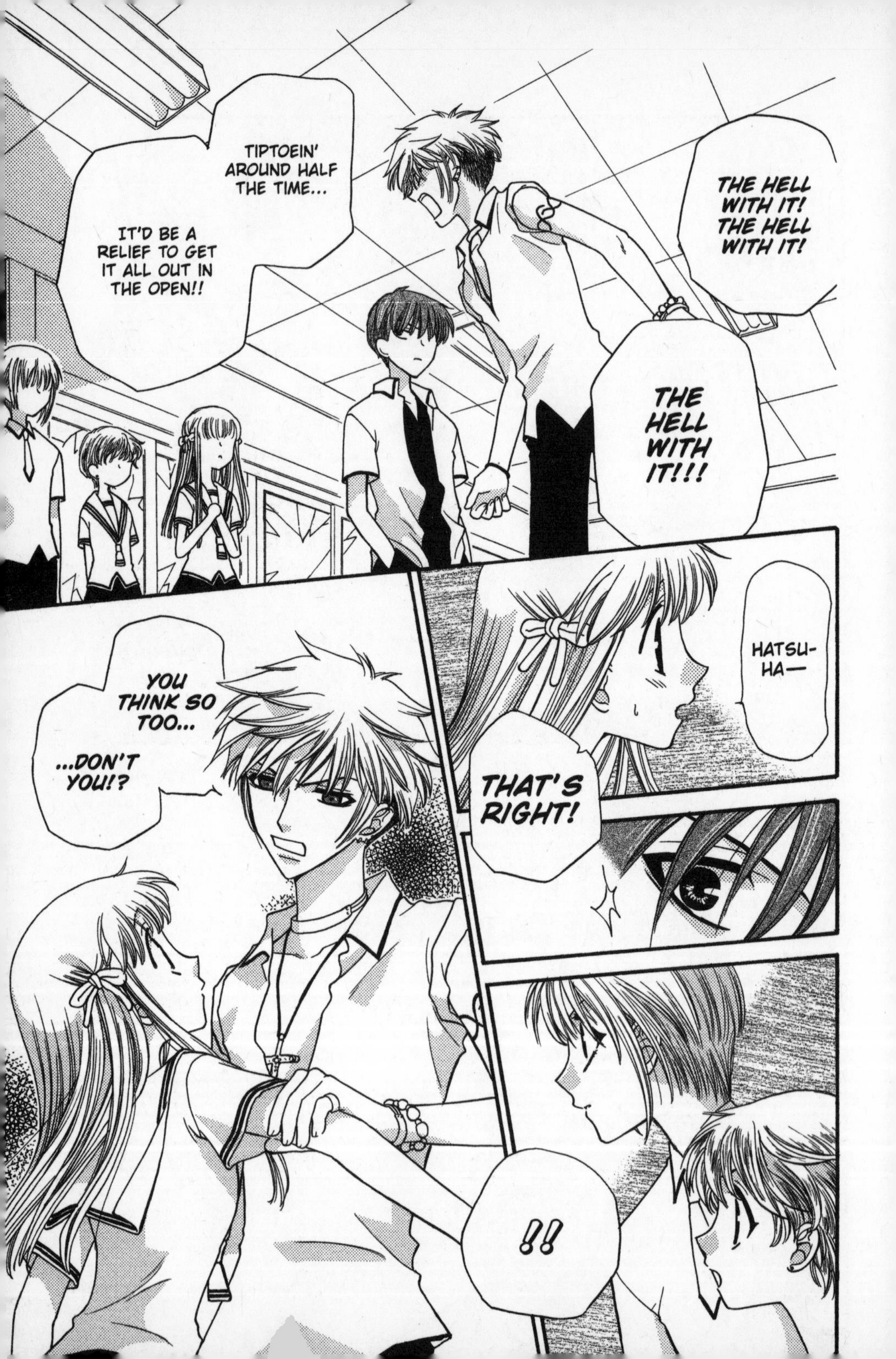
THE HELL WITH IT! THE HELL WITH IT!
THE HELL WITH IT!!!
TIPTOEIN' AROUND HALF THE TIME...
IT'D BE A RELIEF TO GET IT ALL OUT IN THE OPEN!!
HATSU-HA—
THAT'S RIGHT!
!!
YOU THINK SO TOO...
...DON'T YOU!?

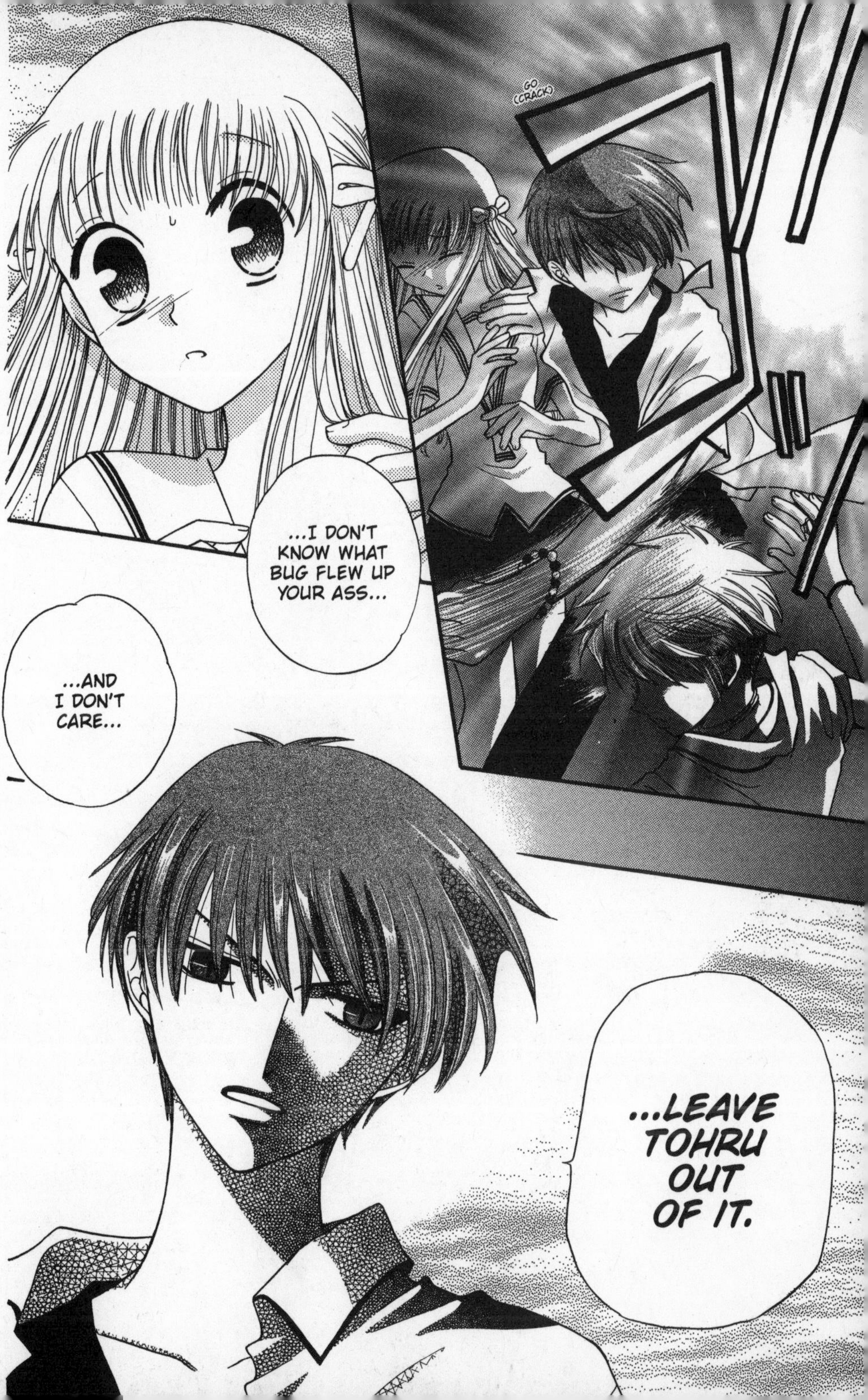
GO (CRACK)
...I DON'T KNOW WHAT BUG FLEW UP YOUR ASS...
...AND I DON'T CARE...
...LEAVE TOHRU OUT OF IT.

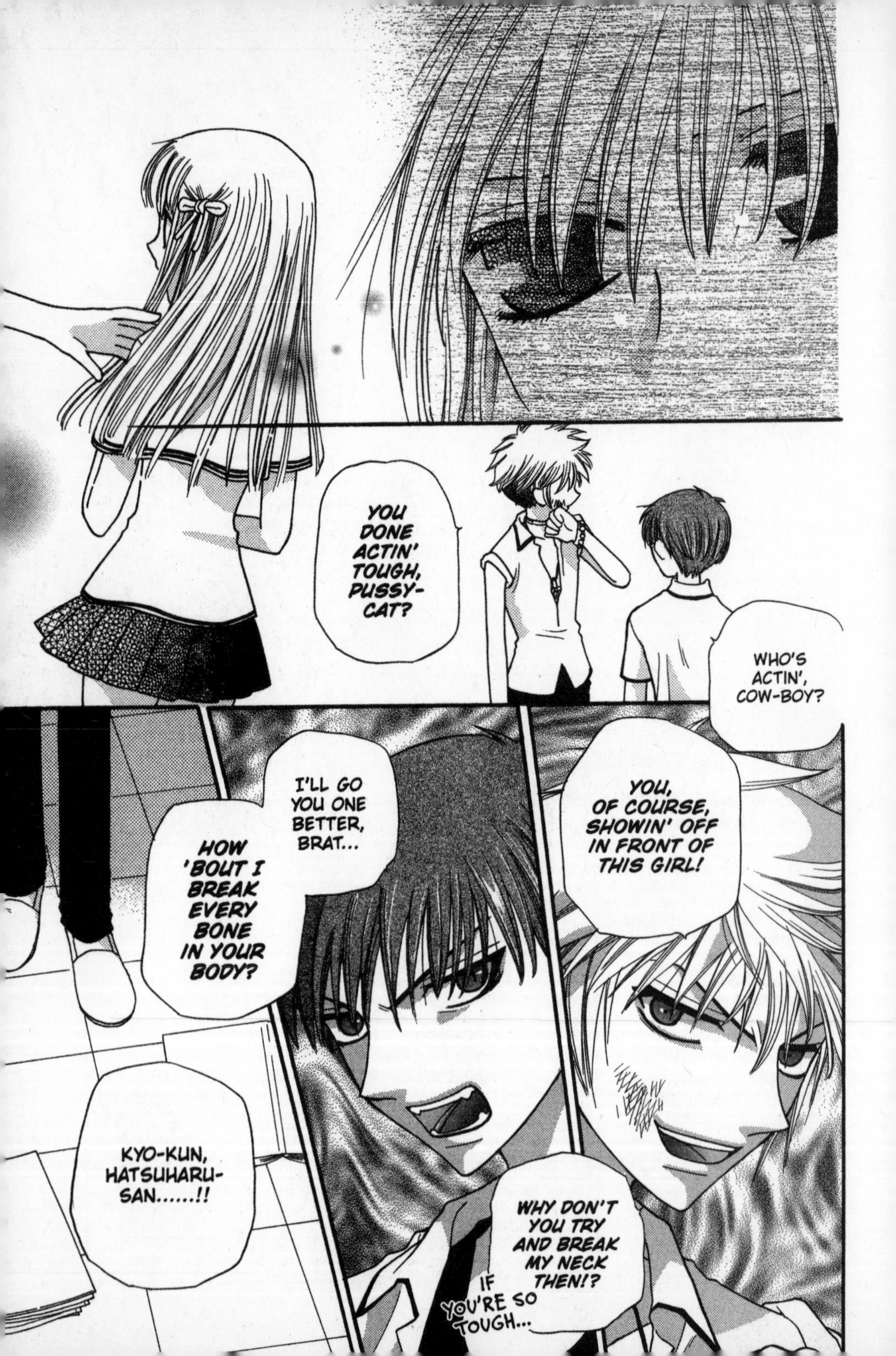
YOU DONE ACTIN' TOUGH, PUSSY-CAT?
WHO'S ACTIN', COW-BOY?
YOU, OF COURSE, SHOWIN' OFF IN FRONT OF THIS GIRL!
I'LL GO YOU ONE BETTER, BRAT...
HOW 'BOUT I BREAK EVERY BONE IN YOUR BODY?
WHY DON'T YOU TRY AND BREAK MY NECK THEN!?
IF YOU'RE SO TOUGH...
KYO-KUN, HATSUHARU-SAN......!!

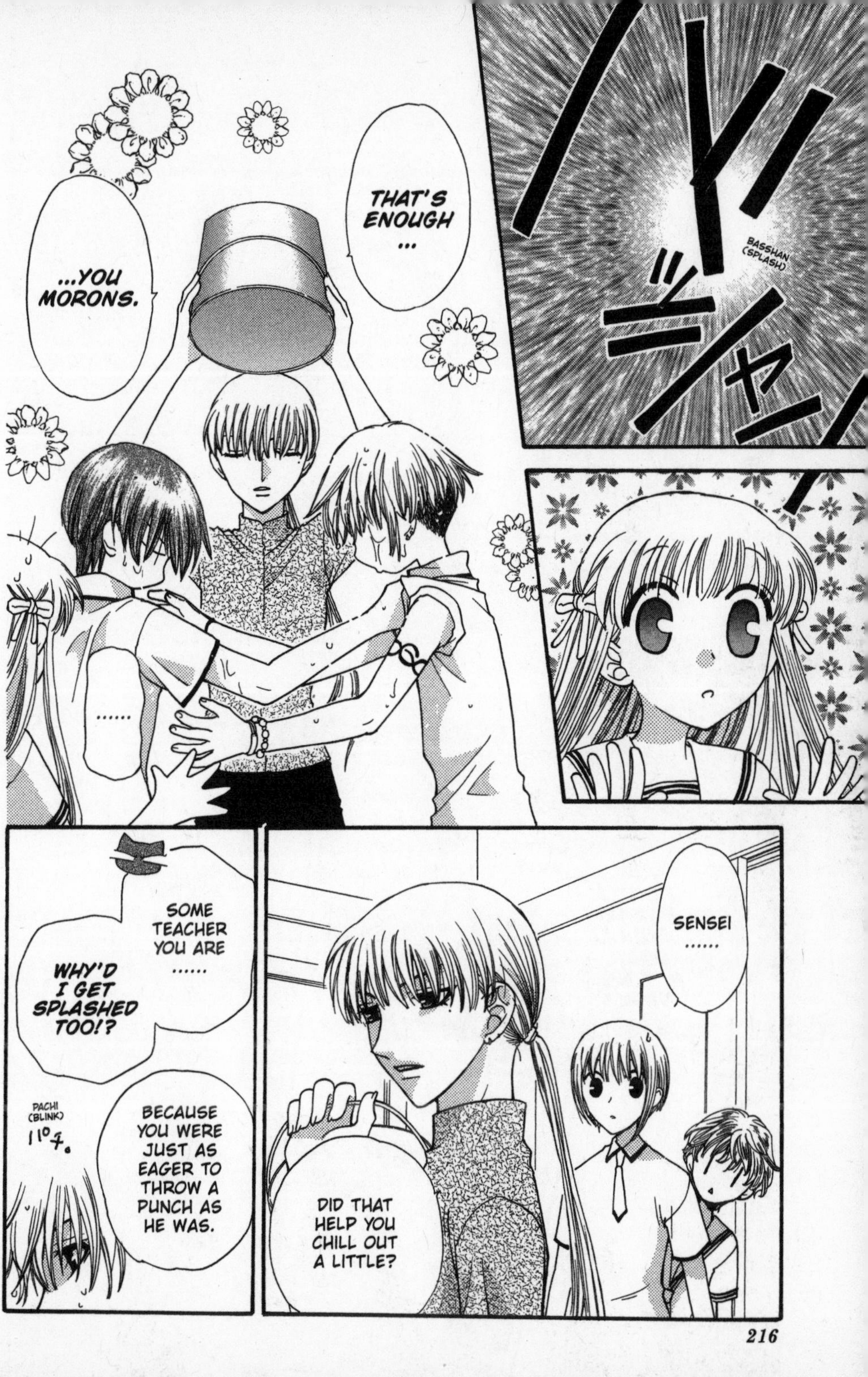
BASSHAN (SPLASH)
THAT'S ENOUGH ...
...YOU MORONS.
......
SENSEI ......
DID THAT HELP YOU CHILL OUT A LITTLE?
SOME TEACHER YOU ARE ......
WHY'D I GET SPLASHED TOO!?
PACHI (BLINK)
BECAUSE YOU WERE JUST AS EAGER TO THROW A PUNCH AS HE WAS.

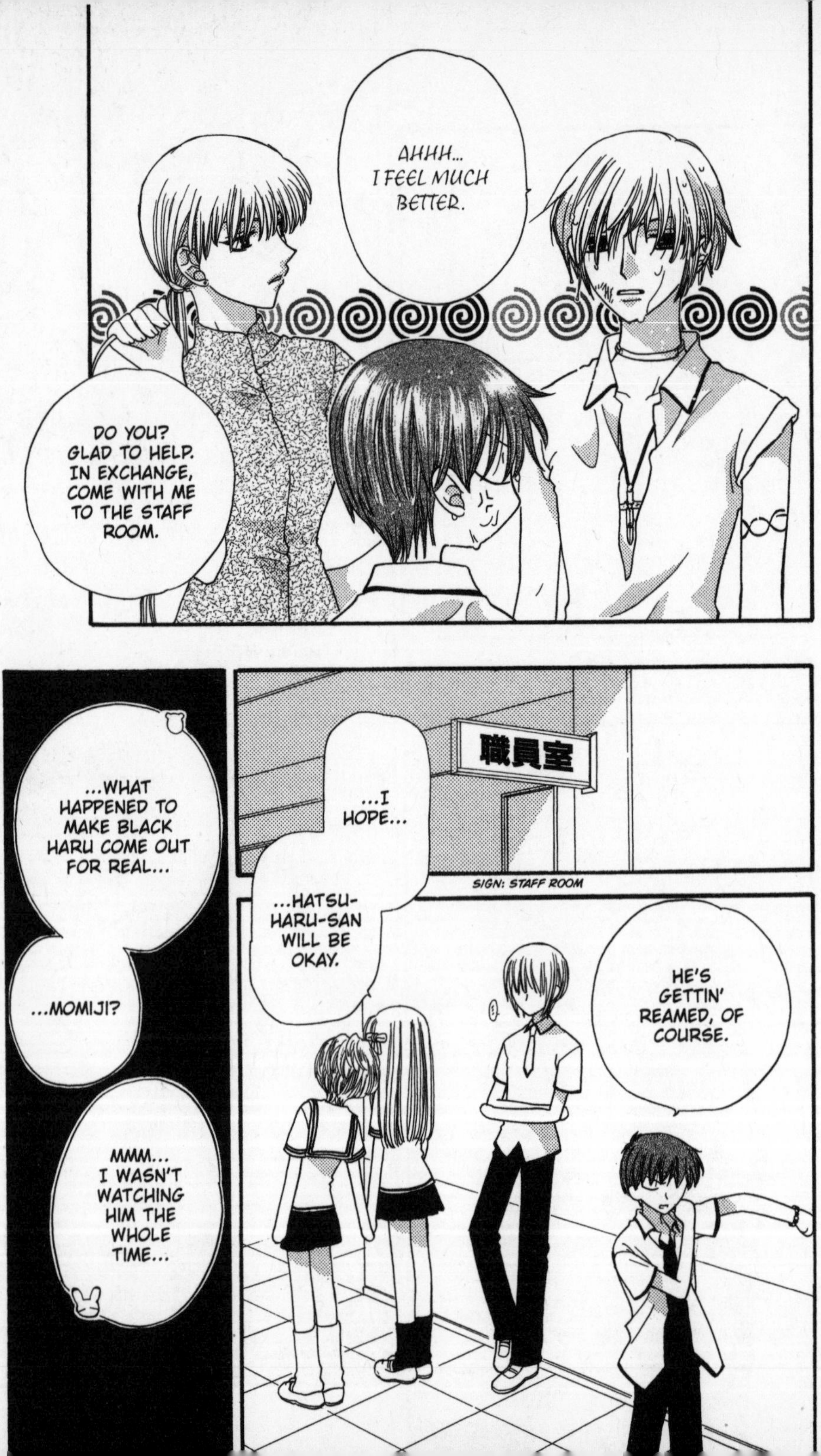
AHHH... I FEEL MUCH BETTER.
DO YOU? GLAD TO HELP. IN EXCHANGE, COME WITH ME TO THE STAFF ROOM.
職員室
...I HOPE...
SIGN: STAFF ROOM
...HATSU-HARU-SAN WILL BE OKAY.
HE'S GETTIN' REAMED, OF COURSE.
...WHAT HAPPENED TO MAKE BLACK HARU COME OUT FOR REAL...
...MOMIJI?
MMM... I WASN'T WATCHING HIM THE WHOLE TIME...

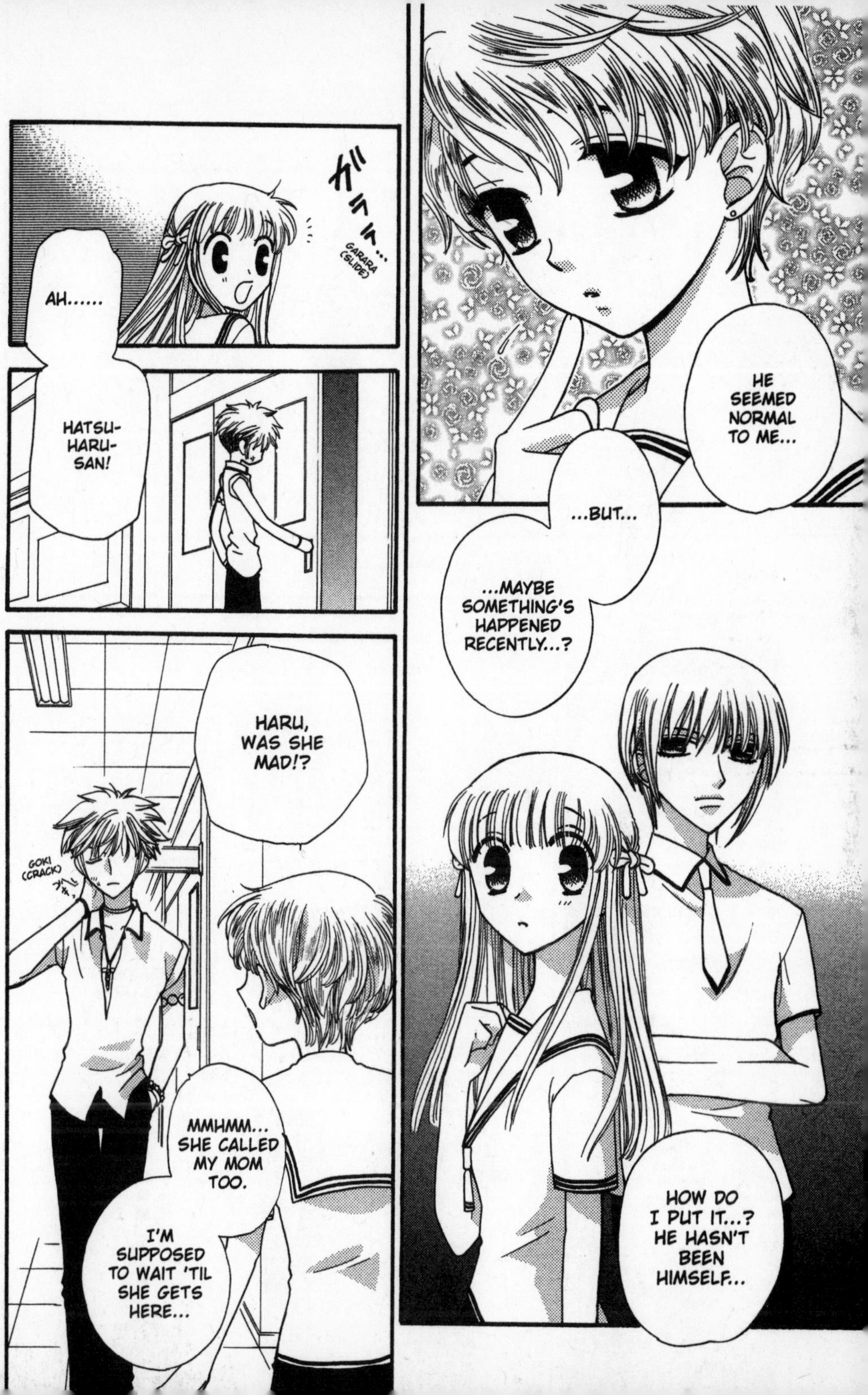
HE SEEMED NORMAL TO ME...
...BUT...
...MAYBE SOMETHING'S HAPPENED RECENTLY...?
HOW DO I PUT IT...? HE HASN'T BEEN HIMSELF...
GARARA (SLIDE)
AH......
HATSU-HARU-SAN!
HARU, WAS SHE MAD!?
GOKI (CRACK)
MMHMM... SHE CALLED MY MOM TOO.
I'M SUPPOSED TO WAIT 'TIL SHE GETS HERE...

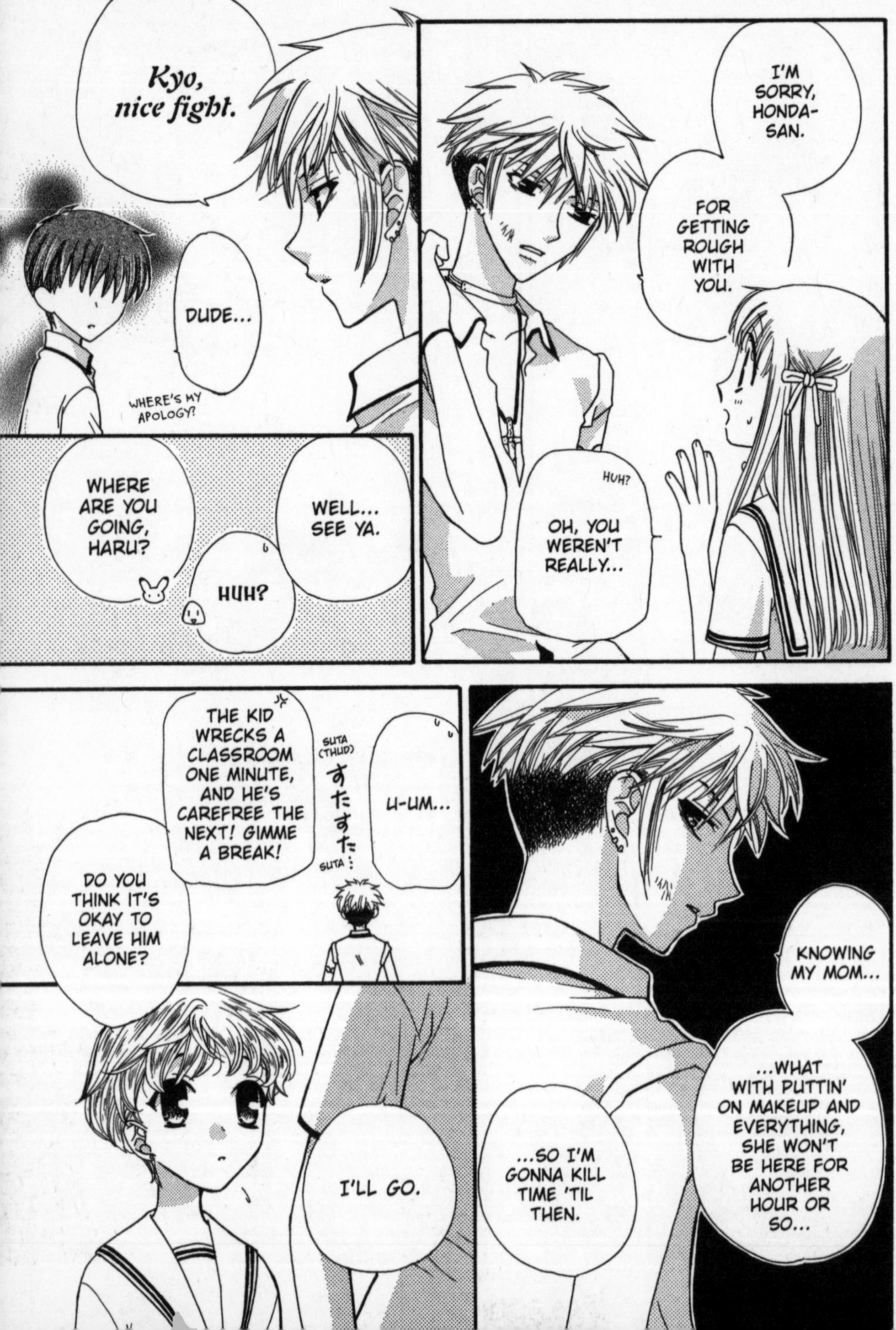
I'M SORRY, HONDA-SAN.
FOR GETTING ROUGH WITH YOU.
HUH?
OH, YOU WEREN'T REALLY...
Kyo, nice fight.
DUDE...
WHERE'S MY APOLOGY?
WELL... SEE YA.
HUH?
WHERE ARE YOU GOING, HARU?
KNOWING MY MOM...
...WHAT WITH PUTTIN' ON MAKEUP AND EVERYTHING, SHE WON'T BE HERE FOR ANOTHER HOUR OR SO...
...SO I'M GONNA KILL TIME 'TIL THEN.
U-UM...
SUTA (THUD) すたすた… SUTA
THE KID WRECKS A CLASSROOM ONE MINUTE, AND HE'S CAREFREE THE NEXT! GIMME A BREAK!
DO YOU THINK IT'S OKAY TO LEAVE HIM ALONE?
I'LL GO.

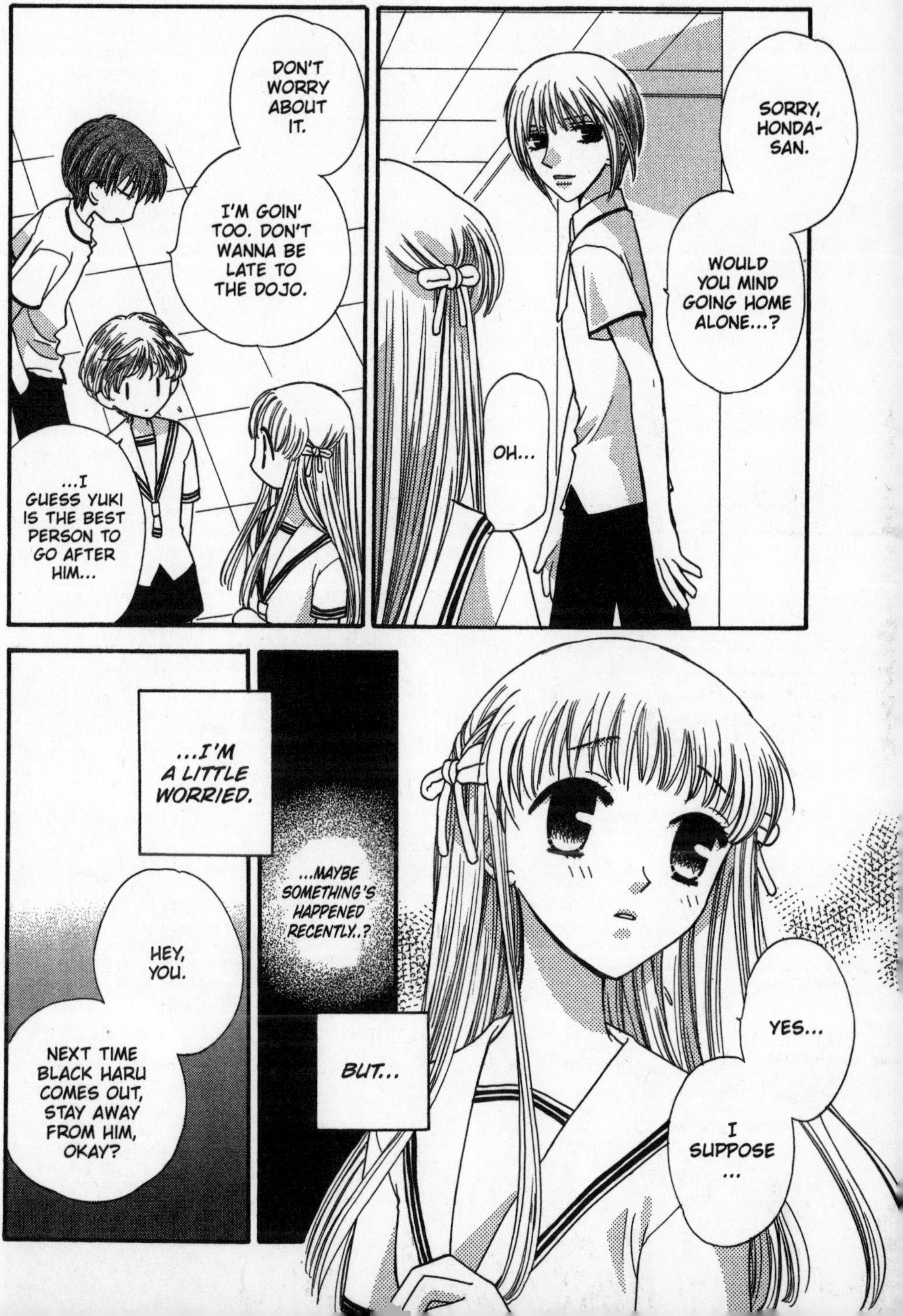
SORRY, HONDA-SAN.
WOULD YOU MIND GOING HOME ALONE...?
OH...
DON'T WORRY ABOUT IT.
I'M GOIN' TOO. DON'T WANNA BE LATE TO THE DOJO.
...I GUESS YUKI IS THE BEST PERSON TO GO AFTER HIM...
YES...
I SUPPOSE ...
BUT...
...MAYBE SOMETHING'S HAPPENED RECENTLY..?
...I'M A LITTLE WORRIED.
HEY, YOU.
NEXT TIME BLACK HARU COMES OUT, STAY AWAY FROM HIM, OKAY?

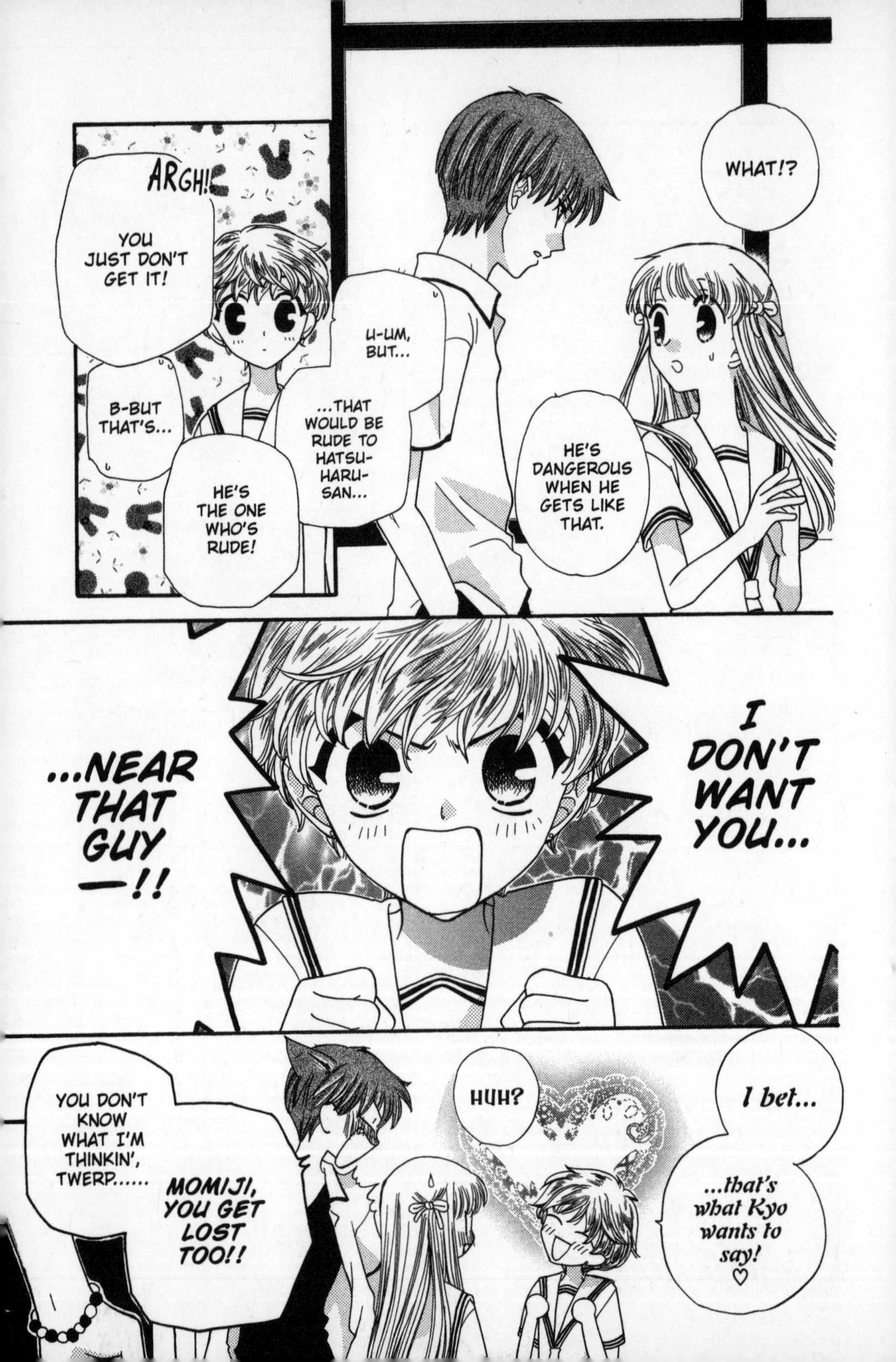
WHAT!?
U-UM, BUT...
HE'S DANGEROUS WHEN HE GETS LIKE THAT.
...THAT WOULD BE RUDE TO HATSU-HARU-SAN...
ARGH!
YOU JUST DON'T GET IT!
B-BUT THAT'S...
HE'S THE ONE WHO'S RUDE!
I DON'T WANT YOU...
...NEAR THAT GUY—!!
I bet...
...that's what Kyo wants to say! ♡
HUH?
YOU DON'T KNOW WHAT I'M THINKIN', TWERP......
MOMIJI, YOU GET LOST TOO!!

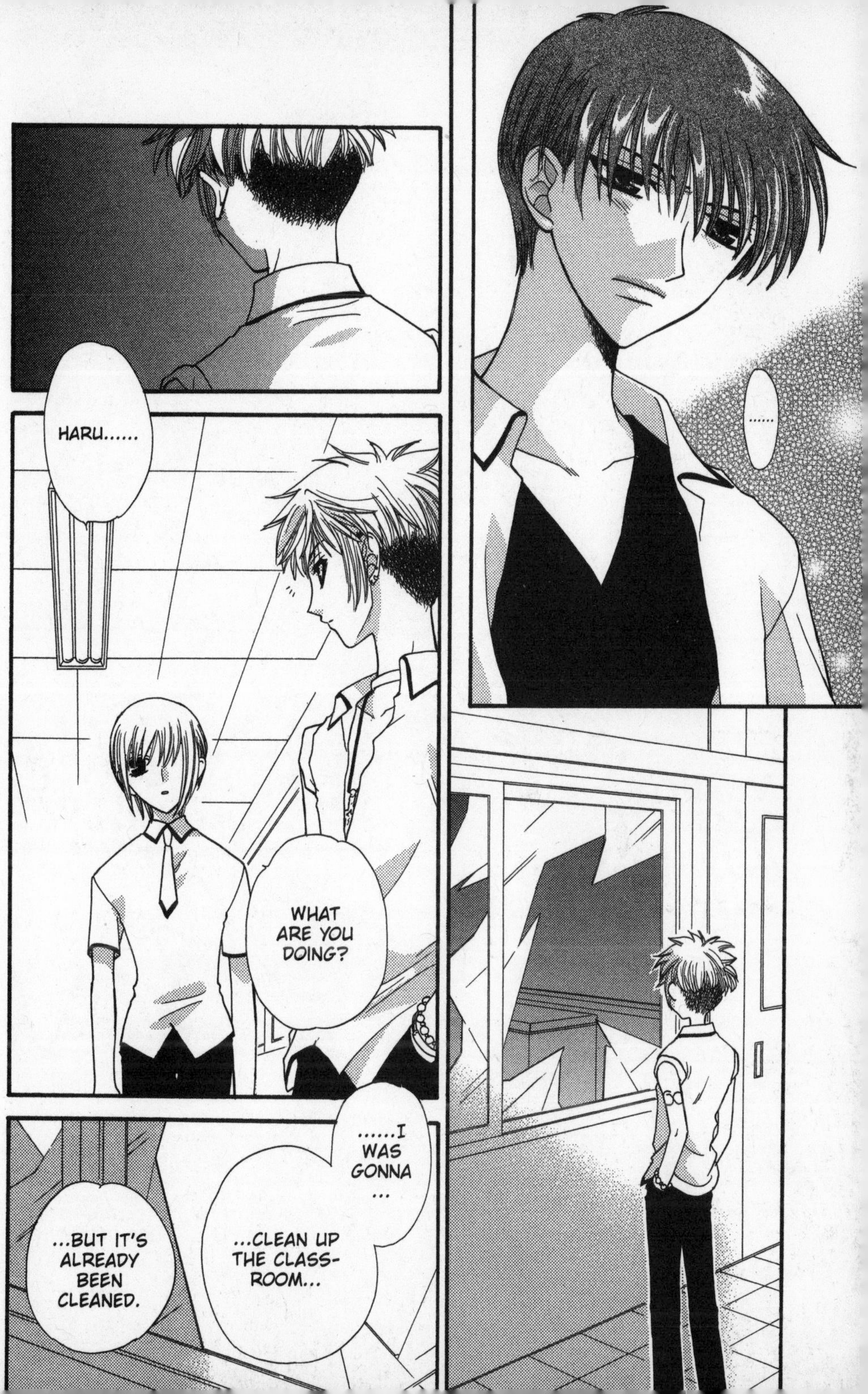
......
HARU......
WHAT ARE YOU DOING?
......I WAS GONNA...
...CLEAN UP THE CLASS-ROOM...
...BUT IT'S ALREADY BEEN CLEANED.

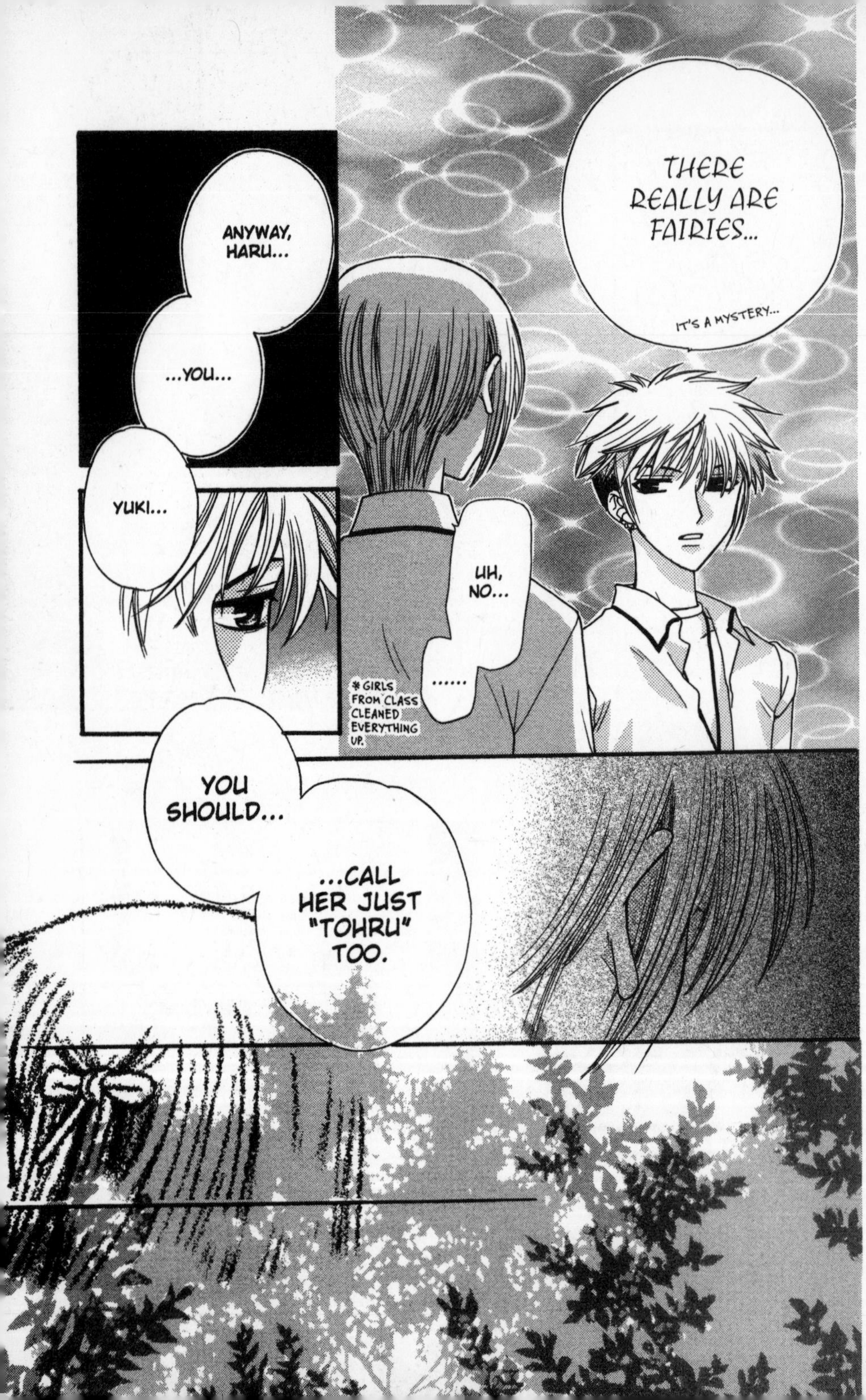

THERE REALLY ARE FAIRIES...
IT'S A MYSTERY...
UH, NO...
......
*GIRLS FROM CLASS CLEANED EVERYTHING UP.
ANYWAY, HARU...
...YOU...
YUKI...
YOU SHOULD...
...CALL HER JUST "TOHRU" TOO.

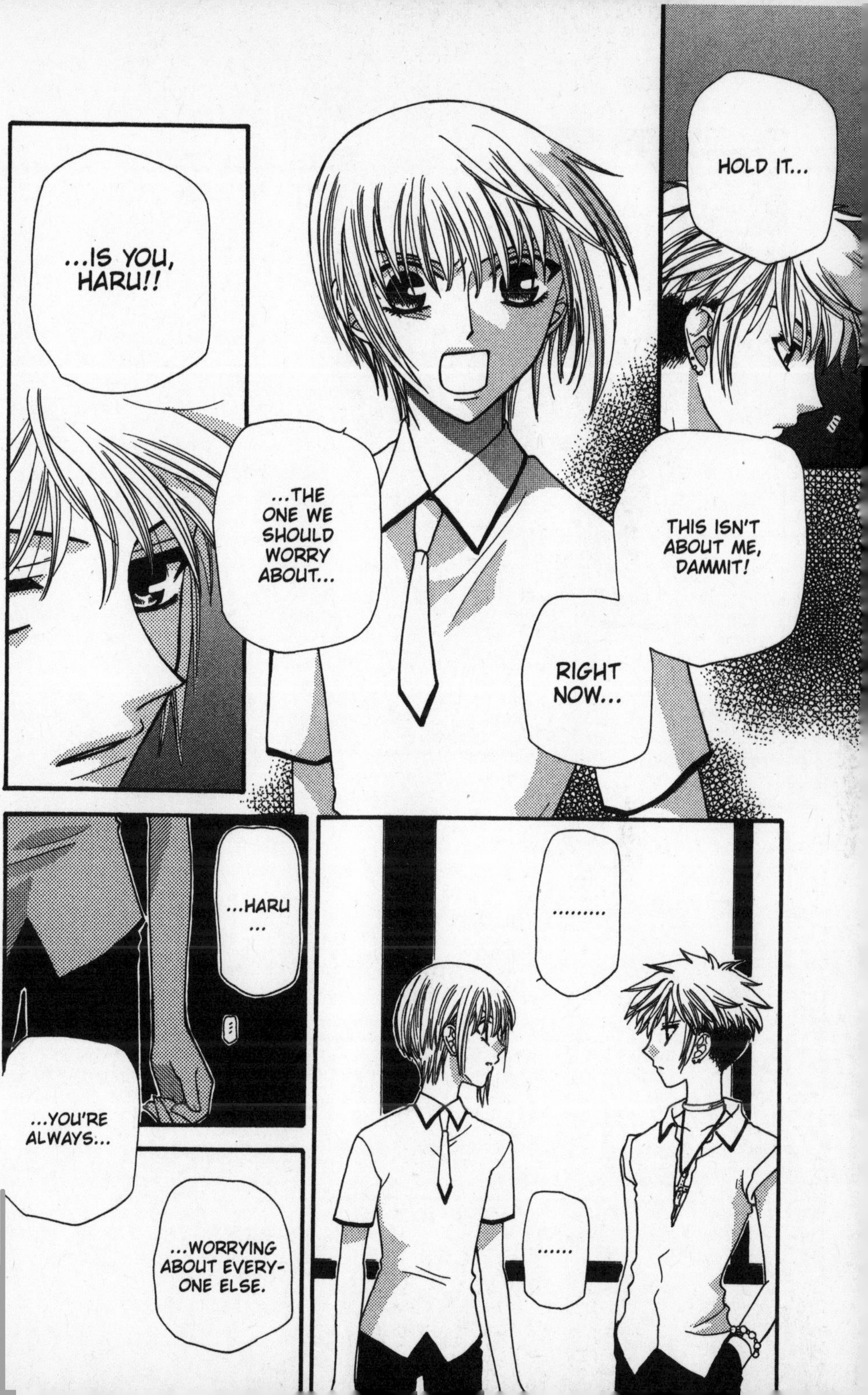
HOLD IT...
THIS ISN'T ABOUT ME, DAMMIT!
RIGHT NOW...
...THE ONE WE SHOULD WORRY ABOUT...
...IS YOU, HARU!!
....
......
...HARU ...
...YOU'RE ALWAYS...
...WORRYING ABOUT EVERY-ONE ELSE.

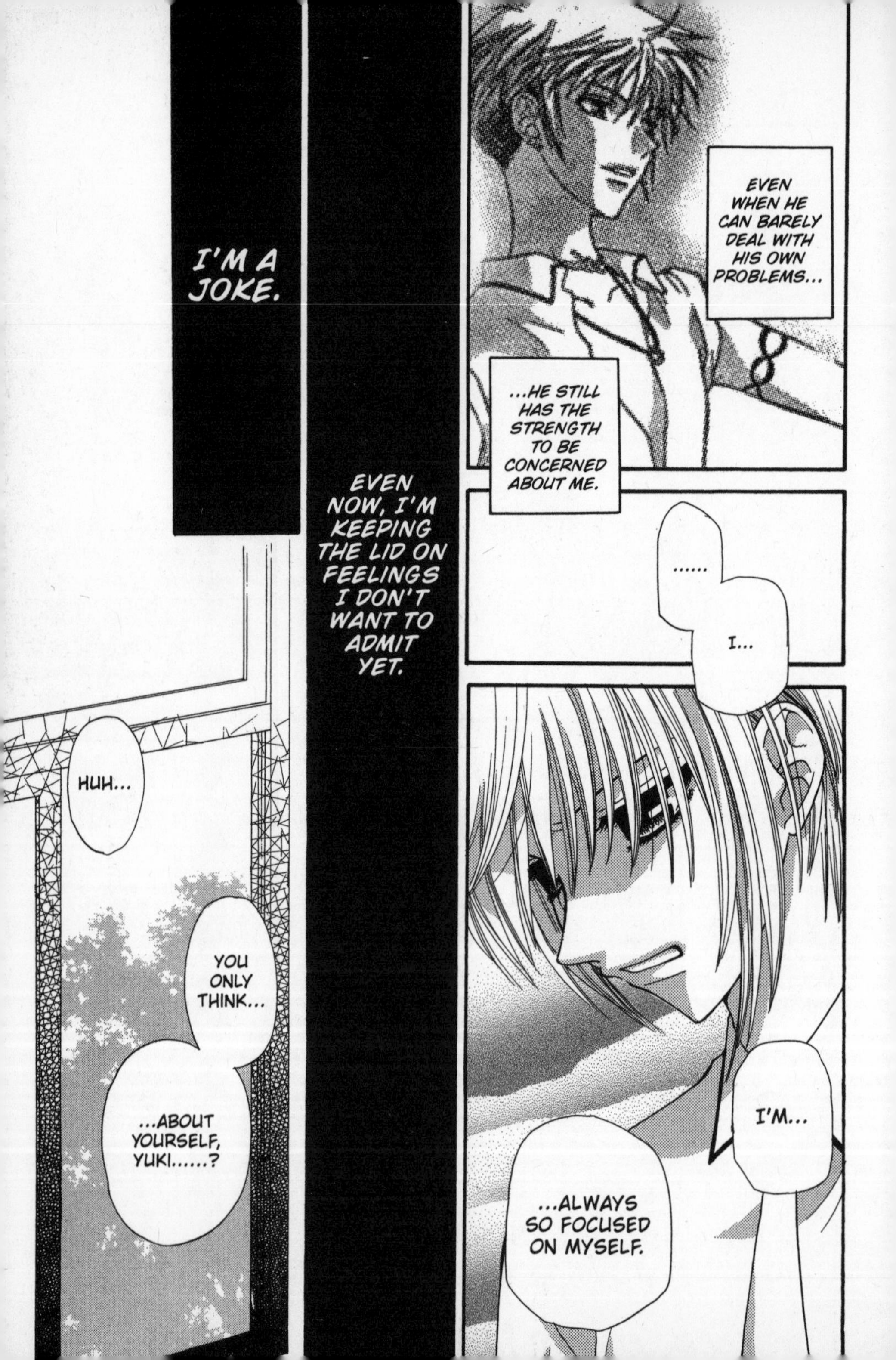
EVEN WHEN HE CAN BARELY DEAL WITH HIS OWN PROBLEMS...
...HE STILL HAS THE STRENGTH TO BE CONCERNED ABOUT ME.
......
I...
I'M...
...ALWAYS SO FOCUSED ON MYSELF.
EVEN NOW, I'M KEEPING THE LID ON FEELINGS I DON'T WANT TO ADMIT YET.
I'M A JOKE.
HUH...
YOU ONLY THINK...
...ABOUT YOURSELF, YUKI......?

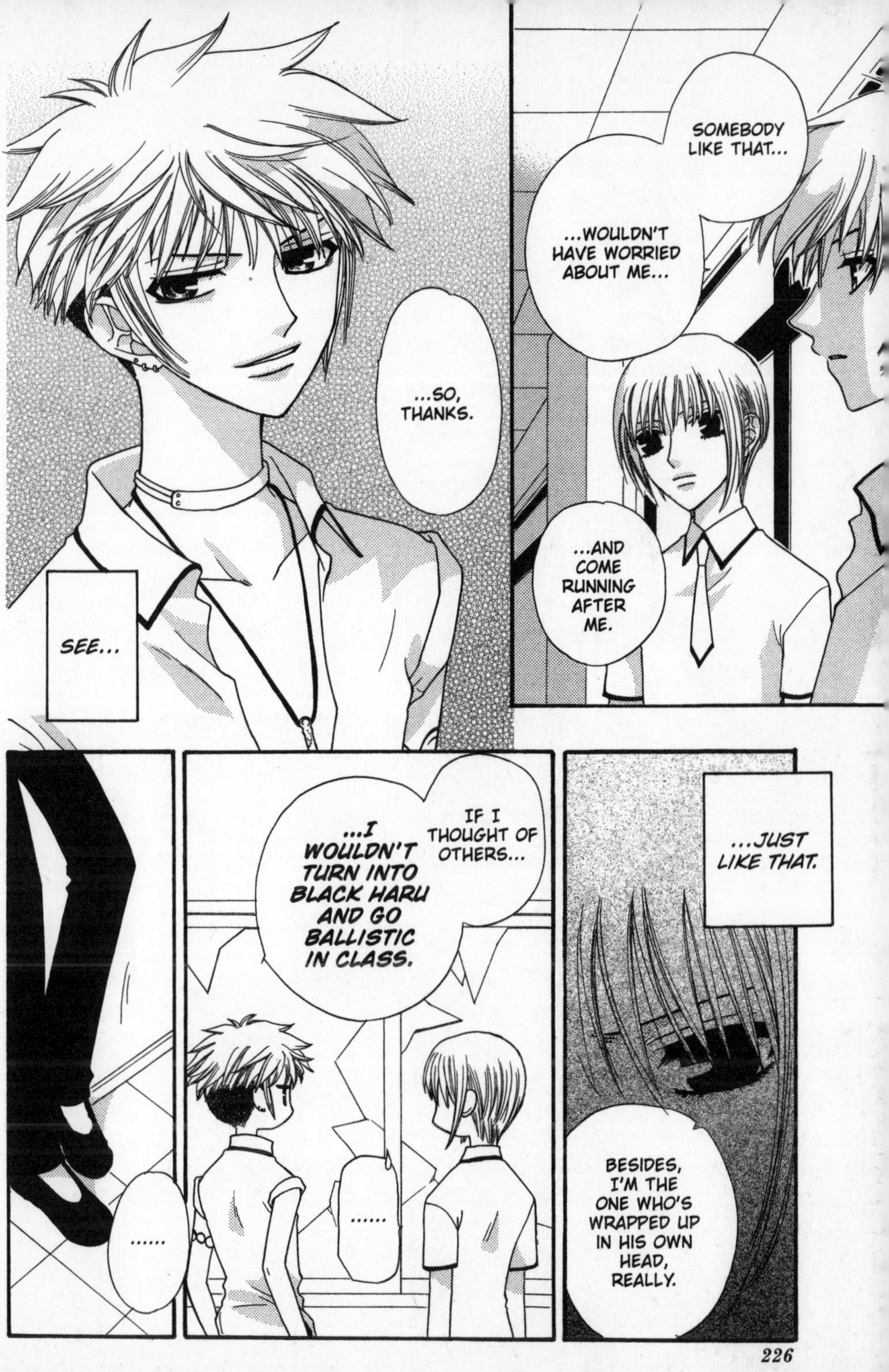
SOMEBODY LIKE THAT...
...WOULDN'T HAVE WORRIED ABOUT ME...
...AND COME RUNNING AFTER ME.
...SO, THANKS.
SEE...
...JUST LIKE THAT.
BESIDES, I'M THE ONE WHO'S WRAPPED UP IN HIS OWN HEAD, REALLY.
IF I THOUGHT OF OTHERS...
...I WOULDN'T TURN INTO BLACK HARU AND GO BALLISTIC IN CLASS.
......
......

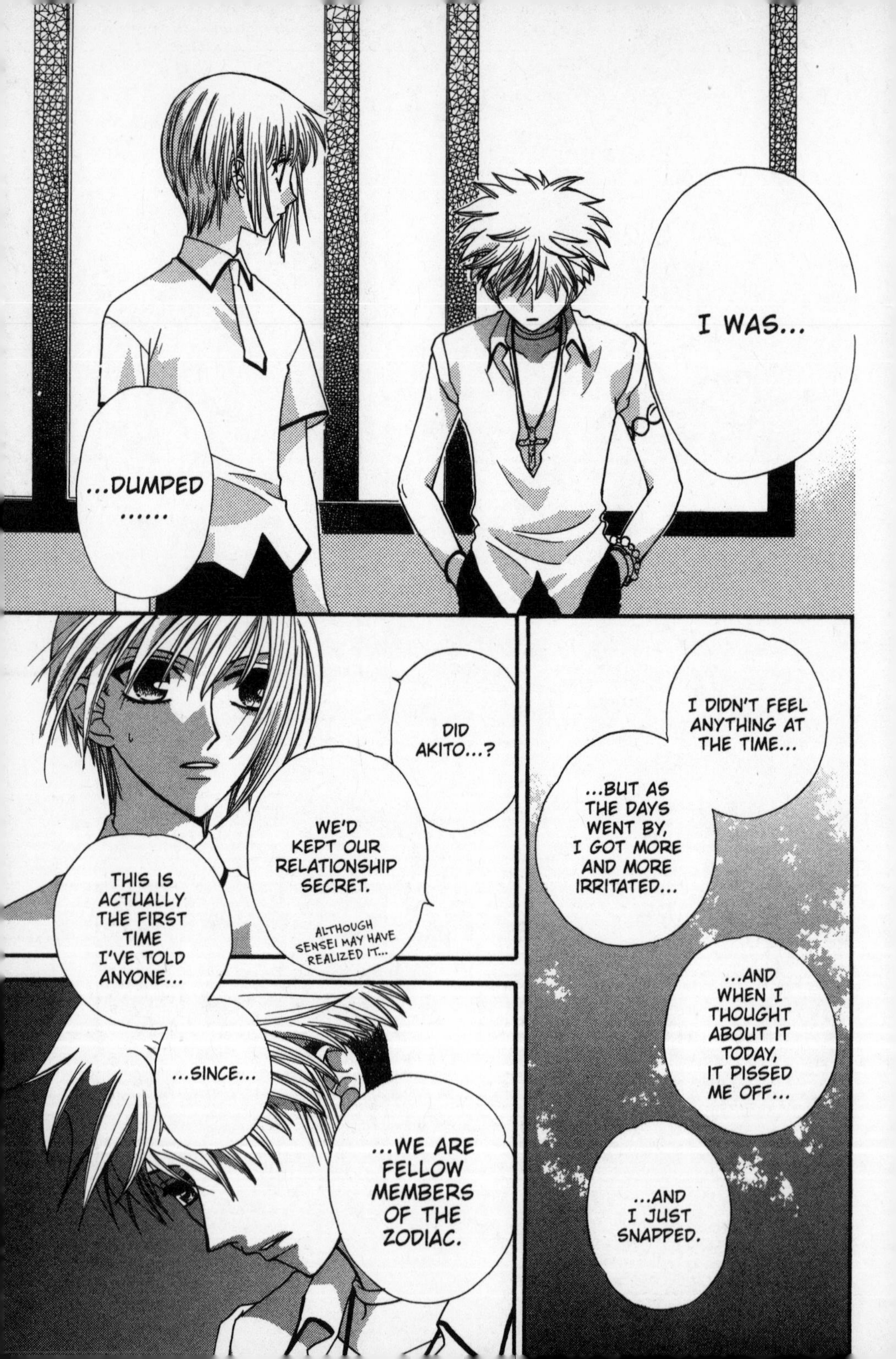
I WAS...
...DUMPED ......
I DIDN'T FEEL ANYTHING AT THE TIME...
...BUT AS THE DAYS WENT BY, I GOT MORE AND MORE IRRITATED...
...AND WHEN I THOUGHT ABOUT IT TODAY, IT PISSED ME OFF...
...AND I JUST SNAPPED.
DID AKITO...?
WE'D KEPT OUR RELATIONSHIP SECRET.
ALTHOUGH SENSEI MAY HAVE REALIZED IT...
THIS IS ACTUALLY THE FIRST TIME I'VE TOLD ANYONE...
...SINCE...
...WE ARE FELLOW MEMBERS OF THE ZODIAC.

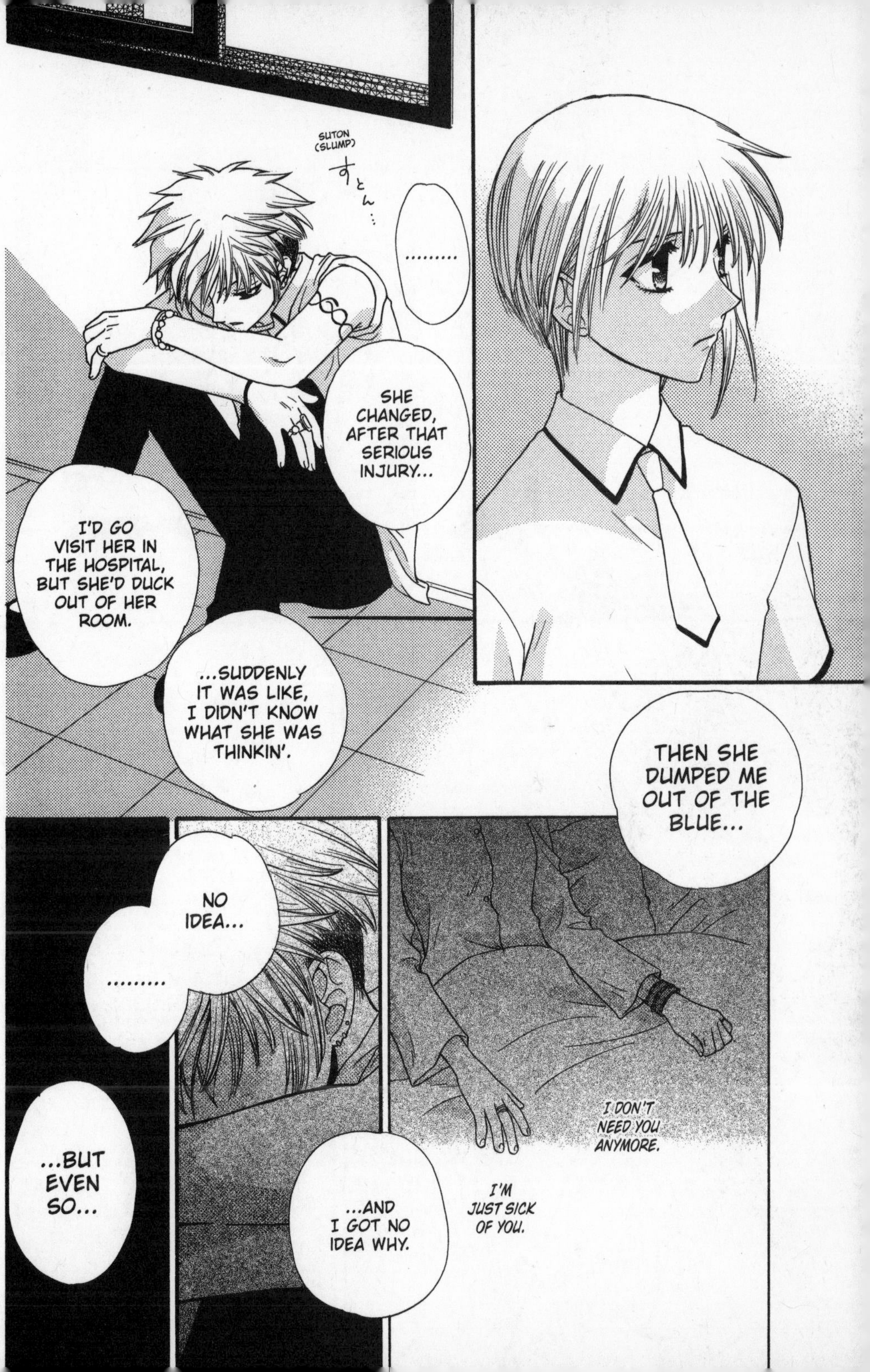

SUTON (SLUMP)
すとん…
………
SHE CHANGED, AFTER THAT SERIOUS INJURY...
I'D GO VISIT HER IN THE HOSPITAL, BUT SHE'D DUCK OUT OF HER ROOM.
...SUDDENLY IT WAS LIKE, I DIDN'T KNOW WHAT SHE WAS THINKIN'.
THEN SHE DUMPED ME OUT OF THE BLUE...
I DON'T NEED YOU ANYMORE.
I'M JUST SICK OF YOU.
...AND I GOT NO IDEA WHY.
NO IDEA...
………
...BUT EVEN SO...

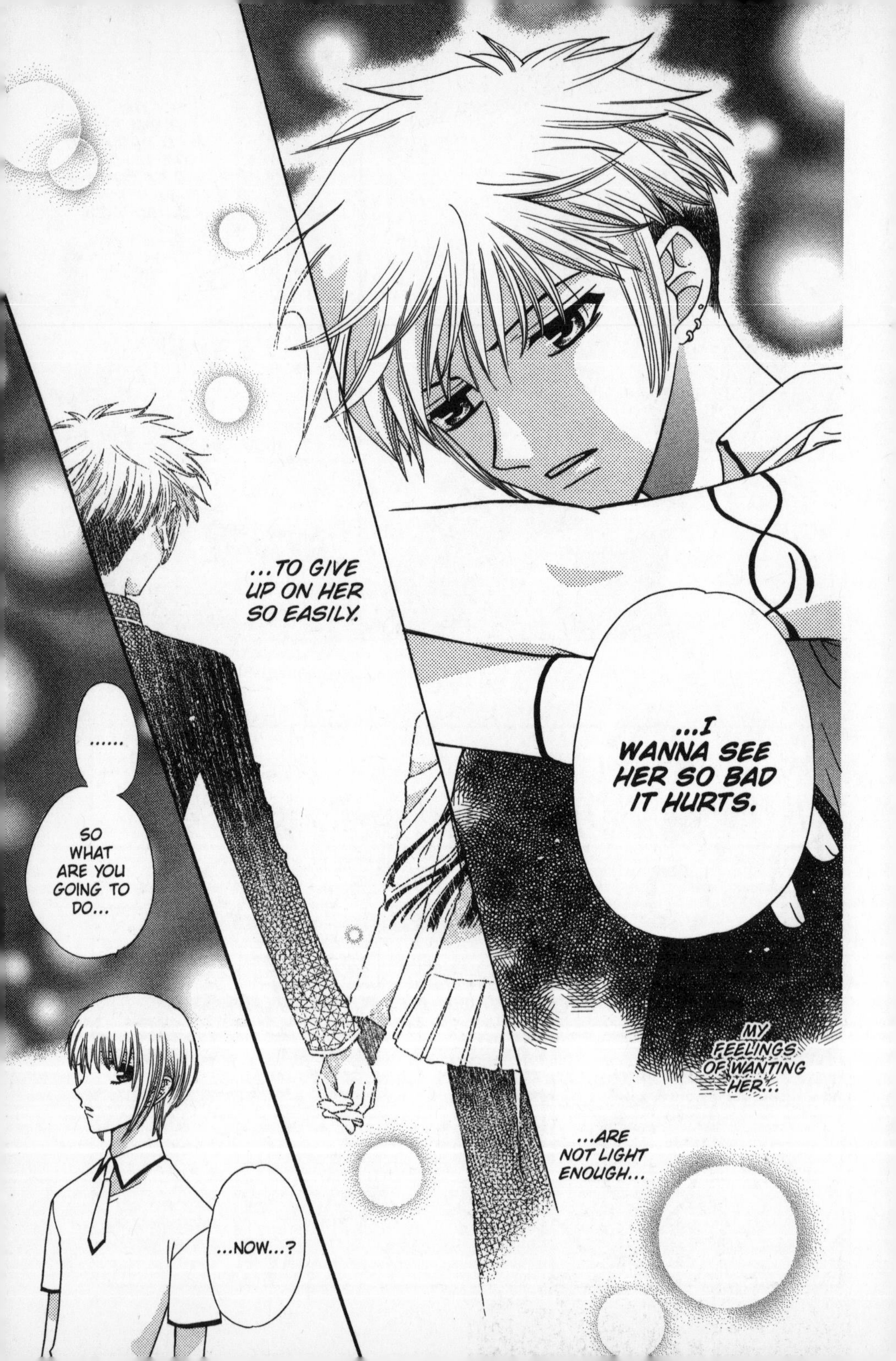
...I WANNA SEE HER SO BAD IT HURTS.
MY FEELINGS OF WANTING HER...
...ARE NOT LIGHT ENOUGH...
...TO GIVE UP ON HER SO EASILY.
......
SO WHAT ARE YOU GOING TO DO...
...NOW...?

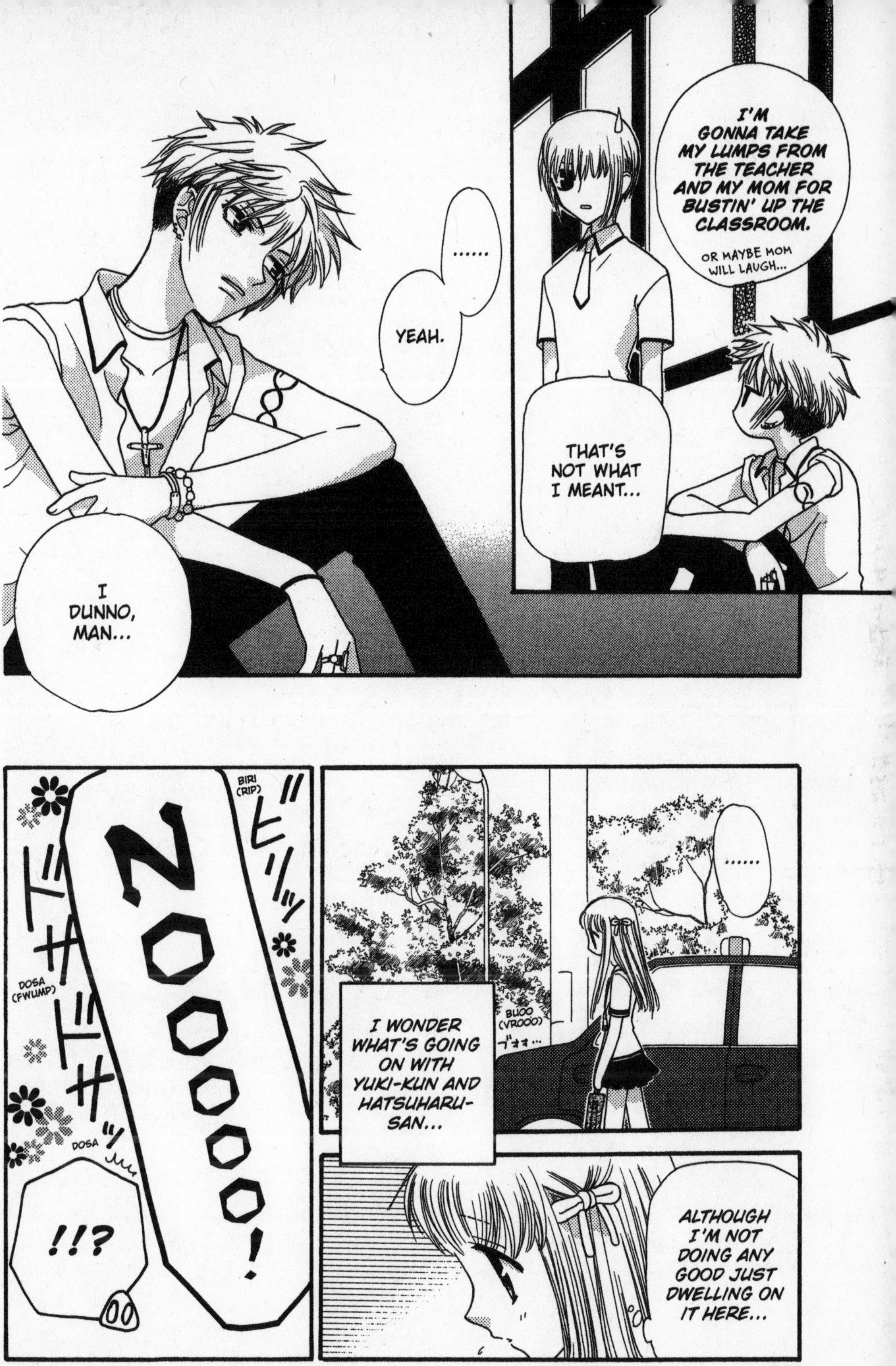
I'M GONNA TAKE MY LUMPS FROM THE TEACHER AND MY MOM FOR BUSTIN' UP THE CLASSROOM.
OR MAYBE MOM WILL LAUGH...
THAT'S NOT WHAT I MEANT...
......
YEAH.
I DUNNO, MAN...
......
BUOO (VROOO)
I WONDER WHAT'S GOING ON WITH YUKI-KUN AND HATSUHARU-SAN...
ALTHOUGH I'M NOT DOING ANY GOOD JUST DWELLING ON IT HERE...
BIRI (RIP)
ZOOOOO!
DOSA (FWUMP)
DOSA
!!?

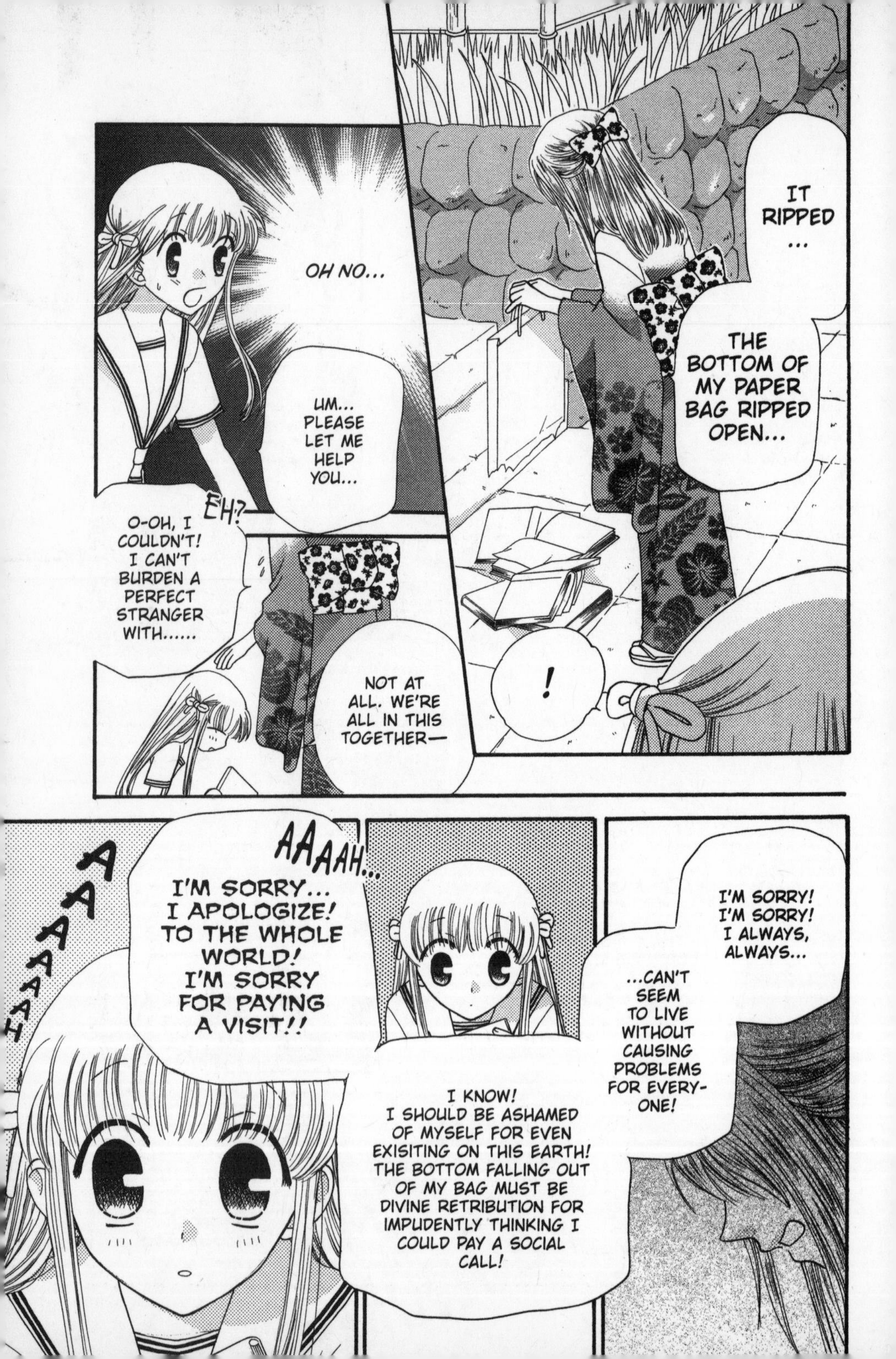
IT RIPPED ...
THE BOTTOM OF MY PAPER BAG RIPPED OPEN...
!
OH NO...
UM... PLEASE LET ME HELP YOU...
EH?
O-OH, I COULDN'T! I CAN'T BURDEN A PERFECT STRANGER WITH......
NOT AT ALL. WE'RE ALL IN THIS TOGETHER—
I'M SORRY! I'M SORRY! I ALWAYS, ALWAYS...
...CAN'T SEEM TO LIVE WITHOUT CAUSING PROBLEMS FOR EVERY-ONE!
I KNOW! I SHOULD BE ASHAMED OF MYSELF FOR EVEN EXISITING ON THIS EARTH! THE BOTTOM FALLING OUT OF MY BAG MUST BE DIVINE RETRIBUTION FOR IMPUDENTLY THINKING I COULD PAY A SOCIAL CALL!
AAAAH...
I'M SORRY... I APOLOGIZE! TO THE WHOLE WORLD! I'M SORRY FOR PAYING A VISIT!!
AAAAAAAH

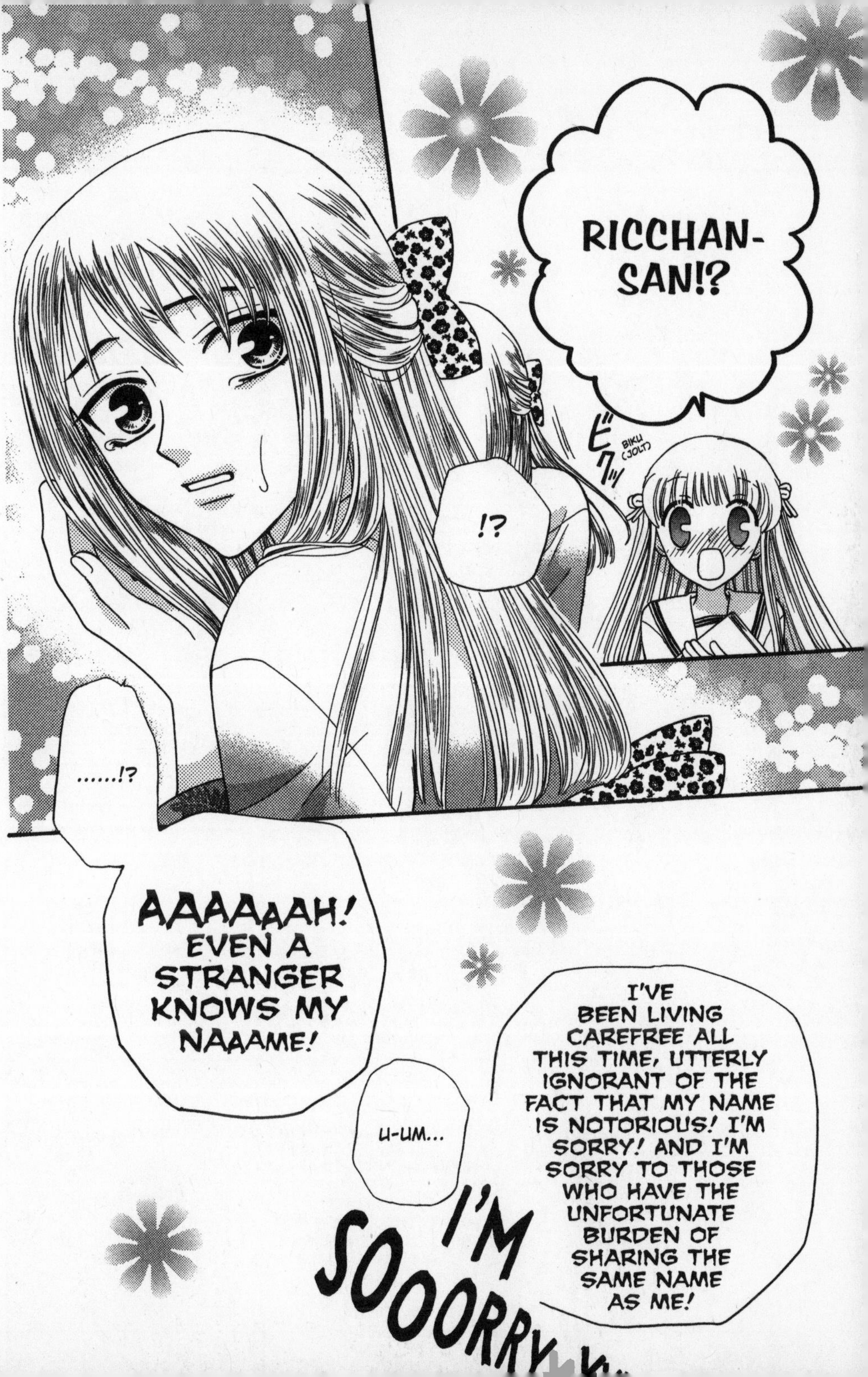
RICCHAN-SAN!?
ビクッ
BIKU (JOLT)
!?
......!?
AAAAAAH! EVEN A STRANGER KNOWS MY NAAAME!
U-UM...
I'VE BEEN LIVING CAREFREE ALL THIS TIME, UTTERLY IGNORANT OF THE FACT THAT MY NAME IS NOTORIOUS! I'M SORRY! AND I'M SORRY TO THOSE WHO HAVE THE UNFORTUNATE BURDEN OF SHARING THE SAME NAME AS ME!
I'M SOOORRY...

Chapter 44

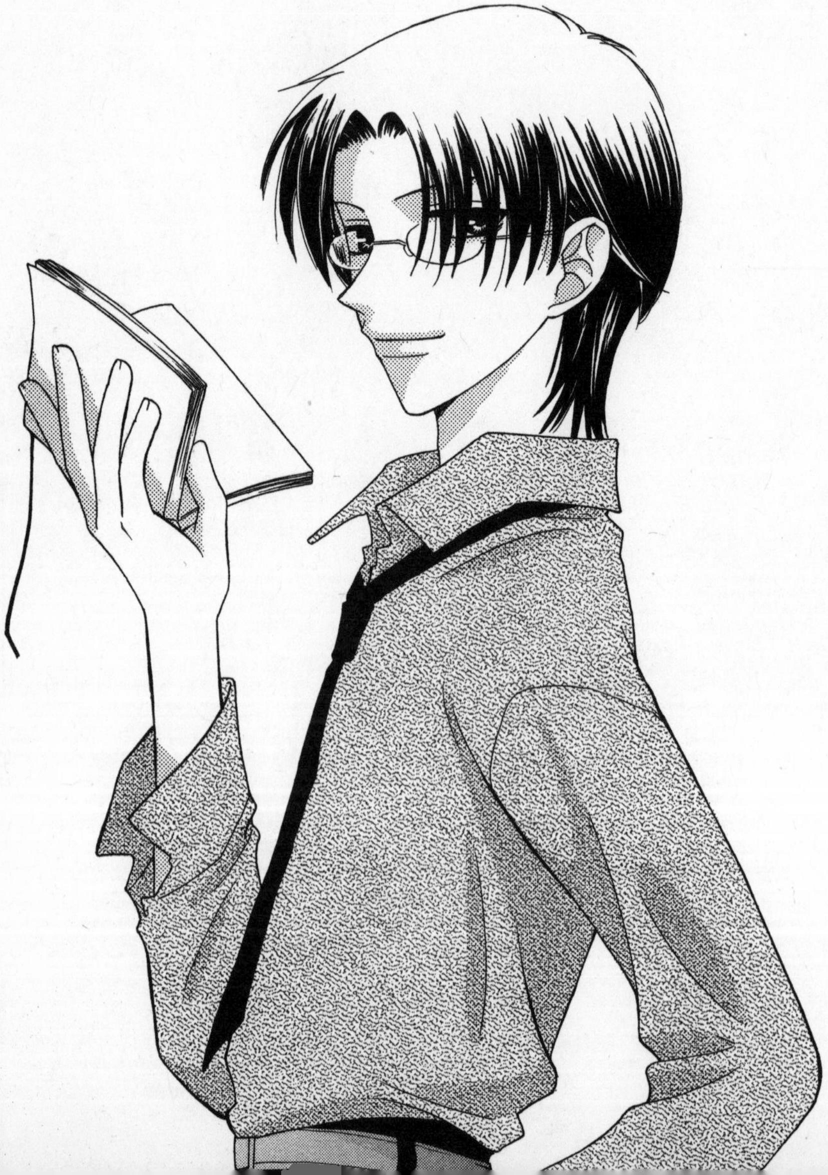

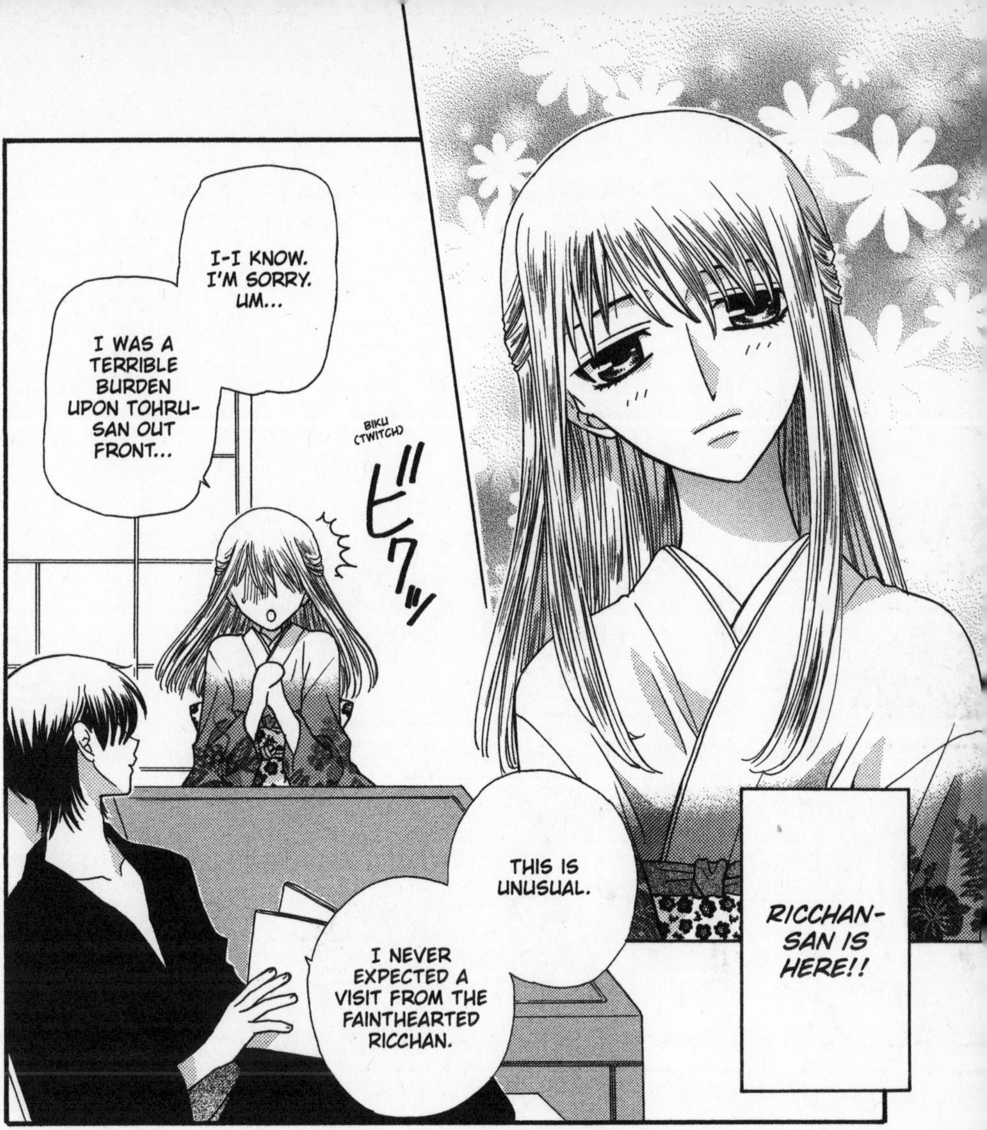
RICCHAN-SAN IS HERE!!
THIS IS UNUSUAL.
I NEVER EXPECTED A VISIT FROM THE FAINTHEARTED RICCHAN.
BIKU (TWITCH)
ビクッ
I-I KNOW. I'M SORRY. UM...
I WAS A TERRIBLE BURDEN UPON TOHRU-SAN OUT FRONT...

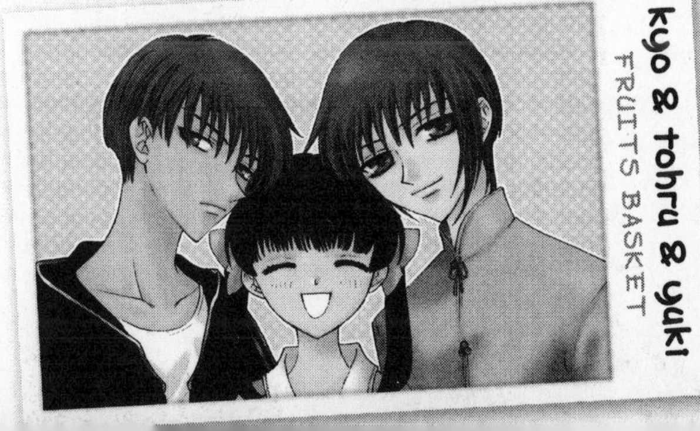
kyo & tohru & yuki
FRUITS BASKET

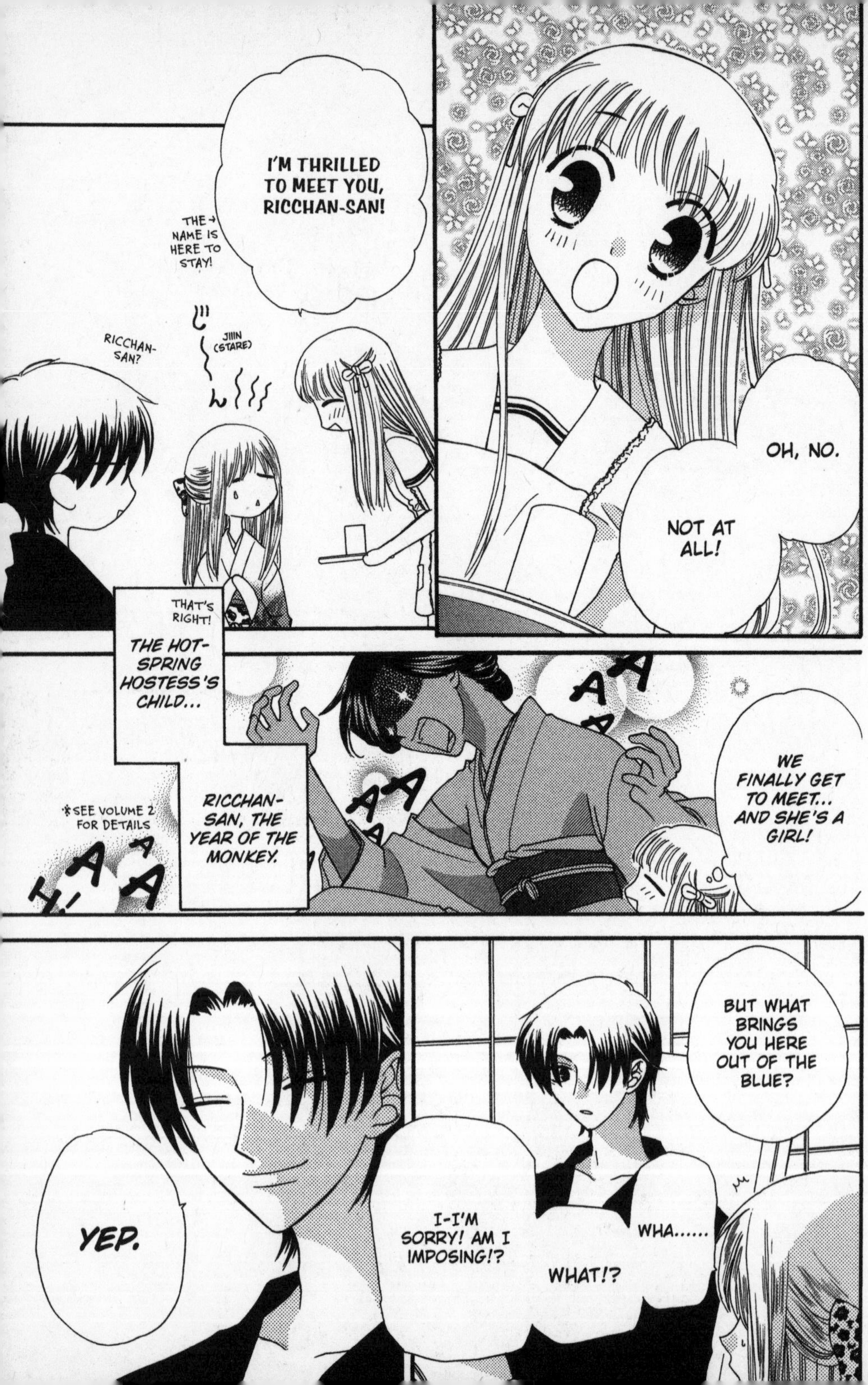
OH, NO.
NOT AT ALL!
I'M THRILLED TO MEET YOU, RICCHAN-SAN!
THE→ NAME IS HERE TO STAY!
JIIIN (STARE)
RICCHAN-SAN?
THAT'S RIGHT!
THE HOT-SPRING HOSTESS'S CHILD...
WE FINALLY GET TO MEET... AND SHE'S A GIRL!
AAAA
RICCHAN-SAN, THE YEAR OF THE MONKEY.
*SEE VOLUME 2 FOR DETAILS
HAAA!
BUT WHAT BRINGS YOU HERE OUT OF THE BLUE?
WHA......
WHAT!?
I-I'M SORRY! AM I IMPOSING!?
YEP.

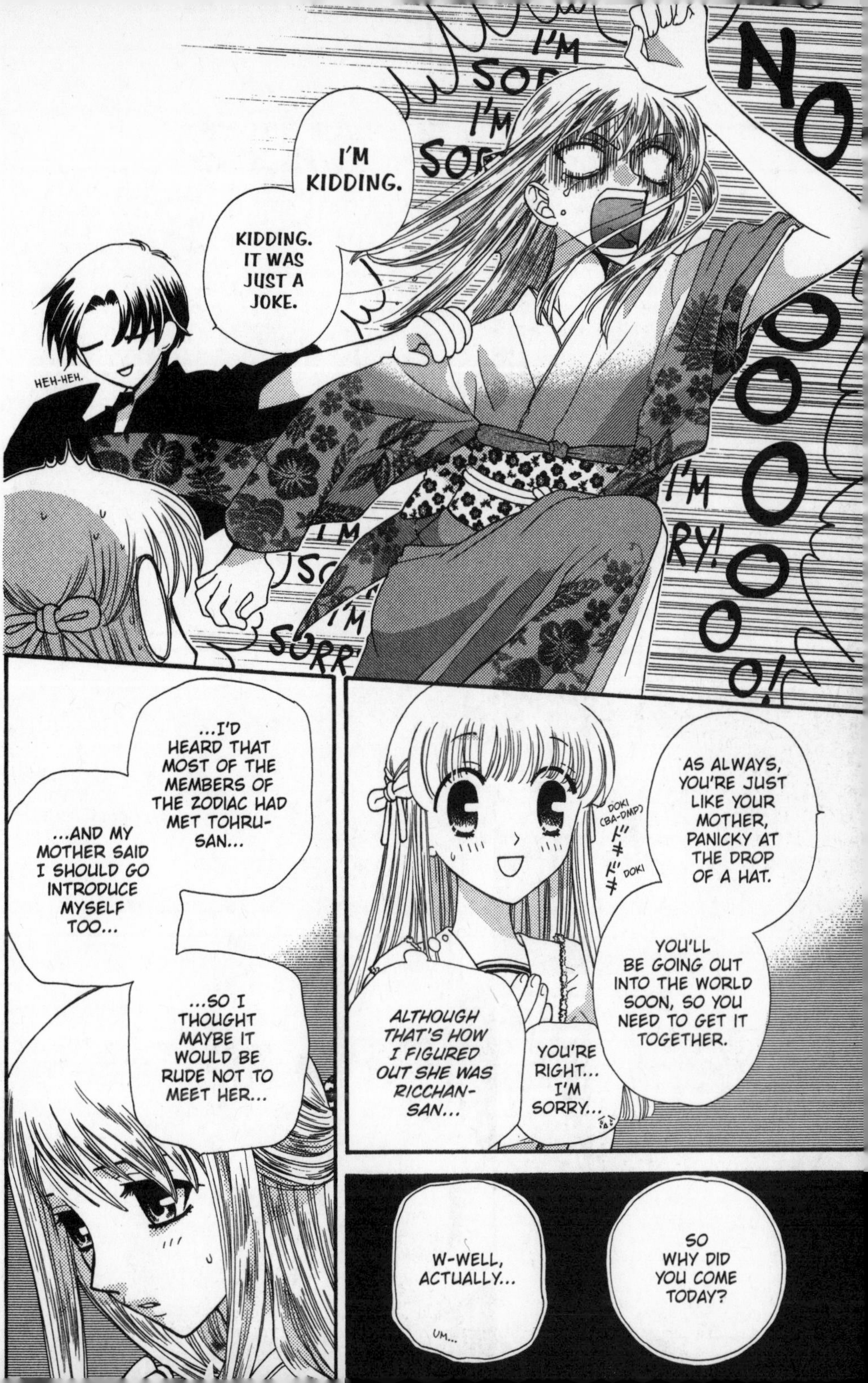

NOOOOOOOO!
I'M SORRY!
I'M SOR
I'M SORR
I'M KIDDING.
KIDDING. IT WAS JUST A JOKE.
HEH-HEH.
I'M SO
I'M SORR
AS ALWAYS, YOU'RE JUST LIKE YOUR MOTHER, PANICKY AT THE DROP OF A HAT.
DOKI (BA-DMP) DOKI
YOU'LL BE GOING OUT INTO THE WORLD SOON, SO YOU NEED TO GET IT TOGETHER.
YOU'RE RIGHT... I'M SORRY...
ALTHOUGH THAT'S HOW I FIGURED OUT SHE WAS RICCHAN-SAN...
SO WHY DID YOU COME TODAY?
W-WELL, ACTUALLY...
UM...
...I'D HEARD THAT MOST OF THE MEMBERS OF THE ZODIAC HAD MET TOHRU-SAN...
...AND MY MOTHER SAID I SHOULD GO INTRODUCE MYSELF TOO...
...SO I THOUGHT MAYBE IT WOULD BE RUDE NOT TO MEET HER...

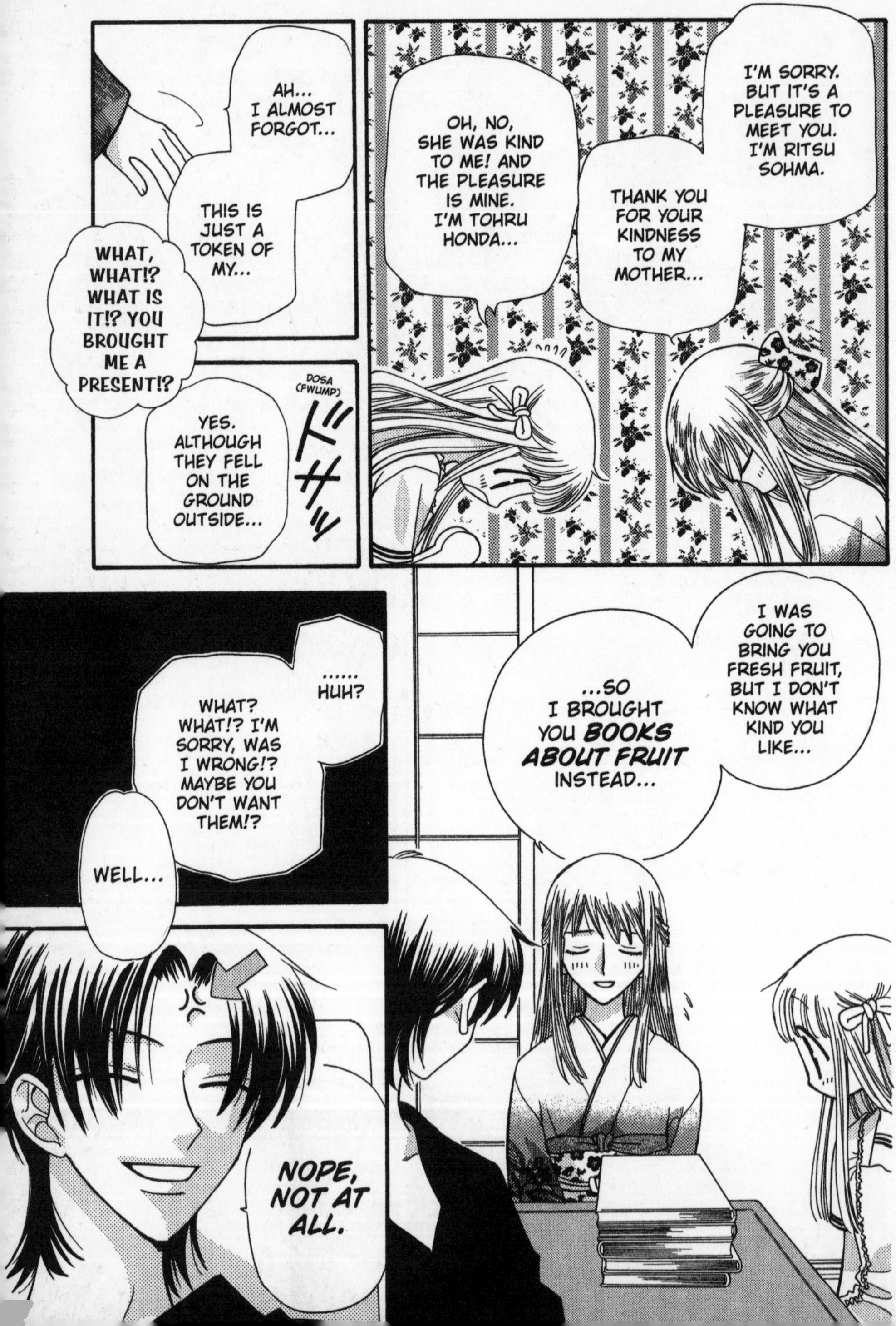
I'M SORRY. BUT IT'S A PLEASURE TO MEET YOU. I'M RITSU SOHMA.
THANK YOU FOR YOUR KINDNESS TO MY MOTHER...
OH, NO, SHE WAS KIND TO ME! AND THE PLEASURE IS MINE. I'M TOHRU HONDA...
AH... I ALMOST FORGOT...
THIS IS JUST A TOKEN OF MY...
WHAT, WHAT!? WHAT IS IT!? YOU BROUGHT ME A PRESENT!?
DOSA (FWUMP)
YES. ALTHOUGH THEY FELL ON THE GROUND OUTSIDE...
I WAS GOING TO BRING YOU FRESH FRUIT, BUT I DON'T KNOW WHAT KIND YOU LIKE...
...SO I BROUGHT YOU **BOOKS ABOUT FRUIT** INSTEAD...
...... HUH?
WHAT? WHAT!? I'M SORRY, WAS I WRONG!? MAYBE YOU DON'T WANT THEM!?
WELL...
NOPE, NOT AT ALL.

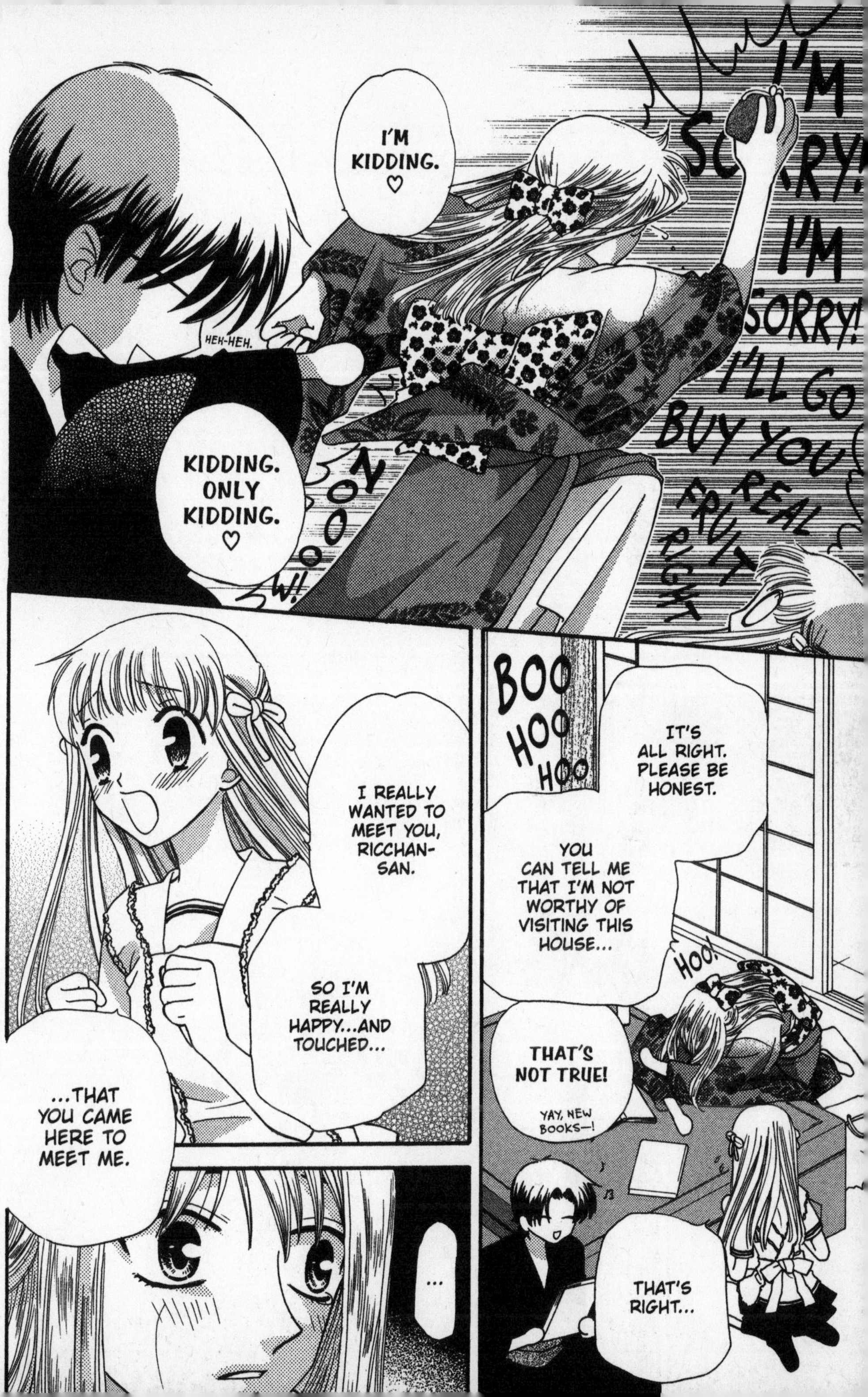
I'M SORRY! I'M SORRY! I'LL GO BUY YOU REAL FRUIT RIGHT
I'M KIDDING. ♡
HEH-HEH.
KIDDING. ONLY KIDDING. ♡
BOO HOO HOO
IT'S ALL RIGHT. PLEASE BE HONEST.
YOU CAN TELL ME THAT I'M NOT WORTHY OF VISITING THIS HOUSE...
HOO!
THAT'S NOT TRUE!
YAY, NEW BOOKS—!
THAT'S RIGHT...
I REALLY WANTED TO MEET YOU, RICCHAN-SAN.
SO I'M REALLY HAPPY...AND TOUCHED...
...THAT YOU CAME HERE TO MEET ME.
...

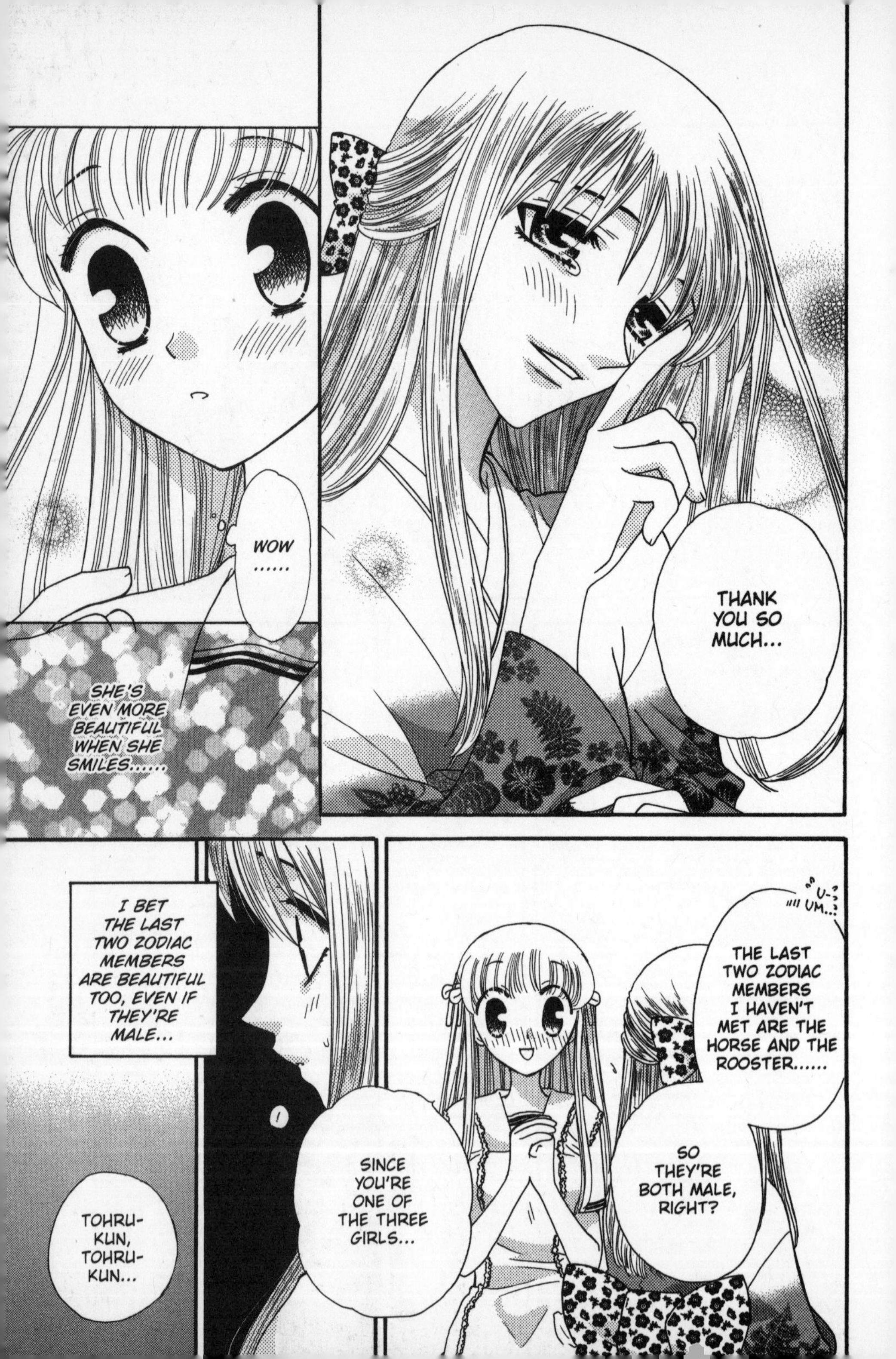
THANK YOU SO MUCH...
WOW ......
SHE'S EVEN MORE BEAUTIFUL WHEN SHE SMILES......
U-? UM..?
THE LAST TWO ZODIAC MEMBERS I HAVEN'T MET ARE THE HORSE AND THE ROOSTER......
SO THEY'RE BOTH MALE, RIGHT?
SINCE YOU'RE ONE OF THE THREE GIRLS...
I BET THE LAST TWO ZODIAC MEMBERS ARE BEAUTIFUL TOO, EVEN IF THEY'RE MALE...
!
TOHRU-KUN, TOHRU-KUN...

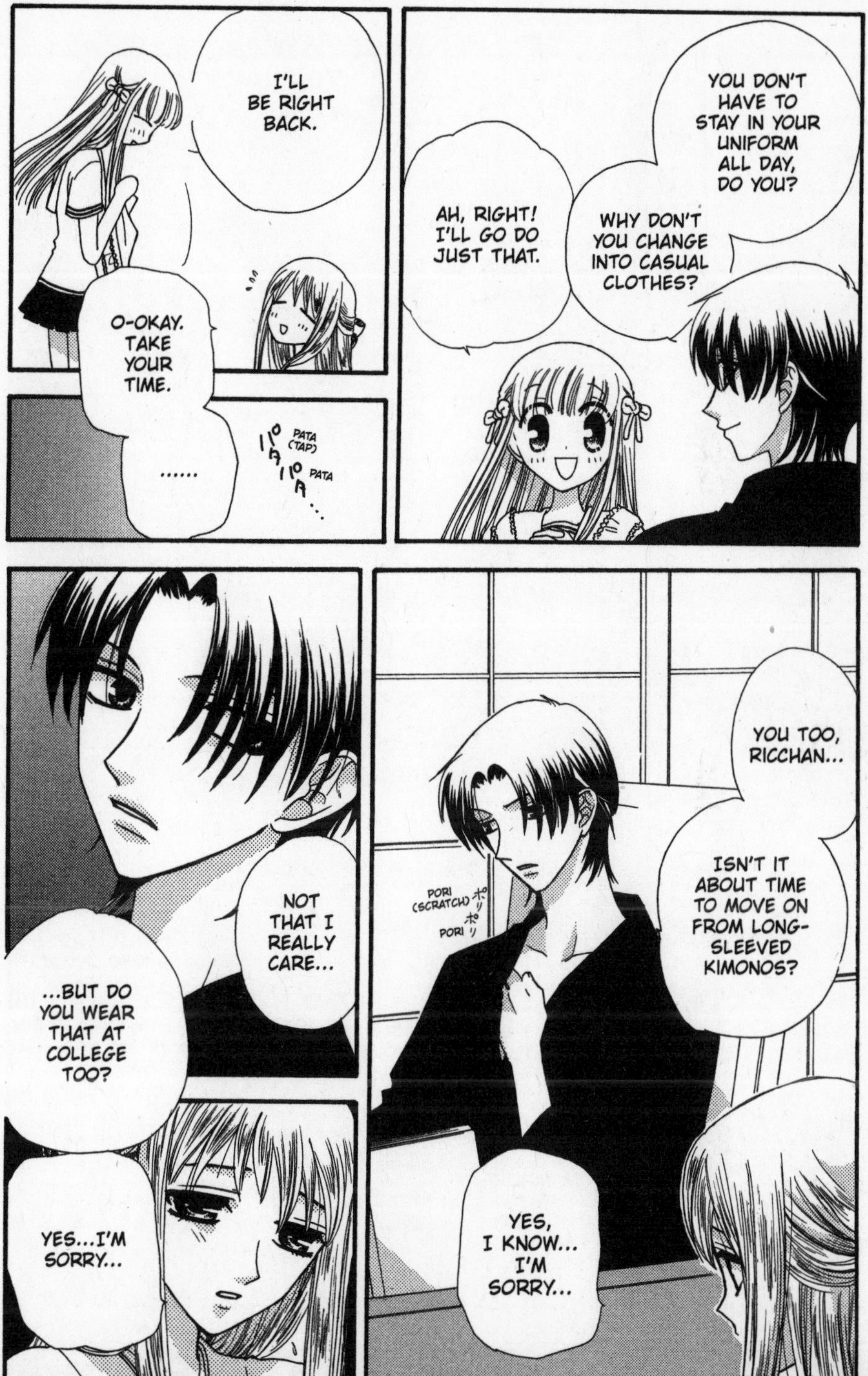
YOU DON'T HAVE TO STAY IN YOUR UNIFORM ALL DAY, DO YOU?
WHY DON'T YOU CHANGE INTO CASUAL CLOTHES?
AH, RIGHT! I'LL GO DO JUST THAT.
I'LL BE RIGHT BACK.
O-OKAY. TAKE YOUR TIME.
PATA (TAP) PATA
......
YOU TOO, RICCHAN...
ISN'T IT ABOUT TIME TO MOVE ON FROM LONG-SLEEVED KIMONOS?
PORI (SCRATCH) PORI
YES, I KNOW... I'M SORRY...
NOT THAT I REALLY CARE...
...BUT DO YOU WEAR THAT AT COLLEGE TOO?
YES...I'M SORRY...

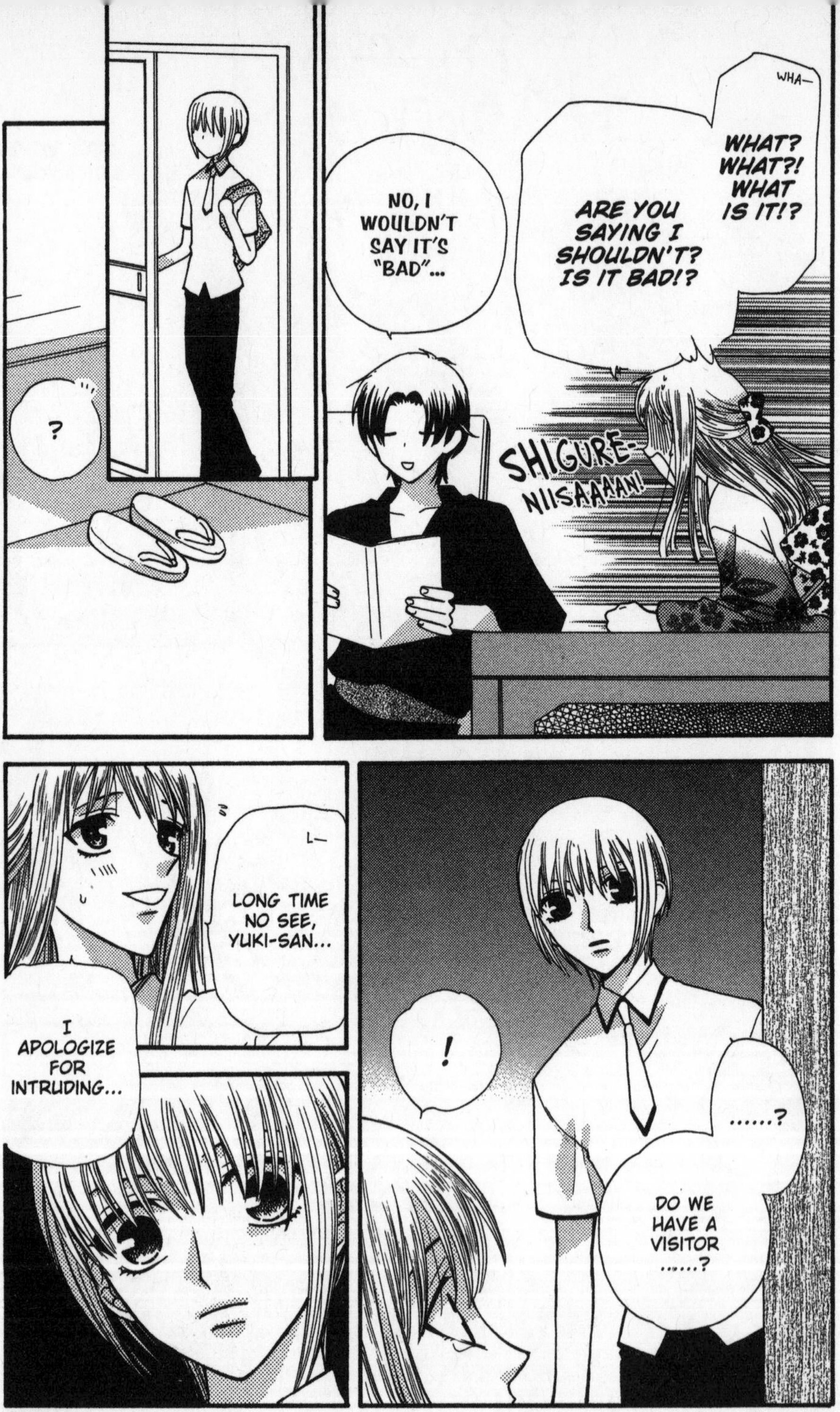
WHA—
WHAT? WHAT?! WHAT IS IT!?
ARE YOU SAYING I SHOULDN'T? IS IT BAD!?
SHIGURE-NIISAAAAN!
NO, I WOULDN'T SAY IT'S "BAD"...
?
......?
DO WE HAVE A VISITOR ......?
!
L—
LONG TIME NO SEE, YUKI-SAN...
I APOLOGIZE FOR INTRUDING...

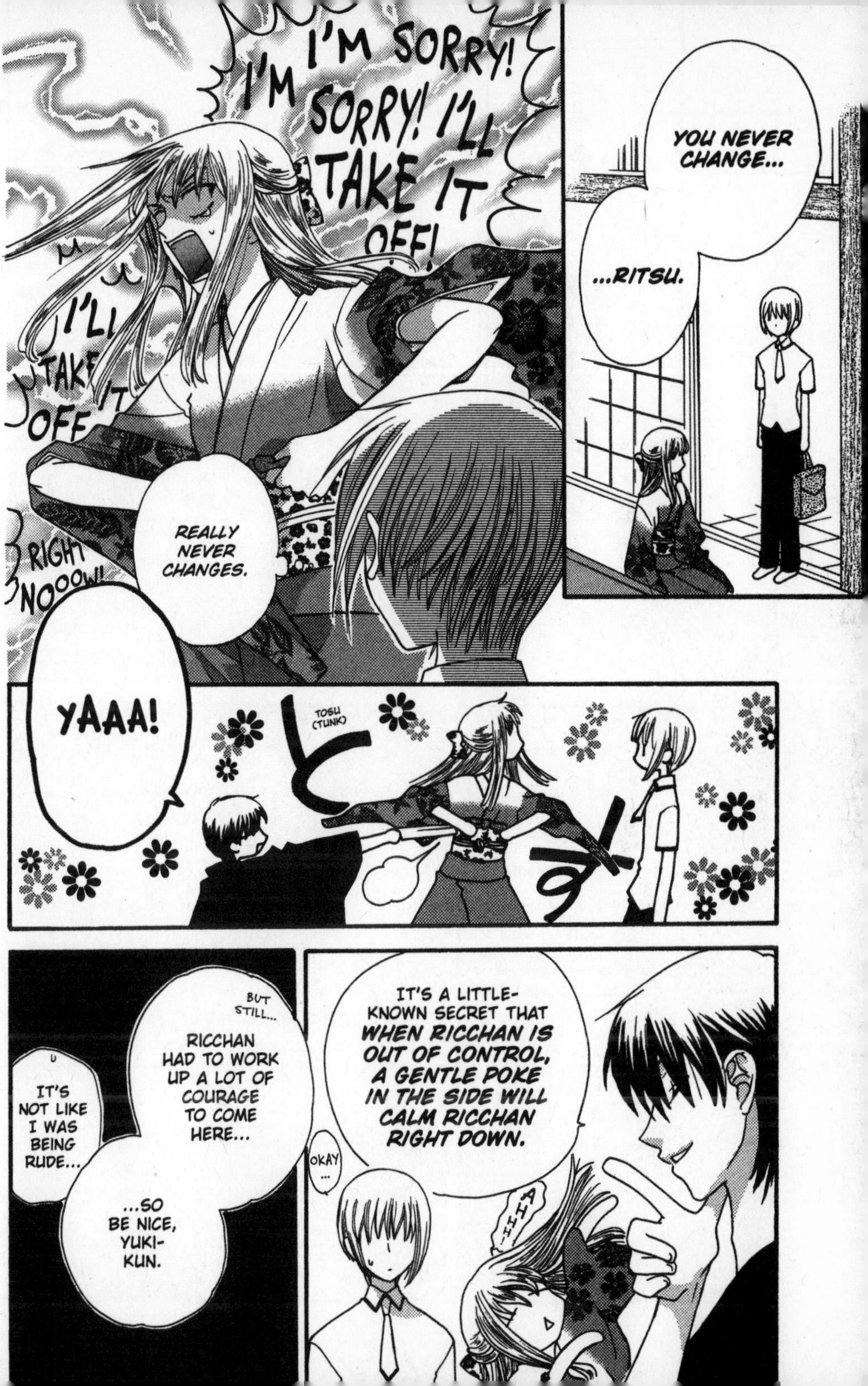
YOU NEVER CHANGE...
...RITSU.
I'M SORRY! I'M SORRY! I'LL TAKE IT OFF!
I'LL TAKE IT OFF
RIGHT NOOOW!
REALLY NEVER CHANGES.
YAAA!
TOSU (TUNK)
IT'S A LITTLE-KNOWN SECRET THAT WHEN RICCHAN IS OUT OF CONTROL, A GENTLE POKE IN THE SIDE WILL CALM RICCHAN RIGHT DOWN.
OKAY...
BUT STILL...
RICCHAN HAD TO WORK UP A LOT OF COURAGE TO COME HERE...
...SO BE NICE, YUKI-KUN.
IT'S NOT LIKE I WAS BEING RUDE...

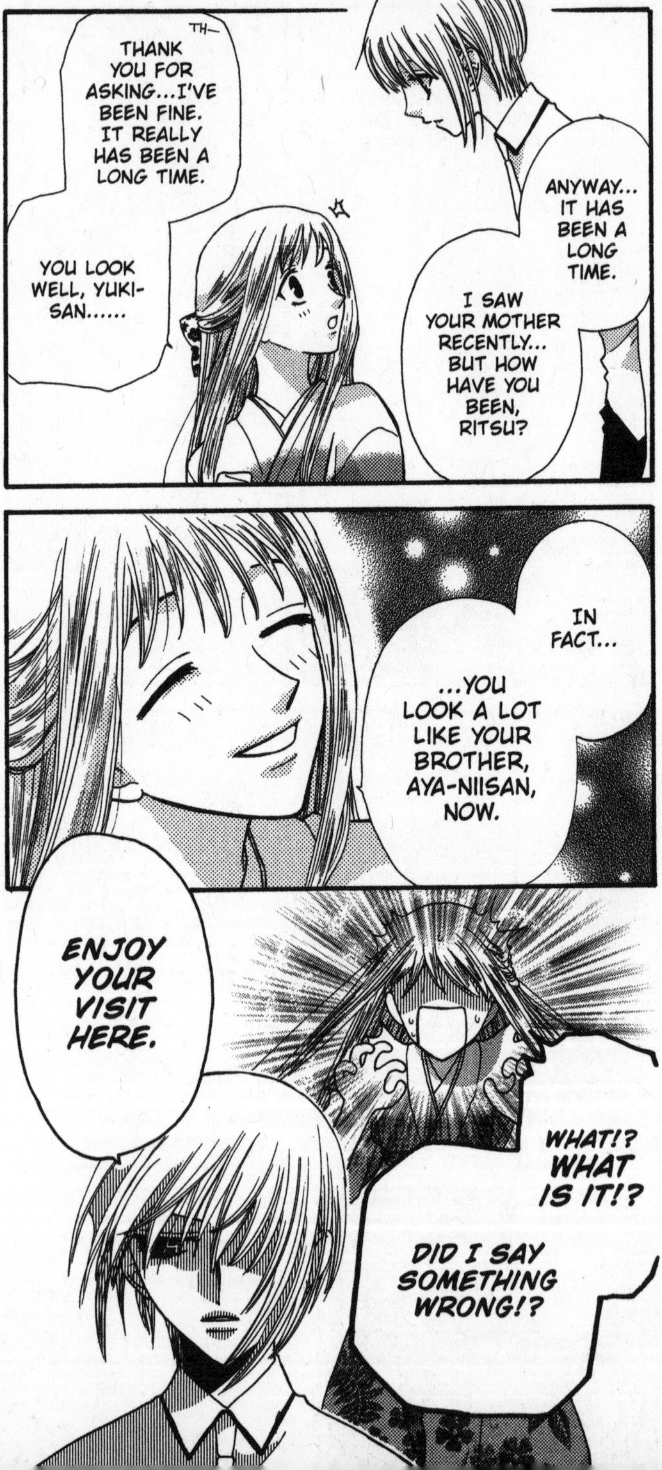
ANYWAY... IT HAS BEEN A LONG TIME.
I SAW YOUR MOTHER RECENTLY... BUT HOW HAVE YOU BEEN, RITSU?
TH—
THANK YOU FOR ASKING...I'VE BEEN FINE. IT REALLY HAS BEEN A LONG TIME.
YOU LOOK WELL, YUKI-SAN......
IN FACT...
...YOU LOOK A LOT LIKE YOUR BROTHER, AYA-NIISAN, NOW.
ENJOY YOUR VISIT HERE.
WHAT!? WHAT IS IT!?
DID I SAY SOMETHING WRONG!?

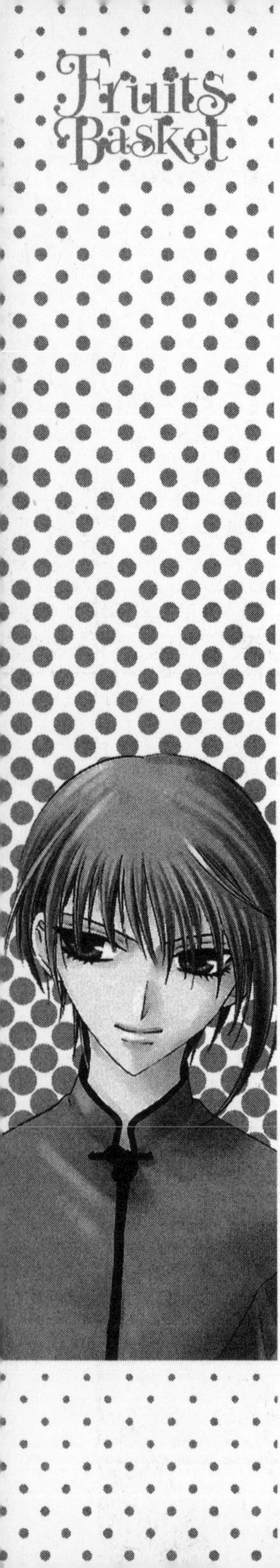
Fruits Basket

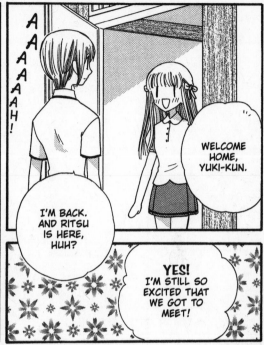

AAAAAAH!
WELCOME HOME, YUKI-KUN.
I'M BACK. AND RITSU IS HERE, HUH?
YES! I'M STILL SO EXCITED THAT WE GOT TO MEET!
BUT YOU MUST BE SURPRISED.
YOU KNOW, THE PANICKY REACTIONS...
HEE HEE.
JUST LIKE THE HOT-SPRING HOSTESS.
AHHH...
YOU NEED TO CALM DOWN!
THIS ISN'T A GEISHA PARTY.
OH!
YUKI-KUN...
...WAS HATSUHARU-SAN ALL RIGHT?
......
GOOD QUES-TION...

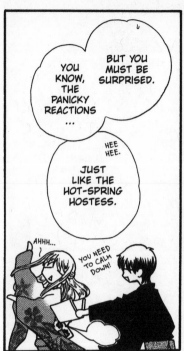

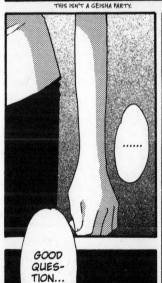

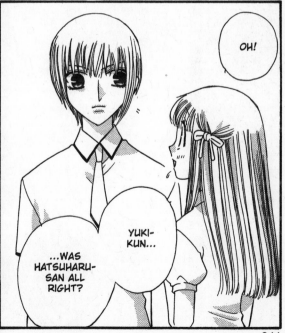

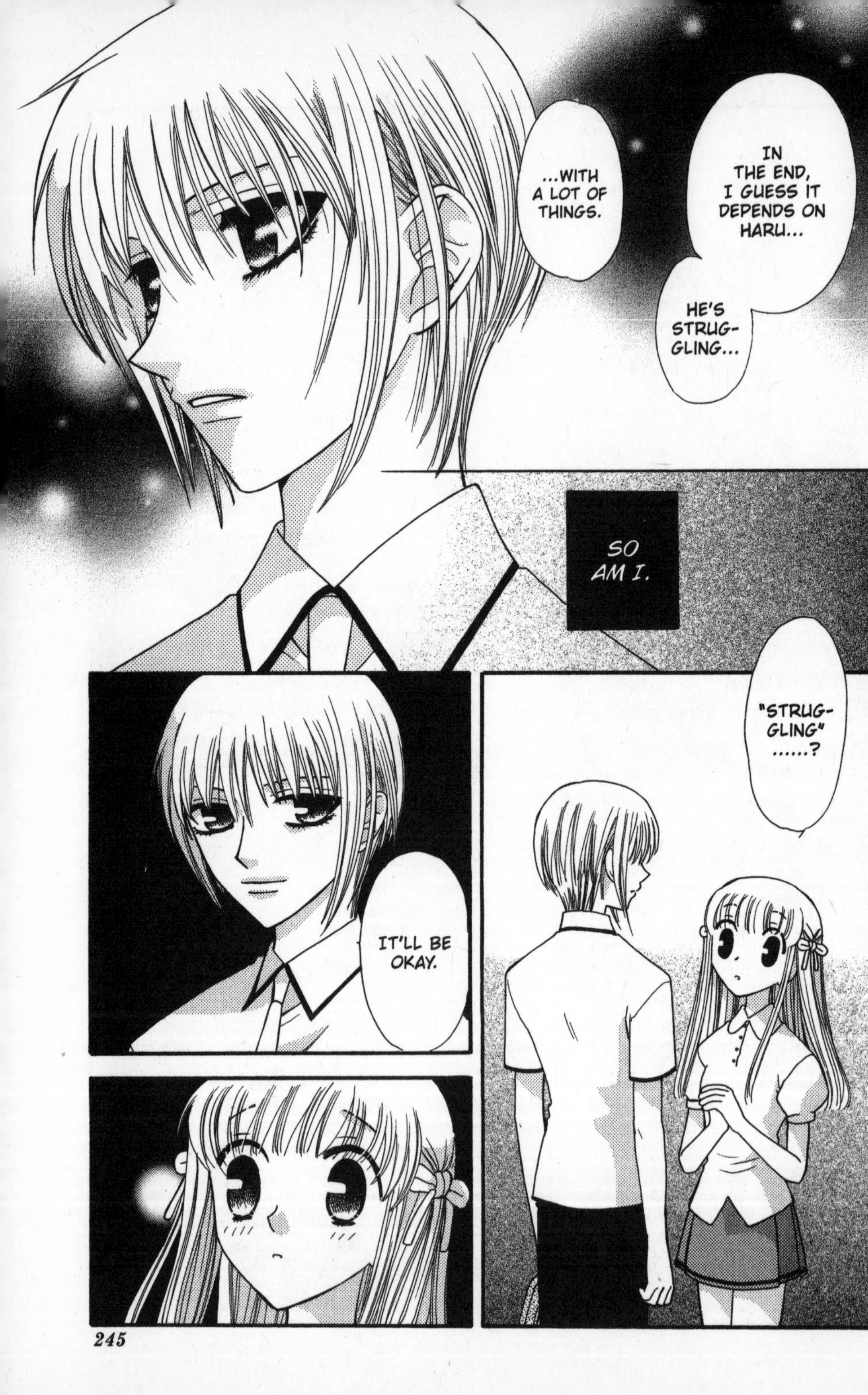
IN THE END, I GUESS IT DEPENDS ON HARU...
HE'S STRUG-GLING...
...WITH A LOT OF THINGS.
SO AM I.
"STRUG-GLING" ......?
IT'LL BE OKAY.

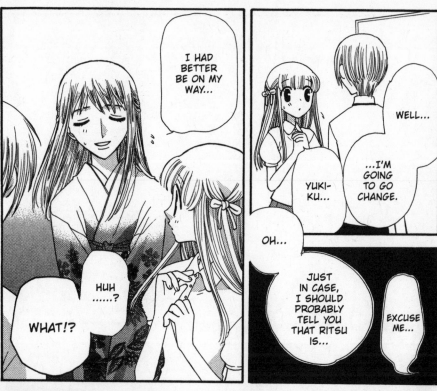

WELL...
...I'M GOING TO GO CHANGE.
YUKI-KU...
OH...
EXCUSE ME...
JUST IN CASE, I SHOULD PROBABLY TELL YOU THAT RITSU IS...
I HAD BETTER BE ON MY WAY...
HUH ......?
WHAT!?
I DON'T WANT TO OVERSTAY MY WELCOME......
Y- YOU'RE NOT! PLEASE STAY. YOU JUST GOT HERE!
I HAVEN'T EVEN SERVED TEA...
OH, I DON'T WANT TO CAUSE YOU ANY TROUBLE. PLEASE DON'T WORRY ABOUT ME...
IT'S REALLY NO TROUBLE. I WANT TO DO IT! SO PLEASE...

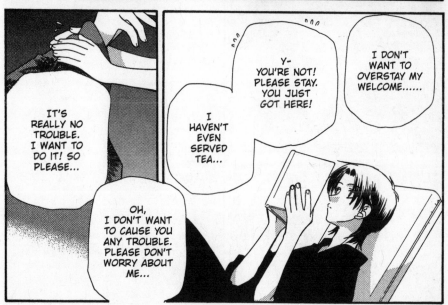

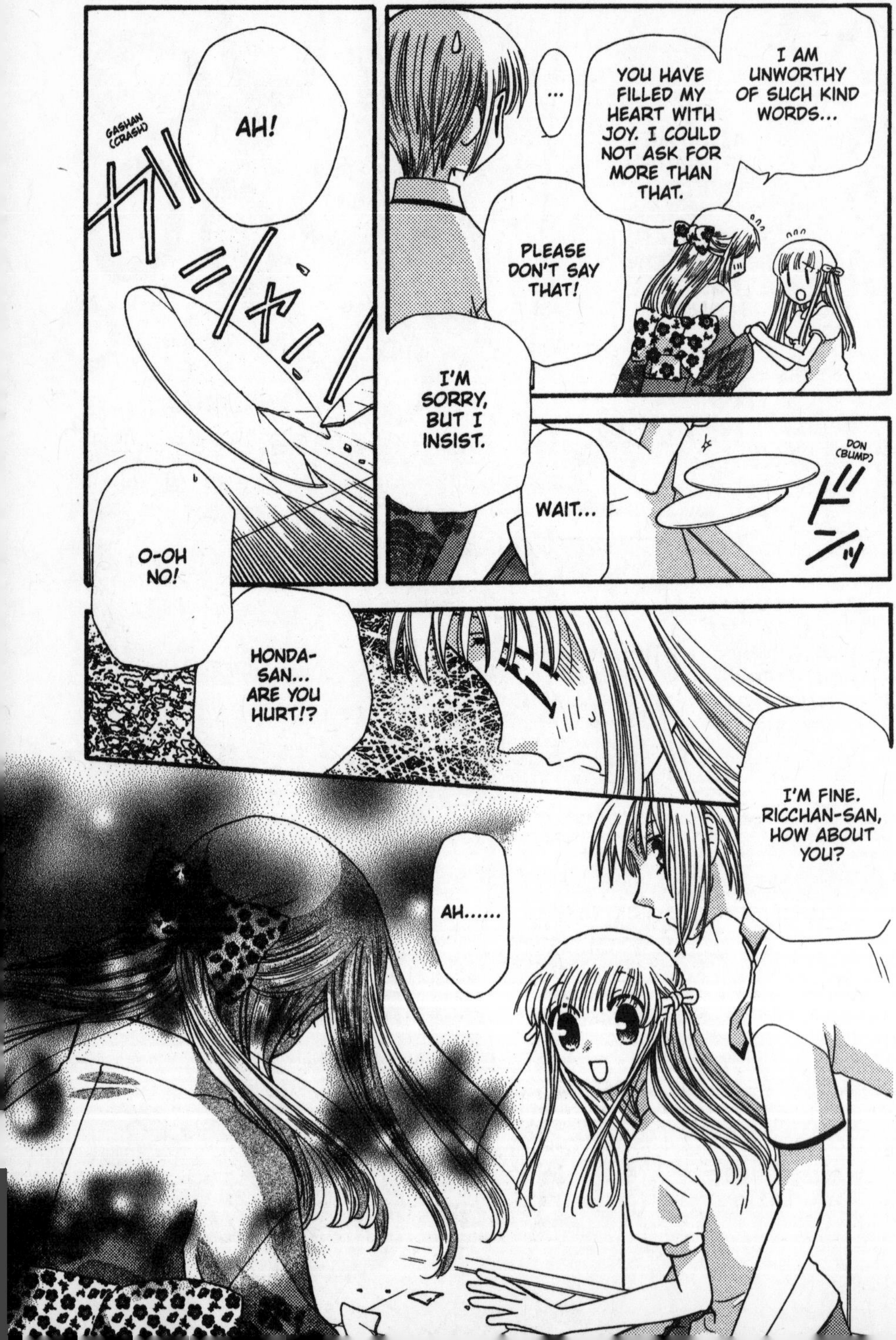
I AM UNWORTHY OF SUCH KIND WORDS...
YOU HAVE FILLED MY HEART WITH JOY. I COULD NOT ASK FOR MORE THAN THAT.
...
PLEASE DON'T SAY THAT!
I'M SORRY, BUT I INSIST.
DON (BUMP)
WAIT...
GASHAN (CRASH)
AH!
O-OH NO!
HONDA-SAN... ARE YOU HURT!?
I'M FINE. RICCHAN-SAN, HOW ABOUT YOU?
AH......

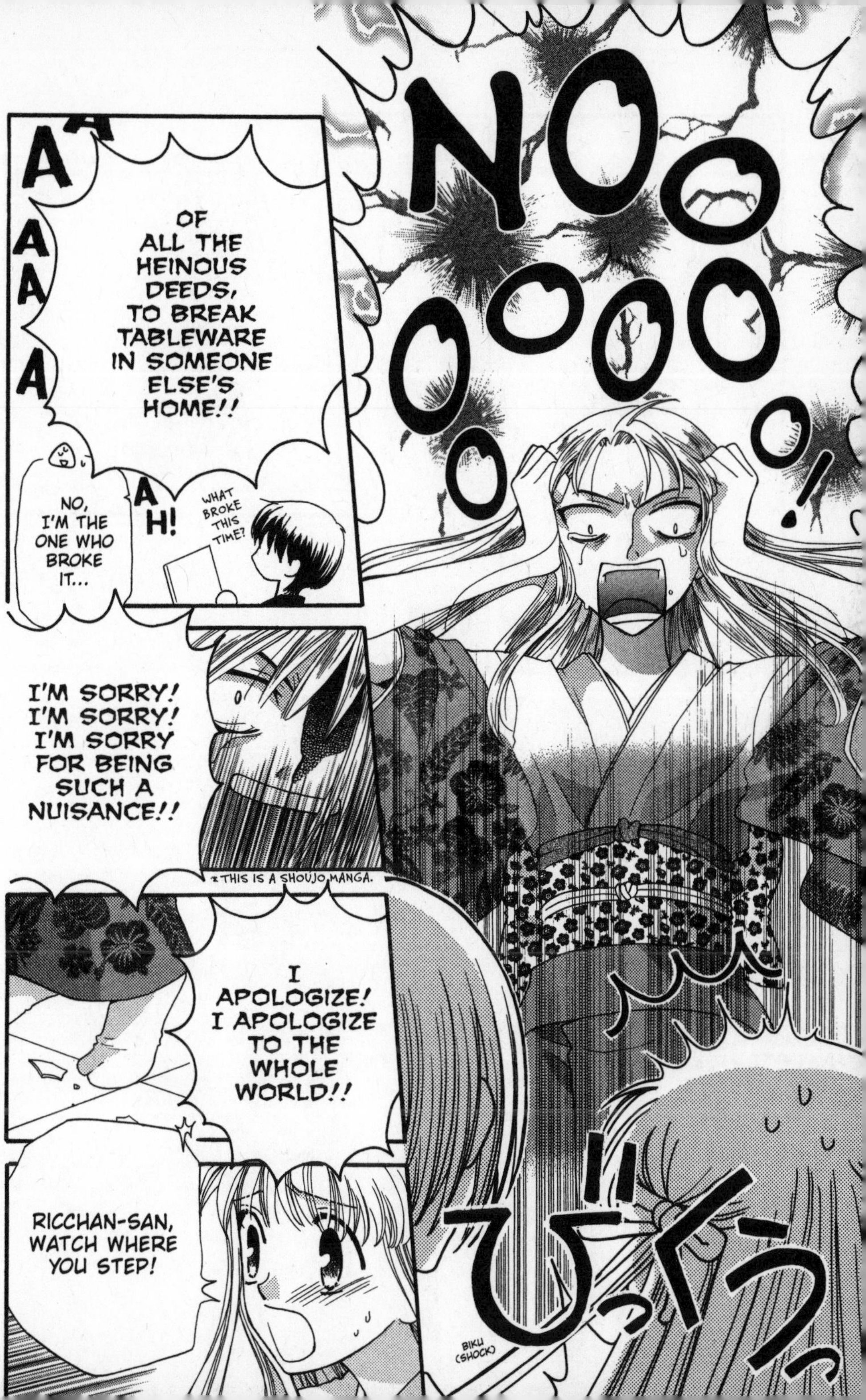

NOOOOOOOOO!
AAAAAAAH!
OF ALL THE HEINOUS DEEDS, TO BREAK TABLEWARE IN SOMEONE ELSE'S HOME!!
WHAT BROKE THIS TIME?
NO, I'M THE ONE WHO BROKE IT...
I'M SORRY! I'M SORRY! I'M SORRY FOR BEING SUCH A NUISANCE!!
* THIS IS A SHOUJO MANGA.
I APOLOGIZE! I APOLOGIZE TO THE WHOLE WORLD!!
BIKU (SHOCK)
RICCHAN-SAN, WATCH WHERE YOU STEP!

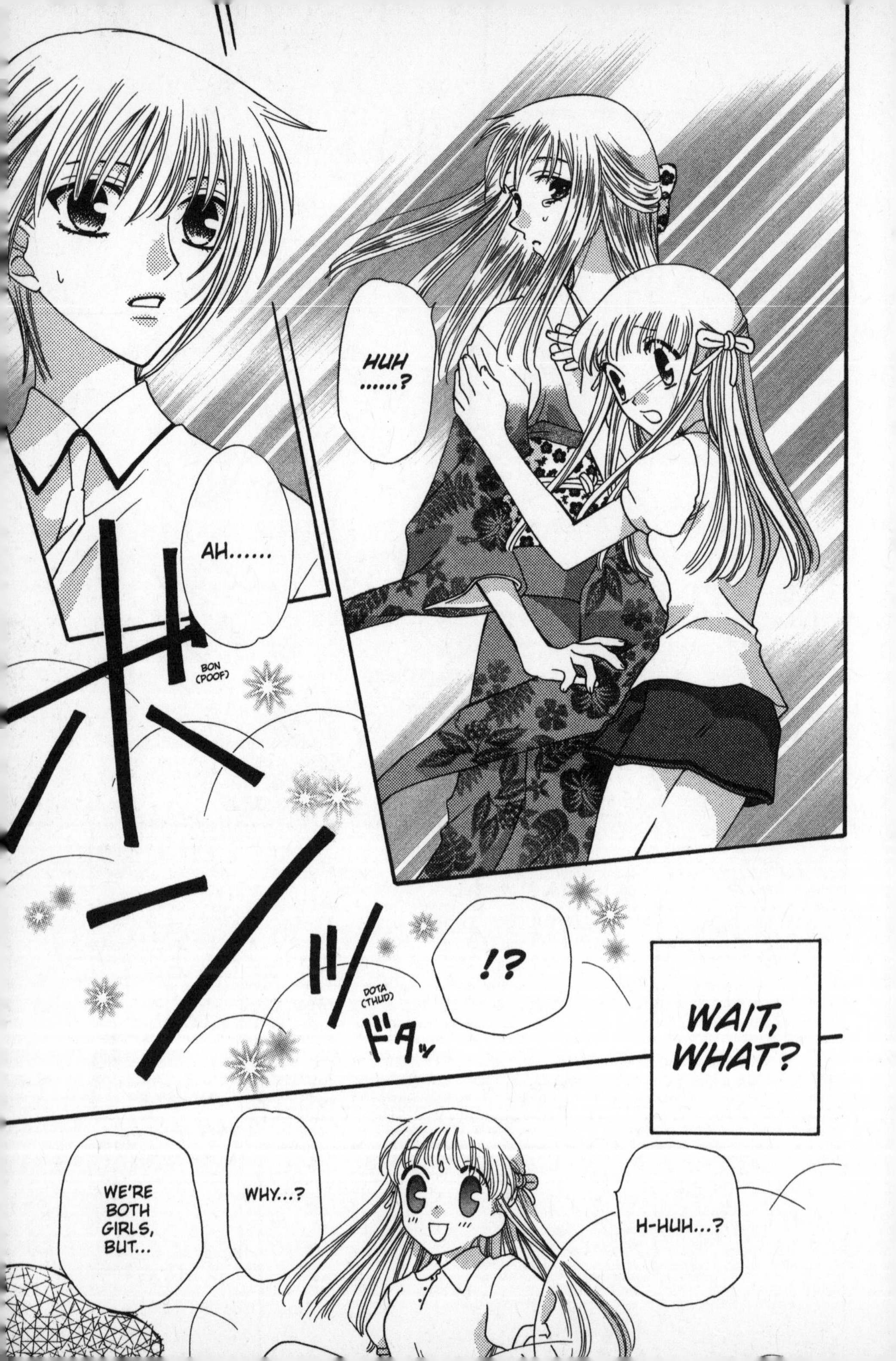

HUH ......?
AH......
BON (POOF)
WAIT, WHAT?
!?
DOTA (THUD)
ドタッ
H-HUH...?
WHY...?
WE'RE BOTH GIRLS, BUT...

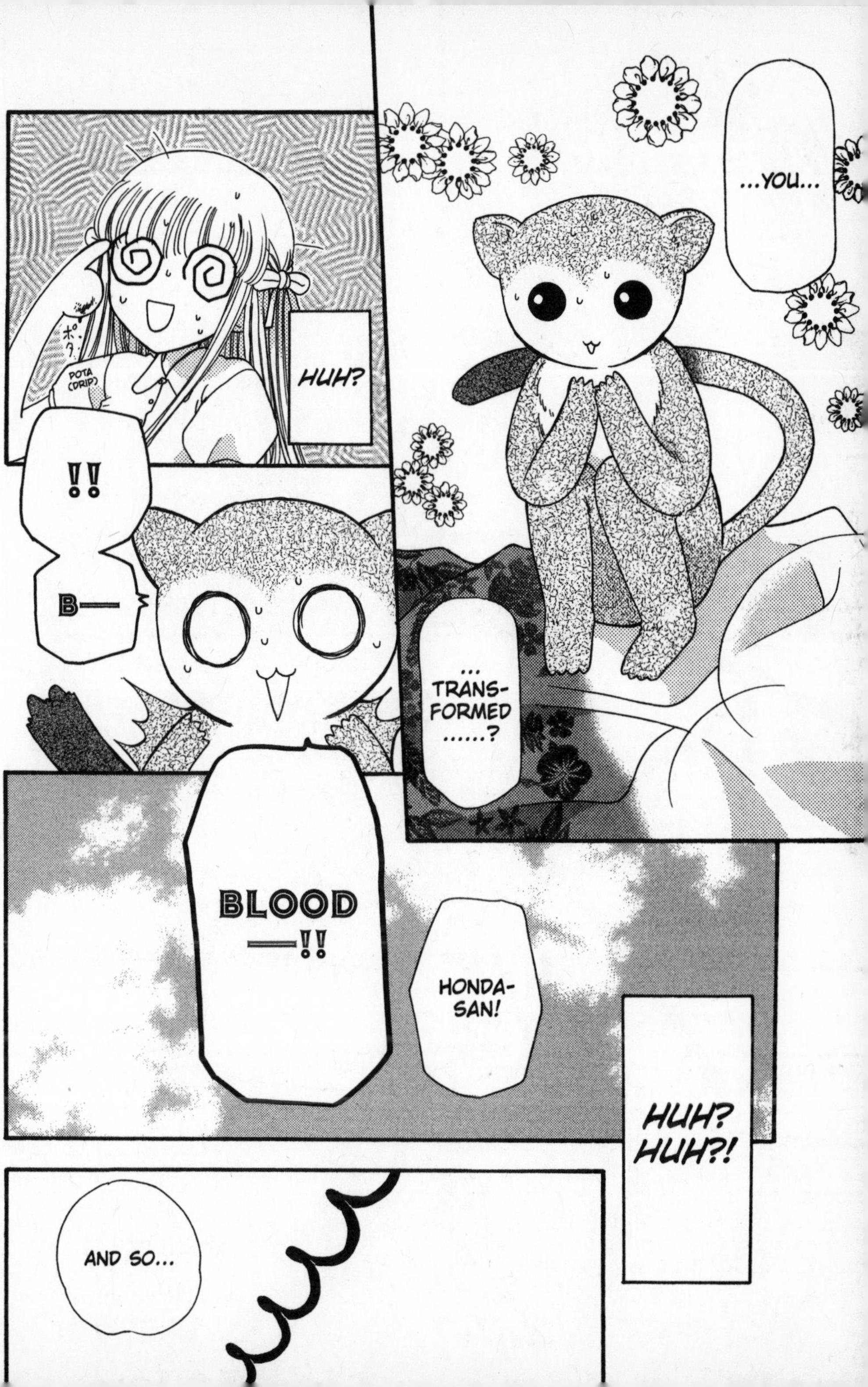
...YOU...
... TRANSFORMED ......?
HUH?
ポタ
POTA (DRIP)
!!
B—
BLOOD —!!
HUH? HUH?!
HONDA-SAN!
AND SO...

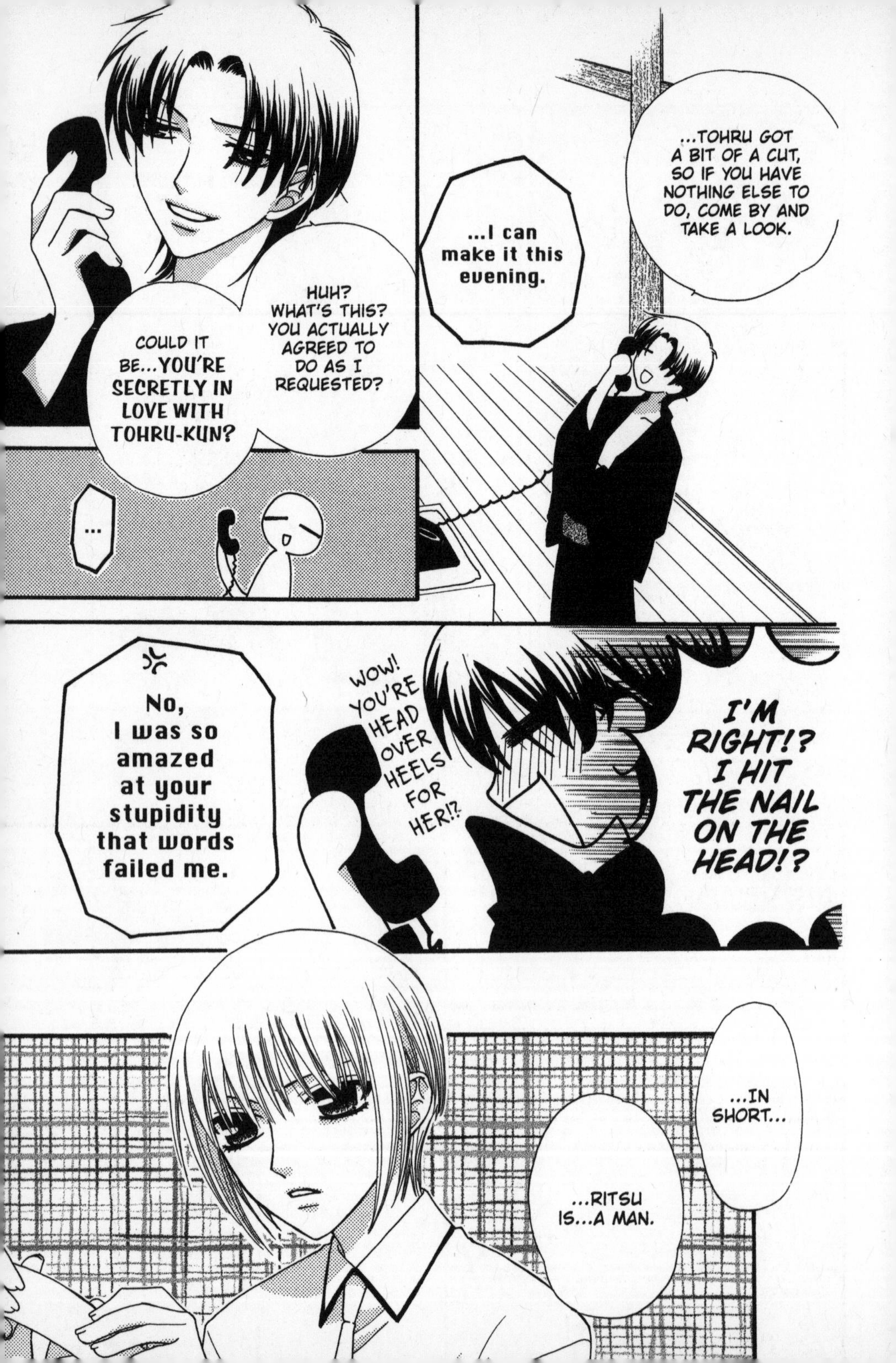
...TOHRU GOT A BIT OF A CUT, SO IF YOU HAVE NOTHING ELSE TO DO, COME BY AND TAKE A LOOK.
...I can make it this evening.
HUH? WHAT'S THIS? YOU ACTUALLY AGREED TO DO AS I REQUESTED?
COULD IT BE...YOU'RE SECRETLY IN LOVE WITH TOHRU-KUN?
...
I'M RIGHT!? I HIT THE NAIL ON THE HEAD!?
WOW! YOU'RE HEAD OVER HEELS FOR HER!?
No, I was so amazed at your stupidity that words failed me.
...IN SHORT...
...RITSU IS...A MAN.

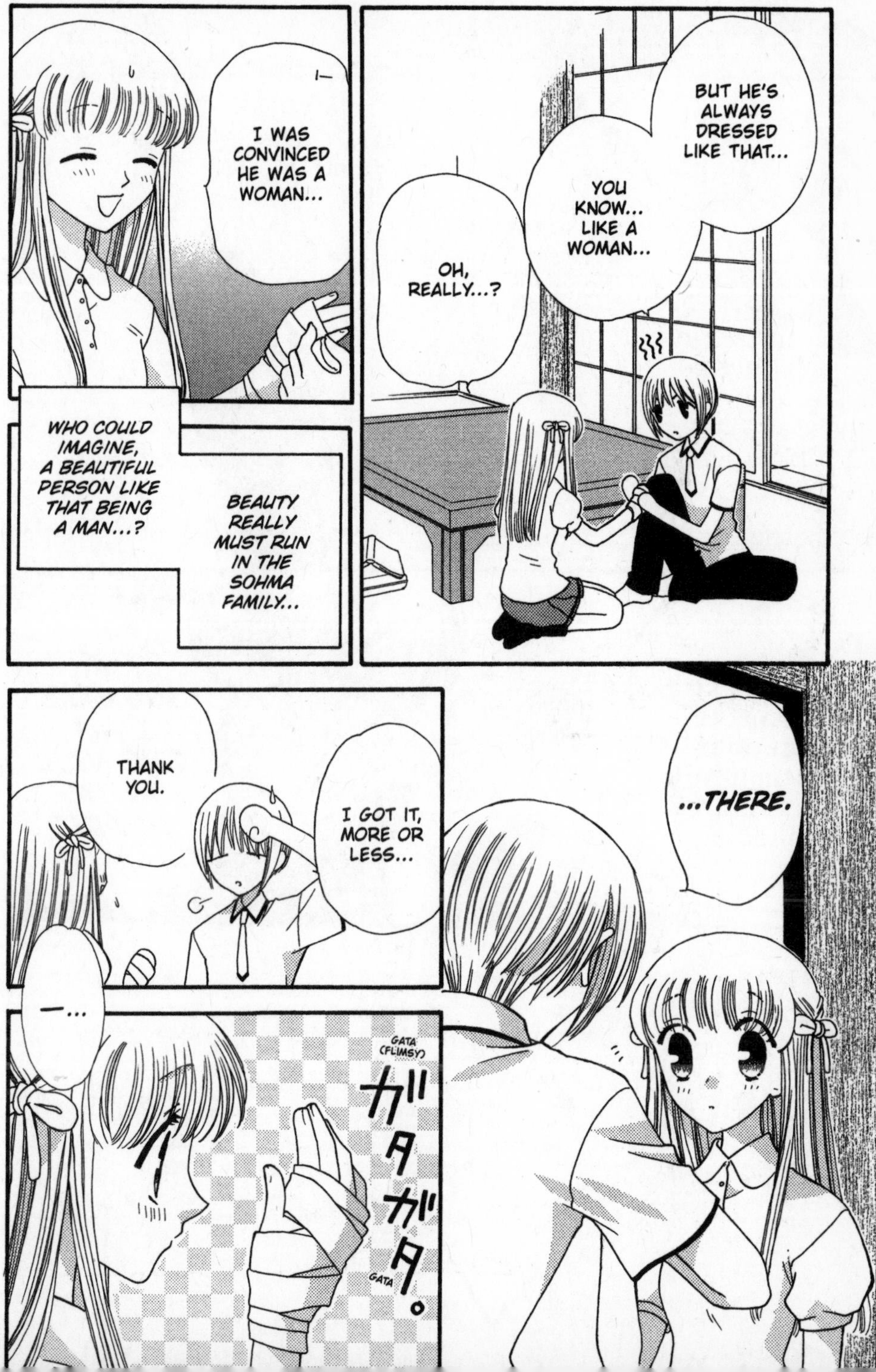
BUT HE'S ALWAYS DRESSED LIKE THAT...
YOU KNOW... LIKE A WOMAN...
OH, REALLY...?
I—
I WAS CONVINCED HE WAS A WOMAN...
WHO COULD IMAGINE, A BEAUTIFUL PERSON LIKE THAT BEING A MAN...?
BEAUTY REALLY MUST RUN IN THE SOHMA FAMILY...
...THERE.
I GOT IT, MORE OR LESS...
THANK YOU.
—...
GATA (FLIMSY)
ガタガタ。
GATA

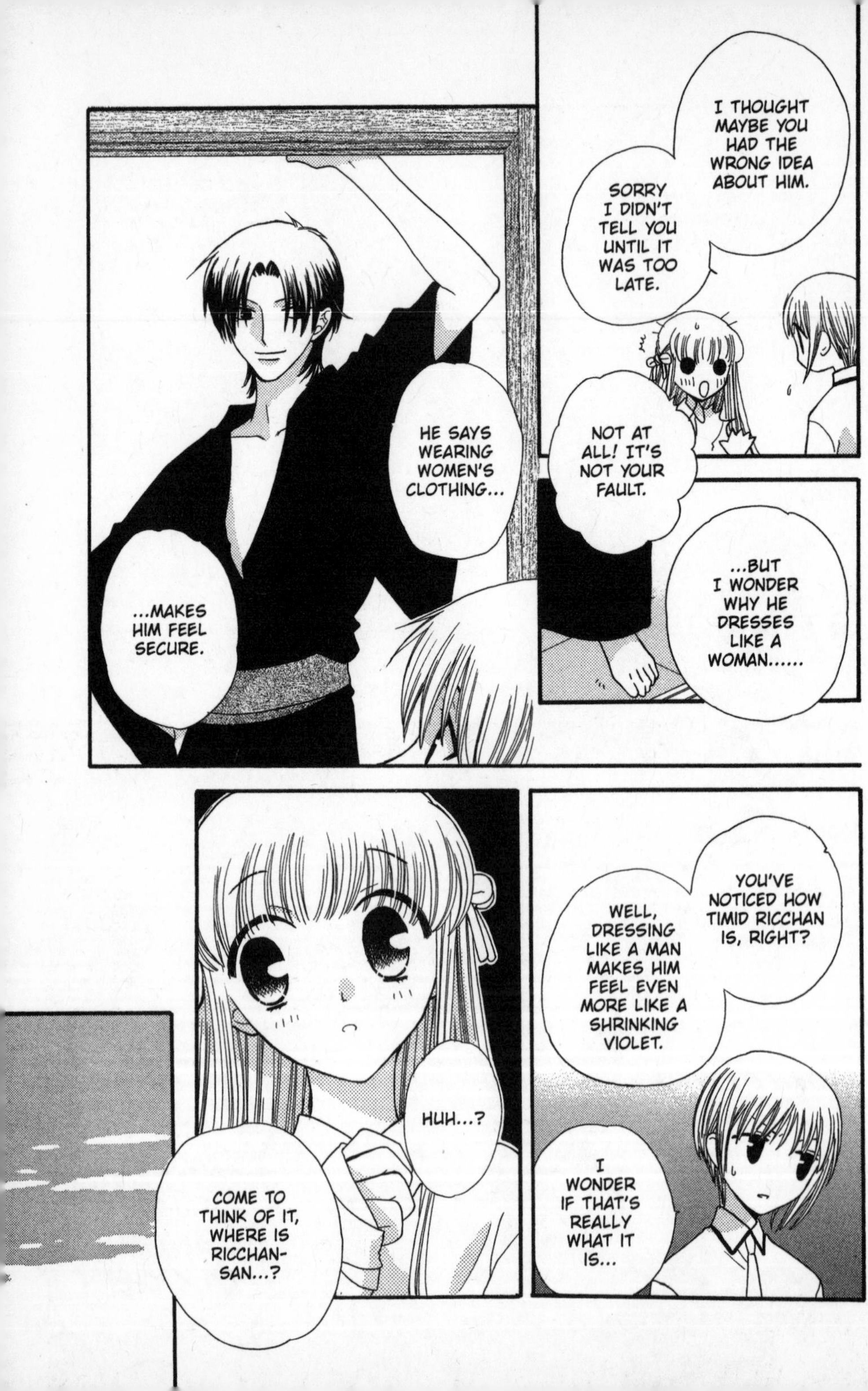
I THOUGHT MAYBE YOU HAD THE WRONG IDEA ABOUT HIM.
SORRY I DIDN'T TELL YOU UNTIL IT WAS TOO LATE.
NOT AT ALL! IT'S NOT YOUR FAULT.
...BUT I WONDER WHY HE DRESSES LIKE A WOMAN......
HE SAYS WEARING WOMEN'S CLOTHING...
...MAKES HIM FEEL SECURE.
YOU'VE NOTICED HOW TIMID RICCHAN IS, RIGHT?
WELL, DRESSING LIKE A MAN MAKES HIM FEEL EVEN MORE LIKE A SHRINKING VIOLET.
I WONDER IF THAT'S REALLY WHAT IT IS...
HUH...?
COME TO THINK OF IT, WHERE IS RICCHAN-SAN...?

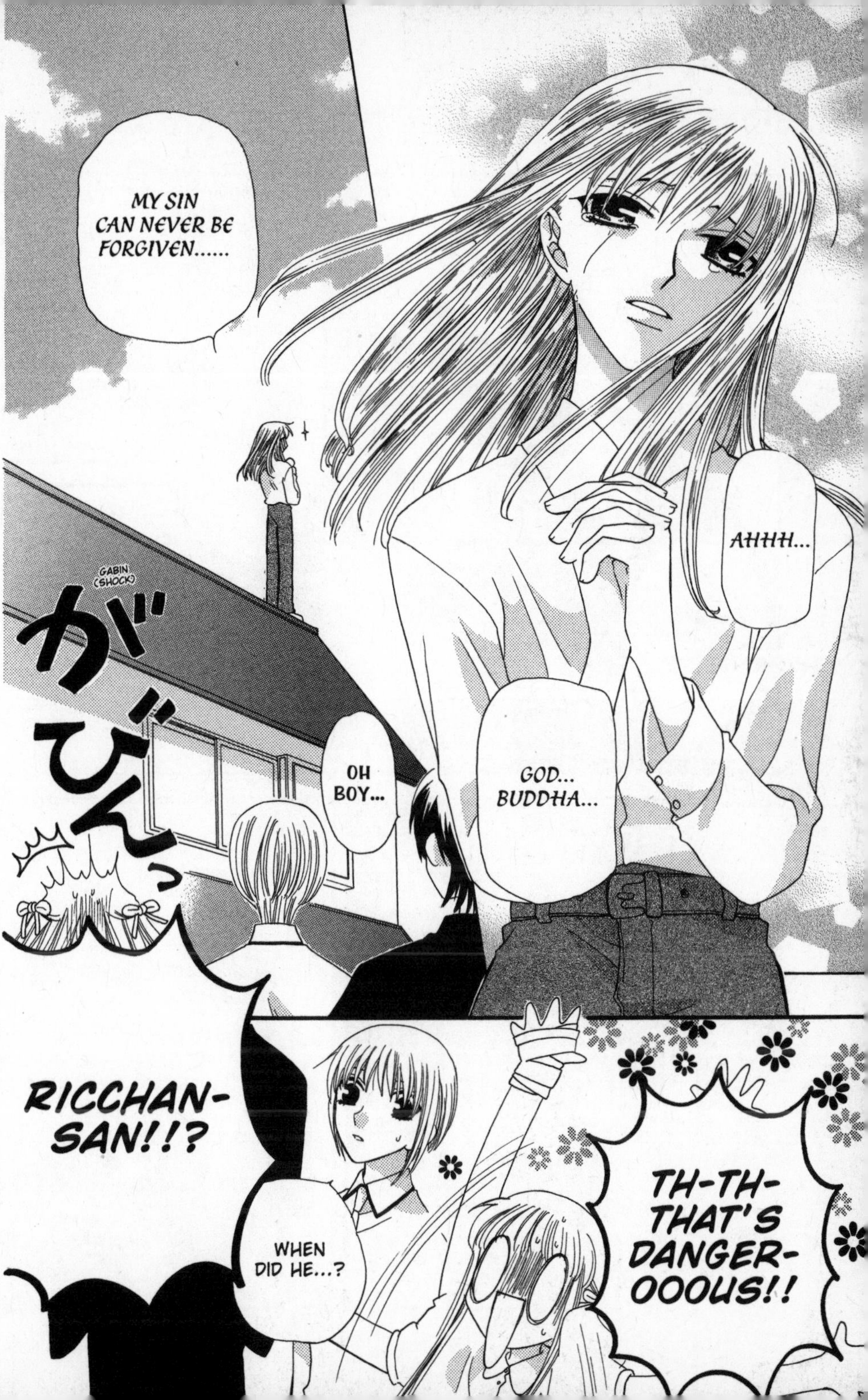
MY SIN CAN NEVER BE FORGIVEN......
AHHH...
GOD... BUDDHA...
OH BOY...
がびんっ
GABIN (SHOCK)
TH-TH-THAT'S DANGER-OOOUS!!
RICCHAN-SAN!!?
WHEN DID HE...?

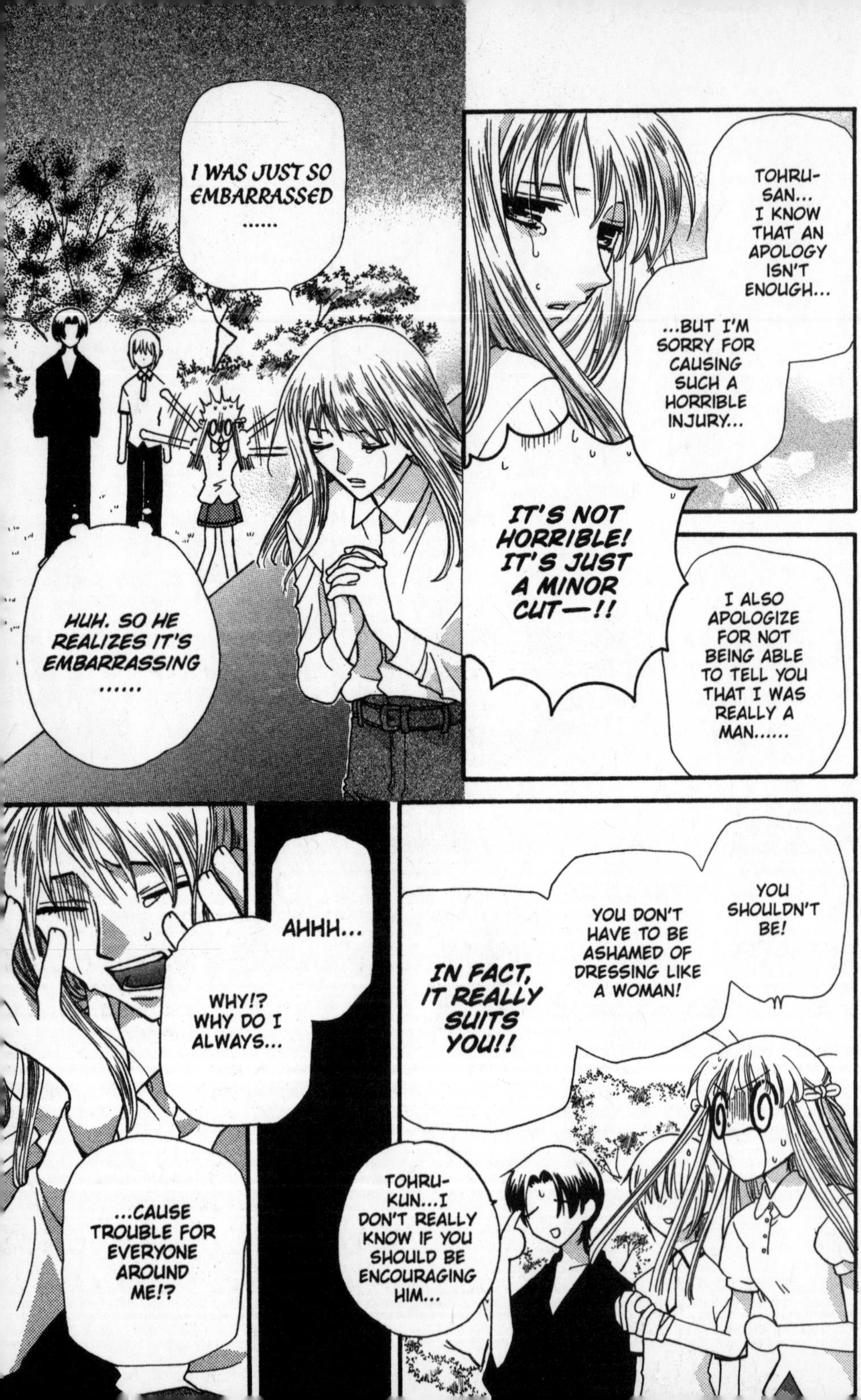
TOHRU-SAN... I KNOW THAT AN APOLOGY ISN'T ENOUGH...
...BUT I'M SORRY FOR CAUSING SUCH A HORRIBLE INJURY...
IT'S NOT HORRIBLE! IT'S JUST A MINOR CUT—!!
I ALSO APOLOGIZE FOR NOT BEING ABLE TO TELL YOU THAT I WAS REALLY A MAN......
I WAS JUST SO EMBARRASSED ......
HUH. SO HE REALIZES IT'S EMBARRASSING ......
YOU SHOULDN'T BE!
YOU DON'T HAVE TO BE ASHAMED OF DRESSING LIKE A WOMAN!
IN FACT, IT REALLY SUITS YOU!!
TOHRU-KUN...I DON'T REALLY KNOW IF YOU SHOULD BE ENCOURAGING HIM...
AHHH...
WHY!? WHY DO I ALWAYS...
...CAUSE TROUBLE FOR EVERYONE AROUND ME!?

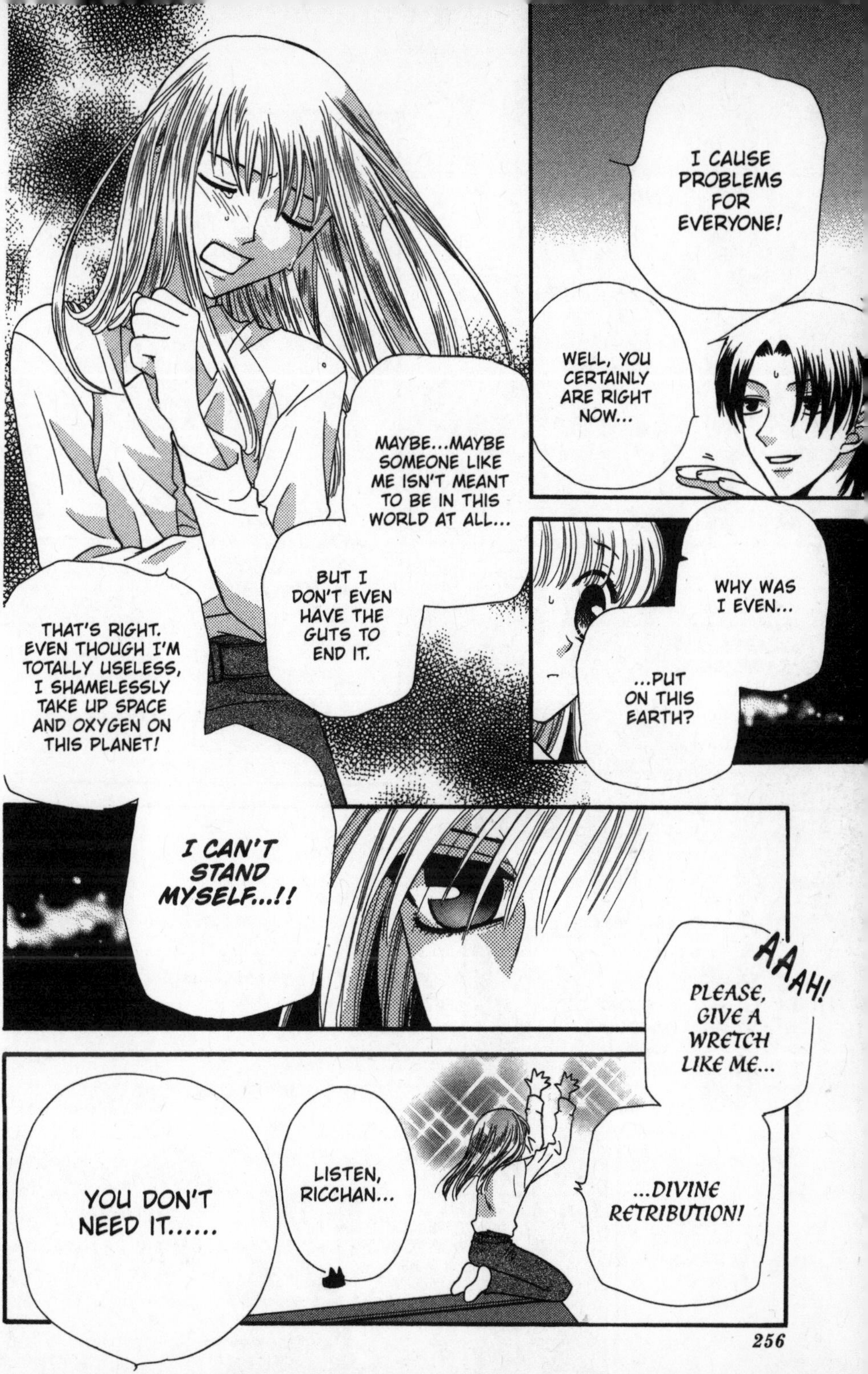
I CAUSE PROBLEMS FOR EVERYONE!
WELL, YOU CERTAINLY ARE RIGHT NOW...
WHY WAS I EVEN...
...PUT ON THIS EARTH?
MAYBE...MAYBE SOMEONE LIKE ME ISN'T MEANT TO BE IN THIS WORLD AT ALL...
BUT I DON'T EVEN HAVE THE GUTS TO END IT.
THAT'S RIGHT. EVEN THOUGH I'M TOTALLY USELESS, I SHAMELESSLY TAKE UP SPACE AND OXYGEN ON THIS PLANET!
I CAN'T STAND MYSELF...!!
AAAAH!
PLEASE, GIVE A WRETCH LIKE ME...
...DIVINE RETRIBUTION!
LISTEN, RICCHAN...
YOU DON'T NEED IT......

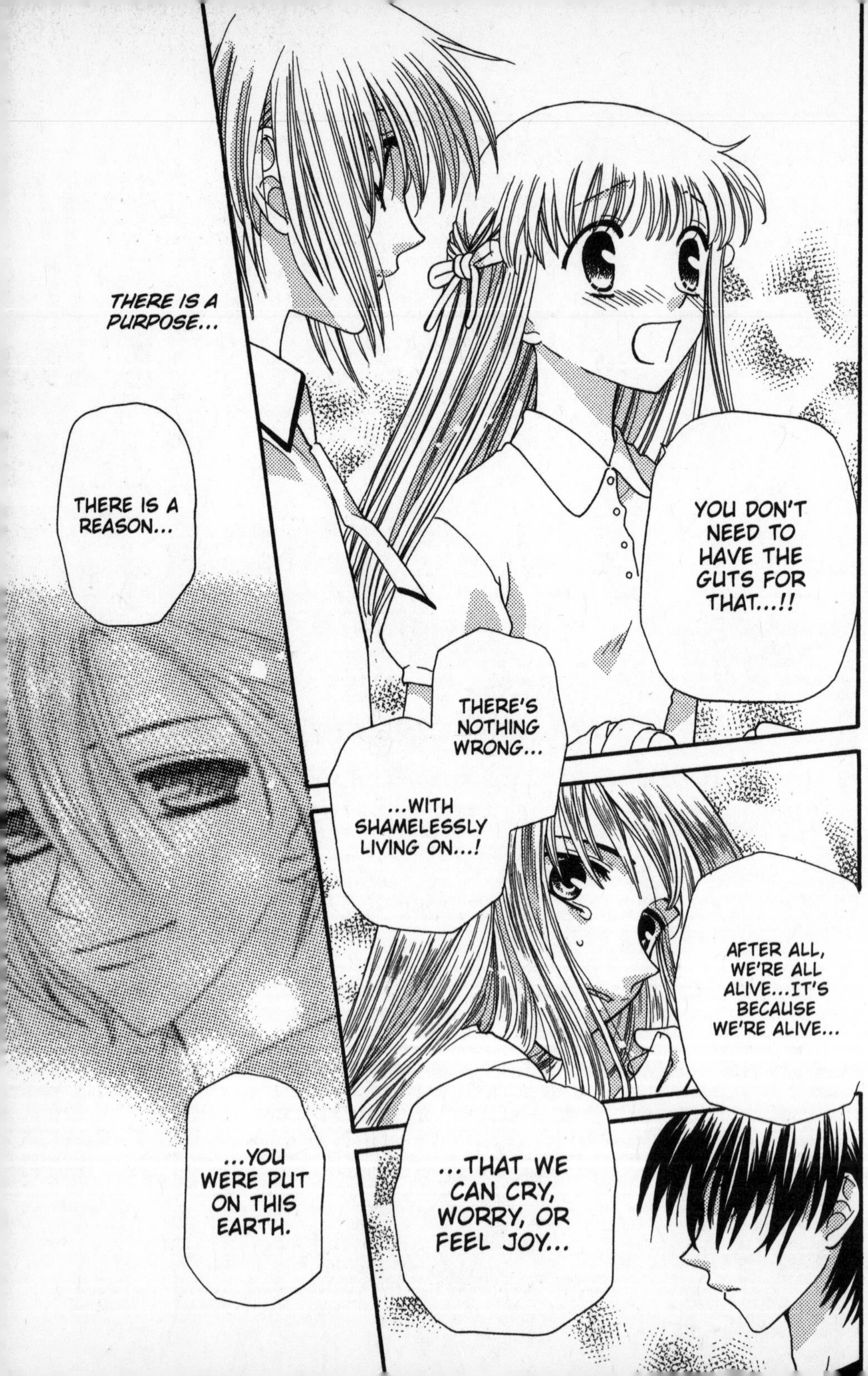
YOU DON'T NEED TO HAVE THE GUTS FOR THAT...!!
THERE'S NOTHING WRONG...
...WITH SHAMELESSLY LIVING ON...!
AFTER ALL, WE'RE ALL ALIVE...IT'S BECAUSE WE'RE ALIVE...
...THAT WE CAN CRY, WORRY, OR FEEL JOY...
THERE IS A PURPOSE...
THERE IS A REASON...
...YOU WERE PUT ON THIS EARTH.

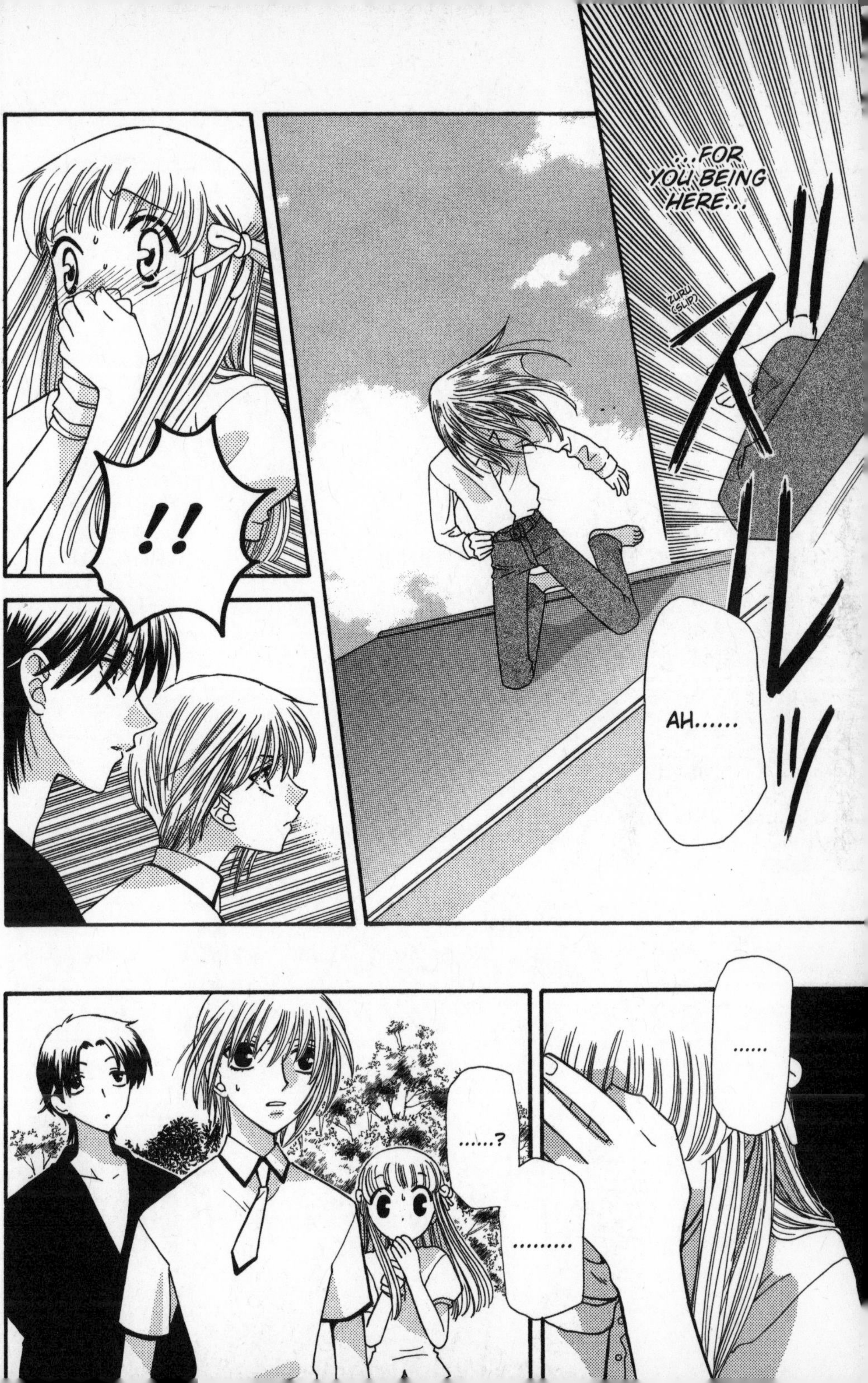
...FOR YOU BEING HERE...
ZURU (SLIP)
AH......
!!
......
......?
....

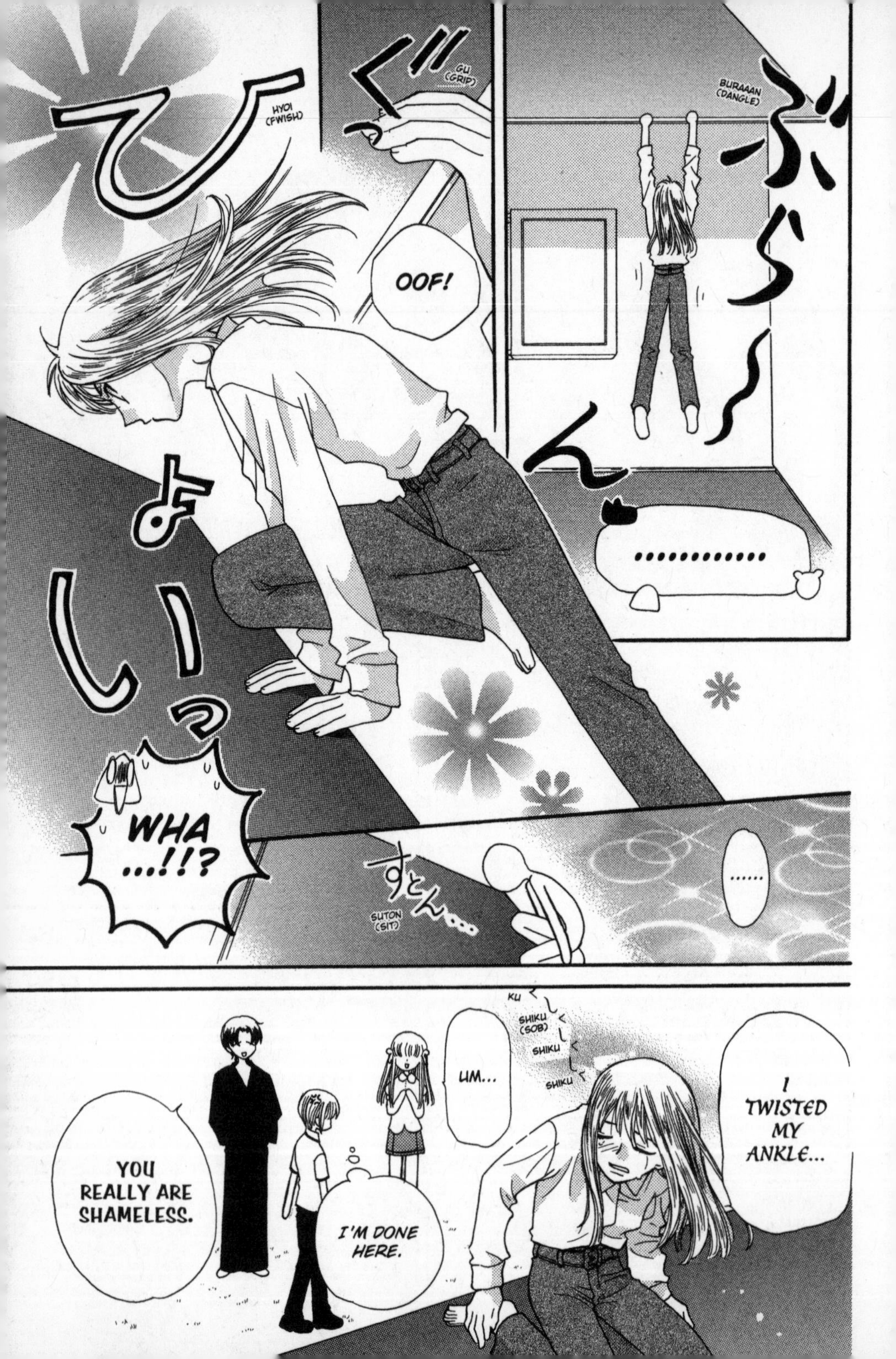

ぶら〜〜ん
BURAAAN (DANGLE)
....
ぐ"
GU (GRIP)
OOF!
HYOI (FWISH)
WHA ...!!?
......
すとん...
SUTON (SIT)
I TWISTED MY ANKLE...
KU SHIKU (SOB) SHIKU SHIKU
UM...
I'M DONE HERE.
YOU REALLY ARE SHAMELESS.

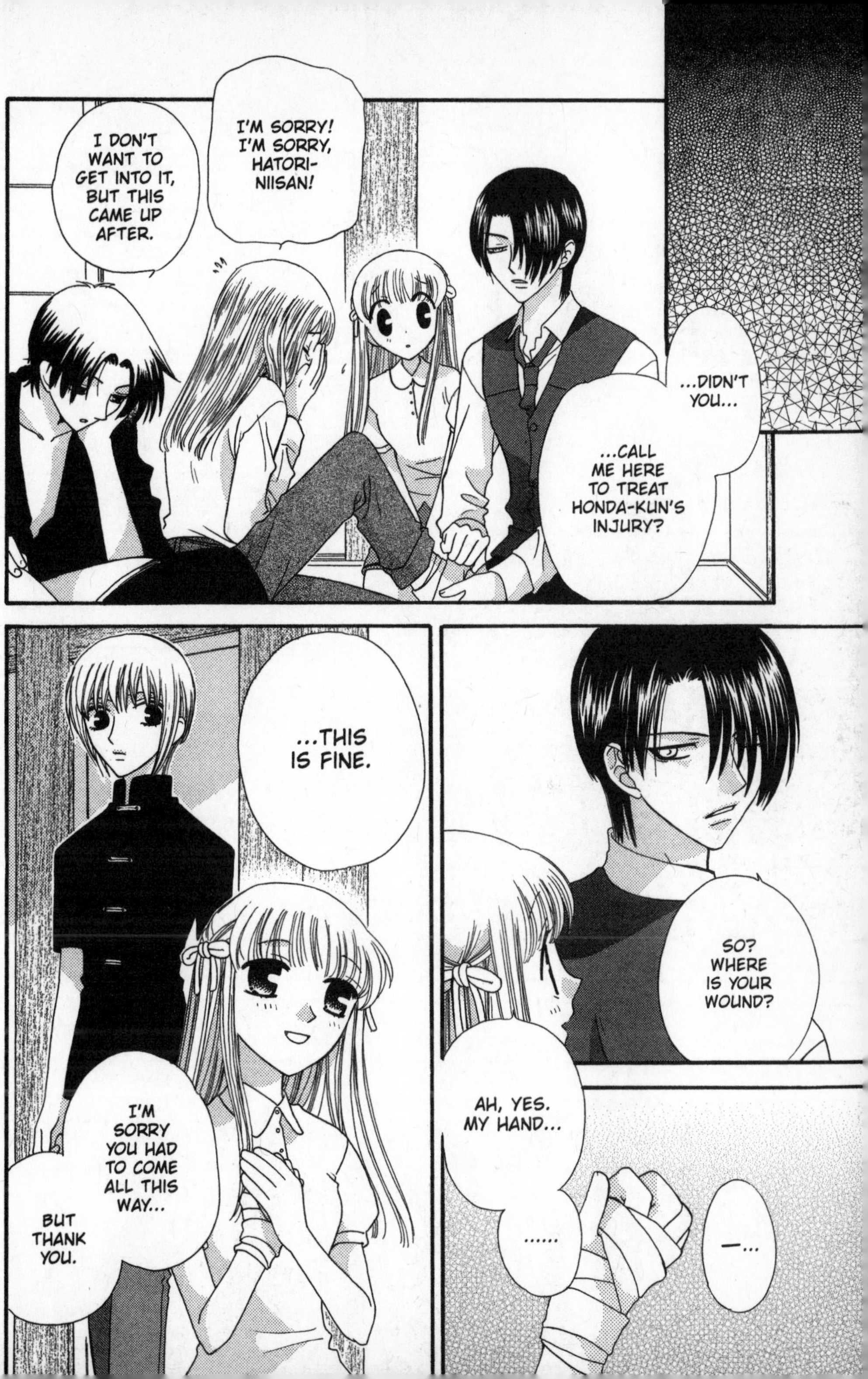
I'M SORRY! I'M SORRY, HATORI-NIISAN!
I DON'T WANT TO GET INTO IT, BUT THIS CAME UP AFTER.
...DIDN'T YOU...
...CALL ME HERE TO TREAT HONDA-KUN'S INJURY?
SO? WHERE IS YOUR WOUND?
AH, YES. MY HAND...
—...
......
...THIS IS FINE.
I'M SORRY YOU HAD TO COME ALL THIS WAY...
BUT THANK YOU.

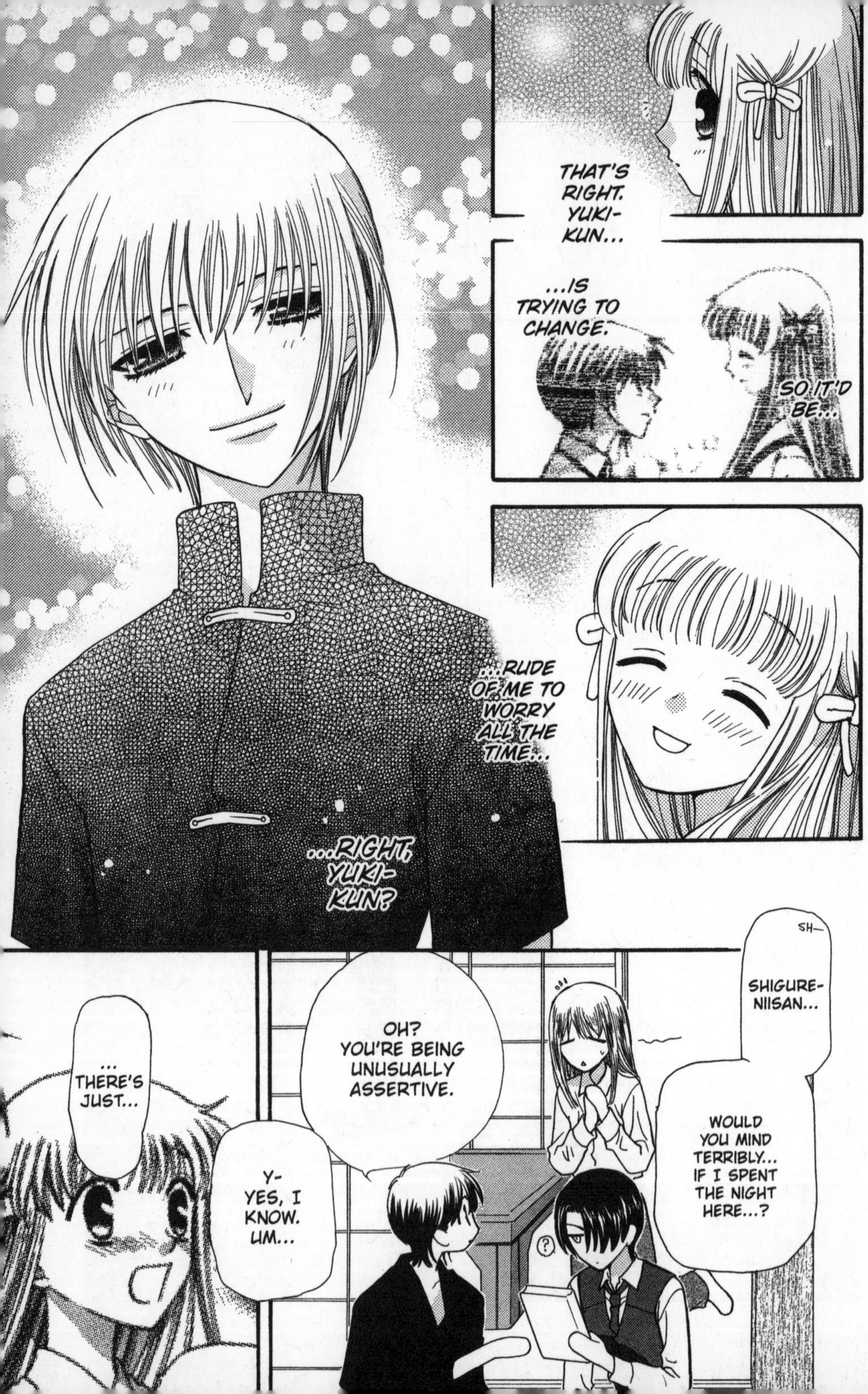
THAT'S RIGHT. YUKI-KUN...
...IS TRYING TO CHANGE.
SO IT'D BE...
...RUDE OF ME TO WORRY ALL THE TIME...
...RIGHT, YUKI-KUN?
SH—
SHIGURE-NIISAN...
WOULD YOU MIND TERRIBLY... IF I SPENT THE NIGHT HERE...?
OH? YOU'RE BEING UNUSUALLY ASSERTIVE.
Y-YES, I KNOW. UM...
... THERE'S JUST...

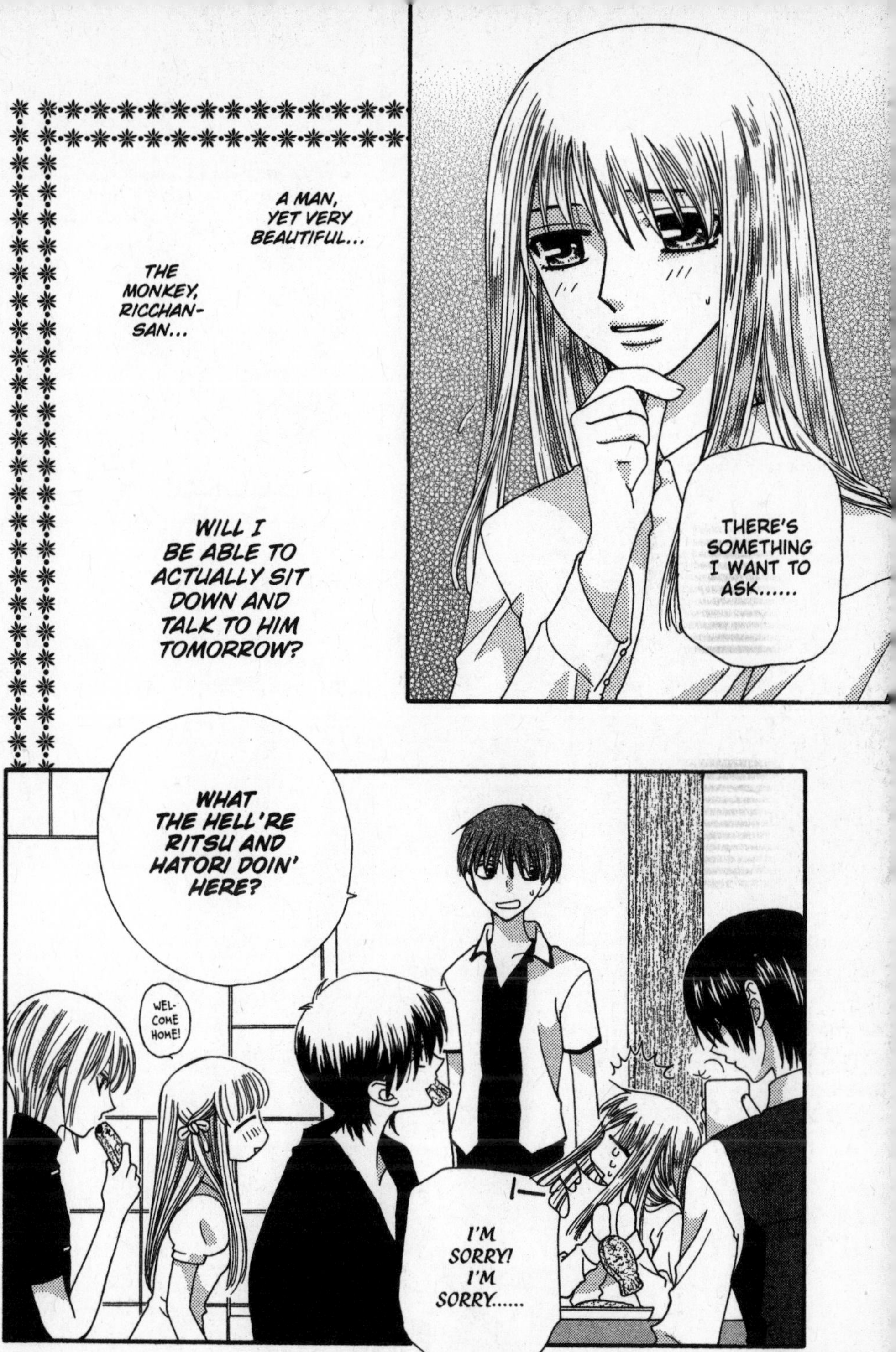
THERE'S SOMETHING I WANT TO ASK......
A MAN, YET VERY BEAUTIFUL...
THE MONKEY, RICCHAN-SAN...
WILL I BE ABLE TO ACTUALLY SIT DOWN AND TALK TO HIM TOMORROW?
WHAT THE HELL'RE RITSU AND HATORI DOIN' HERE?
WEL-COME HOME!
I—
I'M SORRY! I'M SORRY......

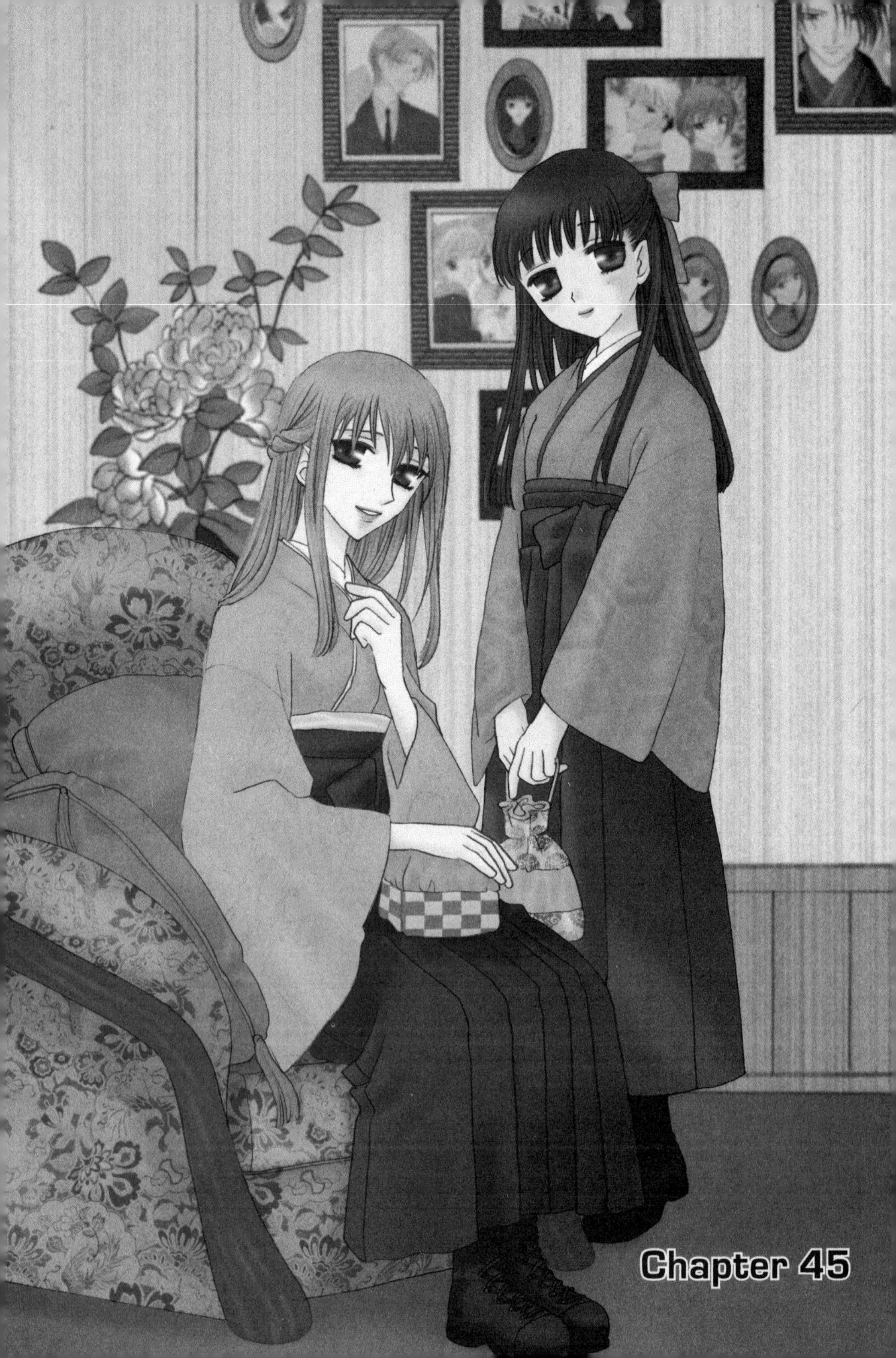
Chapter 45

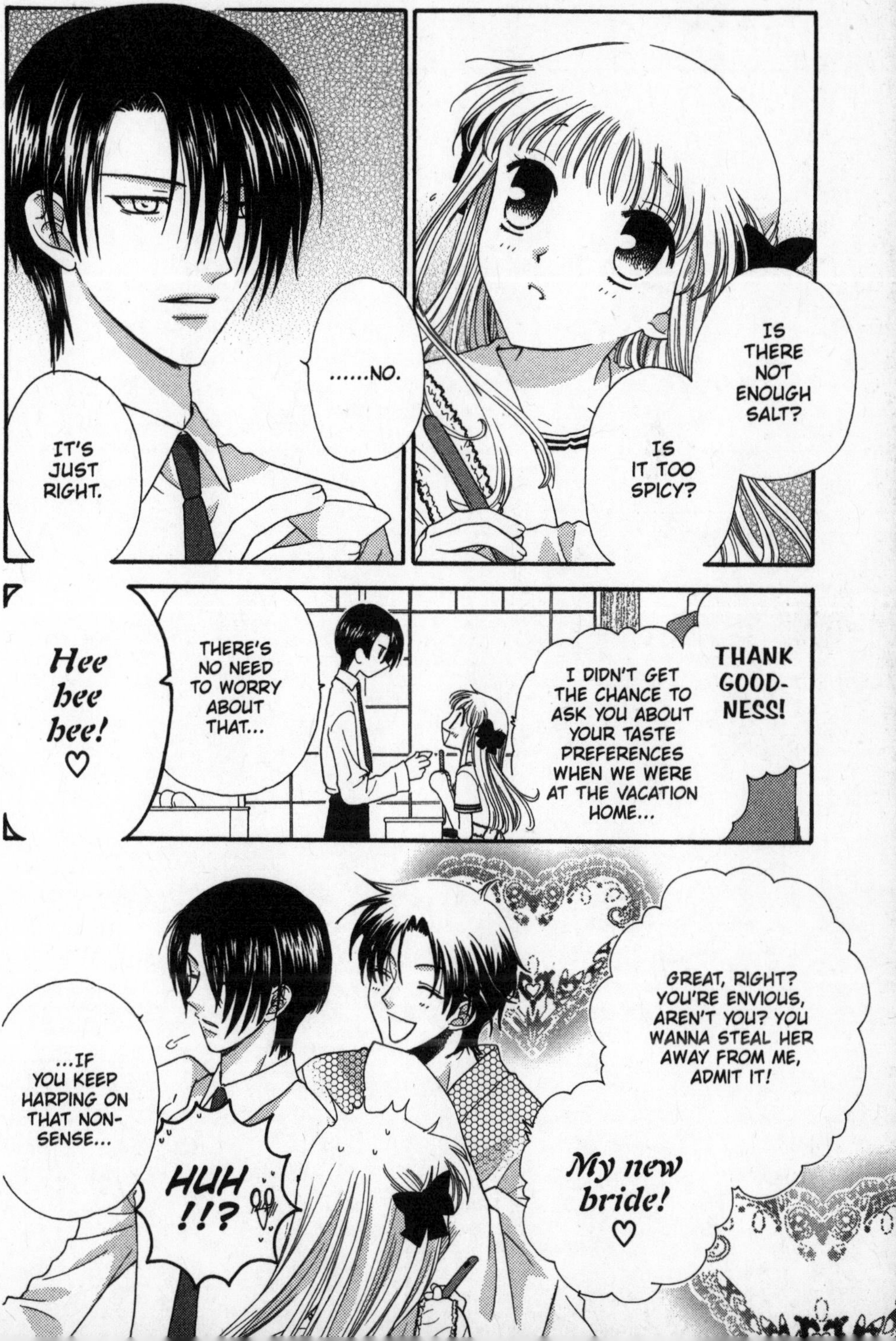
IS THERE NOT ENOUGH SALT?
IS IT TOO SPICY?
......NO.
IT'S JUST RIGHT.
THANK GOODNESS!
I DIDN'T GET THE CHANCE TO ASK YOU ABOUT YOUR TASTE PREFERENCES WHEN WE WERE AT THE VACATION HOME...
THERE'S NO NEED TO WORRY ABOUT THAT...
Hee hee hee! ♡
GREAT, RIGHT? YOU'RE ENVIOUS, AREN'T YOU? YOU WANNA STEAL HER AWAY FROM ME, ADMIT IT!
My new bride! ♡
HUH!!?
...IF YOU KEEP HARPING ON THAT NON-SENSE...

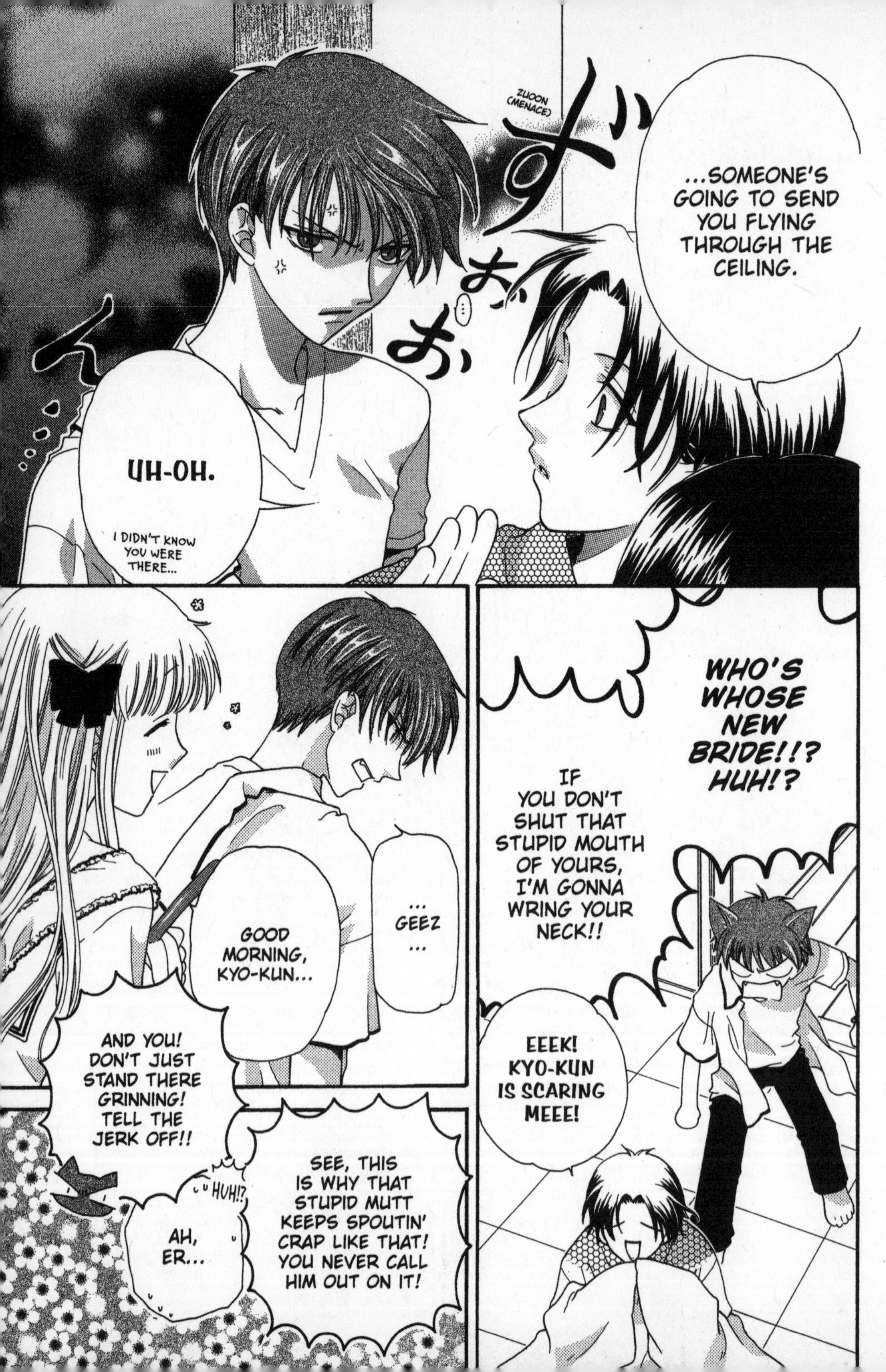
ZUOON (MENACE)
...SOMEONE'S GOING TO SEND YOU FLYING THROUGH THE CEILING.
UH-OH.
I DIDN'T KNOW YOU WERE THERE...
WHO'S WHOSE NEW BRIDE!!? HUH!?
IF YOU DON'T SHUT THAT STUPID MOUTH OF YOURS, I'M GONNA WRING YOUR NECK!!
EEEK! KYO-KUN IS SCARING MEEE!
...GEEZ...
GOOD MORNING, KYO-KUN...
AND YOU! DON'T JUST STAND THERE GRINNING! TELL THE JERK OFF!!
SEE, THIS IS WHY THAT STUPID MUTT KEEPS SPOUTIN' CRAP LIKE THAT! YOU NEVER CALL HIM OUT ON IT!
HUH!?
AH, ER...

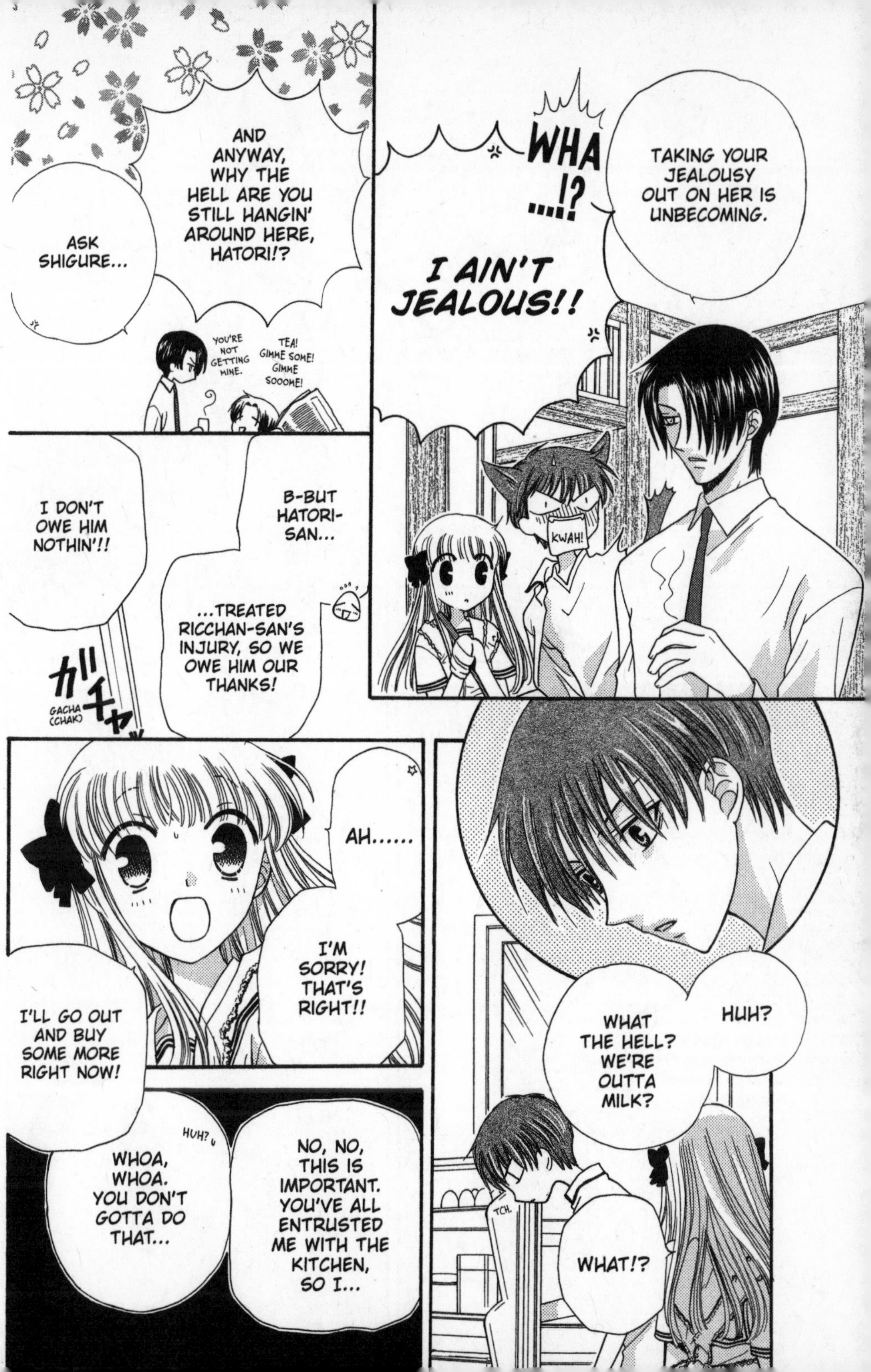
TAKING YOUR JEALOUSY OUT ON HER IS UNBECOMING.
WHA ...!?
I AIN'T JEALOUS!!
AND ANYWAY, WHY THE HELL ARE YOU STILL HANGIN' AROUND HERE, HATORI!?
ASK SHIGURE...
TEA! GIMME SOME! GIMME SOOOME!
YOU'RE NOT GETTING MINE.
KWAH!
B-BUT HATORI-SAN...
...TREATED RICCHAN-SAN'S INJURY, SO WE OWE HIM OUR THANKS!
I DON'T OWE HIM NOTHIN'!!
ガチャ
GACHA (CHAK)
HUH?
WHAT THE HELL? WE'RE OUTTA MILK?
TCH.
WHAT!?
AH......
I'M SORRY! THAT'S RIGHT!!
I'LL GO OUT AND BUY SOME MORE RIGHT NOW!
WHOA, WHOA. YOU DON'T GOTTA DO THAT...
HUH?
NO, NO, THIS IS IMPORTANT. YOU'VE ALL ENTRUSTED ME WITH THE KITCHEN, SO I...

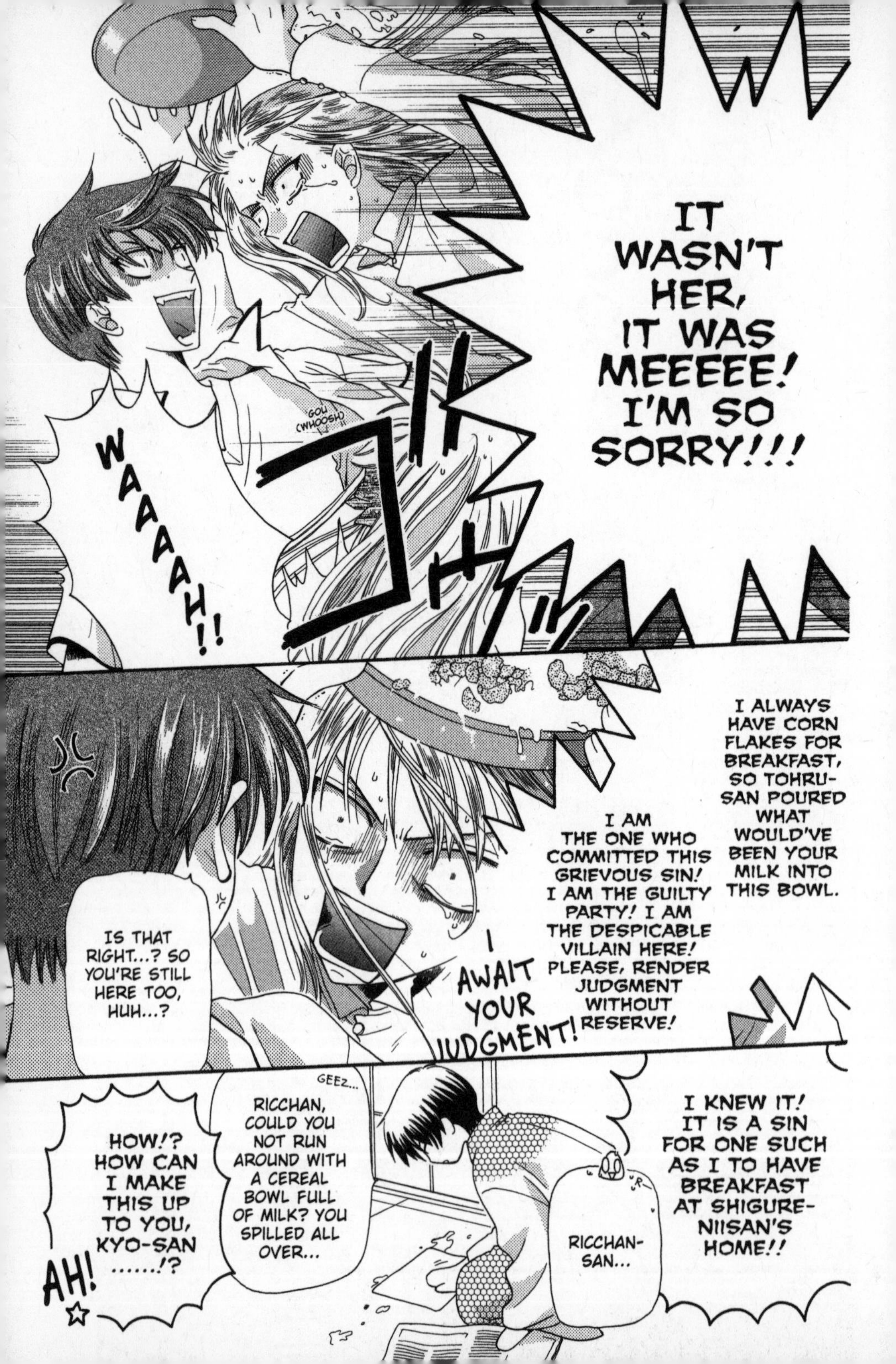
IT WASN'T HER, IT WAS MEEEEE! I'M SO SORRY!!!
GOU (WHOOSH)
WAAAAAH!!
I ALWAYS HAVE CORN FLAKES FOR BREAKFAST, SO TOHRU-SAN POURED WHAT WOULD'VE BEEN YOUR MILK INTO THIS BOWL.
I AM THE ONE WHO COMMITTED THIS GRIEVOUS SIN! I AM THE GUILTY PARTY! I AM THE DESPICABLE VILLAIN HERE! PLEASE, RENDER JUDGMENT WITHOUT RESERVE!
I AWAIT YOUR JUDGMENT!
IS THAT RIGHT...? SO YOU'RE STILL HERE TOO, HUH...?
I KNEW IT! IT IS A SIN FOR ONE SUCH AS I TO HAVE BREAKFAST AT SHIGURE-NIISAN'S HOME!!
RICCHAN-SAN...
GEEZ...
RICCHAN, COULD YOU NOT RUN AROUND WITH A CEREAL BOWL FULL OF MILK? YOU SPILLED ALL OVER...
HOW!? HOW CAN I MAKE THIS UP TO YOU, KYO-SAN ....!?
AH!

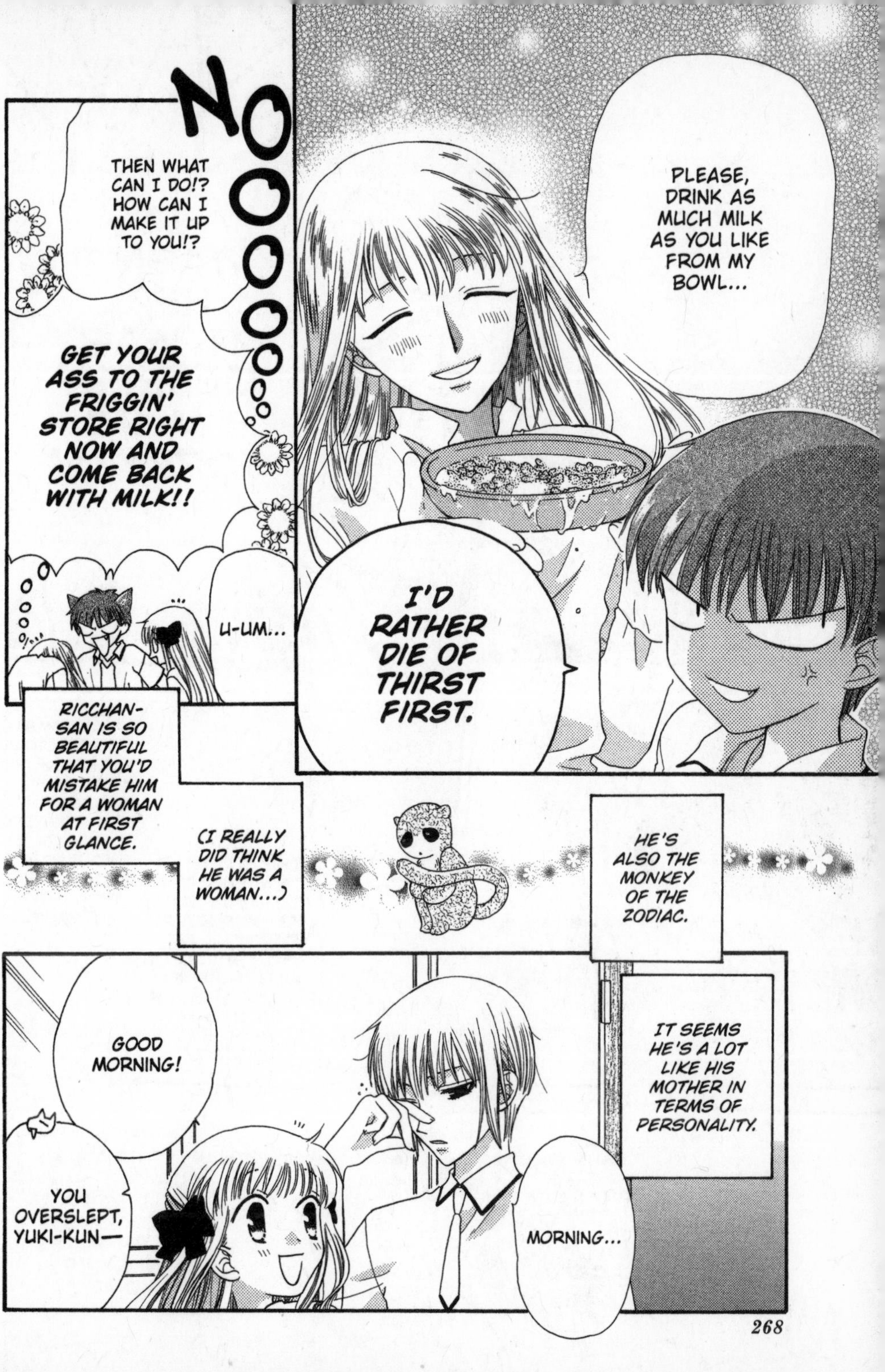
PLEASE, DRINK AS MUCH MILK AS YOU LIKE FROM MY BOWL...
I'D RATHER DIE OF THIRST FIRST.
NOOOOOOO
THEN WHAT CAN I DO!? HOW CAN I MAKE IT UP TO YOU!?
GET YOUR ASS TO THE FRIGGIN' STORE RIGHT NOW AND COME BACK WITH MILK!!
U-UM...
RICCHAN-SAN IS SO BEAUTIFUL THAT YOU'D MISTAKE HIM FOR A WOMAN AT FIRST GLANCE.
(I REALLY DID THINK HE WAS A WOMAN...)
HE'S ALSO THE MONKEY OF THE ZODIAC.
IT SEEMS HE'S A LOT LIKE HIS MOTHER IN TERMS OF PERSONALITY.
GOOD MORNING!
YOU OVERSLEPT, YUKI-KUN—
MORNING...

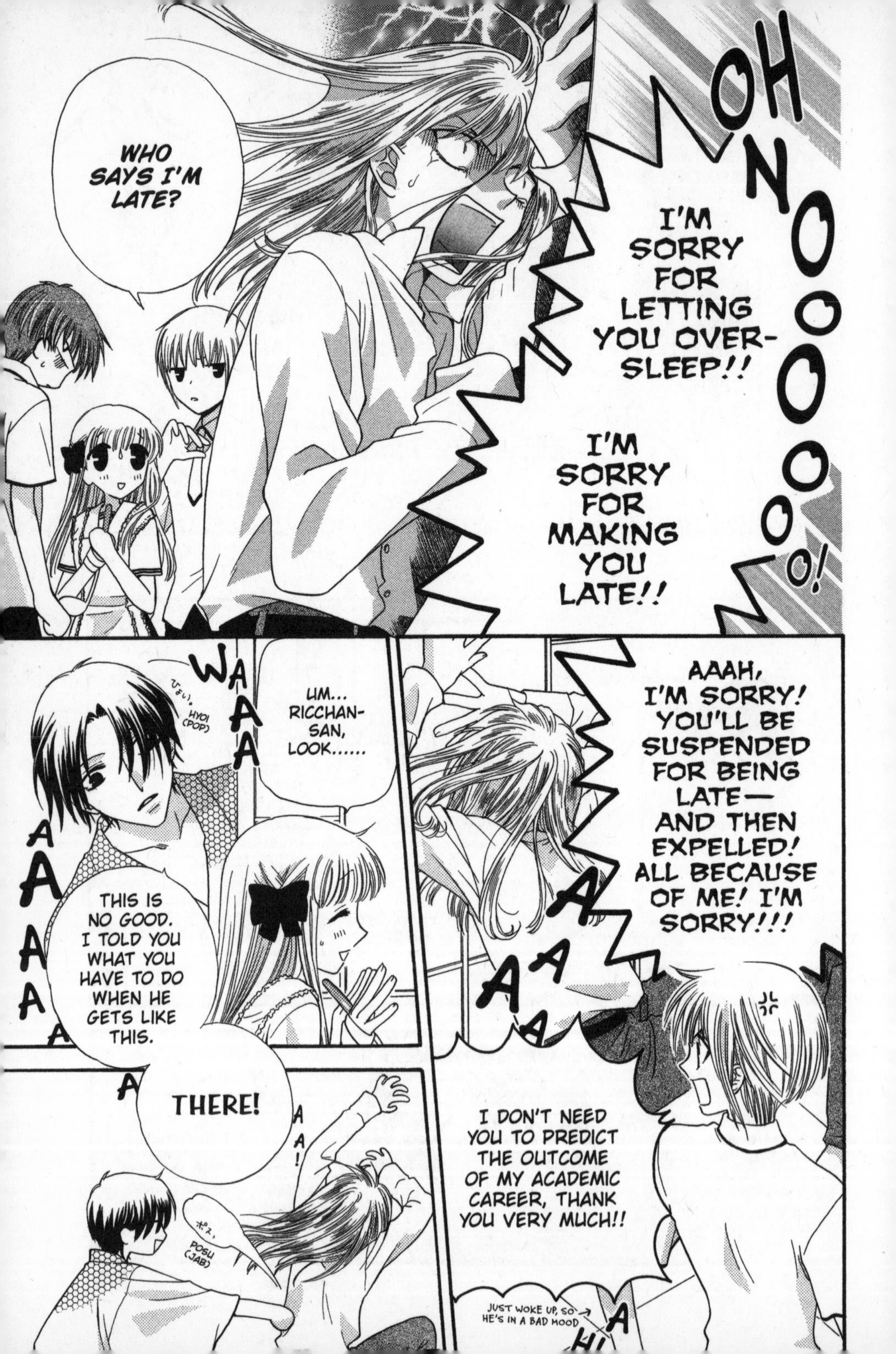
OH NOOOOOOO!
I'M SORRY FOR LETTING YOU OVER-SLEEP!!
I'M SORRY FOR MAKING YOU LATE!!
WHO SAYS I'M LATE?
AAAH, I'M SORRY! YOU'LL BE SUSPENDED FOR BEING LATE— AND THEN EXPELLED! ALL BECAUSE OF ME! I'M SORRY!!!
I DON'T NEED YOU TO PREDICT THE OUTCOME OF MY ACADEMIC CAREER, THANK YOU VERY MUCH!!
JUST WOKE UP, SO HE'S IN A BAD MOOD
UM... RICCHAN-SAN, LOOK......
HYOI (POP)
WAAAA
THIS IS NO GOOD. I TOLD YOU WHAT YOU HAVE TO DO WHEN HE GETS LIKE THIS.
THERE!
POSU (JAB)

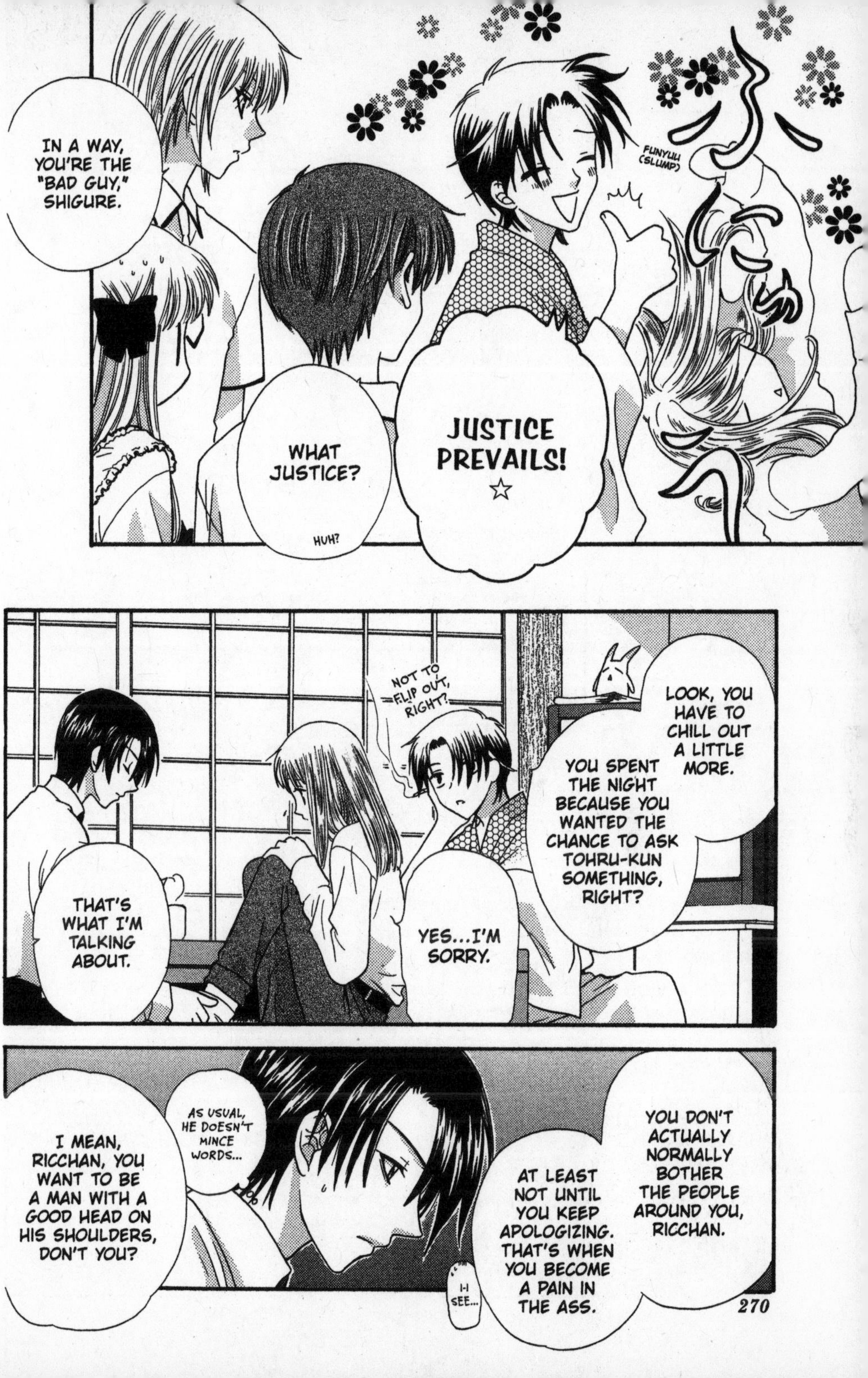
FUNYUU (SLUMP)
JUSTICE PREVAILS! ☆
WHAT JUSTICE?
HUH?
IN A WAY, YOU'RE THE "BAD GUY," SHIGURE.
LOOK, YOU HAVE TO CHILL OUT A LITTLE MORE.
YOU SPENT THE NIGHT BECAUSE YOU WANTED THE CHANCE TO ASK TOHRU-KUN SOMETHING, RIGHT?
NOT TO FLIP OUT, RIGHT?
YES...I'M SORRY.
THAT'S WHAT I'M TALKING ABOUT.
YOU DON'T ACTUALLY NORMALLY BOTHER THE PEOPLE AROUND YOU, RICCHAN.
AT LEAST NOT UNTIL YOU KEEP APOLOGIZING. THAT'S WHEN YOU BECOME A PAIN IN THE ASS.
I-I SEE...
AS USUAL, HE DOESN'T MINCE WORDS...
I MEAN, RICCHAN, YOU WANT TO BE A MAN WITH A GOOD HEAD ON HIS SHOULDERS, DON'T YOU?

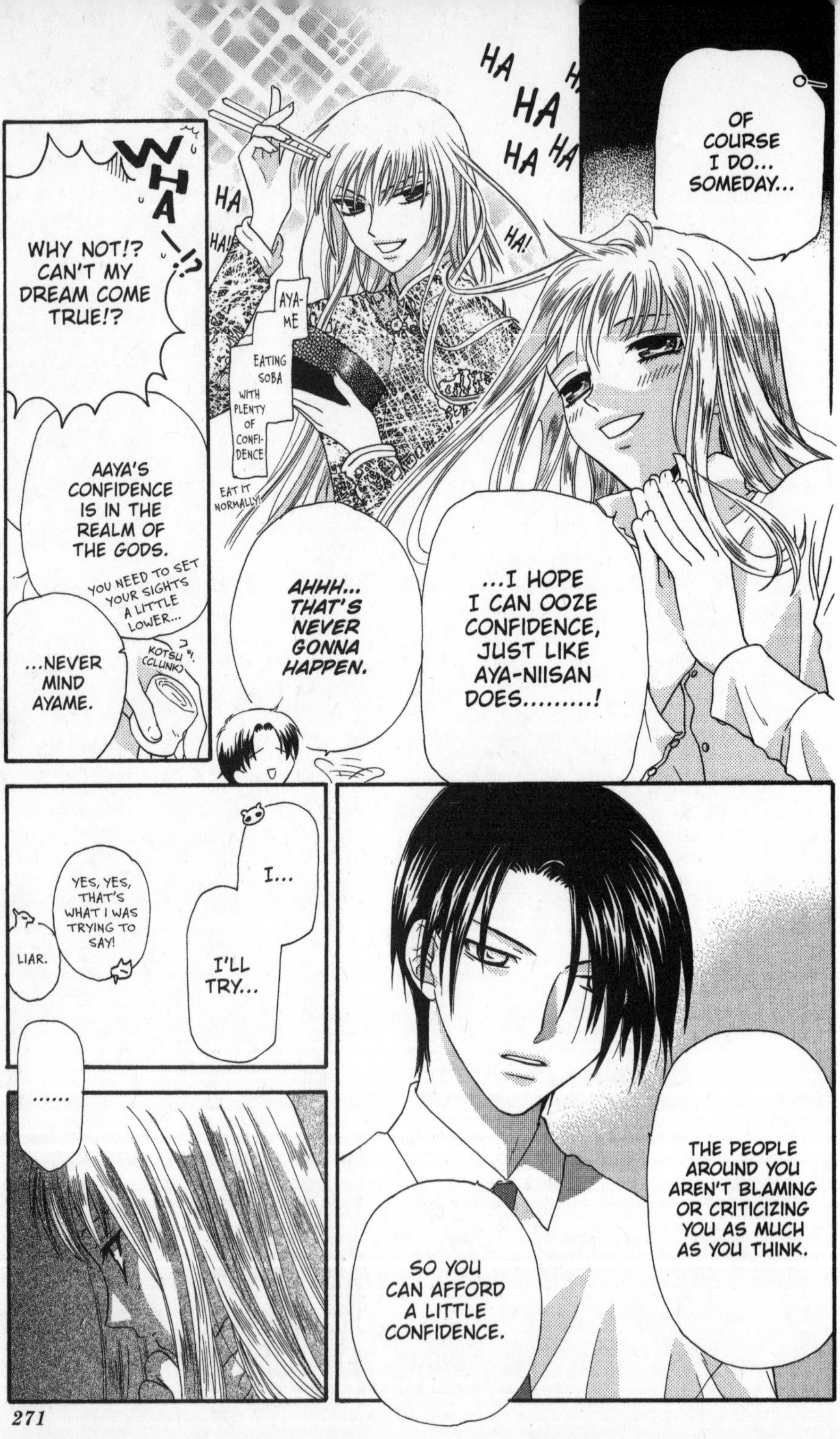
OF COURSE I DO... SOMEDAY...
HA HA HA HA HA HA HA! HA!
AYA-ME
EATING SOBA WITH PLENTY OF CONFIDENCE
EAT IT NORMALLY!
...I HOPE I CAN OOZE CONFIDENCE, JUST LIKE AYA-NIISAN DOES.........!
AHHH... THAT'S NEVER GONNA HAPPEN.
WHA-!?
WHY NOT!? CAN'T MY DREAM COME TRUE!?
AAYA'S CONFIDENCE IS IN THE REALM OF THE GODS.
YOU NEED TO SET YOUR SIGHTS A LITTLE LOWER...
KOTSU (CLUNK)
...NEVER MIND AYAME.
THE PEOPLE AROUND YOU AREN'T BLAMING OR CRITICIZING YOU AS MUCH AS YOU THINK.
SO YOU CAN AFFORD A LITTLE CONFIDENCE.
I...
I'LL TRY...
YES, YES, THAT'S WHAT I WAS TRYING TO SAY!
LIAR.
......

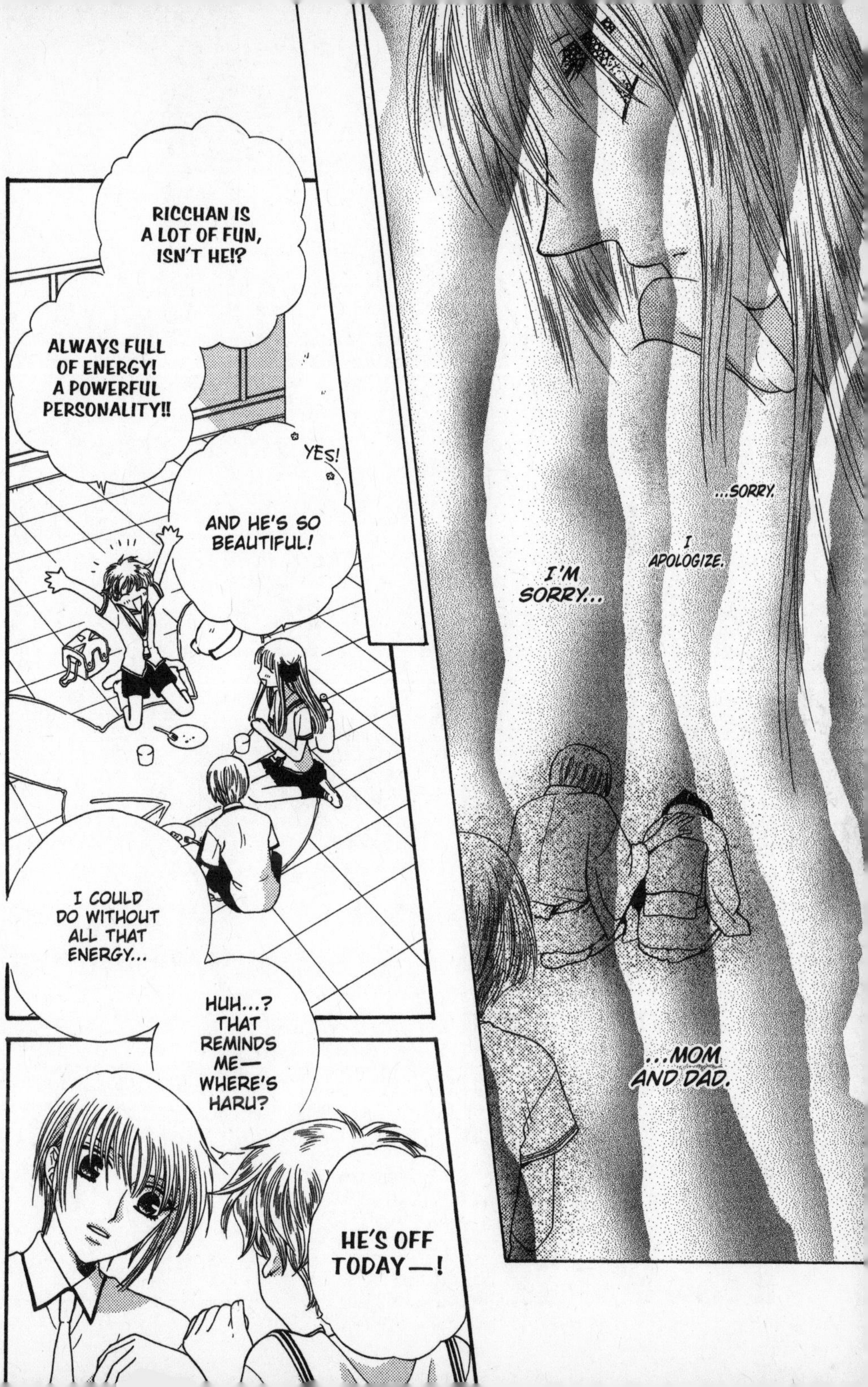
...SORRY.
I APOLOGIZE.
I'M SORRY...
...MOM AND DAD.
RICCHAN IS A LOT OF FUN, ISN'T HE!?
ALWAYS FULL OF ENERGY! A POWERFUL PERSONALITY!!
YES!
AND HE'S SO BEAUTIFUL!
I COULD DO WITHOUT ALL THAT ENERGY...
HUH...? THAT REMINDS ME— WHERE'S HARU?
HE'S OFF TODAY—!

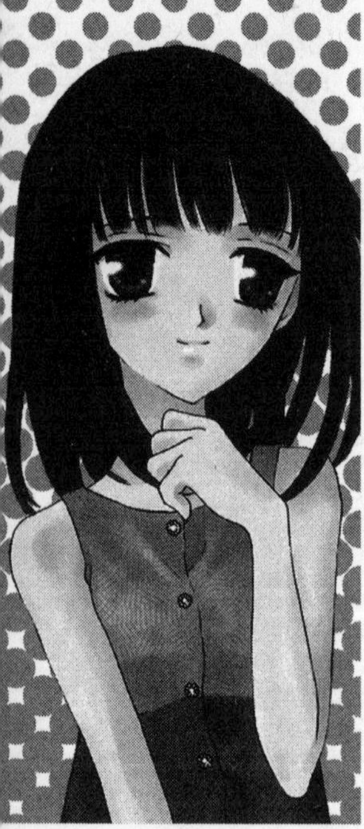

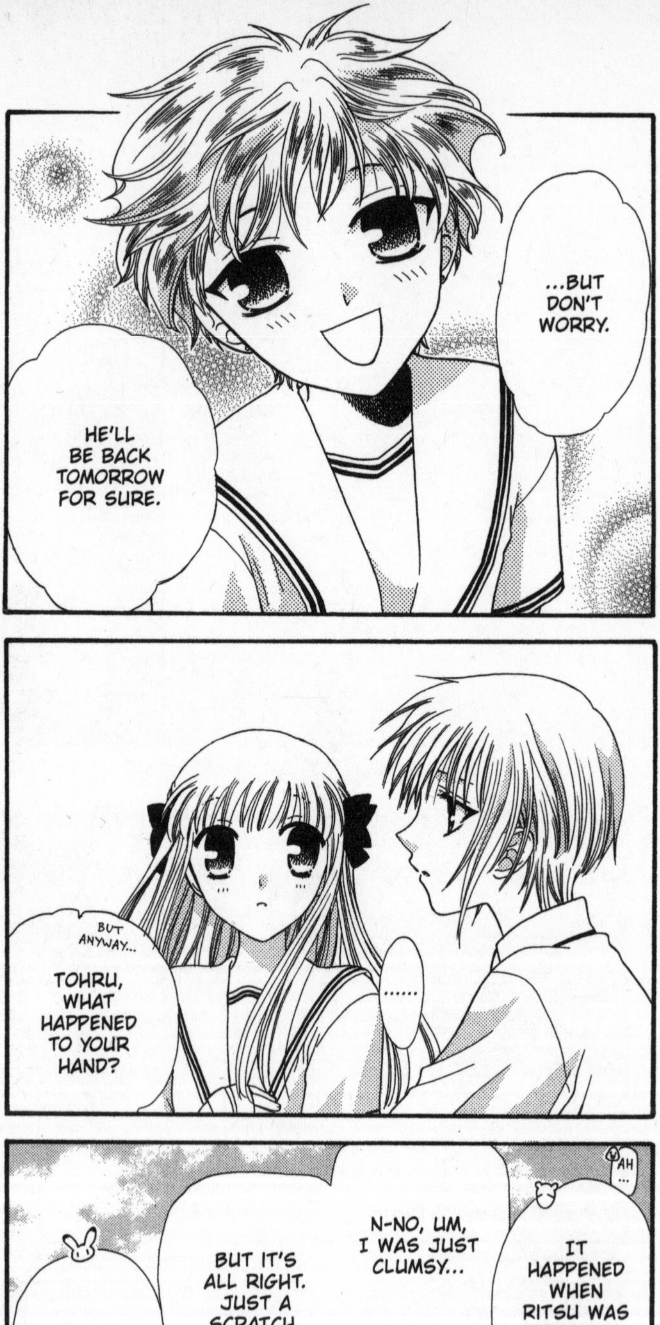
...BUT DON'T WORRY.
HE'LL BE BACK TOMORROW FOR SURE.
......
BUT ANYWAY...
TOHRU, WHAT HAPPENED TO YOUR HAND?
AH...
IT HAPPENED WHEN RITSU WAS FREAKING OUT...
N-NO, UM, I WAS JUST CLUMSY...
BUT IT'S ALL RIGHT. JUST A SCRATCH.
REALLY? FOR SURE?

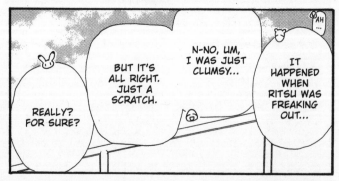

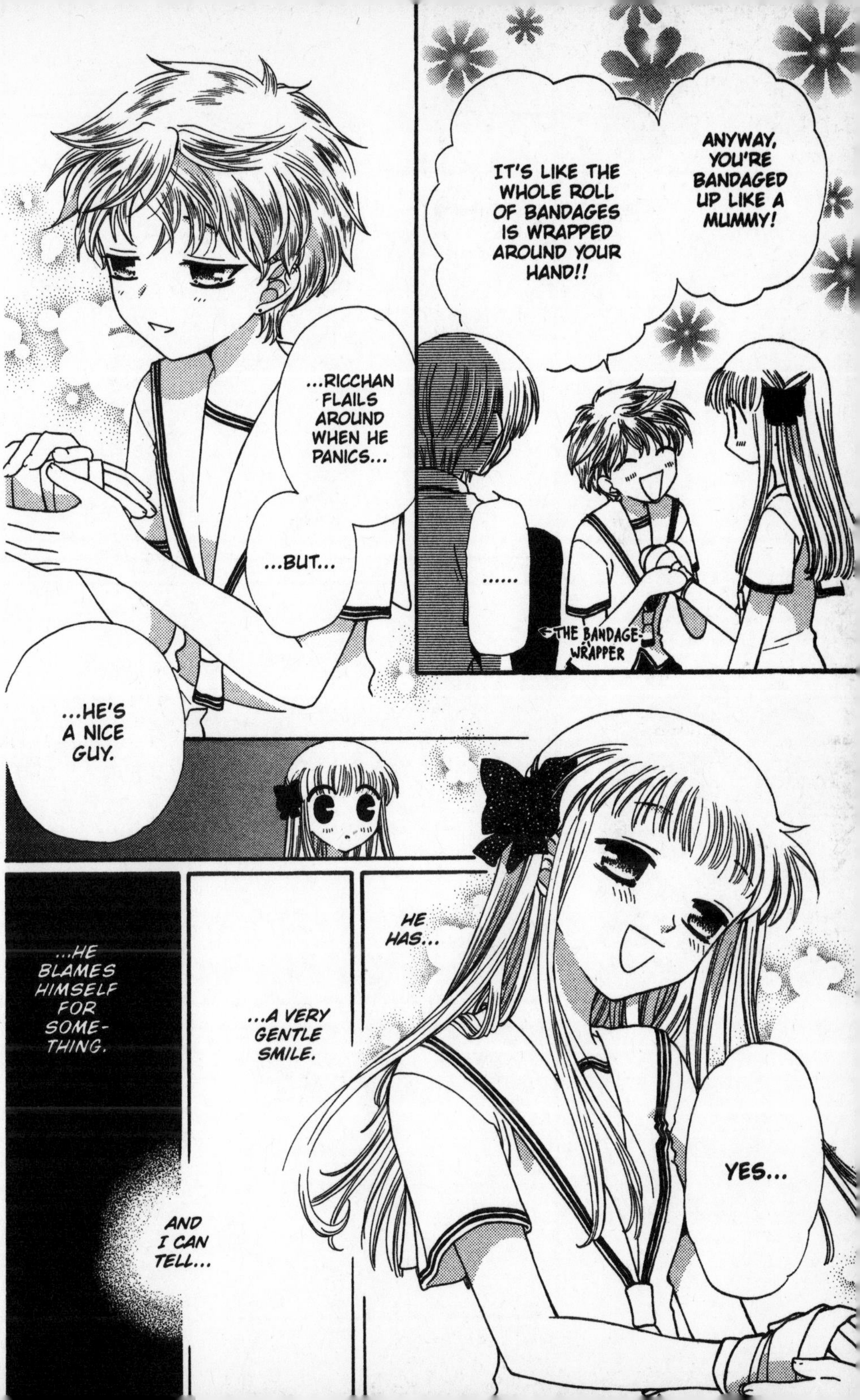
ANYWAY, YOU'RE BANDAGED UP LIKE A MUMMY!
IT'S LIKE THE WHOLE ROLL OF BANDAGES IS WRAPPED AROUND YOUR HAND!!
......
←THE BANDAGE-WRAPPER
...RICCHAN FLAILS AROUND WHEN HE PANICS...
...BUT...
...HE'S A NICE GUY.
YES...
HE HAS...
...A VERY GENTLE SMILE.
AND I CAN TELL...
...HE BLAMES HIMSELF FOR SOME-THING.

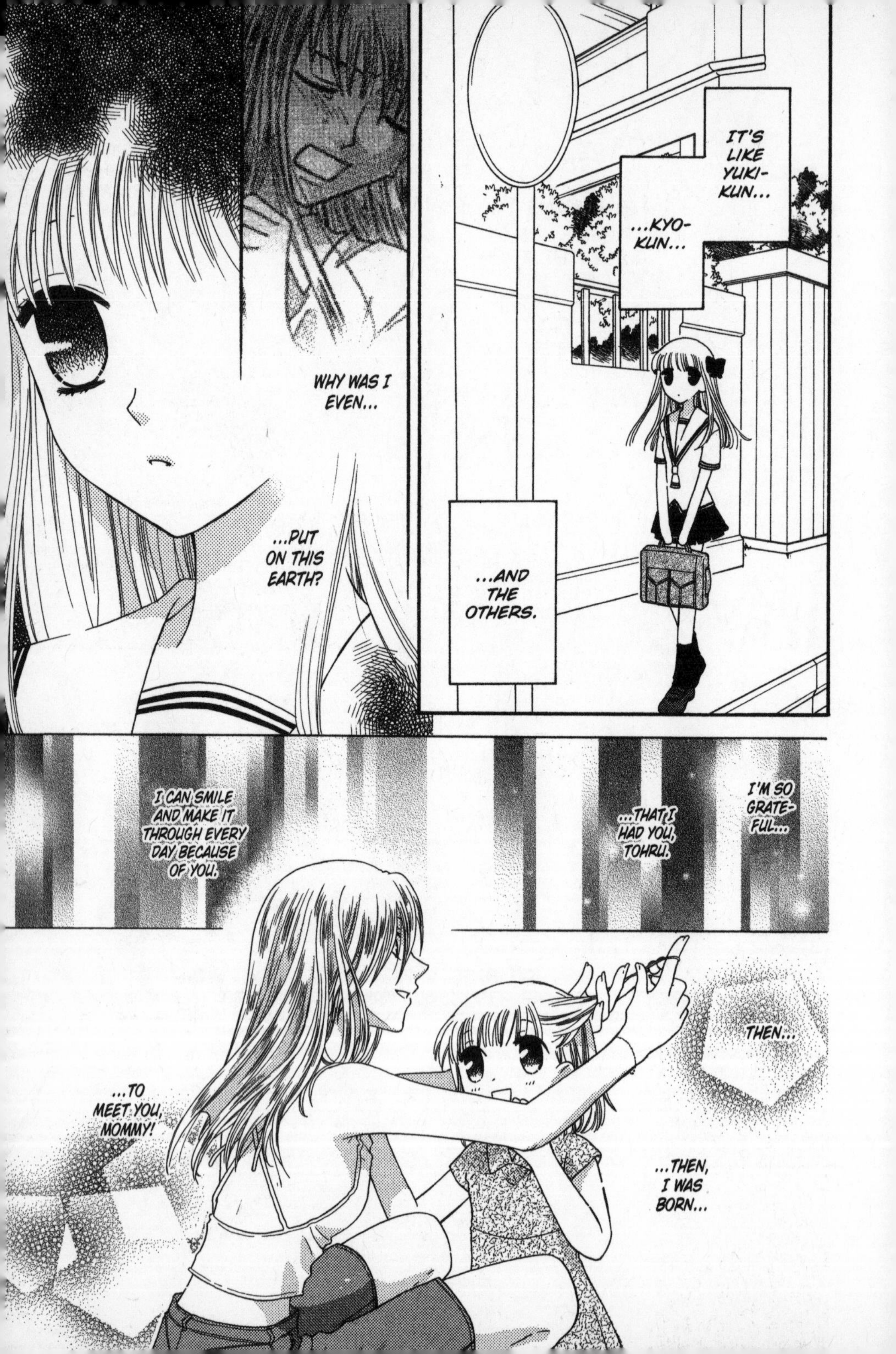
IT'S LIKE YUKI-KUN...
...KYO-KUN...
...AND THE OTHERS.
WHY WAS I EVEN...
...PUT ON THIS EARTH?
I'M SO GRATE-FUL...
...THAT I HAD YOU, TOHRU.
I CAN SMILE AND MAKE IT THROUGH EVERY DAY BECAUSE OF YOU.
THEN...
...THEN, I WAS BORN...
...TO MEET YOU, MOMMY!

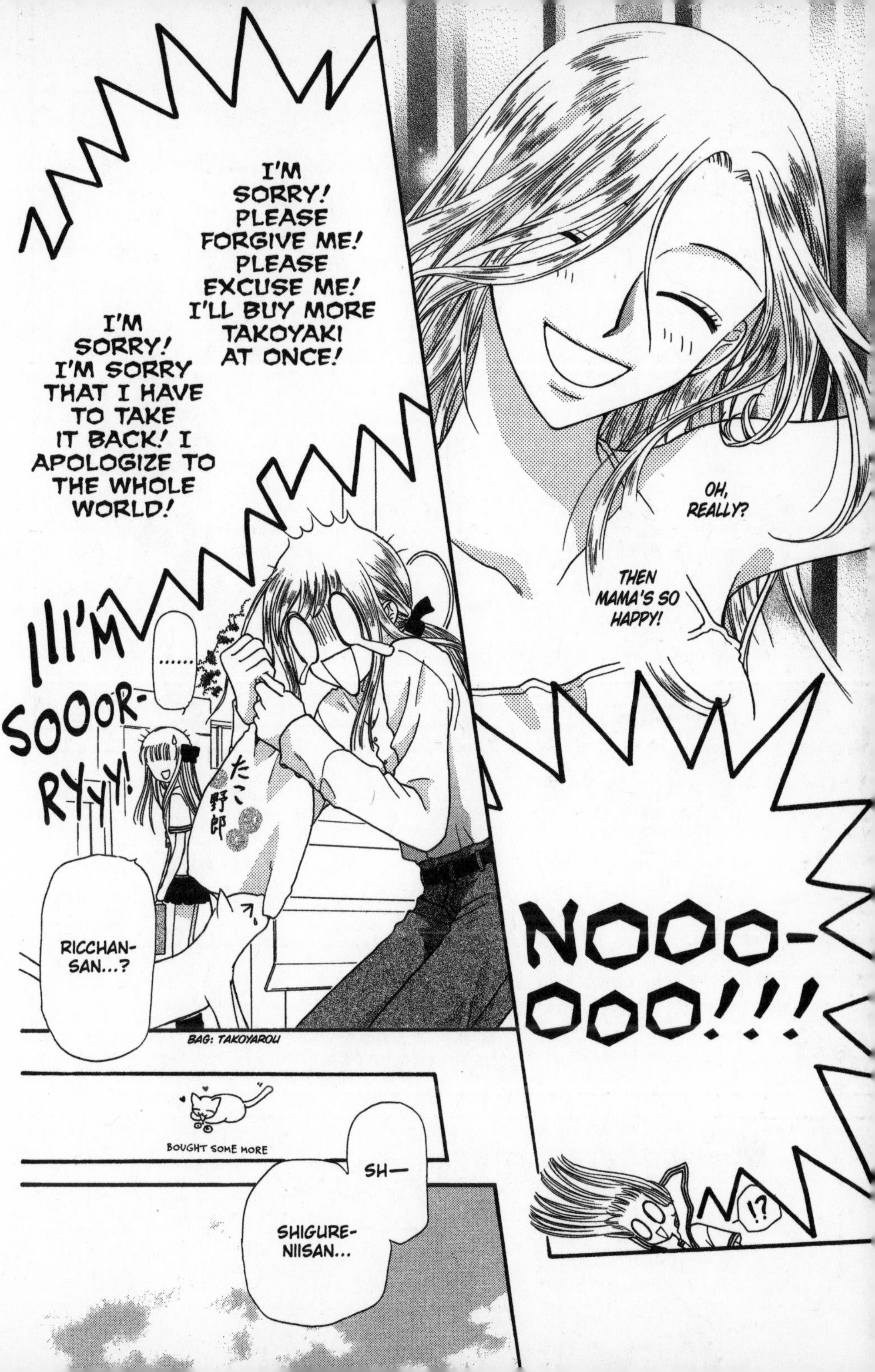
OH, REALLY?
THEN MAMA'S SO HAPPY!
NOOOO-OOO!!!
I'M SORRY! PLEASE FORGIVE ME! PLEASE EXCUSE ME! I'LL BUY MORE TAKOYAKI AT ONCE!
I'M SORRY! I'M SORRY THAT I HAVE TO TAKE IT BACK! I APOLOGIZE TO THE WHOLE WORLD!
IIII'M SOOOR-RYYY!
......
たこ野郎
RICCHAN-SAN...?
BAG: TAKOYAROU
BOUGHT SOME MORE
!?
SH—
SHIGURE-NIISAN...

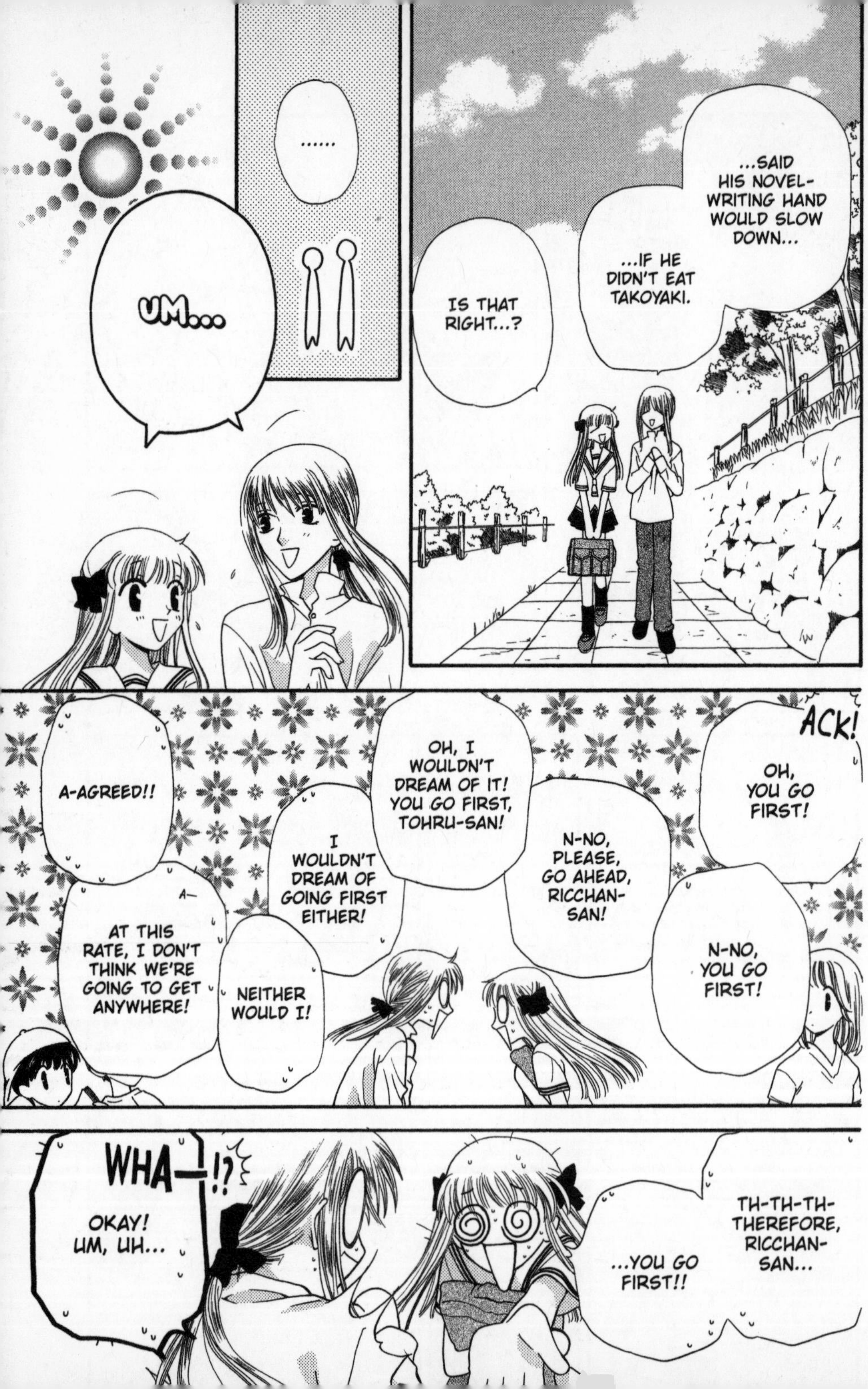
...SAID HIS NOVEL-WRITING HAND WOULD SLOW DOWN...
...IF HE DIDN'T EAT TAKOYAKI.
IS THAT RIGHT...?
......
UM...
ACK!
OH, YOU GO FIRST!
N-NO, YOU GO FIRST!
N-NO, PLEASE, GO AHEAD, RICCHAN-SAN!
OH, I WOULDN'T DREAM OF IT! YOU GO FIRST, TOHRU-SAN!
I WOULDN'T DREAM OF GOING FIRST EITHER!
NEITHER WOULD I!
A-AGREED!!
A—
AT THIS RATE, I DON'T THINK WE'RE GOING TO GET ANYWHERE!
TH-TH-TH-THEREFORE, RICCHAN-SAN...
...YOU GO FIRST!!
WHA—!?
OKAY! UM, UH...

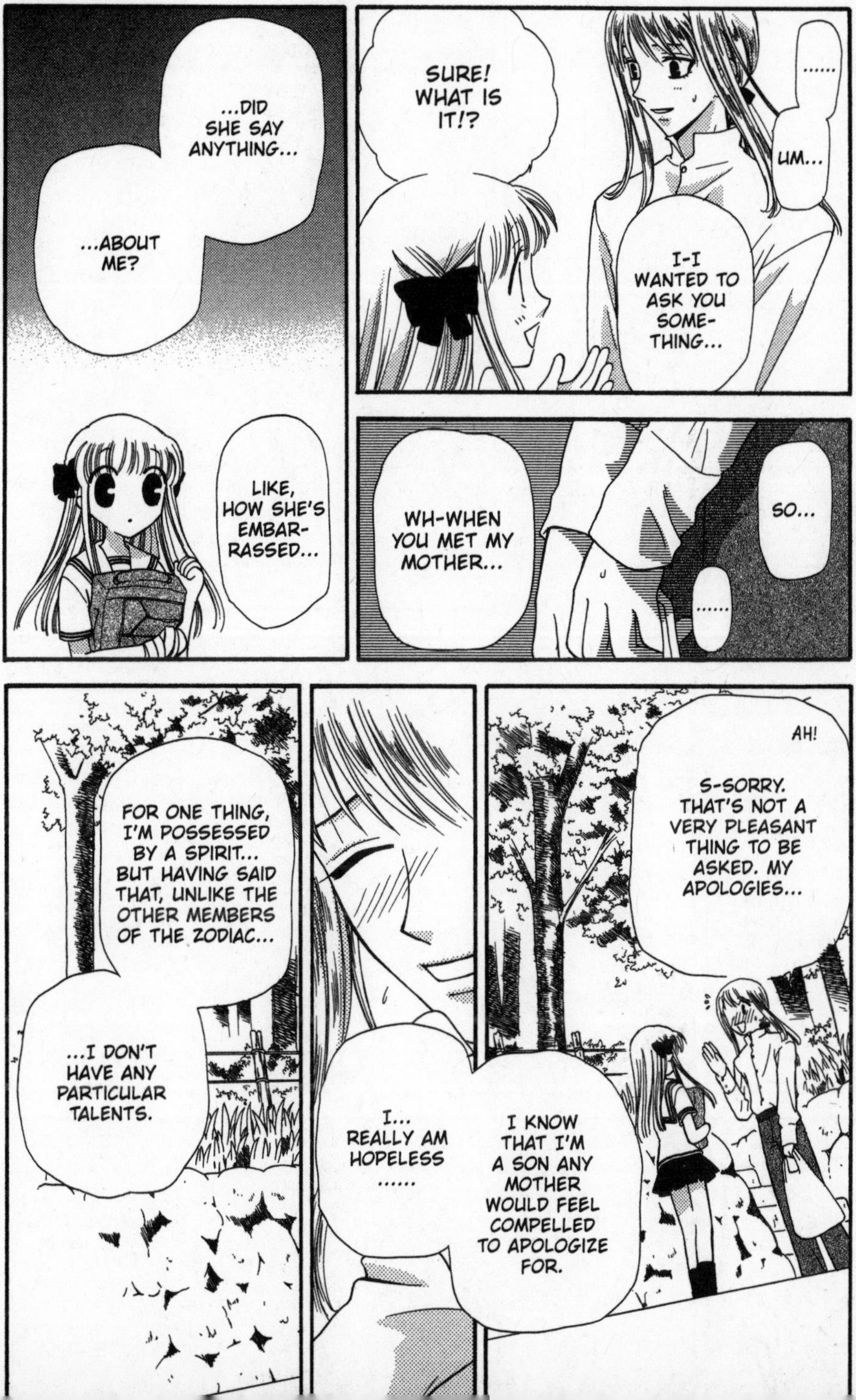
......
UM...
I-I WANTED TO ASK YOU SOME-THING...
SURE! WHAT IS IT!?
SO...
......
WH-WHEN YOU MET MY MOTHER...
...DID SHE SAY ANYTHING...
...ABOUT ME?
LIKE, HOW SHE'S EMBAR-RASSED...
AH!
S-SORRY. THAT'S NOT A VERY PLEASANT THING TO BE ASKED. MY APOLOGIES...
I KNOW THAT I'M A SON ANY MOTHER WOULD FEEL COMPELLED TO APOLOGIZE FOR.
I... REALLY AM HOPELESS ......
FOR ONE THING, I'M POSSESSED BY A SPIRIT... BUT HAVING SAID THAT, UNLIKE THE OTHER MEMBERS OF THE ZODIAC...
...I DON'T HAVE ANY PARTICULAR TALENTS.

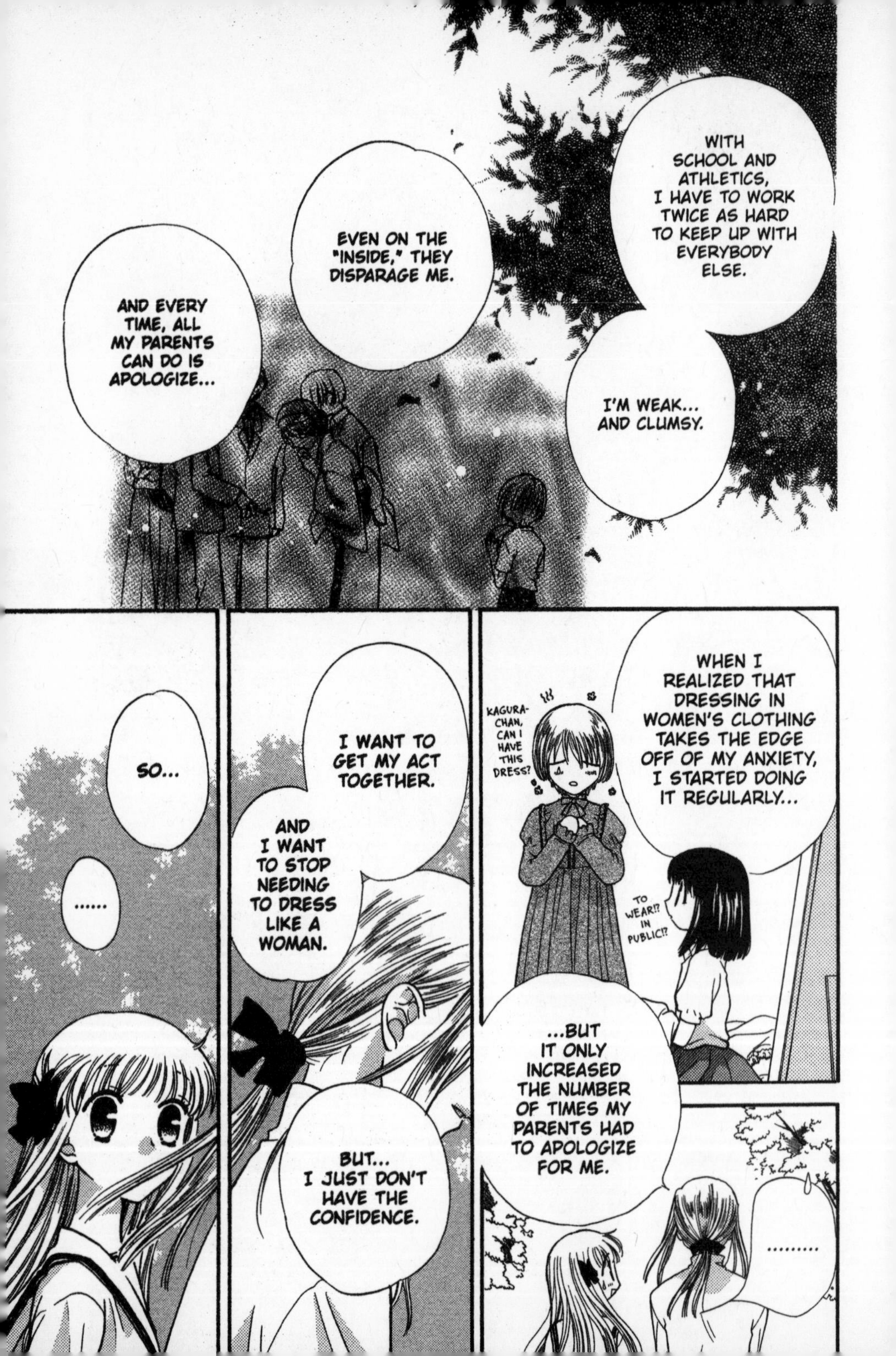
WITH SCHOOL AND ATHLETICS, I HAVE TO WORK TWICE AS HARD TO KEEP UP WITH EVERYBODY ELSE.
I'M WEAK... AND CLUMSY.
EVEN ON THE "INSIDE," THEY DISPARAGE ME.
AND EVERY TIME, ALL MY PARENTS CAN DO IS APOLOGIZE...
WHEN I REALIZED THAT DRESSING IN WOMEN'S CLOTHING TAKES THE EDGE OFF OF MY ANXIETY, I STARTED DOING IT REGULARLY...
KAGURA-CHAN, CAN I HAVE THIS DRESS?
TO WEAR!? IN PUBLIC!?
...BUT IT ONLY INCREASED THE NUMBER OF TIMES MY PARENTS HAD TO APOLOGIZE FOR ME.
....
I WANT TO GET MY ACT TOGETHER.
AND I WANT TO STOP NEEDING TO DRESS LIKE A WOMAN.
BUT... I JUST DON'T HAVE THE CONFIDENCE.
SO...
......

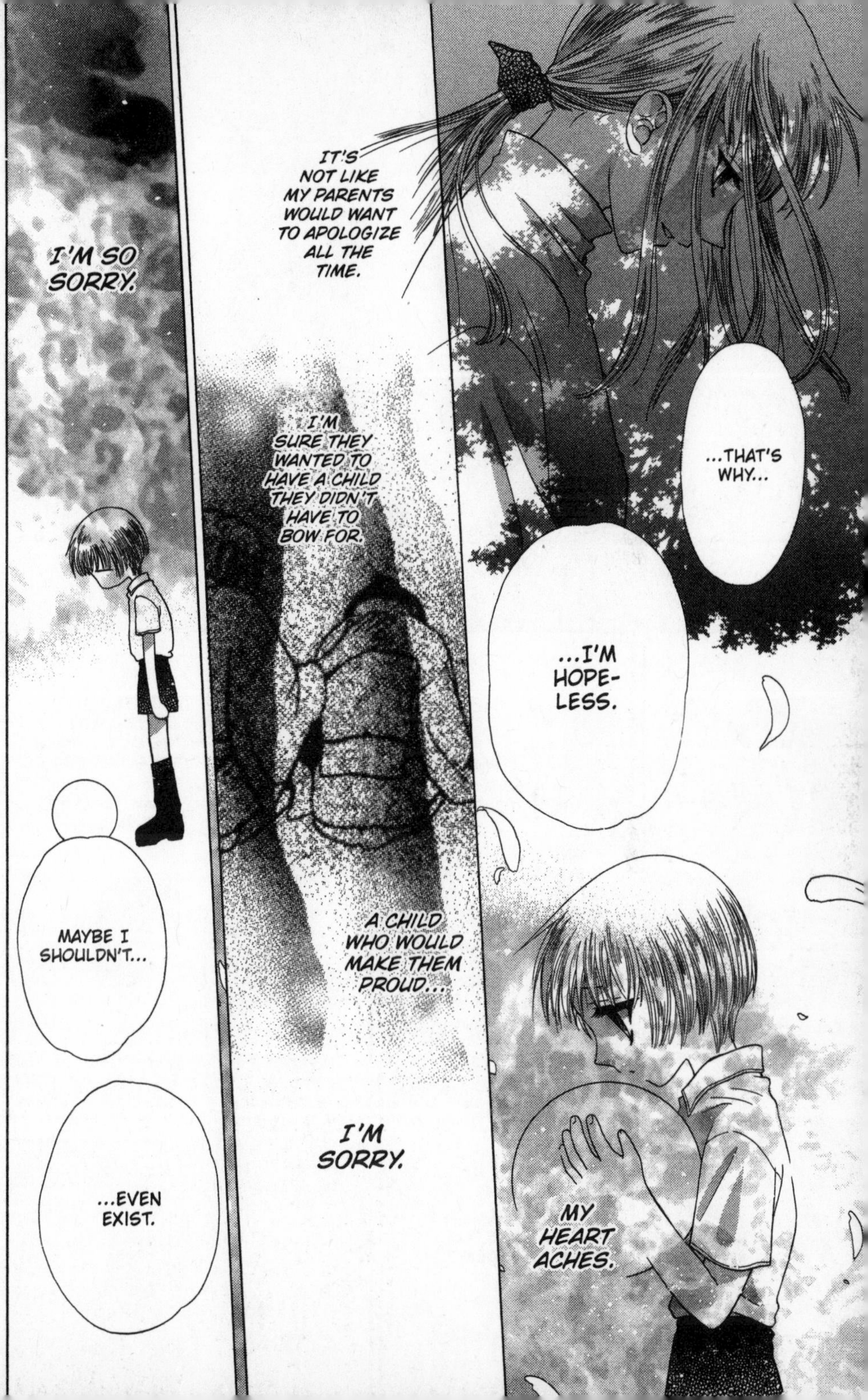
...THAT'S WHY...
...I'M HOPELESS.
MY HEART ACHES.
IT'S NOT LIKE MY PARENTS WOULD WANT TO APOLOGIZE ALL THE TIME.
I'M SURE THEY WANTED TO HAVE A CHILD THEY DIDN'T HAVE TO BOW FOR.
A CHILD WHO WOULD MAKE THEM PROUD...
I'M SORRY.
I'M SO SORRY.
MAYBE I SHOULDN'T...
...EVEN EXIST.

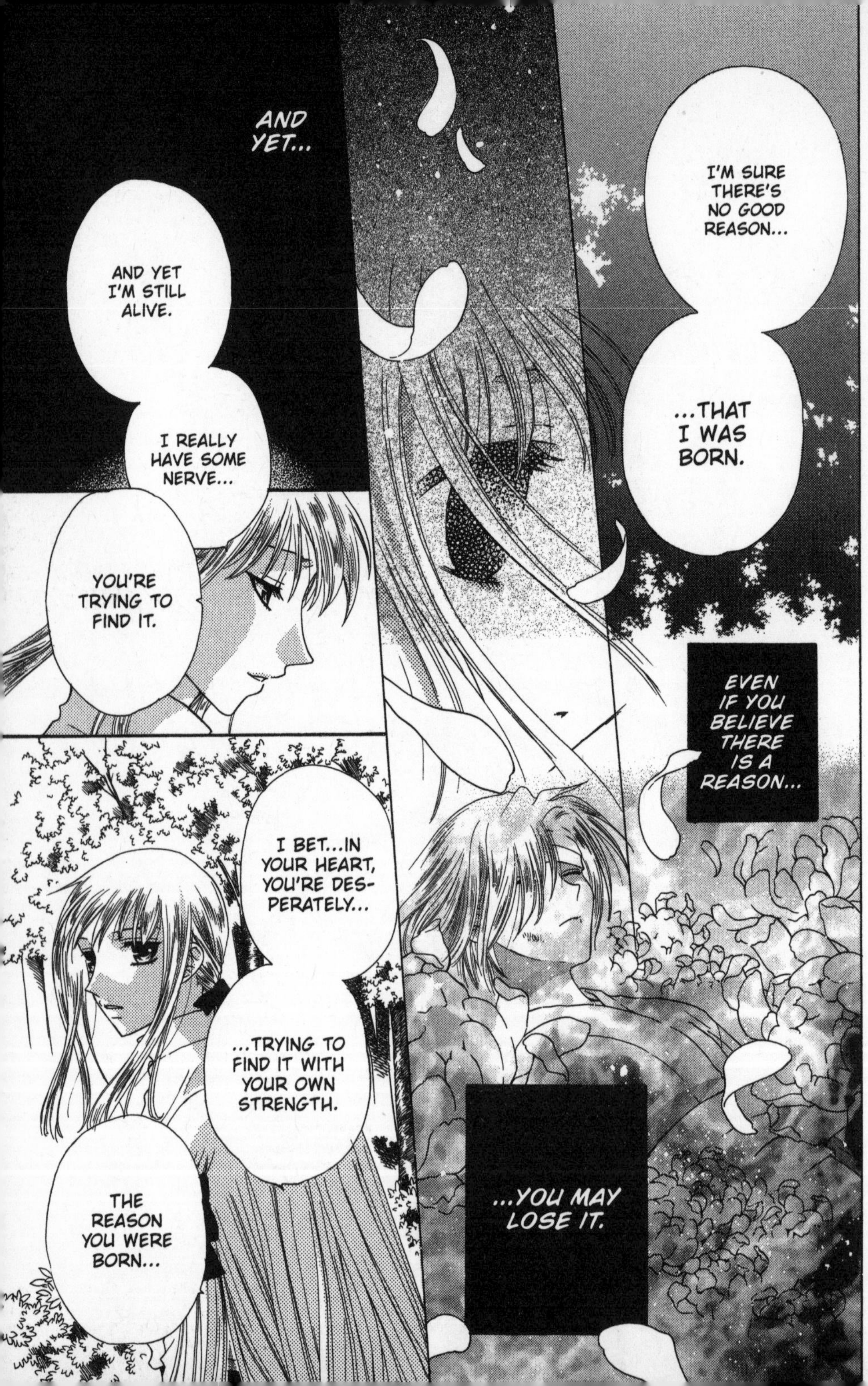
I'M SURE THERE'S NO GOOD REASON...
...THAT I WAS BORN.
AND YET...
AND YET I'M STILL ALIVE.
I REALLY HAVE SOME NERVE...
EVEN IF YOU BELIEVE THERE IS A REASON...
...YOU MAY LOSE IT.
YOU'RE TRYING TO FIND IT.
I BET...IN YOUR HEART, YOU'RE DES-PERATELY...
...TRYING TO FIND IT WITH YOUR OWN STRENGTH.
THE REASON YOU WERE BORN...

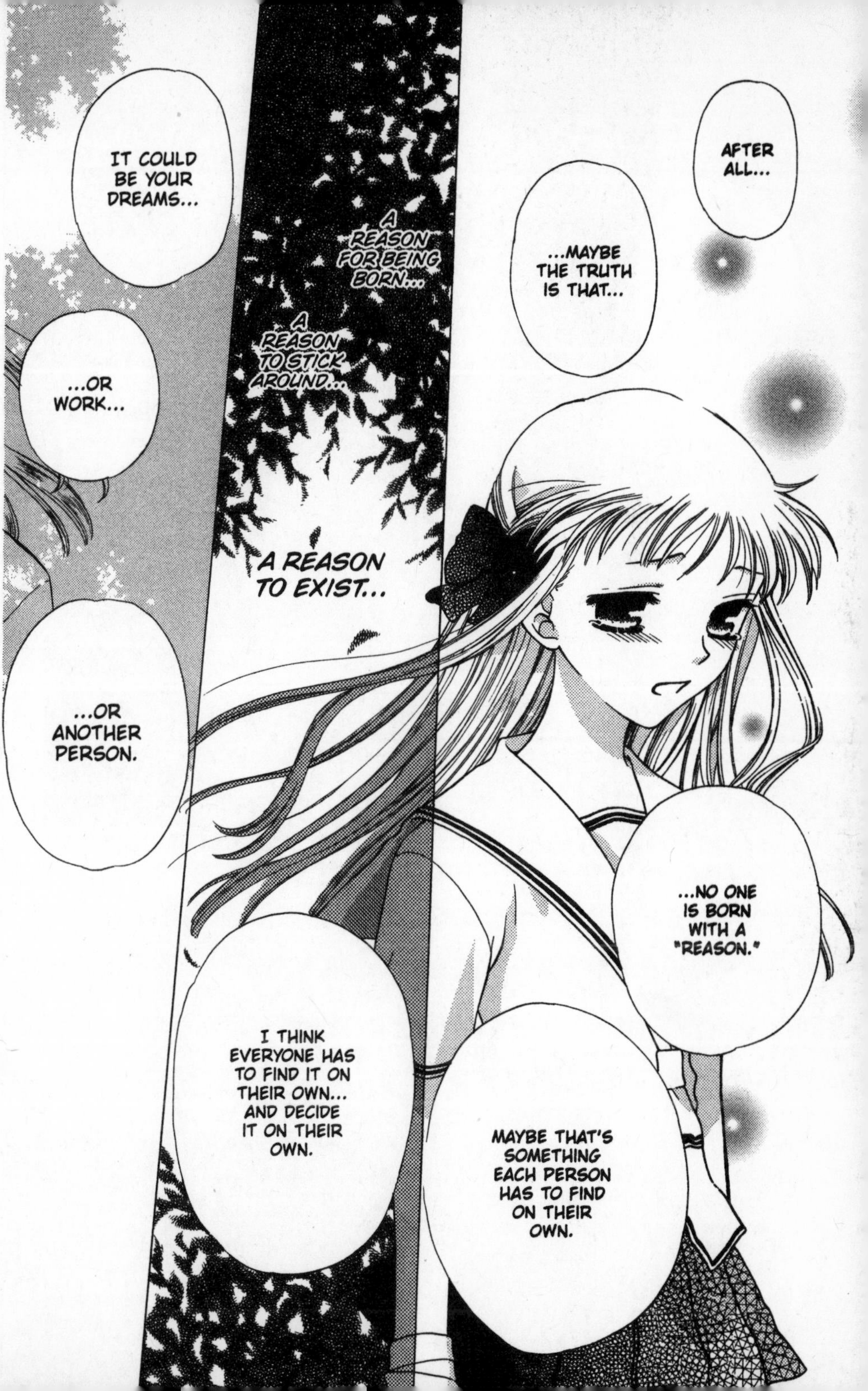
AFTER ALL...
...MAYBE THE TRUTH IS THAT...
...NO ONE IS BORN WITH A "REASON."
MAYBE THAT'S SOMETHING EACH PERSON HAS TO FIND ON THEIR OWN.
A REASON FOR BEING BORN...
A REASON TO STICK AROUND...
A REASON TO EXIST...
I THINK EVERYONE HAS TO FIND IT ON THEIR OWN... AND DECIDE IT ON THEIR OWN.
IT COULD BE YOUR DREAMS...
...OR WORK...
...OR ANOTHER PERSON.

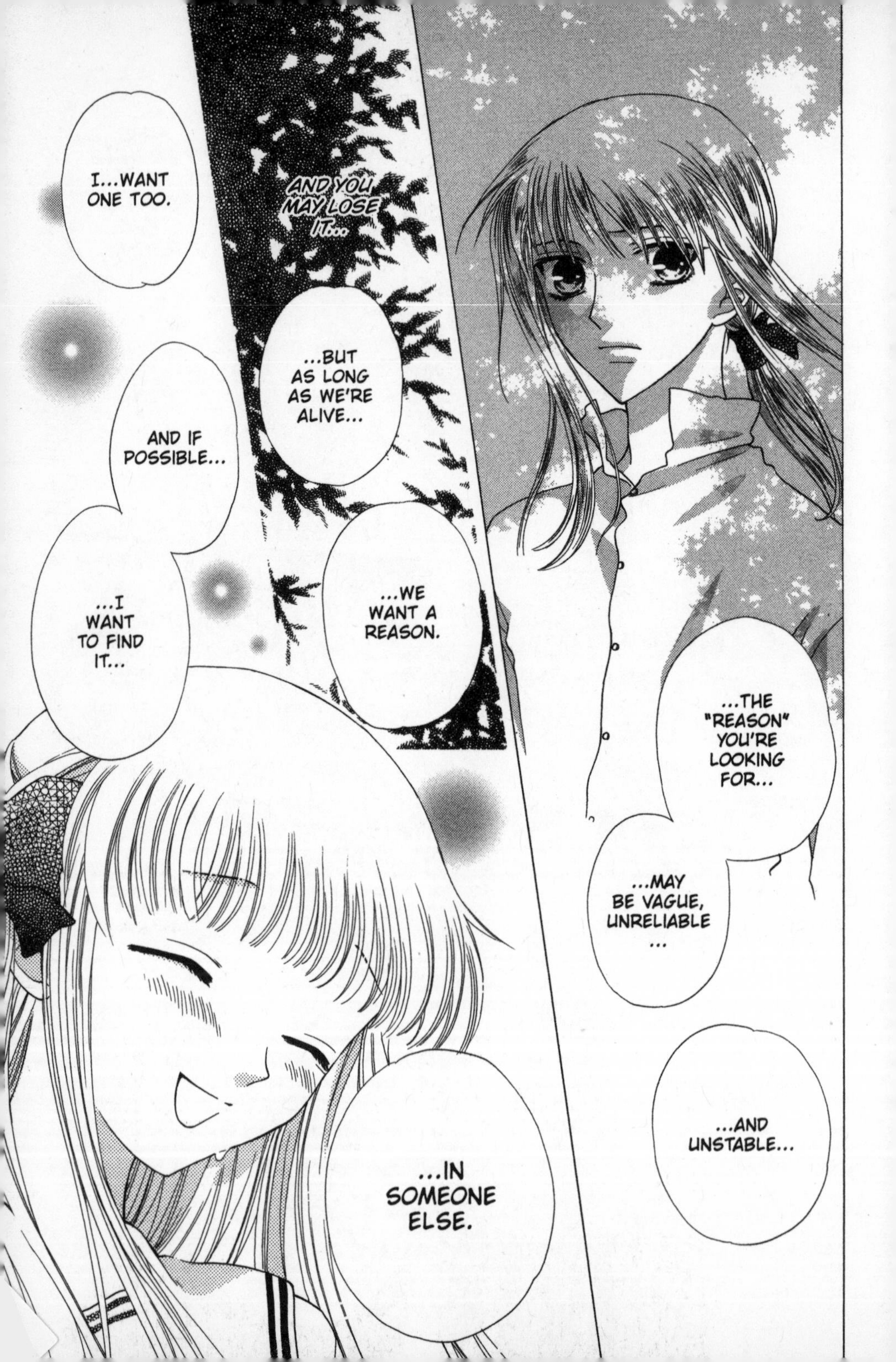
...THE "REASON" YOU'RE LOOKING FOR...
...MAY BE VAGUE, UNRELIABLE ...
...AND UNSTABLE...
AND YOU MAY LOSE IT...
...BUT AS LONG AS WE'RE ALIVE...
...WE WANT A REASON.
I...WANT ONE TOO.
AND IF POSSIBLE...
...I WANT TO FIND IT...
...IN SOMEONE ELSE.

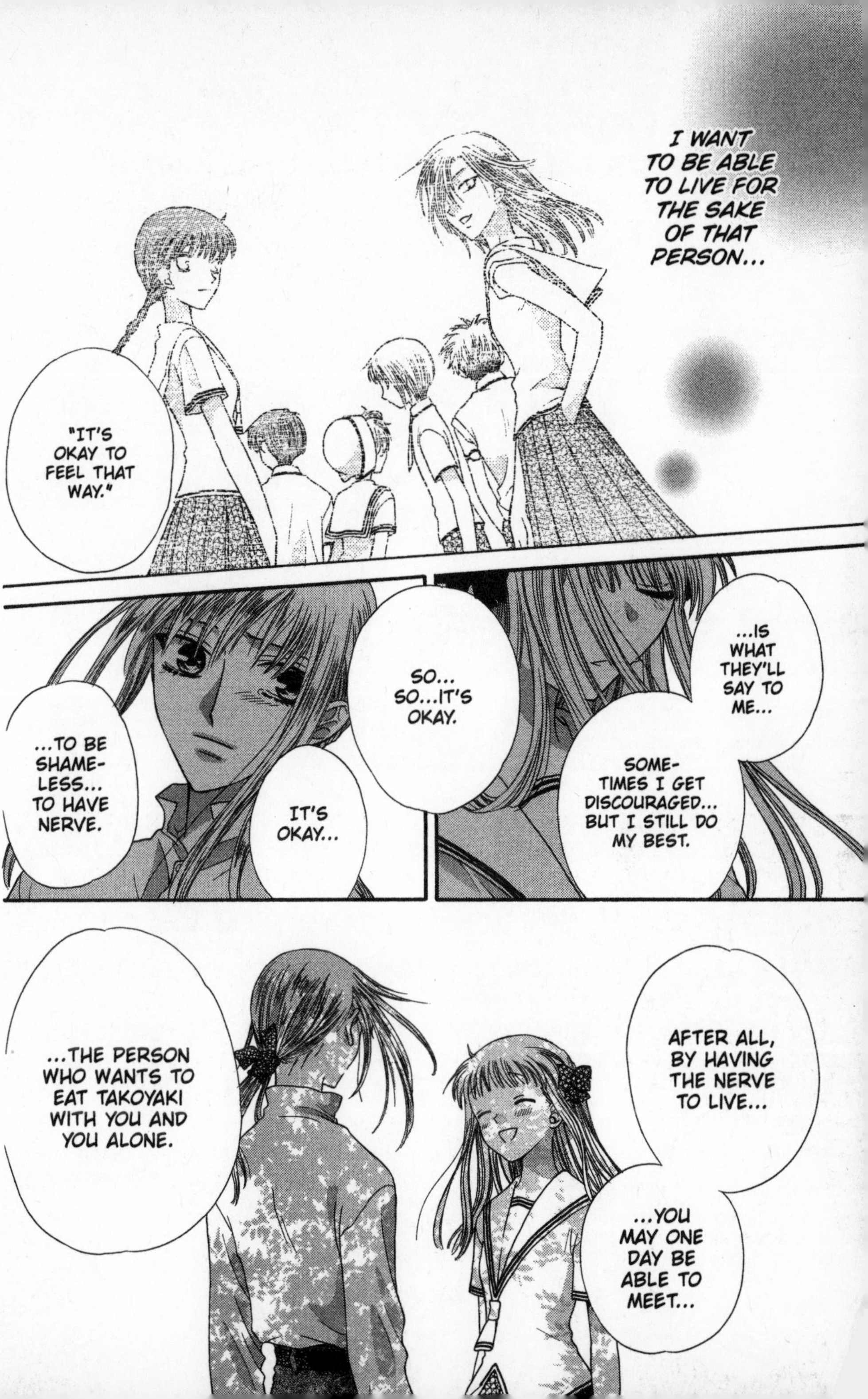
I WANT TO BE ABLE TO LIVE FOR THE SAKE OF THAT PERSON...
"IT'S OKAY TO FEEL THAT WAY."
...IS WHAT THEY'LL SAY TO ME...
SOME-TIMES I GET DISCOURAGED... BUT I STILL DO MY BEST.
SO... SO...IT'S OKAY.
IT'S OKAY...
...TO BE SHAME-LESS... TO HAVE NERVE.
AFTER ALL, BY HAVING THE NERVE TO LIVE...
...YOU MAY ONE DAY BE ABLE TO MEET...
...THE PERSON WHO WANTS TO EAT TAKOYAKI WITH YOU AND YOU ALONE.

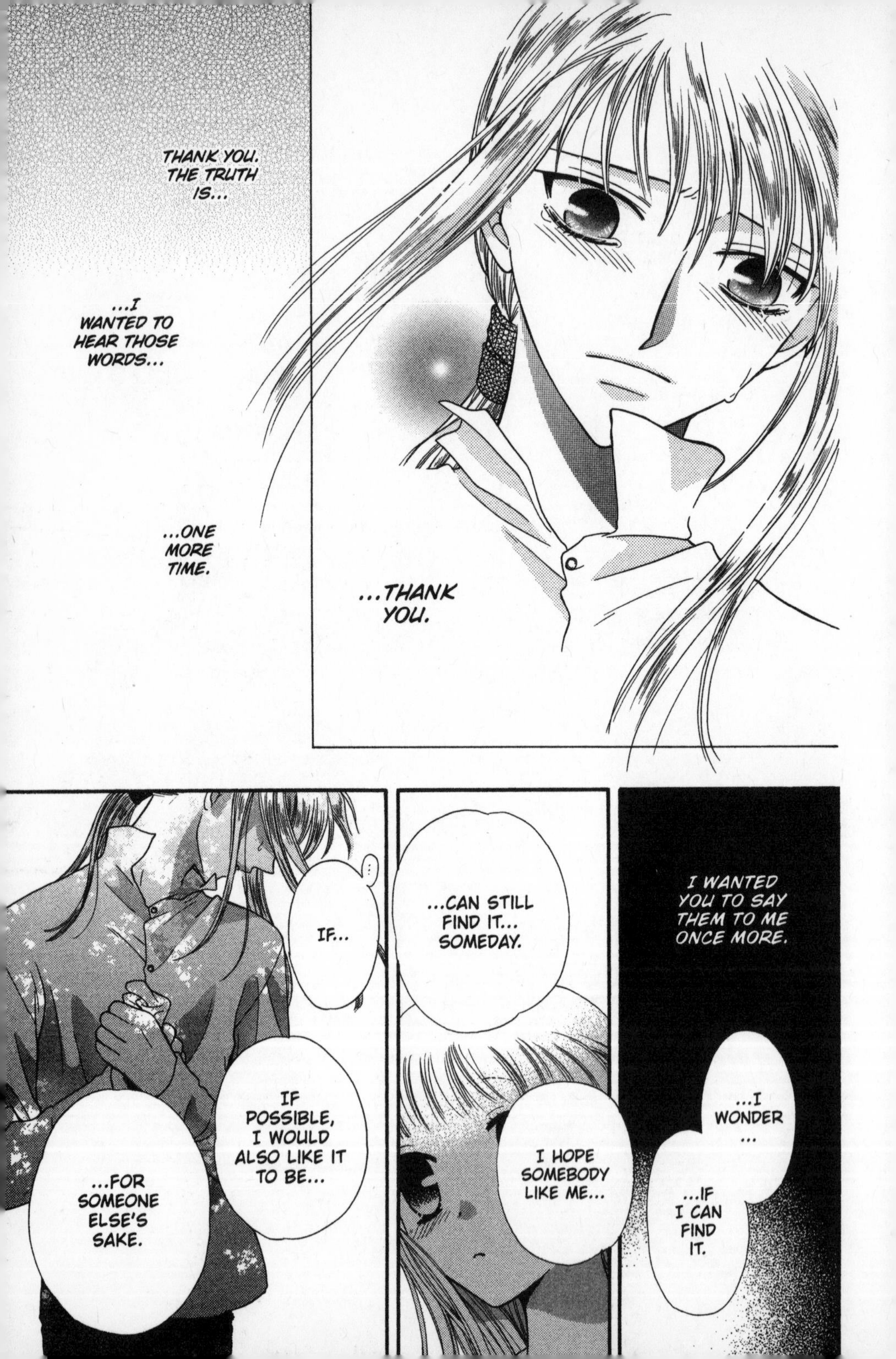
...THANK YOU.
THANK YOU. THE TRUTH IS...
...I WANTED TO HEAR THOSE WORDS...
...ONE MORE TIME.
I WANTED YOU TO SAY THEM TO ME ONCE MORE.
...I WONDER...
...IF I CAN FIND IT.
I HOPE SOMEBODY LIKE ME...
...CAN STILL FIND IT... SOMEDAY.
...
IF...
IF POSSIBLE, I WOULD ALSO LIKE IT TO BE...
...FOR SOMEONE ELSE'S SAKE.

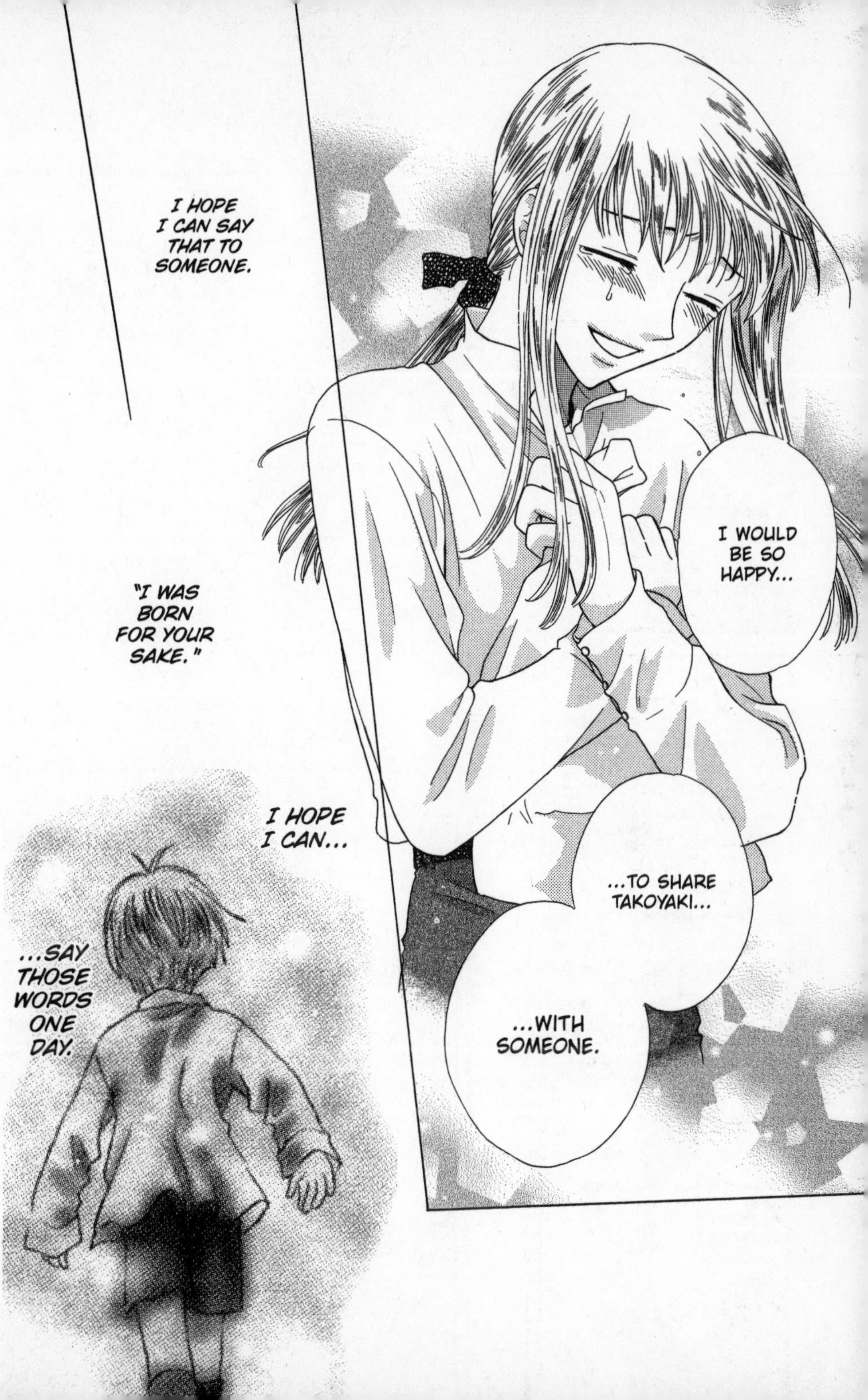
I WOULD BE SO HAPPY...
...TO SHARE TAKOYAKI...
...WITH SOMEONE.
I HOPE I CAN SAY THAT TO SOMEONE.
"I WAS BORN FOR YOUR SAKE."
I HOPE I CAN...
...SAY THOSE WORDS ONE DAY.

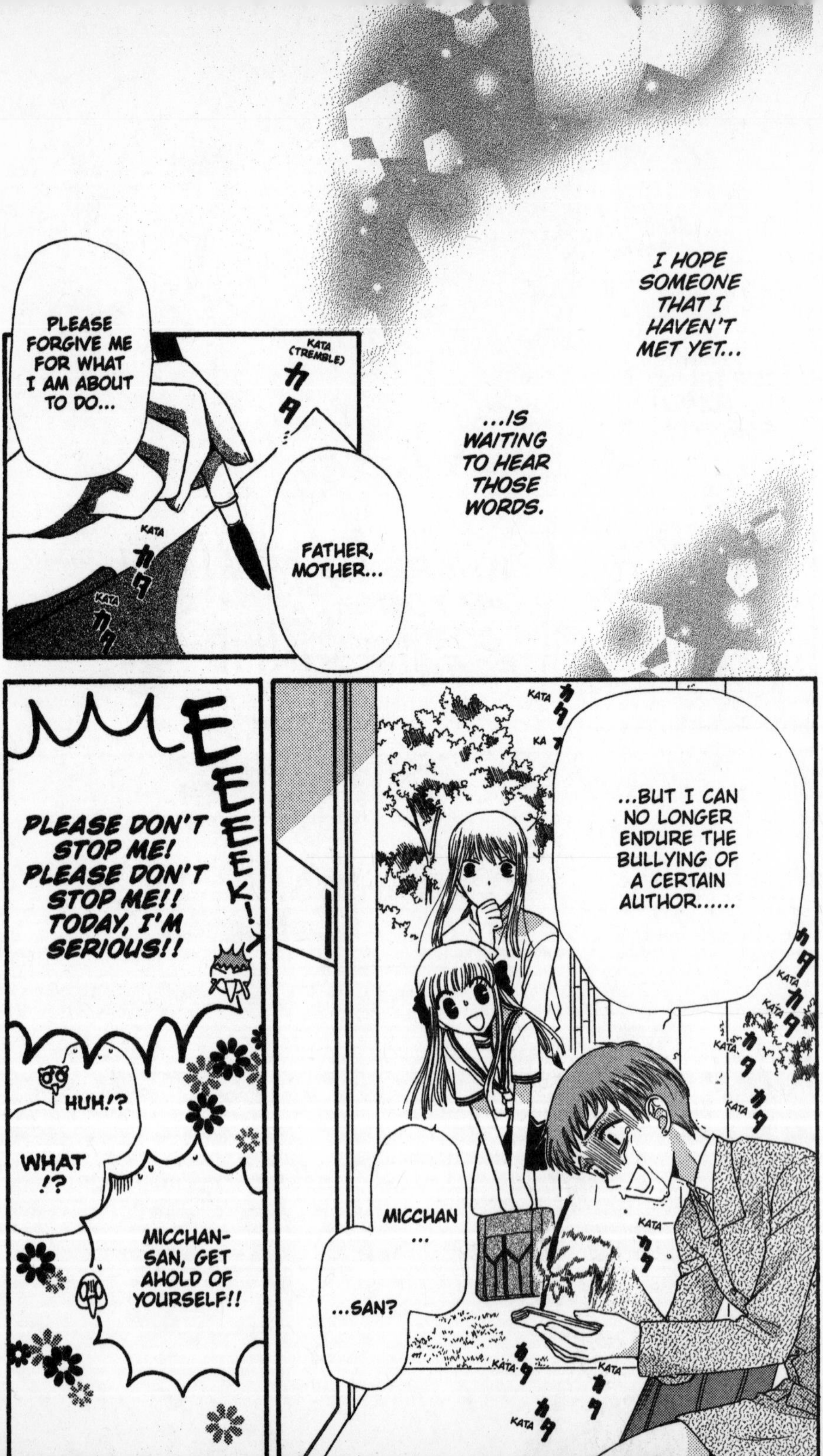
I HOPE SOMEONE THAT I HAVEN'T MET YET...
...IS WAITING TO HEAR THOSE WORDS.
FATHER, MOTHER...
KATA (TREMBLE)
カタ
PLEASE FORGIVE ME FOR WHAT I AM ABOUT TO DO...
KATA
カタ
KATA
カタ
KATA
カタ
KA
...BUT I CAN NO LONGER ENDURE THE BULLYING OF A CERTAIN AUTHOR......
MICCHAN ...
...SAN?
MEEEEEK!
PLEASE DON'T STOP ME! PLEASE DON'T STOP ME!! TODAY, I'M SERIOUS!!
HUH!?
WHAT !?
MICCHAN-SAN, GET AHOLD OF YOURSELF!!

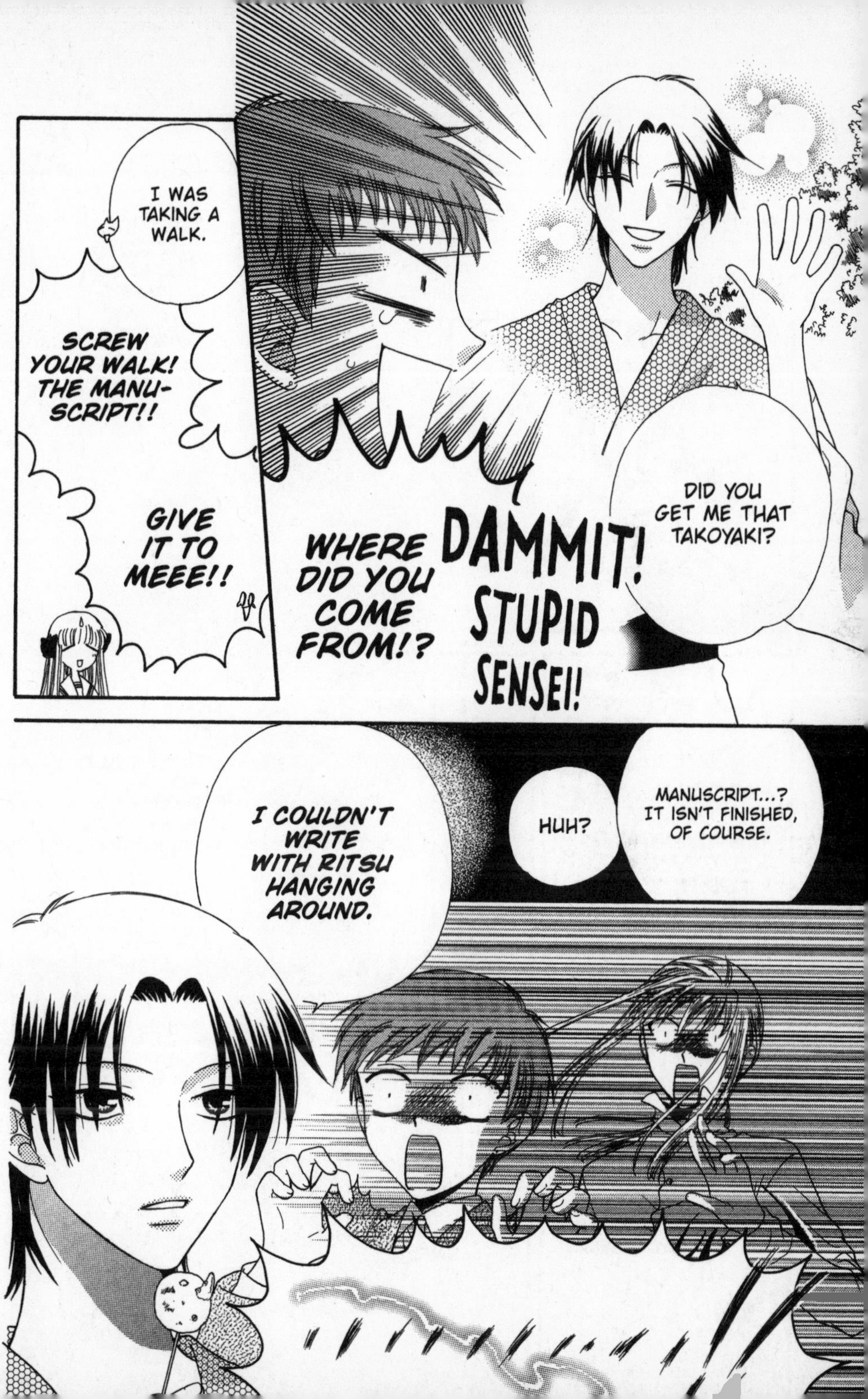
DID YOU GET ME THAT TAKOYAKI?
DAMMIT! STUPID SENSEI!
WHERE DID YOU COME FROM!?
I WAS TAKING A WALK.
SCREW YOUR WALK! THE MANU-SCRIPT!!
GIVE IT TO MEEE!!
MANUSCRIPT...? IT ISN'T FINISHED, OF COURSE.
HUH?
I COULDN'T WRITE WITH RITSU HANGING AROUND.

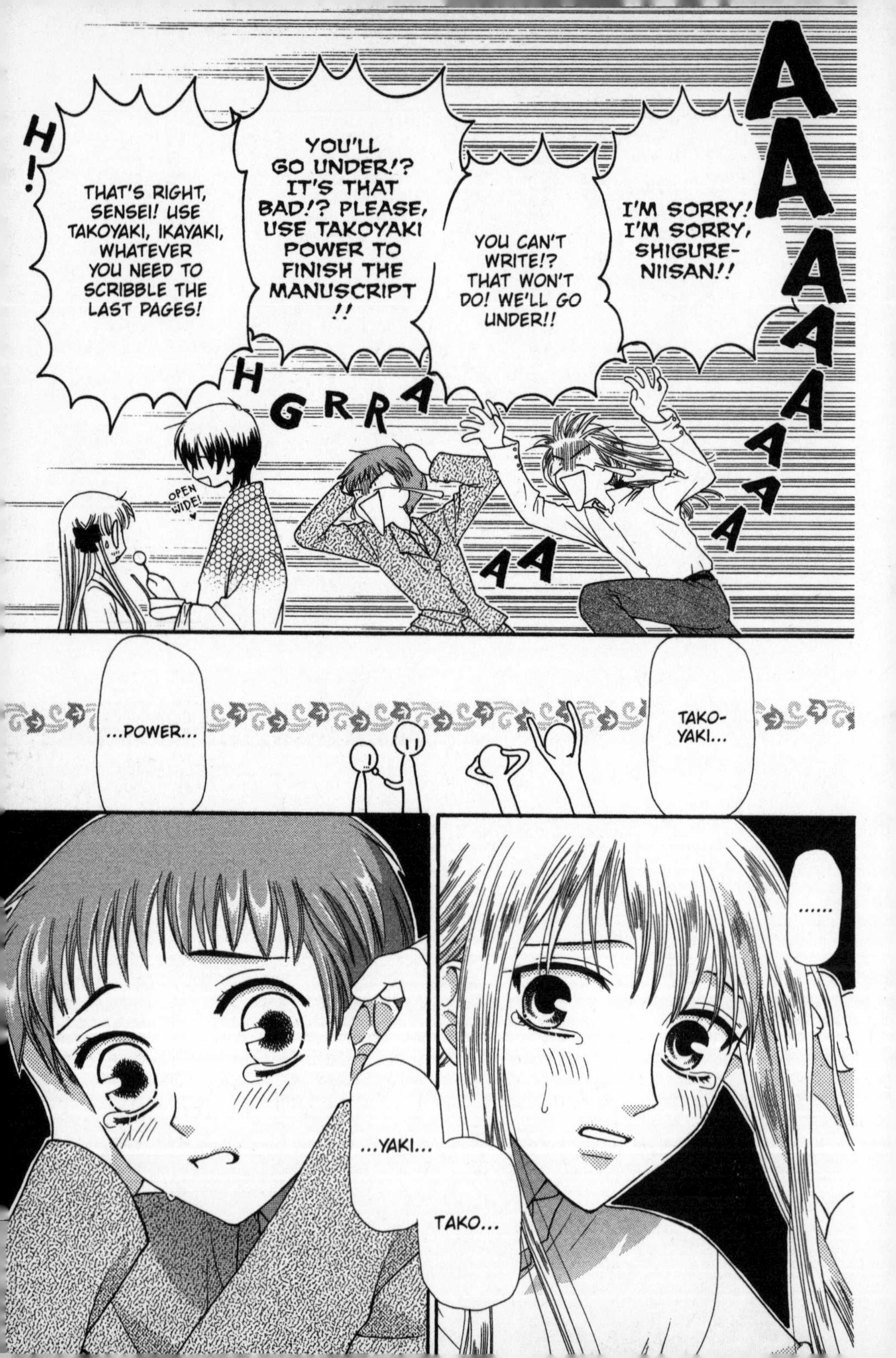
AAAAAAAAAA
I'M SORRY! I'M SORRY, SHIGURE-NIISAN!!
AA
YOU CAN'T WRITE!? THAT WON'T DO! WE'LL GO UNDER!!
YOU'LL GO UNDER!? IT'S THAT BAD!? PLEASE, USE TAKOYAKI POWER TO FINISH THE MANUSCRIPT!!
HGRRA
H!
THAT'S RIGHT, SENSEI! USE TAKOYAKI, IKAYAKI, WHATEVER YOU NEED TO SCRIBBLE THE LAST PAGES!
OPEN WIDE!
TAKO-YAKI...
...POWER...
......
TAKO...
...YAKI...

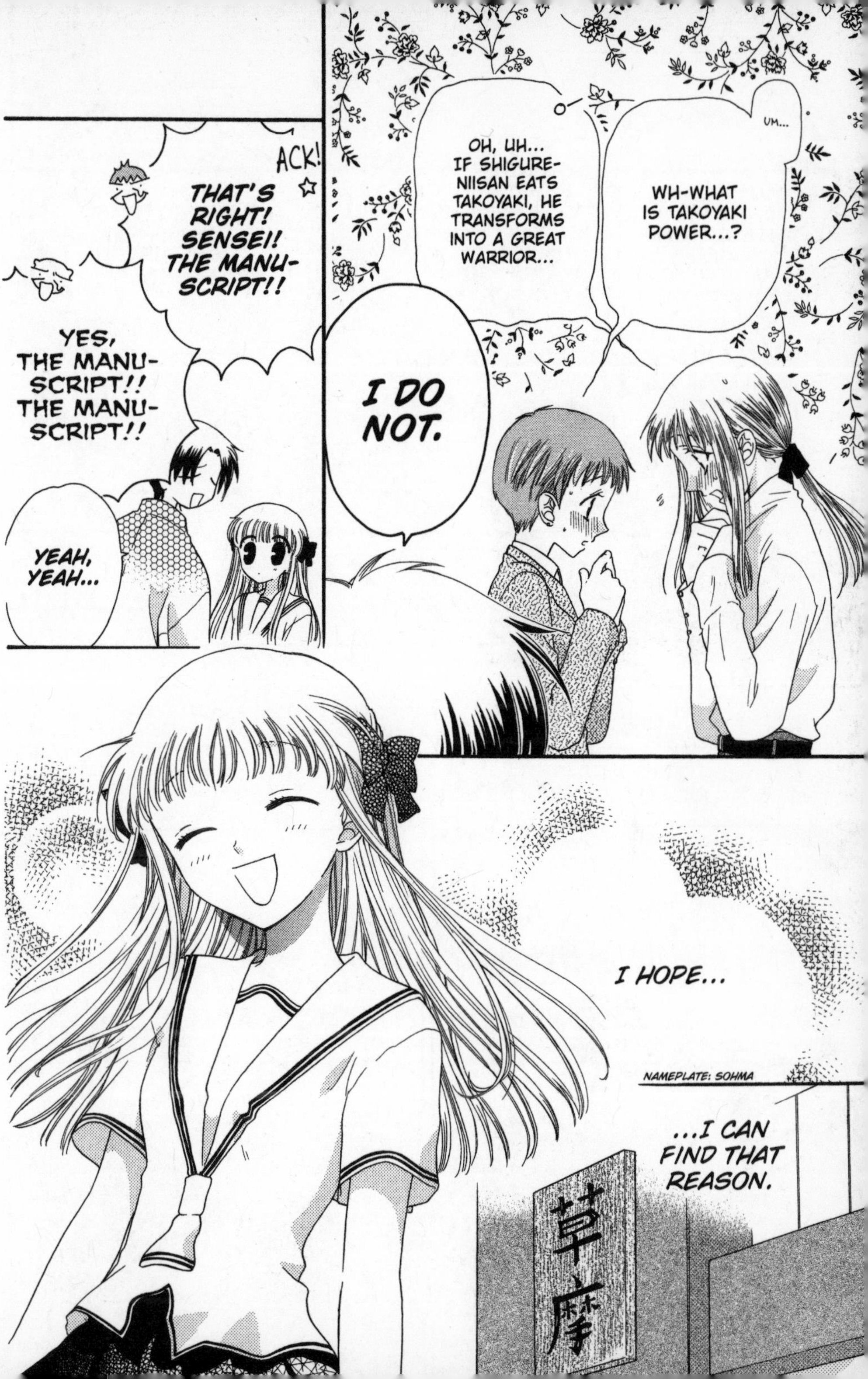
UM...
WH-WHAT IS TAKOYAKI POWER...?
OH, UH... IF SHIGURE-NIISAN EATS TAKOYAKI, HE TRANSFORMS INTO A GREAT WARRIOR...
I DO NOT.
ACK!
THAT'S RIGHT! SENSEI! THE MANU-SCRIPT!!
YES, THE MANU-SCRIPT!! THE MANU-SCRIPT!!
YEAH, YEAH...
I HOPE...
NAMEPLATE: SOHMA
...I CAN FIND THAT REASON.
草摩

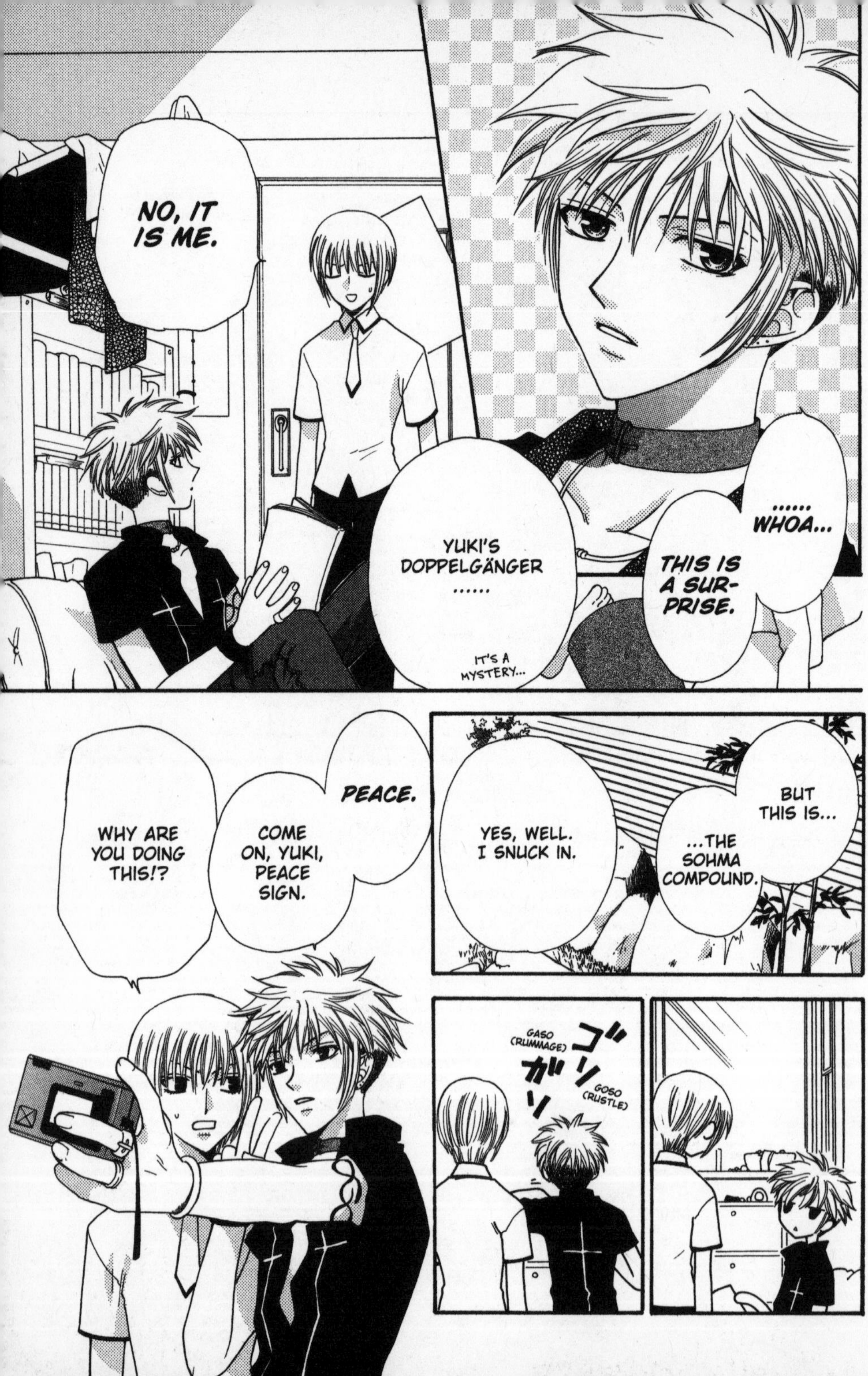

......WHOA...
THIS IS A SUR-PRISE.
YUKI'S DOPPELGÄNGER ......
IT'S A MYSTERY...
NO, IT IS ME.
BUT THIS IS...
...THE SOHMA COMPOUND.
YES, WELL. I SNUCK IN.
ゴソ
ガソ
GASO (RUMMAGE)
GOSO (RUSTLE)
PEACE.
COME ON, YUKI, PEACE SIGN.
WHY ARE YOU DOING THIS!?

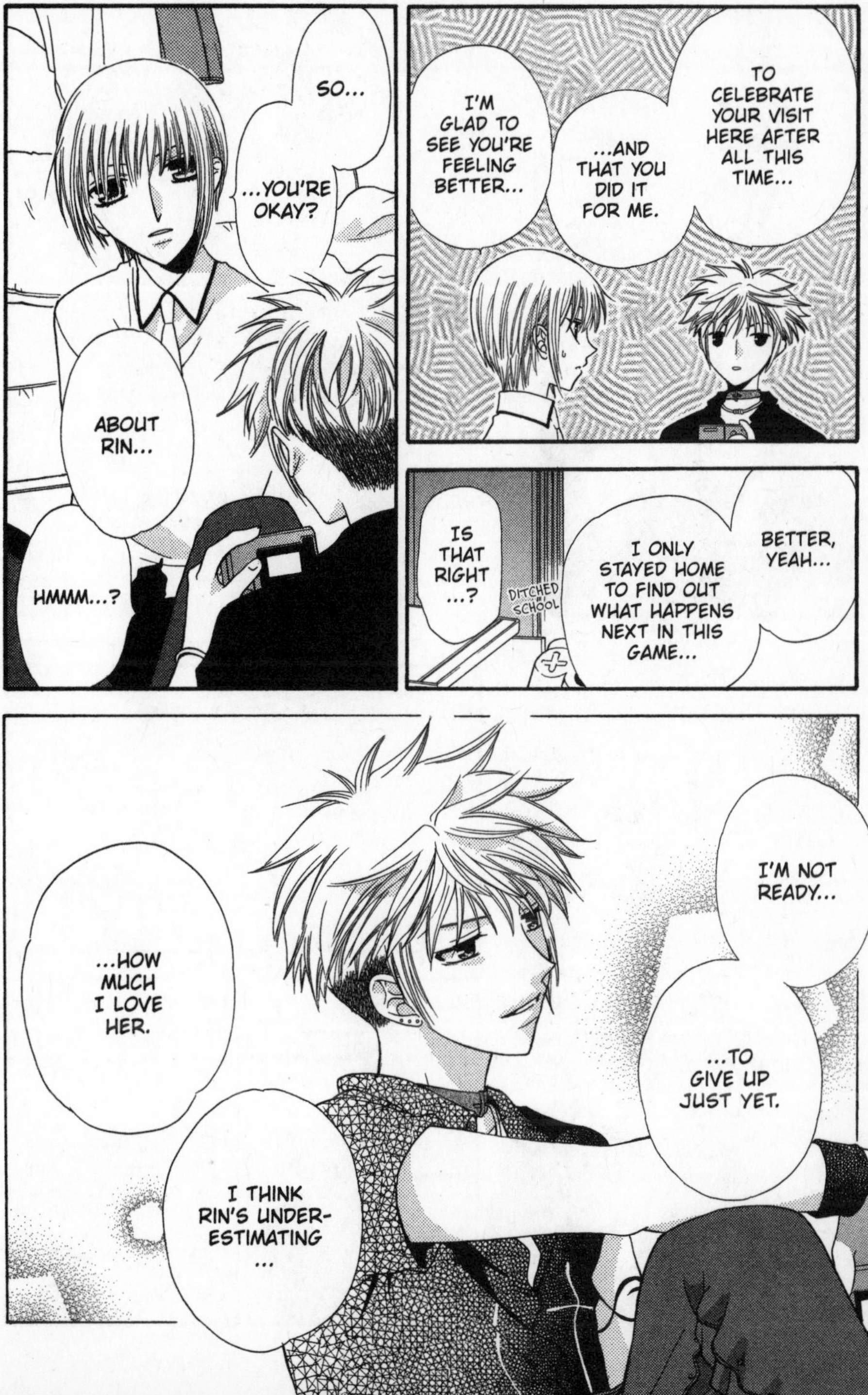
TO CELEBRATE YOUR VISIT HERE AFTER ALL THIS TIME...
...AND THAT YOU DID IT FOR ME.
I'M GLAD TO SEE YOU'RE FEELING BETTER...
BETTER, YEAH...
I ONLY STAYED HOME TO FIND OUT WHAT HAPPENS NEXT IN THIS GAME...
DITCHED SCHOOL
IS THAT RIGHT ...?
SO...
...YOU'RE OKAY?
ABOUT RIN...
HMMM...?
I'M NOT READY...
...TO GIVE UP JUST YET.
...HOW MUCH I LOVE HER.
I THINK RIN'S UNDER-ESTIMATING ...

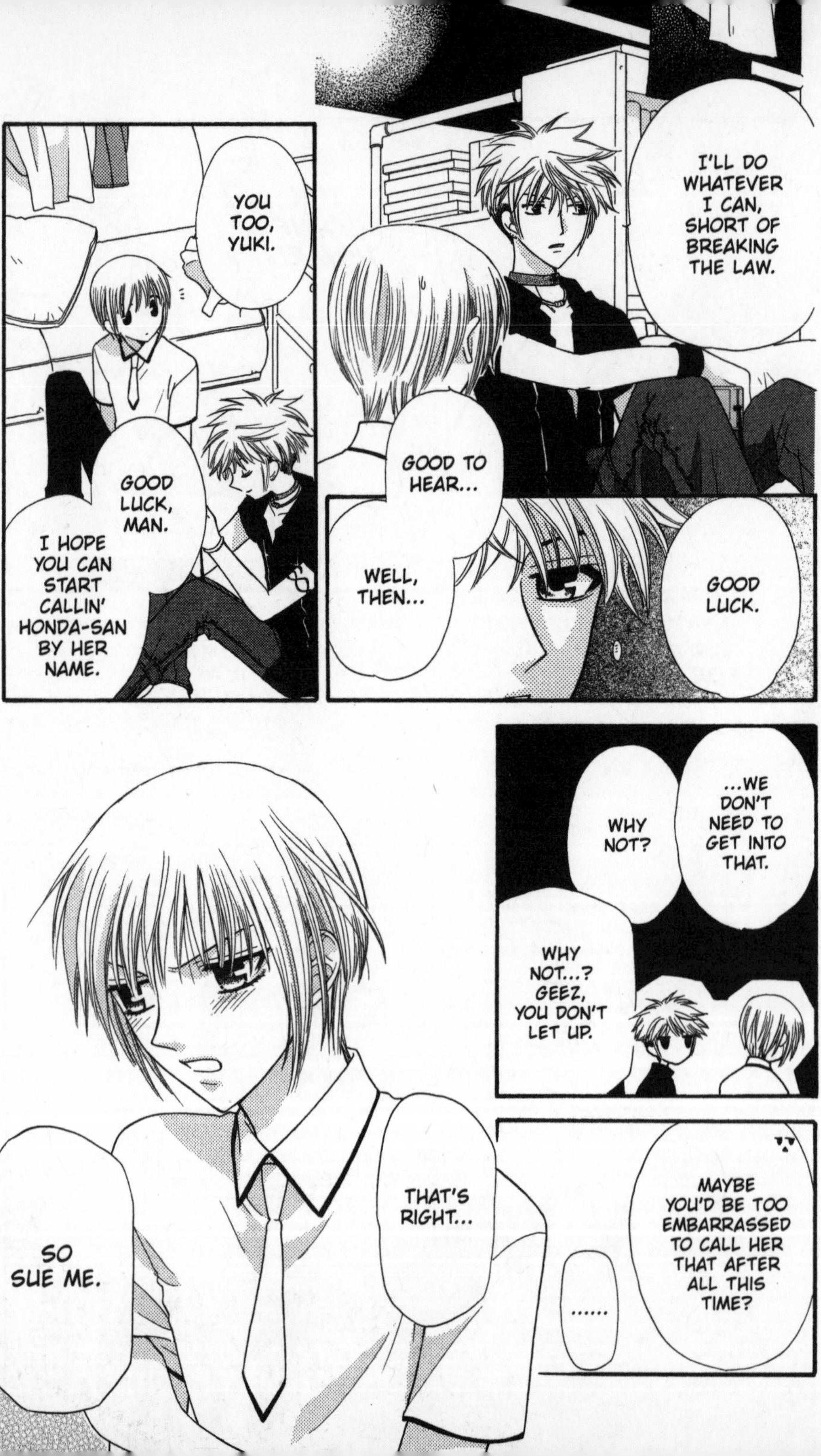
I'LL DO WHATEVER I CAN, SHORT OF BREAKING THE LAW.
GOOD TO HEAR...
GOOD LUCK.
WELL, THEN...
YOU TOO, YUKI.
GOOD LUCK, MAN.
I HOPE YOU CAN START CALLIN' HONDA-SAN BY HER NAME.
...WE DON'T NEED TO GET INTO THAT.
WHY NOT?
WHY NOT...? GEEZ, YOU DON'T LET UP.
MAYBE YOU'D BE TOO EMBARRASSED TO CALL HER THAT AFTER ALL THIS TIME?
......
THAT'S RIGHT...
SO SUE ME.

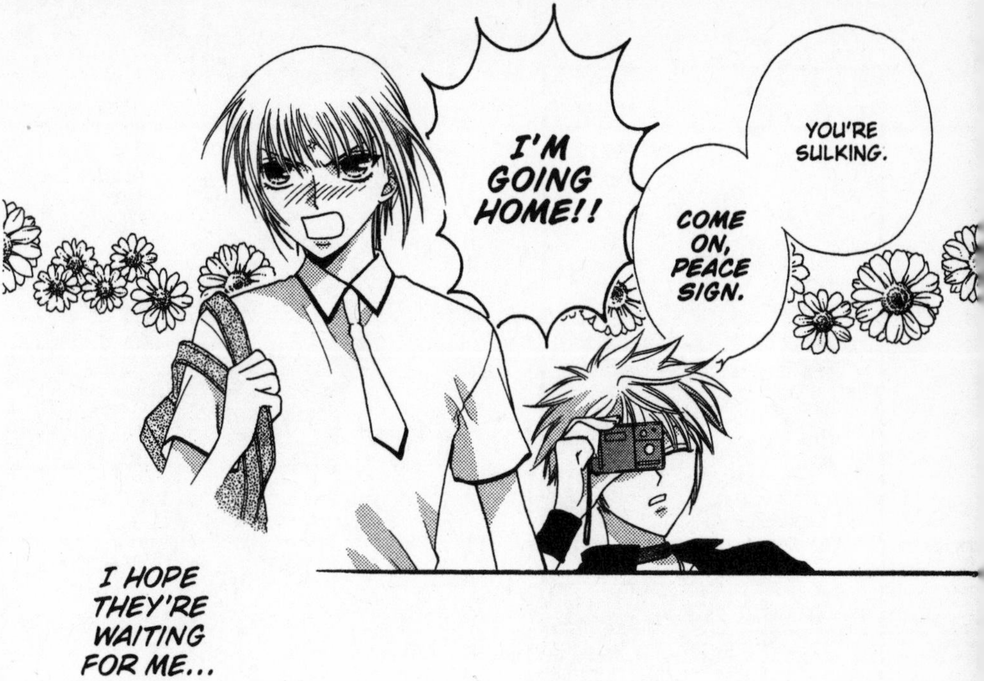
YOU'RE SULKING.
COME ON, PEACE SIGN.
I'M GOING HOME!!
I HOPE THEY'RE WAITING FOR ME...

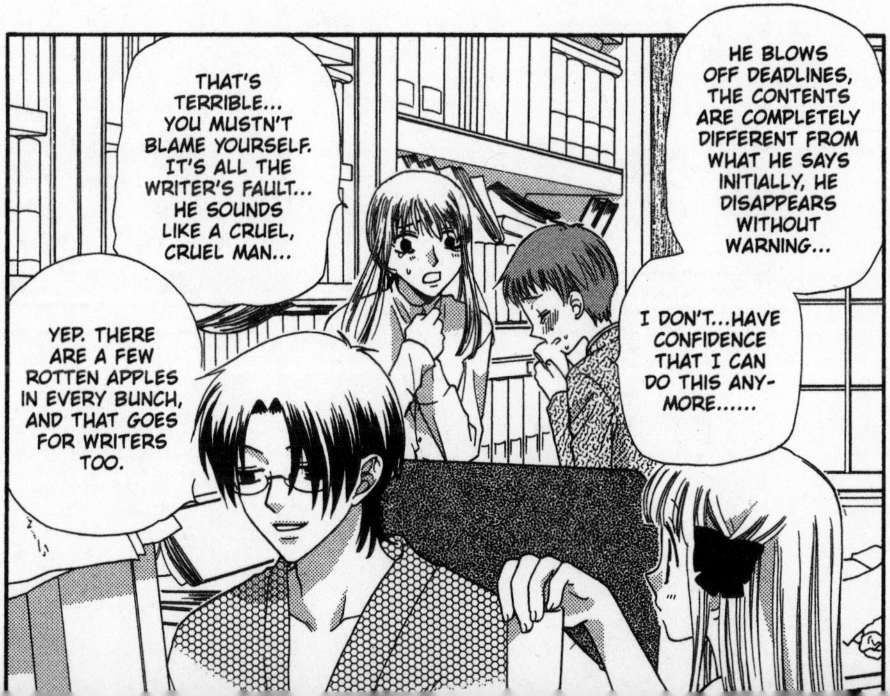
HE BLOWS OFF DEADLINES, THE CONTENTS ARE COMPLETELY DIFFERENT FROM WHAT HE SAYS INITIALLY, HE DISAPPEARS WITHOUT WARNING...
THAT'S TERRIBLE... YOU MUSTN'T BLAME YOURSELF. IT'S ALL THE WRITER'S FAULT... HE SOUNDS LIKE A CRUEL, CRUEL MAN...
I DON'T...HAVE CONFIDENCE THAT I CAN DO THIS ANY-MORE......
YEP. THERE ARE A FEW ROTTEN APPLES IN EVERY BUNCH, AND THAT GOES FOR WRITERS TOO.

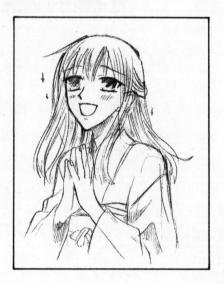

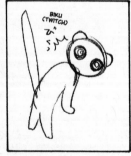

BIKU
(TWITCH)

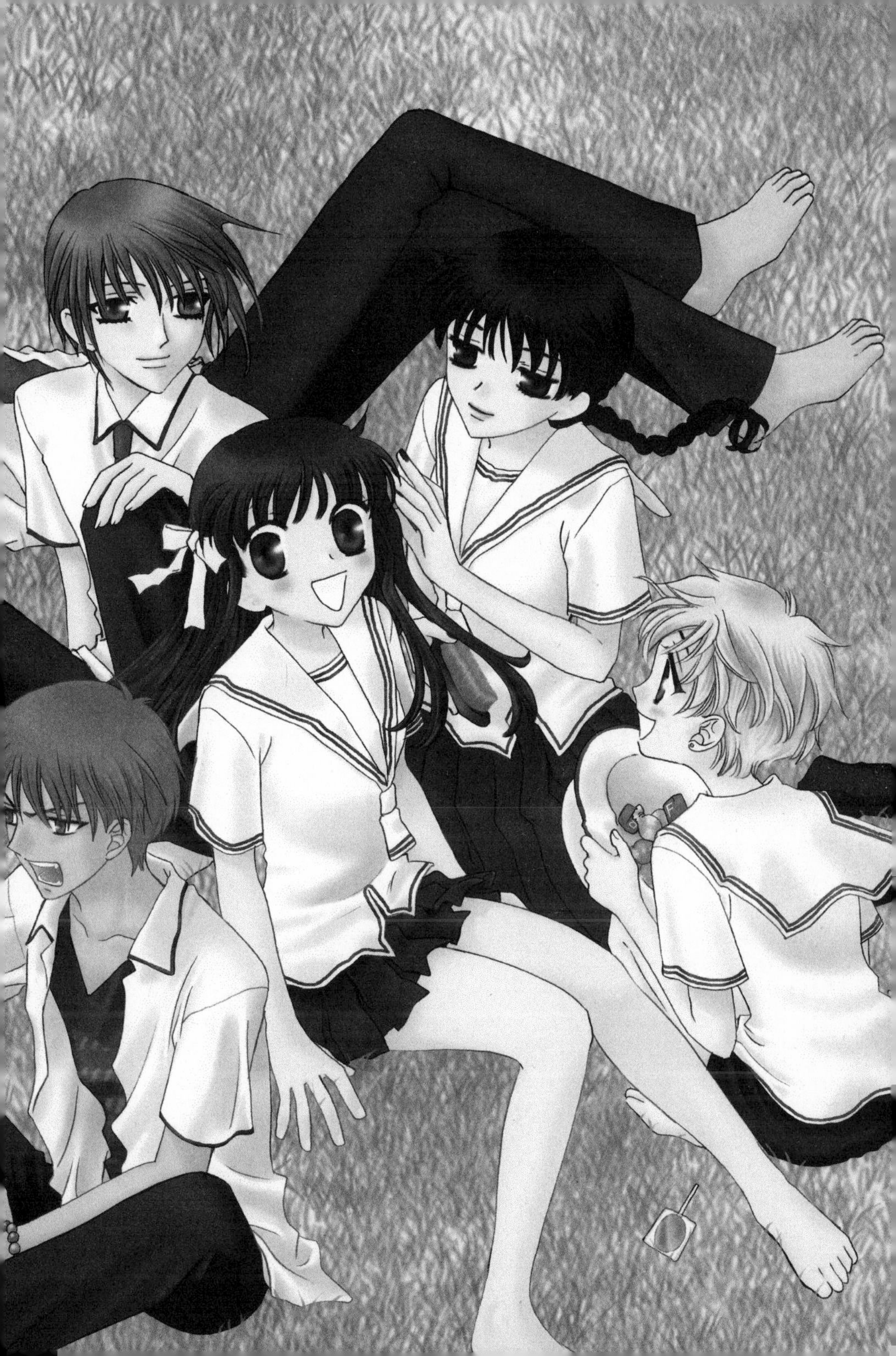

Chapter 46

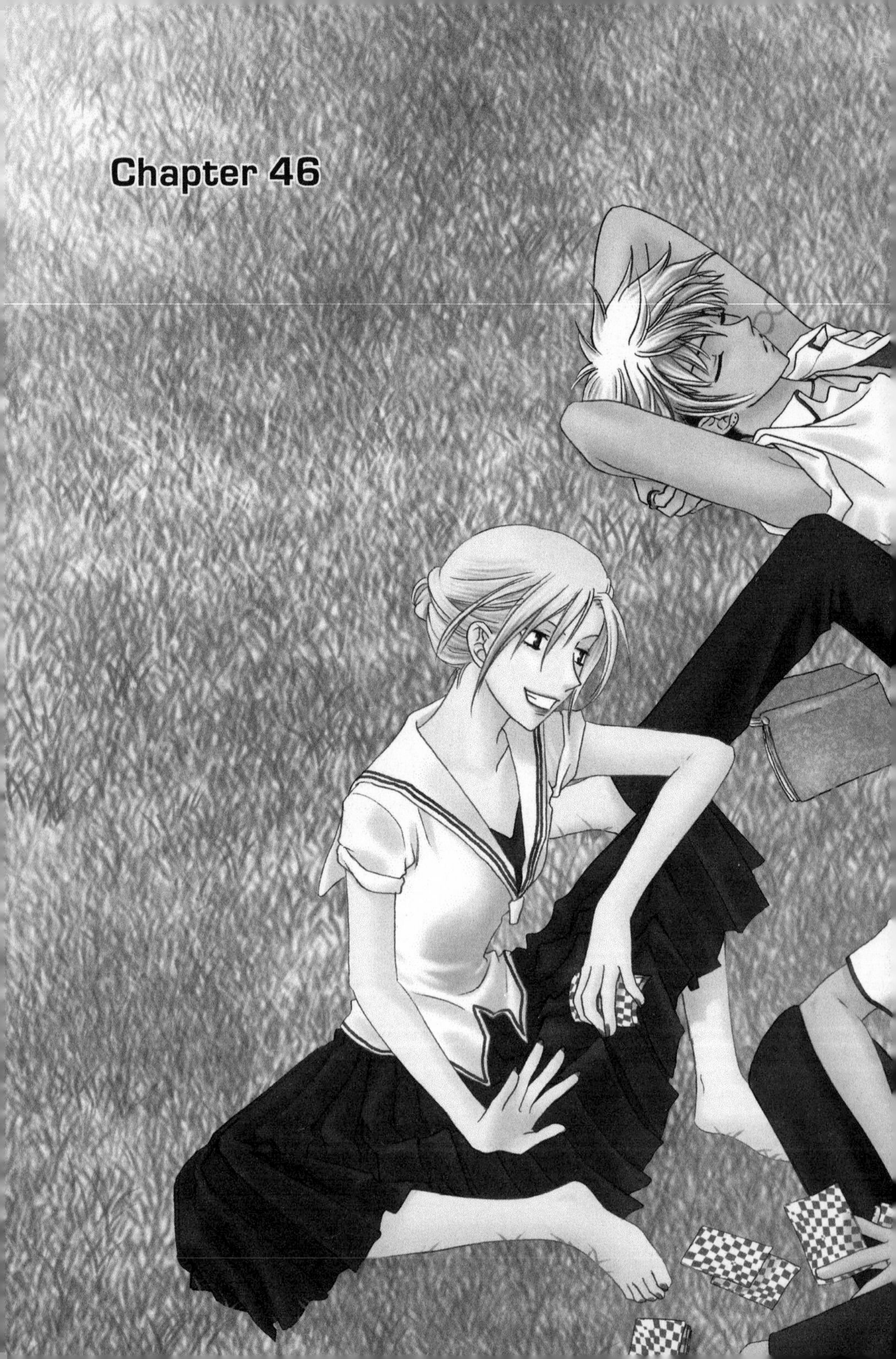

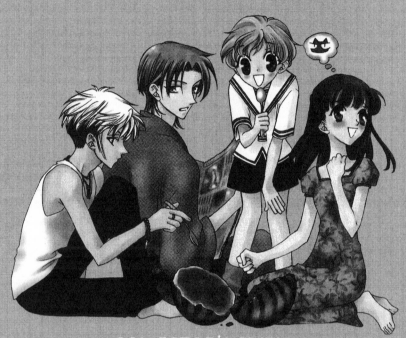

COLLECTOR'S EDITION

Fruits Basket

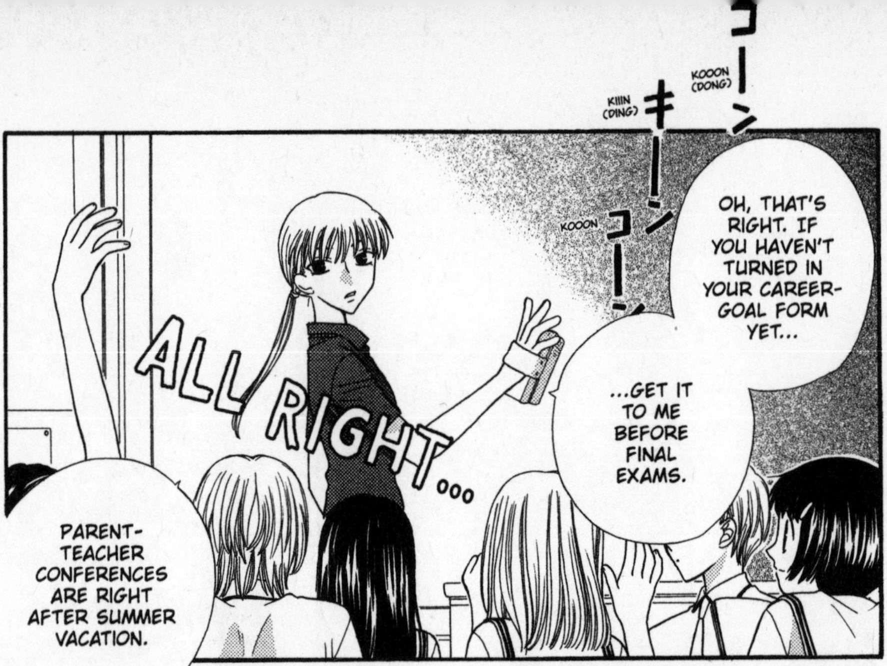
KOOON (DONG)
KIIIN (DING)
KOOON
OH, THAT'S RIGHT. IF YOU HAVEN'T TURNED IN YOUR CAREER-GOAL FORM YET...
...GET IT TO ME BEFORE FINAL EXAMS.
ALL RIGHT...
PARENT-TEACHER CONFERENCES ARE RIGHT AFTER SUMMER VACATION.
BE SURE TO LET YOUR PARENT OR GUARDIAN KNOW.
THAT'S ALL.
DISMISSED!

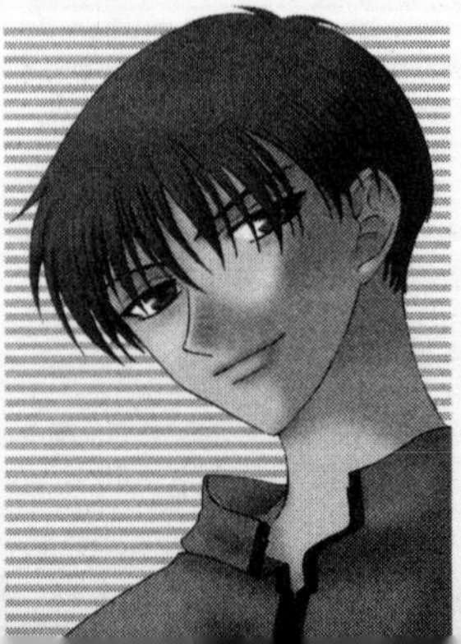

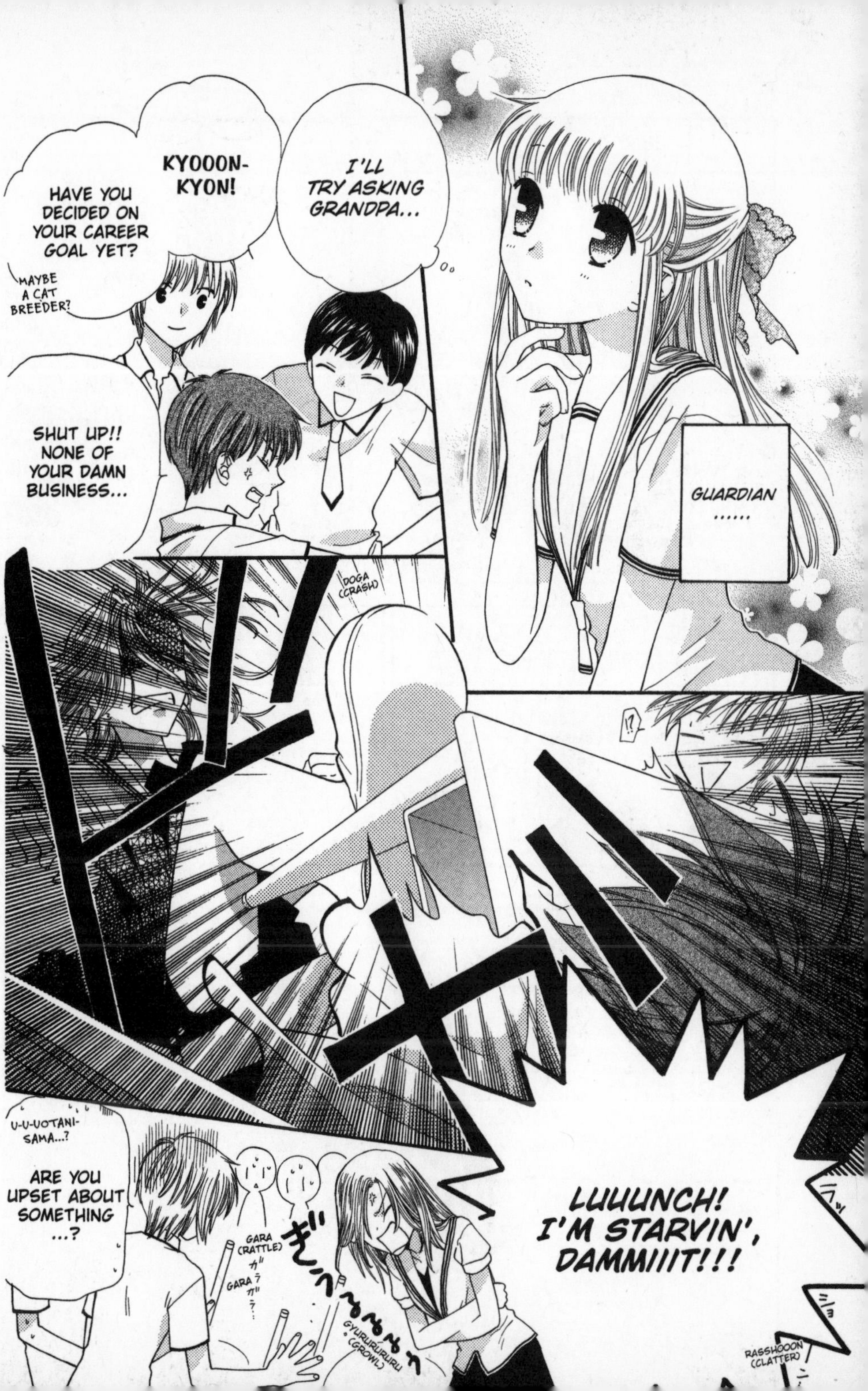
GUARDIAN ......
I'LL TRY ASKING GRANDPA...
KYOOON-KYON!
HAVE YOU DECIDED ON YOUR CAREER GOAL YET?
MAYBE A CAT BREEDER?
SHUT UP!! NONE OF YOUR DAMN BUSINESS...
DOGA (CRASH)
!?
LUUUNCH! I'M STARVIN', DAMMIIIT!!!
RASSHOOON (CLATTER)
GYURURURURU (GROWL)
GARA (RATTLE)
GARA
U-U-UOTANI-SAMA...?
ARE YOU UPSET ABOUT SOMETHING ...?

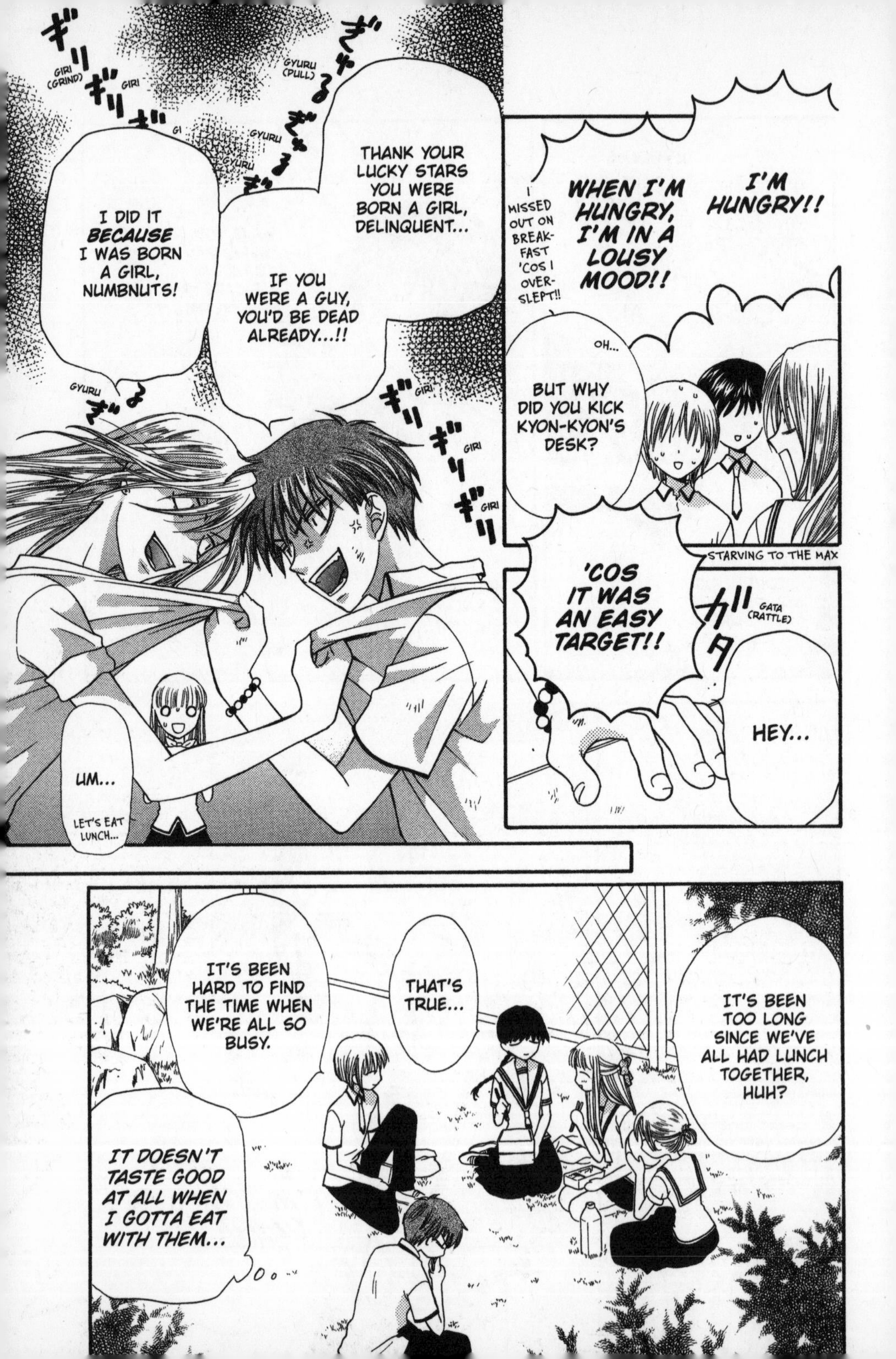
I'M HUNGRY!!
WHEN I'M HUNGRY, I'M IN A LOUSY MOOD!!
I MISSED OUT ON BREAKFAST 'COS I OVERSLEPT!!
OH...
BUT WHY DID YOU KICK KYON-KYON'S DESK?
STARVING TO THE MAX
'COS IT WAS AN EASY TARGET!!
GATA (RATTLE)
HEY...
GYURU (PULL)
GYURU
GYURU
GIRI (GRIND)
GIRI
GI
THANK YOUR LUCKY STARS YOU WERE BORN A GIRL, DELINQUENT...
IF YOU WERE A GUY, YOU'D BE DEAD ALREADY...!!
I DID IT *BECAUSE* I WAS BORN A GIRL, NUMBNUTS!
GYURU
GIRI
GIRI
GIRI
UM...
LET'S EAT LUNCH...
IT'S BEEN TOO LONG SINCE WE'VE ALL HAD LUNCH TOGETHER, HUH?
THAT'S TRUE...
IT'S BEEN HARD TO FIND THE TIME WHEN WE'RE ALL SO BUSY.
IT DOESN'T TASTE GOOD AT ALL WHEN I GOTTA EAT WITH THEM...

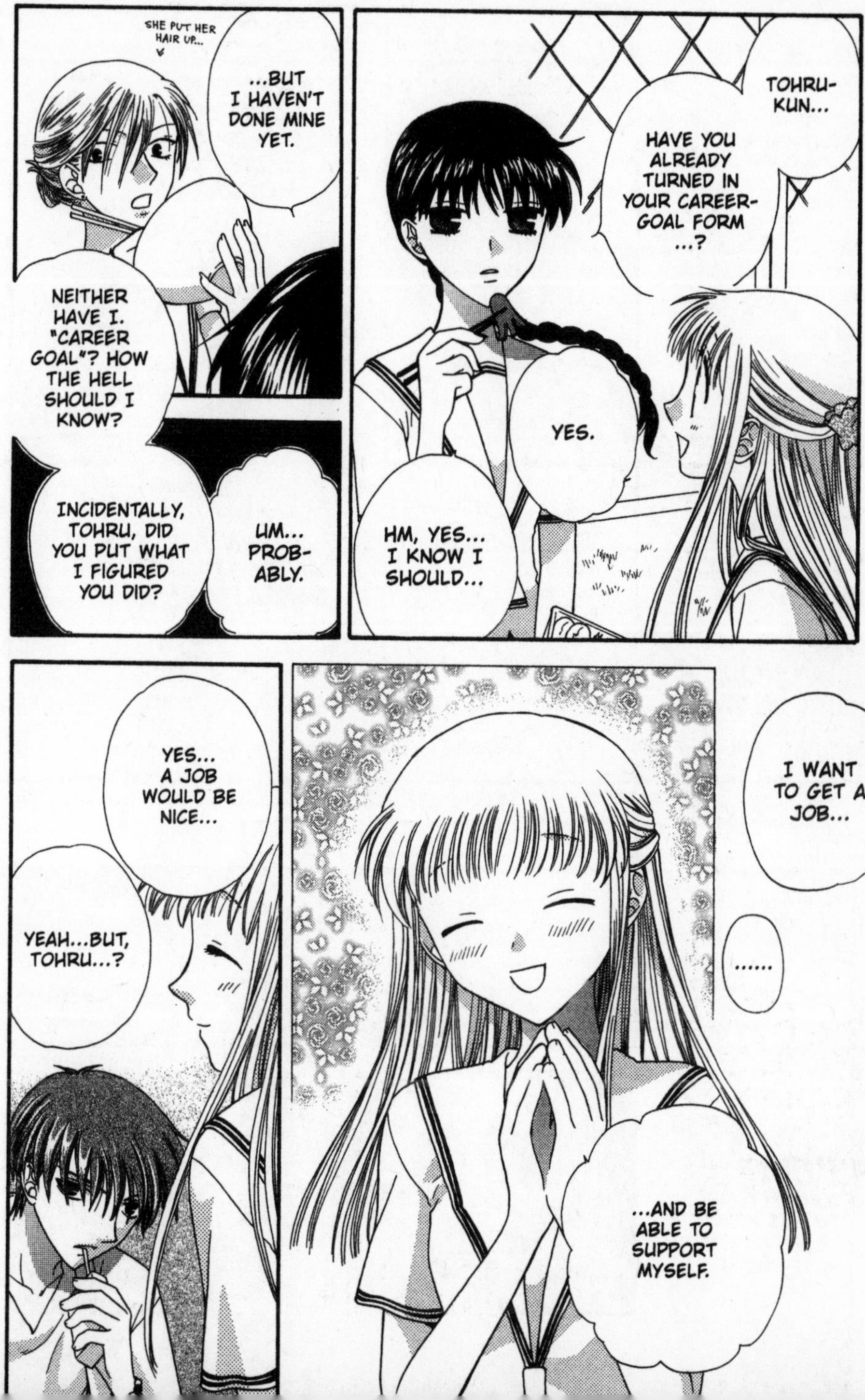
TOHRU-KUN...
HAVE YOU ALREADY TURNED IN YOUR CAREER-GOAL FORM ...?
YES.
HM, YES... I KNOW I SHOULD...
...BUT I HAVEN'T DONE MINE YET.
SHE PUT HER HAIR UP...
NEITHER HAVE I. "CAREER GOAL"? HOW THE HELL SHOULD I KNOW?
INCIDENTALLY, TOHRU, DID YOU PUT WHAT I FIGURED YOU DID?
UM... PROB-ABLY.
I WANT TO GET A JOB...
......
...AND BE ABLE TO SUPPORT MYSELF.
YES... A JOB WOULD BE NICE...
YEAH...BUT, TOHRU...?

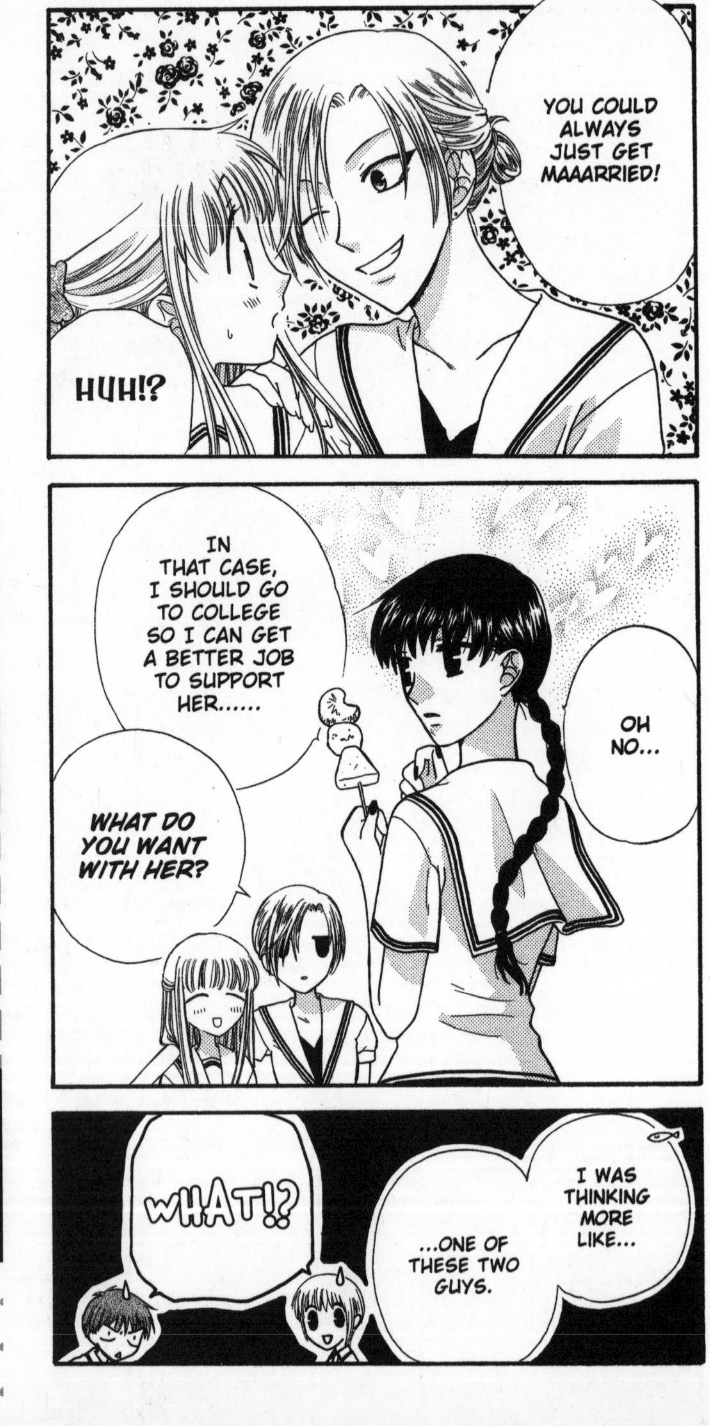
YOU COULD ALWAYS JUST GET MAAARRIED!
HUH!?
IN THAT CASE, I SHOULD GO TO COLLEGE SO I CAN GET A BETTER JOB TO SUPPORT HER......
OH NO...
WHAT DO YOU WANT WITH HER?
I WAS THINKING MORE LIKE...
...ONE OF THESE TWO GUYS.
WHAT!?

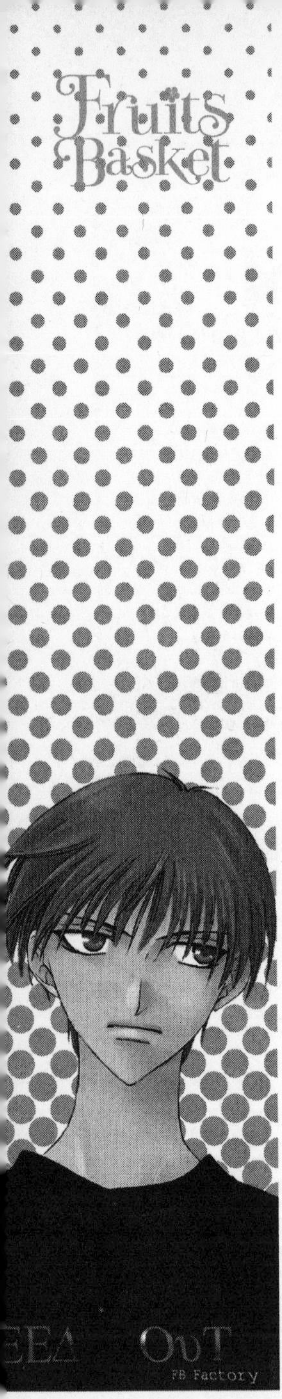
Fruits Basket
FB Factory

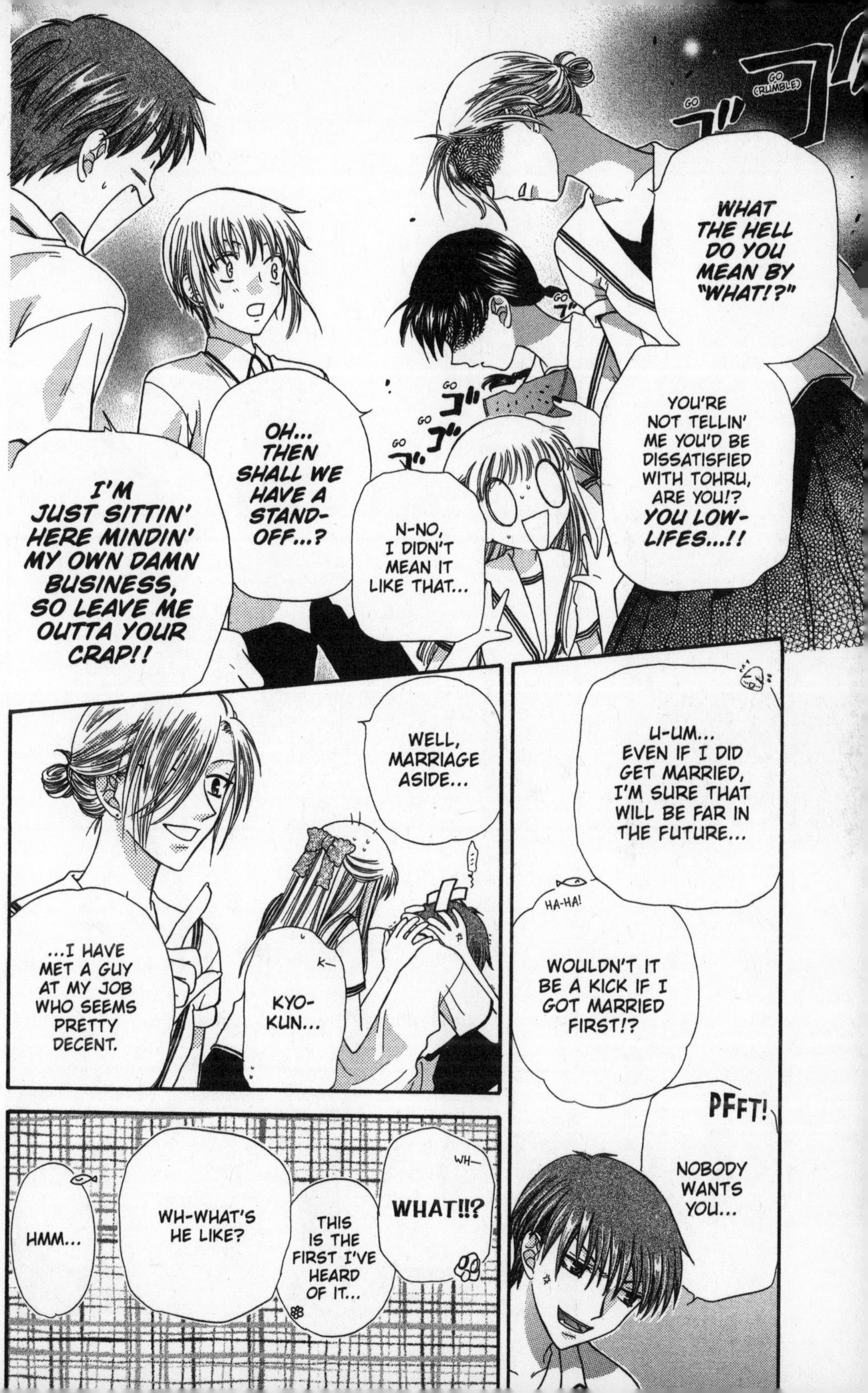
GO
GO (RUMBLE)
WHAT THE HELL DO YOU MEAN BY "WHAT!?"
GO
YOU'RE NOT TELLIN' ME YOU'D BE DISSATISFIED WITH TOHRU, ARE YOU!? YOU LOW-LIFES...!!
GO
GO
GO
N-NO, I DIDN'T MEAN IT LIKE THAT...
OH... THEN SHALL WE HAVE A STAND-OFF...?
I'M JUST SITTIN' HERE MINDIN' MY OWN DAMN BUSINESS, SO LEAVE ME OUTTA YOUR CRAP!!
U-UM... EVEN IF I DID GET MARRIED, I'M SURE THAT WILL BE FAR IN THE FUTURE...
HA-HA!
WOULDN'T IT BE A KICK IF I GOT MARRIED FIRST!?
PFFT!
NOBODY WANTS YOU...
WELL, MARRIAGE ASIDE...
...I HAVE MET A GUY AT MY JOB WHO SEEMS PRETTY DECENT.
K—
KYO-KUN...
WH—
WHAT!!?
THIS IS THE FIRST I'VE HEARD OF IT...
WH-WHAT'S HE LIKE?
HMM...

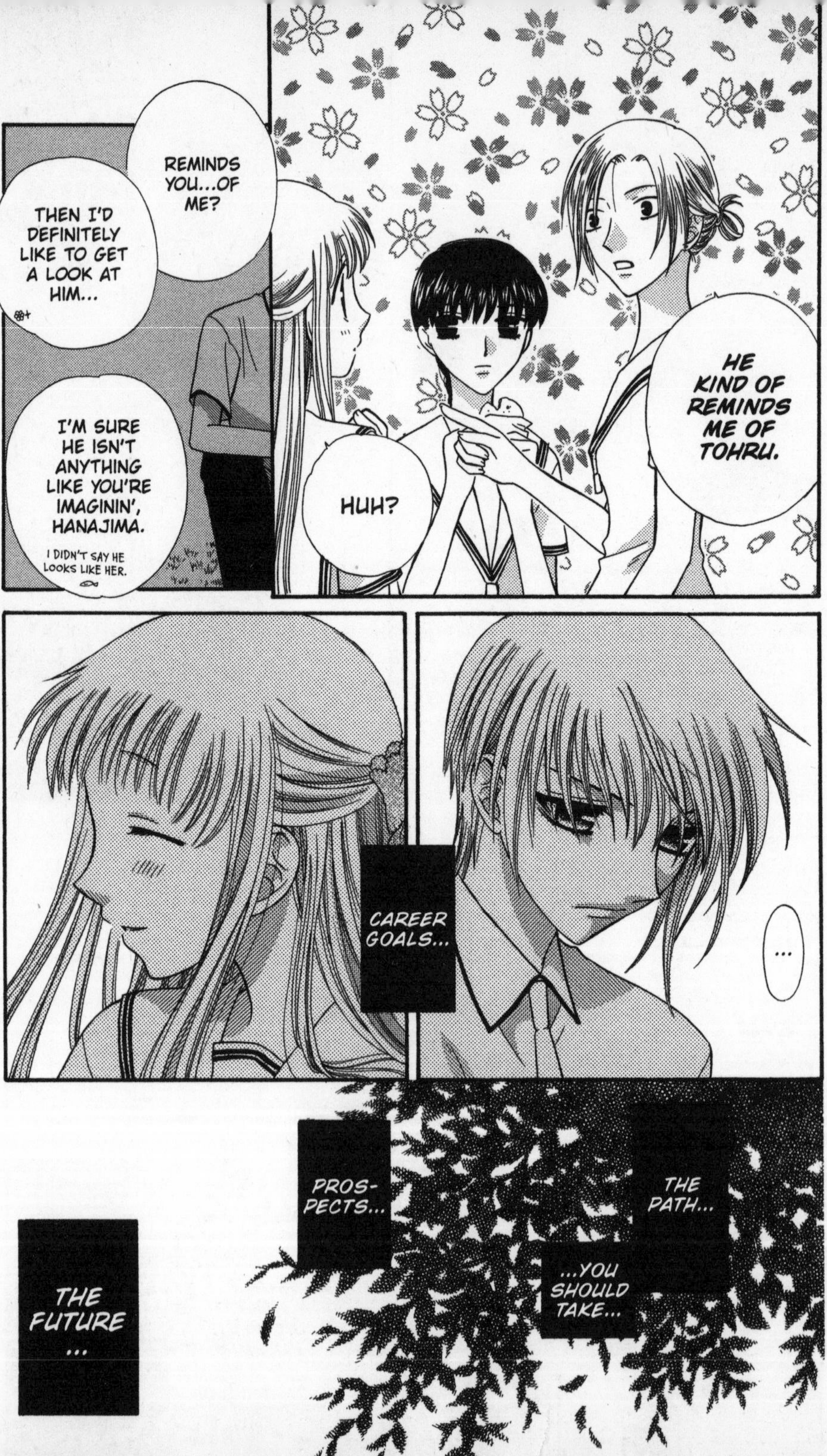
HE KIND OF REMINDS ME OF TOHRU.
HUH?
REMINDS YOU...OF ME?
THEN I'D DEFINITELY LIKE TO GET A LOOK AT HIM...
I'M SURE HE ISN'T ANYTHING LIKE YOU'RE IMAGININ', HANAJIMA.
I DIDN'T SAY HE LOOKS LIKE HER.
...
CAREER GOALS...
THE PATH...
PROSPECTS...
...YOU SHOULD TAKE...
THE FUTURE ...

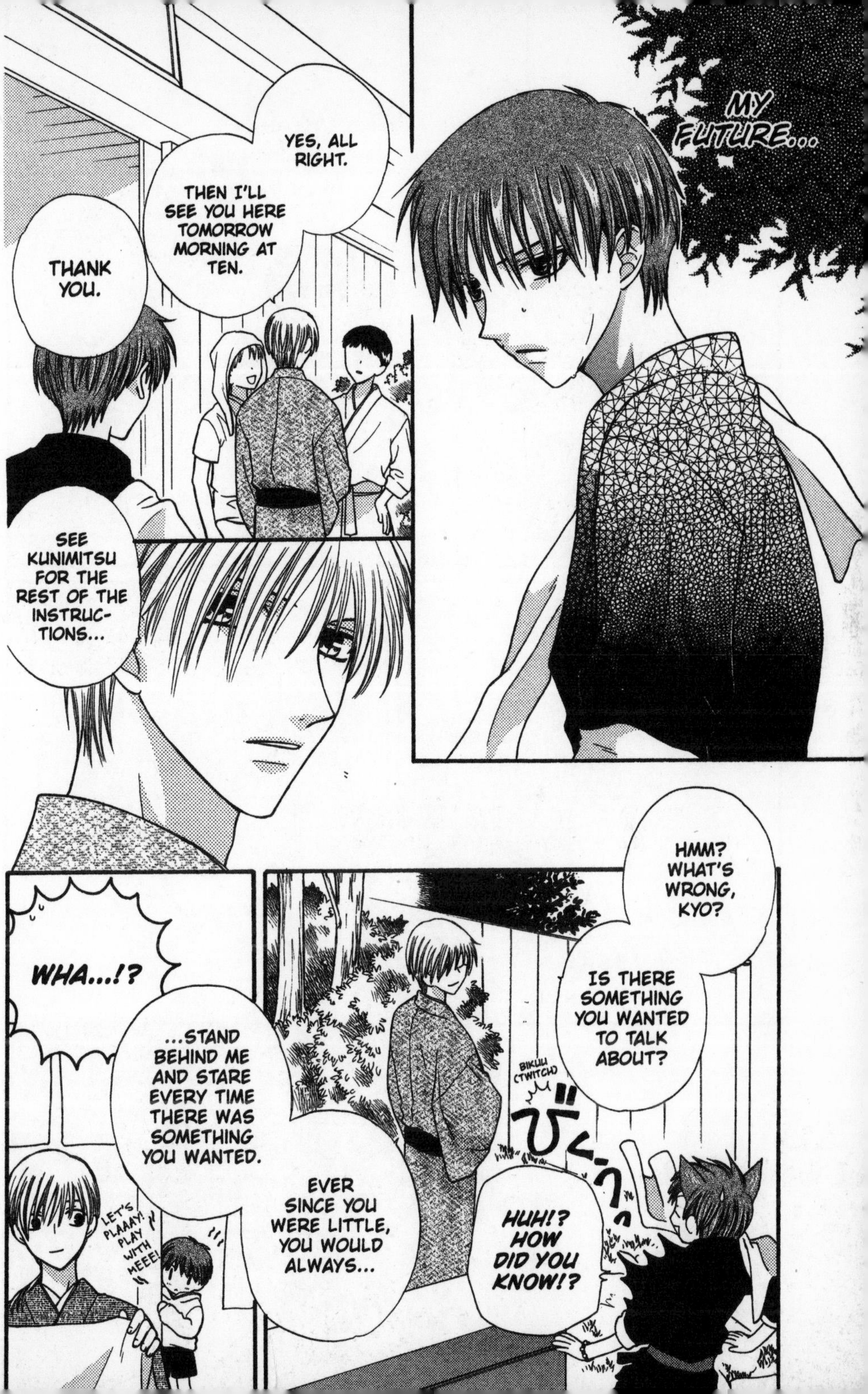
MY FUTURE...
YES, ALL RIGHT.
THEN I'LL SEE YOU HERE TOMORROW MORNING AT TEN.
THANK YOU.
SEE KUNIMITSU FOR THE REST OF THE INSTRUCTIONS...
HMM? WHAT'S WRONG, KYO?
IS THERE SOMETHING YOU WANTED TO TALK ABOUT?
BIKUU (TWITCH)
HUH!? HOW DID YOU KNOW!?
EVER SINCE YOU WERE LITTLE, YOU WOULD ALWAYS...
...STAND BEHIND ME AND STARE EVERY TIME THERE WAS SOMETHING YOU WANTED.
WHA...!?
LET'S PLAAAY! PLAY WITH MEEE!

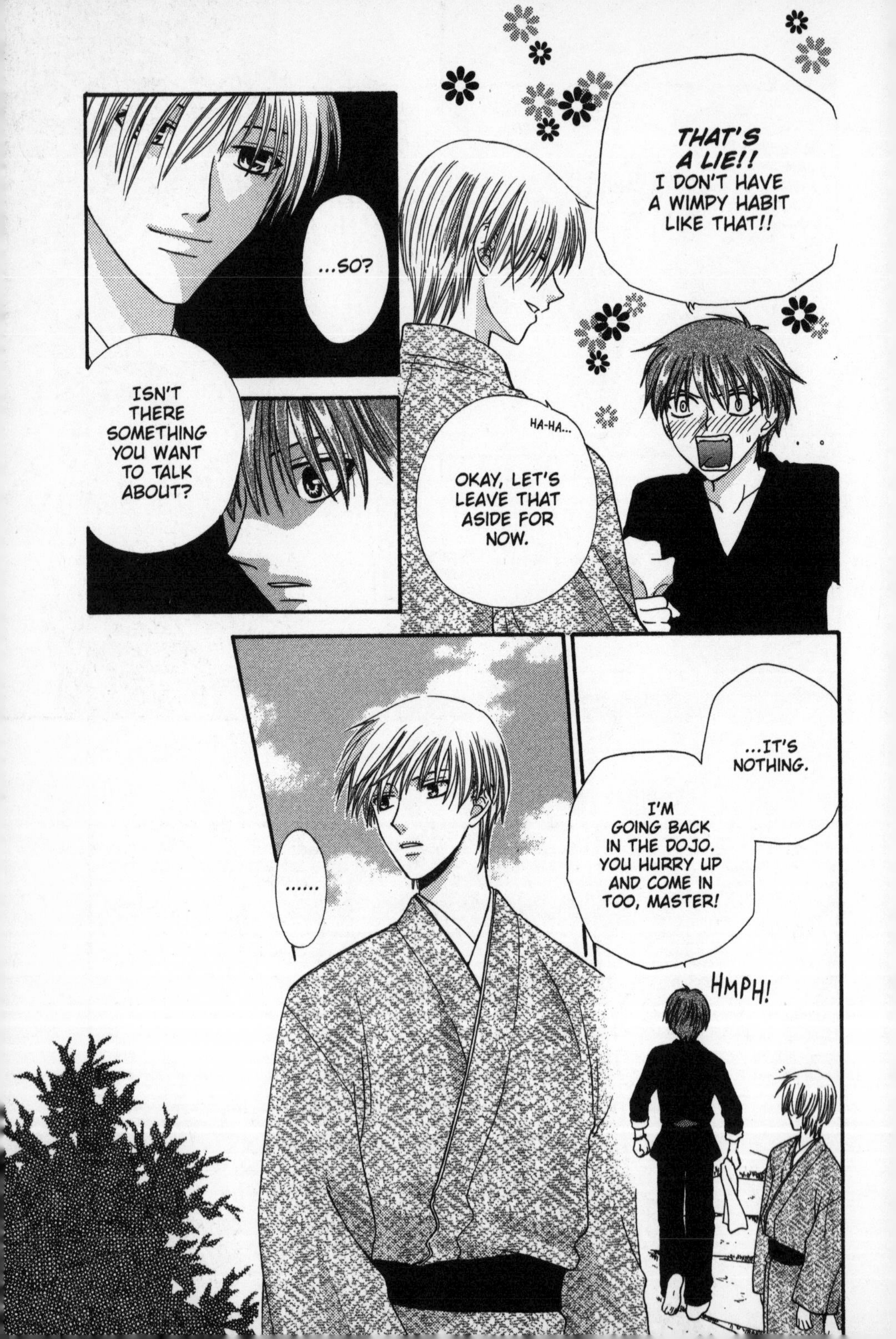
THAT'S A LIE!! I DON'T HAVE A WIMPY HABIT LIKE THAT!!
HA-HA...
OKAY, LET'S LEAVE THAT ASIDE FOR NOW.
...SO?
ISN'T THERE SOMETHING YOU WANT TO TALK ABOUT?
...IT'S NOTHING.
I'M GOING BACK IN THE DOJO. YOU HURRY UP AND COME IN TOO, MASTER!
HMPH!
......

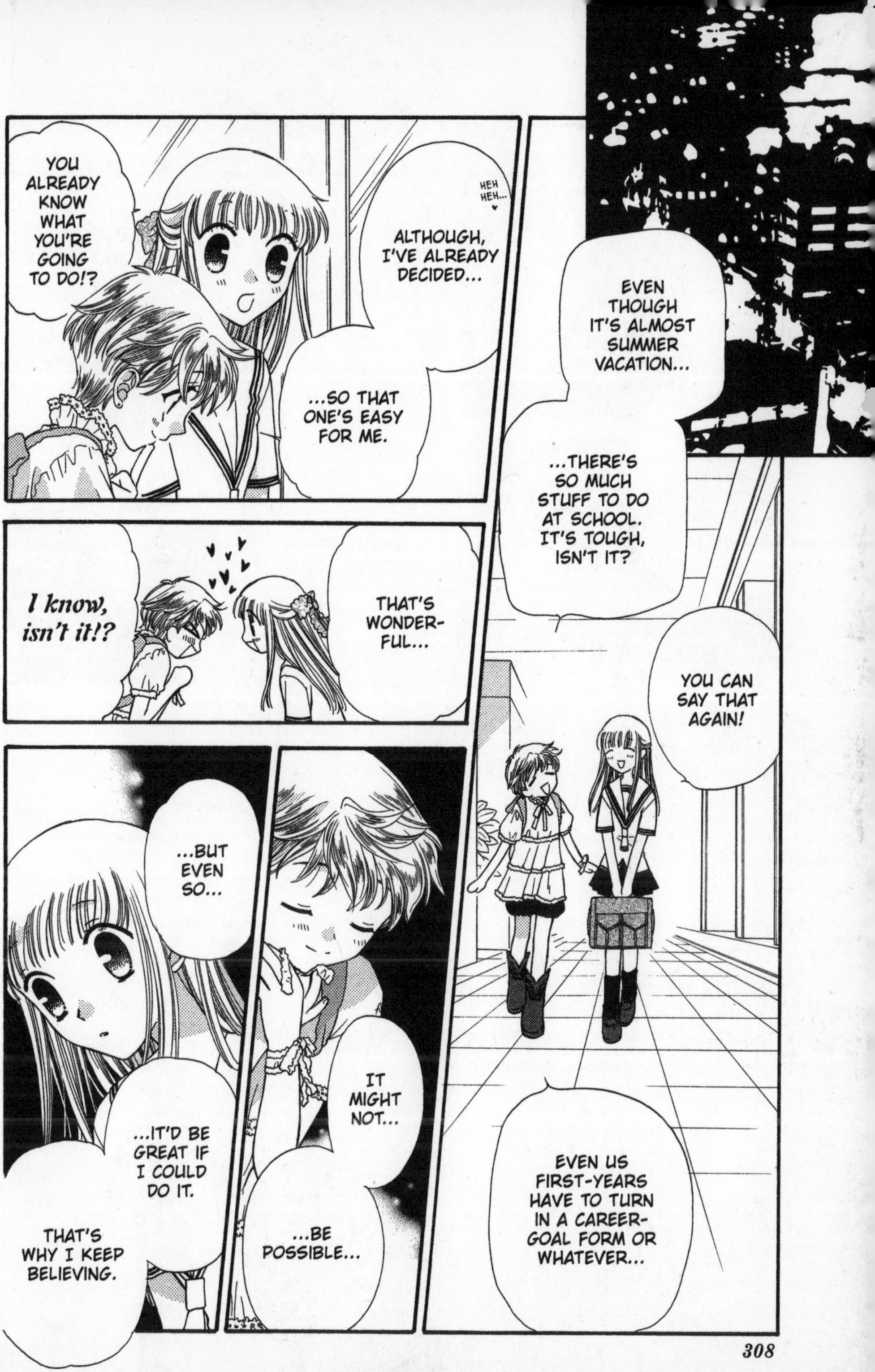
EVEN THOUGH IT'S ALMOST SUMMER VACATION...
...THERE'S SO MUCH STUFF TO DO AT SCHOOL. IT'S TOUGH, ISN'T IT?
YOU CAN SAY THAT AGAIN!
EVEN US FIRST-YEARS HAVE TO TURN IN A CAREER-GOAL FORM OR WHATEVER...
HEH HEH...
ALTHOUGH, I'VE ALREADY DECIDED...
...SO THAT ONE'S EASY FOR ME.
YOU ALREADY KNOW WHAT YOU'RE GOING TO DO!?
THAT'S WONDERFUL...
I know, isn't it!?
IT MIGHT NOT...
...BE POSSIBLE...
...BUT EVEN SO...
...IT'D BE GREAT IF I COULD DO IT.
THAT'S WHY I KEEP BELIEVING.

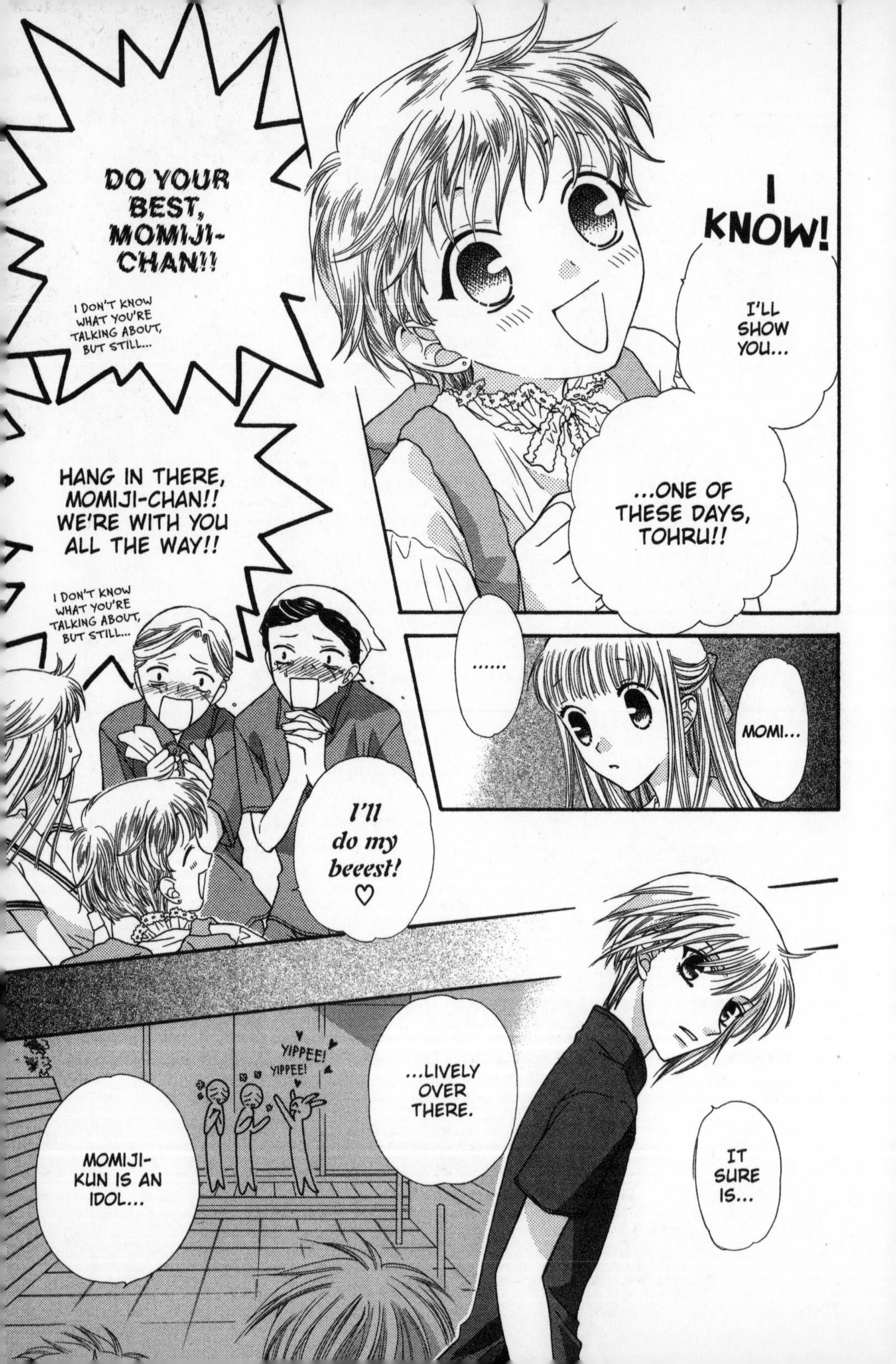
I KNOW!
I'LL SHOW YOU...
...ONE OF THESE DAYS, TOHRU!!
MOMI...
......
DO YOUR BEST, MOMIJI-CHAN!!
I DON'T KNOW WHAT YOU'RE TALKING ABOUT, BUT STILL...
HANG IN THERE, MOMIJI-CHAN!! WE'RE WITH YOU ALL THE WAY!!
I DON'T KNOW WHAT YOU'RE TALKING ABOUT, BUT STILL...
I'll do my beeest! ♡
...LIVELY OVER THERE.
IT SURE IS...
YIPPEE!
YIPPEE!
MOMIJI-KUN IS AN IDOL...

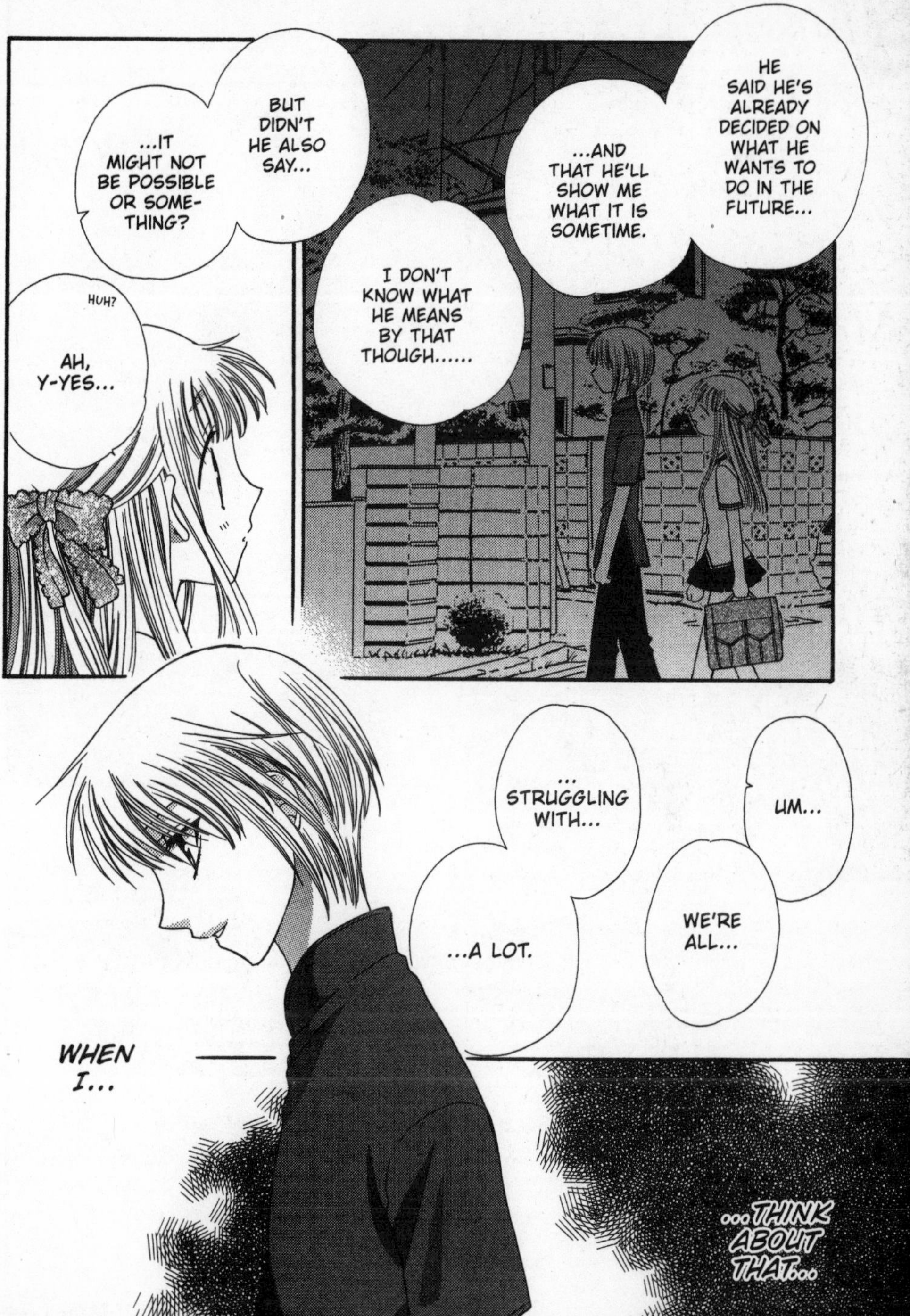

HE SAID HE'S ALREADY DECIDED ON WHAT HE WANTS TO DO IN THE FUTURE...
...AND THAT HE'LL SHOW ME WHAT IT IS SOMETIME.
I DON'T KNOW WHAT HE MEANS BY THAT THOUGH......
BUT DIDN'T HE ALSO SAY...
...IT MIGHT NOT BE POSSIBLE OR SOME-THING?
HUH?
AH, Y-YES...
UM...
WE'RE ALL...
...STRUGGLING WITH...
...A LOT.
WHEN I...
...THINK ABOUT THAT...

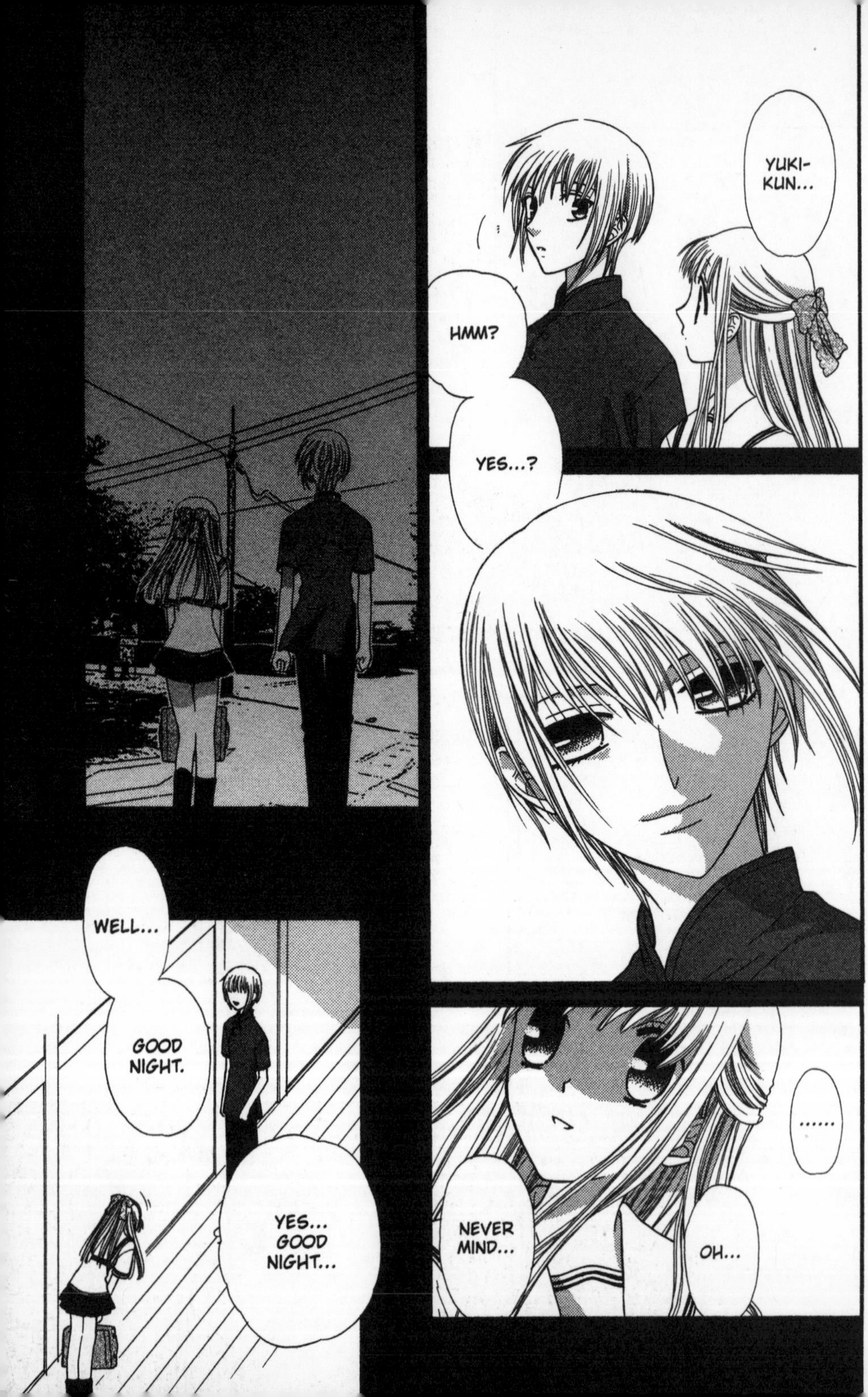
YUKI-KUN...
HMM?
YES...?
......
OH...
NEVER MIND...
WELL...
GOOD NIGHT.
YES... GOOD NIGHT...

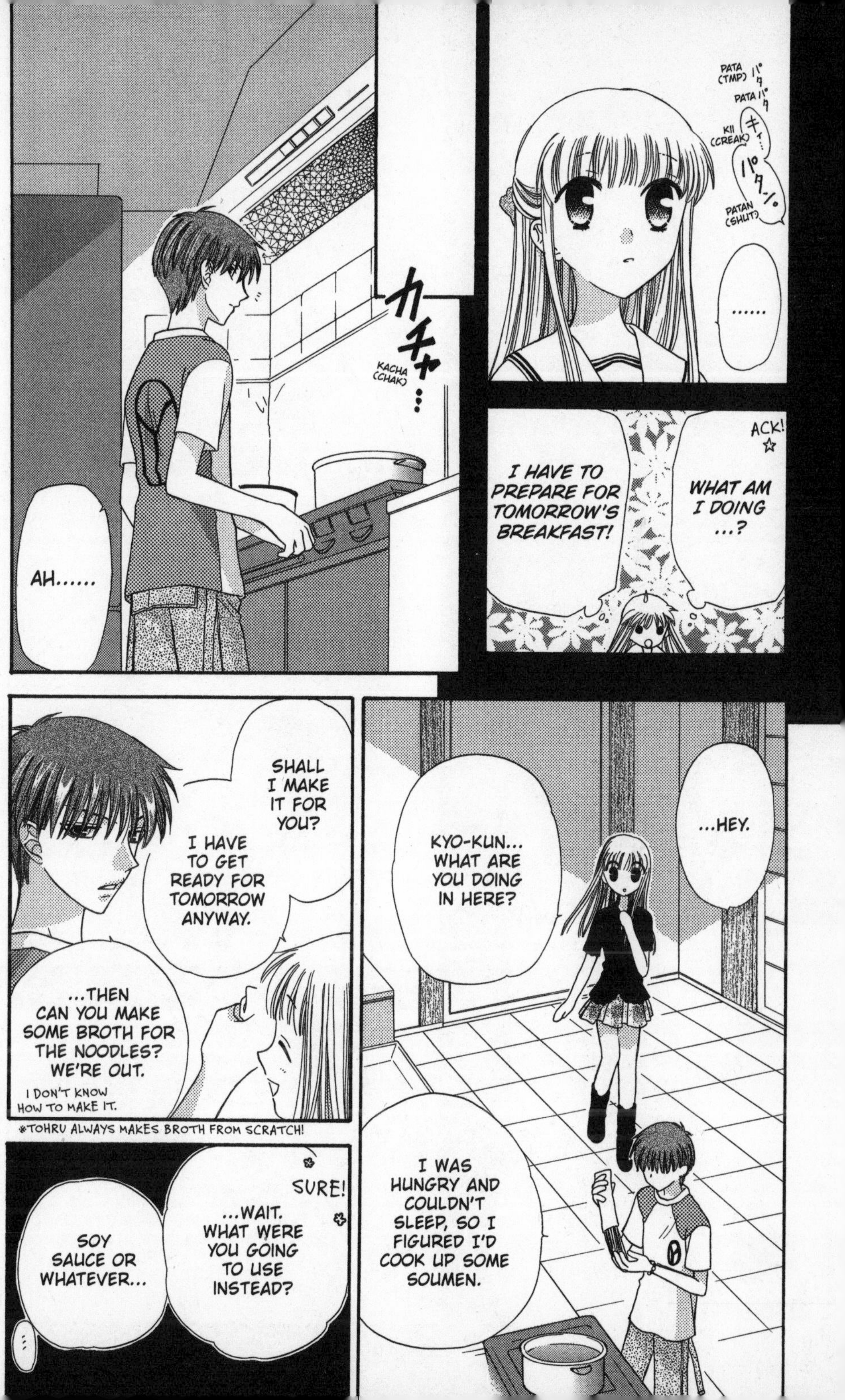
PATA (TMP) パタ
PATA パタ
KII (CREAK) キィ…
パタン。
PATAN (SHUT)
......
WHAT AM I DOING ...?
ACK! ☆
I HAVE TO PREPARE FOR TOMORROW'S BREAKFAST!
カチャ…
KACHA (CHAK)
AH......
...HEY.
KYO-KUN... WHAT ARE YOU DOING IN HERE?
I WAS HUNGRY AND COULDN'T SLEEP, SO I FIGURED I'D COOK UP SOME SOUMEN.
SHALL I MAKE IT FOR YOU?
I HAVE TO GET READY FOR TOMORROW ANYWAY.
...THEN CAN YOU MAKE SOME BROTH FOR THE NOODLES? WE'RE OUT.
I DON'T KNOW HOW TO MAKE IT.
*TOHRU ALWAYS MAKES BROTH FROM SCRATCH!
SURE!
...WAIT. WHAT WERE YOU GOING TO USE INSTEAD?
SOY SAUCE OR WHATEVER...
...

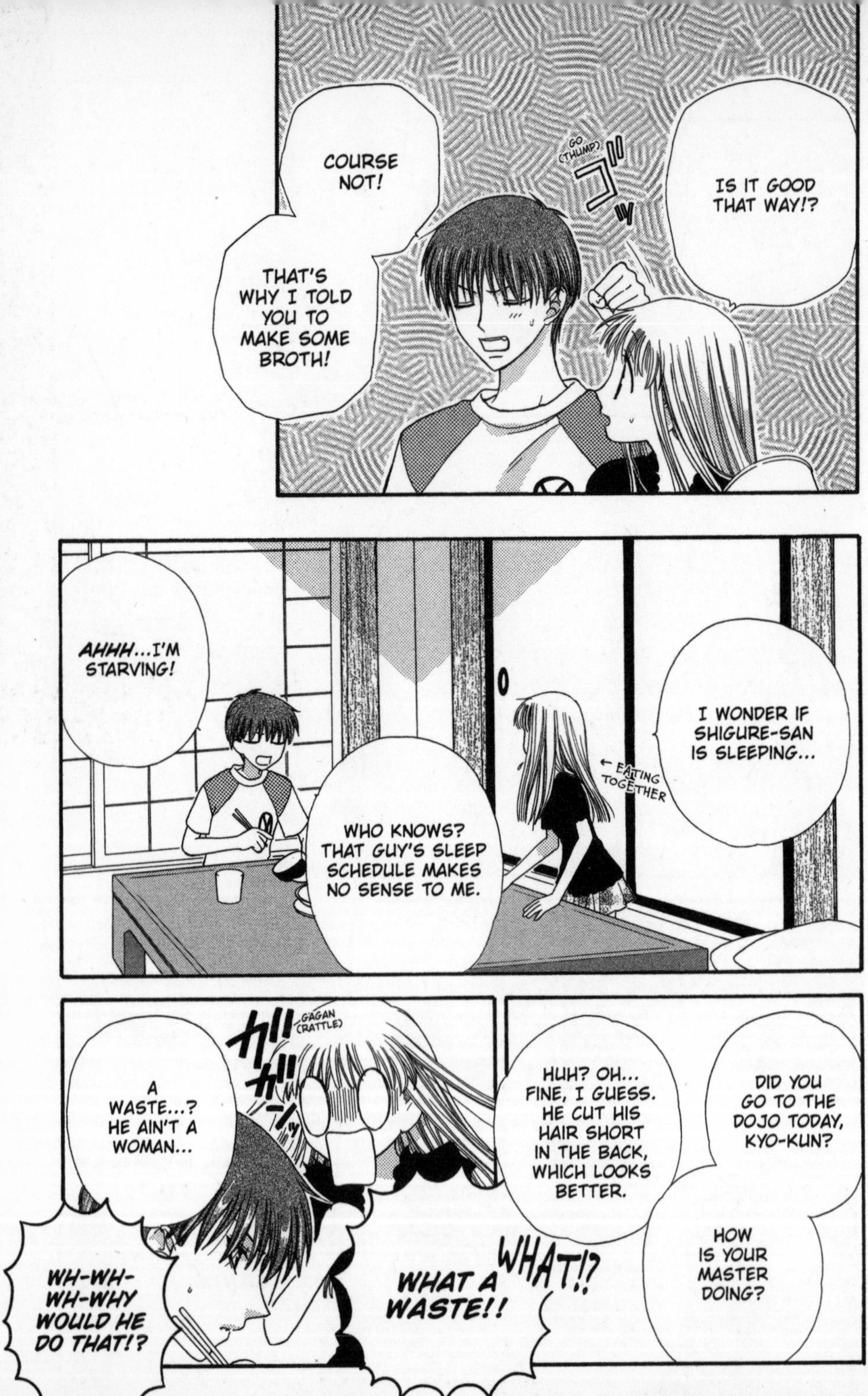
IS IT GOOD THAT WAY!?
GO (THUMP)
COURSE NOT!
THAT'S WHY I TOLD YOU TO MAKE SOME BROTH!
I WONDER IF SHIGURE-SAN IS SLEEPING...
← EATING TOGETHER
WHO KNOWS? THAT GUY'S SLEEP SCHEDULE MAKES NO SENSE TO ME.
AHHH...I'M STARVING!
DID YOU GO TO THE DOJO TODAY, KYO-KUN?
HOW IS YOUR MASTER DOING?
HUH? OH... FINE, I GUESS. HE CUT HIS HAIR SHORT IN THE BACK, WHICH LOOKS BETTER.
WHAT!?
WHAT A WASTE!!
GAGAN (RATTLE)
A WASTE...? HE AIN'T A WOMAN...
WH-WH-WH-WHY WOULD HE DO THAT!?

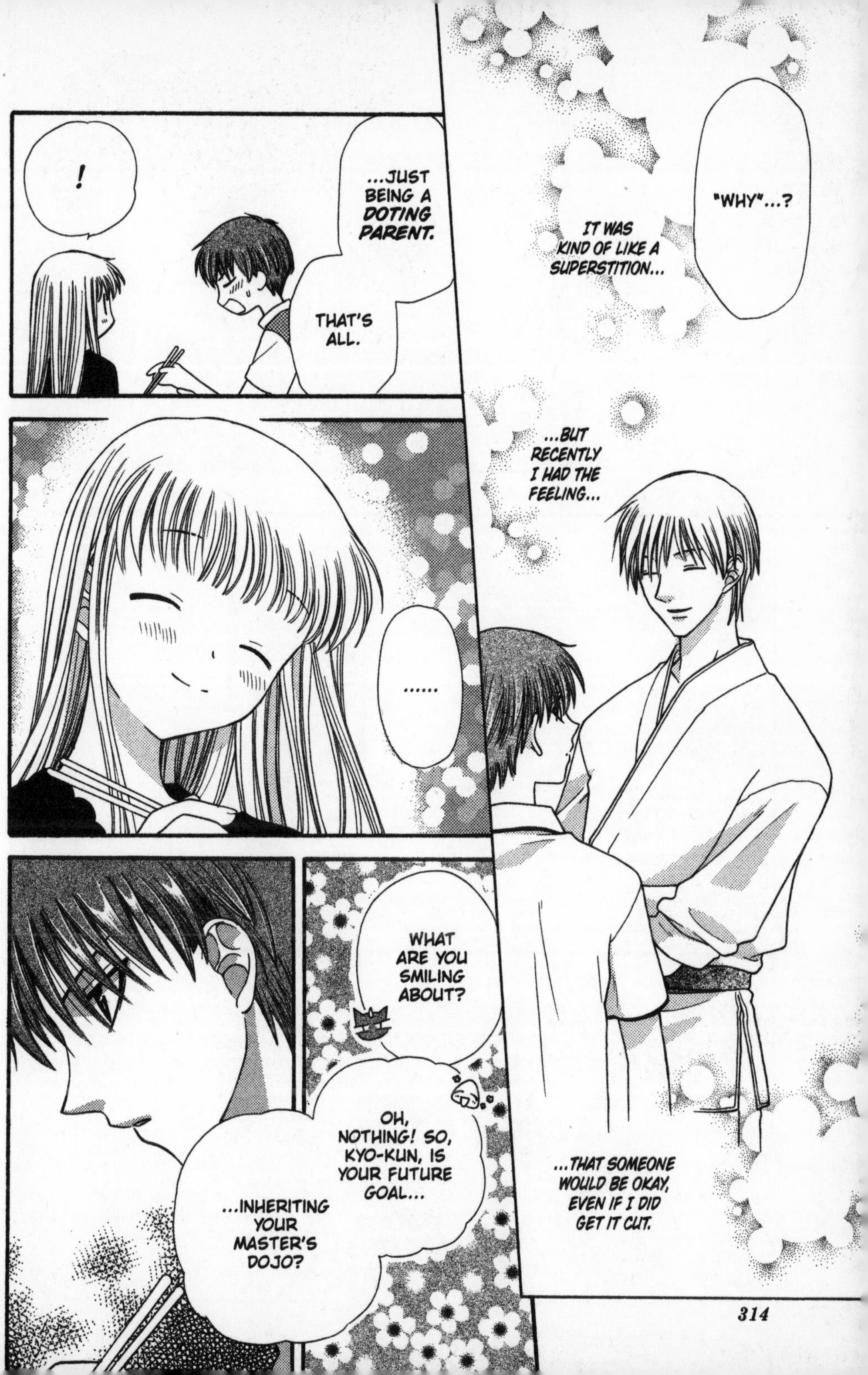
"WHY"...?
IT WAS KIND OF LIKE A SUPERSTITION...
...BUT RECENTLY I HAD THE FEELING...
...THAT SOMEONE WOULD BE OKAY, EVEN IF I DID GET IT CUT.
...JUST BEING A DOTING PARENT.
THAT'S ALL.
!
......
WHAT ARE YOU SMILING ABOUT?
OH, NOTHING! SO, KYO-KUN, IS YOUR FUTURE GOAL...
...INHERITING YOUR MASTER'S DOJO?

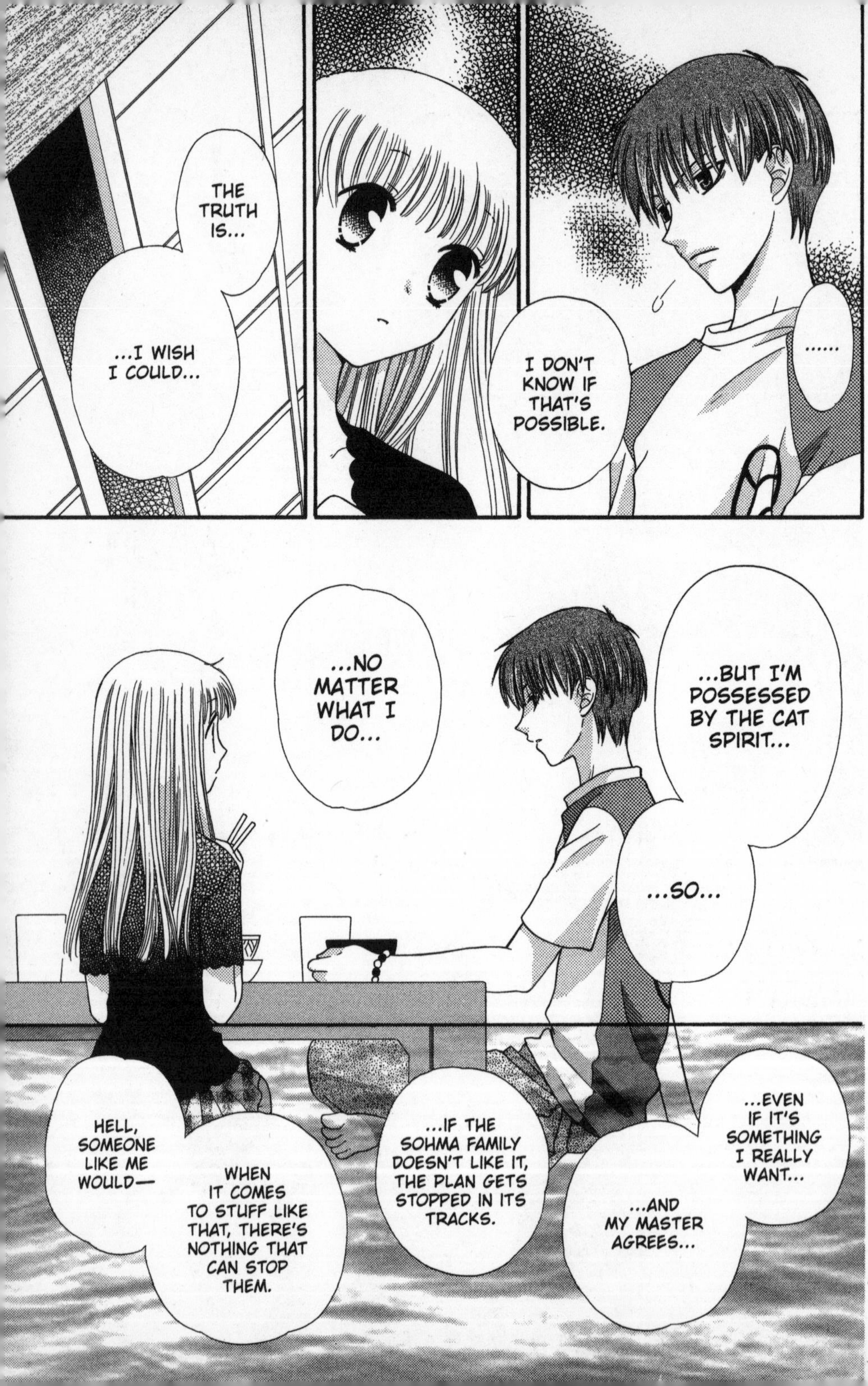
......
I DON'T KNOW IF THAT'S POSSIBLE.
THE TRUTH IS...
...I WISH I COULD...
...BUT I'M POSSESSED BY THE CAT SPIRIT...
...SO...
...NO MATTER WHAT I DO...
...EVEN IF IT'S SOMETHING I REALLY WANT...
...AND MY MASTER AGREES...
...IF THE SOHMA FAMILY DOESN'T LIKE IT, THE PLAN GETS STOPPED IN ITS TRACKS.
WHEN IT COMES TO STUFF LIKE THAT, THERE'S NOTHING THAT CAN STOP THEM.
HELL, SOMEONE LIKE ME WOULD—

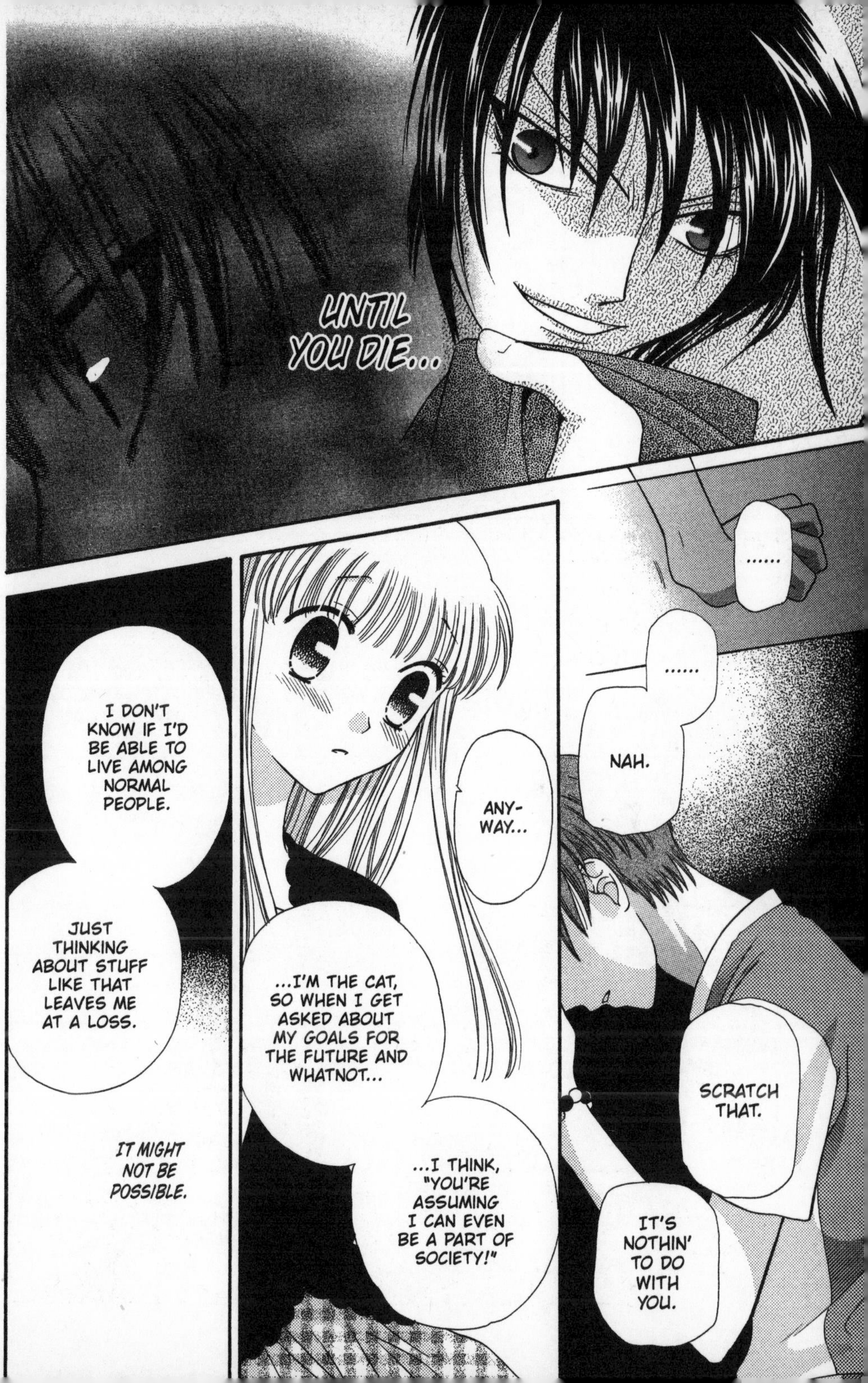
UNTIL YOU DIE...
......
......
NAH.
SCRATCH THAT.
IT'S NOTHIN' TO DO WITH YOU.
ANY-WAY...
...I'M THE CAT, SO WHEN I GET ASKED ABOUT MY GOALS FOR THE FUTURE AND WHATNOT...
...I THINK, "YOU'RE ASSUMING I CAN EVEN BE A PART OF SOCIETY!"
I DON'T KNOW IF I'D BE ABLE TO LIVE AMONG NORMAL PEOPLE.
JUST THINKING ABOUT STUFF LIKE THAT LEAVES ME AT A LOSS.
IT MIGHT NOT BE POSSIBLE.

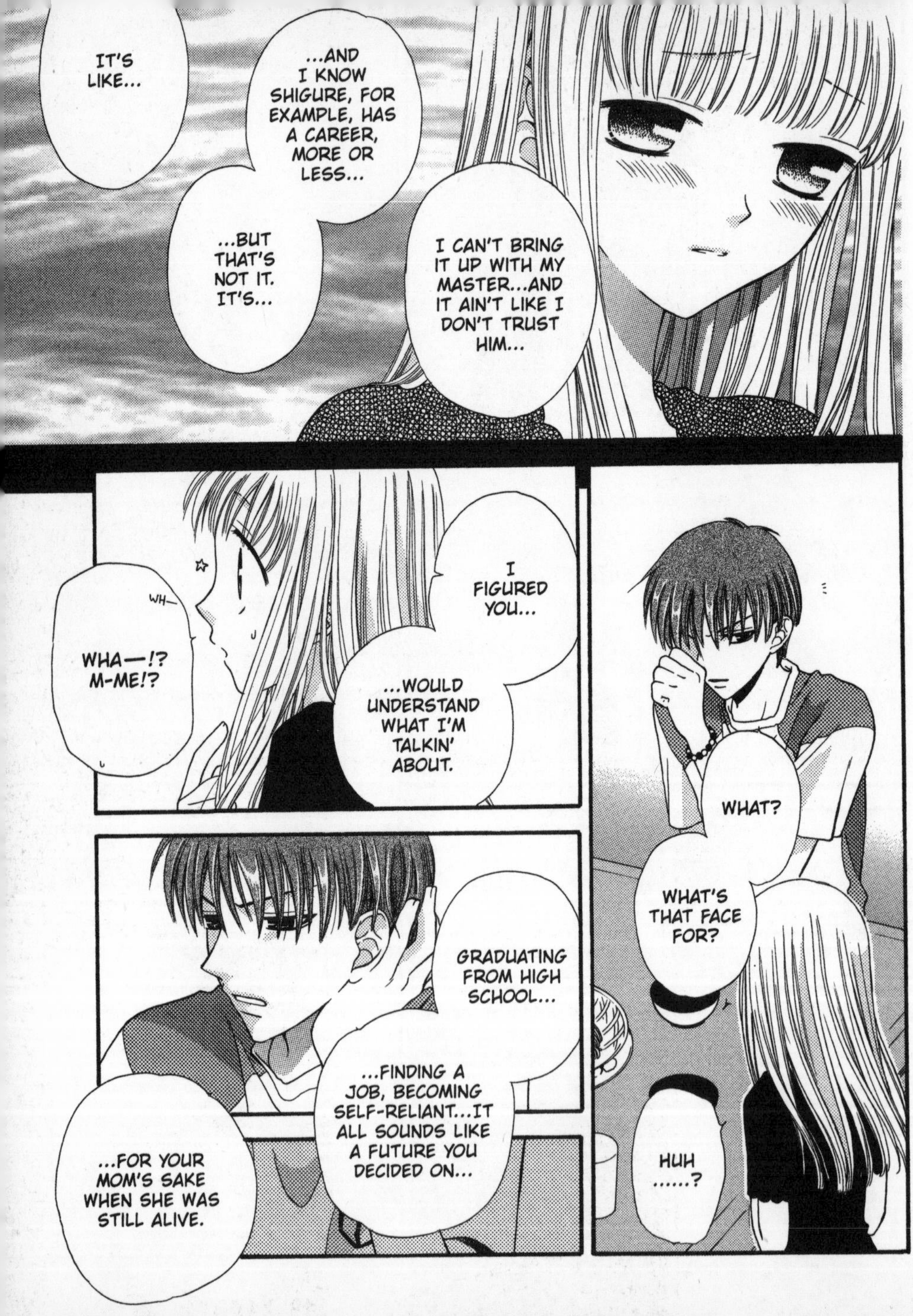
I CAN'T BRING IT UP WITH MY MASTER...AND IT AIN'T LIKE I DON'T TRUST HIM...
...AND I KNOW SHIGURE, FOR EXAMPLE, HAS A CAREER, MORE OR LESS...
...BUT THAT'S NOT IT. IT'S...
IT'S LIKE...
WHAT?
WHAT'S THAT FACE FOR?
HUH ......?
I FIGURED YOU...
...WOULD UNDERSTAND WHAT I'M TALKIN' ABOUT.
WH—
WHA—!? M-ME!?
GRADUATING FROM HIGH SCHOOL...
...FINDING A JOB, BECOMING SELF-RELIANT...IT ALL SOUNDS LIKE A FUTURE YOU DECIDED ON...
...FOR YOUR MOM'S SAKE WHEN SHE WAS STILL ALIVE.

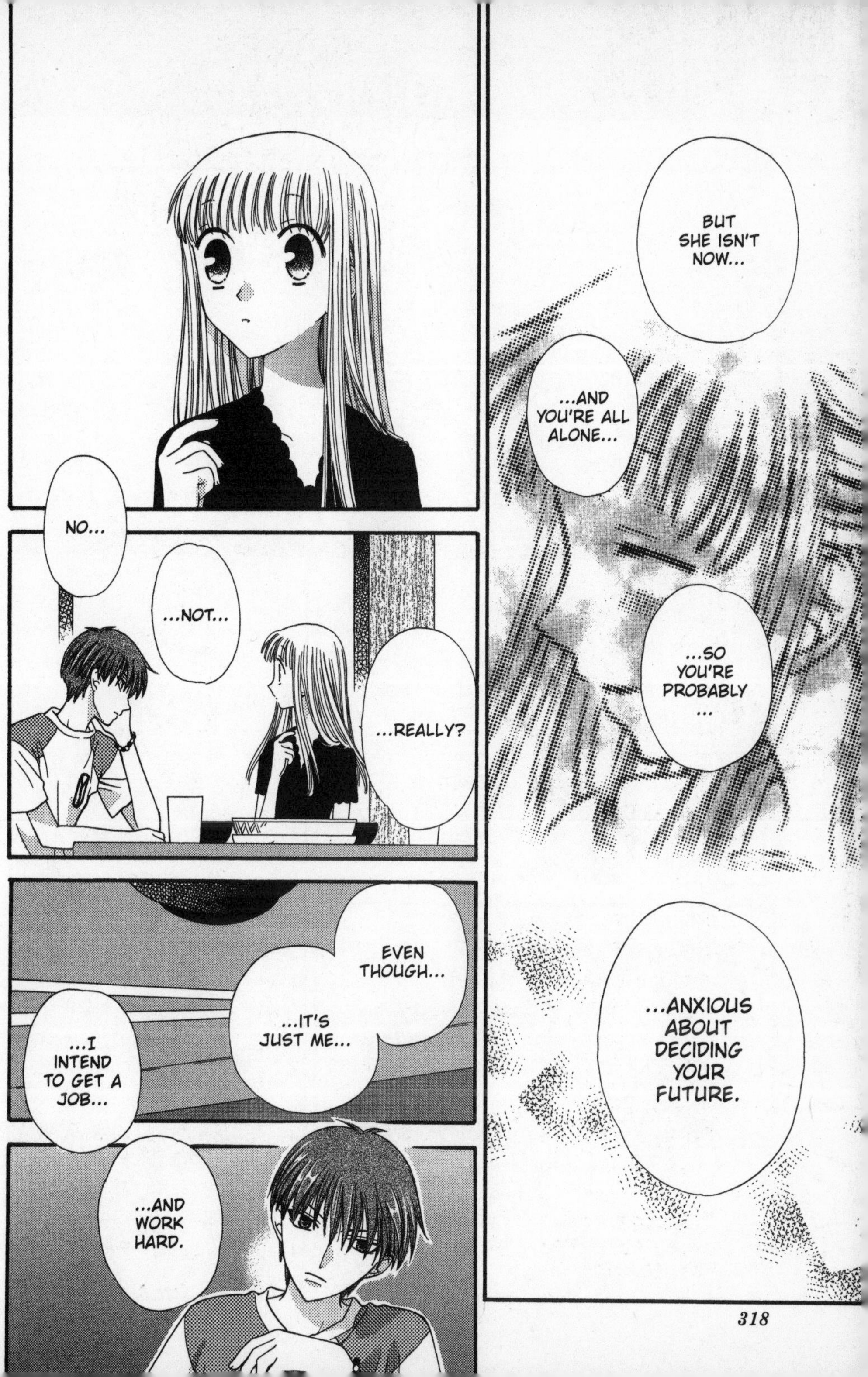
BUT SHE ISN'T NOW...
...AND YOU'RE ALL ALONE...
...SO YOU'RE PROBABLY ...
...ANXIOUS ABOUT DECIDING YOUR FUTURE.
NO...
...NOT...
...REALLY?
EVEN THOUGH...
...IT'S JUST ME...
...I INTEND TO GET A JOB...
...AND WORK HARD.

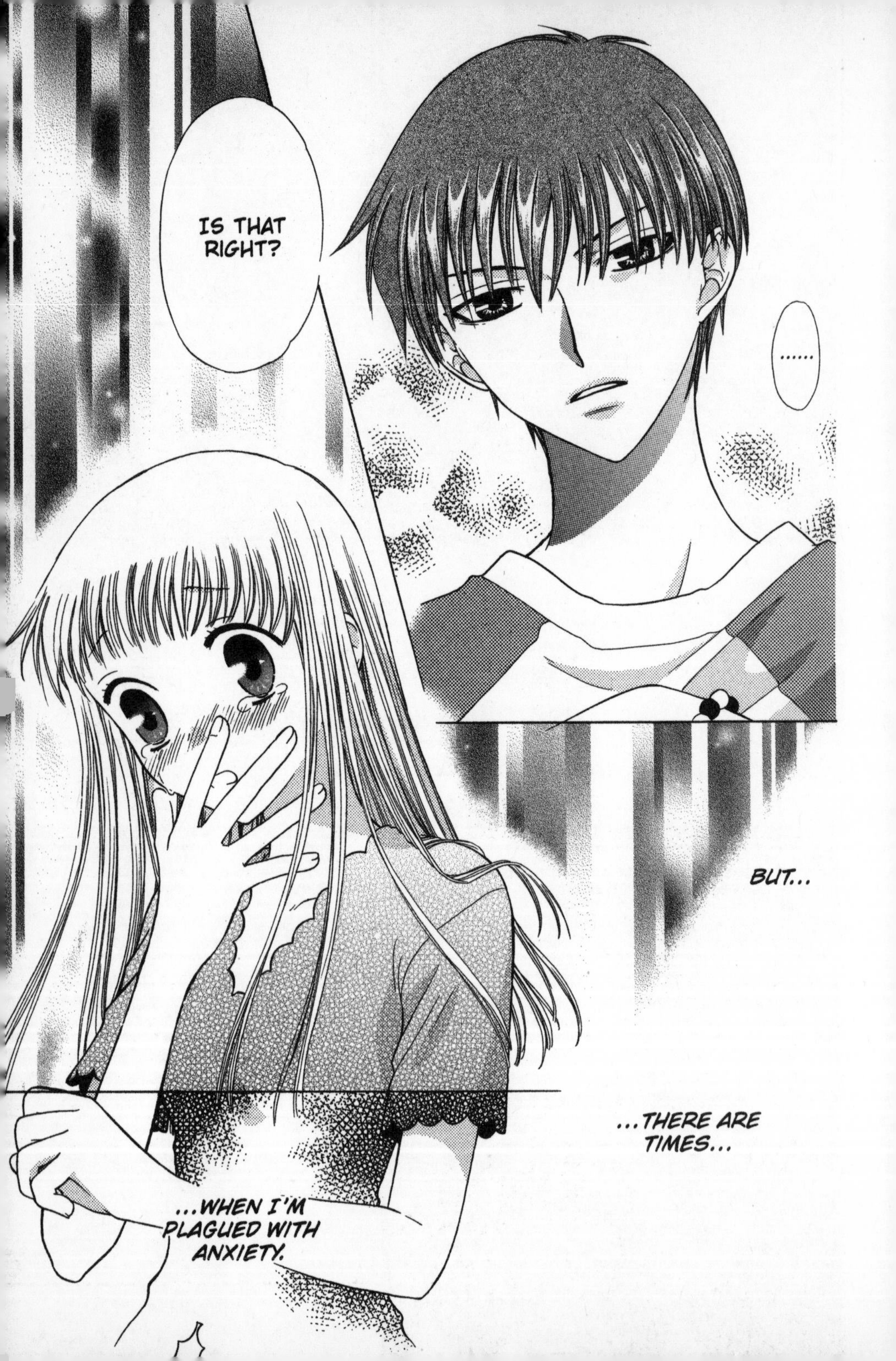
IS THAT RIGHT?
......
BUT...
...THERE ARE TIMES...
...WHEN I'M PLAGUED WITH ANXIETY.

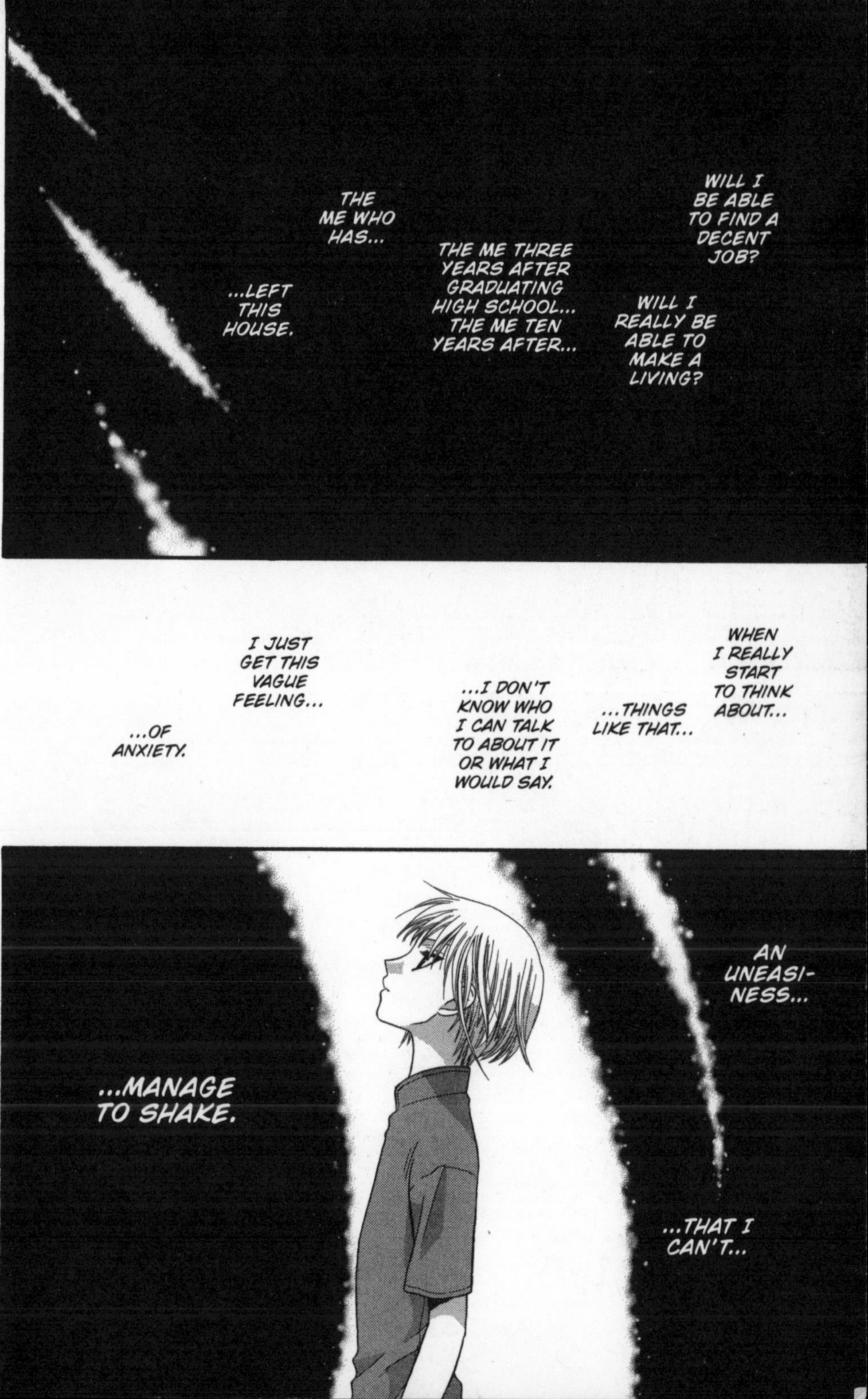
WILL I BE ABLE TO FIND A DECENT JOB?
WILL I REALLY BE ABLE TO MAKE A LIVING?
THE ME THREE YEARS AFTER GRADUATING HIGH SCHOOL... THE ME TEN YEARS AFTER...
THE ME WHO HAS...
...LEFT THIS HOUSE.
WHEN I REALLY START TO THINK ABOUT...
...THINGS LIKE THAT...
...I DON'T KNOW WHO I CAN TALK TO ABOUT IT OR WHAT I WOULD SAY.
I JUST GET THIS VAGUE FEELING...
...OF ANXIETY.
AN UNEASI-NESS...
...THAT I CAN'T...
...MANAGE TO SHAKE.

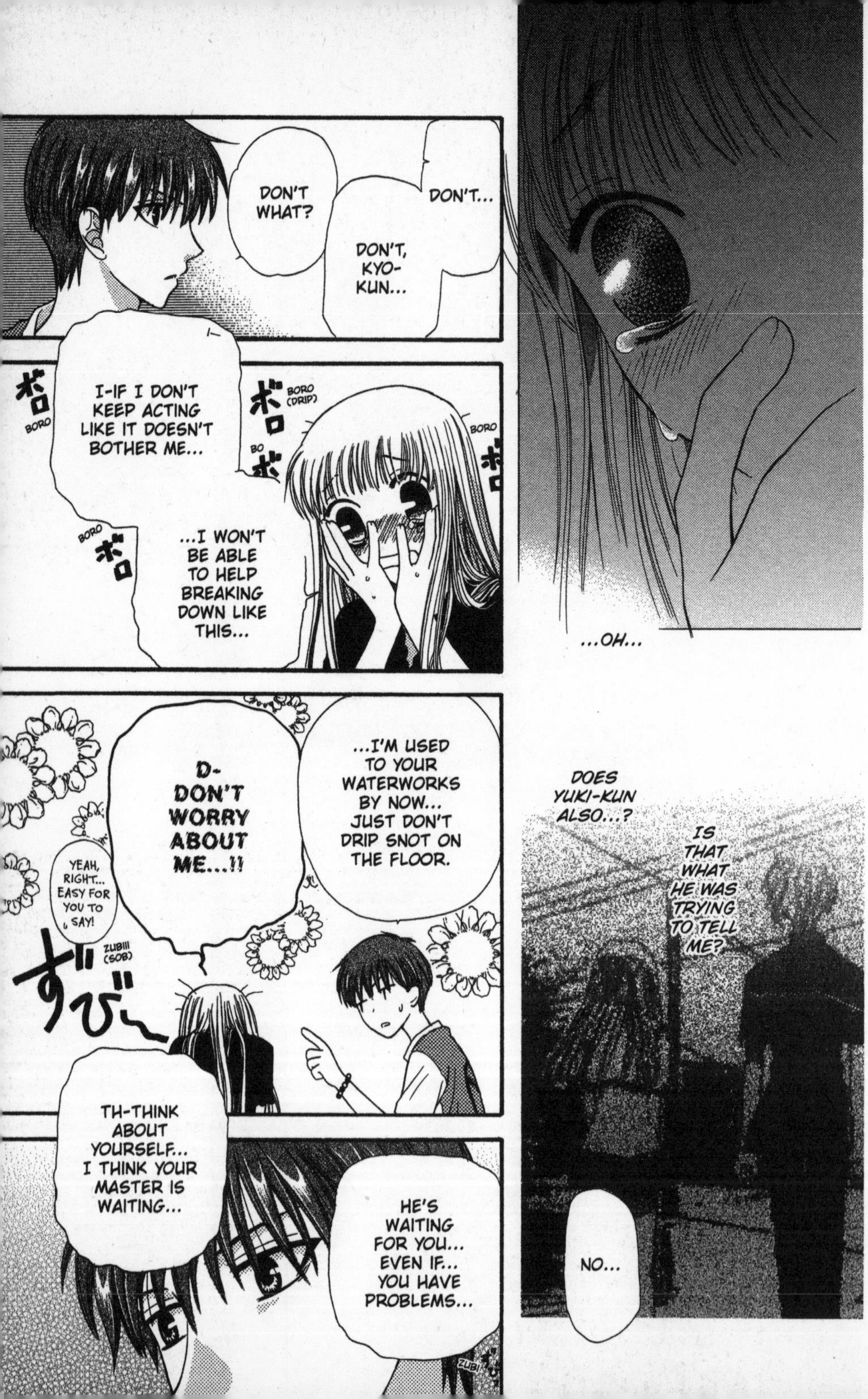

...OH...
DOES YUKI-KUN ALSO...?
IS THAT WHAT HE WAS TRYING TO TELL ME?
NO...
DON'T...
DON'T, KYO-KUN...
DON'T WHAT?
BORO (DRIP)
BORO
BORO
BO
I-IF I DON'T KEEP ACTING LIKE IT DOESN'T BOTHER ME...
BORO
...I WON'T BE ABLE TO HELP BREAKING DOWN LIKE THIS...
...I'M USED TO YOUR WATERWORKS BY NOW... JUST DON'T DRIP SNOT ON THE FLOOR.
D-DON'T WORRY ABOUT ME...!!
YEAH, RIGHT... EASY FOR YOU TO SAY!
ZUBIII (SOB)
HE'S WAITING FOR YOU... EVEN IF... YOU HAVE PROBLEMS...
TH-THINK ABOUT YOURSELF... I THINK YOUR MASTER IS WAITING...
ZUBI

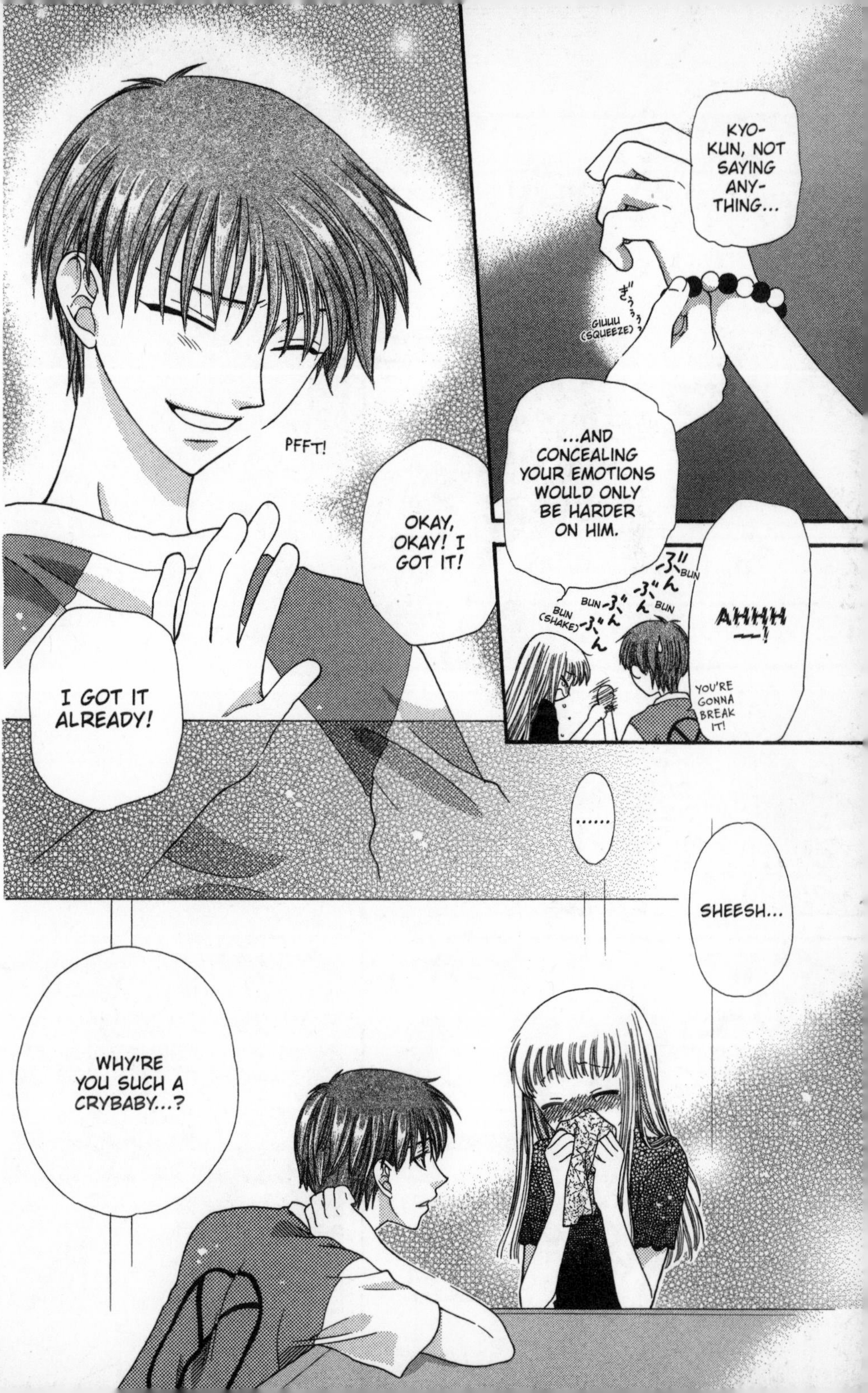
KYO-KUN, NOT SAYING ANY-THING...
GIUUU (SQUEEZE)
...AND CONCEALING YOUR EMOTIONS WOULD ONLY BE HARDER ON HIM.
BUN BUN BUN BUN (SHAKE)
AHHH—!
YOU'RE GONNA BREAK IT!
PFFT!
OKAY, OKAY! I GOT IT!
I GOT IT ALREADY!
......
SHEESH...
WHY'RE YOU SUCH A CRYBABY...?

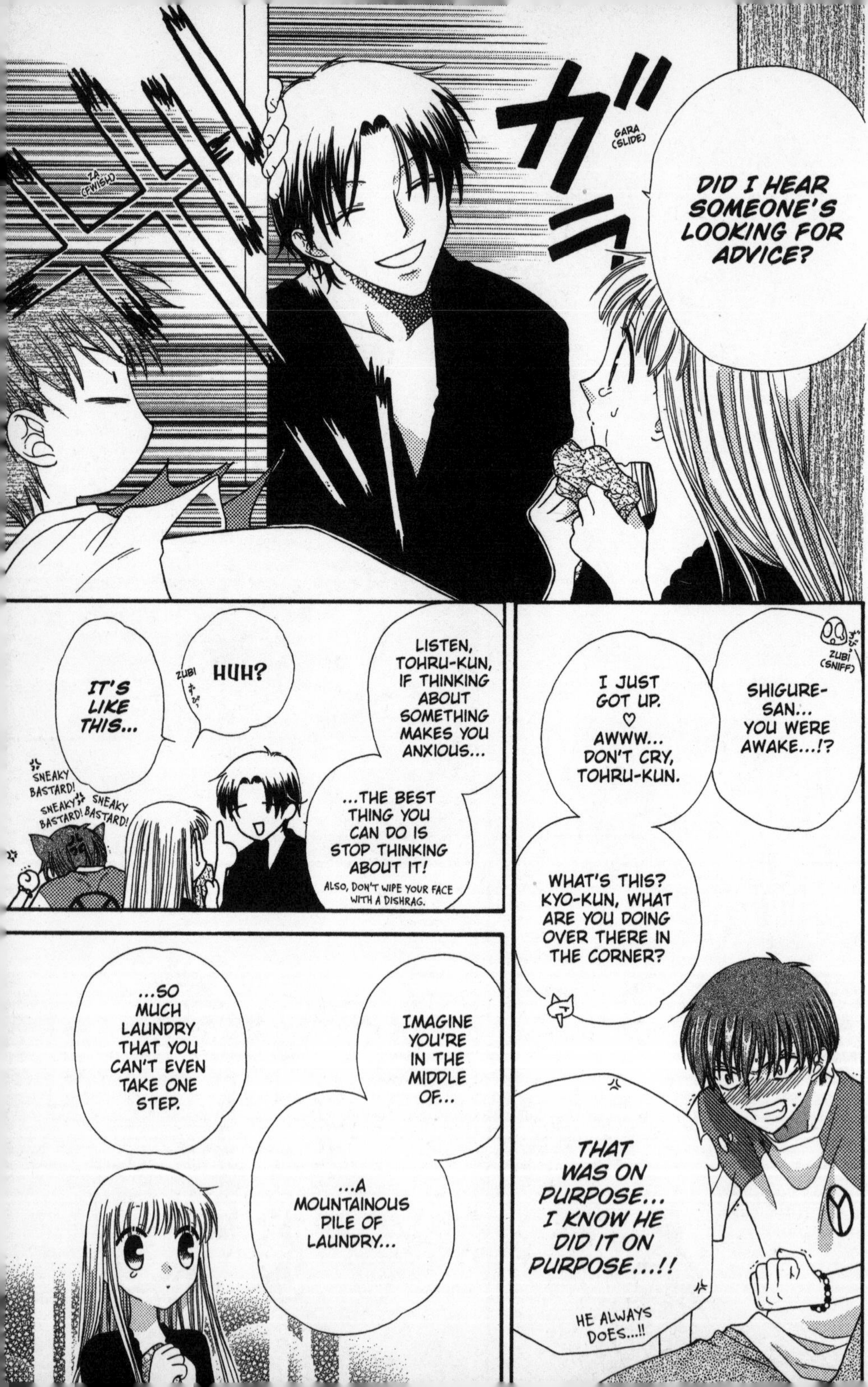
DID I HEAR SOMEONE'S LOOKING FOR ADVICE?
GARA (SLIDE)
ZA (FWISH)
ZUBI (SNIFF)
SHIGURE-SAN... YOU WERE AWAKE...!?
I JUST GOT UP. ♡ AWWW... DON'T CRY, TOHRU-KUN.
WHAT'S THIS? KYO-KUN, WHAT ARE YOU DOING OVER THERE IN THE CORNER?
THAT WAS ON PURPOSE... I KNOW HE DID IT ON PURPOSE...!!
HE ALWAYS DOES...!!
LISTEN, TOHRU-KUN, IF THINKING ABOUT SOMETHING MAKES YOU ANXIOUS...
...THE BEST THING YOU CAN DO IS STOP THINKING ABOUT IT!
ALSO, DON'T WIPE YOUR FACE WITH A DISHRAG.
HUH?
ZUBI
IT'S LIKE THIS...
SNEAKY BASTARD!
SNEAKY BASTARD!
SNEAKY BASTARD!
IMAGINE YOU'RE IN THE MIDDLE OF...
...A MOUNTAINOUS PILE OF LAUNDRY...
...SO MUCH LAUNDRY THAT YOU CAN'T EVEN TAKE ONE STEP.

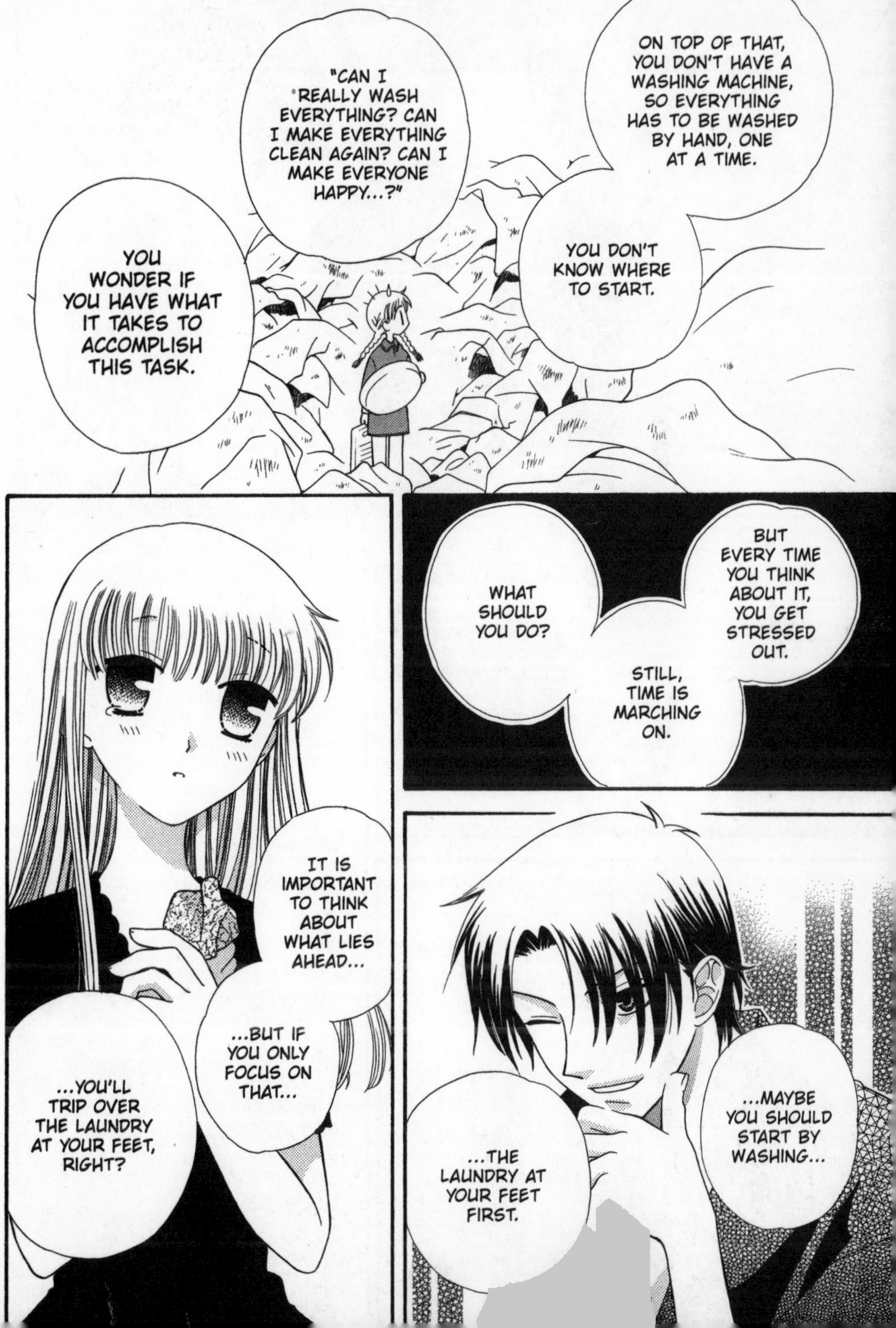
ON TOP OF THAT, YOU DON'T HAVE A WASHING MACHINE, SO EVERYTHING HAS TO BE WASHED BY HAND, ONE AT A TIME.
YOU DON'T KNOW WHERE TO START.
"CAN I REALLY WASH EVERYTHING? CAN I MAKE EVERYTHING CLEAN AGAIN? CAN I MAKE EVERYONE HAPPY...?"
YOU WONDER IF YOU HAVE WHAT IT TAKES TO ACCOMPLISH THIS TASK.
BUT EVERY TIME YOU THINK ABOUT IT, YOU GET STRESSED OUT.
WHAT SHOULD YOU DO?
STILL, TIME IS MARCHING ON.
...MAYBE YOU SHOULD START BY WASHING...
...THE LAUNDRY AT YOUR FEET FIRST.
IT IS IMPORTANT TO THINK ABOUT WHAT LIES AHEAD...
...BUT IF YOU ONLY FOCUS ON THAT...
...YOU'LL TRIP OVER THE LAUNDRY AT YOUR FEET, RIGHT?

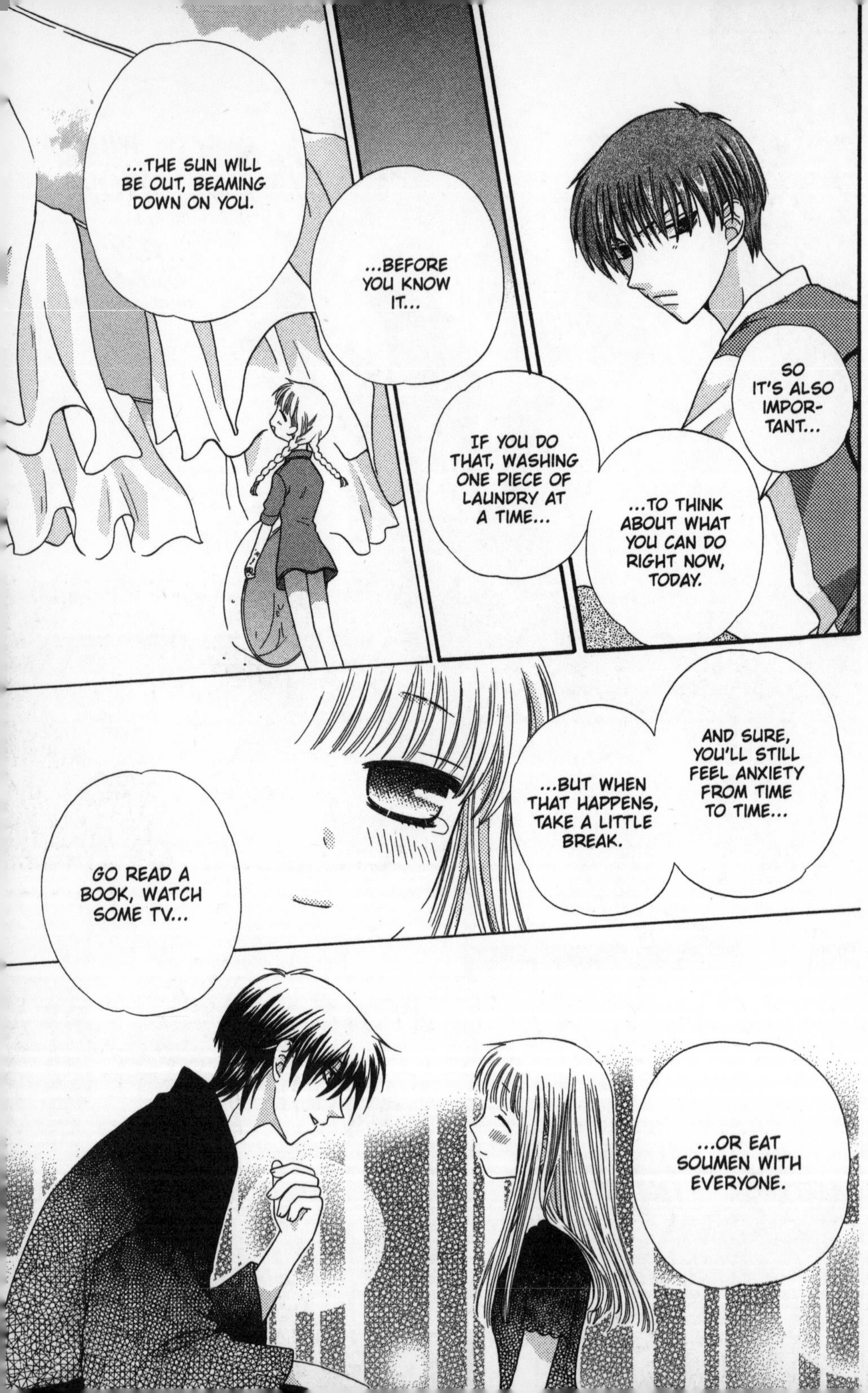
SO IT'S ALSO IMPORTANT...
...TO THINK ABOUT WHAT YOU CAN DO RIGHT NOW, TODAY.
IF YOU DO THAT, WASHING ONE PIECE OF LAUNDRY AT A TIME...
...BEFORE YOU KNOW IT...
...THE SUN WILL BE OUT, BEAMING DOWN ON YOU.
AND SURE, YOU'LL STILL FEEL ANXIETY FROM TIME TO TIME...
...BUT WHEN THAT HAPPENS, TAKE A LITTLE BREAK.
GO READ A BOOK, WATCH SOME TV...
...OR EAT SOUMEN WITH EVERYONE.

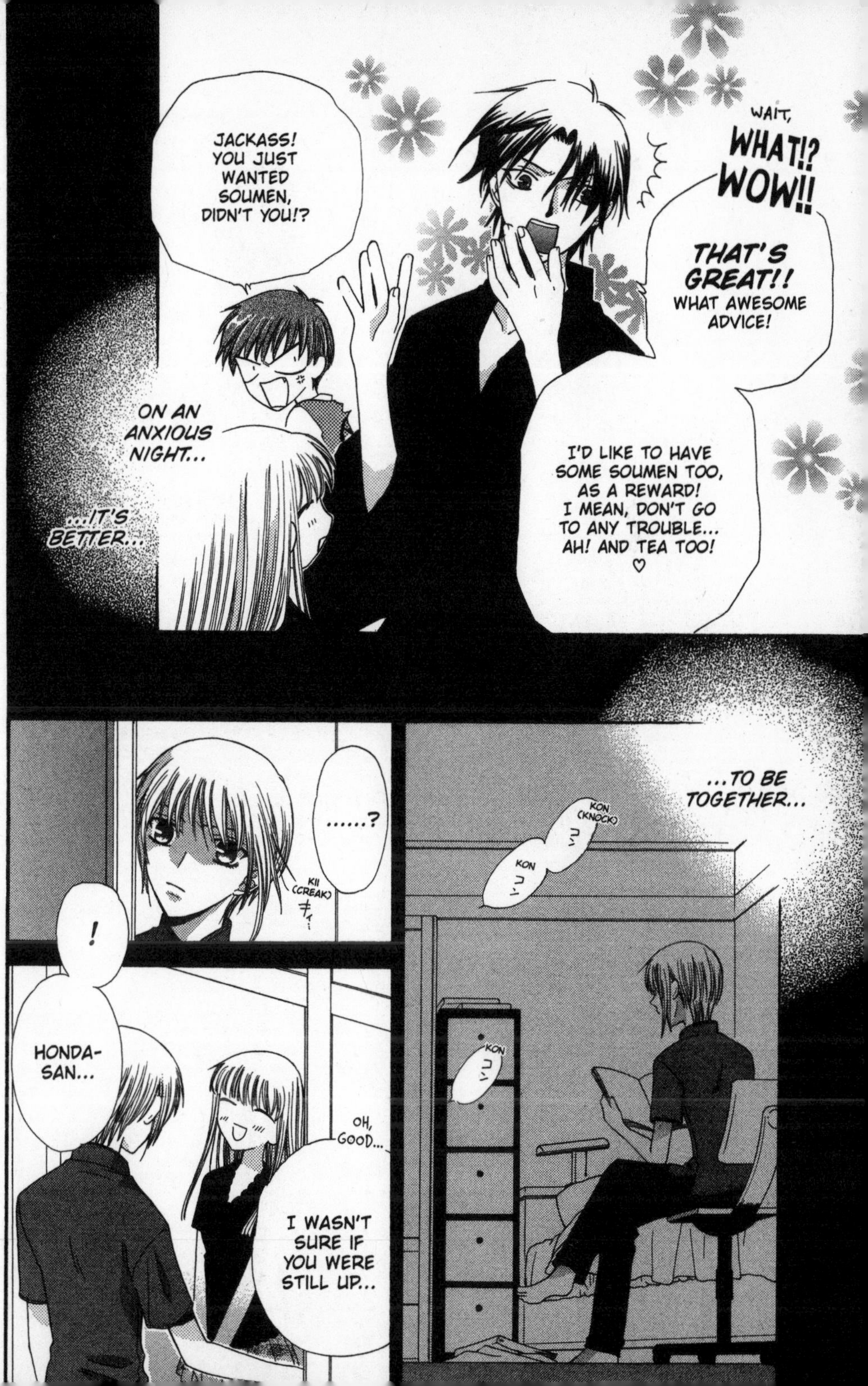
WAIT, WHAT!? WOW!!
THAT'S GREAT!! WHAT AWESOME ADVICE!
I'D LIKE TO HAVE SOME SOUMEN TOO, AS A REWARD! I MEAN, DON'T GO TO ANY TROUBLE... AH! AND TEA TOO! ♡
JACKASS! YOU JUST WANTED SOUMEN, DIDN'T YOU!?
ON AN ANXIOUS NIGHT...
...IT'S BETTER...
...TO BE TOGETHER...
KON (KNOCK)
KON
KON
......?
KII (CREAK)
!
HONDA-SAN...
OH, GOOD...
I WASN'T SURE IF YOU WERE STILL UP...

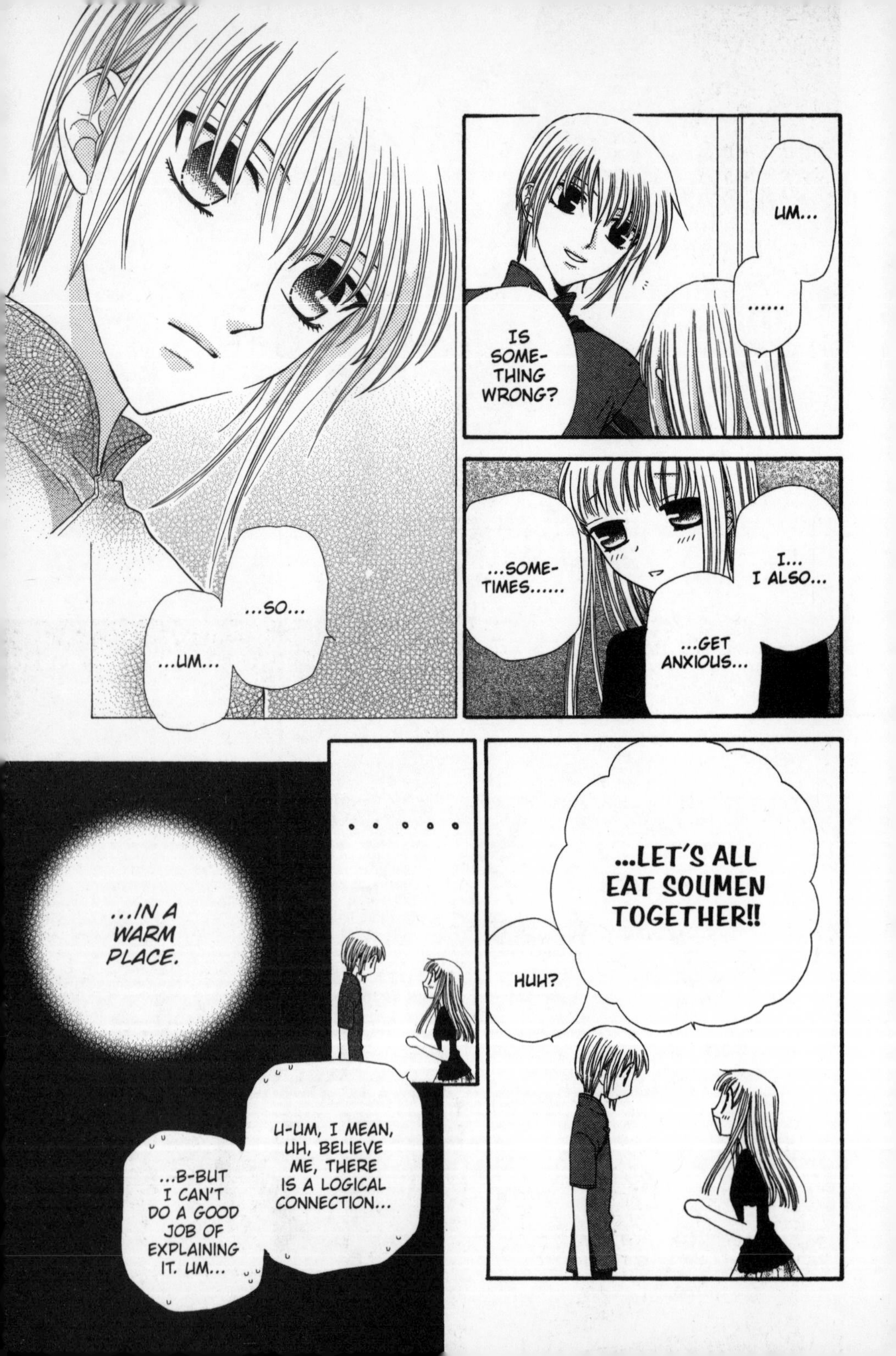
UM...
......
IS SOMETHING WRONG?
I... I ALSO...
...GET ANXIOUS...
...SOMETIMES......
...SO...
...UM...
...LET'S ALL EAT SOUMEN TOGETHER!!
HUH?
.....
...IN A WARM PLACE.
U-UM, I MEAN, UH, BELIEVE ME, THERE IS A LOGICAL CONNECTION...
...B-BUT I CAN'T DO A GOOD JOB OF EXPLAINING IT. UM...

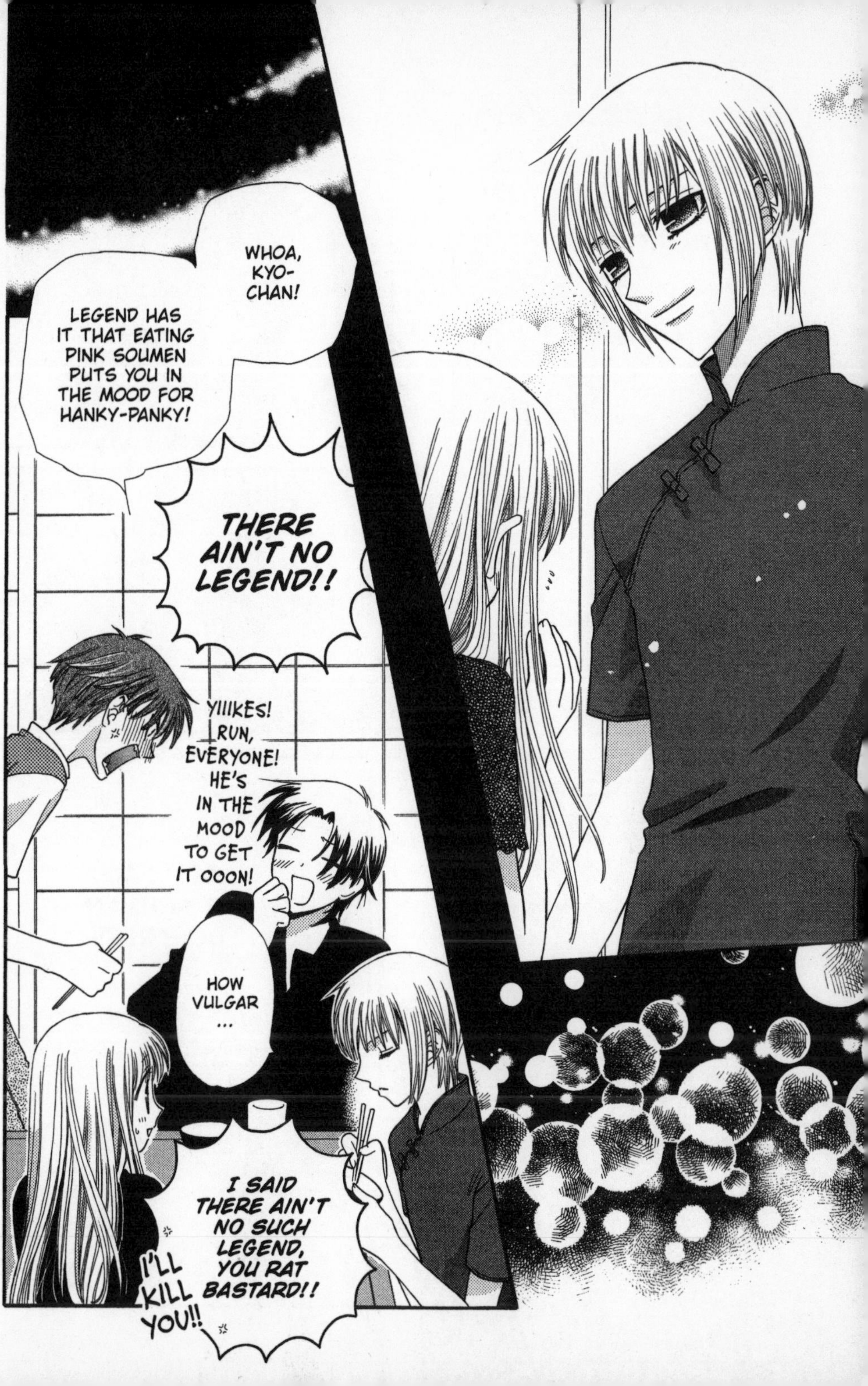
WHOA, KYO-CHAN!
LEGEND HAS IT THAT EATING PINK SOUMEN PUTS YOU IN THE MOOD FOR HANKY-PANKY!
THERE AIN'T NO LEGEND!!
YIIIKES! RUN, EVERYONE! HE'S IN THE MOOD TO GET IT OOON!
HOW VULGAR...
I SAID THERE AIN'T NO SUCH LEGEND, YOU RAT BASTARD!!
I'LL KILL YOU!!

Chapter 47

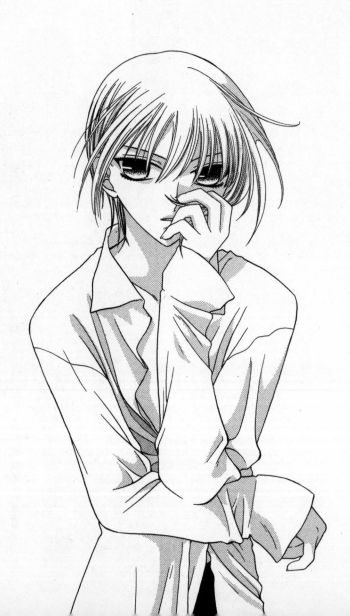

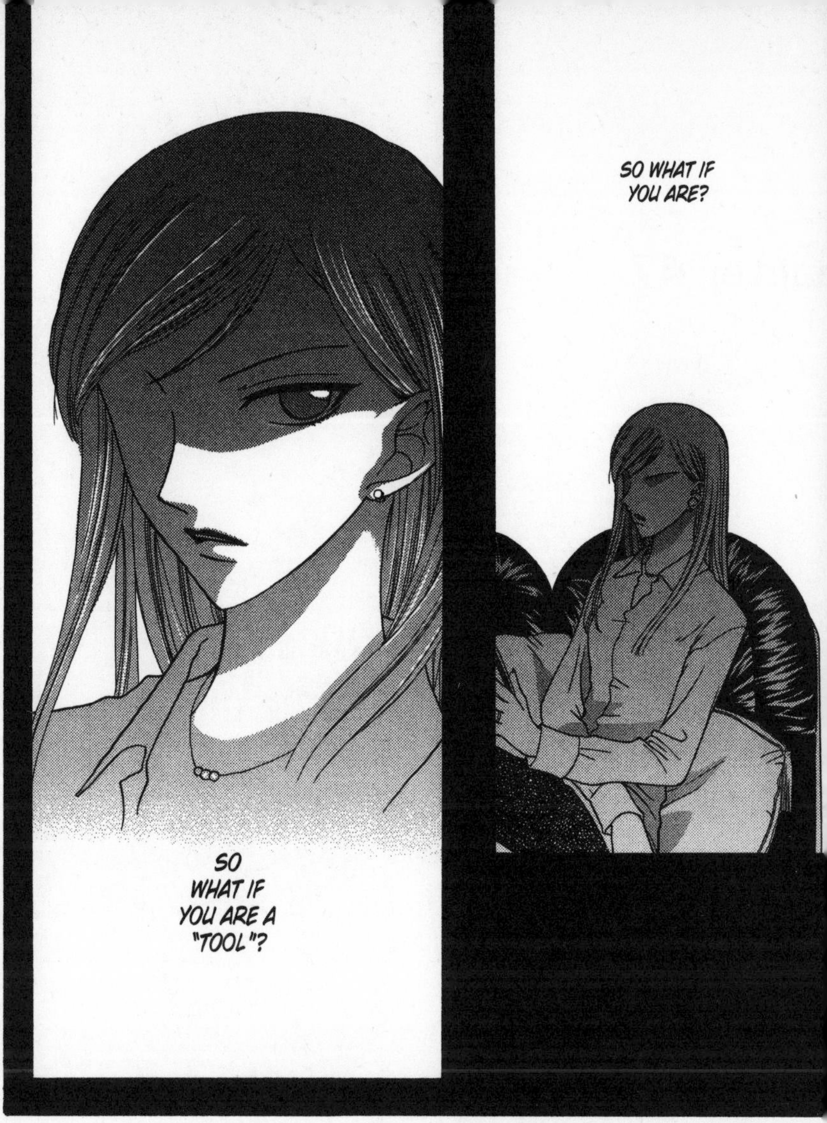
SO WHAT IF YOU ARE?
SO WHAT IF YOU ARE A "TOOL"?

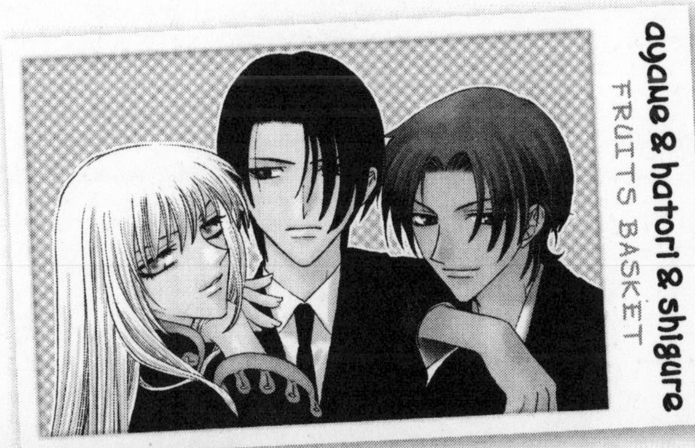
ayame & hatori & shigure
FRUITS BASKET

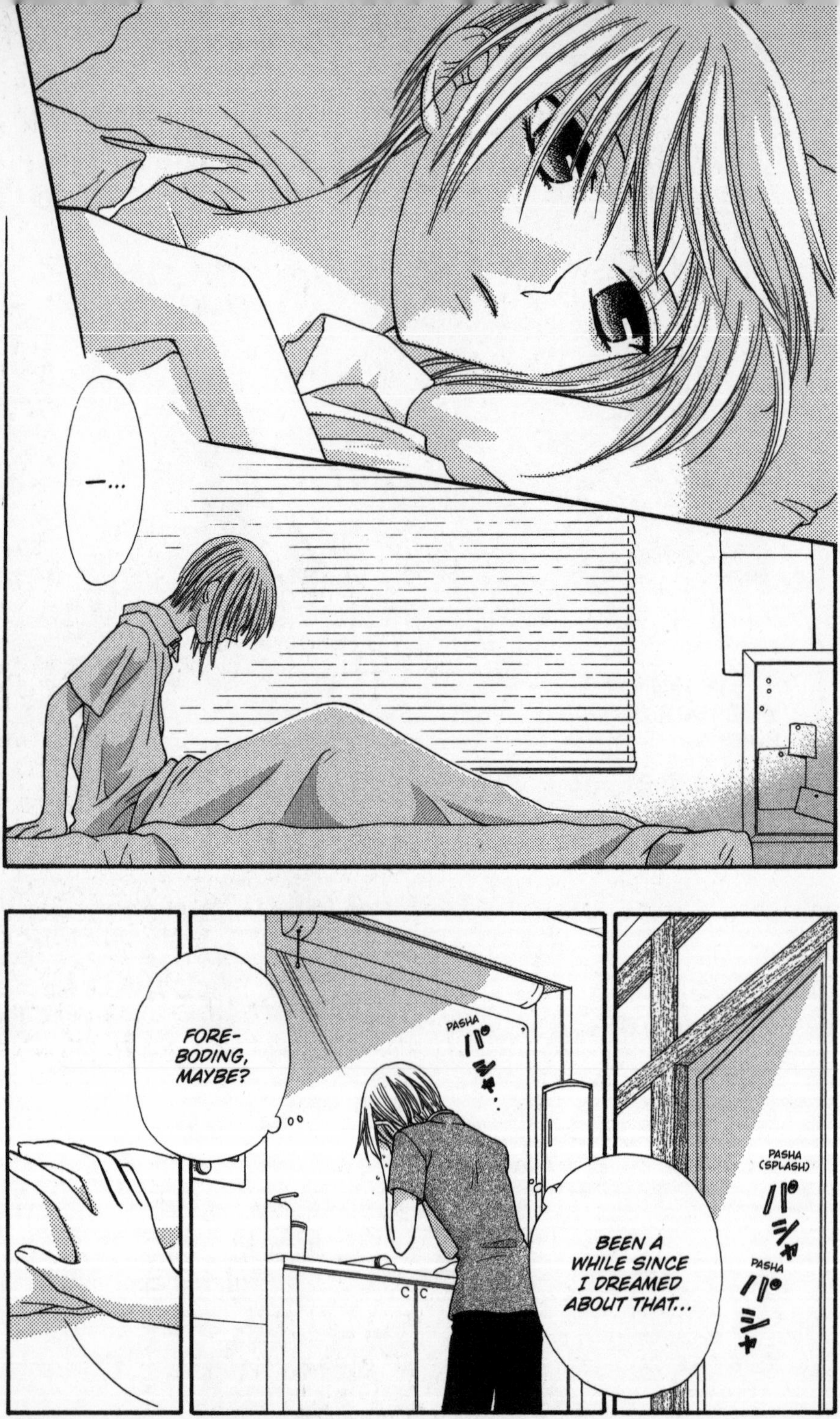
—...
PASHA (SPLASH)
パシャ
PASHA
パシャ
BEEN A WHILE SINCE I DREAMED ABOUT THAT...
PASHA
パシャ..
FORE-BODING, MAYBE?

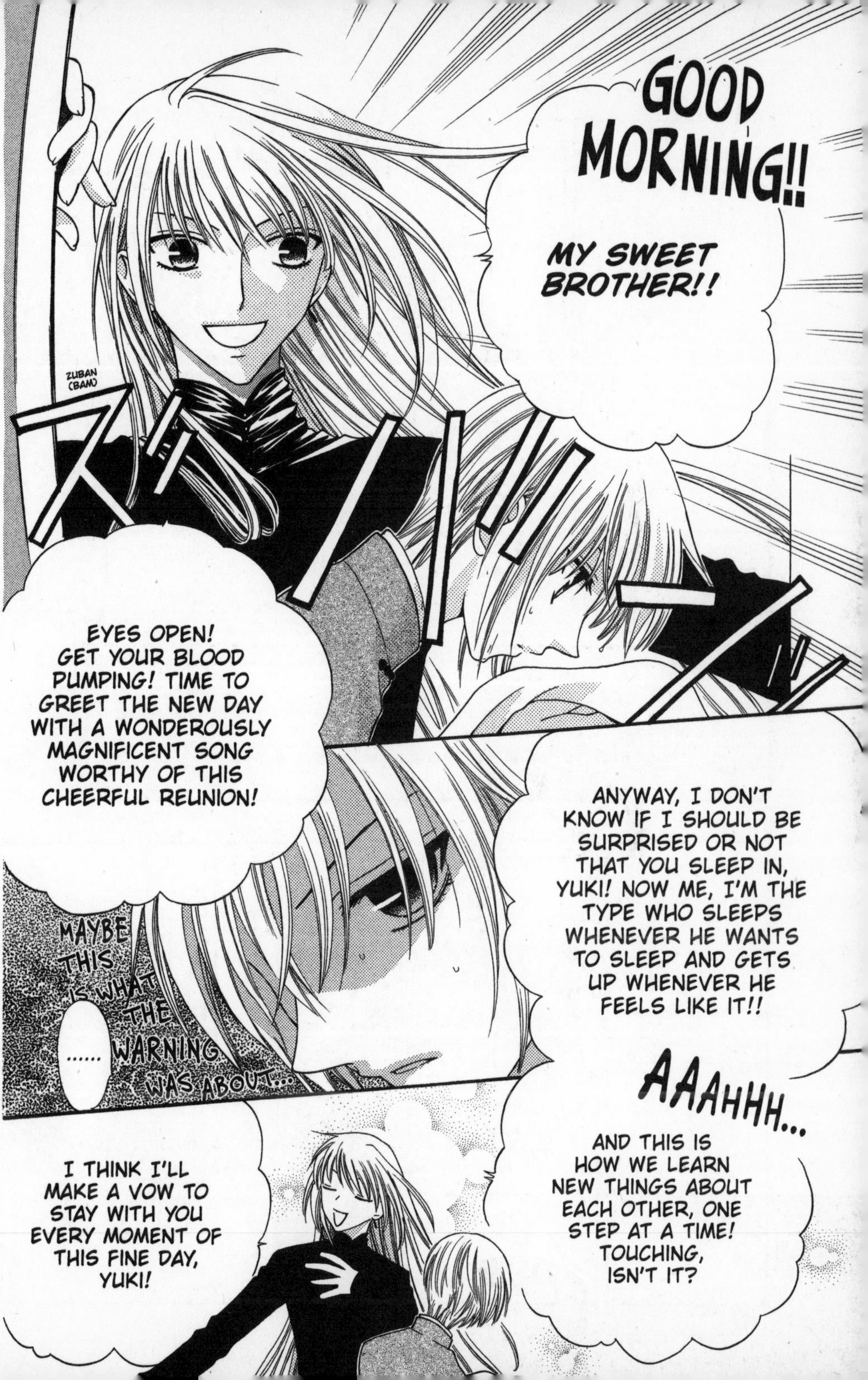
GOOD MORNING!!
MY SWEET BROTHER!!
ZUBAN (BAM)
EYES OPEN! GET YOUR BLOOD PUMPING! TIME TO GREET THE NEW DAY WITH A WONDEROUSLY MAGNIFICENT SONG WORTHY OF THIS CHEERFUL REUNION!
ANYWAY, I DON'T KNOW IF I SHOULD BE SURPRISED OR NOT THAT YOU SLEEP IN, YUKI! NOW ME, I'M THE TYPE WHO SLEEPS WHENEVER HE WANTS TO SLEEP AND GETS UP WHENEVER HE FEELS LIKE IT!!
MAYBE THIS IS WHAT THE WARNING WAS ABOUT...
......
AAAHHH...
AND THIS IS HOW WE LEARN NEW THINGS ABOUT EACH OTHER, ONE STEP AT A TIME! TOUCHING, ISN'T IT?
I THINK I'LL MAKE A VOW TO STAY WITH YOU EVERY MOMENT OF THIS FINE DAY, YUKI!

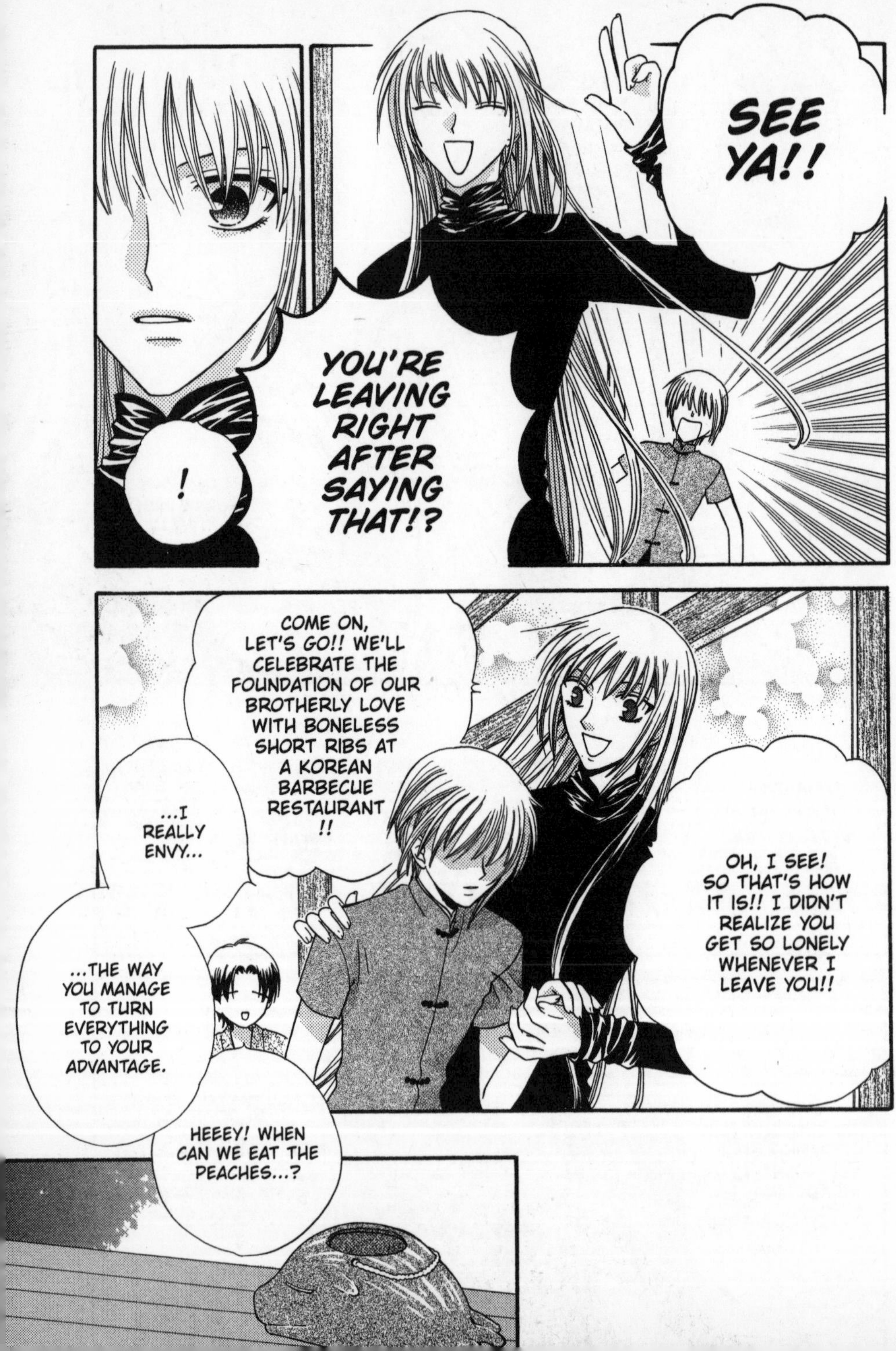
SEE YA!!
YOU'RE LEAVING RIGHT AFTER SAYING THAT!?
!
OH, I SEE! SO THAT'S HOW IT IS!! I DIDN'T REALIZE YOU GET SO LONELY WHENEVER I LEAVE YOU!!
COME ON, LET'S GO!! WE'LL CELEBRATE THE FOUNDATION OF OUR BROTHERLY LOVE WITH BONELESS SHORT RIBS AT A KOREAN BARBECUE RESTAURANT!!
...I REALLY ENVY...
...THE WAY YOU MANAGE TO TURN EVERYTHING TO YOUR ADVANTAGE.
HEEEY! WHEN CAN WE EAT THE PEACHES...?

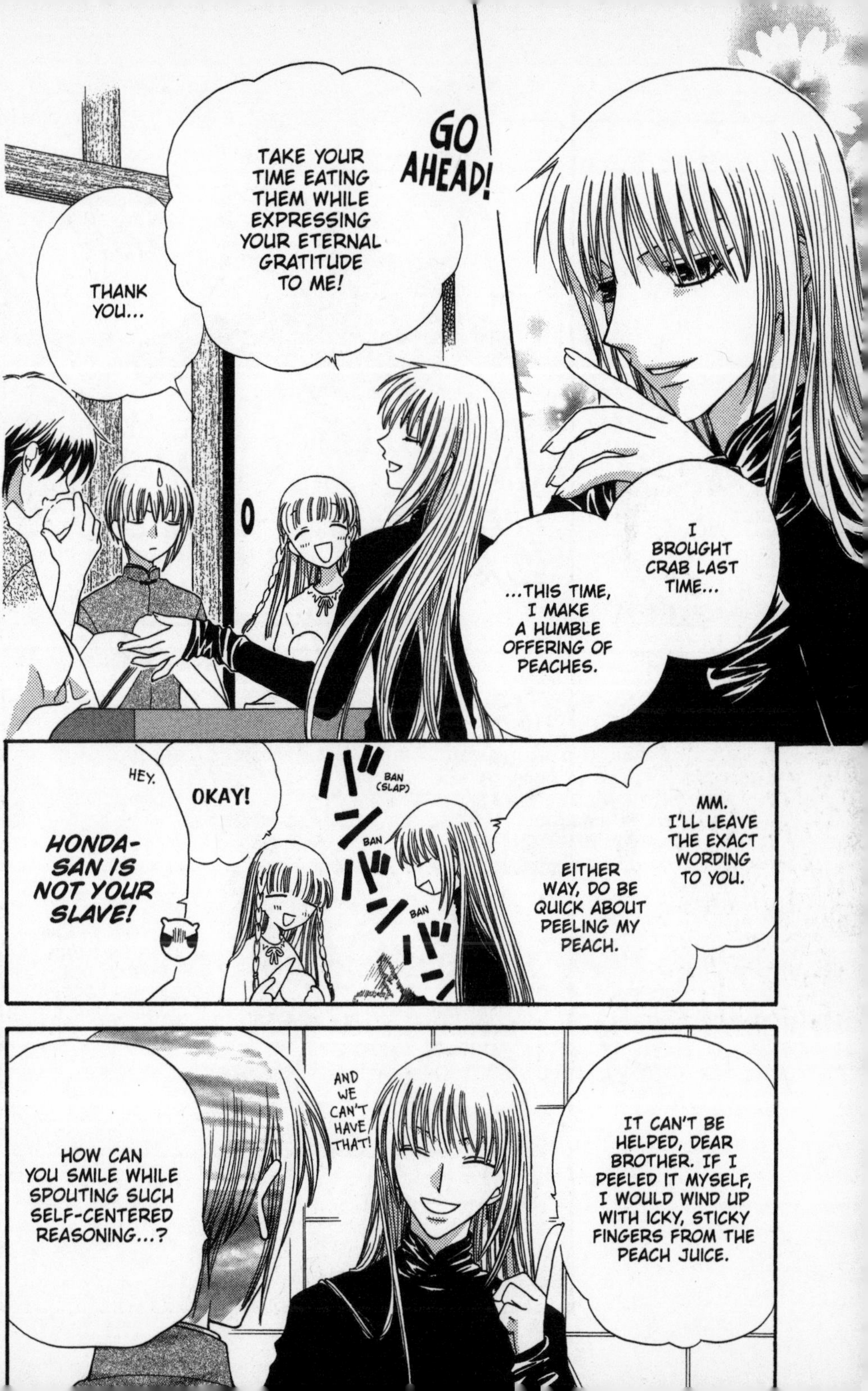
I BROUGHT CRAB LAST TIME...
...THIS TIME, I MAKE A HUMBLE OFFERING OF PEACHES.
GO AHEAD!
TAKE YOUR TIME EATING THEM WHILE EXPRESSING YOUR ETERNAL GRATITUDE TO ME!
THANK YOU...
MM. I'LL LEAVE THE EXACT WORDING TO YOU.
EITHER WAY, DO BE QUICK ABOUT PEELING MY PEACH.
バ BAN (SLAP)
ン バン BAN
バン BAN
OKAY!
HEY.
HONDA-SAN IS NOT YOUR SLAVE!
IT CAN'T BE HELPED, DEAR BROTHER. IF I PEELED IT MYSELF, I WOULD WIND UP WITH ICKY, STICKY FINGERS FROM THE PEACH JUICE.
AND WE CAN'T HAVE THAT!
HOW CAN YOU SMILE WHILE SPOUTING SUCH SELF-CENTERED REASONING...?

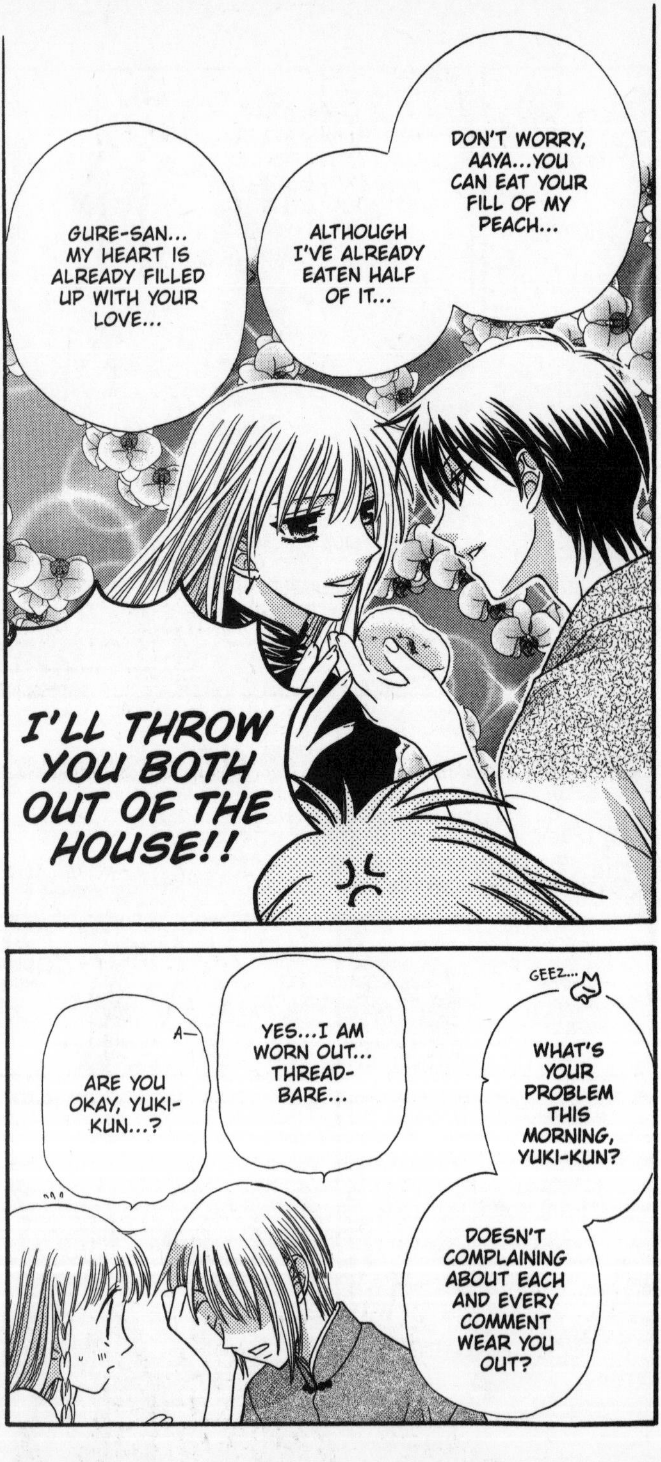
DON'T WORRY, AAYA...YOU CAN EAT YOUR FILL OF MY PEACH...
ALTHOUGH I'VE ALREADY EATEN HALF OF IT...
GURE-SAN... MY HEART IS ALREADY FILLED UP WITH YOUR LOVE...
I'LL THROW YOU BOTH OUT OF THE HOUSE!!
GEEZ...
WHAT'S YOUR PROBLEM THIS MORNING, YUKI-KUN?
DOESN'T COMPLAINING ABOUT EACH AND EVERY COMMENT WEAR YOU OUT?
YES...I AM WORN OUT... THREAD-BARE...
A—
ARE YOU OKAY, YUKI-KUN...?

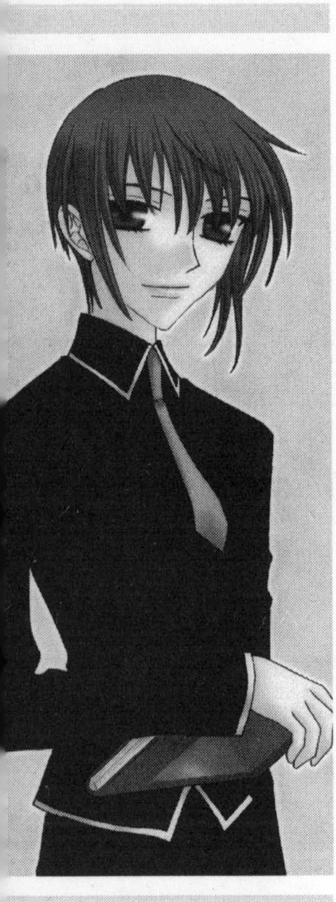

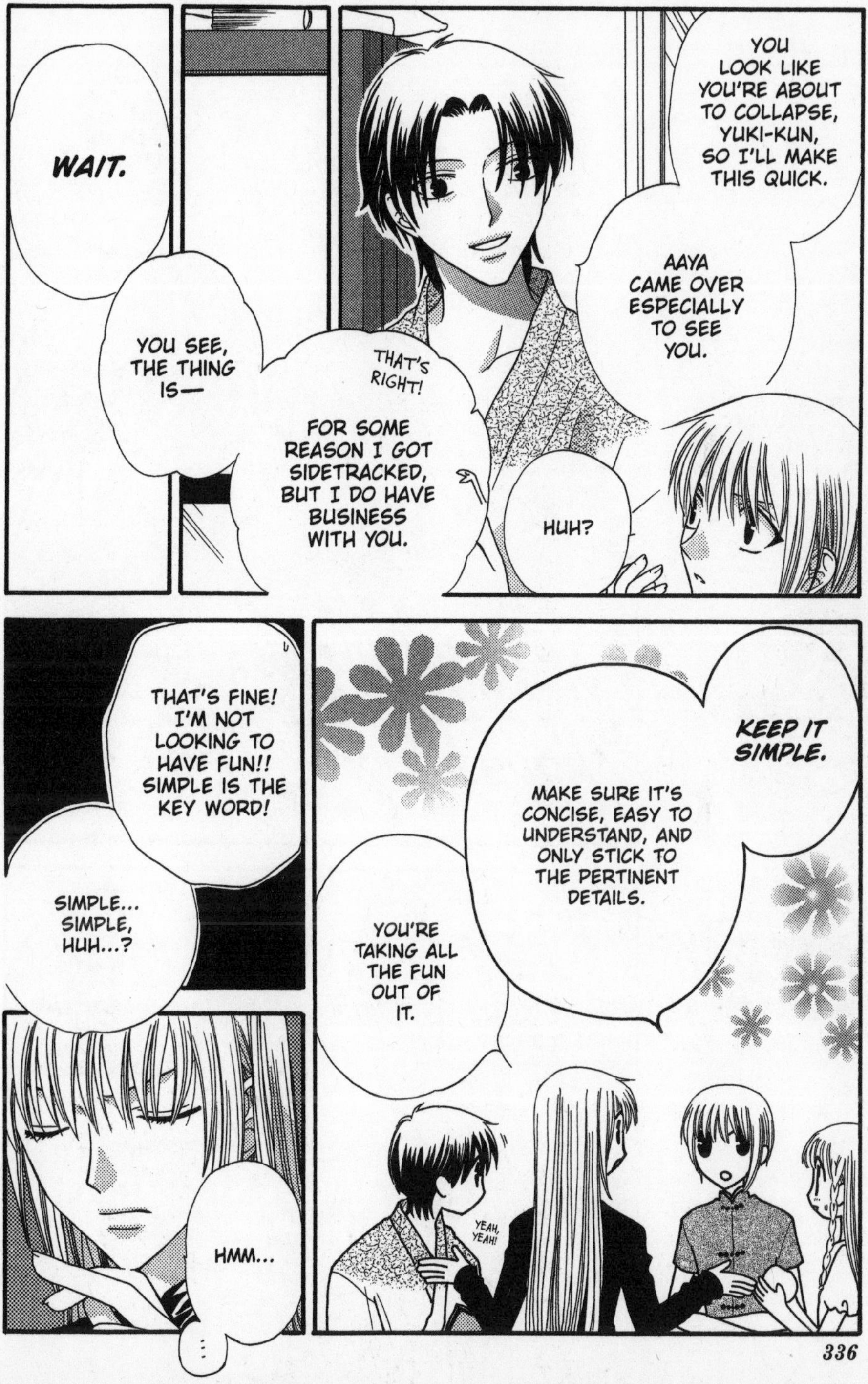
YOU LOOK LIKE YOU'RE ABOUT TO COLLAPSE, YUKI-KUN, SO I'LL MAKE THIS QUICK.
AAYA CAME OVER ESPECIALLY TO SEE YOU.
HUH?
THAT'S RIGHT!
FOR SOME REASON I GOT SIDETRACKED, BUT I DO HAVE BUSINESS WITH YOU.
YOU SEE, THE THING IS—
WAIT.
KEEP IT SIMPLE.
MAKE SURE IT'S CONCISE, EASY TO UNDERSTAND, AND ONLY STICK TO THE PERTINENT DETAILS.
YOU'RE TAKING ALL THE FUN OUT OF IT.
YEAH, YEAH!
THAT'S FINE! I'M NOT LOOKING TO HAVE FUN!! SIMPLE IS THE KEY WORD!
SIMPLE... SIMPLE, HUH...?
HMM...
...

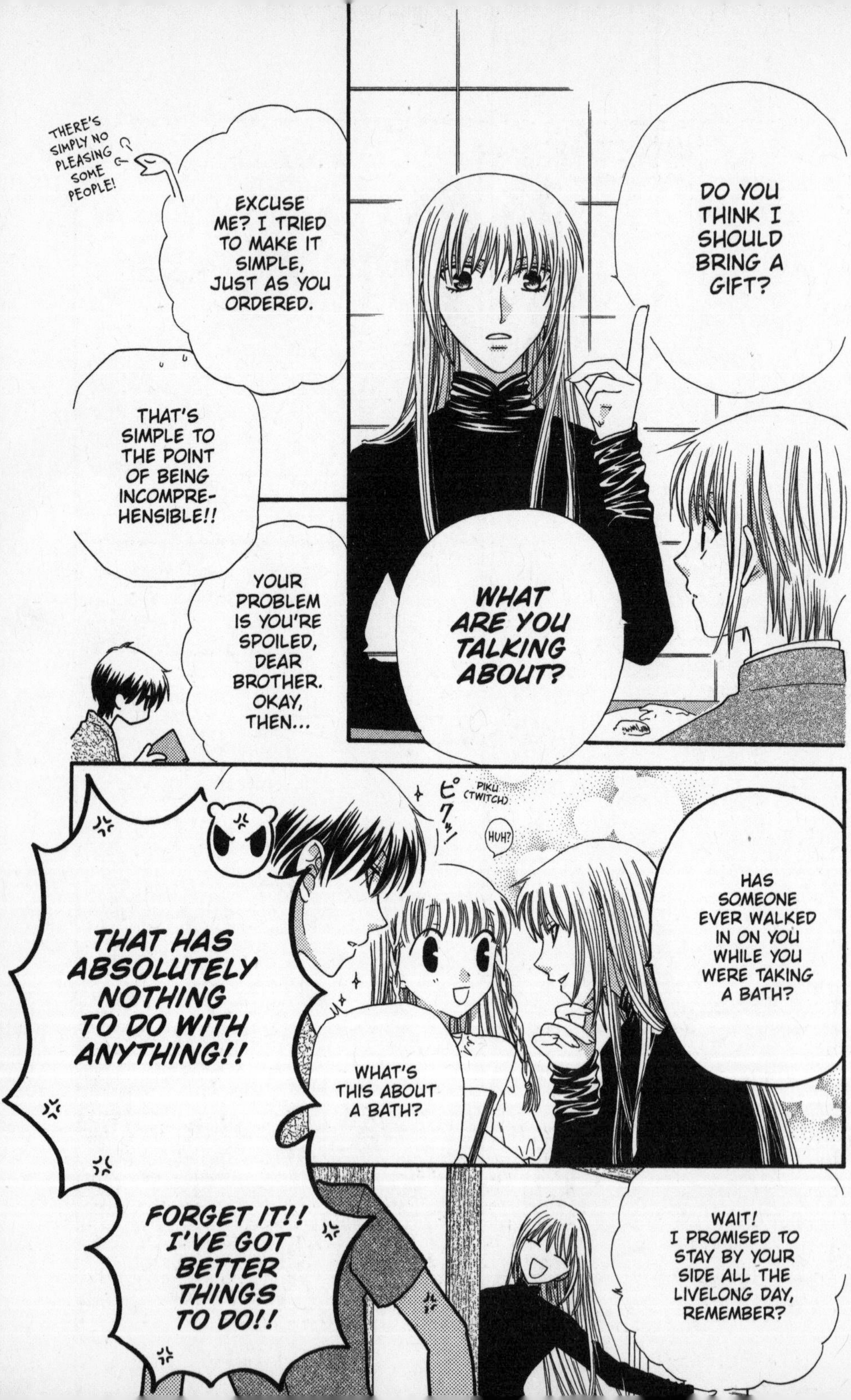
DO YOU THINK I SHOULD BRING A GIFT?
WHAT ARE YOU TALKING ABOUT?
EXCUSE ME? I TRIED TO MAKE IT SIMPLE, JUST AS YOU ORDERED.
THERE'S SIMPLY NO PLEASING SOME PEOPLE!
THAT'S SIMPLE TO THE POINT OF BEING INCOMPRE-HENSIBLE!!
YOUR PROBLEM IS YOU'RE SPOILED, DEAR BROTHER. OKAY, THEN...
HAS SOMEONE EVER WALKED IN ON YOU WHILE YOU WERE TAKING A BATH?
HUH?
ピクッ
PIKU (TWITCH)
WHAT'S THIS ABOUT A BATH?
THAT HAS ABSOLUTELY NOTHING TO DO WITH ANYTHING!!
WAIT! I PROMISED TO STAY BY YOUR SIDE ALL THE LIVELONG DAY, REMEMBER?
FORGET IT!! I'VE GOT BETTER THINGS TO DO!!

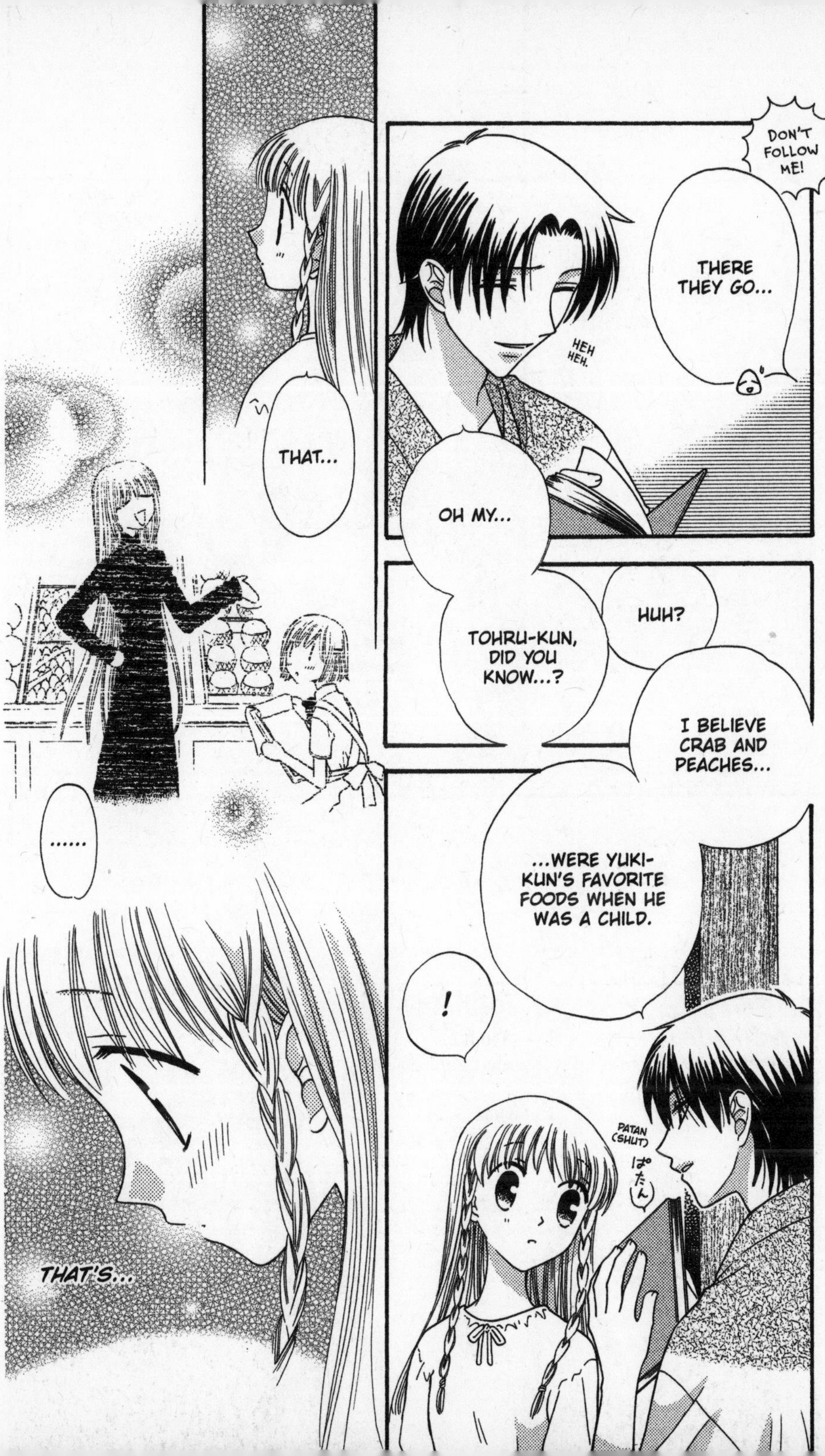
DON'T FOLLOW ME!
THERE THEY GO...
HEH HEH.
OH MY...
TOHRU-KUN, DID YOU KNOW...?
HUH?
I BELIEVE CRAB AND PEACHES...
...WERE YUKI-KUN'S FAVORITE FOODS WHEN HE WAS A CHILD.
!
PATAN (SHUT)
ぱたん
THAT...
......
THAT'S...

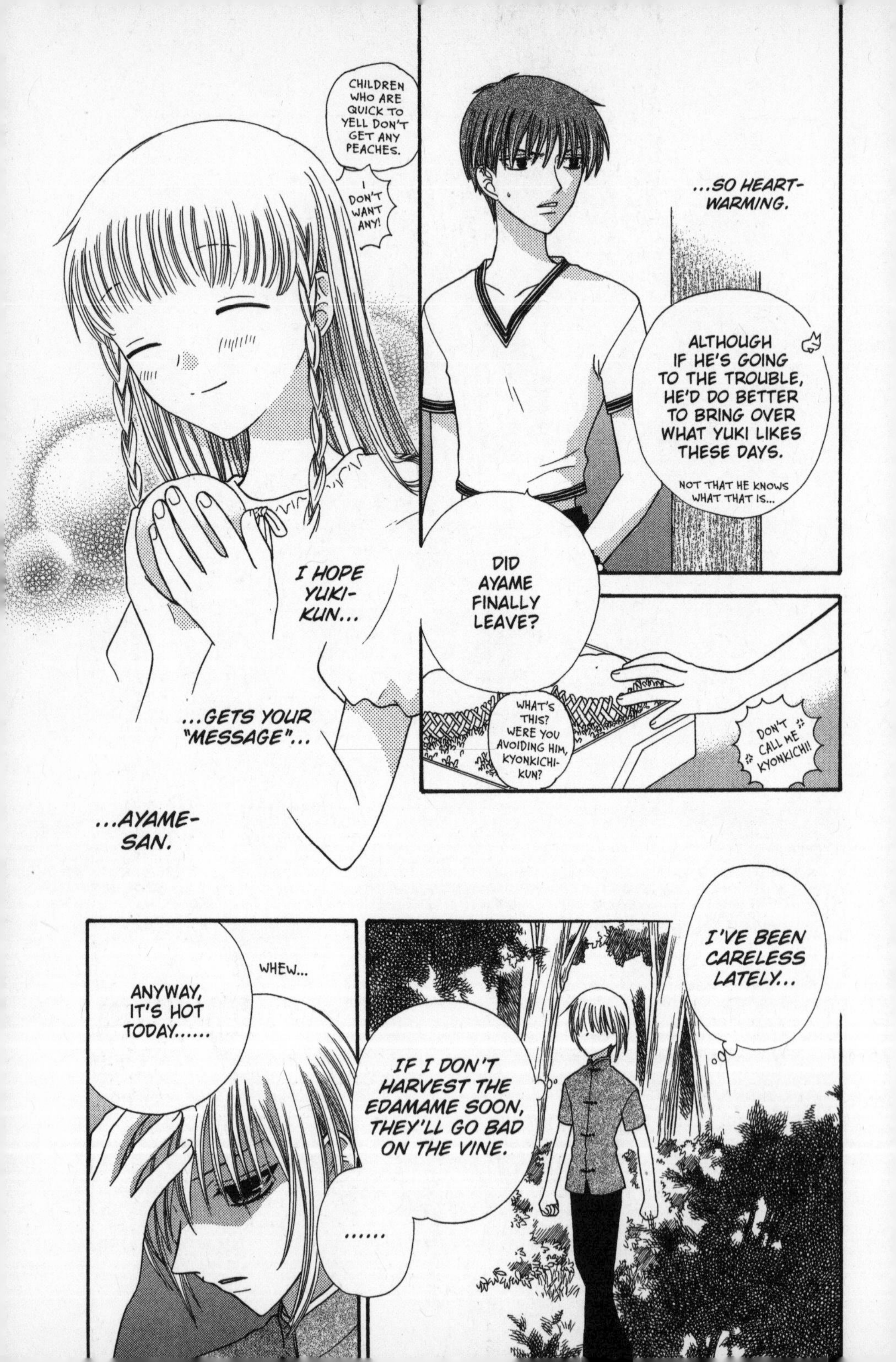
...SO HEART-WARMING.
ALTHOUGH IF HE'S GOING TO THE TROUBLE, HE'D DO BETTER TO BRING OVER WHAT YUKI LIKES THESE DAYS.
NOT THAT HE KNOWS WHAT THAT IS...
CHILDREN WHO ARE QUICK TO YELL DON'T GET ANY PEACHES.
I DON'T WANT ANY!
DID AYAME FINALLY LEAVE?
WHAT'S THIS? WERE YOU AVOIDING HIM, KYONKICHI-KUN?
DON'T CALL ME KYONKICHI!!
I HOPE YUKI-KUN...
...GETS YOUR "MESSAGE"...
...AYAME-SAN.
I'VE BEEN CARELESS LATELY...
IF I DON'T HARVEST THE EDAMAME SOON, THEY'LL GO BAD ON THE VINE.
......
WHEW...
ANYWAY, IT'S HOT TODAY......

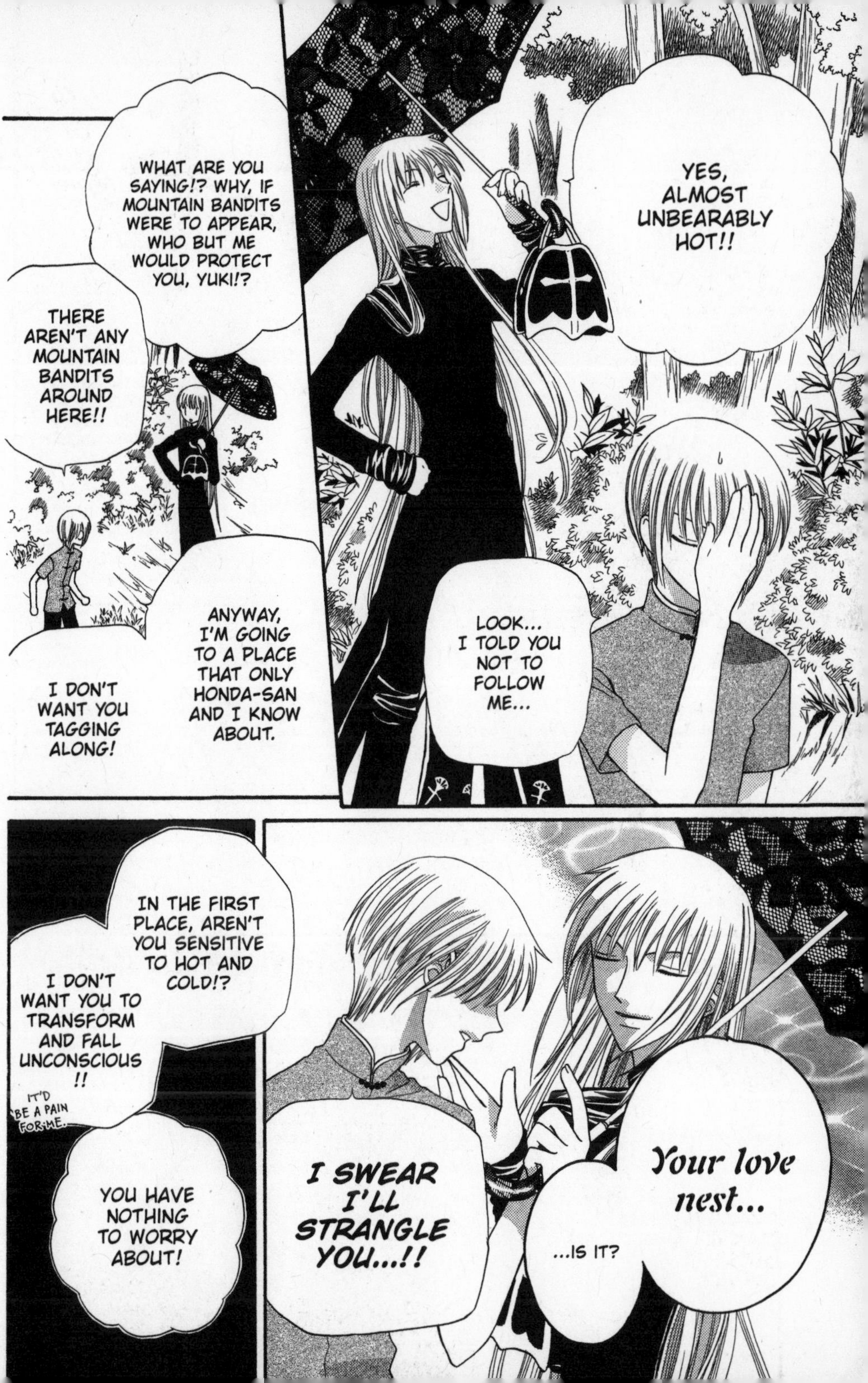

YES, ALMOST UNBEARABLY HOT!!
LOOK... I TOLD YOU NOT TO FOLLOW ME...
WHAT ARE YOU SAYING!? WHY, IF MOUNTAIN BANDITS WERE TO APPEAR, WHO BUT ME WOULD PROTECT YOU, YUKI!?
THERE AREN'T ANY MOUNTAIN BANDITS AROUND HERE!!
ANYWAY, I'M GOING TO A PLACE THAT ONLY HONDA-SAN AND I KNOW ABOUT.
I DON'T WANT YOU TAGGING ALONG!
Your love nest...
...IS IT?
I SWEAR I'LL STRANGLE YOU...!!
IN THE FIRST PLACE, AREN'T YOU SENSITIVE TO HOT AND COLD!?
I DON'T WANT YOU TO TRANSFORM AND FALL UNCONSCIOUS!!
IT'D BE A PAIN FOR ME.
YOU HAVE NOTHING TO WORRY ABOUT!

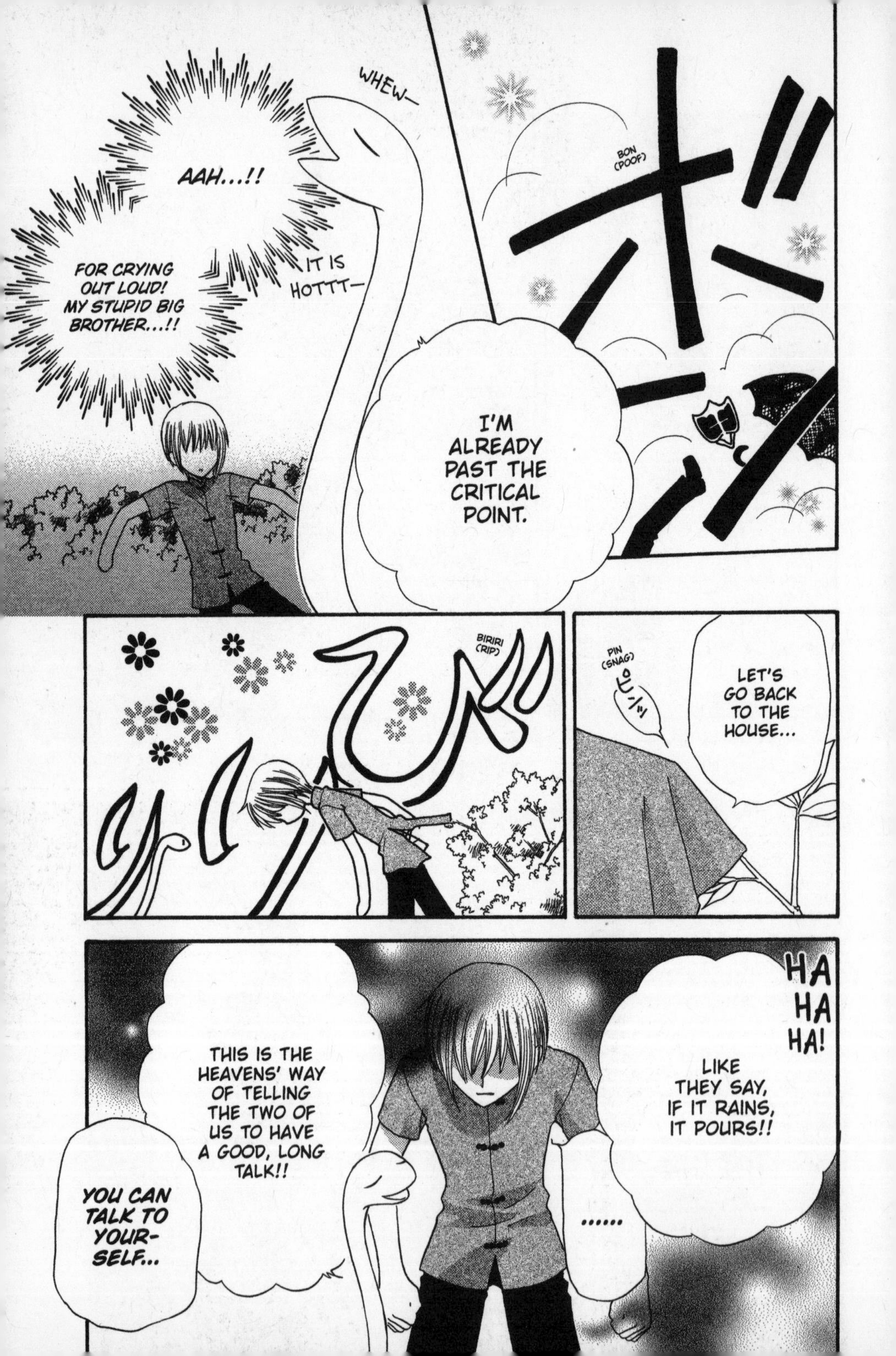
BON (POOF)
WHEW—
AAH...!!
IT IS HOTTT—
FOR CRYING OUT LOUD! MY STUPID BIG BROTHER...!!
I'M ALREADY PAST THE CRITICAL POINT.
PIN (SNAG)
LET'S GO BACK TO THE HOUSE...
BIRIRI (RIP)
HA HA HA!
LIKE THEY SAY, IF IT RAINS, IT POURS!!
......
THIS IS THE HEAVENS' WAY OF TELLING THE TWO OF US TO HAVE A GOOD, LONG TALK!!
YOU CAN TALK TO YOURSELF...

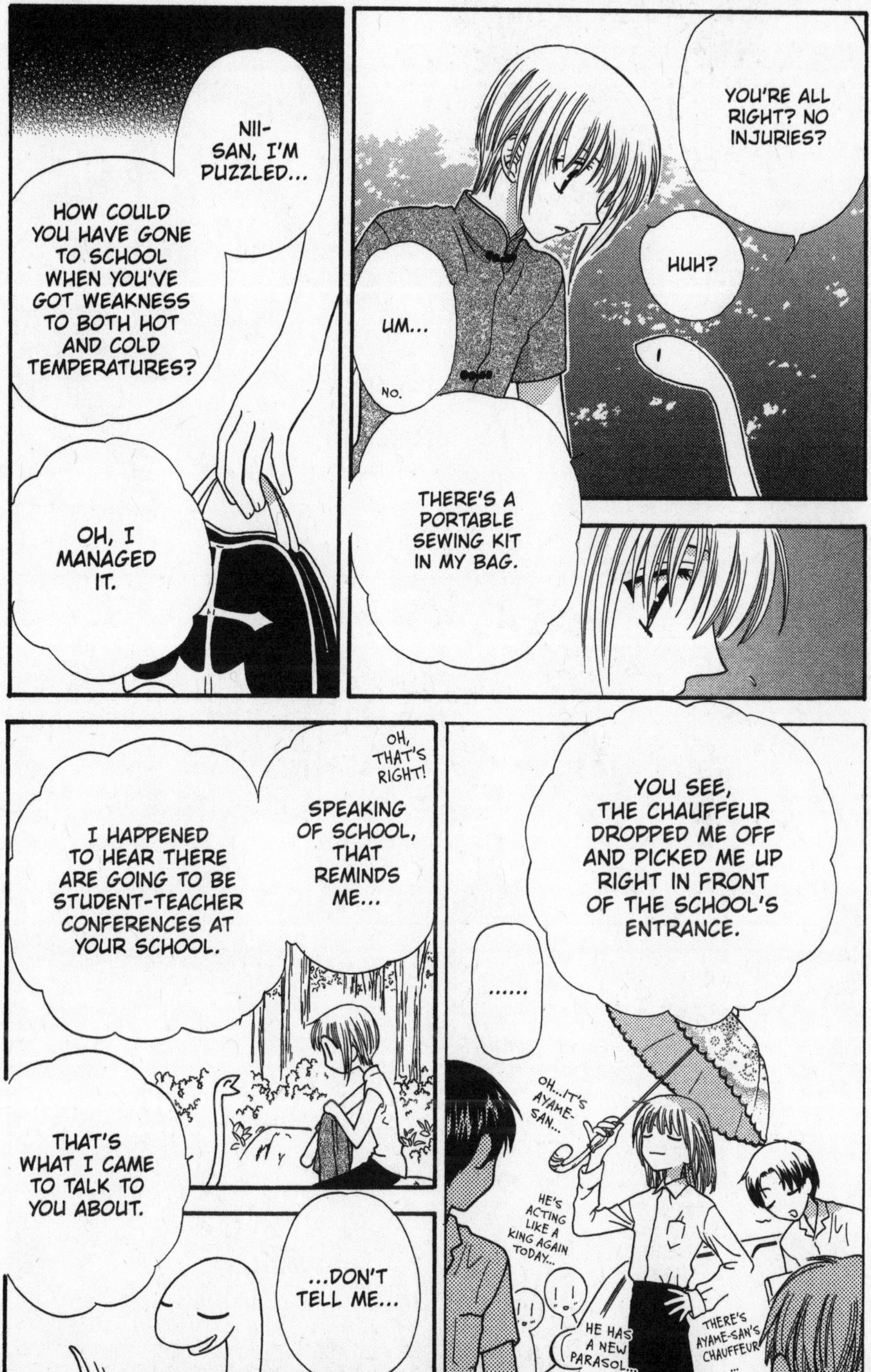
YOU'RE ALL RIGHT? NO INJURIES?
HUH?
UM...
NO.
THERE'S A PORTABLE SEWING KIT IN MY BAG.
NII-SAN, I'M PUZZLED...
HOW COULD YOU HAVE GONE TO SCHOOL WHEN YOU'VE GOT WEAKNESS TO BOTH HOT AND COLD TEMPERATURES?
OH, I MANAGED IT.
YOU SEE, THE CHAUFFEUR DROPPED ME OFF AND PICKED ME UP RIGHT IN FRONT OF THE SCHOOL'S ENTRANCE.
......
OH...IT'S AYAME-SAN...
HE'S ACTING LIKE A KING AGAIN TODAY...
THERE'S AYAME-SAN'S CHAUFFEUR...
HE HAS A NEW PARASOL...
OH, THAT'S RIGHT!
SPEAKING OF SCHOOL, THAT REMINDS ME...
I HAPPENED TO HEAR THERE ARE GOING TO BE STUDENT-TEACHER CONFERENCES AT YOUR SCHOOL.
THAT'S WHAT I CAME TO TALK TO YOU ABOUT.
...DON'T TELL ME...

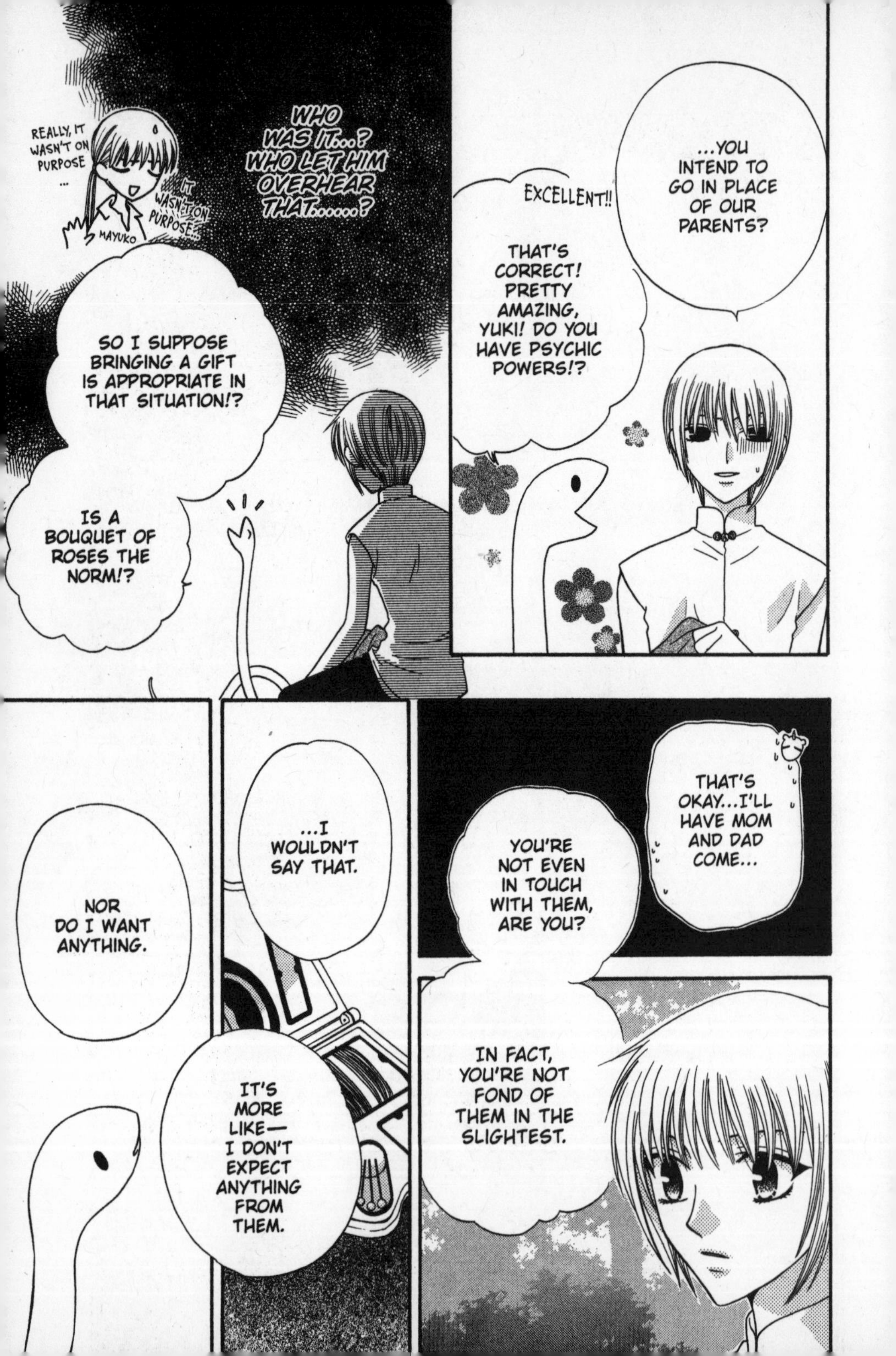
...YOU INTEND TO GO IN PLACE OF OUR PARENTS?
EXCELLENT!!
THAT'S CORRECT! PRETTY AMAZING, YUKI! DO YOU HAVE PSYCHIC POWERS!?
WHO WAS IT...? WHO LET HIM OVERHEAR THAT......?
REALLY, IT WASN'T ON PURPOSE ...
IT WASN'T ON PURPOSE...
MAYUKO
SO I SUPPOSE BRINGING A GIFT IS APPROPRIATE IN THAT SITUATION!?
IS A BOUQUET OF ROSES THE NORM!?
THAT'S OKAY...I'LL HAVE MOM AND DAD COME...
YOU'RE NOT EVEN IN TOUCH WITH THEM, ARE YOU?
IN FACT, YOU'RE NOT FOND OF THEM IN THE SLIGHTEST.
...I WOULDN'T SAY THAT.
IT'S MORE LIKE— I DON'T EXPECT ANYTHING FROM THEM.
NOR DO I WANT ANYTHING.

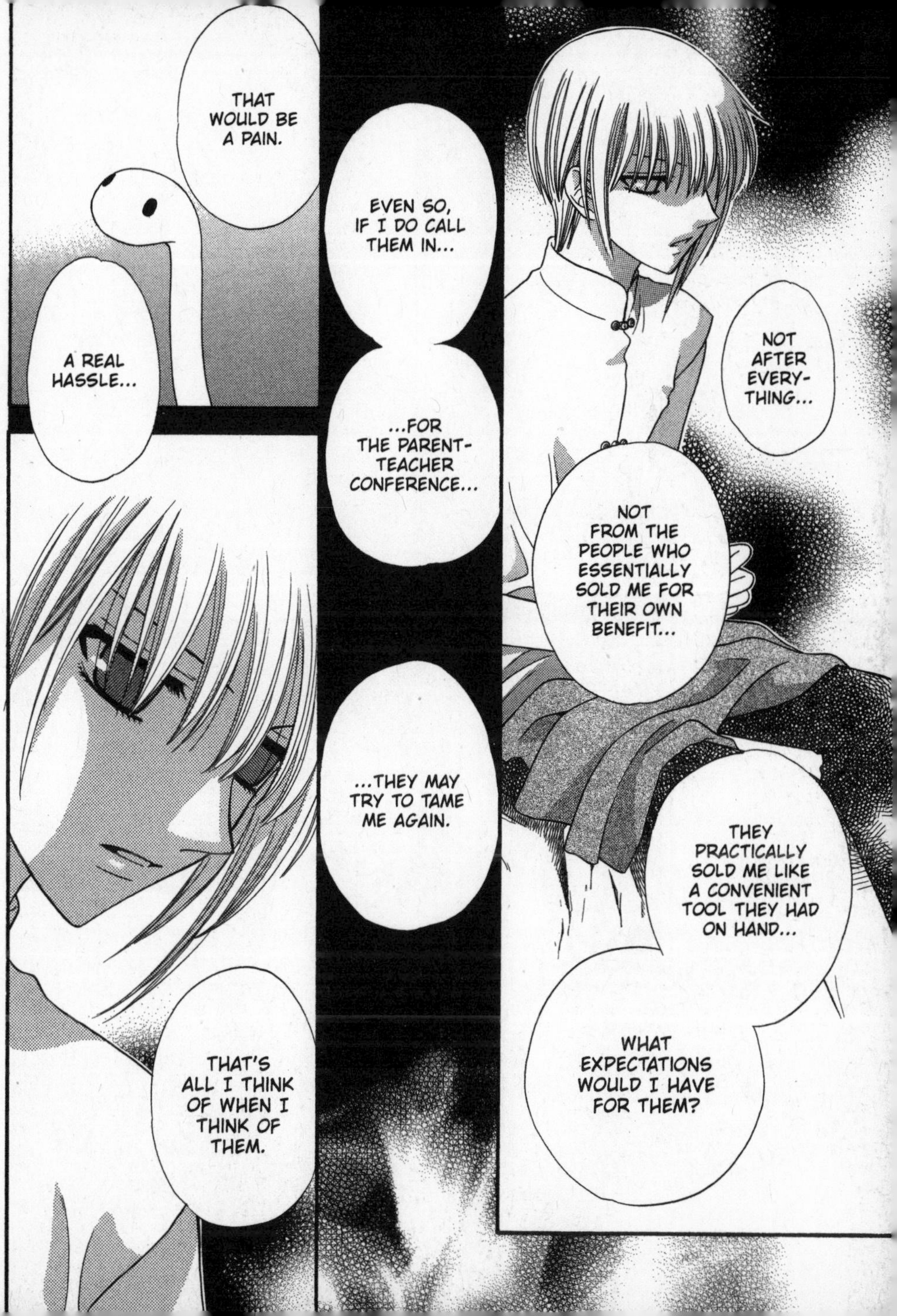
NOT AFTER EVERY-THING...
NOT FROM THE PEOPLE WHO ESSENTIALLY SOLD ME FOR THEIR OWN BENEFIT...
THEY PRACTICALLY SOLD ME LIKE A CONVENIENT TOOL THEY HAD ON HAND...
WHAT EXPECTATIONS WOULD I HAVE FOR THEM?
EVEN SO, IF I DO CALL THEM IN...
...FOR THE PARENT-TEACHER CONFERENCE...
...THEY MAY TRY TO TAME ME AGAIN.
THAT WOULD BE A PAIN.
A REAL HASSLE...
THAT'S ALL I THINK OF WHEN I THINK OF THEM.

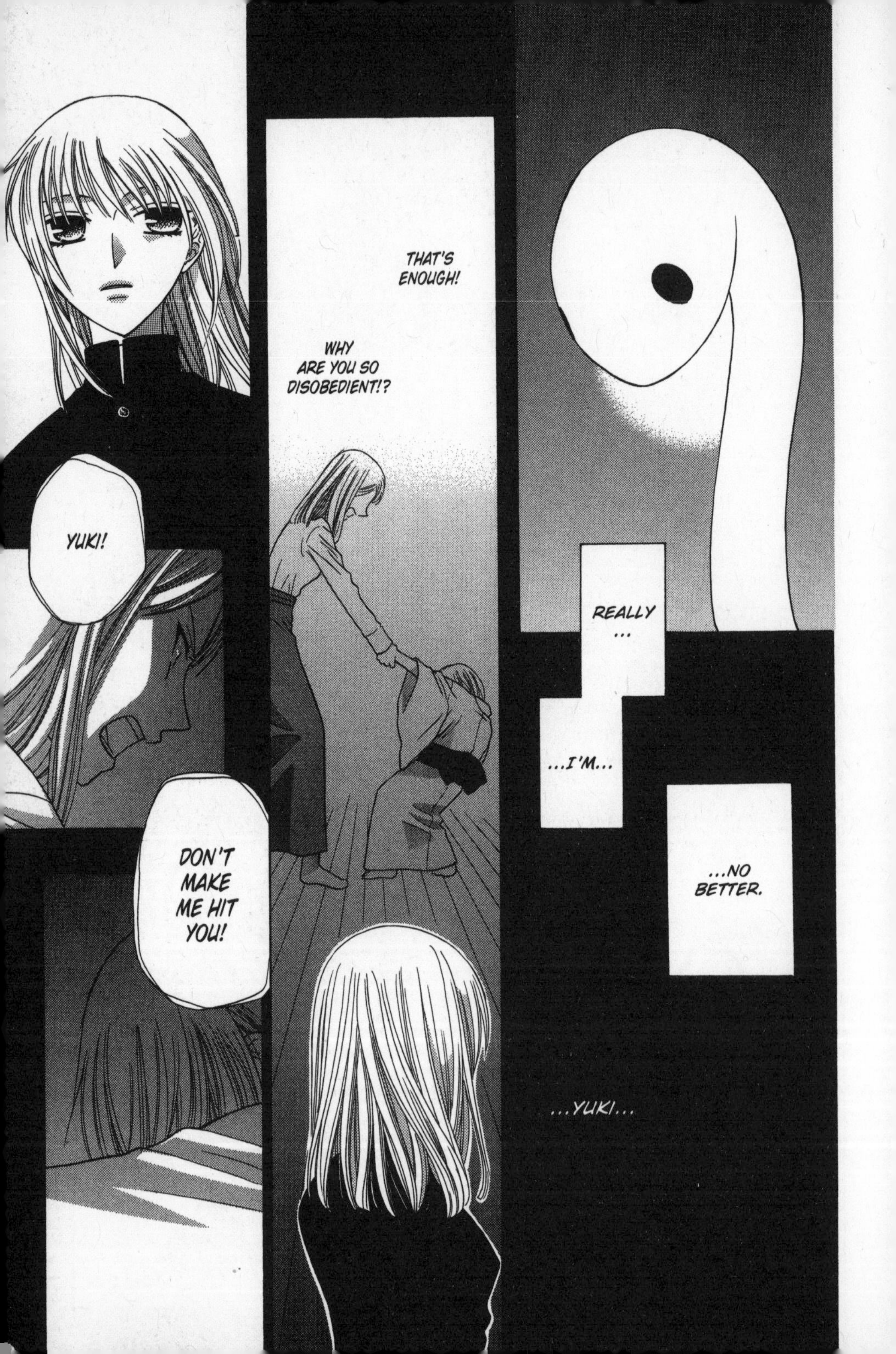
REALLY...
...I'M...
...NO BETTER.
...YUKI...
THAT'S ENOUGH!
WHY ARE YOU SO DISOBEDIENT!?
YUKI!
DON'T MAKE ME HIT YOU!

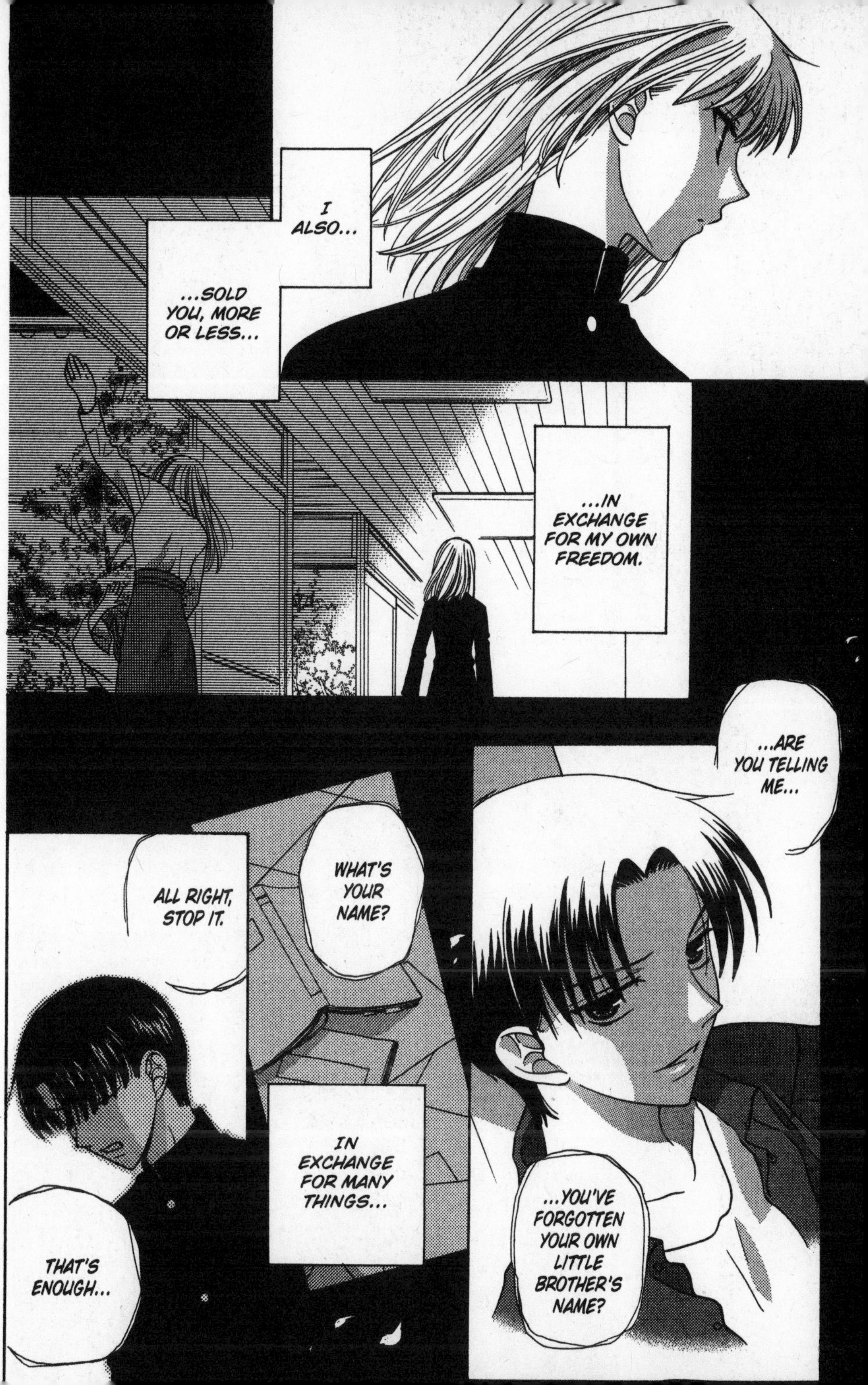
I ALSO...
...SOLD YOU, MORE OR LESS...
...IN EXCHANGE FOR MY OWN FREEDOM.
...ARE YOU TELLING ME...
...YOU'VE FORGOTTEN YOUR OWN LITTLE BROTHER'S NAME?
WHAT'S YOUR NAME?
IN EXCHANGE FOR MANY THINGS...
ALL RIGHT, STOP IT.
THAT'S ENOUGH...

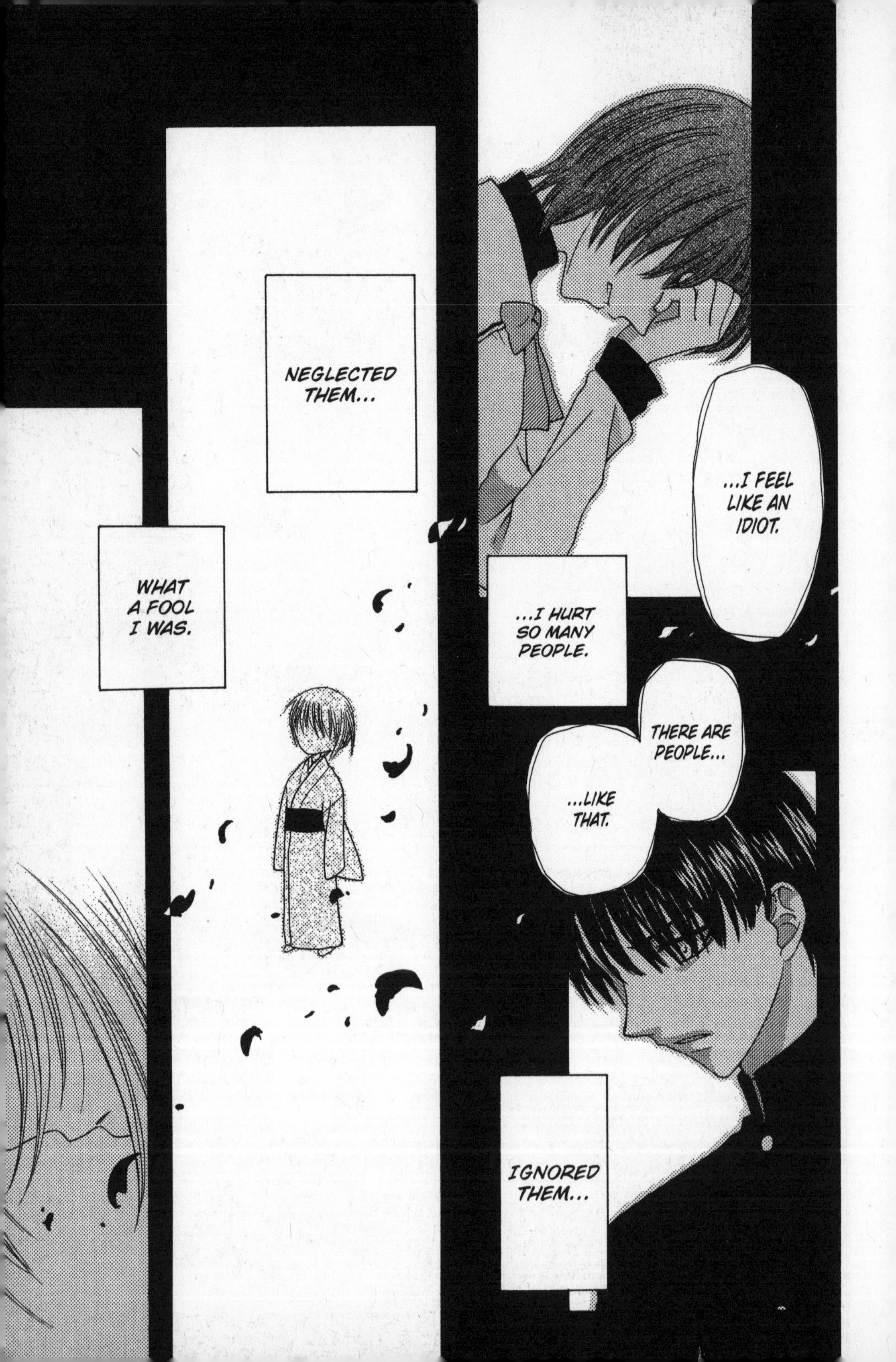
...I FEEL LIKE AN IDIOT.
...I HURT SO MANY PEOPLE.
THERE ARE PEOPLE...
...LIKE THAT.
IGNORED THEM...
NEGLECTED THEM...
WHAT A FOOL I WAS.

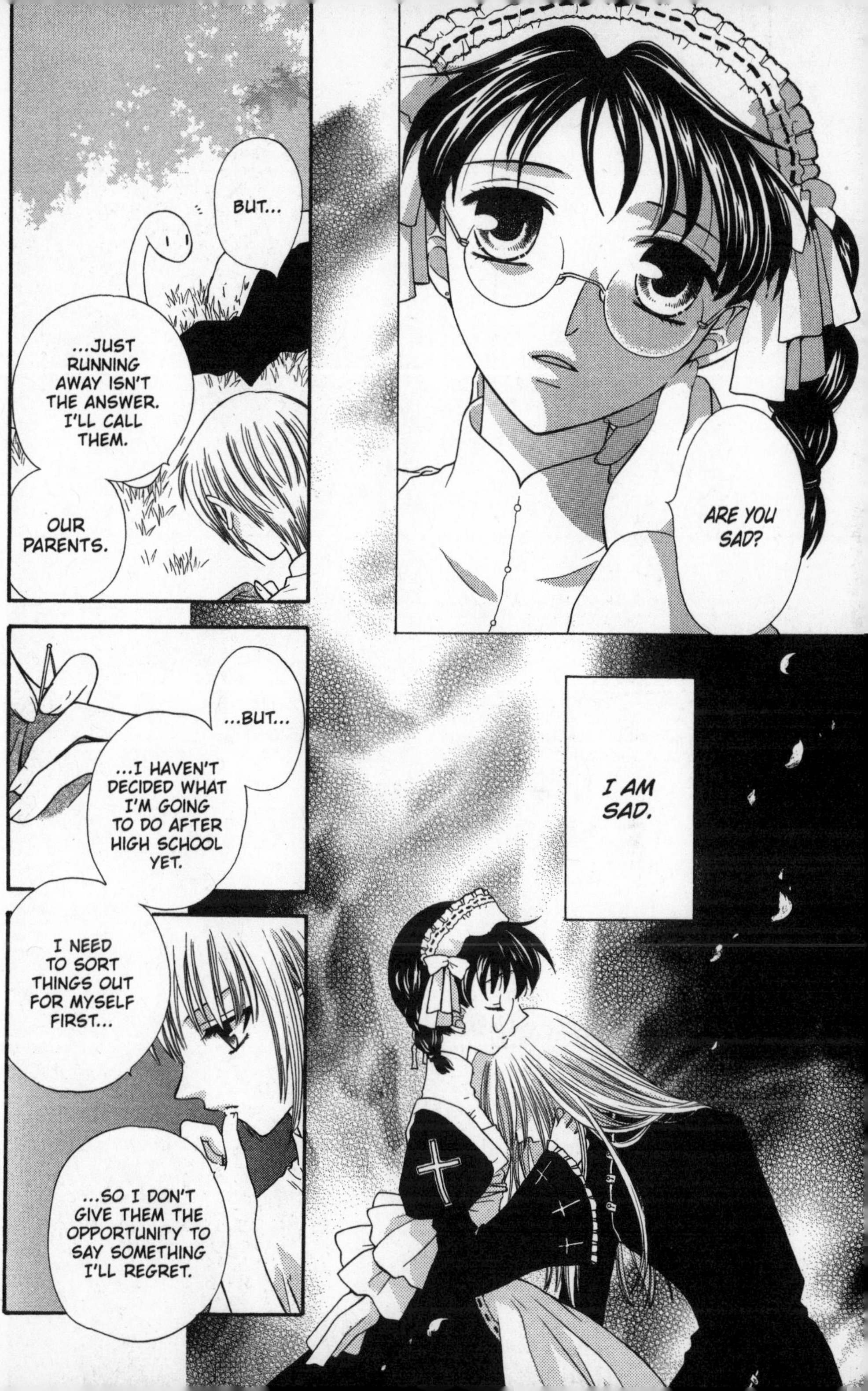
ARE YOU SAD?
BUT...
...JUST RUNNING AWAY ISN'T THE ANSWER. I'LL CALL THEM.
OUR PARENTS.
I AM SAD.
...BUT...
...I HAVEN'T DECIDED WHAT I'M GOING TO DO AFTER HIGH SCHOOL YET.
I NEED TO SORT THINGS OUT FOR MYSELF FIRST...
...SO I DON'T GIVE THEM THE OPPORTUNITY TO SAY SOMETHING I'LL REGRET.

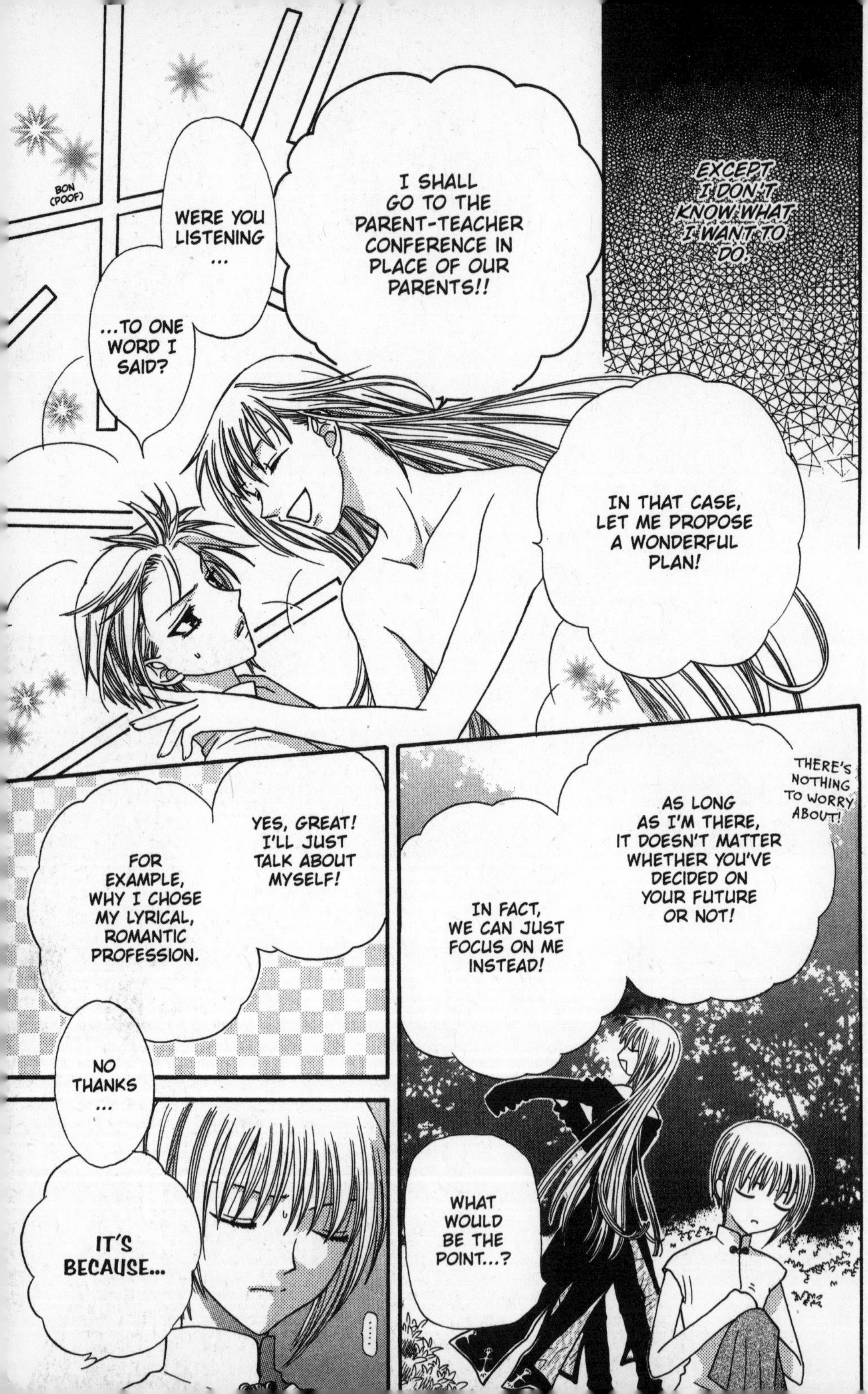
EXCEPT I DON'T KNOW WHAT I WANT TO DO.
IN THAT CASE, LET ME PROPOSE A WONDERFUL PLAN!
I SHALL GO TO THE PARENT-TEACHER CONFERENCE IN PLACE OF OUR PARENTS!!
BON (POOF)
WERE YOU LISTENING ...
...TO ONE WORD I SAID?
THERE'S NOTHING TO WORRY ABOUT!
AS LONG AS I'M THERE, IT DOESN'T MATTER WHETHER YOU'VE DECIDED ON YOUR FUTURE OR NOT!
IN FACT, WE CAN JUST FOCUS ON ME INSTEAD!
WHAT WOULD BE THE POINT...?
YES, GREAT! I'LL JUST TALK ABOUT MYSELF!
FOR EXAMPLE, WHY I CHOSE MY LYRICAL, ROMANTIC PROFESSION.
NO THANKS ...
IT'S BECAUSE...
...

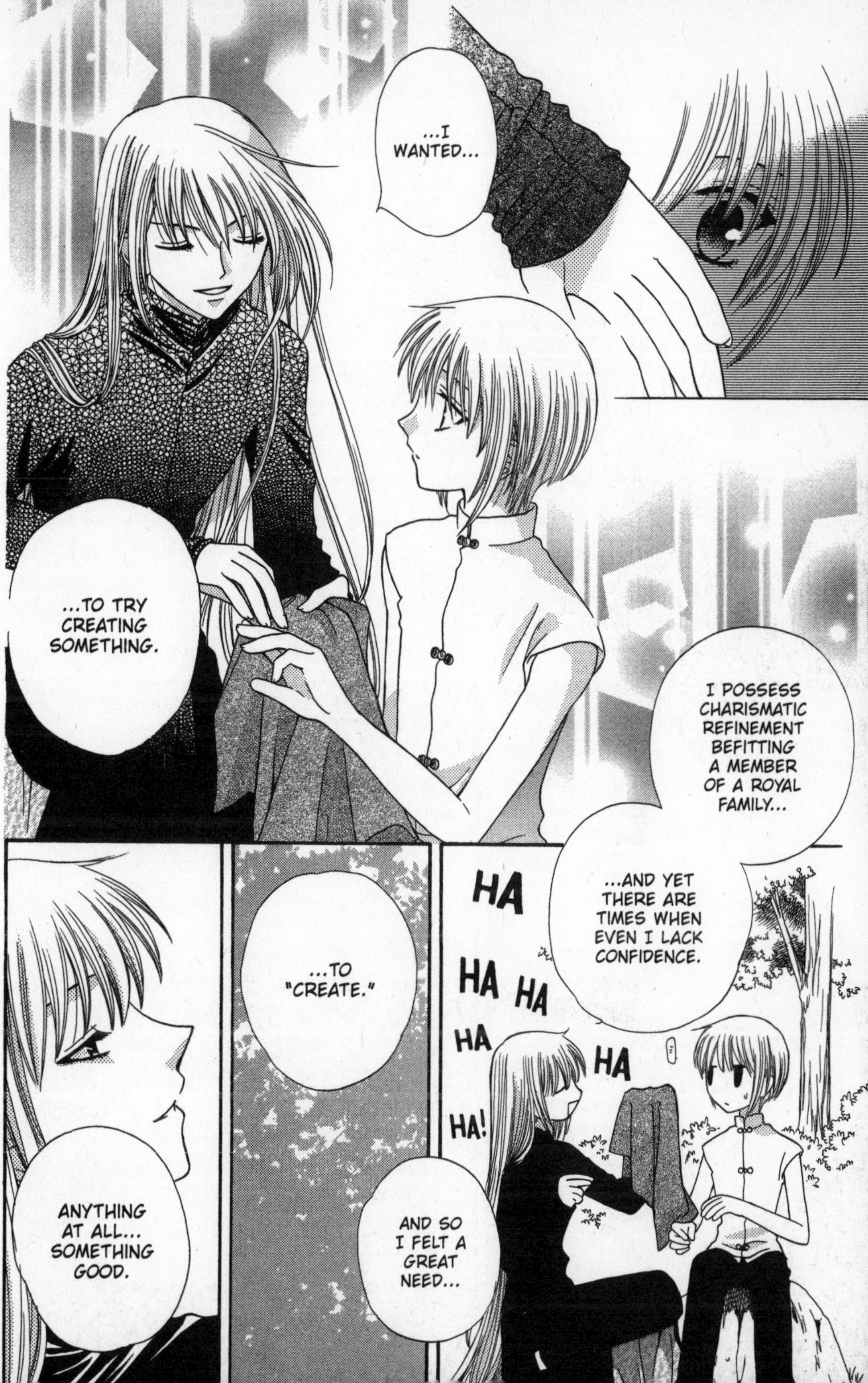

...I WANTED...
...TO TRY CREATING SOMETHING.
I POSSESS CHARISMATIC REFINEMENT BEFITTING A MEMBER OF A ROYAL FAMILY...
...AND YET THERE ARE TIMES WHEN EVEN I LACK CONFIDENCE.
HA HA HA HA HA HA!
AND SO I FELT A GREAT NEED...
...TO "CREATE."
ANYTHING AT ALL... SOMETHING GOOD.

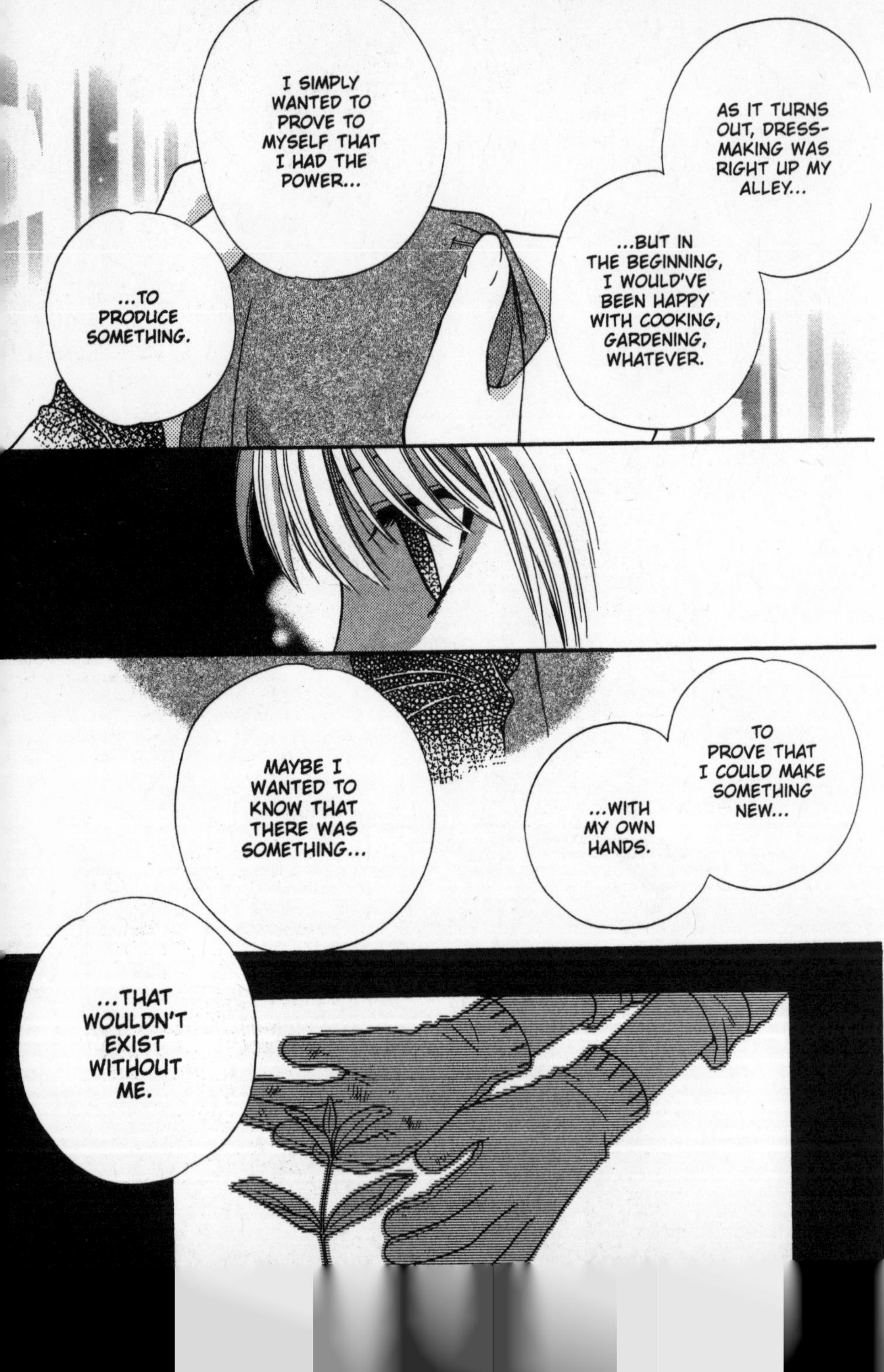
AS IT TURNS OUT, DRESS-MAKING WAS RIGHT UP MY ALLEY...
...BUT IN THE BEGINNING, I WOULD'VE BEEN HAPPY WITH COOKING, GARDENING, WHATEVER.
I SIMPLY WANTED TO PROVE TO MYSELF THAT I HAD THE POWER...
...TO PRODUCE SOMETHING.
TO PROVE THAT I COULD MAKE SOMETHING NEW...
...WITH MY OWN HANDS.
MAYBE I WANTED TO KNOW THAT THERE WAS SOMETHING...
...THAT WOULDN'T EXIST WITHOUT ME.

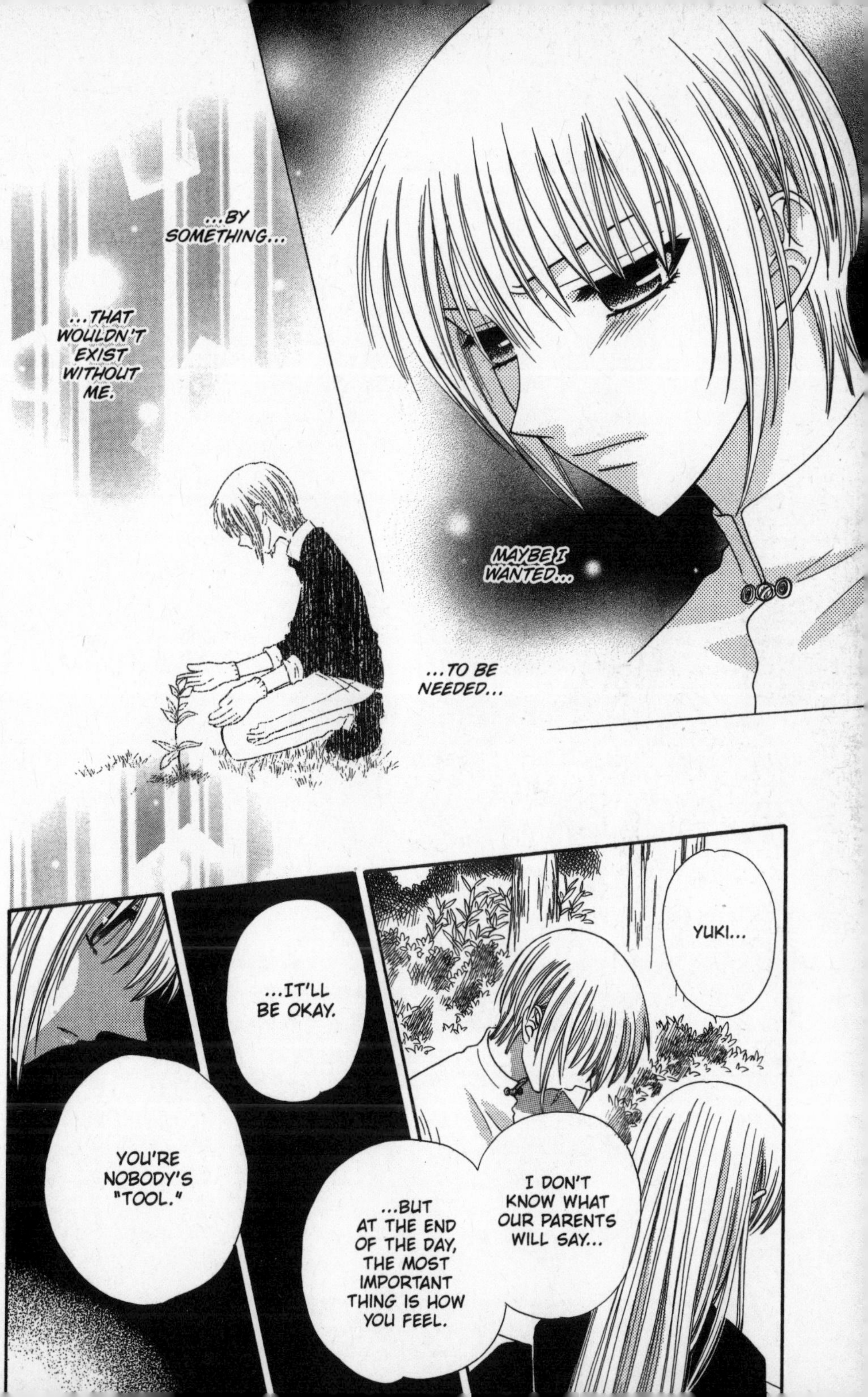
MAYBE I WANTED...
...TO BE NEEDED...
...BY SOMETHING...
...THAT WOULDN'T EXIST WITHOUT ME.
YUKI...
I DON'T KNOW WHAT OUR PARENTS WILL SAY...
...BUT AT THE END OF THE DAY, THE MOST IMPORTANT THING IS HOW YOU FEEL.
...IT'LL BE OKAY.
YOU'RE NOBODY'S "TOOL."

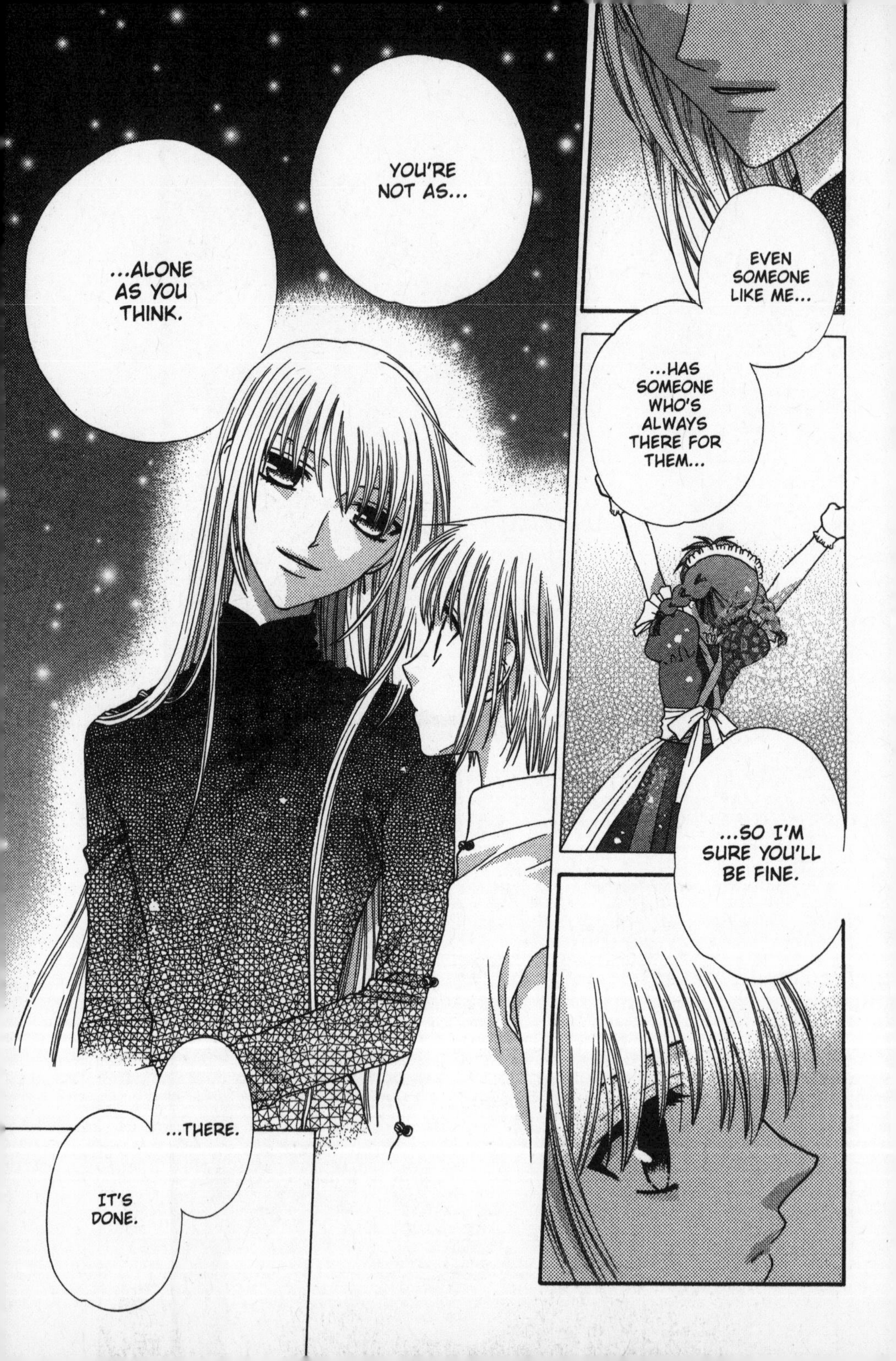
EVEN SOMEONE LIKE ME...
...HAS SOMEONE WHO'S ALWAYS THERE FOR THEM...
...SO I'M SURE YOU'LL BE FINE.
YOU'RE NOT AS...
...ALONE AS YOU THINK.
...THERE.
IT'S DONE.

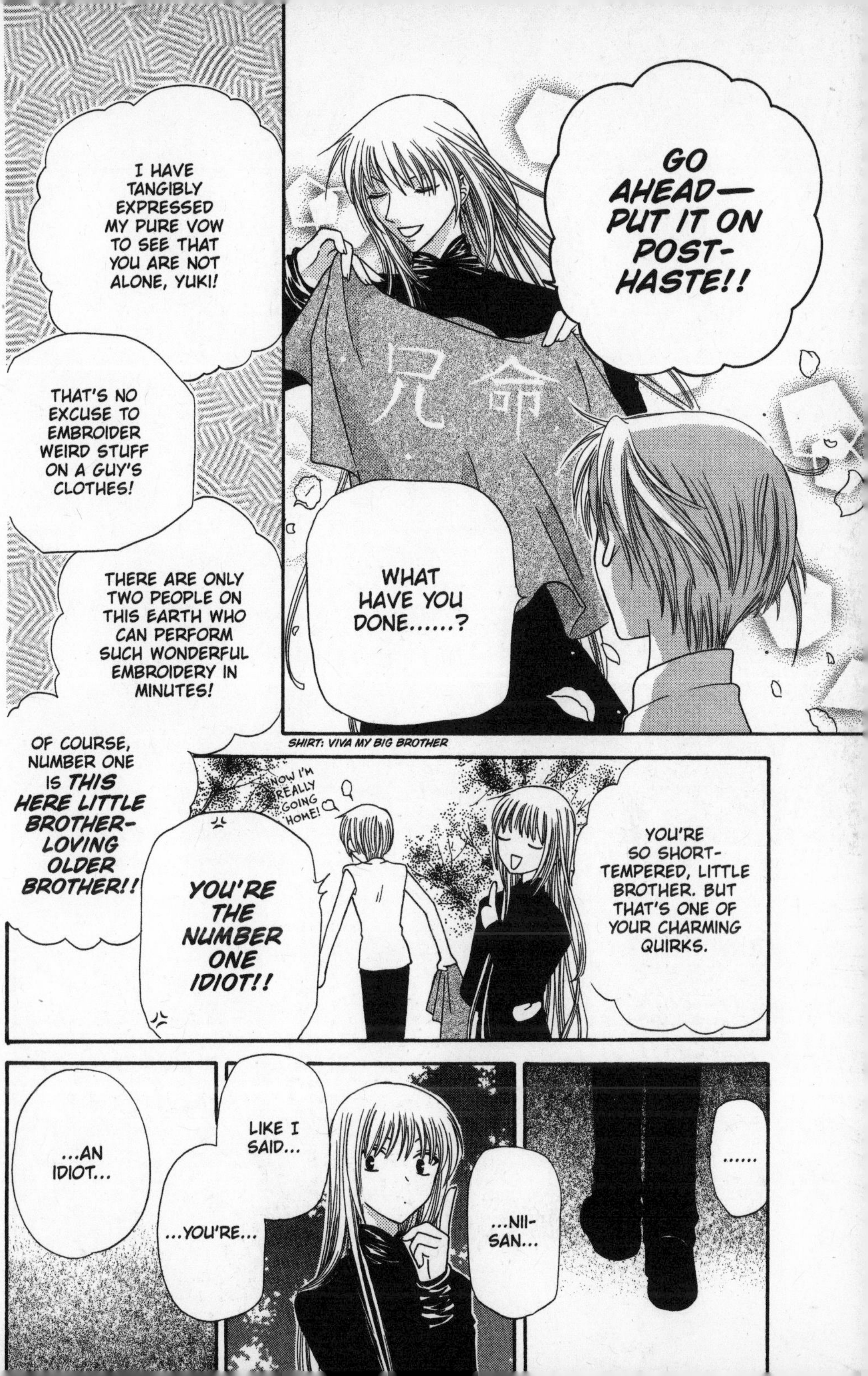
GO AHEAD— PUT IT ON POST-HASTE!!
WHAT HAVE YOU DONE......?
I HAVE TANGIBLY EXPRESSED MY PURE VOW TO SEE THAT YOU ARE NOT ALONE, YUKI!
THAT'S NO EXCUSE TO EMBROIDER WEIRD STUFF ON A GUY'S CLOTHES!
THERE ARE ONLY TWO PEOPLE ON THIS EARTH WHO CAN PERFORM SUCH WONDERFUL EMBROIDERY IN MINUTES!
SHIRT: VIVA MY BIG BROTHER
OF COURSE, NUMBER ONE IS THIS HERE LITTLE BROTHER-LOVING OLDER BROTHER!!
YOU'RE THE NUMBER ONE IDIOT!!
NOW I'M REALLY GOING HOME!
YOU'RE SO SHORT-TEMPERED, LITTLE BROTHER. BUT THAT'S ONE OF YOUR CHARMING QUIRKS.
......
...NII-SAN...
LIKE I SAID...
...YOU'RE...
...AN IDIOT...

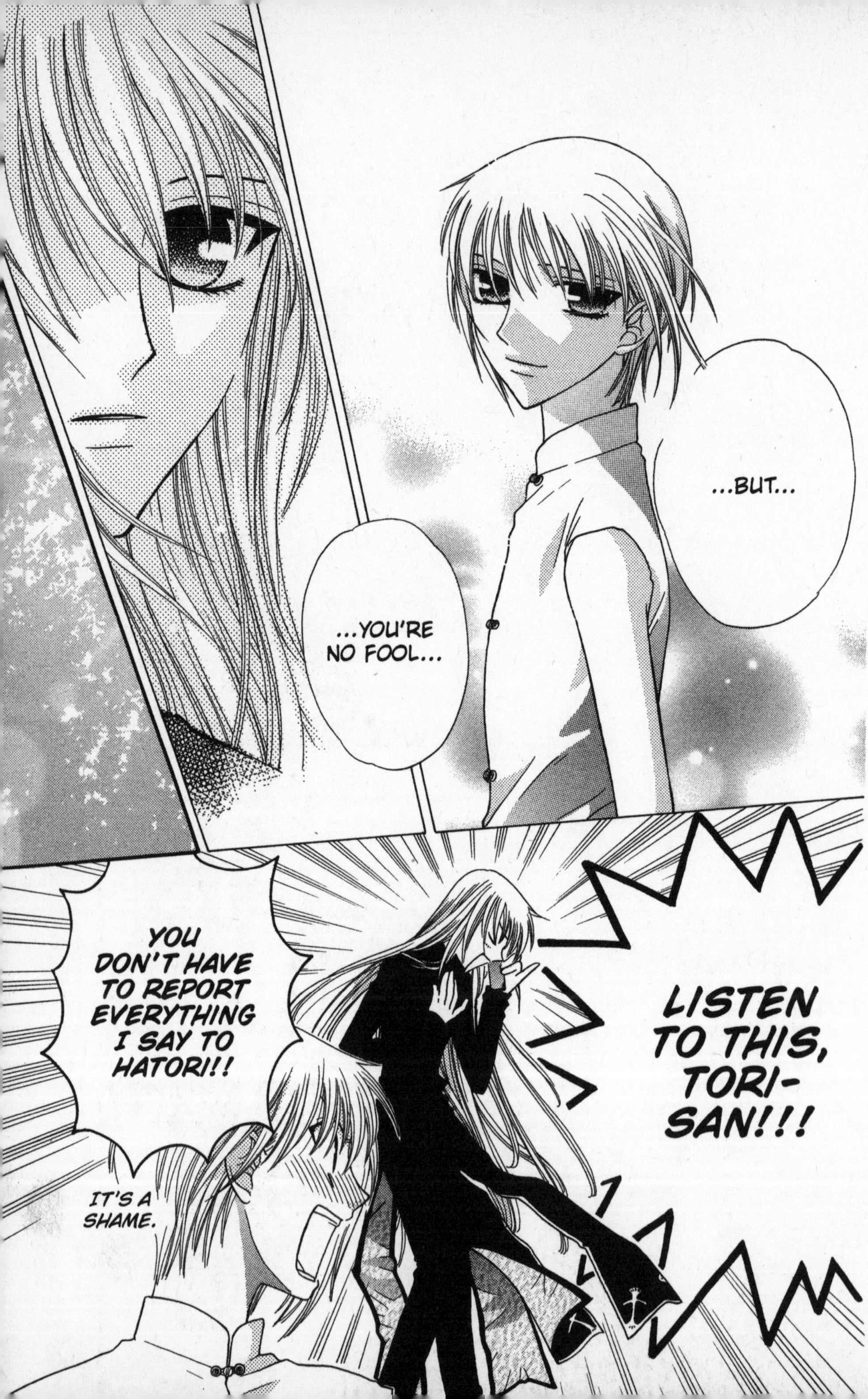

...BUT...
...YOU'RE NO FOOL...
LISTEN TO THIS, TORI-SAN!!!
YOU DON'T HAVE TO REPORT EVERYTHING I SAY TO HATORI!!
IT'S A SHAME.

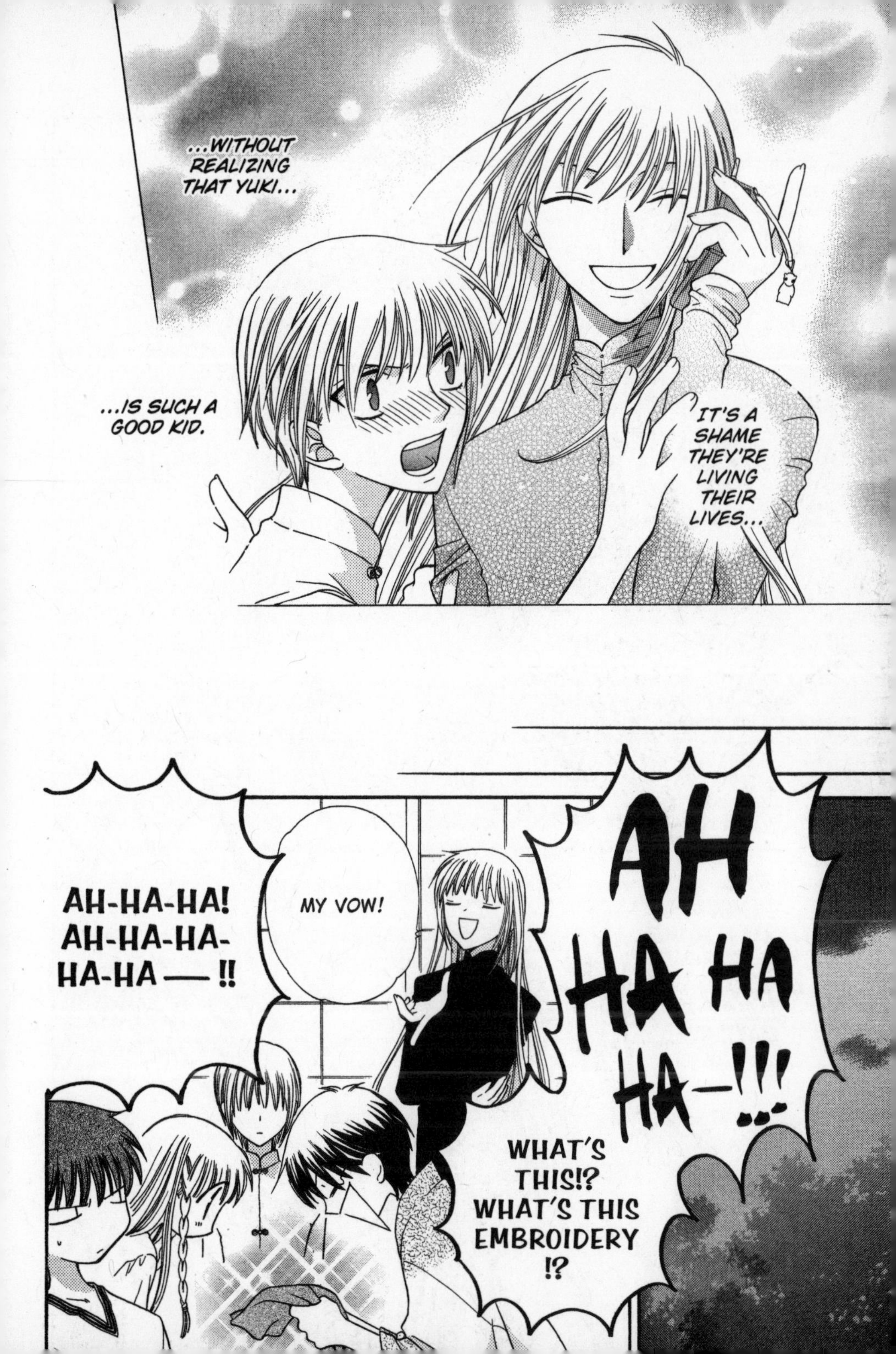

IT'S A SHAME THEY'RE LIVING THEIR LIVES...
...WITHOUT REALIZING THAT YUKI...
...IS SUCH A GOOD KID.
AH HA HA HA HA—!!!
WHAT'S THIS!? WHAT'S THIS EMBROIDERY !?
MY VOW!
AH-HA-HA! AH-HA-HA-HA-HA— !!

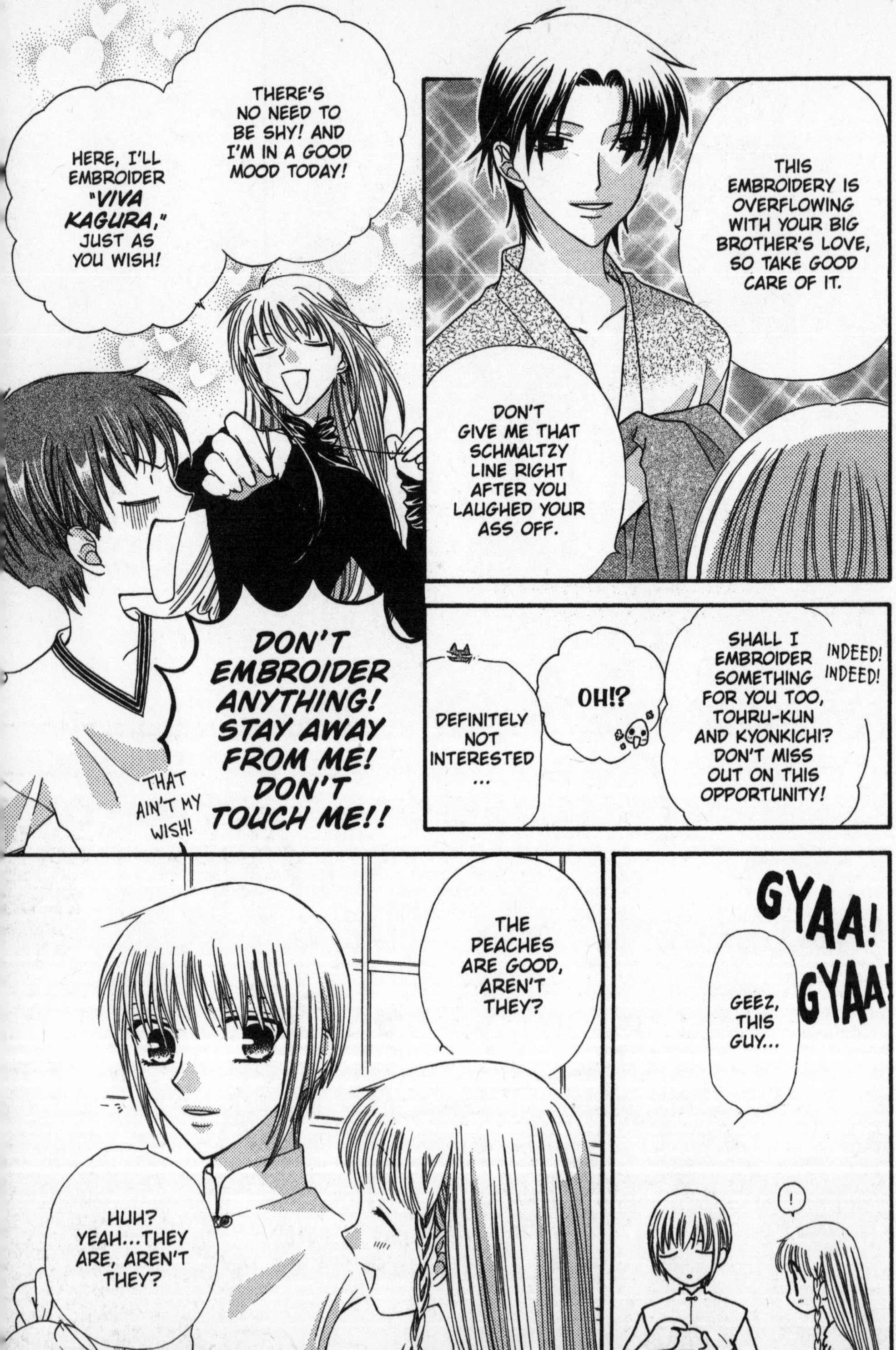
THIS EMBROIDERY IS OVERFLOWING WITH YOUR BIG BROTHER'S LOVE, SO TAKE GOOD CARE OF IT.
DON'T GIVE ME THAT SCHMALTZY LINE RIGHT AFTER YOU LAUGHED YOUR ASS OFF.
INDEED! INDEED!
SHALL I EMBROIDER SOMETHING FOR YOU TOO, TOHRU-KUN AND KYONKICHI? DON'T MISS OUT ON THIS OPPORTUNITY!
OH!?
DEFINITELY NOT INTERESTED ...
THERE'S NO NEED TO BE SHY! AND I'M IN A GOOD MOOD TODAY!
HERE, I'LL EMBROIDER "VIVA KAGURA," JUST AS YOU WISH!
DON'T EMBROIDER ANYTHING! STAY AWAY FROM ME! DON'T TOUCH ME!!
THAT AIN'T MY WISH!
GYAA! GYAA!
GEEZ, THIS GUY...
!
THE PEACHES ARE GOOD, AREN'T THEY?
HUH? YEAH...THEY ARE, AREN'T THEY?

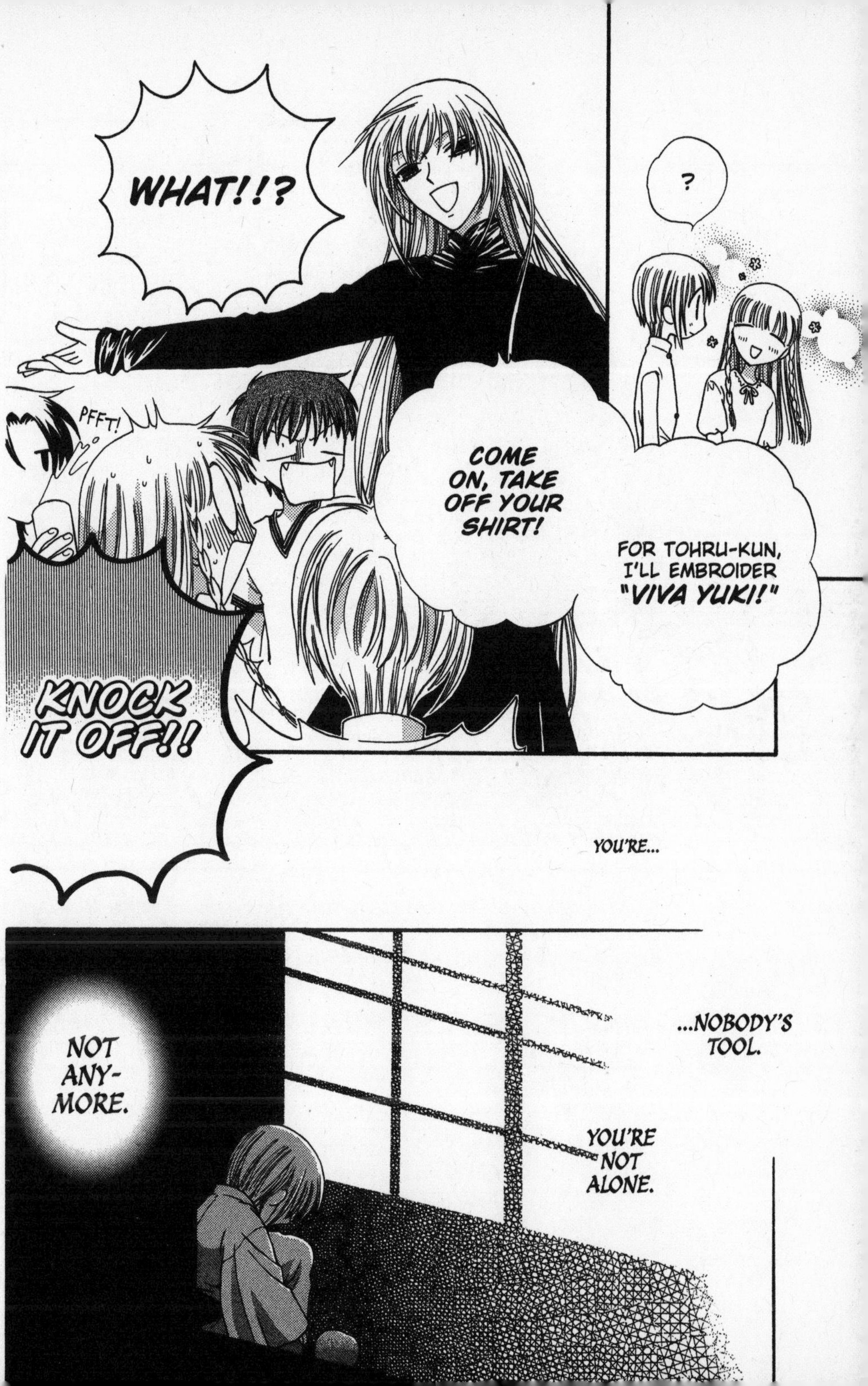
?
FOR TOHRU-KUN, I'LL EMBROIDER "VIVA YUKI!"
COME ON, TAKE OFF YOUR SHIRT!
WHAT!!?
PFFT!
KNOCK IT OFF!!
YOU'RE...
...NOBODY'S TOOL.
YOU'RE NOT ALONE.
NOT ANY-MORE.

COLLECTOR'S EDITION

Fruits Basket

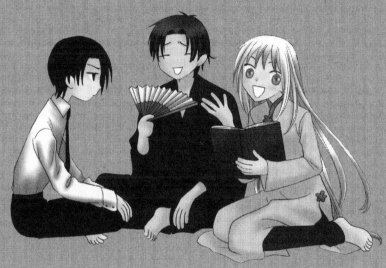

COLLECTOR'S EDITION

Fruits
Basket

Chapter 48

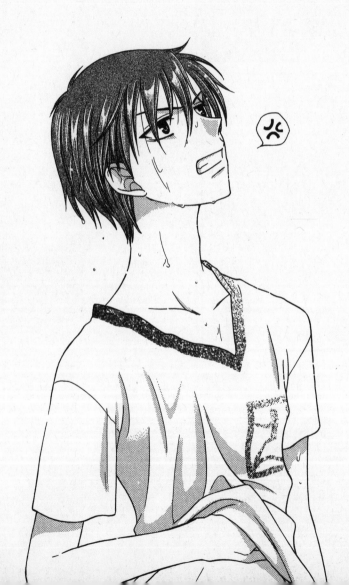

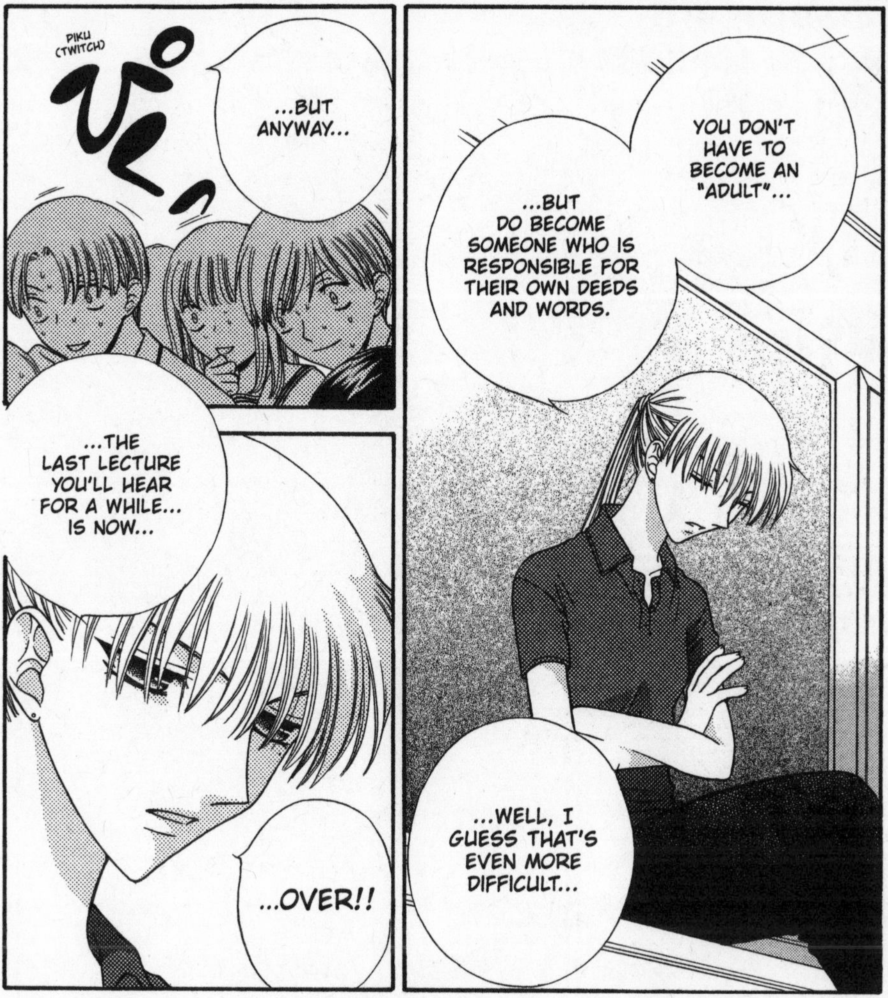
YOU DON'T HAVE TO BECOME AN "ADULT"...
...BUT DO BECOME SOMEONE WHO IS RESPONSIBLE FOR THEIR OWN DEEDS AND WORDS.
...WELL, I GUESS THAT'S EVEN MORE DIFFICULT...
PIKU (TWITCH)
...BUT ANYWAY...
...THE LAST LECTURE YOU'LL HEAR FOR A WHILE... IS NOW...
...OVER!!

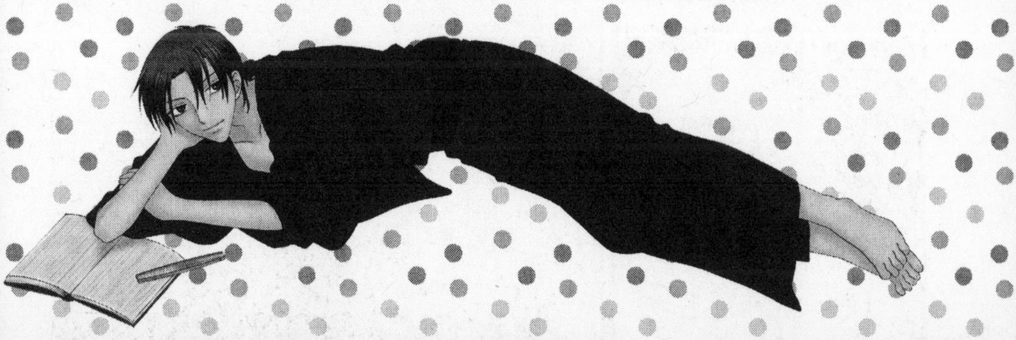

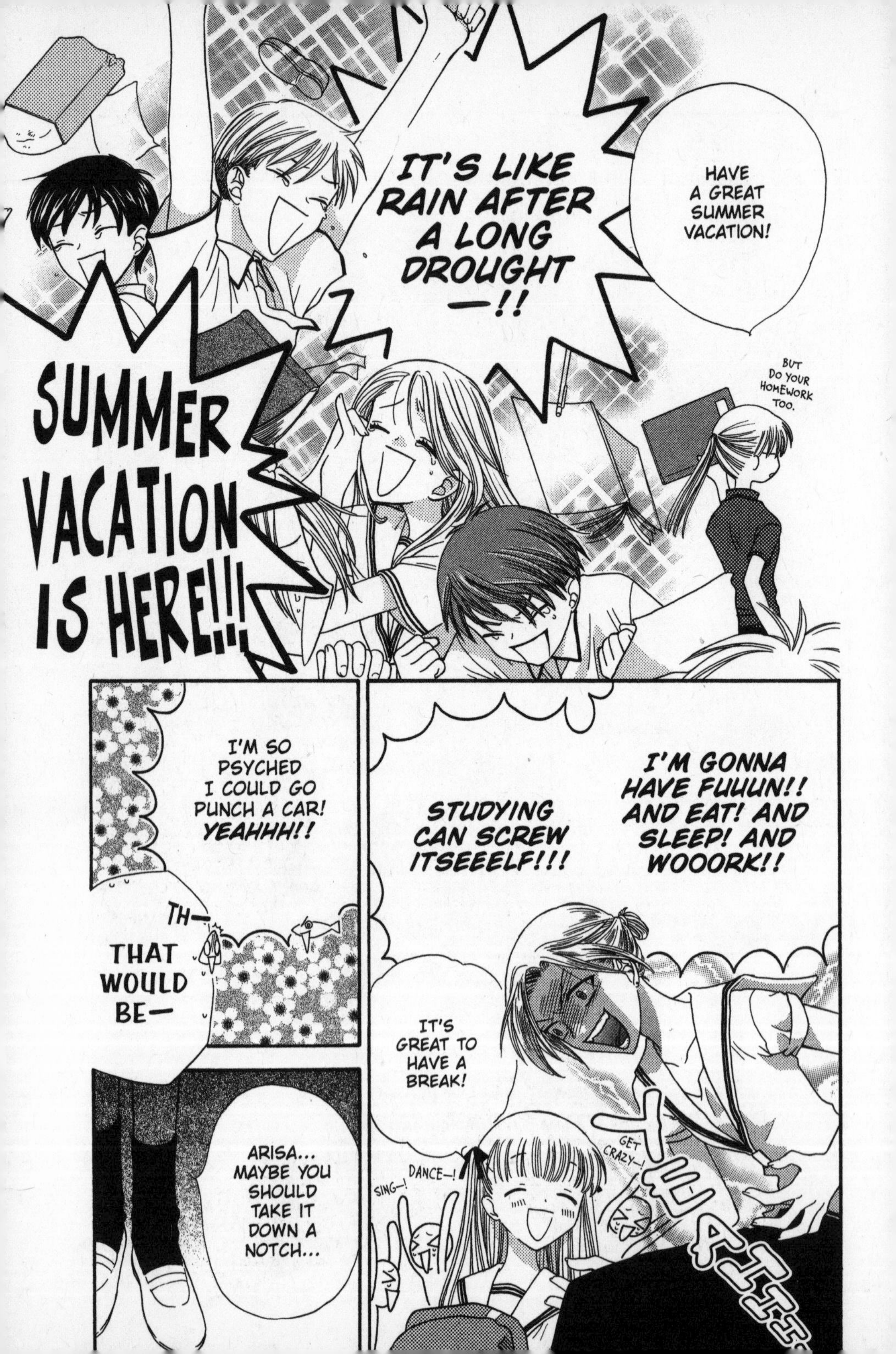
HAVE A GREAT SUMMER VACATION!
BUT DO YOUR HOMEWORK TOO.
IT'S LIKE RAIN AFTER A LONG DROUGHT—!!
SUMMER VACATION IS HERE!!!
I'M GONNA HAVE FUUUN!! AND EAT! AND SLEEP! AND WOOORK!!
STUDYING CAN SCREW ITSEEELF!!!
GET CRAZY—!
IT'S GREAT TO HAVE A BREAK!
DANCE—!
SING—!
I'M SO PSYCHED I COULD GO PUNCH A CAR! YEAHHH!!
TH— THAT WOULD BE—
ARISA... MAYBE YOU SHOULD TAKE IT DOWN A NOTCH...

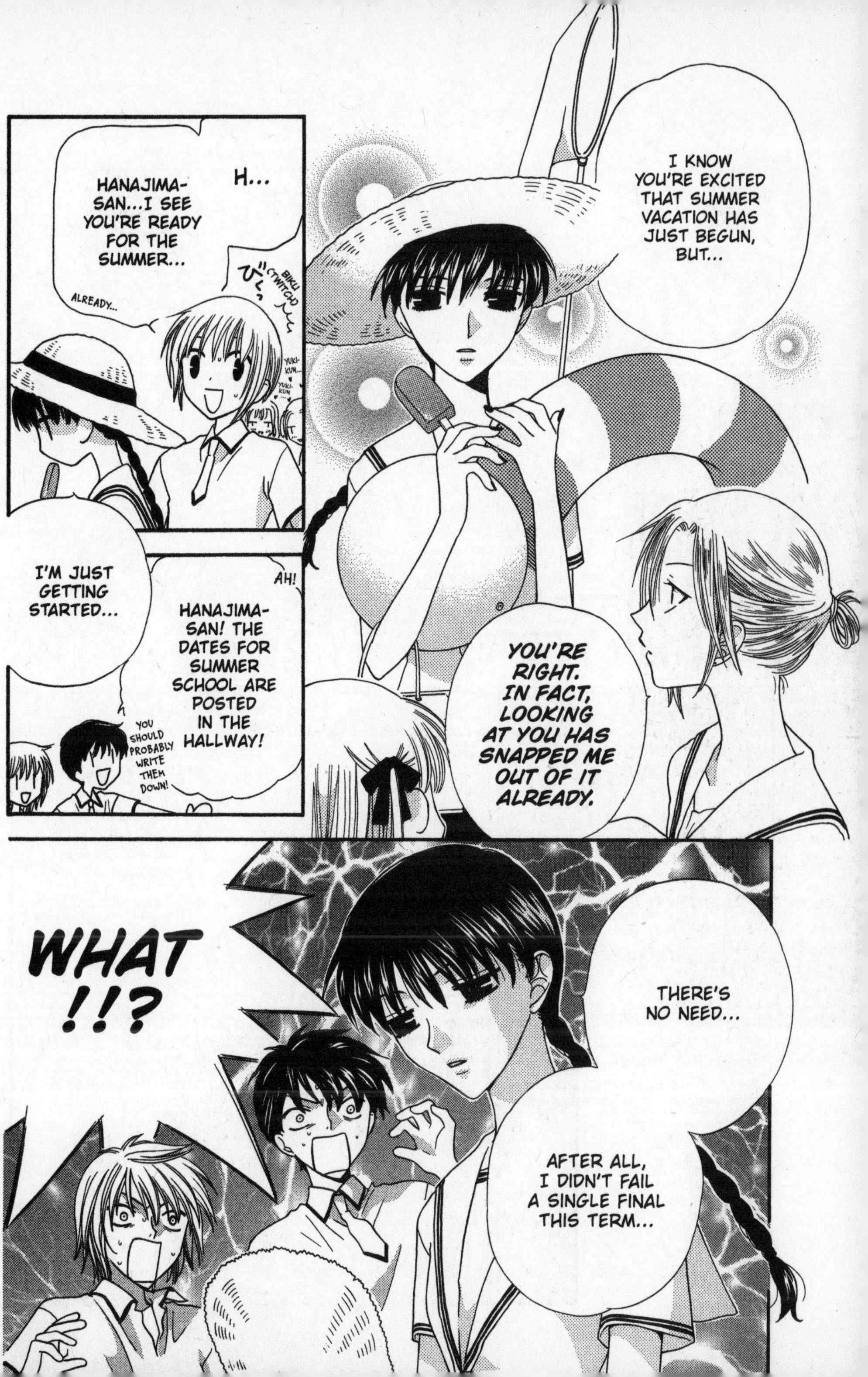
I KNOW YOU'RE EXCITED THAT SUMMER VACATION HAS JUST BEGUN, BUT...
YOU'RE RIGHT. IN FACT, LOOKING AT YOU HAS SNAPPED ME OUT OF IT ALREADY.
I'M JUST GETTING STARTED...
H...
HANAJIMA-SAN...I SEE YOU'RE READY FOR THE SUMMER...
ALREADY...
BIKU (TWITCH)
YUKI-KUN
YUKI-KUN
AH!
HANAJIMA-SAN! THE DATES FOR SUMMER SCHOOL ARE POSTED IN THE HALLWAY!
YOU SHOULD PROBABLY WRITE THEM DOWN!
THERE'S NO NEED...
AFTER ALL, I DIDN'T FAIL A SINGLE FINAL THIS TERM...
WHAT !!?

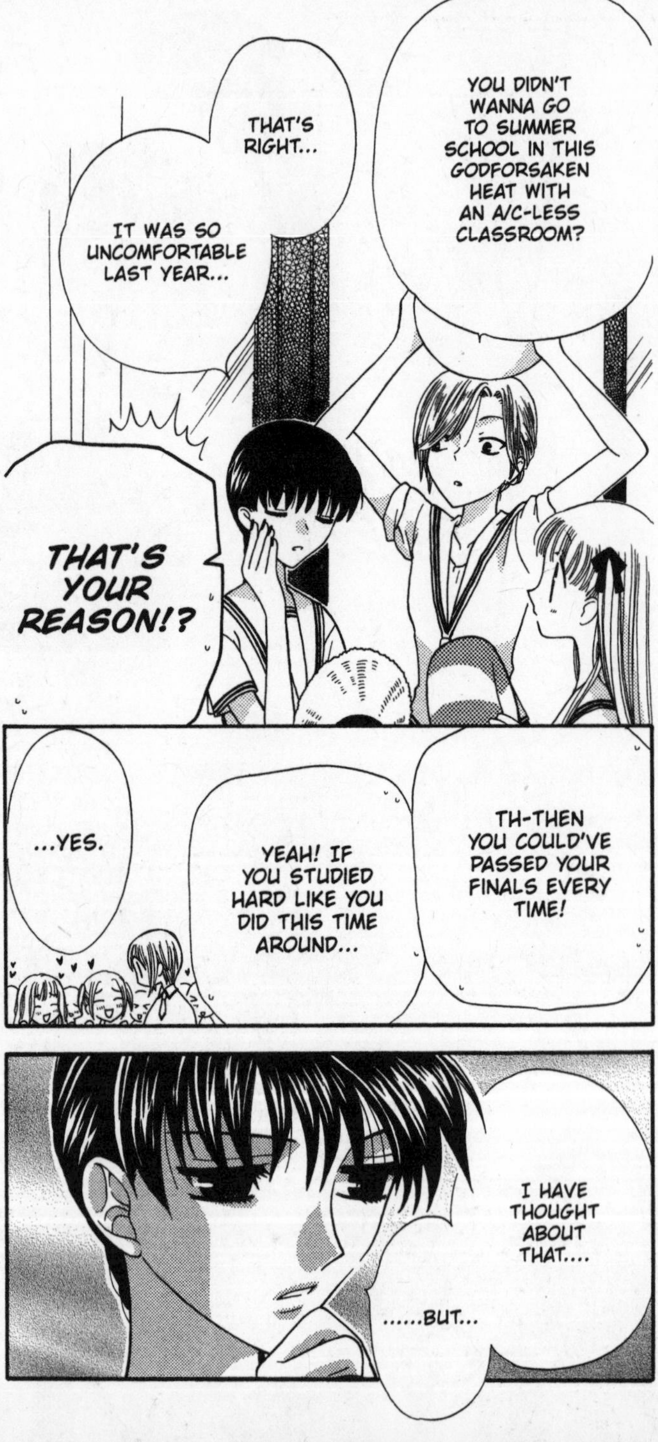
YOU DIDN'T WANNA GO TO SUMMER SCHOOL IN THIS GODFORSAKEN HEAT WITH AN A/C-LESS CLASSROOM?
THAT'S RIGHT...
IT WAS SO UNCOMFORTABLE LAST YEAR...
THAT'S YOUR REASON!?
TH-THEN YOU COULD'VE PASSED YOUR FINALS EVERY TIME!
YEAH! IF YOU STUDIED HARD LIKE YOU DID THIS TIME AROUND...
...YES.
I HAVE THOUGHT ABOUT THAT....
......BUT...

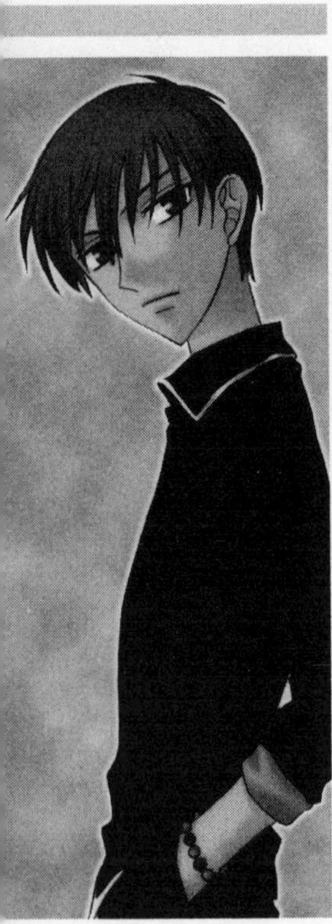

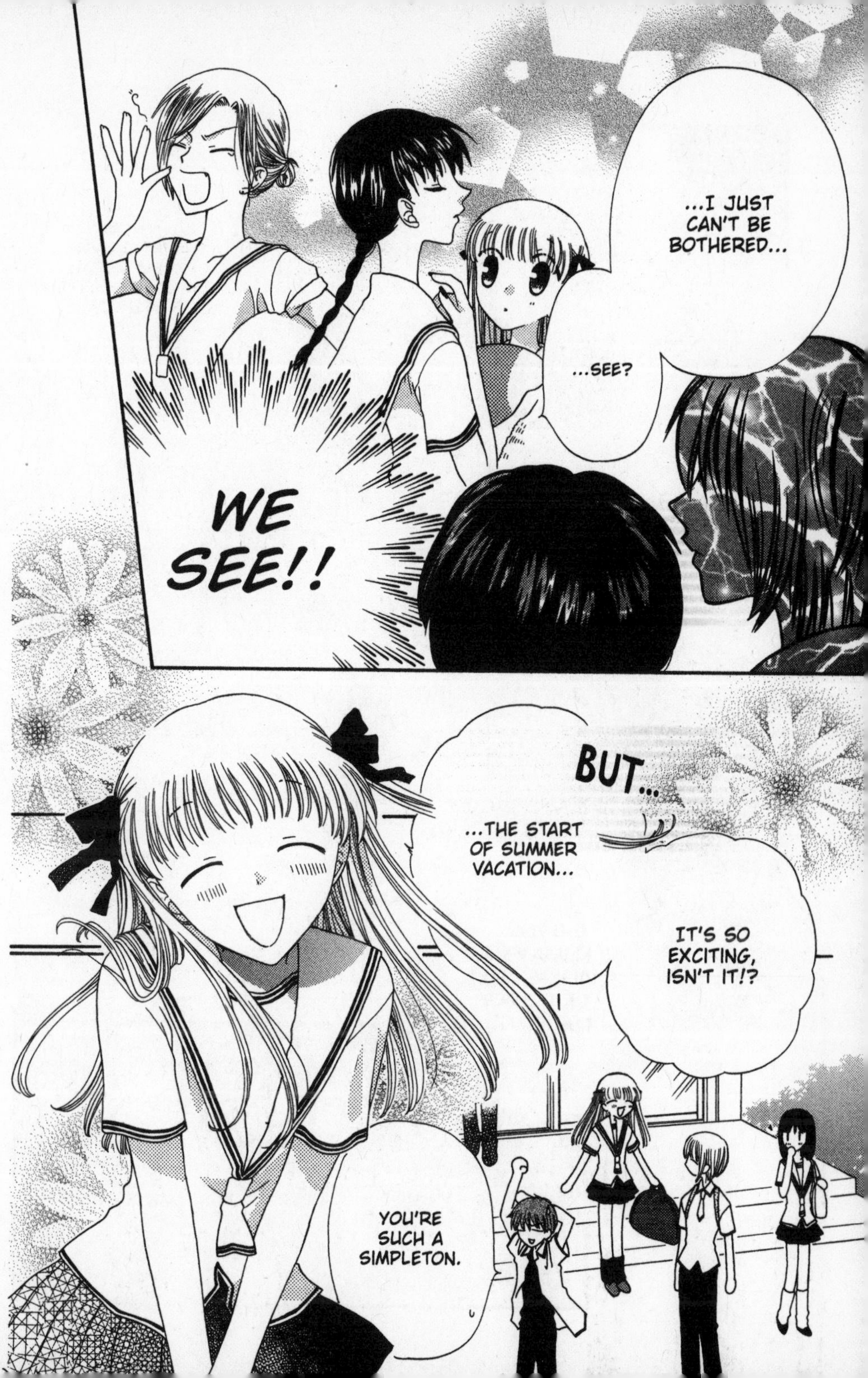
...I JUST CAN'T BE BOTHERED...
...SEE?
WE SEE!!
BUT...
...THE START OF SUMMER VACATION...
IT'S SO EXCITING, ISN'T IT!?
YOU'RE SUCH A SIMPLETON.

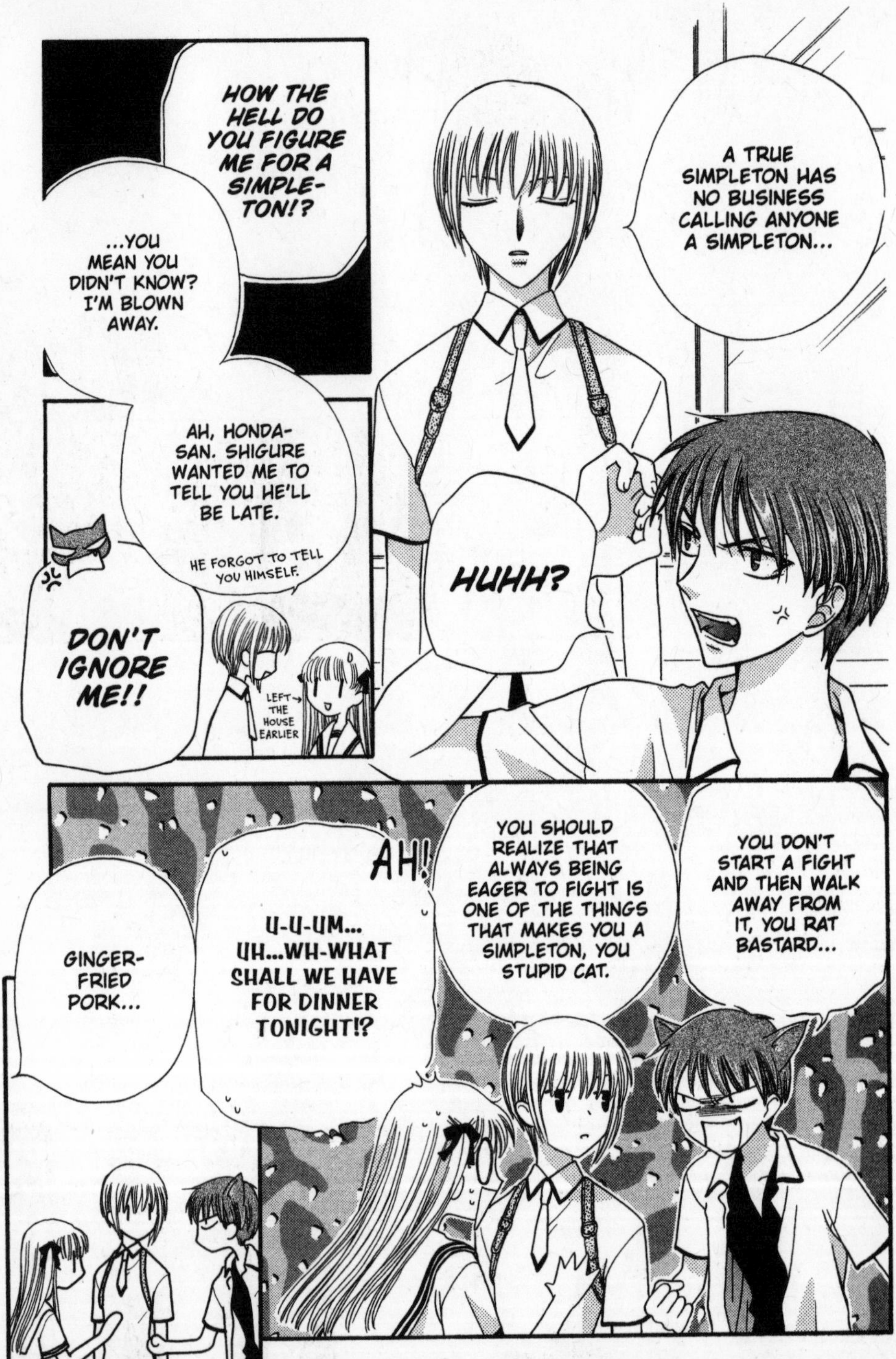
A TRUE SIMPLETON HAS NO BUSINESS CALLING ANYONE A SIMPLETON...
HUHH?
HOW THE HELL DO YOU FIGURE ME FOR A SIMPLE-TON!?
...YOU MEAN YOU DIDN'T KNOW? I'M BLOWN AWAY.
AH, HONDA-SAN. SHIGURE WANTED ME TO TELL YOU HE'LL BE LATE.
HE FORGOT TO TELL YOU HIMSELF.
DON'T IGNORE ME!!
LEFT THE HOUSE EARLIER
YOU DON'T START A FIGHT AND THEN WALK AWAY FROM IT, YOU RAT BASTARD...
YOU SHOULD REALIZE THAT ALWAYS BEING EAGER TO FIGHT IS ONE OF THE THINGS THAT MAKES YOU A SIMPLETON, YOU STUPID CAT.
AH!
U-U-UM... UH...WH-WHAT SHALL WE HAVE FOR DINNER TONIGHT!?
GINGER-FRIED PORK...

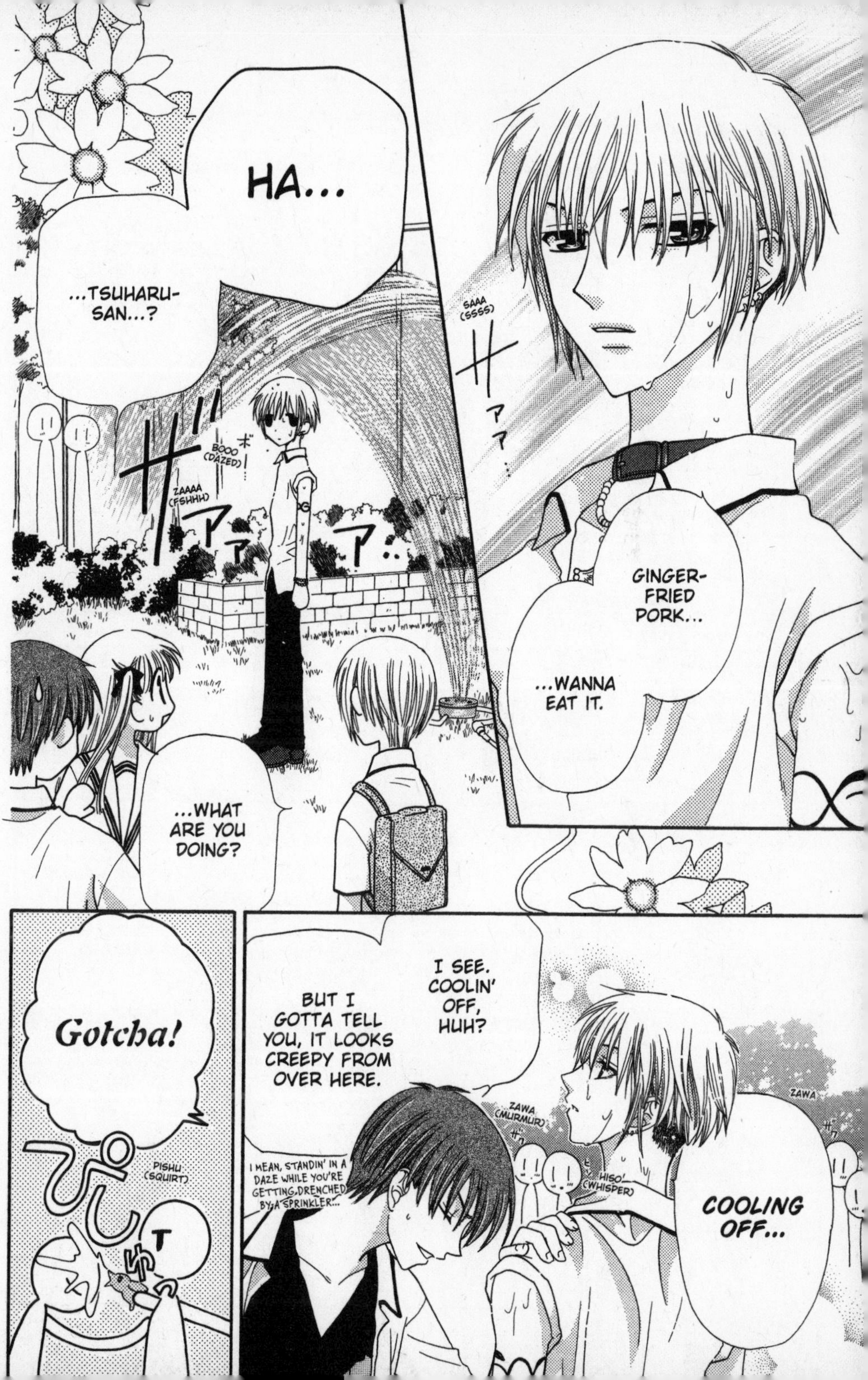
SAAA (SSSSS)
GINGER-FRIED PORK...
...WANNA EAT IT.
HA...
...TSUHARU-SAN...?
BOOO (DAZED)
ZAAAA (FSHHH)
...WHAT ARE YOU DOING?
ZAWA
COOLING OFF...
I SEE. COOLIN' OFF, HUH?
HISO (WHISPER)
ZAWA (MURMUR)
BUT I GOTTA TELL YOU, IT LOOKS CREEPY FROM OVER HERE.
I MEAN, STANDIN' IN A DAZE WHILE YOU'RE GETTING DRENCHED BY A SPRINKLER...
Gotcha!
PISHU (SQUIRT)

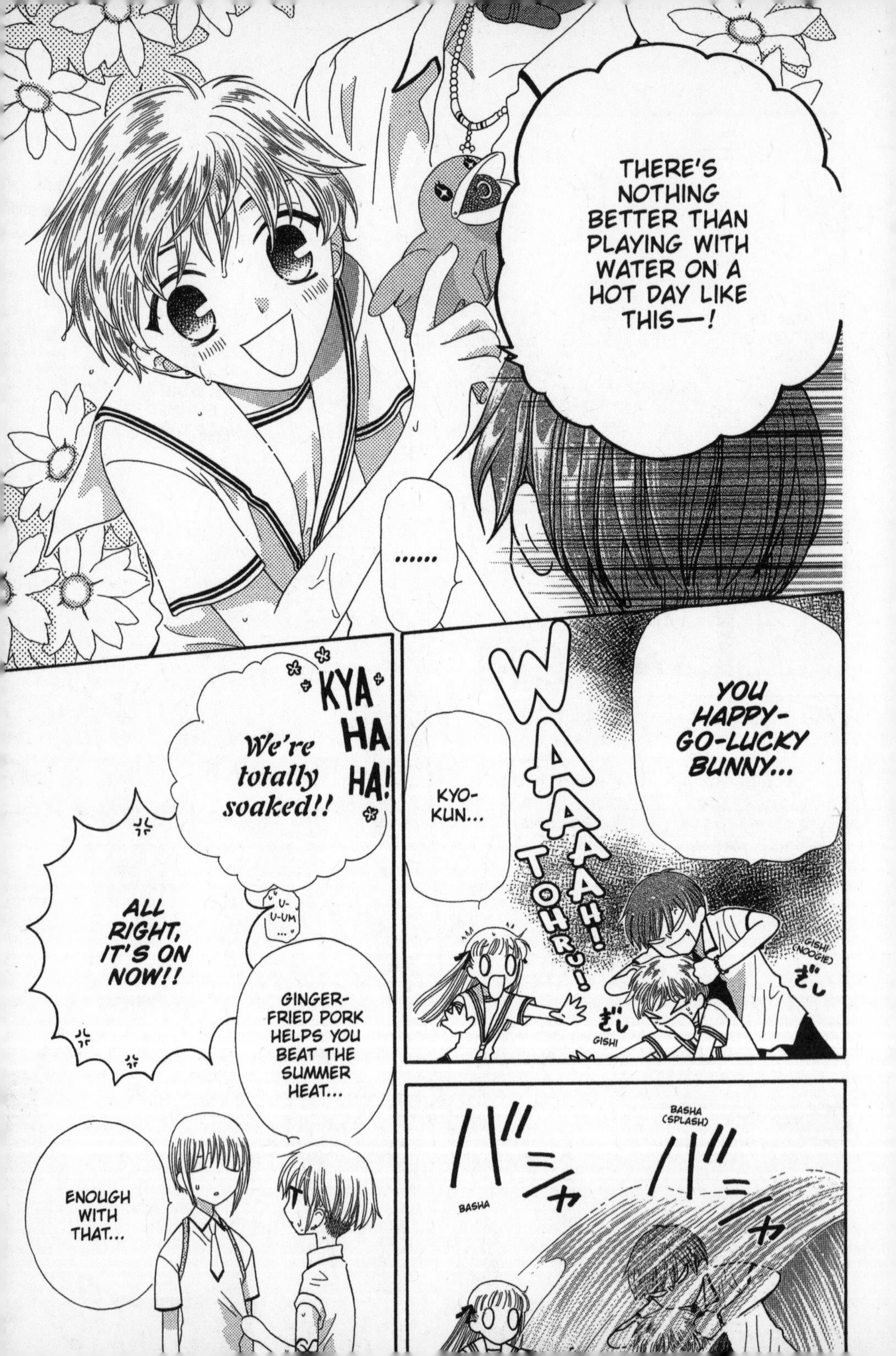
THERE'S NOTHING BETTER THAN PLAYING WITH WATER ON A HOT DAY LIKE THIS—!
......
YOU HAPPY-GO-LUCKY BUNNY...
WAAAAAH!
TOHRU!
KYO-KUN...
GISHI (NOOGIE)
ぎし
ぎし
GISHI
BASHA (SPLASH)
バシャ
バシャ
BASHA
KYA HA HA!
We're totally soaked!!
ALL RIGHT, IT'S ON NOW!!
U-U-UM...
GINGER-FRIED PORK HELPS YOU BEAT THE SUMMER HEAT...
ENOUGH WITH THAT...

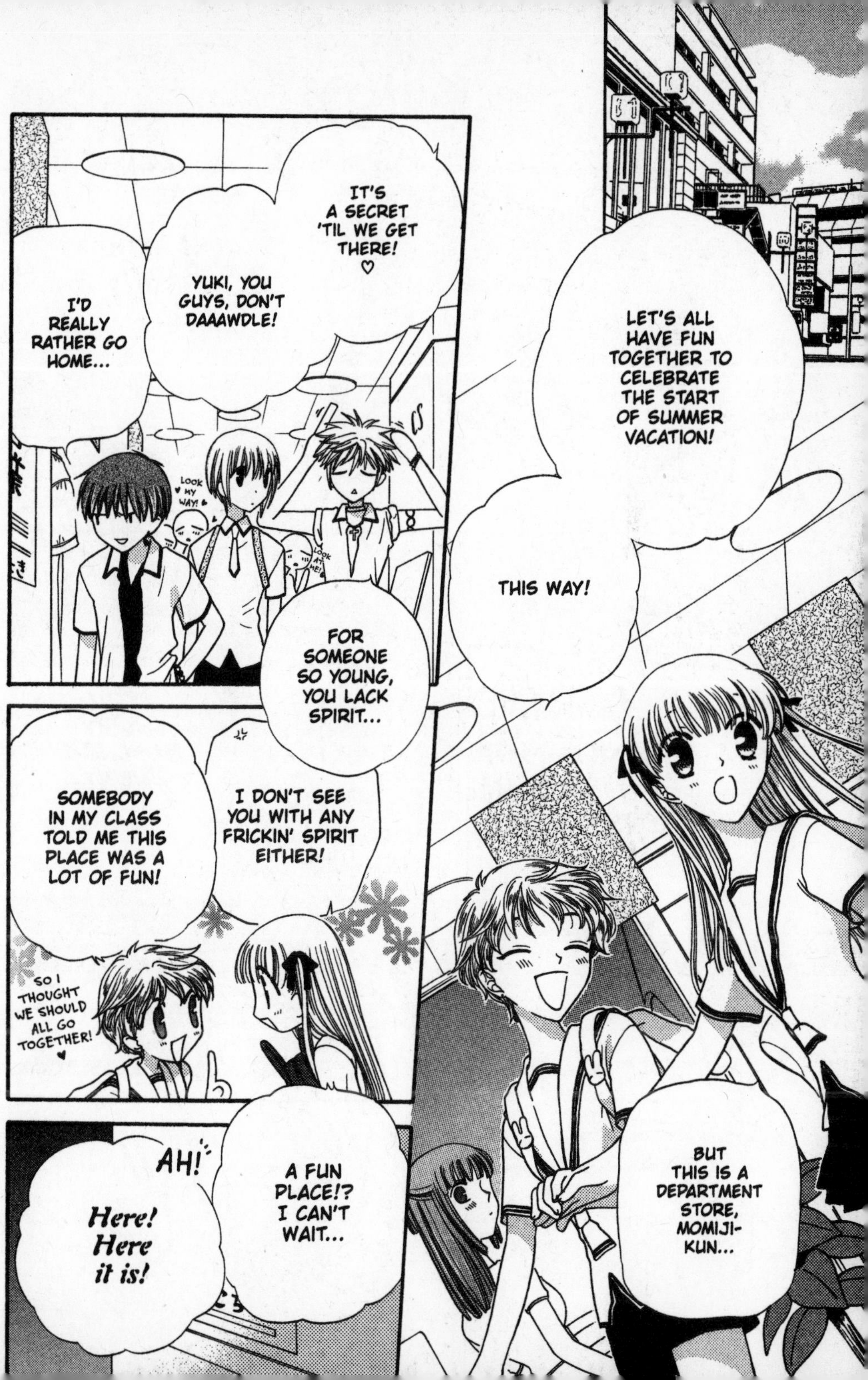
LET'S ALL HAVE FUN TOGETHER TO CELEBRATE THE START OF SUMMER VACATION!
THIS WAY!
BUT THIS IS A DEPARTMENT STORE, MOMIJI-KUN...
IT'S A SECRET 'TIL WE GET THERE! ♡
YUKI, YOU GUYS, DON'T DAAAWDLE!
I'D REALLY RATHER GO HOME...
LOOK MY WAY! ♥
LOOK AT ME!
FOR SOMEONE SO YOUNG, YOU LACK SPIRIT...
I DON'T SEE YOU WITH ANY FRICKIN' SPIRIT EITHER!
SOMEBODY IN MY CLASS TOLD ME THIS PLACE WAS A LOT OF FUN!
SO I THOUGHT WE SHOULD ALL GO TOGETHER! ♥
A FUN PLACE!? I CAN'T WAIT...
AH!
Here! Here it is!

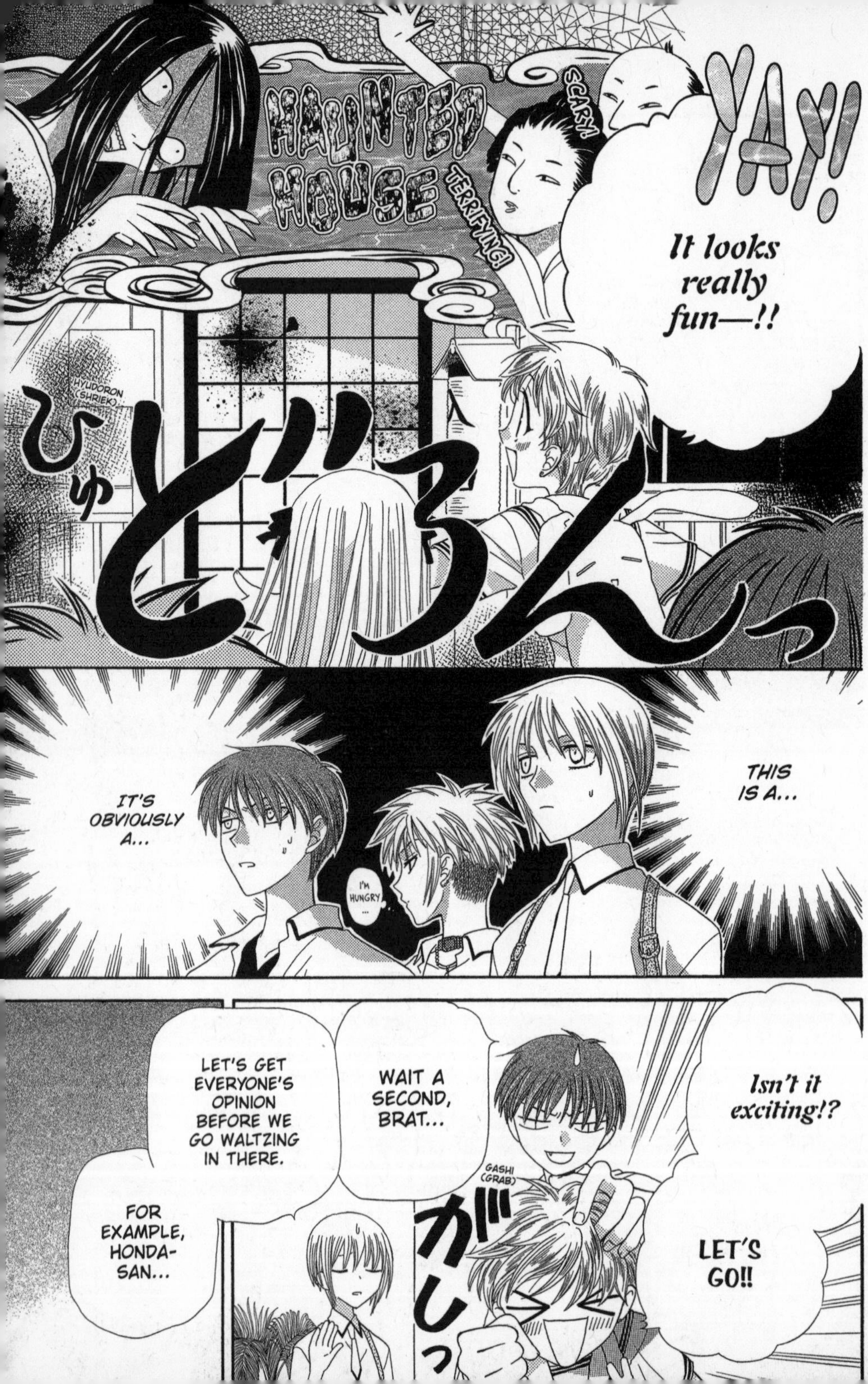
YAY!
It looks really fun—!!
SCARY!
HAUNTED HOUSE
TERRIFYING!
HYUDORON (SHRIEK)
ひゅどろんっ
THIS IS A...
I'M HUNGRY...
IT'S OBVIOUSLY A...
Isn't it exciting!?
LET'S GO!!
GASHI (GRAB)
がしっ
WAIT A SECOND, BRAT...
LET'S GET EVERYONE'S OPINION BEFORE WE GO WALTZING IN THERE.
FOR EXAMPLE, HONDA-SAN...

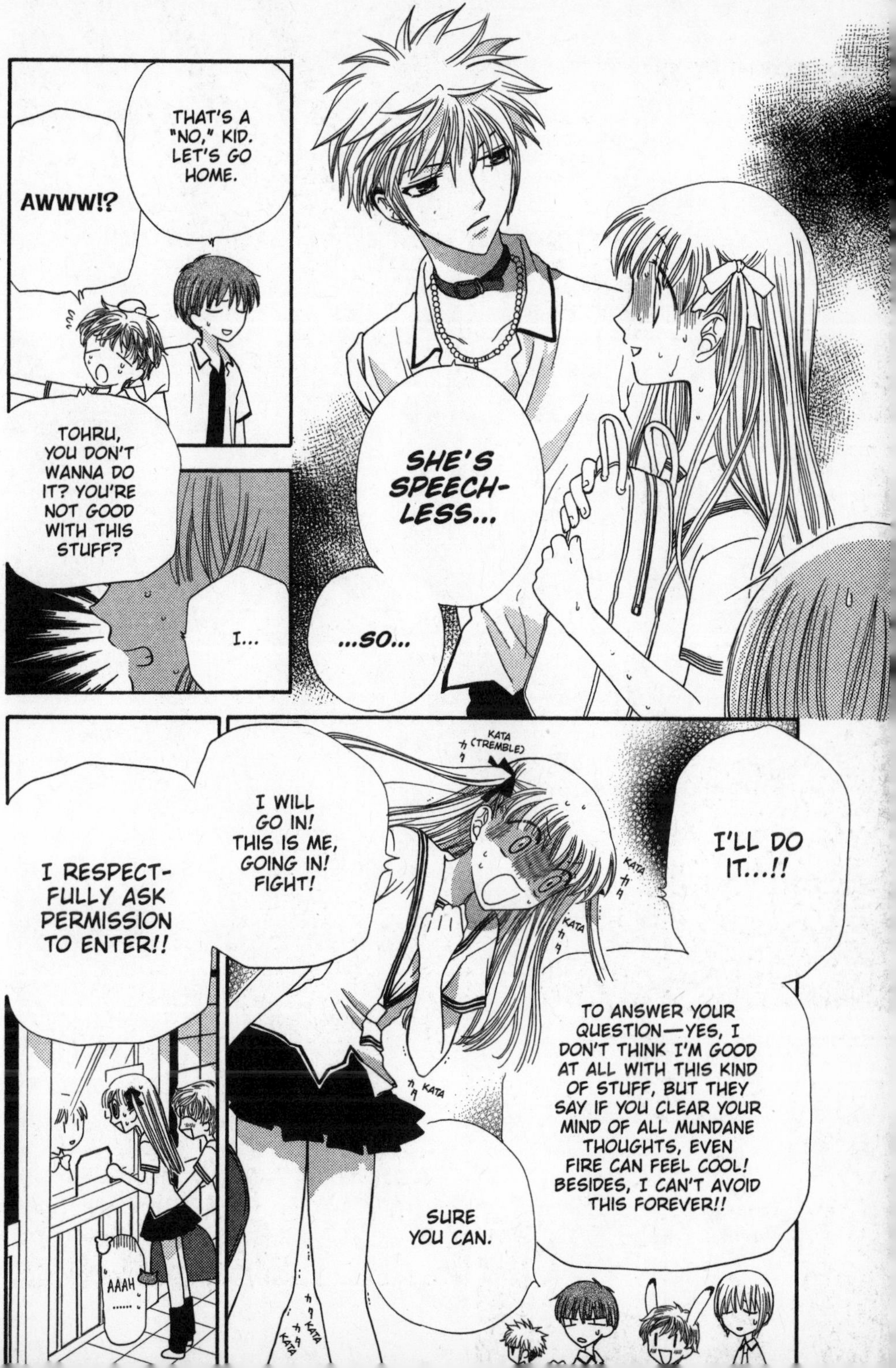
SHE'S SPEECH-LESS...
...SO...
THAT'S A "NO," KID. LET'S GO HOME.
AWWW!?
TOHRU, YOU DON'T WANNA DO IT? YOU'RE NOT GOOD WITH THIS STUFF?
I...
KATA (TREMBLE)
I'LL DO IT...!!
KATA
KATA
TO ANSWER YOUR QUESTION—YES, I DON'T THINK I'M GOOD AT ALL WITH THIS KIND OF STUFF, BUT THEY SAY IF YOU CLEAR YOUR MIND OF ALL MUNDANE THOUGHTS, EVEN FIRE CAN FEEL COOL! BESIDES, I CAN'T AVOID THIS FOREVER!!
KATA
SURE YOU CAN.
KATA KATA
I WILL GO IN! THIS IS ME, GOING IN! FIGHT!
I RESPECT-FULLY ASK PERMISSION TO ENTER!!
AAAH ......

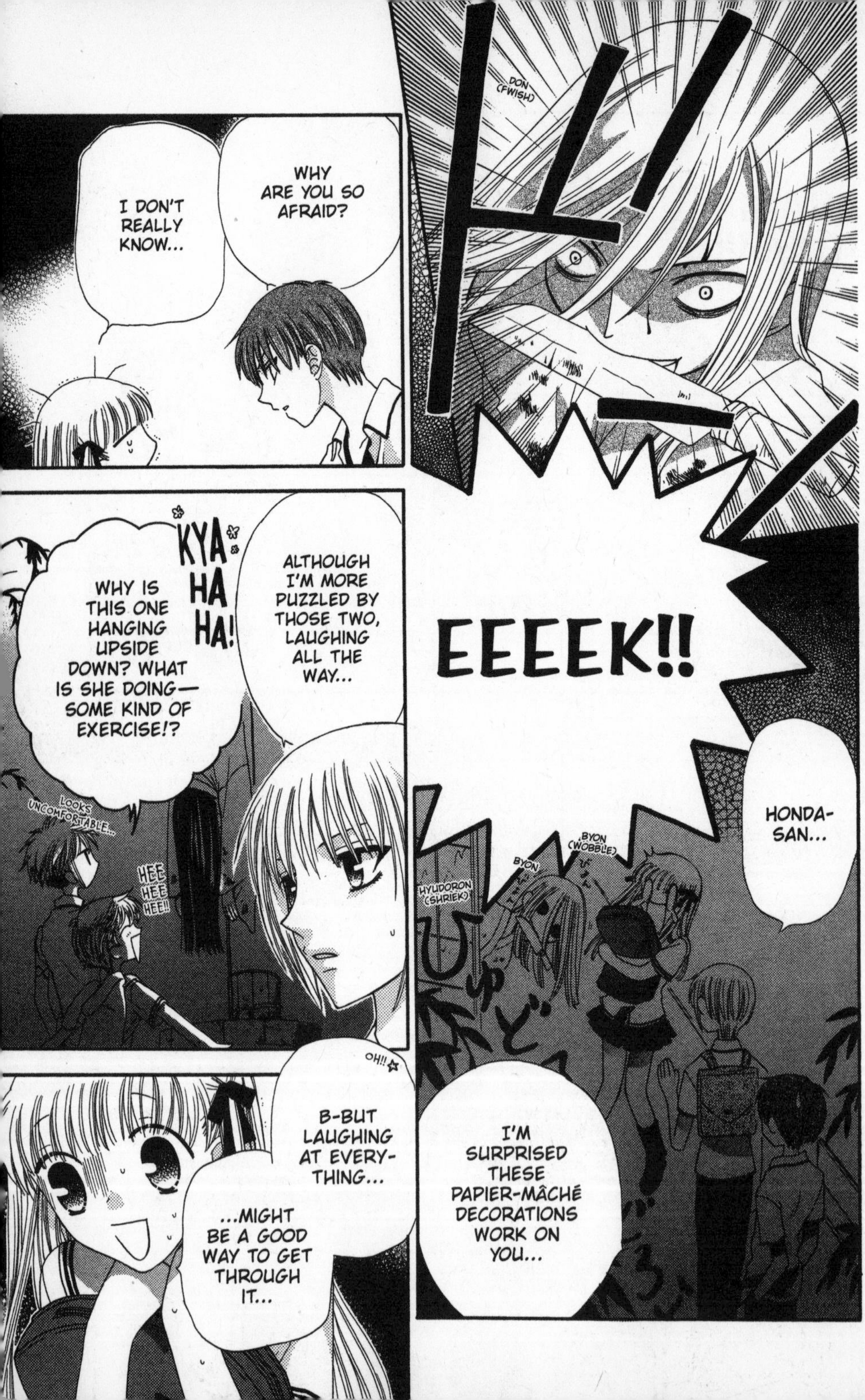
DON (FWISH)
EEEEK!!
HONDA-SAN...
BYON (WOBBLE)
BYON
HYUDORON (SHRIEK)
I'M SURPRISED THESE PAPIER-MÂCHÉ DECORATIONS WORK ON YOU...
WHY ARE YOU SO AFRAID?
I DON'T REALLY KNOW...
ALTHOUGH I'M MORE PUZZLED BY THOSE TWO, LAUGHING ALL THE WAY...
KYA HA HA HA!
WHY IS THIS ONE HANGING UPSIDE DOWN? WHAT IS SHE DOING— SOME KIND OF EXERCISE!?
LOOKS UNCOMFORTABLE...
HEE HEE HEE!!
OH!!
B-BUT LAUGHING AT EVERY-THING...
...MIGHT BE A GOOD WAY TO GET THROUGH IT...

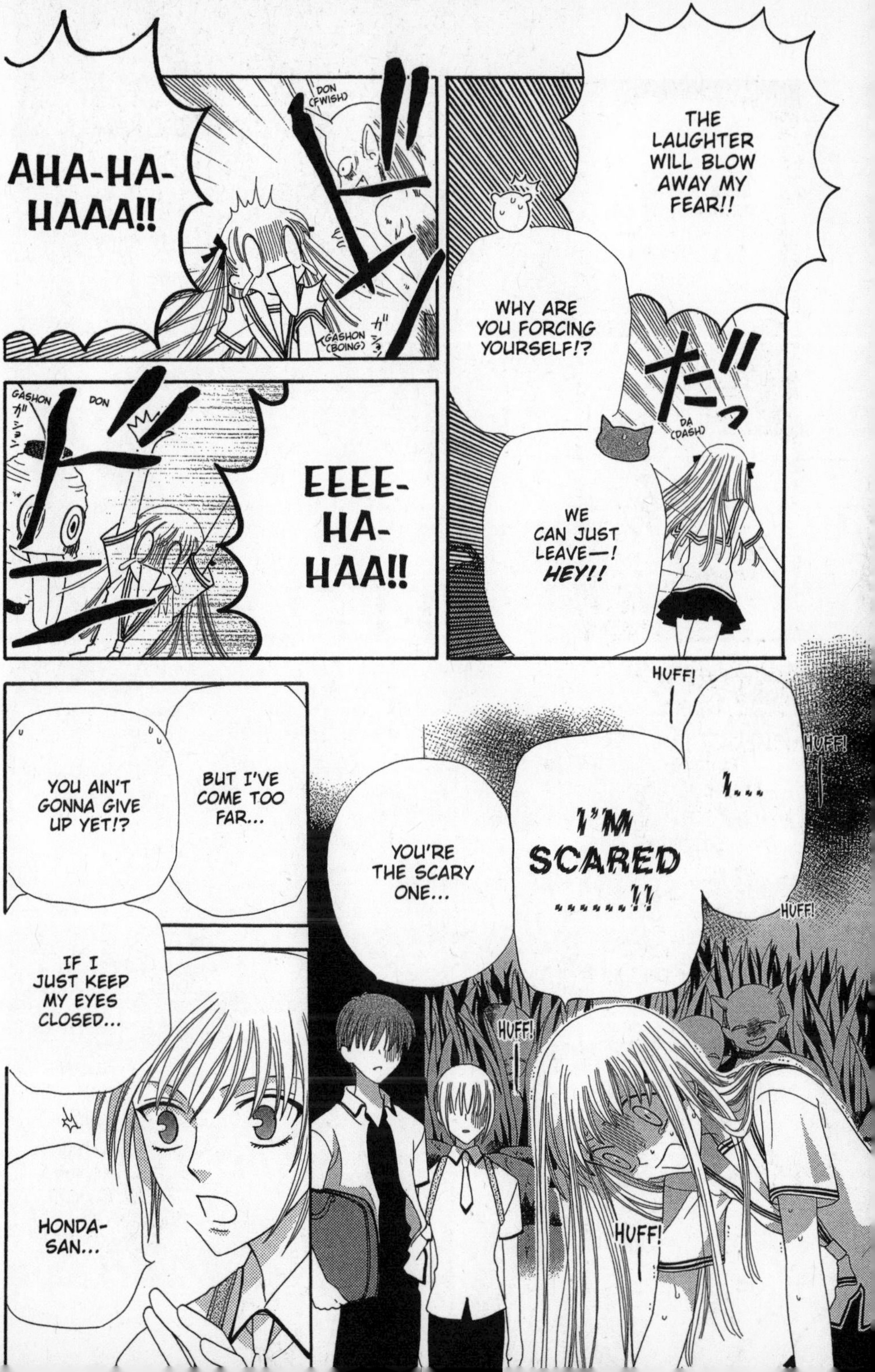
THE LAUGHTER WILL BLOW AWAY MY FEAR!!
WHY ARE YOU FORCING YOURSELF!?
DA (DASH)
WE CAN JUST LEAVE—! HEY!!
DON (FWISH)
AHA-HA-HAAA!!
GASHON (BOING)
GASHON
DON
EEEE-HA-HAA!!
HUFF!
HUFF!
I...
I'M SCARED ......!!
HUFF!
YOU'RE THE SCARY ONE...
HUFF!
HUFF!
BUT I'VE COME TOO FAR...
YOU AIN'T GONNA GIVE UP YET!?
IF I JUST KEEP MY EYES CLOSED...
HONDA-SAN...

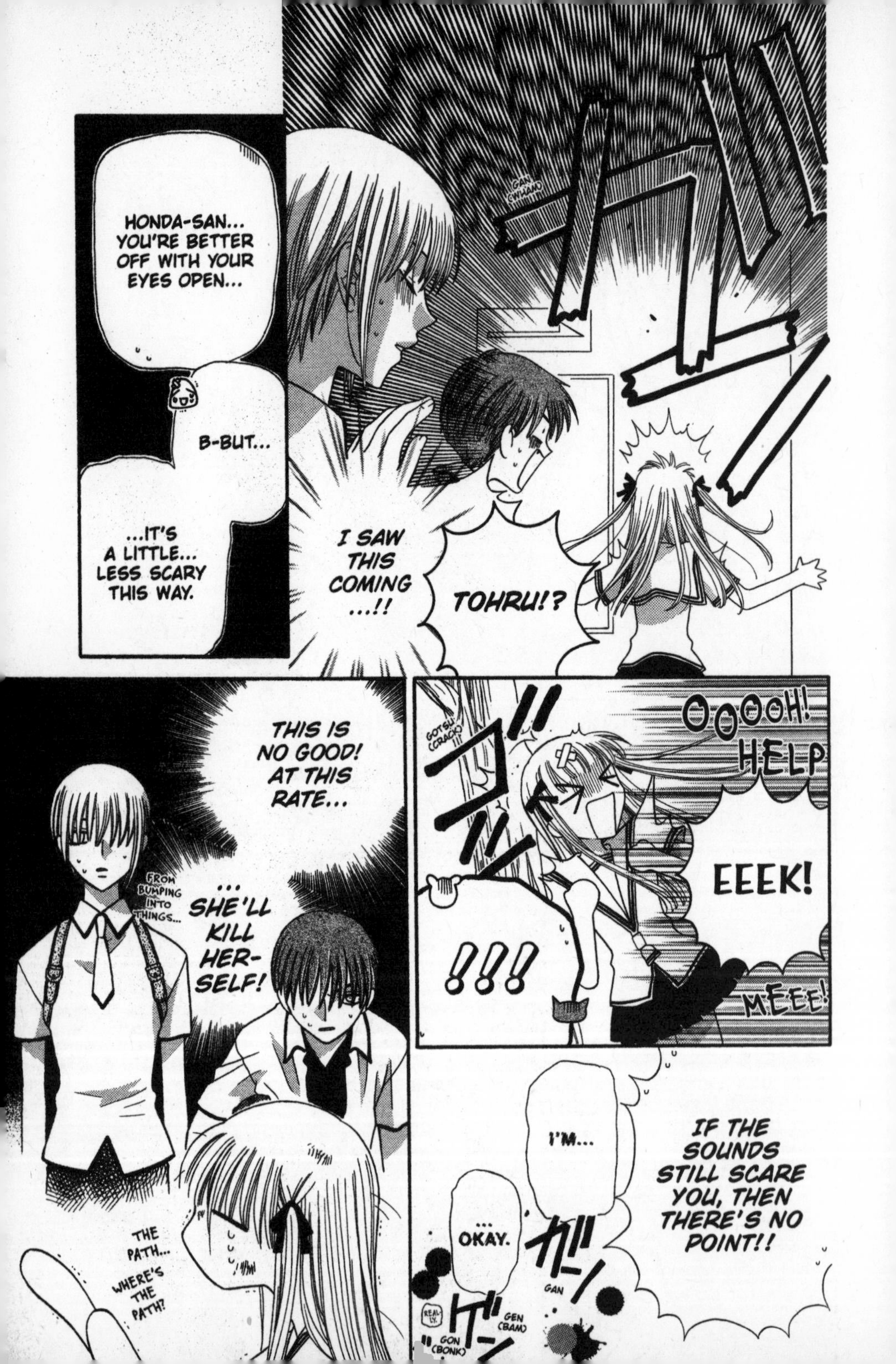
GAN (WHAM)
TOHRU!?
I SAW THIS COMING ...!!
HONDA-SAN... YOU'RE BETTER OFF WITH YOUR EYES OPEN...
B-BUT...
...IT'S A LITTLE... LESS SCARY THIS WAY.
OOOOH! HELP
GOTSU (CRACK)
EEEK!
MEEE!
!!!
IF THE SOUNDS STILL SCARE YOU, THEN THERE'S NO POINT!!
I'M...
... OKAY.
GAN
GEN (BAM)
GON (BONK)
REALLY.
THIS IS NO GOOD! AT THIS RATE...
... SHE'LL KILL HER-SELF!
FROM BUMPING INTO THINGS...
THE PATH... WHERE'S THE PATH?

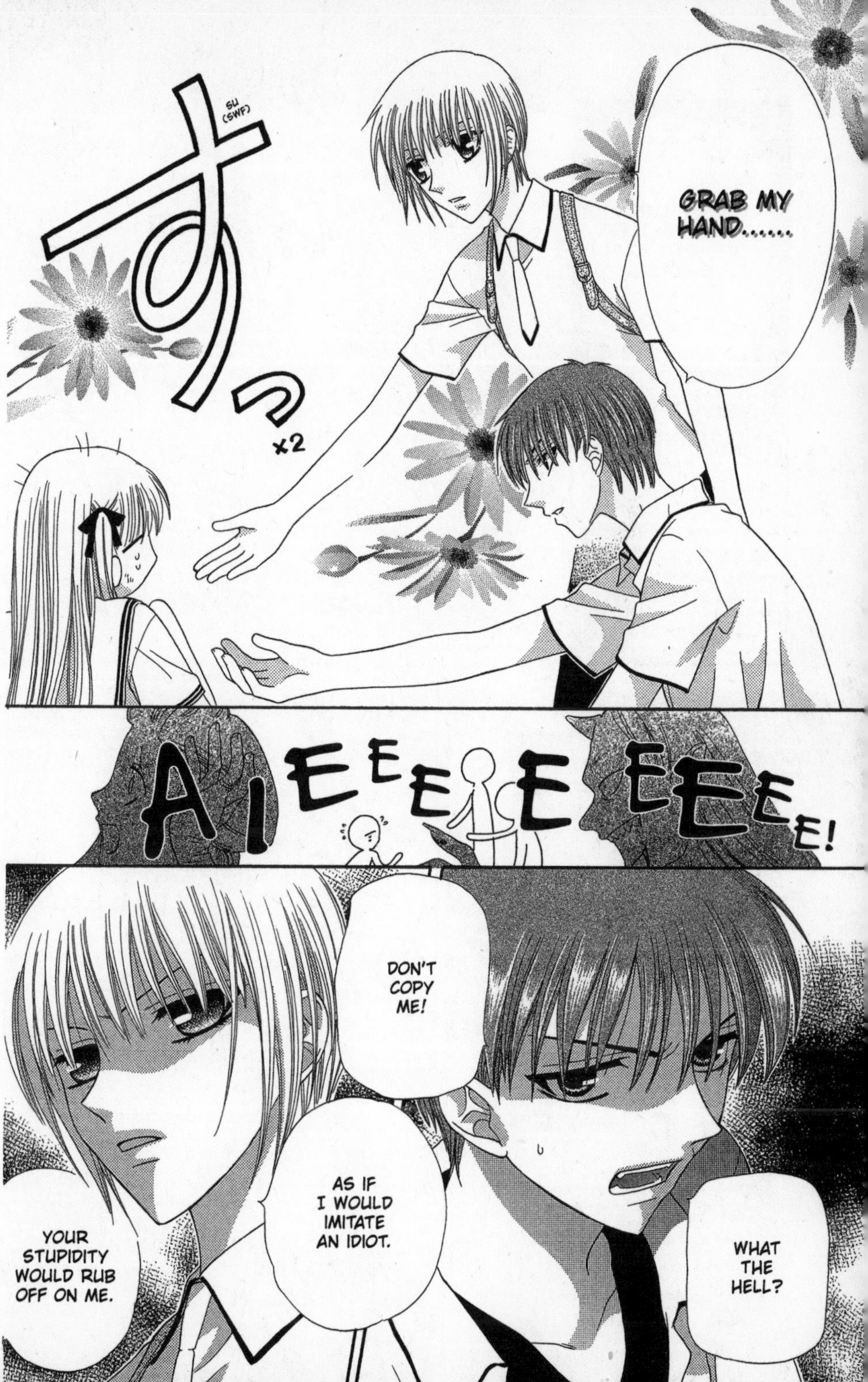
GRAB MY HAND.......
すっ
SU (SWF)
×2
AIEEEEEEEEEEE!
DON'T COPY ME!
WHAT THE HELL?
AS IF I WOULD IMITATE AN IDIOT.
YOUR STUPIDITY WOULD RUB OFF ON ME.

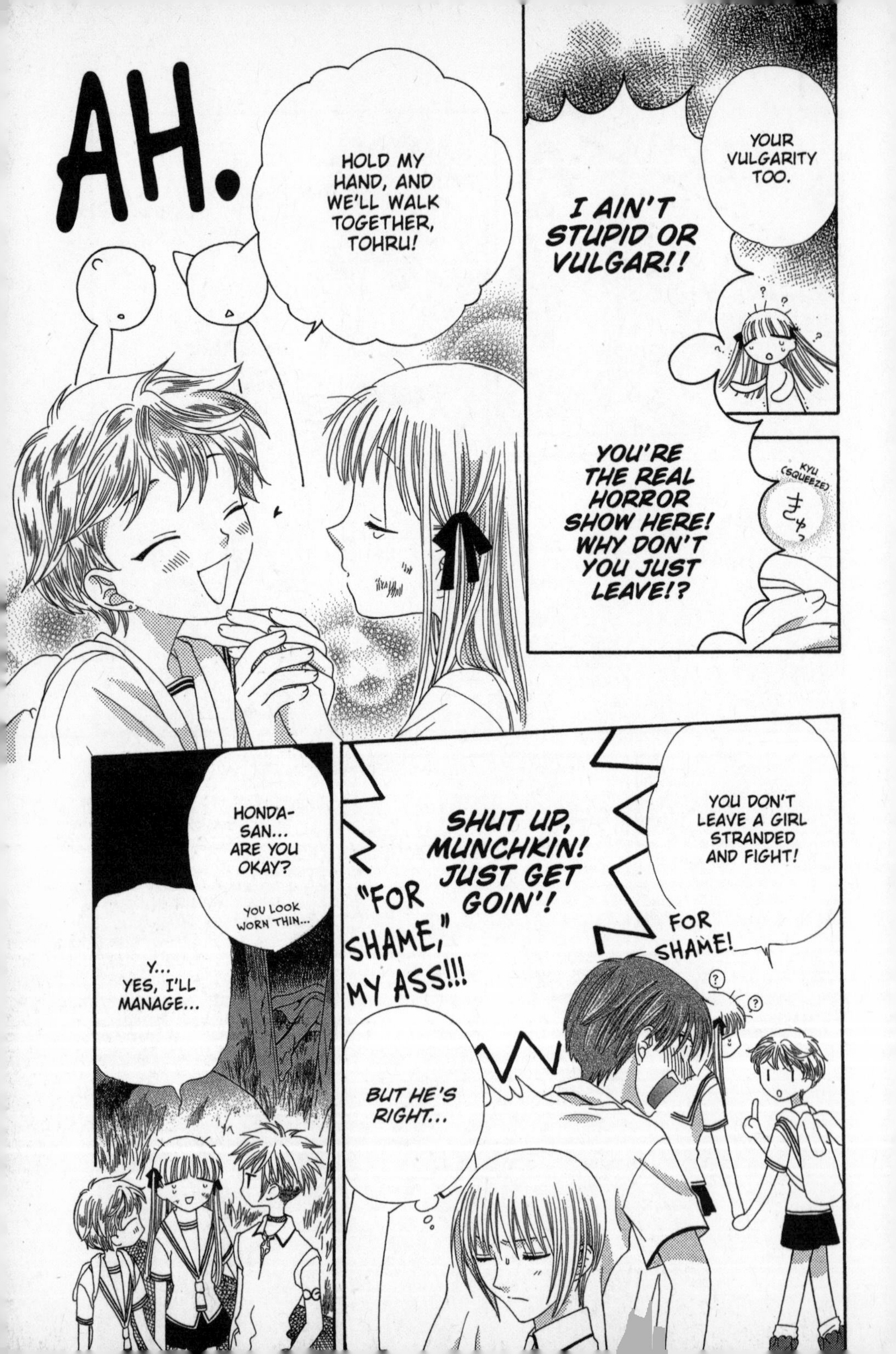
YOUR VULGARITY TOO.
I AIN'T STUPID OR VULGAR!!
YOU'RE THE REAL HORROR SHOW HERE! WHY DON'T YOU JUST LEAVE!?
KYU (SQUEEZE)
きゅっ
HOLD MY HAND, AND WE'LL WALK TOGETHER, TOHRU!
AH.
YOU DON'T LEAVE A GIRL STRANDED AND FIGHT!
FOR SHAME!
SHUT UP, MUNCHKIN! JUST GET GOIN'!
"FOR SHAME," MY ASS!!!
BUT HE'S RIGHT...
HONDA-SAN... ARE YOU OKAY?
YOU LOOK WORN THIN...
Y... YES, I'LL MANAGE...

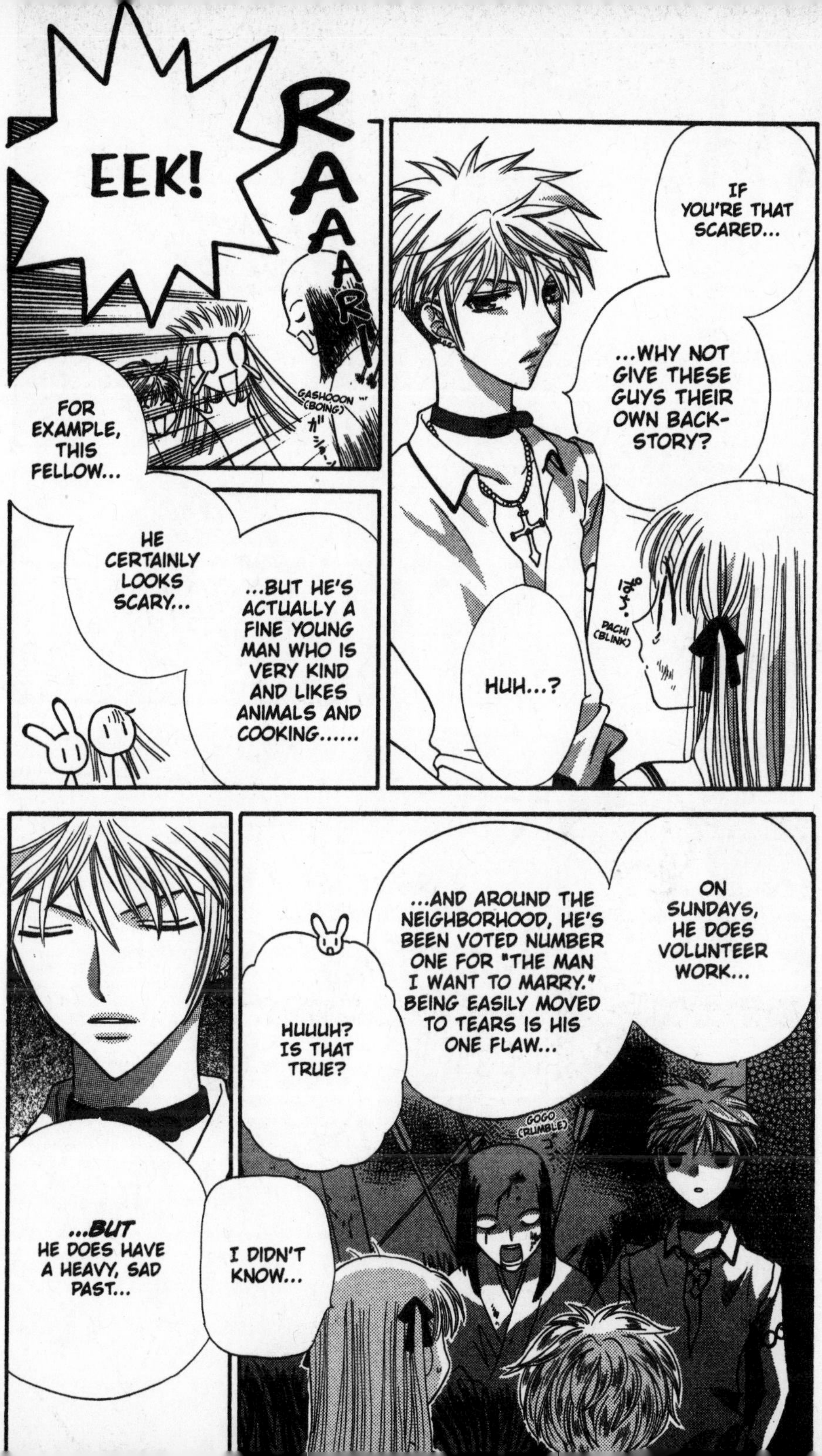
IF YOU'RE THAT SCARED...
...WHY NOT GIVE THESE GUYS THEIR OWN BACK-STORY?
PACHI (BLINK)
HUH...?
EEK!
RAAARI!
GASHOOON (BOING)
FOR EXAMPLE, THIS FELLOW...
HE CERTAINLY LOOKS SCARY...
...BUT HE'S ACTUALLY A FINE YOUNG MAN WHO IS VERY KIND AND LIKES ANIMALS AND COOKING......
ON SUNDAYS, HE DOES VOLUNTEER WORK...
...AND AROUND THE NEIGHBORHOOD, HE'S BEEN VOTED NUMBER ONE FOR "THE MAN I WANT TO MARRY." BEING EASILY MOVED TO TEARS IS HIS ONE FLAW...
HUUUH? IS THAT TRUE?
GOGO (RUMBLE)
...BUT HE DOES HAVE A HEAVY, SAD PAST...
I DIDN'T KNOW...

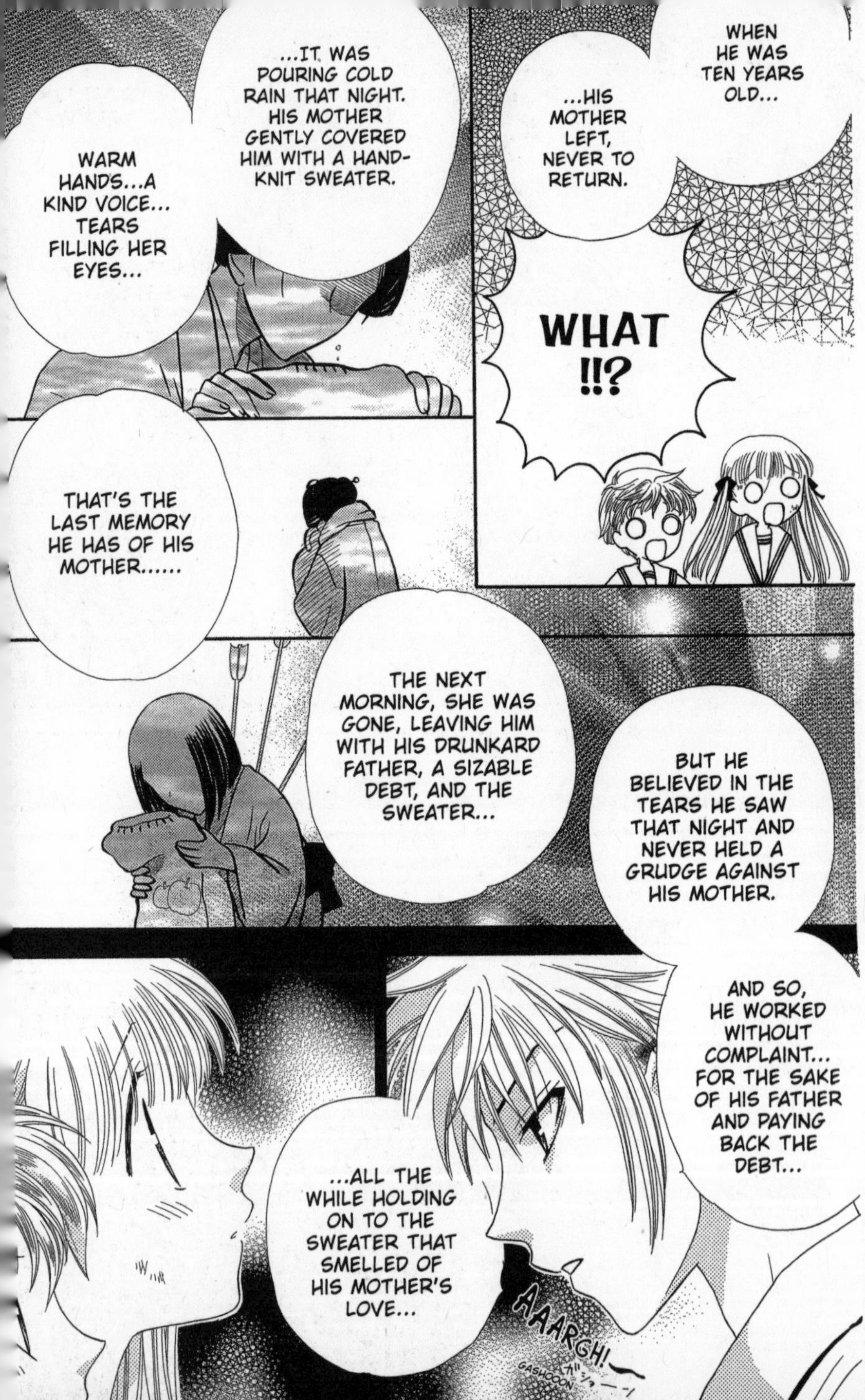
WHEN HE WAS TEN YEARS OLD...
...HIS MOTHER LEFT, NEVER TO RETURN.
WHAT !!?
...IT WAS POURING COLD RAIN THAT NIGHT. HIS MOTHER GENTLY COVERED HIM WITH A HAND-KNIT SWEATER.
WARM HANDS...A KIND VOICE... TEARS FILLING HER EYES...
THAT'S THE LAST MEMORY HE HAS OF HIS MOTHER......
BUT HE BELIEVED IN THE TEARS HE SAW THAT NIGHT AND NEVER HELD A GRUDGE AGAINST HIS MOTHER.
THE NEXT MORNING, SHE WAS GONE, LEAVING HIM WITH HIS DRUNKARD FATHER, A SIZABLE DEBT, AND THE SWEATER...
AND SO, HE WORKED WITHOUT COMPLAINT... FOR THE SAKE OF HIS FATHER AND PAYING BACK THE DEBT...
AAARGH!
GASHOOON
...ALL THE WHILE HOLDING ON TO THE SWEATER THAT SMELLED OF HIS MOTHER'S LOVE...

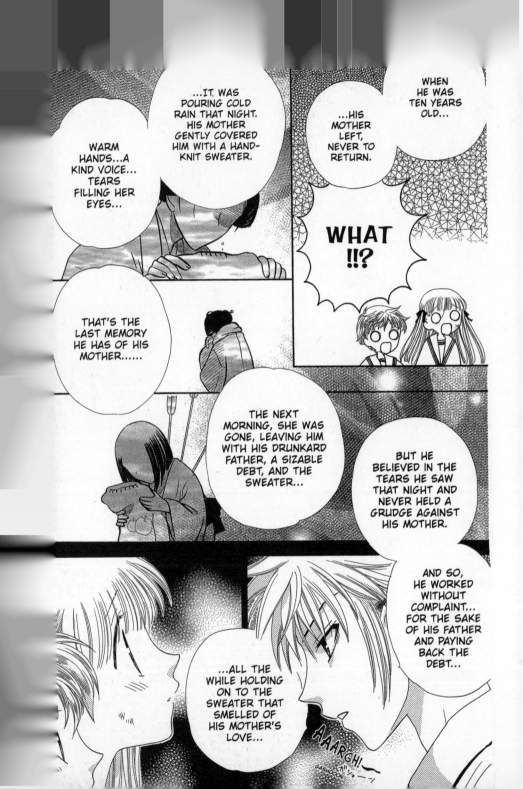

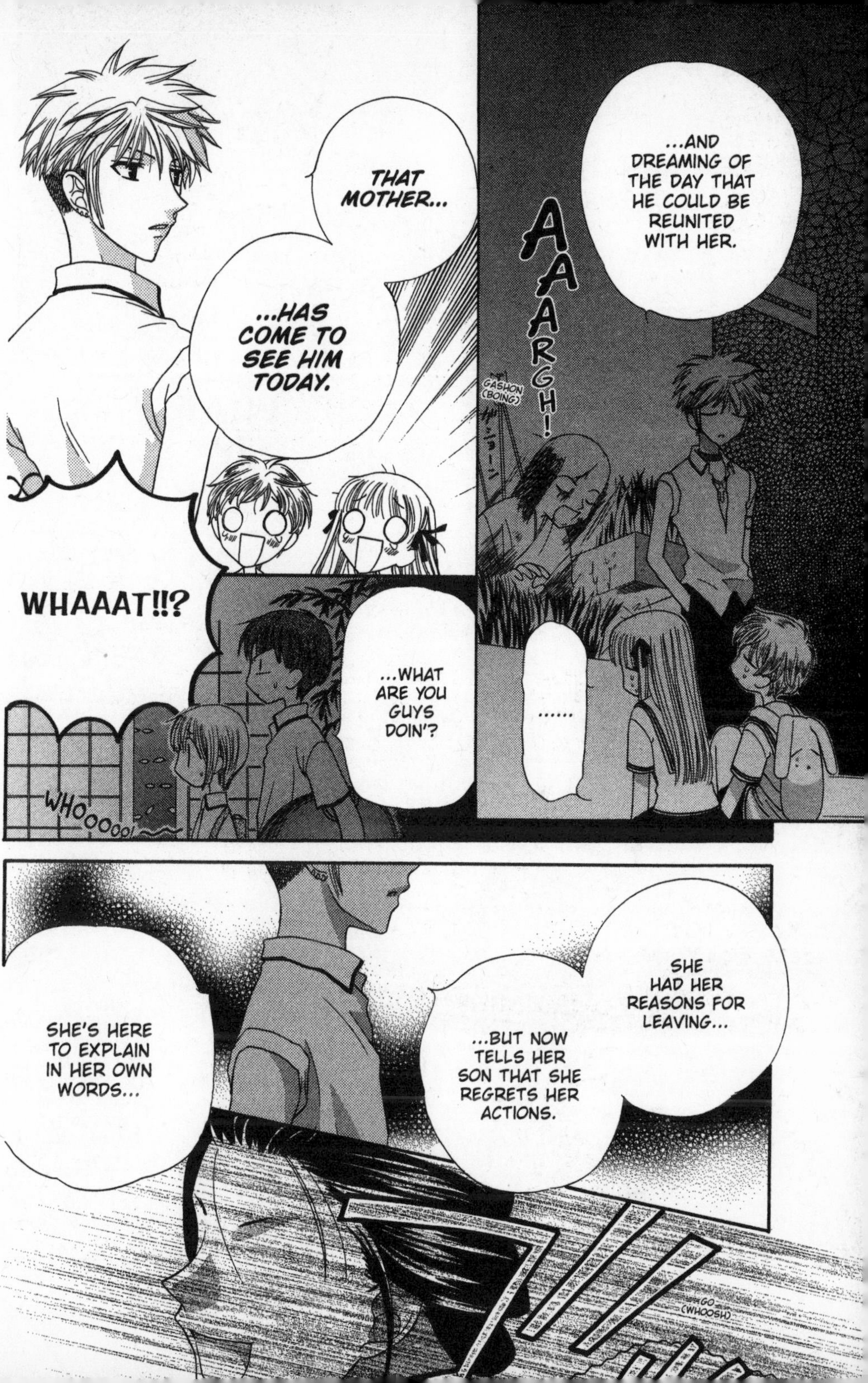
...AND DREAMING OF THE DAY THAT HE COULD BE REUNITED WITH HER.
AAAARGH!
GASHON (BOING)
......
THAT MOTHER...
...HAS COME TO SEE HIM TODAY.
WHAAAT!!?
...WHAT ARE YOU GUYS DOIN'?
WHOOOOO!
SHE HAD HER REASONS FOR LEAVING...
...BUT NOW TELLS HER SON THAT SHE REGRETS HER ACTIONS.
SHE'S HERE TO EXPLAIN IN HER OWN WORDS...
GO (WHOOSH)

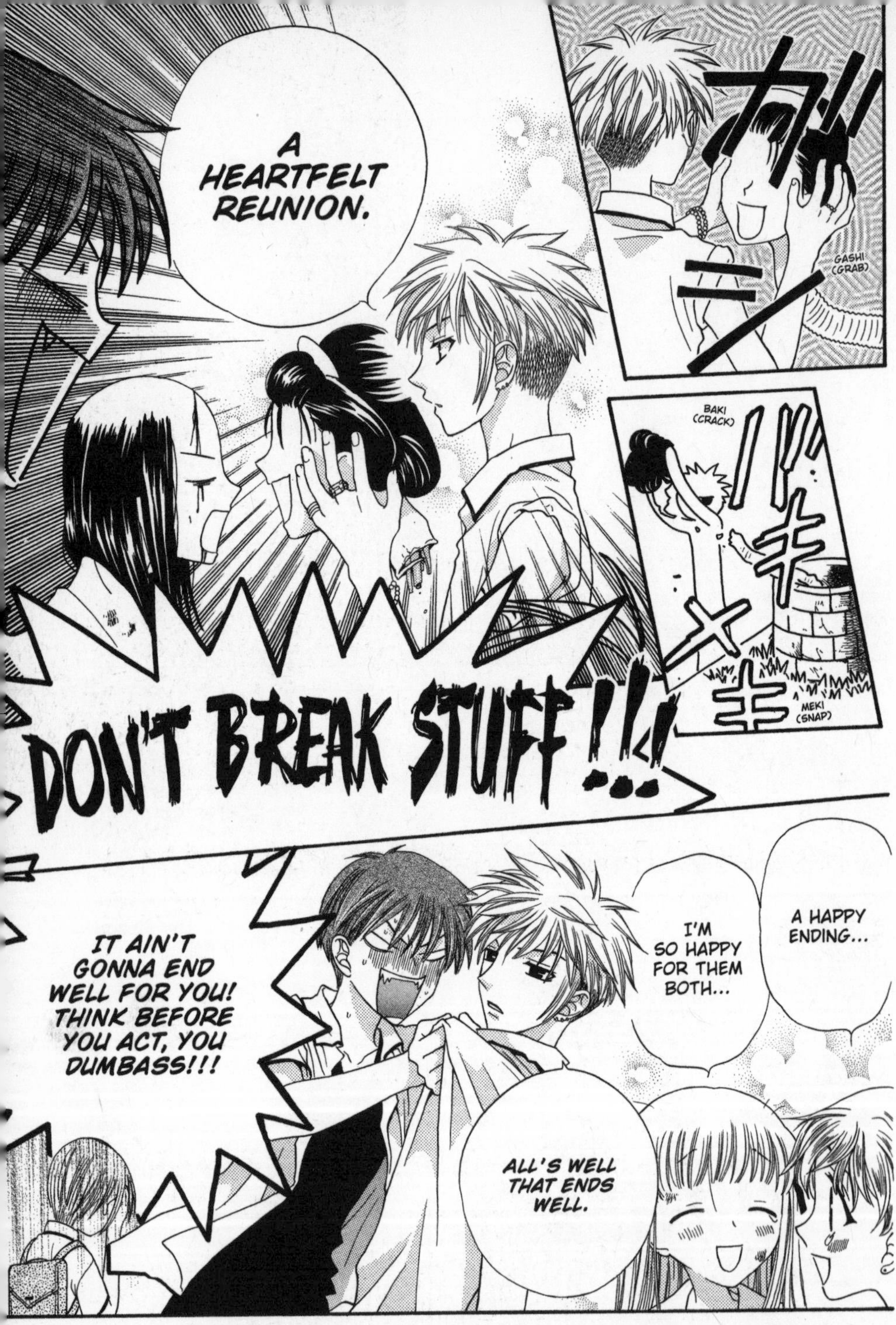
GASHI (GRAB)
BAKI (CRACK)
MEKI (SNAP)
A HEARTFELT REUNION.
DON'T BREAK STUFF!!!
A HAPPY ENDING...
I'M SO HAPPY FOR THEM BOTH...
ALL'S WELL THAT ENDS WELL.
IT AIN'T GONNA END WELL FOR YOU! THINK BEFORE YOU ACT, YOU DUMBASS!!!

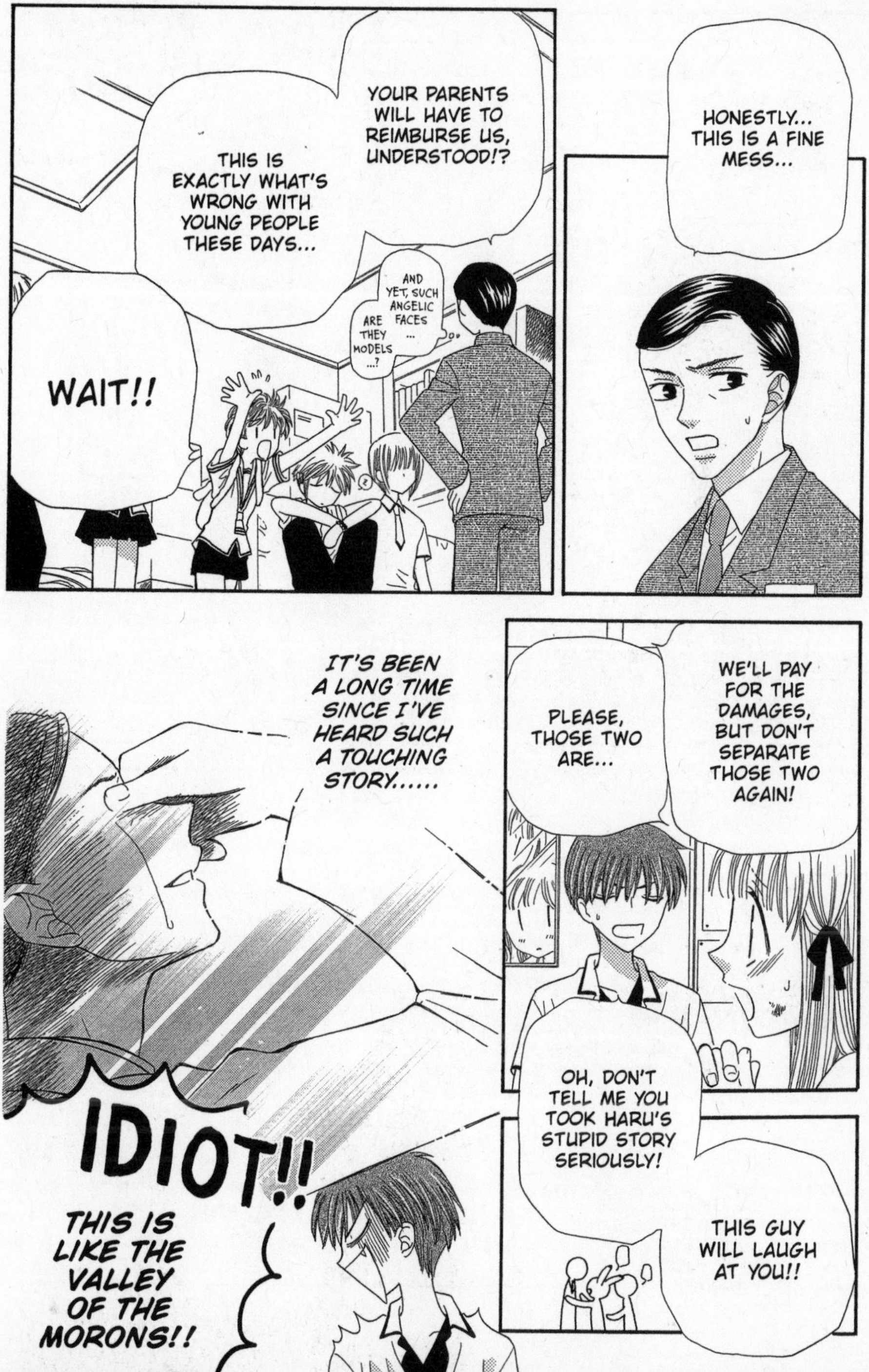

HONESTLY... THIS IS A FINE MESS...
YOUR PARENTS WILL HAVE TO REIMBURSE US, UNDERSTOOD!?
THIS IS EXACTLY WHAT'S WRONG WITH YOUNG PEOPLE THESE DAYS...
AND YET, SUCH ANGELIC FACES ...
ARE THEY MODELS ...?
WAIT!!
WE'LL PAY FOR THE DAMAGES, BUT DON'T SEPARATE THOSE TWO AGAIN!
PLEASE, THOSE TWO ARE...
OH, DON'T TELL ME YOU TOOK HARU'S STUPID STORY SERIOUSLY!
THIS GUY WILL LAUGH AT YOU!!
IT'S BEEN A LONG TIME SINCE I'VE HEARD SUCH A TOUCHING STORY......
IDIOT!!
THIS IS LIKE THE VALLEY OF THE MORONS!!

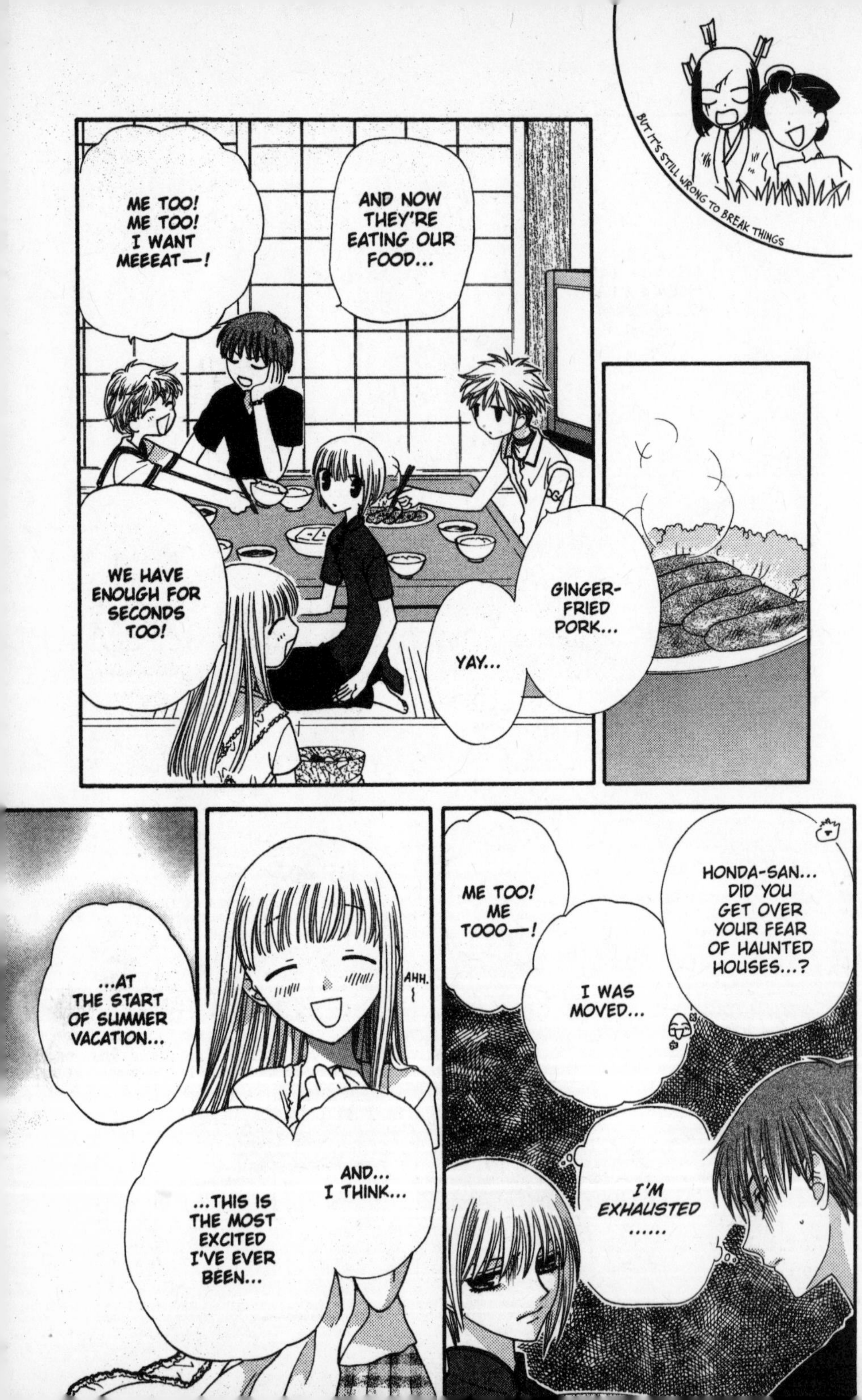
BUT IT'S STILL WRONG TO BREAK THINGS
GINGER-FRIED PORK...
YAY...
AND NOW THEY'RE EATING OUR FOOD...
ME TOO! ME TOO! I WANT MEEEAT—!
WE HAVE ENOUGH FOR SECONDS TOO!
HONDA-SAN... DID YOU GET OVER YOUR FEAR OF HAUNTED HOUSES...?
ME TOO! ME TOOO—!
I WAS MOVED...
I'M EXHAUSTED ......
AHH.
AND... I THINK...
...THIS IS THE MOST EXCITED I'VE EVER BEEN...
...AT THE START OF SUMMER VACATION...

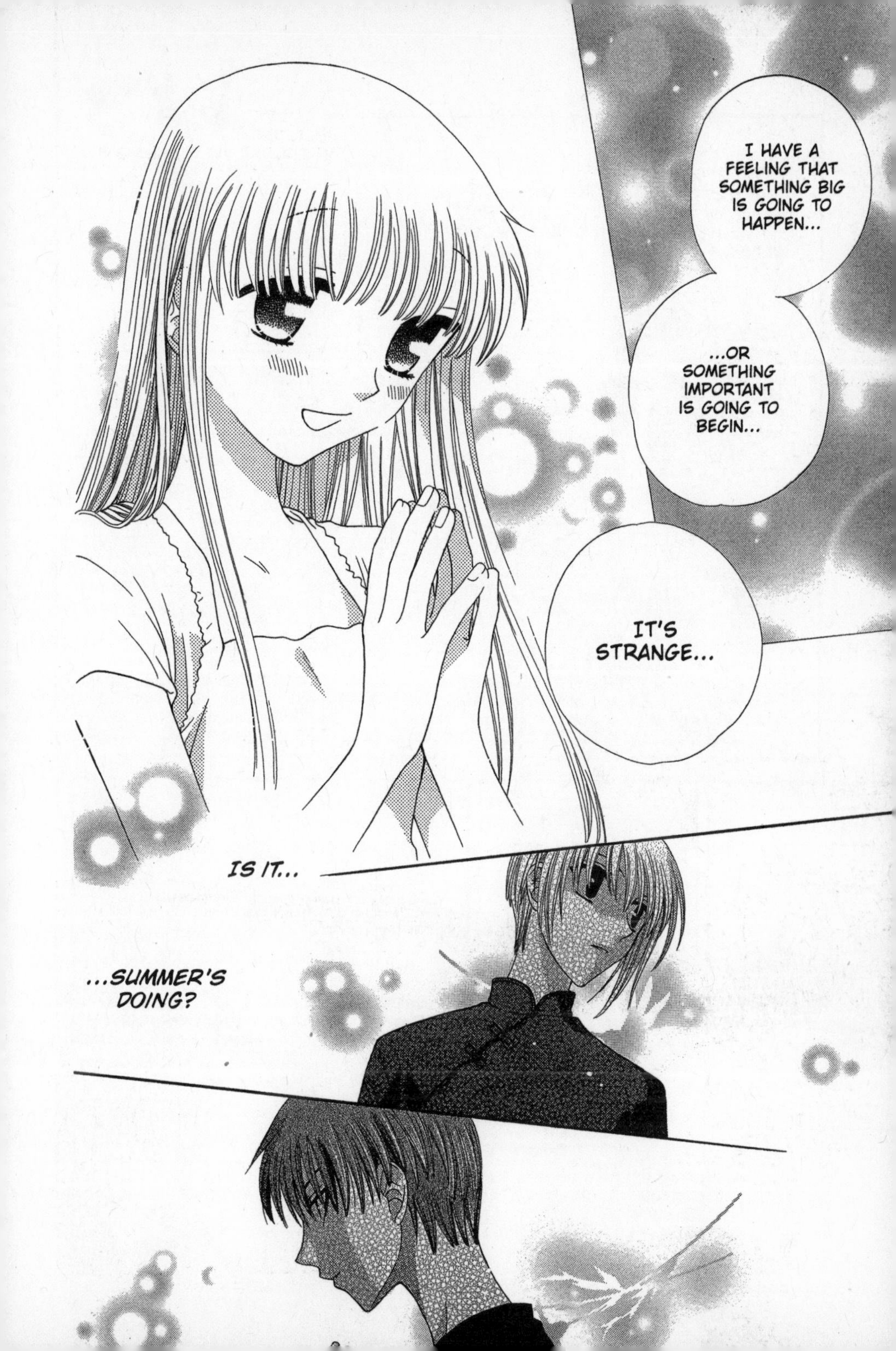
I HAVE A FEELING THAT SOMETHING BIG IS GOING TO HAPPEN...
...OR SOMETHING IMPORTANT IS GOING TO BEGIN...
IT'S STRANGE...
IS IT...
...SUMMER'S DOING?

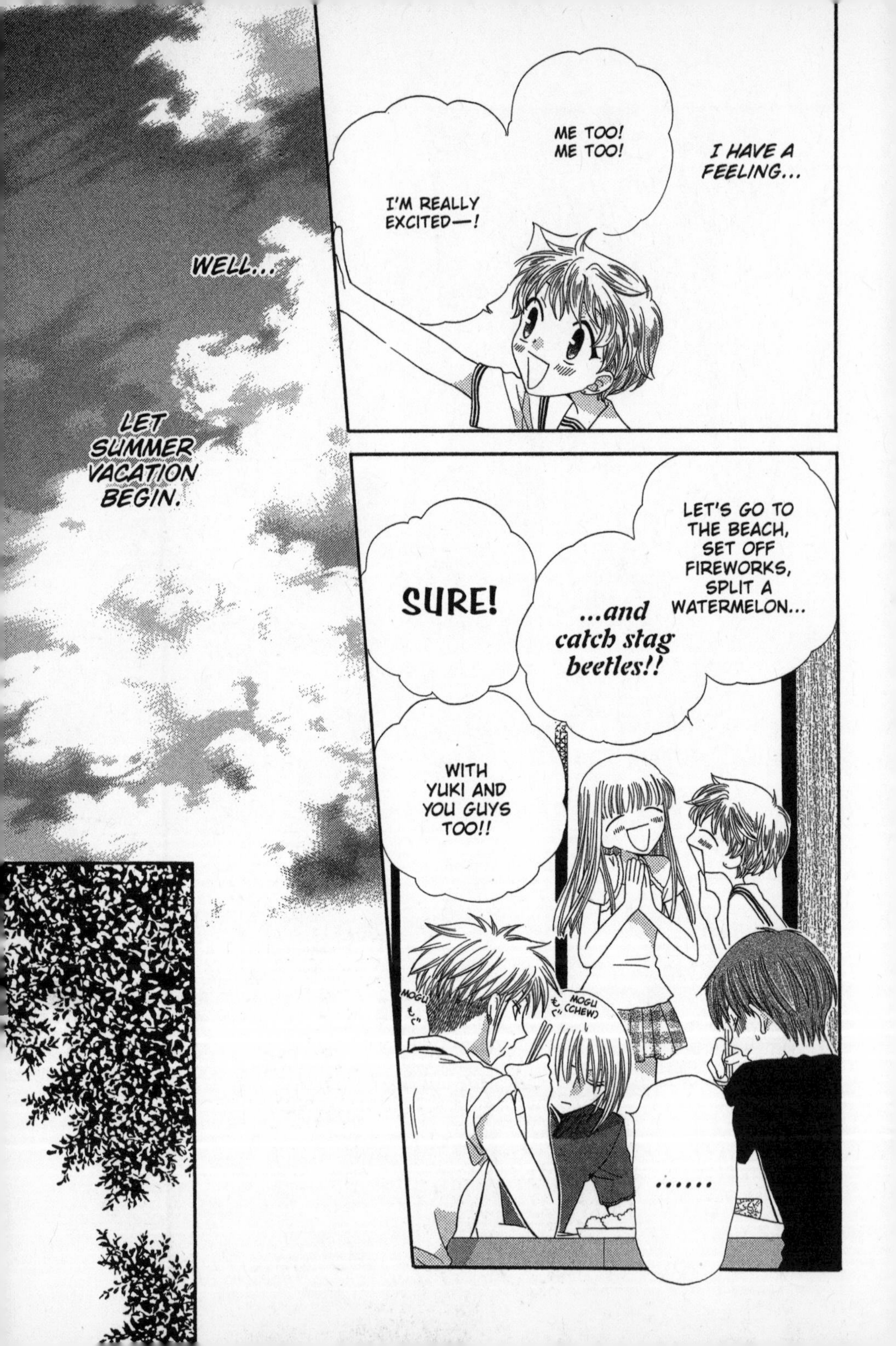
I HAVE A FEELING...
ME TOO! ME TOO!
I'M REALLY EXCITED—!
LET'S GO TO THE BEACH, SET OFF FIREWORKS, SPLIT A WATERMELON...
...and catch stag beetles!!
SURE!
WITH YUKI AND YOU GUYS TOO!!
MOGU (CHEW)
MOGU
......
WELL...
LET SUMMER VACATION BEGIN.

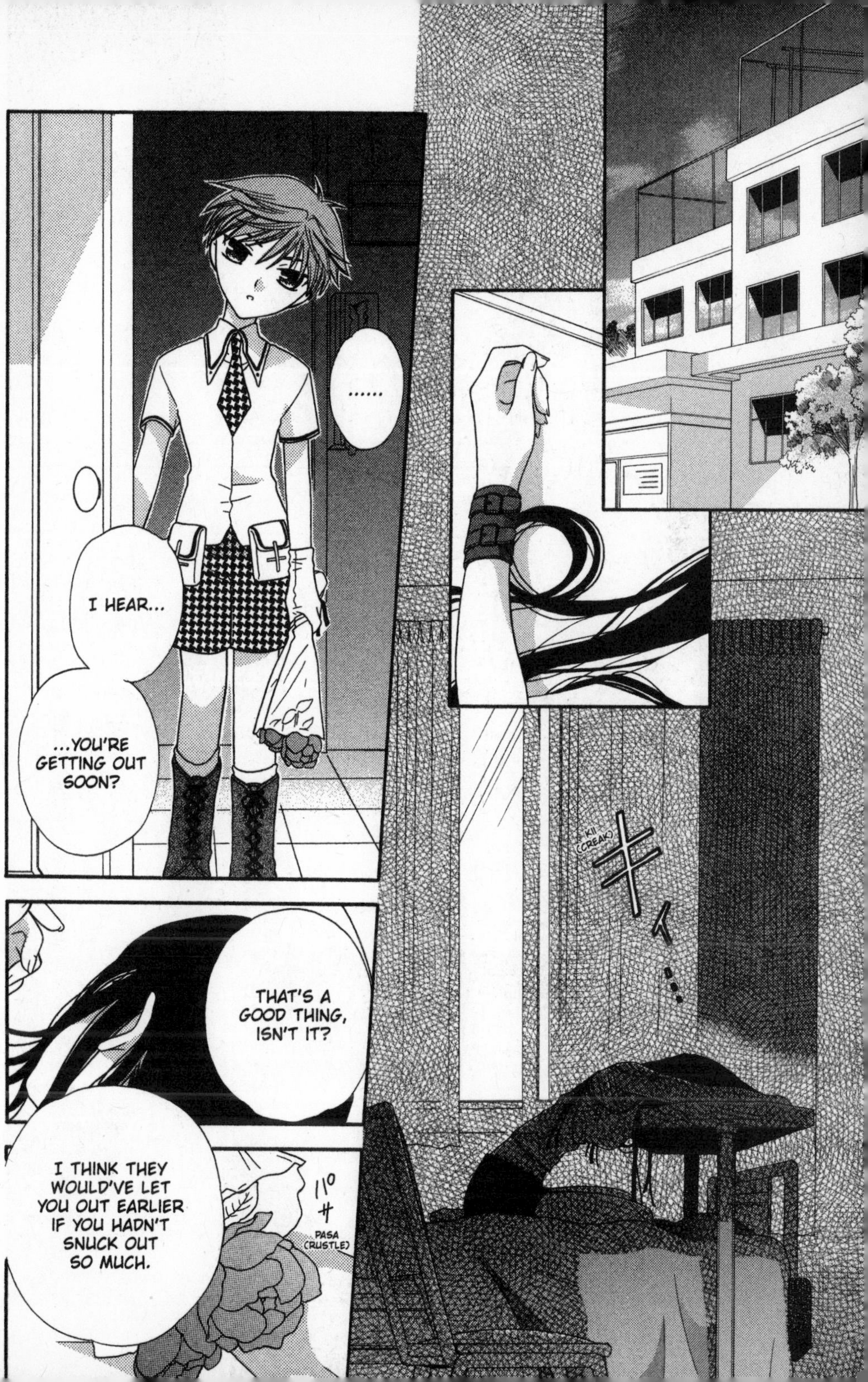
KII (CREAK)
......
I HEAR...
...YOU'RE GETTING OUT SOON?
THAT'S A GOOD THING, ISN'T IT?
I THINK THEY WOULD'VE LET YOU OUT EARLIER IF YOU HADN'T SNUCK OUT SO MUCH.
PASA (RUSTLE)

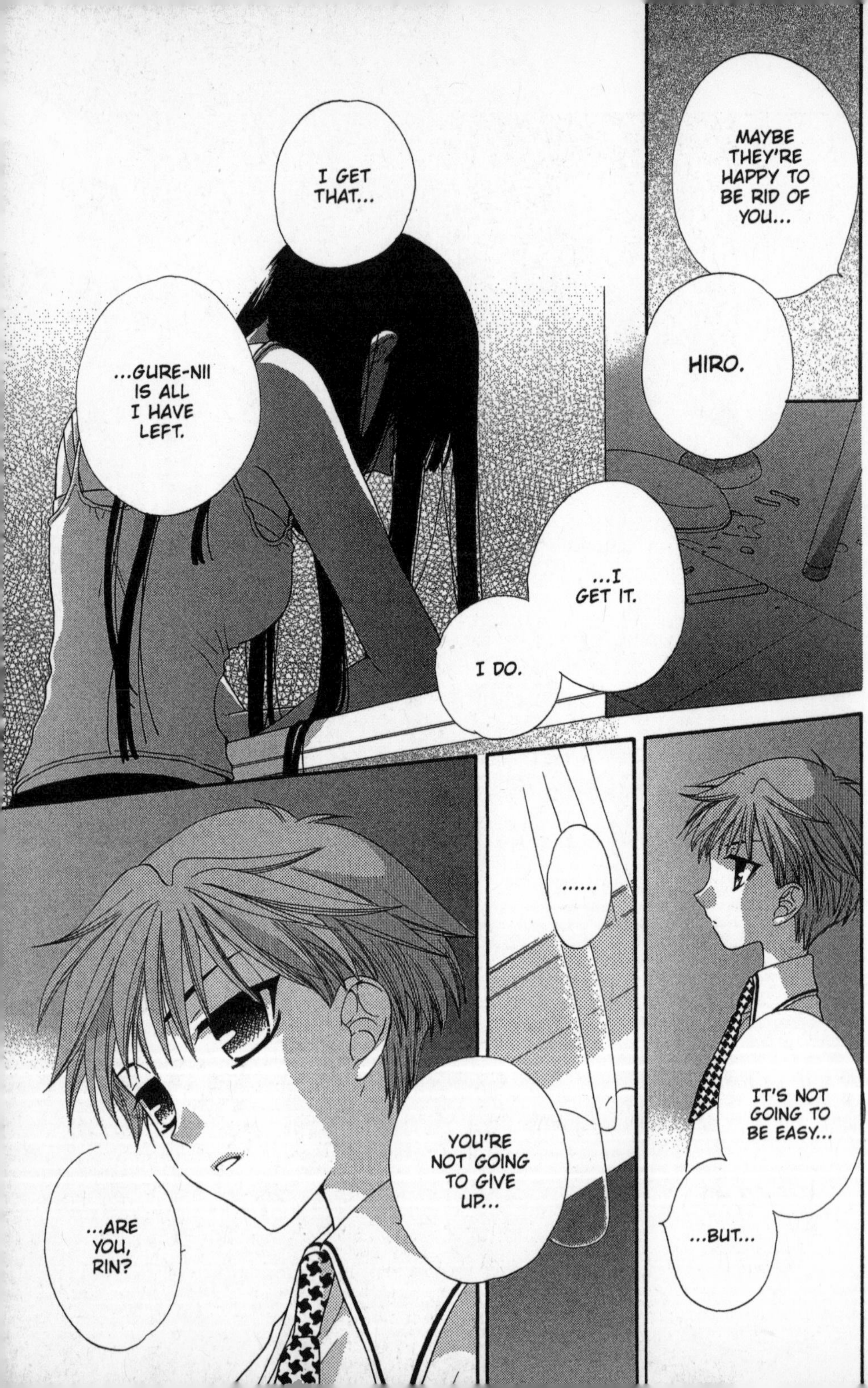
MAYBE THEY'RE HAPPY TO BE RID OF YOU...
HIRO.
I GET THAT...
...GURE-NII IS ALL I HAVE LEFT.
...I GET IT.
I DO.
IT'S NOT GOING TO BE EASY...
...BUT...
......
YOU'RE NOT GOING TO GIVE UP...
...ARE YOU, RIN?

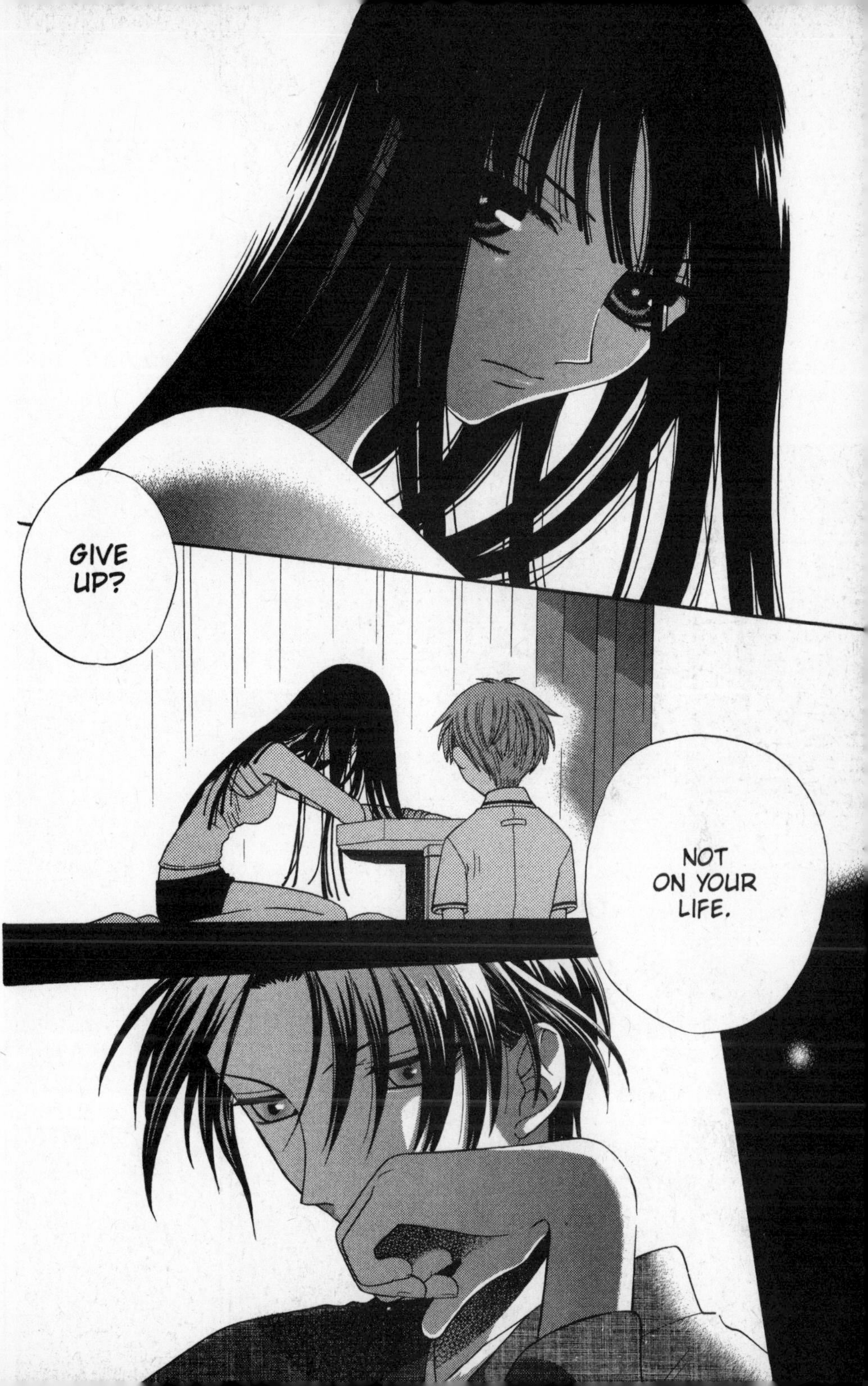
GIVE UP?
NOT ON YOUR LIFE.

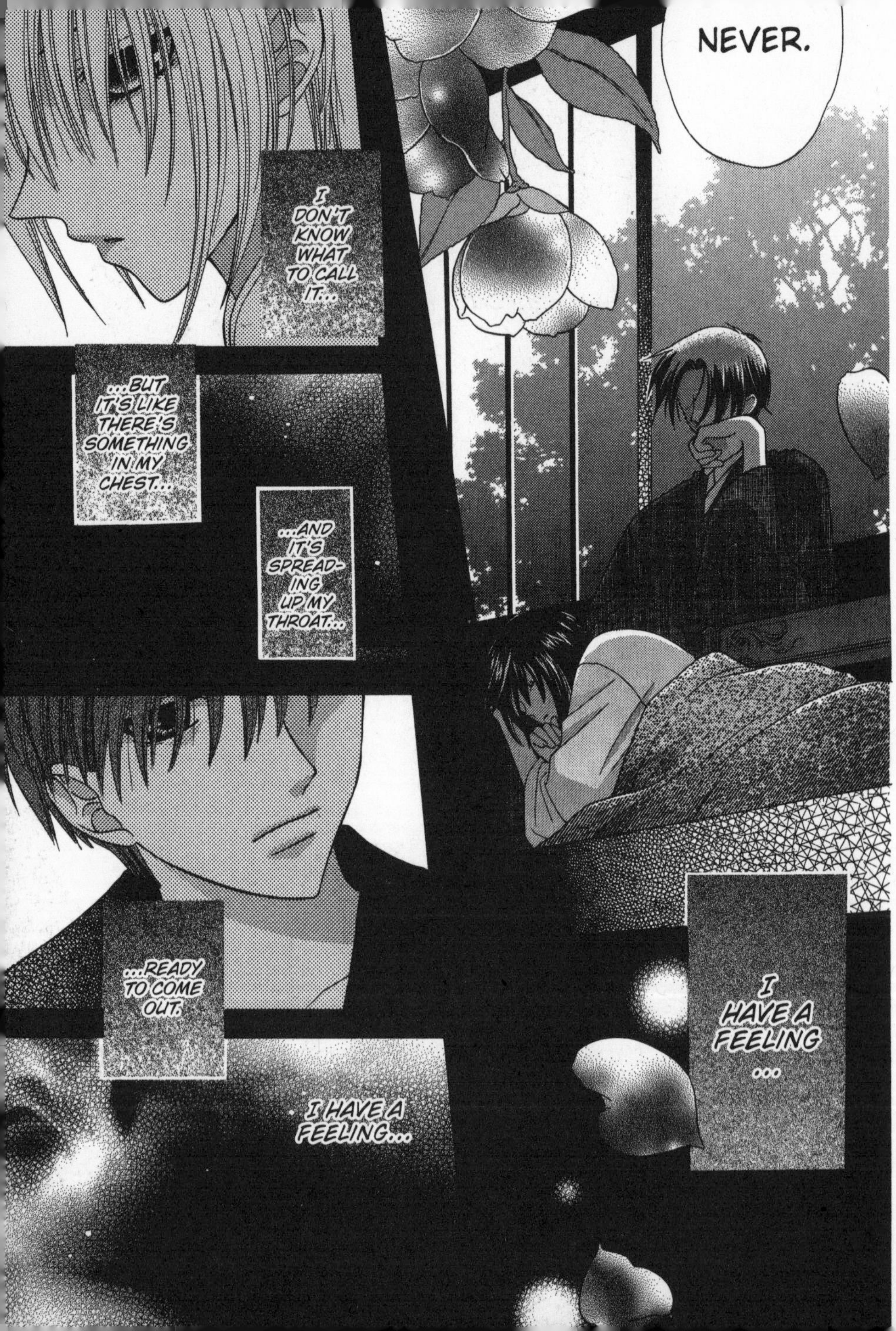
NEVER.
I DON'T KNOW WHAT TO CALL IT...
...BUT IT'S LIKE THERE'S SOMETHING IN MY CHEST...
...AND IT'S SPREADING UP MY THROAT...
...READY TO COME OUT.
I HAVE A FEELING...
I HAVE A FEELING...

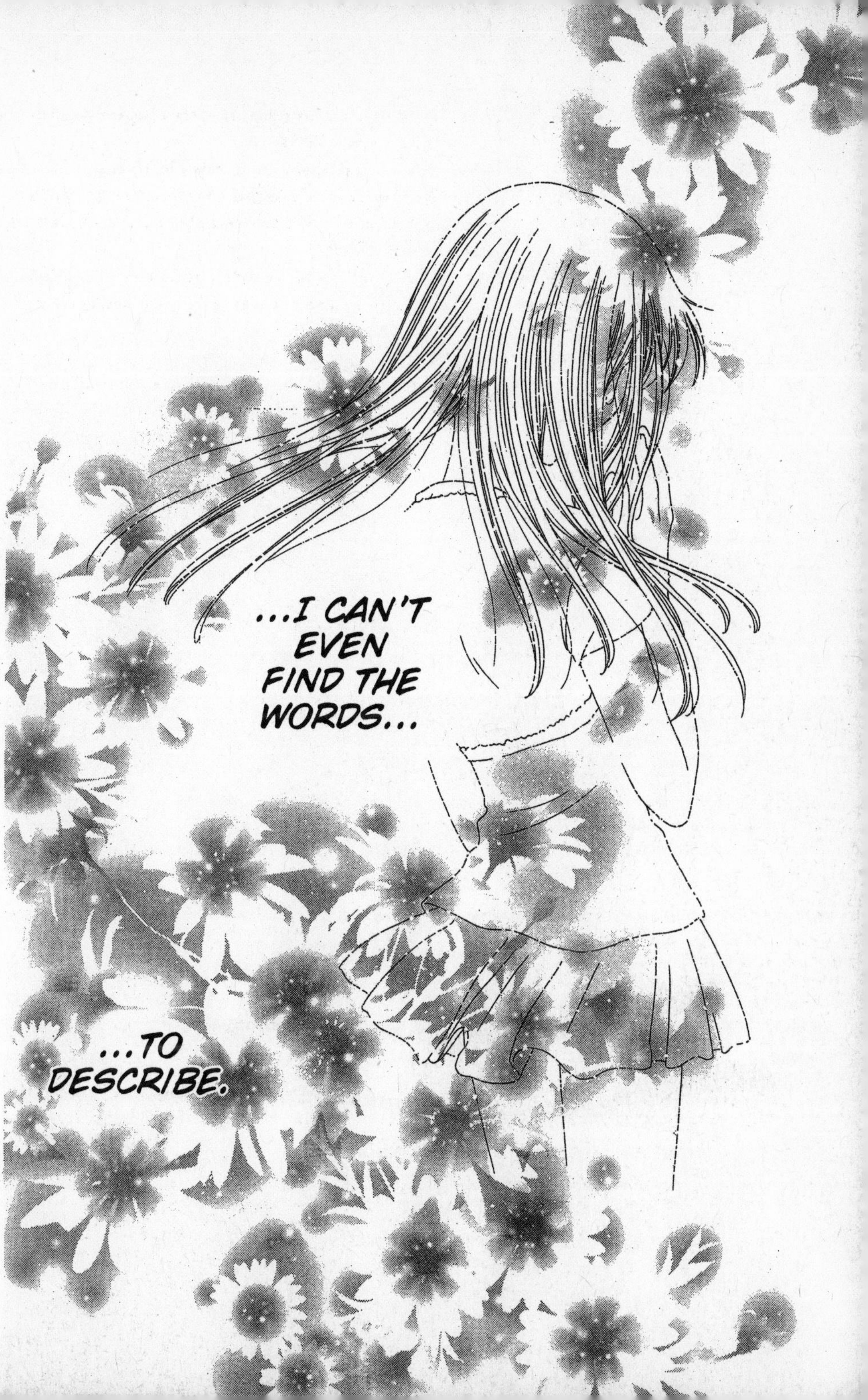
...I CAN'T EVEN FIND THE WORDS...
...TO DESCRIBE.

FEELING OF GRATITUDE

FURUBA went on a long hiatus after chapter 44, in which Ritsu made his debut.
The reason was a problem with my left hand.
It started somewhere around chapters 34–35, but I kept working and tried to downplay it, until at last the hand went kaput.
It took over half a year before I got a clear diagnosis.
Between surgery and recovery time, the series was paused for about a year.

It was so hard for me until I knew the name of the disorder. I hated my left hand, which wouldn't move at all. I've already written about this in the art book, but at the time, I felt like I was alone and struggling to stay afloat in a pitch-dark sea.

In the end, thanks to all of you, I had surgery and was eventually able to use my hand again, but......
My story will continue in Volume 5 of the collector's edition!
With an unexpected twist!

Thank you for getting this collector's edition!

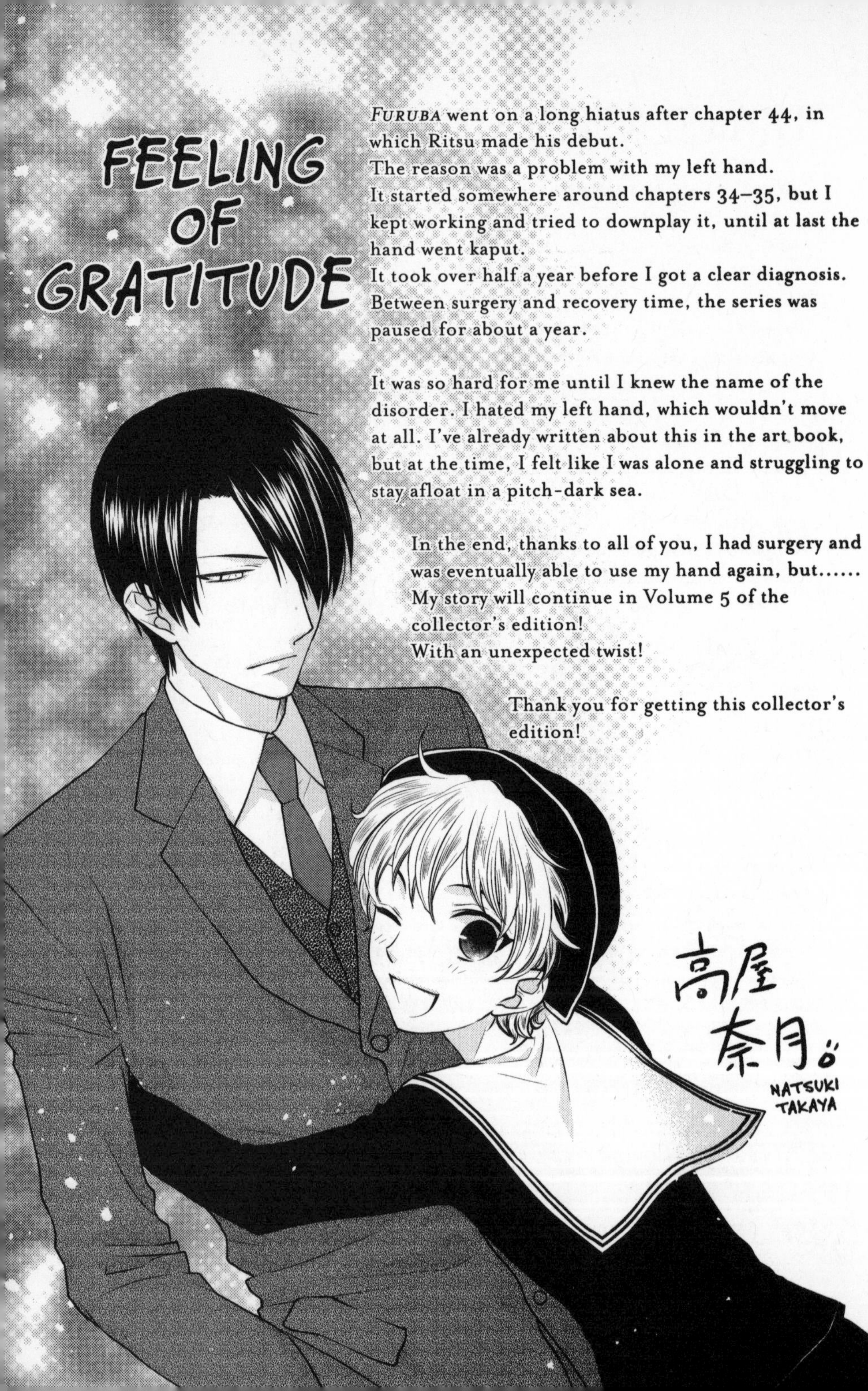

高屋奈月

NATSUKI TAKAYA

TRANSLATION NOTES

COMMON HONORIFICS

no honorific: Indicates familiarity or closeness; if used without permission or reason, addressing someone in this manner would constitute an insult.

-san: The Japanese equivalent of Mr./Mrs./Miss. If a situation calls for politeness, this is the fail-safe honorific.

-sama: Conveys great respect; may also indicate that the social status of the speaker is lower than that of the addressee.

-dono: A very polite honorific, more formal (and sometimes distant) than -san.

-kun: Used most often when referring to boys, this indicates affection or familiarity. Occasionally used by older men among their peers, but it may also be used by anyone referring to a person of lower standing.

-chan: An affectionate honorific indicating familiarity used mostly in reference to girls; also used in reference to cute persons or animals of either gender.

-senpai: A suffix used to address upperclassmen or more experienced coworkers.

-kouhai: A suffix used to address underclassmen or less experienced coworkers.

-sensei: A respectful term for teachers, artists, or high-level professionals.

Page 13

Oba-san: This is the Japanese term for one's aunt, as well as an older woman (as old as one's mother or older). It is often used when speaking directly to a friend's mother, as in this case.

Page 21

The characters in "youth": The Japanese word for "youth" is *seishun*, which can also mean the "springtime of one's life," or "adolescence." As Yuki explains, there are two characters in the word. The first is *sei*, which is the kanji for "blue" or "green" in the sense of "immature." The second character, *shun*, means "spring." Hence "green spring."

Page 35

Das ist keine Art!: This is a German idiom meaning "That's no way to behave!"

Page 49

Onee-chan: This term is the familiar form of "older sister" in Japanese and can also be used to refer to older females (in their teens to early twenties) whom one respects or admires.

Page 94

Girl gangs: Colloquially known as *sukeban*, the girl gangs referred to here are

groups of middle schoolers or high schoolers who engage in delinquent behavior.

Page 135
Clothing: Kyoko's clothing says "Red Butterfly," "The Butterfly in Black Has Arrived," and "I Live for Tohru." Uotani's jacket is a little more complicated. Japanese biker gangs often wear personalized jackets called *tokkoufuku* ("special attack uniforms"), which are reminiscent of the kamikaze units from World War II, *tokkoutai* ("special attack forces"). These jackets are often adorned with military/nationalistic slogans, Buddhist chants, or whatever the owner thinks is badass enough to use to express themselves. Uotani's jacket combines the phrases "Take on all comers" and "Achieving salvation by entering Nirvana" (which rhyme in Japanese). Her left sleeve is a collection of cool-sounding kanji such as "quake," "piercing attack," and "spitting blood."

Page 164
Ane-san: This is a respectful term for "older sister" and includes older females for whom one has respectful or adulatory "big sister" feelings. *Onee-san* means the same thing, but *ane-san* is more commonly used in female delinquent culture, as it is here—with the younger "bad girl" showing respect and admiration to Uotani.

Page 186
Nimono: This word refers to dishes made by simmering the ingredients (usually vegetables, chicken, and fish) in a seasoned broth.

Page 186
Natto: This traditional, often polarizing, Japanese food consists of gooey, sticky, smelly fermented soybeans that are very nutritious and high in protein.

Page 204
Kyoto and Nara: Kyoto is Japan's former capital and was the imperial family's residence from 794 to 1868. The city is full of historical and picturesque shrines, temples, and gardens. Nara also has many historical and natural points of interest. Both are frequent destinations for class trips from Tokyo-area schools—in both reality and in anime/manga—hence the "cliché" appellation.

Page 241
-Niisan: *Nii-san* is a respectful term for an older brother but can also be used for an older brother figure, as it is in this situation.

Page 276
Takoyaki: This popular snack, which hails from Osaka, is essentially a ball-shaped mini-pancake with a small piece of octopus inside and is usually garnished with sauce and mayonnaise.

Page 276

Takoyarou: Translated literally as "Octopus Bastard," this name combines the Japanese word for "octopus" (*tako*) with a rude way of referring to someone (*yarou*).

Page 289

Ikayaki: Grilled squid on a stick typically served with soy sauce, this snack is often sold at Japanese festivals from street food vendors.

Page 309

"Momiji-kun is an idol": Well, maybe he's not literally a pop idol, but he is so adorable that even old women tend to go giddy in his presence.

Page 312

Soumen: These thin white noodles are especially popular in the summer. They can be cooked simply as in this scene or made more fancily by having them flow down a long bamboo "water slide," where they're caught with diners' chopsticks along the way.

Page 332

"Ukiuki Watching": In Japanese, the song Ayame is referring to is "Ukiuki Watching" (*ukiuki* means "to do something excitedly"), the theme song of the long-lived (1982–2014) weekday variety show *Waratte Iitomo!* (literally, "It's Okay to Laugh!"). This song is Ayame's way of telling Yuki that it's noon, the time *Waratte Iitomo!* always aired.

Page 371

Japanese haunted houses: Haunted houses are popular in Japan during the summer, the idea being that getting scared sends shivers down the spine—a great antidote to summer's sweltering heat!

Fruits Basket

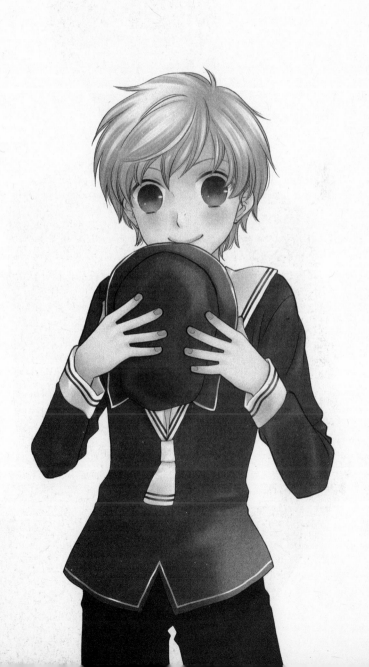

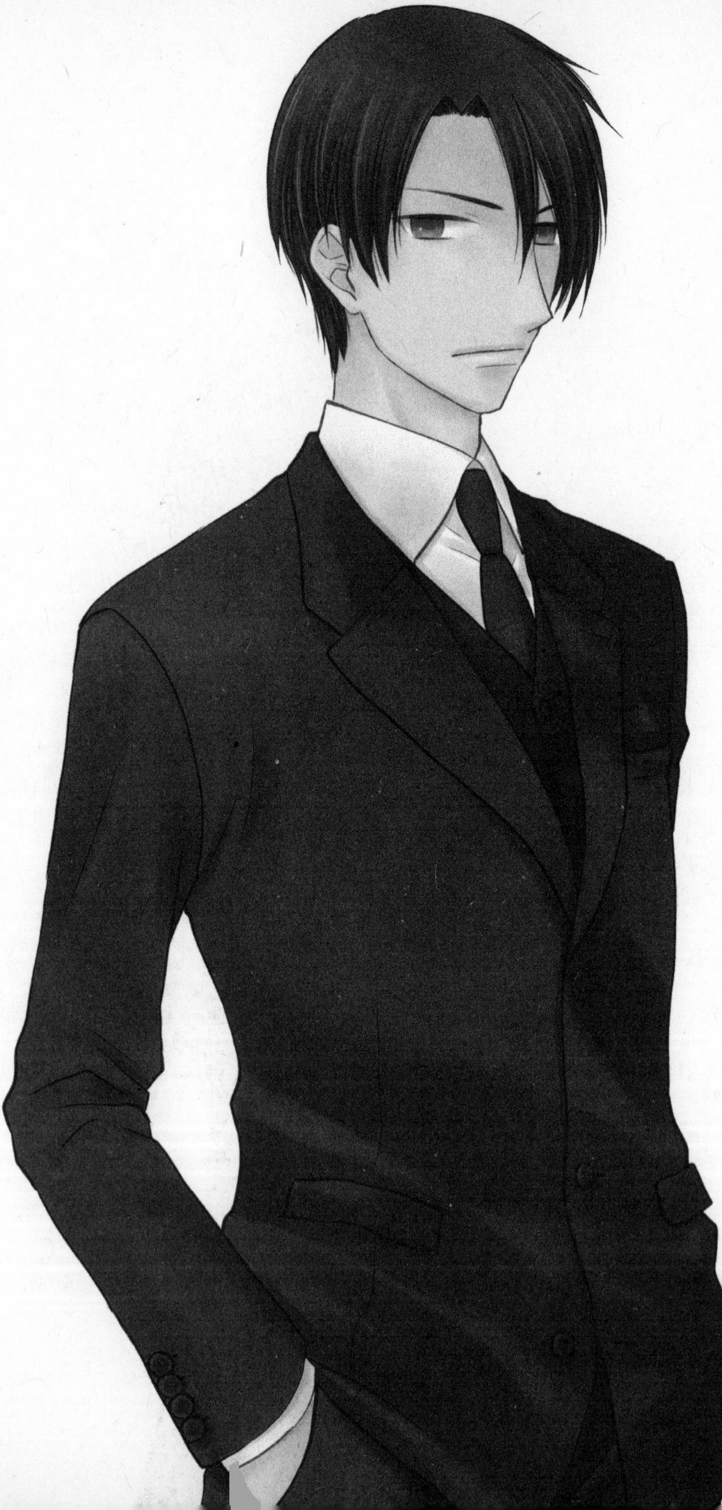

Love Natsuki Takaya?
Don't forget to check out her other works
also available from Yen Press!

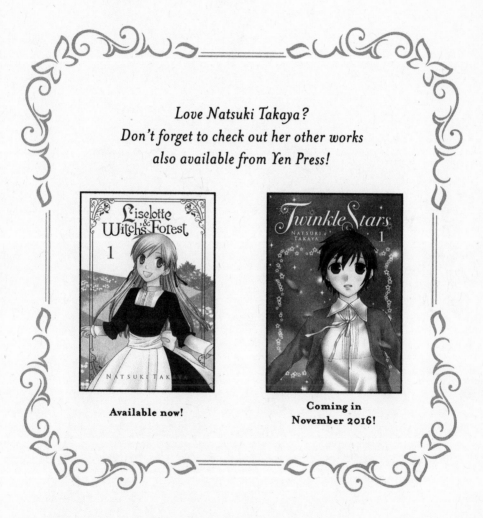

Available now!

**Coming in
November 2016!**

COLLECTOR'S EDITION

Fruits Basket

COLLECTOR'S EDITION

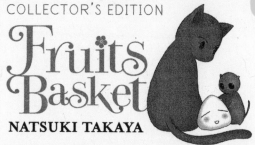

Fruits Basket

NATSUKI TAKAYA

Translation: Sheldon Drzka • Lettering: Lys Blakeslee

Fruits Basket Collector's Edition, Vol. 4 by Natsuki Takaya
© Natsuki Takaya 2015
All rights reserved.
First published in Japan in 2015 by HAKUSENSHA, INC., Tokyo.
English language translation rights in U.S.A., Canada and U.K. arranged with
HAKUSENSHA, INC., Tokyo through Tuttle-Mori Agency, Inc., Tokyo.

English Translation © 2016 by Yen Press, LLC

Yen Press
1290 Avenue of the Americas
New York, NY 10104

Visit us at yenpress.com
facebook.com/yenpress
twitter.com/yenpress
yenpress.tumblr.com

First Yen Press Edition: August 2016

Yen Press is an imprint of Yen Press, LLC.
The Yen Press name and logo are trademarks of Yen Press, LLC.

The publisher is not responsible for websites (or their content) that are not owned by the publisher.

Library of Congress Control Number: 2016932692

ISBN: 978-0-316-36065-4

10 9 8 7 6 5 4 3 2 1

BVG

Printed in the United States of America